MW00962651

LaSalle Banks Guide

A Scholl Corporate Guide®   **1997-98**

Major publicly held corporations and financial institutions
headquartered in Illinois

Published by:
Scholl Communications Incorporated
P.O. Box 560
Deerfield, IL 60015

Telephone: 847.945.1891

Also from Scholl Corporate Guides®

LaSalle Banks Guide / Electronic Edition

The computer database version of the *LaSalle Banks Guide* is available for personal computers.

© Copyright 1997

Scholl Communications Incorporated
Deerfield, Illinois 60015

ISBN: 0-912-51919-3
Library of Congress Catalog Card Number 86-640098

Printed in U.S.A.

LaSalle
THE BANK THAT WORKS℠

To Our Valued Clients and Friends:

The LaSalle Banks are pleased to bring you this guide to major publicly held corporations and financial institutions headquartered in Illinois. This is the first year that our organization is sponsoring the production of this valuable resource, which includes current company profiles, financial and investment facts, and personnel information on leading area businesses.

After extensive economic restructuring following the Rust Belt recession of the early 1980s, Illinois and the Midwest are now recognized as national economic leaders. Illinois, in particular, has developed a strong combination of service firms, modern manufacturing companies, and an active small business community. The state has positioned itself to anticipate and respond to the economic opportunities of the present and future.

In the pages immediately following is a broad overview of our organization and our capabilities. As a full-service financial institution serving the Midwest, with access to an expansive worldwide network, LaSalle is the partner of choice for many businesses. To learn more about how we can help you, please contact us at any of the phone numbers listed at the end of this overview on LaSalle.

Sincerely,

Norman Bobins

Norman Bobins
President and CEO, LaSalle National Corporation
President and CEO, LaSalle National Bank

LaSalle
THE BANK THAT WORKS℠

LaSalle has an unwavering commitment to be the best in the Midwest among banking organizations serving individuals and middle-market businesses. To meet that commitment, LaSalle relies on the combined strengths of our banking network, our advanced technology, and our outstanding personnel.

Our network has over 100 banking offices and 180 ATMs serving customers throughout the Chicago area. You may know us by a few names: LaSalle National Bank, LaSalle Bank N.A., LaSalle Bank NI or LaSalle Bank FSB. But underlying the various names is a unified focus to make our superior services clearly accessible to our customers.

We are further distinguished by our capable, customer-oriented team of banking professionals. Our tellers, personal bankers, and behind the scenes staff join our business banking relationship managers in their dedication to understanding our customers' needs and working to meet their objectives.

ABN AMRO Bank N.V., our parent bank, is an exceptional performer with an impressive history of strength and stability. Established in 1824, ABN AMRO is recognized as one of the most powerful and credit-worthy financial institutions in the world with $341 billion in assets.

Commercial Banking

In 1997, we celebrate the 70th anniversary of our flagship LaSalle National Bank which specializes in commercial lending services. From working lines of credit, to capital equipment and machinery financing to real estate loans, LaSalle's bankers are experts at looking beyond the numbers to structure financing packages that are flexible and competitive.

Our bankers draw on LaSalle's vast resources to provide competitive financing to customers throughout the Midwest. Whether for a working capital line of $200 thousand or $200 million, LaSalle can arrange financing. If a customer is considering purchasing machinery or expanding a plant, LaSalle can provide tax-exempt financing through a local industrial development authority for capital projects for middle-market manufacturing companies.

LaSalle also provides special industry expertise. For example, businesses in the mortgage banking, short line railroad, health care, insurance, construction and engineering, and consumer finance industries can rely on our in-depth knowledge of their markets and competitive financing. We also support our commercial customers with real estate and equipment financing, international banking, treasury management services and asset based financing, to name only a few key areas.

We can provide financing for leveraged buyouts and acquisitions, as well as recapitalizations and employee stock option plans (ESOPs).

LaSalle's Trust and Asset Management Group provides financial services to a wide variety of clients throughout the country. We provide a complete complement of products and services to our institutional market customers including: corporate trust services, 401(k) services, ESOP related services, custody services and master trust, and investment management services. LaSalle Asset-Backed

Securities Trust Services Group has established itself as the market leader in Trustee appointments in the growing market for commercial real estate securitizations.

As part of Trust and Asset Management, our Wealth Management Group is dedicated to fulfilling the personal trust and private banking needs of high net worth individuals. This group of professionals provides access to the many specialized services available throughout the LaSalle and ABN AMRO organizations. These include high-quality investment management, brokerage, and a full range of trust capabilities, in addition to our competitive deposit and credit products.

In 1996, we dramatically increased our equipment leasing capabilities. When customers and relationship managers agree that the decision makes sense, LaSalle National Leasing Corporation works to optimize the tax benefits of equipment leasing.

Beyond the delivery of high-quality financial services, we are committed to supporting local economies and civic efforts. We play an active role in nurturing the health and well-being of those communities, and are determined to make a difference for the people, businesses, and neighborhoods we serve.

Investment Banking

Through our affiliate, ABN AMRO Chicago Corporation, we have enhanced our ability to provide a full range of investment banking, brokerage and securities services. ABN AMRO Chicago Corporation also provides enhanced capabilities in domestic equities, exchange-traded futures, securities clearing, and mergers and acquisitions.

Retail and Community Banking

Our retail customers can choose from a full complement of products and services, from checking to money market accounts, to certificates of deposit and IRAs. We offer individualized solutions to every credit need as well. Our credit services range from mortgages and home equity lines of credit, to overdraft protection.

Our community banking network is designed to bring the strength and sophistication of "downtown banking" to customers throughout the Midwest. From our outstanding lending capabilities to our rapidly growing number of ATMs, LaSalle's local bankers provide the services our customers require where they live and work. Our goal is to build a fully integrated banking network that enables our customers to bank at any LaSalle location, no matter where they established their relationship.

Our affiliate, LaSalle Home Mortgage Corporation, is the single largest provider of home mortgages in the State of Illinois. Throughout Chicagoland, families rely on LaSalle affiliates to make their home-ownership dreams a reality.

The LaSalle Banks Chicago Marathon is known throughout the world as a premier running event. As the race wends its way through the city's neighborhoods, it brings many of our communities together for a day of celebration.

But our commitment to our communities goes far beyond marathon sponsorship. We support economic development, affordable housing, and job creation in the communities we serve. For example, LaSalle provided loan funding for rehabilitation of low-income, multi-family housing in Chicago's Austin and Lawndale communities. And we are partner and mentor to the minority-owned Highland Community Bank in Maywood.

For More Information

To find out more about The Bank That Works, or one of its affiliates, please call:

ABN AMRO Bank	312.904.2400
ABN AMRO Chicago Corporation	312.855.7600
LaSalle National Bank	312.904.2000
LaSalle Bank NI	312.525.2180
LaSalle Bank N.A.	773.777.7700
LaSalle Bank FSB	773.434.3322
LaSalle Mortgage Corporation	708.583.7300

Foreword

Welcome to the 33rd annual edition of the *Guide*. The book is sponsored by the LaSalle Banks and published by Scholl Communications Incorporated. Originally published in 1965 by A.G. Becker & Co. Incorporated, the book was acquired in 1984 by Scholl Communications Incorporated. First Chicago Corporation and its successor sponsored the *Guide* from 1984 to 1997, and we are pleased to welcome the LaSalle Banks as the new sponsor. Editorial management has remained unchanged throughout the book's history.

The new edition provides information on 296 publicly held corporations headquartered in Illinois, as well as information on 24 of the state's largest banks and savings institutions. These organizations were selected principally on the basis of their total revenues and total assets, and the information is intended to be of general interest.

Directory Organization
Companies are listed in alphabetical order, with a separate listing for banks and savings institutions beginning on page 299. Beginning on page 325 is a listing of companies indexed according to Standard Industrial Classification (S.I.C.) business code numbers prepared by the Office of Management and Budget of the Executive Office of the President. The S.I.C. codes listed in this edition are based on the latest version of the revised classification manual.

An ordinal ranking of industrial, retail, transportation, utility, and diversified financial companies by revenues and total assets begins on page 341. Bank and savings institution holding companies are ranked separately, as are commercial banks and savings institutions. For comparative purposes, these lists include rankings from the 1996-97 edition.

Changes from Prior Year
A list of company changes from last year's edition begins on page 349. It includes companies whose names have changes during the year, as well as a summary of companies that have been added to and deleted from the book.

Sources of Information
The information contained in this book was obtained principally from the companies included, and from annual reports, proxy statements, prospectuses, and 10-Ks. Unless otherwise indicated, earnings per share are reported on a primary basis.

While this information has been collected from sources believed to be reliable, and due care and caution have been exercised in preparing and producing this book, its accuracy and completeness are not guaranteed, and liability cannot be assumed for the correctness of the data contained herein. The descriptions are not to be construed as an offer to sell or the solicitation of an offer to buy any of the securities of these companies. Because of the abbreviated nature of the data, the *Guide* is designed as a general source of reference rather than a basis for investment decisions.

Businesses in Illinois are constantly changing. Therefore, some of the data, particularly lists of directors and officers, may have changed since compilation.

Readers who find this publication useful may be interested in the **LaSalle Banks Guide/Electronic Edition**, a self-contained computer database version of the book. For information about the Electronic Edition, please contact the publisher at the address or phone number on the back cover of this book.

Contents

Company	Page	Company	Page

Company	Page	Company	Page

Banks and Savings Institutions

Index and Rankings

Industrial, Commercial and Financial Corporations

AAR CORP.

One AAR Place, 1100 North Wood Dale Road, Wood Dale, Illinois 60191
Telephone: (630) 227-2000

AAR CORP. and its worldwide network of companies, located in the United States, Europe, and the Asia/Pacific region, provide products and services to the aviation industry. Principal products and services include: the purchase, sale, and lease of turbine aircraft engines and engine parts to airlines and independent overhaul facilities; and the supply of aircraft aftermarket parts and equipment. Additionally, the company's technical service capabilities include the overhaul, repair, and exchange of aviation components and systems such as avionics, instrumentation, electronics, accessories, and landing gear; restoration of turbine engine components; and maintenance, modification, and refurbishment of aircraft for airframe manufacturers, airlines, and corporate operators. Manufacturing expertise encompasses air cargo handling equipment; air cargo pallets and containers; aerospace and aircraft structures; bonded composite panels; nuclear shielding products; and floor maintenance equipment. The company also provides financial services, primarily the leasing of commercial aircraft. In January 1997, the company's headquarters moved from Elk Grove Village to Wood Dale. In May 1997, the company agreed to acquire Cooper Aviation Industries Inc., an Elk Grove Village, Illinois-based distributor of aviation parts and accessories. Incorporated in Illinois in 1955; reincorporated in Delaware in 1966.

Directors (In addition to indicated officers)

A. Robert Abboud	Erwin E. Schulze
Howard B. Bernick	Joel D. Spungin
Edgar D. Jannotta	Lee B. Stern
Robert D. Judson	Richard D. Tabery

Officers (Directors*)

*Ira A. Eichner, Chm.	A. Lee Hall, V.P.—Strategic Planning
*David P. Storch, Pres. & C.E.O.	Douglas S. Hara, V.P.—Facilities & Procurement
William A. Bailey, V.P.—Oper.	John C. Mache, V.P.—Mgt. Info. Systems
Ann T. Baldwin, V.P.—Corp. Comm.	Howard A. Pulsifer, V.P., Gen. Coun. & Secy.
Michael K. Carr, V.P.—Tax	Timothy J. Romenesko, V.P., C.F.O. & Treas.
Peter K. Chapman, V.P.—Mktg. & Bus. Dev.	Philip C. Slapke, V.P.—Engine Grp.

Consolidated Balance Sheet   As of May 31, 1997 (000 omitted)

Assets		Liabilities & Stockholders' Equity	
Current assets	$414,100	Current liabilities	$ 99,981
Net property, plant & equipment	71,108	Long-term debt	116,818
Other assets	44,376	Deferred items	37,232
		Other liabilities	6,294
		*Stockholders' equity	269,259
Total	$529,584	Total	$529,584

*18,204,000 shares common stock outstanding.

Consolidated Income Statement

Years Ended May 31	Thousands — — — — — Net Sales	Net Income	Per Share — — — Earnings	Cash Dividends	Common Stock Price Range Fiscal Year
1997	$589,328	$23,025	$1.38	$ .48	31-7/8 — 18-3/8
1996	504,990	16,012	1.00	.48	23-5/8 — 14-7/8
1995	451,395	10,463	.66	.48	15-1/4 — 12
1994	407,754	9,494	.60	.48	17-3/8 — 12-5/8
1993	382,780	283[a]	.02[a]	.48	14-5/8 — 11

[a]Includes $7,200,000 of aftertax expenses primarily related to the write-down of certain inventories to reflect the impact of market conditions and a reduction in income tax expense of $1,200,000.

Transfer Agent & Registrar: First Chicago Trust Co. of New York; The First National Bank of Chicago

Special Counsel:	Schiff, Hardin & Waite	Auditors:	KPMG Peat Marwick LLP
Investor Relations:	Ann T. Baldwin, V.P.	Traded (Symbol):	NYSE, CSE (AIR)
		Stockholders:	14,500
Human Resources:	Robert J. Naughton, Dir.	Employees:	2,196
Mgt. Info. Svcs.:	John C. Mache, V.P.	Annual Meeting:	In October

Aasche Transportation Services, Inc.

10214 North Mt. Vernon Road, Shannon, Illinois 61078-9415
Telephone: (815) 864-2421

Aasche Transportation Services, Inc., through its Asche Transfer, Inc. subsidiary, is a 58 year-old truckload carrier that operates exclusively in the temperature-controlled segment of the transportation services industry. The company transports a variety of foods, including processed and frozen foods, and products which require temperature-sensitive service and "just-in-time" delivery. Incorporated in Delaware in 1994.

Directors   (In addition to indicated officers)

Richard S. Baugh
Gary I. Goldberg

Steven R. Green

Officers   (Directors*)

*Larry L. Asche, Chm. & C.E.O.
*Kevin M. Clark, Pres.
*Diane L. Asche, V.P. & Secy.

*Leon M. Monachos, Treas. & C.F.O.
Daniel R. Wright, C.O.O.

Consolidated Balance Sheet   As of December 31, 1996 (000 omitted)

Assets		Liabilities & Stockholders' Equity	
Current assets	$ 8,715	Current liabilities	$20,316
Net property, plant & equipment	29,552	Long-term debt	14,802
Other assets	11,059	Deferred items	3,677
		*Stockholders' equity	10,531
Total	$49,326	Total	$49,326

*3,953,077 shares common stock outstanding.

Consolidated Income Statement

Years Ended Dec. 31	Thousands		Per Share[a]		Common Stock Price Range[a] Calendar Year
	Revenues	Net Income	Earnings	Cash Dividends	
1996	$77,365	$(2,620)	$ (.67)	$ .00	7-1/8 — 3-1/8
1995	67,748	(1,326)	(.34)	.00	9-1/2 — 4-7/8
1994	34,034	(1,079)	(.57)[b]	.00	8-7/8 — 7-1/4
1993	19,335	332	.26[b]		
1992	16,999	488			

[a]Initial public offering in September 1994.
[b]Pro forma.

Transfer Agent & Registrar:	Continental Stock Transfer & Trust Co.		
General Counsel:	Sachnoff & Weaver, Ltd.	Auditors:	Ernst & Young LLP
Investor Relations:	Leon M. Monachos, C.F.O.	Traded (Symbol):	NASDAQ (ASHE)
Human Resources:	Diane L. Asche, V.P.	Stockholders:	1,700
		Employees:	680
Mgt. Info. Svcs.:	Mike Ossi	Annual Meeting:	In May

Abbott Laboratories
100 Abbott Park Road, Abbott Park, Illinois 60064-3500
Telephone: (847) 937-6100

Abbott Laboratories discovers, develops, manufactures, and sells a broad and diversified line of health care products and services. Pharmaceutical and nutritional products account for 57 percent of total sales and include adult and pediatric pharmaceuticals, nutritionals, and vitamins. Hospital and laboratory products account for 43 percent of total sales and include diagnostic systems for blood banks, hospital and commercial laboratories, and alternate care and testing sites; intravenous and irrigation fluids, and related administration equipment, drugs and drug delivery systems; and anesthetics, critical care products, and other medical specialty products for hospitals, commercial laboratories, and alternate care sites. The company also develops, manufactures, and sells other lines of personal care, agricultural and chemical products, and bulk pharmaceuticals. Products are marketed in about 130 countries through affiliates and distributors. Incorporated in Illinois in 1900.

Directors (In addition to indicated officers)

K. Frank Austen, M.D.	David A. Jones	Addison Barry Rand	John R. Walter
H. Laurance Fuller	Lord Owen	W. Ann Reynolds, Ph.D.	William L. Weiss
Allen F. Jacobson	Boone Powell, Jr.	William D. Smithburg	

Officers (Directors*)

*Duane L. Burnham, Chm. & C.E.O.
*Thomas R. Hodgson, Pres. & C.O.O.
Joy A. Amundson, Sr. V.P.—Chem./Agri. Prods.
Paul N. Clark, Sr. V.P.—Pharm. Oper.
Gary P. Coughlan, Sr. V.P.—Fin. & C.F.O.
José M. de Lasa, Sr. V.P., Secy. & Gen. Coun.
John G. Kringel, Sr. V.P.—Hosp. Prods.
Thomas M. McNally, Sr. V.P.—Ross Prods.
Robert L. Parkinson, Jr., Sr. V.P.—Intl. Oper.
Ellen M. Walvoord, Sr. V.P.—Hum. Res.
Miles D. White, Sr. V.P.—Diagnostic Oper.
Catherine V. Babington, V.P.—Inv. Rel. & Pub. Aff.
Patrick J. Balthrop, V.P.—Diag. Oper.
Mark E. Barmak, V.P.—Litig. & Govt. Aff.
Christopher B. Begley, V.P.—Hosp. Prods. Bus.
Thomas D. Brown, V.P.—Diag. Commerc. Oper.
Gary R. Byers, V.P.—Int. Audit
William G. Dempsey, V.P.—Hosp. Prod. Bus. Sector
Kenneth W. Farmer, V.P.—M.I.S.

Thomas C. Freyman, V.P. & Treas.
David B. Goffredo, V.P.—Pharm. Prods. Mktg. & Sales
Richard A. Gonzales, V.P.—Health Syst.
Guillermo A. Herrera, V.P.—Latin Amer. Oper.
Arthur J. Higgins, V.P.—Pacific, Asia & Africa Oper.
Jay B. Johnston, V.P.—Diag. Assays & Oper.
James J. Koziarz, Ph.D., V.P.—Diag. Prods. R&D
John F. Lussen, V.P.—Taxes
Edward L. Michael, V.P.—Diag. Oper.
Theodore A. Olson, V.P. & Cont.
Andre G. Pernet, Ph.D., V.P.—Pharm. Prods. R&D
Carl A. Spalding, V.P.—Ross Pediatric Prods.
William H. Stadtlander, V.P.—Ross Med. Nut. Prods.
Marcia A. Thomas, V.P.—Corp. Qual. Assur. & Reg. Aff.
H. Thomas Watkins, V.P.—Diag. Oper.
Steven J. Weger, V.P.—Corp. Planning & Dev.
Josef Wendler, V.P.—Eur. Oper.
Lance B. Wyatt, V.P.—Eng.

Consolidated Balance Sheet   As of December 31, 1996 (000 omitted)

Assets		Liabilities & Stockholders' Equity	
Current assets	$ 4,480,902	Current liabilities	$ 4,343,717
Net property, plant & equipment	4,461,543	Long-term debt	932,898
Other assets	2,183,155	Deferred items	153,279
		Other liabilities	875,524
		*Stockholders' equity	4,820,182
Total	$11,125,600	Total	$11,125,600

*774,449,226 shares common stock outstanding.

Consolidated Income Statement

Years Ended Dec. 31	Thousands — — — — Net Sales	Net Income	Per Share[a] — — — Earnings	Cash Dividends	Common Stock Price Range[a] Calendar Year
1996	$11,013,460	$1,882,033	$2.41	$ .93	57-3/8 — 38-1/8
1995	10,012,194	1,688,700	2.12	.82	44-3/4 — 30-5/8
1994	9,156,009	1,516,683	1.87	.74	34 — 25-3/8
1993	8,407,843	1,399,126	1.69	.66	30-7/8 — 22-5/8
1992	7,851,912	1,239,057	1.47	.56[b]	34-1/8 — 26-1/8

[a]Adjusted to reflect a 2-for-1 stock split in May 1992.
[b]Includes one-time payment of $.0025 per share for rights redemption in August 1992.

Transfer Agent & Registrar: The First National Bank of Boston

General Counsel:	José M. de Lasa, Sr. V.P.
Investor Relations:	Catherine V. Babington, V.P.
Human Resources:	Ellen M. Walvoord, Sr. V.P.
Mgt. Info. Svcs.:	Kenneth W. Farmer, V.P.
Auditors:	Arthur Andersen LLP

Traded (Symbol):
   NYSE, CSE, PSE, PHL, BOS, CIN, LON, SWISS (ABT)

Stockholders:	99,513
Employees:	52,817
Annual Meeting:	In April
Internet:	www.abbott.com

ABC Rail Products Corporation

200 South Michigan Avenue, #1300, Chicago, Illinois 60604-2402
Telephone: (312) 322-0360

ABC Rail Products Corporation is a leader in the engineering, manufacturing, and marketing of replacement products and original equipment for the freight railroad and rail transit industries. The company's products include specialty trackwork, such as rail crossings and switches, and mechanical products, such as railcar, locomotive, and idler wheels, mounted wheel sets, and metal brake shoes. In December 1996, the company acquired American Systems Technologies, Inc., a Verona, Wisconsin-based railway signal installation and maintenance company. Incorporated in Delaware in 1987; present name adopted in 1993.

Directors (In addition to indicated officers)

Norman M. Doerr
Jean-Pierre M. Ergas
Donald R. Gant

Clarence E. Johnson
James E. Martin
George W. Peck IV

Officers (Directors*)

*Donald W. Grinter, Chm. & C.E.O.
*D. Chisholm MacDonald, Sr. V.P. & C.F.O.

David G. Kleeschulte, Pres.—China Inv. Corp.;
V.P.& Gen. Mgr.—Wheel Oper.

Consolidated Balance Sheet As of July 31, 1996 (000 omitted)

Assets		Liabilities & Stockholders' Equity	
Current assets	$ 76,268	Current liabilities	$ 48,406
Net property, plant & equipment	72,749	Long-term debt	49,443
Other assets	21,087	Other liabilities	9,581
		*Stockholders' equity	62,674
Total	$170,104	Total	$170,104

*8,271,026 shares common stock outstanding.

Consolidated Income Statement

Years Ended July 31	Thousands — — — — Net Sales	Net Income	Per Share[a] — — — Earnings	Cash Dividends	Common Stock Price Range[ab] Calendar Year
1996	$240,664	$ 6,726	$ .81	$ .00	25-1/2 — 14-3/8
1995	243,229	9,657[c]	1.21[c]	.00	27-5/8 — 19-3/8
1994	187,176	5,197[d]	.79[d]	.00	23-1/4 — 14-1/8
1993	148,676	3,555	.81	.00	15 — 12
1992	143,412	(79)[e]	(.02)[e]	.00	

[a]Adjusted to reflect a 2,000-for-1 stock split in September 1993.
[b]Initial public offering in December 1993.
[c]Includes cumulative effect of accounting change of $1,214,000 and an extraordinary charge of $814,000 ($.25 per share).
[d]Includes an extraordinary charge of $1,690,000 ($.26 per share).
[e]Includes the cumulative gain of an accounting change of $1,079,000 ($.27 per share).

Transfer Agent & Registrar: American Stock Transfer & Trust Co.	
General Counsel: Jones, Day, Reavis & Pogue	**Auditors:** Arthur Andersen LLP
Investor Relations: D. Chisholm MacDonald, Sr. V.P.	**Traded (Symbol):** NASDAQ (ABCR)
	Stockholders: 60
Human Resources: Joseph A. Parsons, V.P.	**Employees:** 1,449
Mgt. Info. Svcs.: Thomas F. Coleman	**Annual Meeting:** In November

AccuMed International, Inc.

920 North Franklin Street, Suite 402, Chicago, Illinois 60610
Telephone: (312) 642-9200

AccuMed International Inc. designs, manufactures, and markets diagnostic screening products for clinical laboratories serving the cytopathology and microbiology markets. The company's primary focus is on the development of cytopathology products that support the review and analysis of Pap smears in order to improve the quality of cell analysis and increase accuracy and productivity in the laboratory. The company's major products include AcCell® Series 2000 automated slide handling and microscopy workstation. The company is headquartered in Chicago, Illinois, with additional facilities in Westlake, Ohio, and East Grinstead, Sussex, England. In October 1996, the company acquired RADCO Ventures, Inc. and a two-thirds equity interest in Oncometrics Imaging Corp. Incorporated in California in 1988 as Alamar Biosciences, Inc. Reincorporated in Delaware in 1995; present name adopted in 1995.

Directors   (In addition to indicated officers)

Don Gaines
Jack H. Halperin
Paul F. Lavallee

Joseph W. Plandowski
Robert L. Priddy
Leonard M. Schiller

Officers   (Directors*)

* Peter P. Gombrich, Chm., Pres. & C.E.O.
Michael D. Burke, Sr. V.P. & Pres.—
  Microbiology Div.
Richard A. Domanik, Ph.D., Sr. V.P.

Norman J. Pressman, Ph.D., Sr. V.P. &
  Pres.—Cytopathology Div.
Leonard R. Prange, V.P., C.O.O. & C.F.O.
Joyce L. Wallach, Gen. Coun. & Secy.

Consolidated Balance Sheet   As of December 31, 1996 (000 omitted)

Assets		Liabilities & Stockholders' Equity	
Current assets	$ 7,035	Current liabilities	$ 3,656
Fixed assets, net	1,696	Long-term debt	231
Notes receivable	214	Minority interest	457
Other assets	5,535	*Stockholders' equity	10,136
Total	$14,480	Total	$14,480

*20,854,157 shares common stock outstanding.

Consolidated Income Statement

Years Ended Dec. 31	Thousands — — — — Net Sales	Net Income	Per Share — — — Earnings	Cash Dividends	Common Stock Price Range Calendar Year
1996	$6,222	$(11,574)[a]	$ (.68)[a]	$ .00	9-3/8 — 1-1/8
1995[b]	100	(5,472)	(.49)	.00	1-3/4 — 1/2
1995[c]	515	(3,760)	(.59)	.00	

[a]Includes a write-off of $5,957,927 ($.35 per share) for acquired in-process research and development costs.
[b]Three months ended December 31, 1995. In 1995, the company changed to calendar year reporting.
[c]Twelve months ended September 30, 1995.

Transfer Agent & Registrar: American Stock Transfer & Trust Co.

General Counsel:	Joyce L. Wallach	Traded (Symbol):	NASDAQ (ACMI)
		Stockholders:	1,536
Human Resources:	Lynn Fleischhacker	Employees:	170
Auditors:	KPMG Peat Marwick LLP	Annual Meeting:	In May

Acme Metals Incorporated

13500 South Perry Avenue, Riverdale, Illinois 60627-1182
Telephone: (708) 849-2500

Acme Metals Incorporated, a holding company for four subsidiaries, is an integrated manufacturer of steel and steel products, including steel strapping products, sheet and strip products, semi-finished steel, iron products, welded steel tube, and auto and truck jacks. Acme Steel Company sells flat-rolled steel strip and related products primarily to industrial equipment, processor, automotive, agricultural, and pipe and tube converter markets. Acme Packaging Corporation markets strapping products, consisting mainly of steel strapping, strapping tools, seals, and stitching wire to industrial customers. Universal Tool & Stamping Company, Inc. is a manufacturer and distributor of automotive and truck jacks and related equipment to domestic and foreign automobile producers operating in the United States. Alpha Tube Corporation is a leading producer of high-quality welded carbon steel tubing for a variety of consumer and industrial markets. Reincorporated in Delaware in 1992.

Directors (In addition to indicated officers)

Buddy Davis	Reynold C. MacDonald
Edward G. Jordan	Allan L. Rayfield
Andrew R. Laidlaw	William P. Sovey
John T. Lane	L. Frederick Sutherland
Frank A. LePage	William R. Wilson

Officers (Directors*)

*Brian W.H. Marsden, Chm.
*Stephen D. Bennett, Pres. & C.E.O.
Gerald J. Shope, V.P.—Hum. Res.
Edward P. Weber, Jr., V.P., Gen. Coun. & Secy.

Jerry F. Williams, V.P.—Fin. & Admin. & C.F.O.
James W. Hoekwater, Treas.
Gregory J. Pritz, Cont.

Consolidated Balance Sheet As of December 31, 1996 (000 omitted)

Assets		Liabilities & Stockholders' Equity	
Current assets	$182,837	Current liabilities	$115,940
Net property, plant & equipment	560,725	Long-term liabilities	429,108
Investments & other assets	62,187	*Stockholders' equity	260,701
Total	$805,749	Total	$805,749

*11,632,551 shares common stock outstanding.

Consolidated Income Statement

Years Ended Abt. Dec. 31	Thousands — — — — Net Sales	Net Income	Per Share — — — Earnings	Cash Dividends	Common Stock Price Range Calendar Year
1996	$498,242	$ 2,667	$ .23	$ .00	21-5/8 — 13-7/8
1995	521,619	28,246	2.44	.00	19-1/4 — 13-3/4
1994	522,880	16,971a	2.16a	.00	27-1/4 — 15
1993	457,406	6,259	1.15	.00	20-3/4 — 12-1/4
1992b	391,562	(53,172)c	(9.85)c	.00	19-3/4 — 11

aIncludes an extraordinary charge of $1,787,000 ($.22 per share).
bReclassified to conform to the current year's presentation.
cIncludes FAS 106 and FAS 109, resulting in a one-time, non-cash charge of $50,323,000 ($9.32 per share).

Transfer Agent & Registrar: First Chicago Trust Co. of New York; Montreal Trust Co.

General Counsel:	Edward P. Weber, Jr., V.P.	Traded (Symbol):	NYSE (AMI)
Investor Relations:	Joel L. Hawthorne, Dir.	Stockholders:	6,000
Human Resources:	Gerald J. Shope, V.P.	Employees:	2,840
Mgt. Info. Svcs.:	Gregory J. Pritz, Cont.	Annual Meeting:	In April
Auditors:	Price Waterhouse LLP	Internet:	www.acmemetals.com

Aerial Communications, Inc.

8410 West Bryn Mawr Avenue, Suite 1100, Chicago, Illinois 60631-3486
Telephone: (773) 399-4200

Aerial Communications, Inc. (formerly American Portable Telecom, Inc.) is a development stage company engaged in acquiring personal communications service (PCS) licenses from the Federal Communications Commission, constructing PCS networks in major trading areas, and offering wireless PCS communications in these areas. Aerial, an 82.8 percent-owned subsidiary of Telephone and Data Systems, Inc., has licenses to provide PCS in areas covering 27.3 million of the U.S. population. The company's markets include Columbus, Houston, Kansas City, Minneapolis-St. Paul, Pittsburgh, and Tampa-St. Petersburg-Orlando. In April 1996, the company completed an initial public offering of 12,250,000 shares of common stock. In March 1997, Aerial began offering PCS to its customers in the Columbus market, and plans to launch service in the other markets by the end of the second quarter. Incorporated in Delaware in 1991; present name adopted in 1996.

Directors (In addition to indicated officers)

James Barr III
LeRoy T. Carlson
Walter C.D. Carlson
John D. Foster

Rudolph E. Hornacek
Murray L. Swanson
Thomas W. Wilson

Officers (Directors*)

*LeRoy T. Carlson, Jr., Chm.
*Donald W. Warkentin, Pres. & C.E.O.
Joseph E. Griffin, V.P.—Bus. Dev.
David B. Lowry, V.P.—Eng. & Oper.
David E. McCarthy, V.P.—Info. Tech.

Carol J. Ogren, V.P.—Hum. Res.
Gerald N. Rhodes, V.P.—Mktg. & Sales
*J. Clarke Smith, V.P.—Fin. & Admin., C.F.O. & Treas.
Michael G. Hron, Secy.

Consolidated Balance Sheet   As of December 31, 1996 (000 omitted)

Assets		Liabilities & Stockholders' Equity	
Current assets	$ 38,831	Current liabilities	$119,326
Net property, plant & equipment	18,592	Long-term debt	103,743
Other assets	615,404	Deferred items	11,973
		*Stockholders' equity	437,785
Total	$672,827	Total	$672,827

*71,359,460 shares common stock outstanding.

Consolidated Income Statement

Years Ended Dec. 31	Thousands — — — — Total Income	Net Income	Per Share[a] — — — — Earnings	Cash Dividends	Common Stock Price Range[a] Calendar Year
1996	$7,924	$(37,921)	$ (.56)	$ .00	17-3/4 — 6-5/8
1995	49	(6,468)	(.11)		
1994	2	(1,283)	(.02)		
1993	2	(67)			

[a]Initial public offering in April 1996.

Transfer Agent & Registrar:	Harris Trust and Savings Bank			
General Counsel:	Sidley & Austin	Traded (Symbol):	NASDAQ (AERL)
Investor Relations:	J. Clarke Smith, V.P.	Stockholders:	2,836
Human Resources:	Carol J. Ogren, V.P.	Employees:	915
Mgt. Info. Svcs.:	David E. McCarthy, V.P.	Annual Meeting:	In May
Auditors:	Arthur Andersen LLP	Internet:	www.aerial1.com

Alberto-Culver Company

2525 Armitage Avenue, Melrose Park, Illinois 60160-1163
Telephone: (708) 450-3000

Alberto-Culver Company and its subsidiaries manufacture and distribute a varied line of food products and mass-marketed personal use products for men and women, including the Alberto VO5 line of hair care products, as well as the Alberto VO5 Hair Therapy, Consort, St. Ives, Swiss Formula, TRESemmé, TCB, and Indola lines of hair care products. Alberto-Culver's institutional and industrial products segment produces professional hair care products for barbershop and beauty salon suppliers. Household/grocery products include Baker's Joy; SugarTwin; Kleen Guard household products; Static Guard; Mrs. Dash low-sodium products; and Molly McButter products. Manufacturing and warehouse facilities are located in Melrose Park, Illinois, and Chatsworth, California. Subsidiaries include: Sally Beauty Company, Inc., a wholesale distributor of beauty salon and barbershop supplies and equipment; Alberto-Culver USA, Inc.; and Alberto-Culver International, Inc. Alberto-Culver's products are manufactured in seven countries and distributed in more than 100. In July 1996, the company sold its Milani, DiaFoods, Thick-It, and Smithers institutional food service brands to St. Louis-based Precision Foods, Inc. Incorporated in Delaware in 1961.

Directors (In addition to indicated officers)

A. Robert Abboud	Robert P. Gwinn	Allan B. Muchin	Harold M. Visotsky
A.G. Atwater, Jr.	Lee W. Jennings	Robert H. Rock	William W. Wirtz

Officers (Directors*)

*Leonard H. Lavin, Chm.
*Howard B. Bernick, Pres. & C.E.O.
*Bernice E. Lavin, V. Chm., Secy. & Treas.
*Carol L. Bernick, Exec. V.P. & Pres./Alberto-Culver USA
William J. Cernugel, Sr. V.P.—Fin. & Cont.
James J. Chickarello, V.P.—U.S.A. Oper.
Wesley C. Davidson, V.P.—Corp. Dev.
Raymond W. Gass, V.P. & Gen. Coun.
Douglas E. Meneely, V.P.—Hum. Res.
Janice J. Miller, V.P.—Market Res.
Thomas Monaghan, V.P.—New Bus. Dev.

Thomas J. Pallone, V.P.—Res. and Dev.
Richard N. Paulsen, V.P.—Info. Sys.
Daniel B. Stone, V.P.—Commun.
John G. Horsman, Jr., Pres.—Intl. Grp.
Michael H. Renzulli, Pres.—Sally Beauty Co., Inc.
John T. Boone, Grp. V.P.—Domestic Cons. Prod.
Anthony J. Borgese, V.P.—Sales/Consumer Prod. Div.
Stuart A. Fine, V.P.—Mktg./St. Ives
Andrew C. Langert, V.P.—Fin./Alberto-Culver USA
Ronald P. Marconet, V.P.—Oper./St. Ives
Kristin B. Muntean, V.P.—Mktg./Consumer Prod. Div.

Consolidated Balance Sheet As of September 30, 1996 (000 omitted)

Assets		Liabilities & Stockholders' Equity	
Current assets	$512,718	Current liabilities	$286,595
Net property, plant & equipment	175,920	Long-term debt	61,548
Goodwill, net	107,603	Deferred items	16,582
Trade names & other tangible assets, net	76,877	Convertible subordinated debentures	100,000
Other assets	36,148	Other liabilities	19,445
		*Stockholders' equity	425,096
Total	$909,266	Total	$909,266

*11,048,600 shares Class A common and 16,766,240 shares Class B common stock outstanding.

Consolidated Income Statement

Years Ended Sept. 30	Thousands — — — — Net Sales	Net Income	Per Share — — — — Earnings	Cash Dividends[a]	Common Stock Price Range[b] Calendar Year
1996	$1,590,409	$62,744	$2.22[c]	$ .35	50 — 32-1/2
1995	1,358,219	52,651	1.89[d]	.31	32-1/2 — 21-3/4
1994	1,216,119	44,068	1.57	.27	27-3/8 — 19-3/8
1993	1,147,990	41,272	1.44	.27[e]	28-1/4 — 20-1/4
1992	1,091,286	38,616	1.36	.24	32 — 21-1/4

[a]Class A common stock dividends are equal to those of Class B common stock.
[b]Class B common stock.
[c]Fully diluted $2.11 per share. Due to the July 1995 issuance of $100,000,000 of ten-year 5-1/2% convertible subordinated debentures, the company is required to report earnings and weighted average shares outstanding on a primary and fully-diluted basis.
[d]Fully-diluted $1.87 per share.
[e]Includes a one-time extraordinary dividend of $.02 per share.

Transfer Agent & Registrar:	The First National Bank of Boston		
General Counsel:	Raymond W. Gass, V.P.	Auditors:	KPMG Peat Marwick LLP
Investor Relations:	Daniel B. Stone, V.P.	Traded (Symbol): NYSE (ACVA, Class A; ACV, Class B common stock)	
Human Resources:	Douglas E. Meneely, V.P.	Stockholders:	2,328
		Employees:	10,700
Mgt. Info. Svcs.:	Richard N. Paulsen, V.P.	Annual Meeting:	In January

Allegiance Corporation

1430 Waukegan Road, McGaw Park, Illinois 60085-6787
Telephone: (847) 689-8410

Allegiance Corporation is America's largest provider of heathcare products and cost-management services for hospitals and other healthcare providers. Allegiance offers more than 200,000 products manufactured at the company's own 22 plants or obtained from hundreds of independent suppliers. These products are sold through 60 company-owned distribution centers across the country. Allegiance was formed in June 1996 as a wholly owned subsidiary of Baxter International Inc., responsible for Baxter's United States healthcare distribution, surgical and respiratory therapy products, and healthcare cost management businesses. In September 1996, Allegiance was spun off from Baxter through a tax-free dividend of Allegiance common stock to Baxter shareholders, in the form of one Allegiance share for every five shares of Baxter stock owned. In December 1996, Allegiance agreed to acquire West Hudson & Co., a health care consulting firm with revenues of nearly $40 million a year. Incorporated in 1996 in Delaware.

Directors (In addition to indicated officers)

Kenneth D. Bloem	Connie R. Curran	David W. Grainger
Silas S. Cathcart	Arthur F. Golden	Michael D. O'Halleran

Officers (Directors*)

*Lester B. Knight, Chm. & C.E.O.
*Joseph F. Damico, Pres. & C.O.O.
William L. Feather, Sr. V.P., Gen. Coun. & Secy.
Peter B. McKee, Sr. V.P. & C.F.O.
Kathy Brittain White, Sr. V.P. & C.I.O.

Richard C. Adloff, Corp. V.P. & Cont.
Robert B. DeBaun, Corp. V.P.—Hum. Res.
Mark J. Ehlert, Corp. V.P.—Qual. & Reg. Aff.
Leonard G. Kuhr, Corp. V.P. & Treas.

Consolidated Balance Sheet   As of December 31, 1996 (000 omitted)

Assets		Liabilities & Stockholders' Equity	
Current assets	$1,335,500	Current liabilities	$ 698,100
Net property, plant & equipment	837,900	Long-term debt	1,106,600
Other assets	625,800	Deferred income taxes	107,400
		Other liabilities	59,400
		*Stockholders' equity	827,700
Total	$2,799,200	Total	$2,799,200

*54,977,000 shares common stock outstanding.

Consolidated Income Statement

Years Ended Dec. 31	Thousands — — — — Net Sales	Net Income	Per Share[a] — — — — Earnings	Cash Dividends	Common Stock Price Range[a] Calendar Year
1996	$4,387,200	$(477,700)[b]	$(8.70)	$ .10	28-1/8 — 15
1995[c]	4,921,900	272,600			
1994[c]	5,108,600	214,900			
1993[cd]	5,019,300	(68,400)			
1992[c]	4,860,900	242,800			

[a]Spun off from Baxter International Inc. in September 1996.
[b]Includes a charge of $550,000,000 for the writedown of goodwill. Also includes $62,800,000 of non-recurring costs for facility consolidations and other asset writedowns, $13,200,000 of non-recurring costs related to the company's spinoff from Baxter, and $19,500,000 of non-recurring costs related to litigation expenses.
[c]Data for 1992-95 includes certain businesses that were divested in 1994 and 1995.
[d]Includes a pretax charge of $484,000,000 for restructuring.

Transfer Agent & Registrar:	First Chicago Trust Co. of New York		
General Counsel:	William L. Feather, Sr. V.P.	Traded (Symbol):	NYSE, CSE (AEH)
Investor Relations:	Jessica M. Fisher	Stockholders:	58,000
Human Resources:	Robert B. DeBaun, Corp. V.P.	Employees:	20,700
Mgt. Info. Svcs.:	Kathy Brittain White, Sr. V.P.	Annual Meeting:	In May
Auditors:	Price Waterhouse LLP	Internet:	www.allegiance.net

Alliance Bancorp

One Grant Square, Hinsdale, Illinois 60521
Telephone: (630) 323-1776

Alliance Bancorp (formerly Hinsdale Financial Corporation) is the holding company for Liberty Federal Bank. The bank conducts its business through 15 retail banking offices located in Bensenville, Chicago, Clarendon Hills, Elmhurst, Forest Park, Glenview, Hinsdale, Lisle, Morton Grove, Norridge, Oak Park, West Chicago, and Westmont, Illinois. The bank is principally engaged in the business of attracting retail deposits from the general public and investing those funds in mortgage loans and mortgage-backed securities, secured primarily by one- to four-family residential real estate loans, consumer loans, and investment securities. In February 1997, the company (then operating as Hinsdale Financial Corporation) completed a merger with Liberty Bancorp, Inc., with Hinsdale as the surviving company. Upon consumation of the merger, the company changed its name to Alliance Bancorp. Incorporated in Delaware in 1992.

Directors   (In addition to indicated officers)

Edward J. Burns	Edward J. Nusrala
Howard A. Davis	William C. O'Donnell
Whit G. Hughes	William R. Rybak
Howard R. Jones	Russell F. Stephens, Jr.
H. Verne Loeppert	Donald E. Sveen
David D. Mill	Vernon B. Thomas, Jr.

Officers   (Directors*)

*Fredric G. Novy, Chm.
*Kenne P. Bristol, Pres. & C.E.O.

Richard A. Hojnicki, Exec. V.P., C.F.O. & Secy.

Consolidated Balance Sheet[a]   As of December 31, 1996 (000 omitted)

Assets		Liabilities & Stockholders' Equity	
Cash & due from banks	$ 7,645		
Investment securities	1,998	Deposits	$462,869
Interest-bearing deposits	19,596	Borrowings	131,900
Mortgage-backed securities	5,140	Other liabilities	16,569
Loans, net	609,371	*Stockholders' equity	56,626
Net property & equipment	6,592		
Other assets	17,622		
Total	$667,964		
		Total	$667,964

[a]For Hinsdale Financial Corporation.
*2,790,085 shares common stock outstanding.

Consolidated Income Statement[a]

Years Ended Dec. 31	Thousands — — — —		Per Share[b] — — — —		Common Stock
	Total Income	Net Income	Earnings	Cash Dividends	Price Range[b] Calendar Year
1996[c]	$14,254	$1,079	$ .38	$ .00	
1996[d]	58,648	3,074	1.10	.00	27-3/4 — 21
1995[d]	52,692	4,459	1.61	.00	23 — 16-5/8
1994[d]	42,110	4,716	1.69	.00	20-5/8 — 15-3/4
1993[d]	39,820	4,598	1.65	.00	18-3/4 — 12-3/8

[a]For Hinsdale Financial Corporation.
[b]Adjusted to reflect a 25% stock dividend in October 1995.
[c]Three months ended December 31, 1996. Company changed to calendar year reporting in 1996.
[d]Twelve months ended September 30. Stock prices represent calendar years.

Transfer Agent & Registrar:	Harris Trust and Savings Bank		
General Counsel:	Rock Fusco Reynolds & Garvy	**Traded (Symbol):**	NASDAQ (ABCL)
Investor Relations:	Richard A. Hojnicki, Exec. V.P.	**Stockholders:**	410
Human Resources:	Susan Schliep, V.P.	**Employees:**	345
Mgt. Info. Svcs.:	Tony Rosado, V.P.	**Annual Meeting:**	In May
Auditors:	KPMG Peat Marwick LLP	**Internet:**	www.libertyfb.com

Allied Products Corporation

10 South Riverside Plaza, Suite 400, Chicago, Illinois 60606
Telephone: (312) 454-1020

Allied Products Corporation manufactures and markets large metal stamping presses, as well as implements and machinery used in agriculture, landscaping, and ground maintenance businesses. Agricultural equipment includes farm implements and Zero Turn® mowers, landscape tools, and turf and golf course mowing equipment. Industrial products include metal forming presses and custom compounding of thermoplastic resins. The original predecessor of the business was a partnership known as Richard Brothers Die Works, founded in 1915 to manufacture automotive dies. Major divisions include Bush Hog, Verson, and Coz. Incorporated in 1928; reincorporated in Delaware in 1967.

Directors   (In addition to indicated officers)

Lloyd A. Drexler
William D. Fischer
Stanley J. Goldring
John E. Jones

John W. Puth
Mitchell I. Quain
Saul S. Sherman

Officers   (Directors*)

*Richard A. Drexler, Chm., Pres. & C.E.O.
*Kenneth B. Light, Exec. V.P., C.F.O. & C.A.O.
 Martin A. German, Sr. V.P.
 Bobby M. Middlebrooks, Sr. V.P.

David B. Corwine, V.P., Gen. Coun. & Secy.
Robert J. Fleck, V.P.—Acct. & Chf. Acct. Off.
Patrick J. Riley, V.P. & Treas.

Consolidated Balance Sheet   As of December 31, 1996 (000 omitted)

Assets		Liabilities & Stockholders' Equity	
Current assets	$125,260	Current liabilities	$ 74,460
Net property, plant & equipment	38,386	Long-term debt	489
Other assets	8,303	Other liabilities	3,547
		*Stockholders' equity	93,453
Total	$171,949	Total	$171,949

*8,459,773 shares common stock outstanding.

Consolidated Income Statement

Years Ended Dec. 31	Thousands — — — — Net Sales	Net Income	Per Share — — — Earnings	Cash Dividends	Common Stock Price Range Calendar Year
1996	$274,414	$ 19,004	$ 2.11	$ .20	31-1/8 — 20-5/8
1995	260,861	33,989	3.48	.08	24-1/8 — 13-3/8
1994	215,529	14,333	1.37	.00	17-3/8 — 12
1993	217,988	15,284	1.47	.00	15-7/8 — 2-3/4
1992	195,341	(24,954)	(3.32)	.00	4 — 1-1/2

Transfer Agent & Registrar: LaSalle National Trust, N.A.

General Counsel:	David B. Corwine, V.P.	Traded (Symbol):	NYSE(ADP), PSE(ADPP)
Investor Relations:	Kenneth B. Light, Exec. V.P.	Stockholders:	2,200
Human Resources:	Kenneth B. Light, Exec. V.P.	Employees:	1,500
Mgt. Info. Svcs:	Kenneth B. Light, Exec. V.P.	Annual Meeting:	In May
Auditors:	Coopers & Lybrand L.L.P.	Internet:	www.allprod.com

The Allstate Corporation

Allstate Plaza, 2775 Sanders Road, Northbrook, Illinois 60062-6127
Telephone: (847) 402-5000

The Allstate Corporation is the parent of Allstate Insurance Company, a leading U.S. property liability and life insurer. Allstate has more than 20 million customers, and its name and the "You're in Good Hands" trademark are widely recognized. Allstate's primary business is the sale of private passenger automobile and homeowners insurance. It maintains national market shares in each of those lines of approximately 12 percent. The company also sells life insurance, annuity, and group pension products. In 1996, the company sold its independent agent-generated commercial business and its domestic and foreign reinsurance operations. On June 30, 1995, Allstate became a 100 percent publicly owned company when Sears, Roebuck and Co. spun off its 80.3 percent ownership of the company. Incorporated in Delaware in 1992.

Directors (In addition to indicated officers)

James G. Andress
Warren L. Batts
Edward A. Brennan
James M. Denny

Christopher F. Edley
Michael A. Miles
Joshua I. Smith
Mary Alice Taylor

Officers (Directors*)

*Jerry D. Choate, Chm. & C.E.O.
Edward M. Liddy, Pres. & C.O.O.
Casey J. Sylla, Sr. V.P. & Chf. Inv. Off.

Thomas J. Wilson, V.P. & C.F.O.
Robert W. Pike, V.P., Secy. & Gen. Coun.

Consolidated Balance Sheet   As of December 31, 1996 (000 omitted)

Assets		Liabilities & Stockholders' Equity	
Investments	$58,329,000	Insurance reserves	$23,669,000
Premium installment receivables	2,691,000	Contractholder funds	20,120,000
Deferred policy acquisition costs	2,614,000	Unearned premiums	6,174,000
Reinsurance recoverable, net	2,147,000	Debt	1,386,000
Other assets	3,176,000	Other liabilities	3,418,000
Separate accounts	5,551,000	Separate accounts	5,539,000
		Mandatorily redeemable preferred securities	750,000
		*Stockholders' equity	13,452,000
Total	$74,508,000	Total	$74,508,000

*441,458,000 shares common stock outstanding.

Consolidated Income Statement

Years Ended Dec. 31	Thousands — — — — Total Revenues	Net Income	Per Share[a] — — — — Earnings	Cash Dividends	Common Stock Price Range[a] Calendar Year
1996	$24,299,000	$ 2,075,000	$ 4.63	$ .85	60-7/8 — 37-3/8
1995	22,793,000	1,904,000	4.24	.78	42-3/8 — 23-1/2
1994	21,109,000	484,000	1.08	.72	29-7/8 — 22-5/8
1993	20,602,000	1,302,000	2.99[b]	.36[c]	34-1/4 — 27-1/8
1992	19,984,000	(825,000)[d]	(1.91)[bd]		

[a]Initial public offering in June 1993.
[b]Pro forma.
[c]Represents dividends per share since becoming a public company in June 1993.
[d]Includes FAS 106 and FAS 112, resulting in a charge to net earnings of $325,600,000 ($.75 per share).

Transfer Agent & Registrar: Harris Trust and Savings Bank

General Counsel:	Robert W. Pike, V.P.	Traded (Symbol):	NYSE, CSE (ALL)
Investor Relations:	Robert Block, Asst. V.P.	Stockholders:	220,201
Human Resources:	Joan Crockett, Sr. V.P.	Employees:	48,200
Mgt. Info. Svcs.:	Frank Pollard, Sr. V.P.	Annual Meeting:	In May
Auditors:	Deloitte & Touche LLP	Internet:	www.allstate.com

Alternative Resources Corporation

100 Tri-State International, Suite 300, Lincolnshire, Illinois 60069
Telephone: (847) 317-1000

Alternative Resources Corporation is a leading provider of technical services, including component outsourcing and project-based resources, for information technology operations of more than 850 Fortune 1000 and mid-sized companies. The company operates through a network of more than 50 offices in the U.S. and Canada. Alternative Resources' technical employee resource base includes more than 40,000 individuals skilled in the areas of help desk/desktop and workstation (PC/LAN); client server support; voice and data communications (LAN/WAN); and mainframe and mid-range computer operations. Incorporated in Delaware in 1988.

Directors   (In addition to indicated officers)

JoAnne Brandes
Michael E. Harris
Raymond R. Hipp

A. Donald Rully
Bruce R. Smith

Officers   (Directors*)

*Larry I. Kane, Chm. & C.E.O.
*Richard K. Williams, Pres. & C.O.O.
*Robert V. Carlson, Exec. V.P.

Bradley K. Lamers, V.P.—Fin., C.F.O., Treas. & Secy.
Silvia U. Masini, V.P.

Consolidated Balance Sheet   As of December 31, 1996 (000 omitted)

Assets		Liabilities & Stockholders' Equity	
Current assets	$60,203	Current liabilities	$ 8,391
Net property, plant & equipment	2,880	Deferred items	345
Other assets	1,320	*Stockholders' equity	55,667
Total	$64,403	Total	$64,403

*15,347,027 shares common stock outstanding.

Consolidated Income Statement

Years Ended Dec. 31	Thousands ———— Revenues	Net Income	Per Share[a] ———— Earnings	Cash Dividends	Common Stock Price Range[ab] Calendar Year
1996	$196,728	$13,218	$ .83	$ .00	44-1/2 — 13-1/2
1995	154,173	10,358	.65	.00	34 — 14-3/4
1994	94,478	6,190	.51	.00	15-7/8 — 8-1/8
1993	53,061	3,226	.67		
1992	27,948	1,601[c]	.32[c]		

[a]Adjusted to reflect secondary offerings in June 1995 and November 1994, a 2-for-1 stock split in May 1995, and a 7-for-1 stock split in February 1994.
[b]Initial public offering in May 1994.
[c]Includes an extraordinary item (utilization of net operating loss carryforward) of $479,731 ($.11 per share).

Transfer Agent & Registrar:	Harris Trust and Savings Bank		
General Counsel:	McDermott, Will & Emery	Traded (Symbol):	NASDAQ (ALRC)
Investor Relations:	Susan H. Fisher, Dir.	Stockholders:	150
Human Resources:	Sheryl Eshkenazi, Dir.	Employees:	4,500
Mgt. Info. Svcs.:	Mark Lovendahl, Dir.	Annual Meeting:	In April
Auditors:	KPMG Peat Marwick LLP	Internet:	www.alrc.com

AMCOL International Corporation

One North Arlington, 1500 West Shure Drive, Suite 500, Arlington Heights, Illinois 60004-7803
Telephone: (847) 394-8730

AMCOL International Corporation is a supplier of specialty chemicals and minerals, providing products and technologies for a wide range of industrial and consumer-related markets worldwide. Established in 1927 under the name American Colloid Company, AMCOL is a leading supplier of bentonite, a non-metallic clay primarily composed of a mineral called montmorillonite. The absorbent polymers segment, Chemdal International, manufactures and markets absorbent polymers, a specialty chemical. The company is particularly focused on the polymer category known as superabsorbent polymers (SAP), widely used in personal care products such as baby diapers, adult incontinence products, and sanitary napkins. The environmental segment, Colloid Environmental Technologies Co. (CETCO), competes in highly specialized market sectors, many of which utilize bentonite. CETCO supplies building materials, drilling products, landfill liners, and wastewater treatment products. The minerals division, American Colloid Company, mines, processes, and distributes bentonite and products with similar applications to industrial and consumer markets, including metalcasting, well drilling, cat litter, and agriculture. The company also operates a trucking and freight business, which provides services to both the company's plants and outside customers. AMCOL operates 32 processing plants in the United States, nine of which include mining operations, as well as processing plants in Australia, Canada, China, England, and Thailand. AMCOL's newest venture, Nanocor, Inc., is in the field of nanocomposite technologies, where it has developed a patented technology that disperses nanoscale particles of chemically-modified clays into plastic resins, improving strength, heat stability, and barrier properties. Pilot plant began production in 1996; commercial introduction of the technology is anticipated in 1997. Other subsidiaries include: Ameri-Co Carriers, Inc.; Nationwide Freight Services, Inc.; Chemdal, Ltd. (England); American Colloid Company, Ltd. (Canada); Volclay, Ltd.; CETCO Europe Ltd. (England); Volclay De Mexico; CETCO Pty. Ltd.; and Volclay Pty. Ltd. (Australia). Incorporated in South Dakota in 1924 as Bentonite Mining & Manufacturing Co.; reincorporated in Delaware in 1959; present name adopted in 1995.

Directors (In addition to indicated officers)

C. Eugene Ray, Chm.	James A. McClurg	Audrey Weaver
Arthur Brown	Jay D. Proops	Paul C. Weaver
Robert E. Driscoll III	Clarence O. Redman, Secy.	
Raymond A. Foos	Dale E. Stahl	

Officers (Directors*)

*John Hughes, Pres. & C.E.O.
 Roger P. Palmer, Sr. V.P. & Pres.—CETCO
*Paul G. Shelton, Sr. V.P., C.F.O. & Pres.—Trans. Div.

Lawrence E. Washow, Sr. V.P. & Pres.—Chemdal Corp.
Peter L. Maul, V.P. & Pres.—Nanocor, Inc.
Frank B. Wright, Jr., V.P. & Pres.—American Colloid Co.

Consolidated Balance Sheet   As of December 31, 1996 (000 omitted)

Assets		Liabilities & Stockholders' Equity	
Current assets	$148,475	Current liabilities	$ 51,870
Net property, plant & equipment	180,876	Long-term debt	118,855
Intangible assets	15,217	Other liabilities	12,579
Other assets	6,140	*Stockholders' equity	167,404
Total	$350,708	Total	$350,708

*19,529,659 shares common stock outstanding.

Consolidated Income Statement

Years Ended Dec. 31	Thousands — — — — Net Sales	Net Income[a]	Per Share[b] — — — Earnings[a]	Cash Dividends	Common Stock Price Range[b] Calendar Year
1996	$405,347	$15,225	$ .78	$ .28	17 — 10-3/4
1995	347,688	17,771	.90	.26	18-1/4 — 11-7/8
1994	265,443	15,283	.78	.24	25-1/4 — 10-1/2
1993	219,151	13,120	.76	.20	33 — 9-1/8
1992	182,669	8,506	.52	.16	9-3/8 — 3-7/8

[a]Restated to reflect FAS 109.
[b]Adjusted to reflect a 2-for-1 stock split in June 1993 and a 3-for-2 stock split in January 1993.

Transfer Agent & Registrar: Harris Trust and Savings Bank

General Counsel:	Keck, Mahin & Cate	Traded (Symbol):	NASDAQ (ACOL)
Investor Relations:	Jodi L. Warner, Mgr.	Stockholders:	2,344
Human Resources:	Steve Alexander, Mgr.	Employees:	1,328
Mgt. Info. Svcs.:	Russell Petrik, Mgr.	Annual Meeting:	In May
Auditors:	KPMG Peat Marwick LLP	Internet:	www.amcol.com

AMCORE Financial, Inc.

501 Seventh Street, Rockford, Illinois 61104
Telephone: (815) 968-2241

AMCORE Financial, Inc. is a multi-bank holding company that operates six banks and seven diversified financial services subsidiaries. The affiliated banks are: AMCORE Bank N.A., Rockford; AMCORE Bank N.A., Northwest; AMCORE Bank N.A., Rock River Valley; AMCORE Bank, N.A., North Central; AMCORE Bank, N.A., South Central; and AMCORE Bank, Aledo. The financial services subsidiaries are: AMCORE Financial Life Insurance Co., which reinsures credit life, accident, and health insurance; AMCORE Mortgage, Inc., which provides a full range of mortgage banking services; AMCORE Consumer Finance Company, Inc., specializing in consumer lending; AMCORE Investment Group, N.A., which provides personal trust services, employee benefit plans, estate administration, and various other services to corporations and individuals; AMCORE Investment Services, Inc., a broker/dealer providing a full line of retail brokerage products and services; AMCORE Capital Management, Inc., which manages investments for the AMCORE Vintage mutual funds, AMCORE Investment Group, N.A., and bank affiliates; Rockford Mercantile Agency, Inc., a collection agency; and AMCORE Insurance Group, Inc., a full-service insurance agency offering personal and commercial insurance products. Personal and commercial banking services include savings and checking accounts, export/import support, and consumer, agricultural, small business, and mortgage loans. Commercial banking provides services to commercial and government organizations. AMCORE Financial operates in the northern half of Illinois, excluding Cook County and south-central Wisconsin. Incorporated in Nevada in 1982.

Directors   (In addition to indicated officers)

Milton R. Brown
Richard C. Dell
Robert A. Doyle
Theresa P. Gilbert
Lawrence E. Gloyd

William R. McManaman
Ted Ross
Robert J. Smuland
Jack D. Ward
Gary L. Watson

Officers   (Directors*)

*Carl J. Dargene, Chm.
*Robert J. Meuleman, Pres. & C.E.O.
 Kenneth E. Edge, Exec. V.P. & C.O.O.
 James S. Waddell, Exec. V.P., C.A.O. & Corp. Secy.
 Alan W. Kennebeck, Grp. V.P.

Gerald W. Lister, Grp. V.P.
Charie A. Zanck, Grp. V.P.
John R. Hecht, Sr. V.P. & C.F.O.
William T. Hippensteel, Sr. V.P.—Corp. Mktg.

Consolidated Balance Sheet   As of December 31, 1996 (000 omitted)

Assets		Liabilities & Stockholders' Equity	
Current assets	$ 111,854	Current liabilities	$2,434,524
Total securities	1,148,719	Long-term debt	124,095
Net loans & leases	1,441,221	Deferred items	6,454
Net property, plant & equipment	46,060	Other liabilities	28,840
Other assets	66,696	*Stockholders' equity	220,637
Total	$2,814,550	Total	$2,814,550

*14,265,977 shares common stock outstanding.

Consolidated Income Statement[a]

Years Ended Dec. 31	Thousands — — — — Total Income	Net Income	Per Share[b] — — — — Earnings	Cash Dividends	Common Stock Price Range[b] Calendar Year
1996	$231,507	$26,383	$1.86	$ .64	27-1/4 — 18-7/8
1995	196,201	18,271	1.30	.58	24 — 17
1994	169,081	21,801	1.55	.55	22-3/4 — 15-3/4
1993	165,626	21,440	1.53	.41	20 — 13-1/2
1992	163,530	18,556	1.36	.35	14-5/8 — 7-7/8

[a]Restated to reflect a merger with NBM Bancorp, Inc. in May 1995.
[b]Adjusted to reflect a 3-for-2 stock split in December 1993 and a 10% stock dividend in May 1992.

Transfer Agent & Registrar:	Firstar		
General Counsel:	Maggio & Fox	Traded (Symbol):	NASDAQ (AMFI)
Investor Relations:	John R. Hecht, Sr. V.P.	Stockholders:	5,200
Human Resources:	James S. Waddell, Exec. V.P.	Employees:	1,199
Mgt. Info. Svcs.:	Richard M. Brattland, Sr. V.P.	Annual Meeting:	In May
Auditors:	McGladrey & Pullen, LLP	Internet:	www.amcore.com

American Classic Voyages Co.
Two North Riverside Plaza, Suite 200, Chicago, Illinois 60606-2639
Telephone: (312) 258-1890

American Classic Voyages Co. and its subsidiaries are leading providers of overnight passenger cruises on inland waterways in the continental United States and among the Hawaiian Islands. The company operates two cruise lines, The Delta Queen Steamboat Co. and American Hawaii Cruises. Delta Queen currently operates three vessels having 1,026 total passenger berths, providing two- to fourteen-night paddlewheel-driven steamboat cruises on the Mississippi, Ohio, Cumberland, Tennessee, Arkansas, Illinois, and Atchafalaya Rivers, as well as the Intracoastal Waterway. American Hawaii operates one vessel having 817 passenger berths, providing three-, four-, and seven-night inter-island cruises in Hawaii. Incorporated in Delaware in 1985; present name adopted in 1994.

Directors (In addition to indicated officers)

Corinne C. Boggs	Jon E.M. Jacoby
Arthur A. Greenberg	Ann Lurie
Jerry R. Jacob	Sheli Z. Rosenberg

Officers (Directors*)

*Samuel Zell, Chm.	Cornel J. Martin, V.P.—Corp. Affairs
*Philip C. Calian, Pres. & C.E.O.	Kathryn F. Gray, Cont., Chf. Acct. Off. & Treas.
R. Anthony McKinnon, Exec. V.P.—Oper.	Ray Yee, Chf. Info. Off.
Jordan B. Allen, Sr. V.P., Gen. Coun. & Secy.	

Consolidated Balance Sheet   As of December 31, 1997 (000 omitted)

Assets		Liabilities & Stockholders' Equity	
Current assets	$ 32,239	Current liabilities	$ 70,984
Net property, plant & equipment	166,883	Long-term debt	85,898
Other assets	12,742	*Stockholders' equity	54,982
Total	$211,864	Total	$211,864

*13,867,829 shares common stock outstanding.

Consolidated Income Statement

Years Ended Dec. 31	Thousands — — — — Revenues	Net Income	Per Share — — — Earnings	Cash Dividends	Common Stock Price Range Calendar Year
1996	$191,542	$(17,636)[a]	$(1.28)[a]	$ .00	13-1/4 — 6-1/2
1995	189,821	(9,671)[b]	(.70)[b]	.08	14-1/2 — 8-5/8
1994	195,197	(983)[c]	(.07)[c]	.16	19-1/4 — 12
1993[d]	121,689	4,220	.36	.16	22-1/4 — 11-3/8
1993[e]	66,725	9,181	.81	.04	

[a]Includes a write-down of $38,400,000 ($1.89 per share) for the company's decision not to renovate and return to service the ship Constitution and a gain of $11,700,000 ($.57 per share) net of tax, on the sale of the Maison Dupuy Hotel.
[b]Includes a one-time net charge of $5,900,000 ($.28 per share) reflecting costs associated with American Queen pre-inaugural activities and shakedown cruises.
[c]Includes one-time charges of $5,700,000 ($.20 per share).
[d]Includes the results of American Hawaii Cruises since its acquisition in August 1993; results also reflect the impact of the Mississippi River flood.
[e]Fiscal year ended March 31.

Transfer Agent & Registrar:	Bank of Boston			
General Counsel:	Jordan B. Allen, Sr. V.P.	Traded (Symbol):	NASDAQ (AMCV)
Investor Relations:	Karen Brown	Stockholders:	725
Human Resources:	Amy Klein-Alter	Employees:	1,470
Mgt. Info. Svcs.:	Ray Yee, C.I.O.	Annual Meeting:	In June
Auditors:	KPMG Peat Marwick LLP	Internet:	www.cruisehawaii.com

American Disposal Services, Inc.

745 McClintock Drive, Suite 305, Burr Ridge, Illinois 60521
Telephone: (630) 655-1105

American Disposal Services is a regional, integrated, non-hazardous solid waste services holding company that provides solid waste collection, transfer, and disposal services through its principal subsidiaries, ADS, Inc. and County Disposal, Inc. The company owns six solid waste landfills, and owns, operates, or has exclusive contracts to receive waste from 13 transfer stations. The company's landfills and transfer stations are supported by its collection operations, which serve over 226,000 residential, commercial, and industrial customers. The company currently serves customers in 11 states: Arkansas, Connecticut, Illinois, Indiana, Kansas, Massachusetts, Missouri, Ohio, Oklahoma, Pennsylvania, and Rhode Island. In July 1996, the company completed an initial public offering of 3,162,500 shares of common stock. Incorporated in Delaware in 1995.

Directors   (In addition to indicated officers)

David C. Stoller, Chm.
G.T. Blankenship
A. Lawrence Fagan

Merril M. Halpern
Richard T. Henshaw III
Norman Steisel

Officers   (Directors*)

*Richard De Young, Pres.
Lawrence R. Conrath, V.P. & Cont.
Richard Kogler, V.P. & C.O.O.
Stephen P. Lavey, V.P. & C.F.O.

John J. McDonnell, V.P.—Eng.
Mary T. Ryan, V.P.—Corp. Aff.
Ann L. Straw, V.P., Gen. Coun. & Secy

Consolidated Balance Sheet   As of December 31, 1996 (000 omitted)

Assets		Liabilities & Stockholders' Equity	
Current assets	$ 13,644	Current liablities	$ 12,425
Net property, plant & equipment	93,692	Long-term debt	65,445
Other assets	37,650	Deferred items	1,416
		Other liabilities	7,603
		*Stockholders' equity	58,097
Total	$144,986	Total	$144,986

*8,872,381 shares common stock outstanding.

Consolidated Income Statement

Years Ended Dec. 31	Thousands — — — —		Per Share[a] — — — —		Common Stock Price Range[a] Calendar Year
	Revenues	Net Income	Earnings	Cash Dividends	
1996	$56,804	$ (370)[b]	$ (.05)[b]	$ .00	19-1/2 — 9
1995[c]	30,004	(3,743)[d]	(1.06)[d]		
1994[c]	18,517	(2,389)	(.99)		
1993[c]	7,730	(749)[e]	(.53)[e]		
1992[c]	146	(854)	(2.14)		

[a]Initial public offering in July 1996.
[b]Includes an extraordinary loss of $476,000 ($.07 per share) on early retirement of debt.
[c]Pro forma.
[d]Includes an extraordinary loss of $908,000 ($.26 per share) on early retirement of debt.
[e]Includes an extraordinary gain of $74,000 ($.05 per share) on early retirement of debt.

Transfer Agent & Registrar:	Continental Stock Transfer & Trust Co.		
General Counsel:	Ann L. Straw, V.P.	Traded (Symbol):	NASDAQ (ADSI)
Investor Relations:	Mary T. Ryan, V.P.	Stockholders:	65
Human Resources:	Jackie Tylka	Employees:	580
Mgt. Info. Svcs.:	Anson Johnson	Annual Meeting:	In May
Auditors:	Ernst & Young LLP	Internet:	www.AmericanDisposal.com

American Medserve Corporation

184 Shuman Boulevard, Suite 200, Naperville, Illinois 60563
Telephone: (630) 717-2904

American Medserve Corporation is a leading independent provider of pharmacy services to long-term care institutions, including skilled nursing facilities, assisted living facilities, and other long-term health care settings. The company purchases, repackages, and dispenses pharmaceuticals to patients or residents in its client facilities, and provides those facilities with related consultant pharmacist and information services, including formulary management (management of pharmaceuticals dispensed to minimize cost and maximize therapeutic benefit), automated medical record-keeping, drug therapy evaluation, and assistance with regulatory compliance. The company also provides infusion therapy, parenteral and enteral therapy, inhalation and respiratory therapy, and wound care management services. American Medserve was formed in November 1993 and began operation in August 1994. Incorporated in Delaware in 1993.

Directors (In addition to indicated officers)

James H.S. Cooper
Charles C. Halberg

Lee M. Mitchell

Officers (Directors*)

*Bryan C. Cressey, Chm.
*Timothy L. Burfield, Pres. & C.E.O.
Michael B. Freedman, V.P.—Bus. Dev.

J. Jeffrey Gephart, V.P.—Natl. Sales
Charles R. Wallace, V.P.—Fin., C.F.O., Treas. & Secy.

Consolidated Balance Sheet   As of December 31, 1996 (000 omitted)

Assets		Liabilities & Stockholders' Equity	
Current assets	$ 50,868	Current liabilities	$ 12,374
Net property, plant & equipment	5,509	Long-term debt	5,800
Other assets	56,921	Deferred income taxes	641
		Other liabilities	1,484
		*Stockholders' equity	92,999
Total	$113,298	Total	$113,298

*12,000,464 shares common stock outstanding.

Consolidated Income Statement

Years Ended Dec. 31	Thousands — — — —		Per Share[a] — — —		Common Stock Price Range[a]
	Revenues	Net Income	Earnings	Cash Dividends	Calendar Year
1996	$82,027	$(2,571)[b]	$ (.35)[b]	$ .00	18-1/4 — 15
1995[c]	27,347	296	.05		
1995[d]	24,793	92	.02		

[a]Initial public offering in November 1996.
[b]Includes a writeoff of $437,000 ($.06 per share) for deferred financing costs and $2,805,000 ($.38 per share) in non-recurring charges incurred in connection with, or immediately preceding, the company's initial public offering.
[c]Six months ended December 31. In December 1995, the company changed to calendar year reporting.
[d]Twelve months ended June 30.

Transfer Agent & Registrar: LaSalle National Bank

General Counsel:	Gardner, Carton & Douglas	Auditors:	Ernst & Young LLP
Investor Relations:	Charles R. Wallace, V.P.	Traded (Symbol):	NASDAQ (AMCI)
		Stockholders:	40
Human Resources:	Charles R. Wallace, V.P.	Employees:	675
Mgt. Info. Svcs.:	Charles R. Wallace, V.P.	Annual Meeting:	In June

Amerihost Properties, Inc.

2400 East Devon Avenue, Suite 280, Des Plaines, Illinois 60018
Telephone: (847) 298-4500

Amerihost Properties, Inc. and its subsidiaries are engaged in the development, operation, and management of the AmeriHost Inn hotels and a mid-market hotel chain. The company provides a complete product, from site evaluation and selection stages through the operating stages. As of April 1997, the company operated 75 hotels in 16 states. Amerihost conducts its business through four departments: Hotel Development, Hotel Operations, Hotel Management, and Employee Leasing. The company builds, manages, and owns AmeriHost Inn hotels and intends to expand the chain extensively over the next several years. As of April 1997, 47 AmeriHost Inn hotels were open, with 18 more under construction. Amerihost also owns and manages 28 hotels with national franchise or independent affiliations. Amerihost Properties' wholly owned subsidiaries include: Amerihost Lodging Group, Inc.; Amerihost Development, Inc.; Amerihost Renovations, Inc.; Amerihost Management, Inc.; and Amerihost Staffing, Inc. The company's main focus is building AmeriHost Inn hotels in secondary and tertiary markets throughout the United States, with an emphasis in the midwestern region. Incorporated in Delaware in 1984.

Directors   (In addition to indicated officers)

Reno J. Bernardo

Salomon Dayan

Officers   (Directors*)

*H. Andrew Torchia, Chm.
*Michael P. Holtz, Pres. & C.E.O.

*Russell J. Cerqua, Exec. V.P., C.F.O., Treas. & Secy.

Consolidated Balance Sheet   As of December 31, 1996 (000 omitted)

Assets		Liabilities & Stockholders' Equity	
Current assets	$11,957	Current liabilities	$11,004
Net property, plant & equipment	45,836	Long-term debt	32,785
Investments	1,596	Deferred items	631
Other assets	7,512	Other liabilities	1,569
		*Stockholders' equity	20,912
Total	$66,901	Total	$66,901

*6,036,921 shares common stock outstanding.

Consolidated Income Statement

Years Ended Dec. 31	Thousands — — — —		Per Share — — —		Common Stock Price Range Calendar Year
	Revenues	Net Income	Earnings	Cash Dividends	
1996	$68,342	$ 3,395	$ .50	$ .00	10-1/4 — 5-7/8
1995	51,962	2,138	.35	.00	7-1/2 — 3-1/2
1994	43,347	571	.10	.00	6-3/4 — 3-1/2
1993	34,274	(761)	(.15)	.00	12-1/4 — 4
1992	29,411	511	.22	.00	8 — 3

Transfer Agent & Registrar:	Affiliated Stock Transfer Co.		
Legal Counsel:	McDermott, Will & Emery	Traded (Symbol):	NASDAQ (HOST)
Investor Relations:	Karin Rowe	Stockholders:	1,514
Human Resources:	William Roclaw	Employees:	1,920
Mgt. Info. Svcs.: Gary Brookshier, V.P.—Sys. & Tech.		Annual Meeting:	In July
Auditors:	BDO Seidman	Internet:	www.amerihostinn.com

Amerin Corporation
200 East Randolph Drive, 49th Floor, Chicago, Illinois 60601-7125
Telephone: (312) 540-0078

Amerin Corporation is the holding company for two operating subsidiaries: Amerin Guaranty Corporation and Amerin Re Corporation. Amerin Guaranty provides private mortgage insurance to mortgage bankers, savings institutions, commercial banks, and other lenders in all 50 states. Amerin Re Corporation provides reinsurance to Amerin Guaranty to satisfy risk exposure requirements of several states. Incorporated in Delaware in 1991.

Directors (In addition to indicated officers)

Peter H. Gleason
Alan E. Goldberg
Howard I. Hoffen

Timothy A. Holt
Larry E. Swedroe

Officers (Directors*)

*Gerald L. Friedman, Chm., Pres. & C.E.O.
George G. Freudenstein, Sr. V.P., C.F.O. & Treas.

Randolph C. Sailer II, Sr. V.P., Gen. Coun. & Secy.

Consolidated Balance Sheet   As of December 31, 1996 (000 omitted)

Assets		Liabilities & Stockholders' Equity	
Current assets	$340,195	Current liabilities	$ 39,366
Net property, plant & equipment	4,368	Deferred items	289
Deferred policy acquisition costs	5,569	Other liabilities	14,560
Other assets	4,692	*Stockholders' equity	300,609
Total	$354,824	Total	$354,824

*26,080,839 shares common stock outstanding.

Consolidated Income Statement

Years Ended Dec. 31	Thousands — — — — Net Revenues	Net Income[a]	Per Share[b] — — — Earnings	Cash Dividends	Common Stock Price Range[bc] Calendar Year
1996	$79,381	$ 28,229	$ 1.07	$ .00	28-1/2 — 19
1995	35,662	(28,098)[d]	(2.32)[d]	.00	28-1/2 — 18
1994	10,490	(3,059)	(.36)		
1993	5,284	(7,232)	(.99)		
1992	1,395	(5,576)	(1.98)		

[a]Reflects income applicable to common shareholders after dividends on preferred stock.
[b]Reflects 125-for-1 stock split in November 1995.
[c]Initial public offering in November 1995.
[d]Includes compensation charge of $35,741,000 ($2.95 per share) in connection with initial public offering.

Transfer Agent & Registrar:	Wilmington Trust Company			
General Counsel:	Randolph C. Sailer II, Sr. V.P.	Auditors:	Ernst & Young LLP
Investor Relations:	George G. Freudenstein, Sr. V.P.	Traded (Symbol):	NASDAQ (AMRN)
		Stockholders:	4,600
Human Resources:	Joyce Mason	Employees:	95
Mgt. Info. Svcs.:	Sean P. Connelly	Annual Meeting:	In June

Ameritech Corporation

30 South Wacker Drive, Chicago, Illinois 60606
Telephone: (312) 750-5000

Ameritech Corporation, a leading communications company serving more than 13 million customers, operates under 15 customer-focused business units. Eleven of these units are further grouped into two sectors to leverage synergies and help ensure strategic consistency: Communications and Information Products; and Consumer and Business Services. The company provides a wide array of local phone, data, and video services in Illinois, Indiana, Michigan, Ohio, and Wisconsin. Ameritech creates new information, entertainment, and interactive services for homes, businesses, and governments around the world. A leading cellular company, Ameritech serves more than 2.7 million cellular and 1.1 million paging customers, and has cellular interests in telephone companies in Belgium, Hungary, New Zealand, and Norway, and in business directories in Germany and other countries. Incorporated in Delaware in 1983.

Directors   (In addition to indicated officers)

Donald C. Clark	Sheldon B. Lubar	John D. Ong
Melvin R. Goodes	Lynn M. Martin	Addison Barry Rand
Hanna Holborn Gray, Ph.D.	Arthur C. Martinez	Laura D'Andrea Tyson
James A. Henderson	John B. McCoy	James A. Unruh

Officers   (Directors*)

*Richard C. Notebaert, Chm. & C.E.O.
Barry Allen, Exec. V.P.—Consumer & Bus. Svcs.
W. Patrick Campbell, Exec. V.P.—Corp. Strategy & Bus. Dev.
Walter S. Catlow, Exec. V.P. & Pres.—Intl.
Thomas E. Richards, Exec. V.P.—Commun. & Info. Prod.
Oren G. Shaffer, Exec. V.P. & C.F.O.
Kelly R. Welsh, Exec. V.P. & Gen. Coun.
Walter M. Oliver, Sr. V.P.—Hum. Res.

Thomas J. Reiman, Sr. V.P.—State & Gov. Aff.
Joan H. Walker, Sr. V.P.—Corp. Commun.
Joel S. Engel, V.P.—Tech.
Barbara A. Klein, V.P. & Compt.
Gary R. Lytle, V.P.—Fed. Rel.
Sari L. Macrie, V.P.—Inv. Rel.
Richard W. Pehlke, V.P. & Treas.
Ali Shadman, V.P.—Corp. Strategy
Lawrence E. Strickling, V.P.—Public Policy
Bruce B. Howat, Secy.

Consolidated Balance Sheet   As of December 31, 1996 (000 omitted)

Assets		Liabilities & Stockholders' Equity	
Current assets	$ 3,799,000	Current liabilities	$ 6,832,000
Net property, plant & equipment	13,507,000	Long-term debt	4,437,000
Other assets	6,401,000	Deferred items	4,751,000
		*Stockholders' equity	7,687,000
Total	$23,707,000	Total	$23,707,000

*549,928,000 shares common stock outstanding.

Consolidated Income Statement

Years Ended Dec. 31	Thousands — — — — Net Sales	Net Income	Per Share[a] — — — — Earnings	Cash Dividends	Common Stock Price Range[a] Calendar Year
1996	$14,917,000	$ 2,134,000[b]	$ 3.87[b]	$2.12	66-7/8 — 49-5/8
1995	13,427,800	2,007,600[c]	3.63[c]	2.00	59-3/8 — 39-7/8
1994	12,569,500	(1,063,600)[d]	(1.94)[d]	1.92	43-1/8 — 36-1/4
1993	11,864,700	1,512,800	2.78	1.84	45-1/2 — 35
1992	11,284,700	(400,400)[e]	(.75)[e]	1.76	37 — 28-1/8

[a]Adjusted to reflect a 2-for-1 stock split in December 1993.
[b]Includes an after-tax gain of $18,000,000 ($.04 per share) from the sale of Polish cellular interests.
[c]Includes an after-tax gain of $120,000,000 ($.22 per share) associated with restructuring and exchange of cellular interests.
[d]Includes an extraordinary loss of $2,234,000,000 ($4.07 per share).
[e]Includes a charge to reflect FAS 106 and FAS 112, resulting in a cumulative effect of $1,746,400,000 ($3.26 per share).

Transfer Agent & Registrar: First Chicago Trust Co. of New York

General Counsel: Kelly R. Welsh, Exec. V.P.

Investor Relations: Sari L. Macrie, V.P.

Human Resources: Walter M. Oliver, Sr. V.P.

Auditors: Arthur Andersen LLP

Traded (Symbol):
NYSE, BSE, CSE, PSE, PHSE, LON, TOK, AMSTR, 3SWISS (AIT)

Annual Meeting: In April

Stockholders: 837,000

Employees: 66,128

Internet: www.ameritech.com

Amoco Corporation

200 East Randolph Drive, Chicago, Illinois 60601
Telephone: (312) 856-6111

Amoco Corporation and its consolidated subsidiaries form one of the largest international petroleum and chemical companies in the nation. The company engages in exploration, production, and transportation of crude oil and natural gas; and in manufacturing, transporting, and marketing of petroleum and chemical products. Operations are conducted in three major sectors: exploration and production—for exploration and production activities; petroleum products—for refining, transporting, and marketing activities; and chemicals—for the manufacture and sale of chemical products. United States refineries process approximately 1,074,000 barrels of crude oil and natural gas liquids each day. Products are sold through about 3,000 company-owned or leased retail outlets, in addition to about 6,300 other retail outlets. Incorporated in Indiana in 1889.

Directors   (In addition to indicated officers)

Donald R. Beall	Richard J. Ferris	Martha R. Seger
Ruth S. Block	Floris A. Maljers	Theodore M. Solso
John H. Bryan	Arthur C. Martinez	Michael H. Wilson
Erroll B. Davis, Jr.	Walter E. Massey	

Officers   (Directors*)

*H. Laurance Fuller, Chm. & C.E.O.
*William G. Lowrie, Pres.
James E. Fligg, Sr. Exec. V.P.—Strat. Plan. & Intl. Bus. Dev.
John L. Carl, Exec. V.P. & C.F.O.
L. Richard Flury, Exec. V.P.—Exploration & Prod. Sector
W. Douglas Ford, Exec. V.P.—Petroleum Products Sector
Enrique J. Sosa, Exec. V.P.—Chemicals Sector
R. Wayne Anderson, Sr. V.P.—Hum. Res.

George S. Spindler, Sr. V.P.—Law & Corp. Affairs
David F. Work, Sr. V.P.—Shared Services
Judith G. Boynton, V.P. & Cont.
R.C. Carr, V.P.—Plan.
Stephen A. Elbert, V.P.—Govt. Rel.
Stephen F. Gates, V.P., Gen. Coun. & Corp. Secy.
William R. Hutchinson, V.P.—Fin. Oper.
Marshall T. Jones, Acting V.P.—Info. Tech.
Daniel R. Mitchell, V.P. & Gen. Tax Coun.
Walter R. Quanstrom, V.P.—Env., Health & Safety
Donald E. Tornberg, V.P.—Progress
Marsha C. Williams, Treas.

Consolidated Balance Sheet   As of December 31, 1996 (000 omitted)

Assets		Liabilities & Stockholders' Equity	
Current assets	$ 7,063,000	Current liabilities	$ 6,139,000
Net property, plant & equipment	23,400,000	Long-term obligations	4,229,000
Other assets	1,637,000	Deferred items	5,195,000
		Minority interest	129,000
		*Stockholders' equity	16,408,000
Total	$32,100,000	Total	$32,100,000

*497,275,364 shares common stock outstanding.

Consolidated Income Statement

Years Ended Dec. 31	Thousands — — — —		Per Share — — — —		Common Stock
	Total Revenues[a]	Net Income	Earnings	Cash Dividends	Price Range Calendar Year
1996	$36,112,000	$ 2,834,000	$ 5.69	$2.60	83-1/2 — 65
1995	31,004,000	1,862,000	3.76	2.40	72-5/8 — 56-3/8
1994	30,362,000	1,789,000	3.60	2.20	64-1/8 — 50-7/8
1993	28,617,000	1,820,000	3.66	2.20	59-1/4 — 48-1/8
1992	28,219,000	(74,000)[b]	(.15)[b]	2.20	53-3/4 — 41-3/4

[a]Includes consumer excise taxes.
[b]Includes FAS 106 and 109, resulting in cumulative charges of $924,000,000 ($1.86 per share).

Transfer Agent & Registrar: First Chicago Trust Co. of New York; The R-M Trust Co., Toronto; Amoco Corp. Shareholder Services

General Counsel:	Stephen F. Gates, V.P.	Traded (Symbol):	NYSE, CSE, PSE, Toronto, Swiss (AN)
Investor Relations:	Chuck K. Koepke, V.P.		
Human Resources:	R. Wayne Anderson, Sr. V.P.	Stockholders:	134,472
		Employees:	41,723
Mgt. Info. Svcs.:	Marshall T. Jones, Acting V.P.	Annual Meeting:	In April
Auditors:	Price Waterhouse LLP	Internet:	www.amoco.com

Andrew Corporation

10500 West 153rd Street, Orland Park, Illinois 60462
Telephone: (708) 349-3300

Andrew Corporation is a global supplier of communications systems equipment and services. Important markets are wireless communications, including cellular, personal communications systems, land mobile radio and common carrier, along with broadcast, corporate, and government institutions. The Commercial Products Group supplies complete packages of transmission products and services, including terrestrial microwave, broadcast and earth station antennas and systems, coaxial cables, waveguide, towers, and shelters. The Government Products Group offers electronic radar and communications reconnaissance receiving systems, position finding systems, positioners, cable, waveguide and high frequency, and other antenna systems. The Network Products Group provides computer connectivity equipment including bridges, token ring hardware, printer adapters, and midrange emulation products. Field sales offices are located in Orland Park, Illinois; Atlanta, Georgia; Dallas, Texas; Washington, D.C.; Tokyo; Zurich; and other cities around the world. The company has 17 manufacturing facilities in five countries: United States, Australia, Brazil, Canada, and Great Britain. Principal subsidiaries include: Andrew Canada Inc.; Andrew A.G.; Andrew Data Corp.; and Andrew SciComm Inc. In March 1996, Andrew Corporation acquired The Antenna Company, an Itasca, Illinois-based maker of wireless phone antennas. Incorporated in Illinois in 1947 as a successor to a partnership formed in 1937; reincorporated in Delaware in 1987.

Directors   (In addition to indicated officers)

John G. Bollinger
Jon L. Boyes, Ph.D.
Kenneth J. Douglas

Jere D. Fluno
Ormand J. Wade

Officers   (Directors*)

*Floyd L. English, Ph.D., Chm., Pres. & C.E.O.
William R. Currer, Grp. Pres.—Comm. Prod.
Thomas E. Charlton, Grp. Pres.—Comm. Sys.
Roger K. Fisher, Grp. Pres.—Wireless Prod.
Charles R. Nicholas, Exec. V.P. & C.F.O.
John E. DeSana, V.P.—Heliax® Cable &
  Accessories
John R.D. Dickson, V.P.—Corp. Mktg./MIS

Barry J. Houlihan, V.P.—Antennas
Robert J. Hudzik, V.P.—Bus. Dev.
Debra Huttenburg, V.P.—Antenna Sys.
Gregory F. Maruszak, V.P. & Cont.
Jose A. Perez, V.P.—Mktg. & Sales—Andrew Telecom
John B. Scott, V.P.—Corp. R&D/Mktg./MIS
M. Jeffrey Gittelman, Treas.
James F. Petelle, Secy. & Gen. Atty.

Consolidated Balance Sheet[a]   As of September 30, 1996 (000 omitted)

Assets		Liabilities & Stockholders' Equity	
Current assets	$401,984	Current liabilities	$117,382
Net property, plant & equipment	132,700	Long-term debt	40,423
Other assets	96,545	Deferred items	7,919
		Other liabilities	9,291
		*Stockholders' equity	456,214
Total	$631,229	Total	$631,229

*60,432,000 shares common stock outstanding.

Consolidated Income Statement

Years Ended Sept. 30	Thousands — — — — Net Sales	Net Income	Per Share[a] — — — — Earnings	Cash Dividends	Common Stock Price Range[a] Calendar Year
1996	$793,575	$90,397	$ .98	$ .00	38-5/8 — 13-7/8
1995[b]	663,960	69,955	.77	.00	28-3/8 — 15-1/8
1994[b]	588,233	45,767	.51	.00	15-7/8 — 7-1/8
1993[b]	451,957	29,403	.33	.00	8-5/8 — 4
1992[b]	453,408	26,151	.26	.00	4-7/8 — 2-3/8

[a]Adjusted to reflect 3-for-2 stock splits in February 1997, 1996, 1995, and 1994, and a 2-for-1 stock split in February 1993.
[b]Restated to reflect the acquisition of The Antenna Company in March 1996 which was accounted for as a pooling-of-interests.

Transfer Agent & Registrar:	Harris Trust and Savings Bank		
General Counsel:	Gardner, Carton & Douglas	Traded (Symbol):	NASDAQ (ANDW)
Investor Relations:	Tami Kamarauskas	Stockholders:	3,642
Human Resources:	Nella Mech	Employees:	4,622
Mgt. Info. Svcs.:	John R.D. Dickson, V.P.	Annual Meeting:	In February
Auditors:	Ernst & Young LLP	Internet:	www.andrew.com

Anicom, Inc.

6133 North River Road, Suite 1000, Rosemont, Illinois 60018
Telephone: (847) 518-8700

Anicom, Inc. specializes in the sale and distribution of communications-related wire, cable, fiber optics, and computer network and connectivity products. The products offered by the company generally fall into four categories: voice and data communications and fiber optics; sound, security, fire, alarm, and energy management systems; electronic cable; and industrial cable. Since its initial public offering in February 1995, Anicom has grown from 7 to 41 locations through acquisitions and internal expansion. Through March 1997, Anicom has successfully completed nine acquisitions. Incorporated in Delaware in 1994.

Directors (In addition to indicated officers)

William R. Anixter
Peter Huizenga
Ira J. Kaufman

Thomas Reiman
Michael Segal
Lee B. Stern

Officers (Directors*)

*Alan B. Anixter, Chm.
*Scott C. Anixter, Co-Chm. & C.E.O.
*Carl E. Putnam, Pres. & C.O.O.
*Robert Brzustewicz, Sr. Exec. V.P.

Glen M. Nast, Sr. Exec. V.P.
Robert L. Swanson, Sr. Exec. V.P.
*Donald C. Welchko, V.P. & C.F.O.

Consolidated Balance Sheet As of December 31, 1996 (000 omitted)

Assets		Liabilities & Stockholders' Equity	
Current assets	$57,539	Current liabilities	$24,143
Net property, plant & equipment	2,820	Long-term debt	3,013
Other assets	27,595	Deferred items	165
		Other liabilities	774
		*Stockholders' equity	59,859
Total	$87,954	Total	$87,954

*15,559,805 shares common stock outstanding.

Consolidated Income Statement

Years Ended Dec. 31	Thousands — — — — Net Sales	Net Income	Per Share[a] — — — — Earnings	Cash Dividends	Common Stock Price Range[ab] Calendar Year
1996	$115,993	$2,623	$ .20	$ .00	10-1/8 — 4-3/8
1995	29,358	764	.14	.00	7-1/4 — 3
1994	17,866	412	.10	.00	

[a]Adjusted to reflect a 2-for-1 stock split in the form of a 100 percent stock dividend in October 1996.
[b]Initial public offering in February 1995.

Transfer Agent & Registrar: Harris Trust and Savings Bank

General Counsel:	Katten Muchin & Zavis	Traded (Symbol):	NASDAQ (ANIC)
Investor Relations:	Donald C. Welchko, V.P.	Stockholders:	736
Human Resources:	Lee Smela	Employees:	490
Mgt. Info. Svcs.:	Paul Adams	Annual Meeting:	In May
Auditors:	Coopers & Lybrand L.L.P.	Internet:	www.anicommm.com

Anixter International Inc.

Two North Riverside Plaza, Suite 1900, Chicago, Illinois 60606
Telephone: (312) 902-1515

Anixter International Inc. (formerly Itel Corporation), is a leading global value-added provider of integrated networking and cabling solutions that support business information and infrastructure requirements. Anixter teams with customers to implement these solutions by combining a variety of customized pre- and post-sale services, products from the world's leading manufacturers, and superior logistics management through a global network in 37 countries and 156 cities. The company's principal subsidiary is Anixter Inc. Anixter International owns approximately 19 percent of ANTEC Corporation. Incorporated in Delaware in 1967; present name adopted in 1995.

Directors   (In addition to indicated officers)

Lord James Blyth	John R. Petty
Robert E. Fowler, Jr.	Sheli Z. Rosenberg
F. Philip Handy	Stuart M. Sloan
Melvyn N. Klein	Thomas C. Theobald

Officers   (Directors*)

*Samuel Zell, Chm.	James M. Froisland, V.P. & Cont.
*Rod F. Dammeyer, Pres. & C.E.O.	Philip F. Meno, V.P.—Taxes
James E. Knox, Sr. V.P., Gen. Coun. & Secy.	*Bob Grubbs, Pres./C.E.O.—Anixter Inc.
Dennis J. Letham, Sr. V.P. & C.F.O.	

Consolidated Balance Sheet   As of December 31, 1996 (000 omitted)

Assets		Liabilities & Stockholders' Equity	
Current assets	$ 868,500	Current liabilities	$ 313,500
Net property, plant & equipment	61,600	Long-term debt	468,400
Other assets	330,900	Deferred items & other long-term liabilities	43,600
		*Stockholders' equity	435,500
Total	$1,261,000	Total	$1,261,000

*48,038,162 shares common stock outstanding.

Consolidated Income Statement[a]

Years Ended Dec. 31	Thousands — — — — Net Sales	Net Income	Per Share[b] — — — — Earnings	Cash Dividends	Common Stock Price Range[b] Calendar Year
1996	$2,475,300	$ 36,100	$ .73	$ .00	20 — 12-5/8
1995	2,194,800	39,100	.71	.00	22-1/8 — 16-5/8
1994	1,732,600	246,900	3.86	.00	18-1/8 — 11-3/8
1993	1,756,200	(1,200)	(.07)	.00	16-7/8 — 10-1/8
1992	1,464,600	(104,300)	(1.90)	.00	12-1/8 — 8

[a]Consolidated results in 1993 included ANTEC, while 1994 consolidated results present ANTEC as an equity investment. Anixter reduced its interest in ANTEC to 30 percent of ANTEC's outstanding shares in 1994. Due to ANTEC's merger with TSX in February 1997, Anixter's interest has been reduced to approximately 19 percent.
[b]Adjusted to reflect a 2-for-1 stock split in October 1995.

Transfer Agent & Registrar: ChaseMellon Shareholder Services, L.L.C.

General Counsel:	James E. Knox, Sr. V.P.	Stockholders:	5,700
		Employees:	5,600
Auditors:	Ernst & Young LLP	Annual Meeting:	In May
Traded (Symbol):	NYSE (AXE)	Internet:	www.anixter.com

ANTEC Corporation

2850 West Golf Road, Rolling Meadows, Illinois 60008
Telephone: (847) 439-4444

ANTEC Corporation is an international communications technology company, with major offices in Atlanta, Georgia, and Denver, Colorado. ANTEC specializes in the manufacturing, design, and engineering of hybrid fiber/coax broadband networks. ANTEC is a leading developer and supplier of optical transmission, construction, rebuild, and maintenance equipment for the broadband communications industry. ANTEC provides a broad range of products and services to cable system operators. ANTEC supplies almost all of the products required in a cable system, including headend, distribution, drop, and in-home subscriber products. In February 1997, ANTEC acquired TSX Corporation of El Paso, Texas, through a 1-for-1 exchange of common stock. Incorporated in Delaware in 1993.

Directors (In addition to indicated officers)

Rod F. Dammeyer	Samuel K. Skinner
William H. Lambert	Bruce Van Wagner
John R. Petty	Mary Agnes Wilderotter

Officers (Directors*)

*John M. Egan, Chm. & C.E.O.	James A. Bauer, V.P.—Comm. & Adm.
*James L. Faust, Exec. V.P. & Pres.—ANTEC Intl.	Daniel J. Distel, V.P. & Cont.
Lawrence A. Margolis, Exec. V.P., C.F.O. & Secy.	James E. Knox, Gen. Coun.
	Gordon E. Halverson, C.E.O.—TeleWire

Consolidated Balance Sheet As of December 31, 1996 (000 omitted)

Assets		Liabilities & Stockholders' Equity	
Current assets	$225,807	Current liabilities	$ 82,046
Net property, plant & equipment	25,521	Long-term debt	102,658
Goodwill	167,128	*Stockholders' equity	252,534
Other assets	18,782		
Total	$437,238	Total	$437,238

*23,000,000 shares common stock outstanding.

Consolidated Income Statement

Years Ended Dec. 31	Thousands — — — — Net Sales	Net Income[a]	Per Share[b] — — — Earnings	Cash Dividends	Common Stock Price Range[b] Calendar Year
1996	$604,382	$ 13,457	$ .59	$ .00	19-5/8 — 8-1/2
1995[c]	658,237	(3,619)	(.16)	.00	26-3/4 — 11-1/8
1994	553,510	18,888	.89	.00	38-1/2 — 15
1993[d]	427,601	11,545	.56	.00	30-1/4 — 21
1992[d]	300,974	6,210	.31		

[a]Includes FAS 109.
[b]Initial public offering in September 1993.
[c]Includes a $21,700,000 pretax non-recurring charge. Before this charge, net income and earnings were $9,400,000 and $.42, respectively.
[d]Pro forma.

Transfer Agent & Registrar: The Bank of New York

General Counsel:	James E. Knox	Traded (Symbol):	NASDAQ (ANTC)
Investor Relations:	James A. Bauer, V.P.	Stockholders:	525
Human Resources:	James A. Bauer, V.P.	Employees:	3,000
		Annual Meeting:	In May
Auditors:	Ernst & Young LLP	Internet:	www.antec.com

Aon Corporation

123 North Wacker Drive, Chicago, Illinois 60606
Telephone: (312) 701-3000

Aon Corporation is a worldwide provider of insurance and consulting services through global distribution networks. Aon provides risk management, insurance services, and consulting solutions for commercial and industrial enterprises, financial institutions, insurance organizations, municipalities, and individuals through Aon Group and Aon's consumer underwriting businesses. Aon Group is the world's fastest growing international and commercial brokerage and consulting organization. Aon's consumer insurance businesses underwrite and market a variety of specialized insurance and extended warranty products, principally through Combined Insurance Company of America and Virginia Surety Co. In early 1997, Aon acquired New York-based Alexander & Alexander Services Inc., a holding firm with risk-management, insurance, and human-resource management consulting operations. Incorporated in Delaware in 1979.

Directors (In addition to indicated officers)

Daniel T. Carroll	Andrew J. McKenna	George A. Schaefer
Franklin A. Cole	Newton N. Minow	Fred L. Turner
Edgar D. Jannotta, Sr.	Peer Pedersen	Arnold R. Weber
Perry J. Lewis	Donald S. Perkins	
Joan D. Manley	John W. Rogers, Jr.	

Officers (Directors*)

*Patrick G. Ryan, Chm., Pres. & C.E.O.
Charles H. Chapman, Exec. V.P.—Systems
Daniel T. Cox, Exec. V.P.
Harvey N. Medvin, Exec. V.P., C.F.O. & Treas.
*Raymond I. Skilling, Exec. V.P. & Chf. Coun.
Michael A. Conway, Sr. V.P. & Sr. Invest. Off.
Richard F. Ferruci, Sr. V.P.

Gary A. Ackland, V.P.—Int. Audit
Jerome I. Baer, V.P.—Tax
William J. Fasel, V.P. & Corp. Secy.
John A. Reschke, V.P.—Comp. & Ben.
Joan E. Steel, V.P.
Stephen C. Taylor, V.P.—Prof. Dev.
James D. White, V.P. & Cont.

Consolidated Balance Sheet   As of December 31, 1996 (000 omitted)

Assets		Liabilities & Stockholders' Equity	
Cash	$ 410,100	Policyholders' liabilities	$ 4,359,600
Investments	5,212,800	General liabilities	6,480,200
Deferred policy acquisition costs	598,800	Redeemable preferred stock	50,000
Receivables	4,624,400	*Stockholders' equity	2,832,900
Other assets	2,876,600		
Total	$13,722,700	Total	$13,722,700

*110,912,000 shares common stock outstanding.

Consolidated Income Statement

Years Ended Dec. 31	Thousands — — — —		Per Share[d] — — — —		Common Stock Price Range[d] Calendar Year
	Total Revenues[a]	Net Income[bc]	Earnings[bc]	Cash Dividends	
1996	$4,181,000	$335,000	$2.87	$1.42	64-3/4 — 47-1/2
1995	4,611,000	403,000	3.48	1.34	50-7/8 — 31-3/8
1994	4,157,000	360,000	3.14	1.26	35-3/4 — 29-1/4
1993	3,845,000	324,000	2.81	1.18	39 — 30-7/8
1992	3,336,000	206,000	1.93	1.11	36 — 26-1/8

[a]From continuing and discontinued operations.
[b]Before cumulative effect of FAS 106 and 109 in 1992.
[c]After realized investment gains.
[d]Adjusted to reflect a 3-for-2 stock split in May 1994.

Transfer Agent & Registrar:	First Chicago Trust Co. of New York		
Chief Counsel:	Raymond I. Skilling, Exec. V.P.	Traded (Symbol):	NYSE, CSE, LONDON (AOC)
Financial Relations:	William J. Fasel, V.P.	Stockholders:	13,000
		Employees:	28,000
Human Resources:	Ginny Schooley, Dir.	Annual Meeting:	In April
Auditors:	Ernst & Young LLP	Internet:	www.aon.com

APAC TeleServices, Inc.

One Parkway North Center, Deerfield, Illinois 60015
Telephone: (847) 945-0055

APAC TeleServices, Inc. is a provider of outsourced telephone-based sales, marketing, and customer management services. The company's client base is comprised of large companies with growing needs for cost-effective means of contacting and servicing current and prospective customers. APAC operates more than 9,000 workstations in 67 telephone call centers located primarily in the Midwest. In October 1995, APAC completed an initial public offering of 4,300,000 shares of common stock. In 1996, the company formed a new, Atlanta-based division to service major relationships with clients in that region. Incorporated in Illinois in 1973.

Directors (In addition to indicated officers)

Thomas M. Collins
George D. Dalton

Morris R. Shechtman
Paul G. Yovovich

Officers (Directors*)

*Theodore G. Schwartz, Chm. & C.E.O.
*Marc S. Simon, C.F.O.
Donald B. Berryman, Sr. V.P. & Gen. Mgr.—Svc. Solutions/Atlanta
Kenneth G. Culver, Sr. V.P.—Facilities
John C. Dontje, Sr. V.P. & Gen. Mgr.—Sales Source
Robert C. Froetscher, Sr. V.P. & Gen. Mgr.—Svc. Solutions/Deerfield
Gregory K. Jones, Sr. V.P.—Strat. Mkts.

Allen A. Kalkstein, Sr. V.P. & Gen. Mgr.—Tech. Sol.
Richard H. Kremer, Sr. V.P.—People & Learning
James M. Nikrant, Sr. V.P. & Gen. Mgr.—Sales Solutions
Daniel Bauer, V.P.—Mktg. & Strat. Planning
James H. Blackburn, V.P.—People & Learning
Ronald R. Hansen, V.P.—Fin.
Elaine R. Klein, V.P.—Emp. Svcs.
Philip B. Wade, V.P. & Cont.
William S. Lipsman, Gen. Coun.

Consolidated Balance Sheet As of December 29, 1996 (000 omitted)

Assets		Liabilities & Stockholders' Equity	
Current assets	$ 62,284	Current liabilities	$ 48,930
Net property, plant & equipment	78,444	Long-term debt	1,325
Other assets	653	Deferred items	2,920
		*Stockholders' equity	88,206
Total	$141,381	Total	$141,381

*46,540,057 shares common stock outstanding.

Consolidated Income Statement

Years Ended Abt. Dec. 31	Thousands — — — — Net Sales	Net Income	Per Share[a][b] — — — Earnings	Cash Dividends	Common Stock Price Range[a][b] Calendar Year
1996	$276,443	$30,550	$ .64	$ .00	59 — 13-3/8
1995	101,667	7,483[c]	.18[c]	.00	16-7/8 — 10
1994	46,618	3,896[c]	.10[c]		
1993	28,912	2,349[c]	.06[c]		
1992	13,529	844[c]	.02[c]		

[a]Adjusted to reflect a 60,000-for-1 stock split in March 1994; a 3.3-for-1 stock split in September 1995; and a 2-for-1 stock split in the form of a dividend in May 1996.
[b]Initial public offering in October 1995.
[c]Pro forma.

Transfer Agent & Registrar: Harris Trust and Savings Bank

General Counsel:	William S. Lipsman	Traded (Symbol):	NASDAQ (APAC)
Investor Relations:	Marc Simon, C.F.O.	Stockholders:	128
Human Resources:	Richard H. Kremer, Sr. V.P.	Employees:	14,000
Mgt. Info. Svcs.:	Allen A. Kalkstein, Sr. V.P.	Annual Meeting:	In May
Auditors:	Arthur Andersen LLP	Internet:	www.apacteleservices.com

AptarGroup, Inc.

475 West Terra Cotta Avenue, Suite E, Crystal Lake, Illinois 60014-9695
Telephone: (815) 477-0424

AptarGroup, Inc. produces three broad categories of dispensing packaging components: pumps, aerosol valves, and dispensing closures, which are sold to the fragrance/cosmetics, personal care, pharmaceutical, household products, and food industries. Manufacturing facilities are located in the United States and Europe. In December 1995, AptarGroup announced the acquisition of a controlling interest in General Plastics S.A., a manufacturer of dispensing closures for the personal care market. General Plastics is headquartered near Paris, and has two manufacturing facilities in France. In October 1995, AptarGroup announced the acquisition of Liquid Molding Systems, Inc., a domestic manufacturer of liquid silicone rubber valves for dispensing closure systems. Incorporated in Delaware in 1992.

Directors   (In addition to indicated officers)

King Harris, Chm.
Eugene L. Barnett
Ralph Gruska
Leo A. Guthart

William W. Harris
Ervin J. LeCoque
Alfred Pilz

Officers   (Directors*)

*Carl A. Siebel, Pres. & C.E.O.
*Peter Pfeiffer, V. Chm.
 Stephen J. Hagge, Exec. V.P., Secy. & Treas.
 Lawrence Lowrimore, V.P.—Hum. Res.
 Ralph Poltermann, V.P.—Risk Mgt.
 Jacques Blanie, Exec. V.P.—Seaquist Perfect
   Dispensing Div.
 Francois Boutan, Fin. Dir.—Eur. Oper.

Pierre Cheru, Gen. Dir.—Valois S.A.
Francesco Mascitelli, Gen. Mgr.—SAR SpA
James R. Reed, Pres.—Seaquist Perfect
   Dispensing Div.
Eric S. Ruskoski, Pres.—Seaquist Closures Div.
Hans-Josef Schutz, Man. Dir.—Pfeiffer Grp.
Alain Vichot, Gen. Dir. Adj.—Valois S.A.

Consolidated Balance Sheet   As of December 31, 1996 (000 omitted)

Assets		Liabilities & Stockholders' Equity	
Current assets	$237,231	Current liabilities	$116,259
Net property, plant & equipment	255,329	Long-term debt	76,569
Other assets	83,576	Deferred items	47,609
		*Stockholders' equity	335,699
Total	$576,136	Total	$576,136

*17,950,000 shares common stock outstanding.

Consolidated Income Statement

Years Ended Dec. 31	Thousands — — — — Net Sales	Net Income	Per Share — — — Earnings	Cash Dividends	Common Stock Price Range Calendar Year
1996	$615,808	$37,548	$2.09	$ .28	43-1/8 — 29
1995	557,455	35,714	1.99	.26	38-1/4 — 24-5/8
1994	474,266	27,258	1.65	.23	29 — 20-1/8
1993[a]	411,525	21,563[b]	1.34[b]	.10	22 — 16[c]
1992	370,293	19,479			

[a]Includes the effects of The Pfeiffer Group and minority interest since acquisition on April 22, 1993.
[b]Before cumulative effect of accounting change for FAS 109, resulting in a net gain of $1,400,000 ($.09 per share).
[c]Trading commenced on April 23, 1993.

Transfer Agent & Registrar: ChaseMellon Shareholder Services, L.L.P.

General Counsel:	Sidley & Austin	Auditors:	Price Waterhouse LLP
Investor Relations:	Stephen J. Hagge, Exec. V.P.	Traded (Symbol):	NYSE (ATR)
		Stockholders:	1,000
Human Resources:	Lawrence Lowrimore, V.P.	Employees:	3,900
Mgt. Info. Svcs.:	Ruth Freer	Annual Meeting:	In May

Archer-Daniels-Midland Company

4666 Faries Parkway, Decatur, Illinois 62526-5666
Telephone: (217) 424-5200

Archer-Daniels-Midland Company (ADM) is in the business of procuring, transporting, storing, processing and merchandising agricultural products. The Oilseed Processing Division operates extraction plants that produce a broad line of vegetable oils including soy, corn, sunflower, peanut, conola, and cottonseed. The ADM Corn Processing Division manufactures and distributes sweeteners, starches, beverage alcohol, and ethanol. The Protein Specialties Division produces soy flours, protein isolates and textured vegetable protein used in processed meat products, convenience foods, and pet food. ADM Milling Co. produces wheat flour used in bakery products, cereals, processed foods, and pasta products. Its grain division handles grain acquisition and merchandising. The Southern Cotton Oil Company processes cottonseed. American River Transportation Company assists the company as a carrier of drybulk and liquid commodities. ADM conducts operations throughout the United States and in Canada, France, Germany, Ireland, the Netherlands, Portugal, Spain, and the United Kingdom. Other major subsidiaries include: ADM/Growmark; Fleischmann Malting Co., Inc.; Gooch Foods, Inc.; Hickory Point Bank & Trust; Tabor Grain Co.; and ADM International Ltd. In December 1996, the company announced an agreement to acquire the world's largest cocoa bean processor, the Grace Cocoa business of Boca Raton, Florida-based W.R. Grace & Co. Incorporated in Delaware in 1923.

Directors   (In addition to indicated officers)

Shreve M. Archer, Jr.	Gaylord O. Coan, V. Chm.	John K. Vanier
John R. Block	F. Ross Johnson	O. Glenn Webb
Richard Burt	M. Brian Mulroney	Andrew Young
Mollie Hale Carter	Robert S. Strauss	

Officers   (Directors*)

*Dwayne O. Andreas, Chm.	Jack McDonald, V.P.
*G. Allen Andreas, Pres. & C.E.O.	Paul Mulhollem, V.P.
Charles T. Bayless, Grp. V.P.	Brian F. Peterson, V.P.
Howard E. Buoy, Grp. V.P.	Raymond V. Preiksaitis, V.P.—Mgmt. Info. Svcs.
Larry H. Cunningham, Grp. V.P.	John G. Reed, Jr., V.P.
Craig L. Hamlin, Grp. V.P.	Richard P. Reising, V.P., Gen. Coun. & Secy.
Burnell D. Kraft, Grp. V.P.	John D. Rice, V.P.
Martin L. Andreas, Sr. V.P. & Exec. Asst. to C.E.O.	Kenneth A. Robinson, V.P.
William H. Camp, V.P.	Douglas J. Schmalz, V.P. & C.F.O.
Barrie R. Cox, V.P.	Stephen Yu, V.P.
Edward A. Harjehausen, V.P.	Charles P. Archer, Treas.
Paul L. Krug, Jr., V.P.	Steven R. Mills, Cont.
John E. Long, V.P.	

Consolidated Balance Sheet   As of June 30, 1996 (000 omitted)

Assets		Liabilities & Stockholders' Equity	
Current assets	$ 4,384,683	Current liabilities	$ 1,633,551
Net property, plant & equipment	4,114,301	Long-term debt	2,002,979
Other assets	1,950,885	Deferred items	668,527
		*Stockholders' equity	6,144,812
Total	$10,449,869	Total	$10,449,869

*545,821,000 shares common stock outstanding.

Consolidated Income Statement

Years Ended June 30	Thousands — — — — — Net Sales	Net Income	Per Share[a] — — — Earnings	Cash Dividends	Common Stock Price Range[a] Calendar Year
1996	$13,314,049	$695,912	$1.27	$ .17	23-1/8 — 15-5/8
1995	12,671,868	795,915	1.40	.08	19 — 13-5/8
1994	11,374,372	484,069	.89	.06	19-1/8 — 12-7/8
1993	9,811,362	567,527[b]	.95[b]	.05	15-7/8 — 12-1/8
1992	9,231,502	503,757	.84	.05	17-1/8 — 11-5/8

[a]Adjusted for annual 5% stock dividends through September 1996 and a 3-for-2 stock split in December 1994.
[b]Includes a gain to reflect FAS 106 and FAS 109, resulting in a cumulative effect of $33,018,000 ($.06 per share).

Transfer Agent & Registrar: Harris Trust and Savings Bank

General Counsel: Richard P. Reising, V.P.

Investor Relations: Charles P. Archer, Treas.

Human Resources: Martin Reed

Mgt. Info. Svcs.: Raymond V. Preiksaitis, V.P.

Auditors: Ernst & Young LLP

Traded (Symbol):
NYSE, CSE, Tokyo, Frankfurt, 3 Swiss (ADM)

Stockholders: 35,431

Employees: 14,811

Annual Meeting: In October

Internet: www.admworld.com

Argosy Gaming Company

219 Piasa Street, Alton, Illinois 62002-6232
Telephone: (618) 474-7500

Argosy Gaming Company is a leading multi-jurisdictional developer, owner, and operator of riverboat casinos and related entertainment facilities in the midwestern and southern United States. The company, through its subsidiaries and joint ventures, owns and operates the Alton Belle Casino in Alton, Illinois, serving the St. Louis metropolitan area; the Argosy Casino in Riverside, Missouri, serving the Kansas City metropolitan market; and the Belle of Baton Rouge in Baton Rouge, Louisiana. The company is also a major partner and operator of the Belle of Sioux City in Sioux City, Iowa, and the Argosy Casino in Lawrenceburg, Indiana, serving the southeast tri-state Cincinnati, Ohio metropolitan market, including Dayton and Columbus, Ohio; Lexington and Louisville, Kentucky; and Indianapolis, Indiana. The company commenced operations in September 1991 with the first gambling riverboat in Alton, Illinois, located roughly 20 miles northeast of downtown St. Louis. Subsidiaries are: Alton Gaming Company; Belle of Sioux City L.P.; Catfish Partnership in Commendam; Missouri Gaming Company; and Indiana Gaming Company. Incorporated in Delaware in 1992.

Directors (In addition to indicated officers)

William F. Cellini, Chm.	Jimmy F. Gallagher
Edward F. Brennan	William J. McEnery
George L. Bristol	John B. Pratt, Sr.
Felix Lance Callis	

Officers (Directors*)

*James B. Perry, Pres., C.E.O. & Acting Treas. G. Dan Marshall, V.P.—Inv. Rel.
 Dale Black, V.P., Cont. & Prin. Acct. Off. Patsy S. Hubbard, Corp. Secy.

Consolidated Balance Sheet As of December 31, 1996 (000 omitted)

Assets		Liabilities & Stockholders' Equity	
Current assets	$ 58,841	Current liabilities	$ 44,966
Net property, plant & equipment	314,480	Long-term debt	377,308
Other assets	158,838	Other liabilities	37,184
		*Stockholders' equity	72,701
Total	$532,159	Total	$532,159

*24,333,333 shares common stock outstanding.

Consolidated Income Statement

Years Ended Dec. 31	Thousands — — — — Net Revenues	Net Income	Per Share[a] — — — Earnings	Cash Dividends	Common Stock Price Range[a] Calendar Year
1996	$244,817	$(24,829)	$(1.02)	$ .00	9-1/4 — 4-1/4
1995	252,691	6,953	.29	.00	17-1/2 — 7-1/4
1994	153,045	9,635	.40	.00	27 — 10
1993[b]	67,525	10,825	.38	.00	36-3/4 — 15-1/4
1992[b]	58,019	15,214	.36	.00	

[a]Initial public offering in February 1993.
[b]Pro forma.

Transfer Agent & Registrar: Harris Trust and Savings Bank

General Counsel:	Winston & Strawn	Traded (Symbol):	NYSE (AGY)
Investor Relations:	G. Dan Marshall, V.P.	Stockholders:	907
Human Resources:	Patricia A. Mathews	Employees:	3,730
Mgt. Info. Svcs.:	Jeff Pour	Annual Meeting:	In April
Auditors:	Ernst & Young LLP	Internet:	www.argosycasinos.com

ARTRA GROUP Incorporated
500 Central Avenue, Northfield, Illinois 60093
Telephone: (847) 441-6650

ARTRA GROUP Incorporated, through its wholly owned subsidiary Bagcraft Corporation of America, a flexible packaging manufacturer, supplies specialty wraps and bags to the food industry. ARTRA also has an approximate 14 percent equity interest in COMFORCE Corp., a growing publicly traded (AMEX: CFS) telecommunications/computer staffing and consulting concern. Incorporated in Pennsylvania in 1933.

Director (In addition to indicated officers)

Edward A. Celano	Gerard M. Kenny
Howard R. Conant	Maynard K. Louis
Robert L. Johnson	

Officers (Directors*)

*John Harvey, Chm. & C.E.O.	James D. Doering, V.P., Treas. & C.F.O.
*Peter R. Harvey, Pres. & C.O.O.	Robert S. Gruber, V.P.—Corp. Rel.
John G. Hamm, Exec. V.P.	Lawrence D. Levin, Cont.
John Conroy, V.P.—Corp. Admin.	Edwin G. Rymek, Secy.

Consolidated Balance Sheet   As of December 26, 1996 (000 omitted)

Assets		Liabilities & Stockholders' Equity	
Current assets	$46,900	Current liabilities	$ 50,292
Net property, plant & equipment	24,934	Long-term debt	34,207
Other assets	5,545	Deferred items	2,135
		Other liabilities	12,335
		*Stockholders' equity[a]	(21,590)
Total	$77,379	Total	$ 77,379

*7,624,766 shares common stock outstanding.
[a]ARTRA GROUP Incorporated is involved in pending litigation to recover its investment in Emerald Acquisition Corp. common stock and Emerald junior debentures. For further information, please refer to ARTRA's Form 10-K.

Consolidated Income Statement

Years Ended Abt. Dec. 31	Thousands — — — — Net Sales[a]	Net Income	Per Share — — — Earnings	Cash Dividends	Common Stock Price Range Calendar Year
1996	$120,699	$ 12,973[b]	$ 1.51[b]	$ .00	9-1/4 — 4-5/8
1995[c]	121,879	(2,903)[b]	(.63)[b]	.00	6 — 3-1/4
1994[c]	111,837	(20,470)[b]	(3.73)[b]	.00	7-3/4 — 3-3/4
1993	113,584	13,514[b]	2.61[b]	.00	8-3/8 — 3
1992	121,084	(37,972)[d]	(8.90)	.00	11-1/4 — 3-3/8

[a]1994-1992 reclassified for discontinued operations.
[b]Includes extraordinary gains of $9,424,000 ($1.23 per share) in 1996; $14,030,000 ($2.06 per share) in 1995; $8,965,000 ($1.57 per share) in 1994; and a non-recurring gain of $22,057,000 ($4.49 per share) in 1993 from extinguished debt of a subsidiary.
[c]Includes a gain on the sale of Arcar Graphics, Inc. in October 1995.
[d]Includes non-recurring charges of $18,150,000.

Transfer Agent & Registrar:	Mellon Securities Transfer Services			
General Counsel:	Kwiatt, Silverman & Ruben Ltd.	Traded (Symbol):	NYSE, PSE (ATA)	
Investor Relations:	Robert S. Gruber, V.P.	Stockholders:	2,500	
Human Resources:	John Conroy, V.P.	Employees:	900	
Auditors:	Coopers & Lybrand L.L.P.	Annual Meeting:	As set by Directors	

Avondale Financial Corp.

20 North Clark Street, Chicago, Illinois 60602-5085
Telephone: (312) 782-6200

Avondale Financial Corp. is the holding company for Avondale Federal Savings Bank, a federally chartered stock savings bank. The bank, founded in 1911, has its headquarters in Chicago. It provides community banking services to the north and northwest sides of the city through five branch offices. The bank also operates a consumer lending business which originates home mortgages, home equity lines of credit, private label credit cards, and a variety of consumer loans, primarily though third-party distribution channels throughout the United States. Incorporated in Delaware in 1993.

Directors (In addition to indicated officers)

Jameson A. Baxter
Sandra P. Guthman
Arthur L. Knight, Jr.

Peter G. Krivkovich
Hipolito (Paul) Roldan
Robert A. Wislow

Officers (Directors*)

*R. Thomas Eiff, Chm.
*Robert S. Engelman, Jr., Pres. & C.E.O.
 Howard A. Jaffe, V.P. & C.F.O.

Anthony Pallante II, V.P.
Doria L. Koros, Secy.

Consolidated Balance Sheet   As of December 31, 1996 (000 omitted)

Assets		Liabilities & Stockholders' Equity	
Cash and cash equivalents	$ 9,074	Deposits	$330,655
Securities owned	240,255	Other liabilities	204,027
Loans, net	317,300	*Stockholders' equity	60,889
Other assets	28,942		
Total	$595,571	Total	$595,571

*3,525,288 shares common stock outstanding.

Consolidated Income Statement

Years Ended Dec. 31	Thousands — — — — Total Income	Net Income	Per Share[a] — — — Earnings	Cash Dividends	Common Stock Price Range[a] Calendar Year
1996	$56,284	$ 4,216	$1.13	$ .00	17-1/2 — 12-1/2
1995[b]	33,875	2,777	.69	.00	15-1/4 — 11-1/4
1995	27,569	(1,420)			
1994	33,854	2,707			
1993	39,488	(3,991)			

[a]Initial public offering in April 1995.
[b]Nine months ended December 31. Company changed to calendar year reporting in 1995; prior years represent March fiscal year end.

Transfer Agent & Registrar:	LaSalle National Bank		
General Counsel:	Silver, Freedman & Taff L.L.P.	Auditors:	Arthur Andersen LLP
Investor Relations:	Howard A. Jaffe, V.P.	Traded (Symbol):	NASDAQ (AVND)
		Stockholders:	1,400
Human Resources:	Howard A. Jaffe, V.P.	Employees:	200
Mgt. Info. Svcs.:	Anthony Pallante II, V.P.	Annual Meeting:	In May

BAB Holdings, Inc.

8501 West Higgins Road, Suite 320, Chicago, Illinois 60631
Telephone: (312) 380-6100

BAB Holdings, Inc. operates and franchises specialty bagel stores under the Big Apple Bagels brand name featuring daily baked "from scratch" bagels, cream cheeses, coffee, and other related products. The company also acts as a licensor of Big Apple Bagels bagel-deli units owned and operated by Host Marriott Services featuring the company's par-baked bagel and other related products in airport and travel plaza locations. In addition, BAB operates and franchises Brewster's Coffee concept specialty retail coffee stores. In November 1995, the company completed an initial public offering of 3,825,000 shares of common stock. In May 1997, the company announced that it had completed its acquisition of New Jersey-based My Favorite Muffin Too, Inc., a privately held operator and franchisor of 59 specialty muffin and bagel cafes primarily on the East Coast. Incorporated in Illinois in 1992.

Directors (In addition to indicated officers)

David L. Epstein
Paul C. Stolzer

Cynthia A. Vahlkamp

Officers (Directors*)

*Michael W. Evans, Pres. & C.E.O.
*Michael K. Murtaugh, V.P. & Gen. Coun.

Thomas J. Fletcher, C.O.O.
Theodore P. Noncek, C.F.O., Secy. & Treas.

Consolidated Balance Sheet As of November 30, 1996 (000 omitted)

Assets		Liabilities & Stockholders' Equity	
Current assets	$ 3,686	Current liabilities	$ 2,351
Net property, plant & equipment	3,534	Long-term debt	2
Other assets	3,928	*Stockholders' equity	8,795
Total	$11,148	Total	$11,148

*7,143,069 shares common stock outstanding.

Consolidated Income Statement

Years Ended Nov. 30	Thousands — — — —		Per Share[a] — — —		Common Stock
	Net Sales	Net Income	Earnings[b]	Cash Dividends	Price Range[ac] Calendar Year
1996	$6,324	$(321)	$ (.04)	$ .00	11-3/4 — 3-1/8
1995	2,033	(436)	(.12)		
1994	979	(372)	(.15)		
1993	187	(325)	(.13)		

[a]Reflects a 3-for-2 stock dividend in April 1996.
[b]Fully diluted.
[c]Initial public offering in November 1995.

Transfer Agent & Registrar: LaSalle National Trust, N.A.

General Counsel:	Michael K. Murtaugh, V.P.	Traded (Symbol):	NASDAQ (BAGL)
Investor Relations:	Theodore P. Noncek, C.F.O.	Stockholders:	185
Mgt. Info. Svcs.:	Paul Lutton	Employees:	399
Auditors:	Ernst & Young LLP	Annual Meeting:	In April

LaSalle Banks Guide

Baker, Fentress & Company

200 West Madison Street, Suite 3510, Chicago, Illinois 60606
Telephone: (312) 236-9190

Baker, Fentress & Company is a non-diversified closed-end investment company which invests primarily for capital appreciation. Until 1960, the company conducted business as an investment banker and a broker/dealer in securities. Since 1970, Baker, Fentress & Company has been registered as an investment company under the Investment Company Act of 1940. The company invests primarily in common stocks and other equity-type securities. Baker, Fentress invests in preferred stocks, bonds, debentures and notes, and short-term obligations. Major investments include: Levin Management; Consolidated-Tomoka Land Co.; WMX Technologies, Inc.; Barnett Banks; MCI Communications; PanEnergy; Echlin, Inc.; Harnischfeger; United Healthcare; and Newell Co. The company has a policy of distributing annually to shareholders amounts equal to at least 8 percent of the company's average net assets. In 1996, the company acquired John A. Levin & Co., Inc. ("Levco"), a New York-based investment advisory firm. Incorporated in Delaware in 1954.

Directors (In addition to indicated officers)

Frederick S. Addy
Bob D. Allen
Jessica M. Bibliowicz
Eugene V. Fife
J. Barton Goodwin
David D. Grumhaus

Jeffrey A. Kigner
Burton G. Malkiel
David D. Peterson
Melody L.P. Sarnell
William H. Springer

Officers (Directors*)

*James P. Gorter, Chm.
*John A. Levin, Pres. & C.E.O.
 James P. Koeneman, V.P., C.F.O. & Secy.
 Scott E. Smith, V.P.

Todd H. Steele, V.P.
Janet Sandona Jones, Treas. & Asst. Secy.
Lana L. Spence, Asst. Treas.

Consolidated Balance Sheet   As of December 31, 1996 (000 omitted)

Assets		Liabilities & Stockholders' Equity	
Current assets	$773,032	Current liabilities	$ 14,527
Net property, plant & equipment	641	Long-term debt	18,000
		*Stockholders' equity	741,146
Total	$773,673	Total	$773,673

*34,042,181 shares common stock outstanding.

Consolidated Income Statement

Years Ended Dec. 31	Thousands — — — — Net Invest. Income	Cash Dividends	Per Share — — — Cap. Gain Distrib.	Net Asset Value	Common Stock Price Range Calendar Year
1996	$10,670	$78	$1.78	$21.77	20-1/4 — 16-1/4
1995	9,419	35	1.20	21.75	17-5/8 — 13-3/4
1994	6,933	35	1.46	17.47	17-7/8 — 13-3/8
1993	7,116	48	1.76	20.42	19-7/8 — 16-3/8
1992	8,430	39	1.42	20.82	19-1/8 — 16-5/8

Transfer Agent & Registrar: Harris Trust and Savings Bank

General Counsel: Bell, Boyd & Lloyd

Investor Relations: James P. Koeneman, V.P.

Human Relations: Lana L. Spence, Mgr.

Mgt. Info. Svcs.: Lana L. Spence, Asst. Treas.

Auditors: Ernst & Young LLP

Traded (Symbol): NYSE (BKF)

Stockholders: 16,000

Employees: 10

Annual Meeting: In April

Bally Total Fitness Holding Corporation

8700 West Bryn Mawr Avenue, Chicago, Illinois 60631
Telephone: (773) 399-1300

Bally Total Fitness Holding Corporation, formerly Bally's Health & Tennis Corporation, is a commercial operator of fitness centers. The company operates approximately 320 fitness centers, concentrated in 27 states and Canada. On a membership basis, the company offers extensive aerobics programs and personal training. Fitness centers offer prospective members the option of financing their initial membership fees. The company was spun off from Bally Entertainment Corporation in January 1996. Incorporated in Delaware in 1983.

Directors (In addition to indicated officers)

Arthur M. Goldberg
Aubrey C. Lewis
J. Kenneth Looloian

James F. Mc Anally, M.D.
Liza M. Walsh

Officers (Directors*)

*Lee S. Hillman, Pres. & C.E.O.
John W. Dwyer, Sr. V.P., C.F.O. & Treas.
Cary A. Gaan, Sr. V.P., Gen. Coun. & Secy.
Harold Morgan, Sr. V.P.—Hum. Res.

David M. Tolmie, Sr. V.P.—New Bus. Dev.
John Wildman, Sr. V.P.—Sales & Mktg.
Julie Adams, V.P. & Cont.

Consolidated Balance Sheet   As of December 31, 1996 (000 omitted)

Assets		Liabilities & Stockholders' Equity	
Current assets	$193,844	Current liabilities	$187,312
Net installment contracts	146,972	Long-term debt	376,397
Net property, plant & equipment	325,459	Deferred items	26,440
Other assets	147,205	Other liabilities	6,824
		*Stockholders' equity	216,507
Total	$813,480	Total	$813,480

*12,495,161 shares common stock outstanding.

Consolidated Income Statement

Years Ended Dec. 31	Thousands — — — — Net Sales	Net Income	Per Share[a] — — — Earnings	Cash Dividends	Common Stock Price Range[a] Calendar Year
1996	$625,640	$(35,545)	$(2.92)	$ .00	9-1/8 — 3-3/4
1995	661,740	(36,497)[b]	(3.08)[b]		
1994	661,505	(76,305)[b]	(6.44)[b]		
1993	694,800	(28,000)[c]			
1992	744,700	(7,500)			

[a]Spun off from Bally Entertainment Corporation in January 1996.
[b]Pro forma.
[c]Excludes an extraordinary after tax loss of $6,000,000 from early redemption of debt and a credit of $20,700,000 for cumulative effect of adopting FAS No.109.

Transfer Agent & Registrar: LaSalle National Bank

General Counsel:	Cary A. Gaan, Sr. V.P.	Auditors:	Ernst & Young LLP
Investor Relations:	Lee S. Hillman, Pres.	Traded (Symbol):	NASDAQ (BFIT)
		Stockholders:	9,000
Human Relations:	Harold Morgan, Sr. V.P.	Employees:	14,400
Mgt. Info. Svcs.:	John W. Dwyer, Sr. V.P.	Annual Meeting:	As set by Directors

Baxter International Inc.

One Baxter Parkway, Deerfield, Illinois 60015
Telephone: (847) 948-2000

Baxter International Inc., through its subsidiaries, is a global medical-products and services company which is a leader in technologies related to the blood and circulatory system. The company has market-leading positions in four global businesses: biotechnology, cardiovascular medicine, renal therapy, and intravenous system/medical products. Baxter subsidiaries include Baxter World Trade Corp. and Baxter Healthcare Corp. In September 1996, the company spun off its healthcare products and cost-management business, Allegiance Corporation, through a tax-free dividend of Allegiance common stock to Baxter shareholders. Incorporated in Delaware in 1931.

Directors (In addition to indicated officers)

Walter Boomer
Pei-yuan Chia
John W. Colloton
Susan Crown
Mary Johnston Evans
Frank R. Frame

Martha R. Ingram
Arnold J. Levine, Ph.D.
Georges C. St. Laurent, Jr.
Monroe E. Trout, M.D.
Reed V. Tuckson, M.D.
Fred L. Turner

Officers (Directors*)

*Vernon R. Loucks, Jr., Chm. & C.E.O.
*Harry M. Jansen Kraemer, Jr., Pres.
 Arthur F. Staubitz, Sr. V.P. & Gen. Coun.
 Michael J. Tucker, Sr. V.P.—Hum. Res.
 Brian P. Anderson, V.P.—Fin.
 Fabrizio Bonanni, V.P.—Qual. Sys.

John F. Gaither, Jr., V.P.—Corp. Dev. & Strategy
David C. McKee, V.P. & Dep. Gen. Coun.
Kshitij Mohan, V.P.—R & D
John L. Quick, V.P.—Qual. Mgmt.
Steven J. Meyer, Treas.

Consolidated Balance Sheet   As of December 31, 1996 (000 omitted)

Assets		Liabilities & Stockholders' Equity	
Current assets	$3,480,000	Current liabilities	$2,445,000
Net property, plant & equipment	1,843,000	Long-term debt	1,695,000
Other assets	2,273,000	Deferred items	255,000
		Other liabilities	697,000
		*Stockholders' equity	2,504,000
Total	$7,596,000	Total	$7,596,000

*334,739,000 shares common stock outstanding.

Consolidated Income Statement

Years Ended Dec. 31	Thousands — — — — Net Sales[a]	Net Income	Per Share — — — Earnings	Cash Dividends	Common Stock Price Range Calendar Year
1996	$5,438,000	$ 669,000	$ 2.11[b]	$1.17	48-1/8 — 39-3/4
1995	5,048,000	649,000	1.34[b]	1.11	44-3/4 — 26-3/4
1994	4,479,000	596,000	1.45[b]	1.02	28-7/8 — 21-5/8
1993	4,116,000	(198,000)[c]	(.72)[c]	1.00	32-3/4 — 20
1992	3,857,000	441,000[d]	1.56[d]	.86	40-1/2 — 30-1/2

[a]Restated to exclude operations discontinued in 1992.
[b]From continuing operations.
[c]Includes a provision for restructuring charges of a pretax amount of $700,000,000 and a provision for litigation charges of a pretax amount of $330,000,000; also includes a gain to reflect FAS 109 and FAS 112, resulting in a cumulative effect of $70,000,000 ($.25 per share).
[d]Includes a charge to reflect FAS 106, resulting in a cumulative effect of $165,000,000 ($.59 per share).

Transfer Agent & Registrar: First Chicago Trust Co. of New York

General Counsel: Arthur F. Staubitz, Sr. V.P.

Investor Relations: Neville Jeharajah, V.P.

Human Resources: Michael J. Tucker, Sr. V.P.

Auditors: Price Waterhouse LLP

Traded (Symbol):
  NYSE, CSE, PSE, LON, Swiss (BAX)

Stockholders: 64,700

Employees: 37,000

Annual Meeting: In May

Internet: www.baxter.com

Bell & Howell Company

5215 Old Orchard Road, Skokie, Illinois 60077-1076
Telephone: (847) 470-7660

Bell & Howell Company (formerly Bell & Howell Holdings Company) is a leading provider of systems and services for information access and dissemination. The company consists of two business segments, information access and mail processing systems. The information access segment develops and markets imaging and information services and systems that provide its customers with access solutions to targeted segments of complex public and private information databases. The mail processing systems segment develops and markets a complete range of high volume mail processing systems, which increasingly utilize the company's proprietary software to expand the capabilities and improve the efficiencies and effectiveness of customers' mailing operations. Principal subsidiaries are: Bell & Howell Operating Company; Bell & Howell Mail Processing Systems Company; UMI Company; Bell & Howell Publication Systems Company; Bell & Howell Document Management Products Company; and Bell & Howell Postal Systems Inc. Incorporated in Delaware in 1993.

Directors   (In addition to indicated officers)

David Bonderman	William E. Oberndorf
David Brown	Gary L. Roubos
J. Taylor Crandall	John H. Scully
Daniel L. Doctoroff	

Officers   (Directors*)

*William J. White, Chm.	Kevin O'Shea, V.P. & Treas.
*James P. Roemer, Pres. & C.E.O.	Maria T. Rubly, V.P.
*Nils A. Johansson, Exec. V.P. & C.F.O.	Gary S. Salit, Gen. Coun. & Secy.
Stuart T. Lieberman, V.P., Cont. & Chf. Acct. Officer	

Consolidated Balance Sheet   As of December 28, 1996 (000 omitted)

Assets		Liabilities & Stockholders' Equity	
Current assets	$352,487	Current liabilities	$ 360,285
Net property, plant & equipment	155,728	Long-term liabilities	547,600
Total investments & other assets	292,303	Deferred items	58,077
		*Stockholders' equity	(165,444)
Total	$800,518	Total	$ 800,518

*18,329,000 shares common stock outstanding.

Consolidated Income Statement

Years Ended Abt. Dec. 31	Thousands — — — — Net Sales	Net Income[a]	Per Share[b] — — — Earnings	Cash Dividends	Common Stock Price Range[bc] Calendar Year
1996	$902,797	$ 23,070	$ 1.24	$ .00	35-1/4 — 22-3/4
1995	819,889	15,991	.96	.00	29-3/8 — 15-1/2
1994[d]	720,340	(9,994)	(.52)		
1993[e]	675,553	(188,047)			
1992	670,039	(22,335)			

[a]Applicable to common stock.
[b]Adjusted to reflect a 4.26-for-1 stock split in May 1995.
[c]Initial public offering in May 1995.
[d]Unaudited pro forma; includes extraordinary losses of $9,193,000.
[e]Includes extraordinary losses of $6,625,000 and a charge to reflect FAS 106, resulting in a cumulative effect of $4,759,000.

Transfer Agent & Registrar:	The First National Bank of Boston		
General Counsel:	Gary S. Salit, Secy.	Traded (Symbol):	NYSE (BHW)
Investor Relations:	Kevin O'Shea, V.P.	Stockholders:	4,000
		Employees:	5,791
Human Resources:	Maria T. Rubly, V.P.	Annual Meeting:	In May
Auditors:	KPMG Peat Marwick LLP	Internet:	www.bellhowell.com

Beverly Bancorporation, Inc.

16345 South Harlem Avenue, Suite 3E, Tinley Park, Illinois 60477
Telephone: (708) 614-5072

Beverly Bancorporation, Inc. is a community-based financial services holding company. Through its subsidiaries, the company provides a full range of banking services and personal and corporate trust services. The company's principal operating subsidiaries are Beverly National Bank and Beverly Trust Company. Beverly Bank was federally chartered in 1863 and is the second oldest active national bank in Illinois. As a community oriented, full-service commercial bank with 12 locations, it provides a full range of banking services to individuals, small- to medium-sized businesses, and not-for-profit organizations. Beverly Trust provides a wide array of trust services for individuals and corporations. In August 1996, the company completed an initial public offering of 1,000,000 shares of common stock. Incorporated in Illinois in 1969. Reincorporated in Delaware in 1996.

Directors (In addition to indicated officers)

Anthony R. Pasquinelli, Chm.
William E. Brazley
David B. Colmar

Christopher M. Cronin
Richard I. Polanek
William C. Waddell

Officers (Directors*)

*John D. Van Winkle, Pres. & C.E.O.
James W. Martin, Jr., Exec. V.P. &
  Mgr.—Consumer Sales
Charles E. Ofenloch, Exec. V.P. &
  Mgr.—Commer. Sales

John T. O'Neill, Exec. V.P. & C.F.O.
Ronald F. Stajkowski, Exec. V.P. & Mgr.—Beverly
  Trust Co.
Mark Spehr, Sr. V.P. & Chf. Lending Off.
Sandra J. Tome, Secy.

Consolidated Balance Sheet As of December 31, 1996 (000 omitted)

Assets		Liabilities & Stockholders' Equity	
Cash and due from banks	$ 25,698	Deposits	$560,146
Investement securities	206,327	Securities sold	2,542
Net loans	368,602	Other liabilities	5,410
Net property, plant & equipment	15,816	*Stockholders' equity	61,946
Other assets	13,601		
Total	$630,044	Total	$630,044

*5,172,182 shares common stock outstanding.

Consolidated Income Statement

Years Ended Dec. 31	Thousands — — — —		Per Share[a] — — — —		Common Stock
	Total Income	Net Income	Earnings	Cash Dividends	Price Range[a] Calendar Year
1996	$51,698	$6,789	$1.50	$ .21	18-1/4 — 15-1/8
1995	47,840	6,204	1.26	.19	
1994	43,223	6,416	1.34	.18	
1993	43,288	5,246	1.13	.17	
1992	47,883	4,404	.96	.17	

[a]Initial public offering in August 1996.

Transfer Agent & Registrar:	Harris Trust and Savings Bank		
General Counsel:	Lord Bissell & Brook	Traded (Symbol):	NASDAQ (BEVB)
Investor Relations:	Sandra J. Tome, Secy.	Stockholders:	328
Human Resources:	Galina Bryant, V.P.	Employees:	338
Mgt. Info. Svcs.:	Thaddeus Witwicki, Sr. V.P.	Annual Meeting:	In May
Auditors:	Grant Thornton LLP	Internet:	www.beverlybank.com

Binks Sames Corporation

9201 West Belmont Avenue, Franklin Park, Illinois 60131-2887
Telephone: (847) 671-3000

Binks Sames Corporation and its subsidiaries design, manufacture, and distribute spray finishing and coating application equipment. The company divides its products into two general groups: standard equipment and industrial equipment. The standard equipment line consists of more than 40 models of spray guns, a wide variety of air and fluid nozzles, a complete line of high and low pressure material handling pumps, pressure tanks, portable and stationary air compressors, and accessories such as siphon cups, pressure cups, oil and water extractors, air and fluid regulators, ball valves, hose connections and fittings, air and fluid hoses, paint heaters, and replacement parts. The industrial equipment line includes spray booths, paint circulating systems, air replacement systems, automatic spray coating machines, electrocoating systems, electrostatic application equipment, spray painting robots, and complete industrial finishing systems involving custom design and engineering services. Binks also manufactures water cooling towers used in connection with air conditioning and water treatment systems. Domestically, the company operates nine branch offices with warehouse facilities, 26 sales offices, and a network of more than 5,200 distributors. Foreign subsidiaries are located in Australia, Belgium, Canada, France, Germany, Italy, Japan, Mexico, Sweden, and the United Kingdom. Major subsidiaries are Binks R&D; Sames Electrostatic; Binks Manufacturing Co. of Canada; Binks International, S.A. (Belgium); Binks-Bullows, Ltd. (England); Sames, S.A. (France); Binks Japan, Ltd.; and Binks Deutschland GmbH. Incorporated in Delaware in 1929.

Directors   (In addition to indicated officers)

Wayne F. Edwards	William W. Roche
Donald G. Meyer	Clifford J. Vaughan
Burke B. Roche, Chm. Emeritus	

Officers   (Directors*)

* John J. Schornack, Chm.
* Doran J. Unschuld, Pres. & C.E.O.
* Terence P. Roche, Exec. V.P., Asst. Secy. & Asst. Treas.
Samuel W. Culbertson, V.P.—Res. & Dev.
Stephen R. Kennedy, V.P.—Hum. Res.

Adrien Lacchia, V.P.—Sames & Co-Managing Dir.—Sames, S.A.
Jeffrey W. Lemajeur, V.P.—Fin., C.F.O. & Treas.
Stephen R. Mathers, V.P.—Corp. Dev.
Carl M. Springer, V.P.—Mfg. & Eng., Asst. Secy. & Asst. Treas.
Ernest F. Watts, V.P.—Mkt. Dev. & Pres./C.E.O. Sames

Consolidated Balance Sheet   As of November 30, 1996 (000 omitted)

Assets		Liabilities & Stockholders' Equity	
Current assets	$190,014	Current liabilities	$ 93,559
Net property, plant & equipment	27,968	Long-term debt	44,634
Other assets	12,247	Deferred items	9,989
		*Stockholders' equity	82,047
Total	$230,229	Total	$230,229

*3,088,837 shares common stock outstanding.

Consolidated Income Statement

Years Ended Nov. 30	Thousands — — — — Net Sales	Net Income	Per Share[a] — — — — Earnings	Cash Dividends	Common Stock Price Range[a] Calendar Year
1996	$296,686	$(11,108)	$(3.60)	$ .40	42-3/4 — 21
1995	266,003	4,306	1.39	.50	26　　— 18-1/2
1994	243,599	3,415	1.11	.30	23-1/4 — 18-1/2
1993	210,405	1,331	.44	.36	26-1/8 — 21-3/4
1992	223,680	1,609[b]	.55[b]	1.00	25-3/4 — 20-1/2

[a]Adjusted to reflect a 2% stock dividend paid in August 1993 and a 3% stock dividend paid in June 1993.
[b]Includes a gain to reflect FAS 109, resulting in a cumulative effect of $194,956 ($.07 per share).

Transfer Agent & Registrar:	Harris Trust and Savings Bank		
General Counsel:	Vedder, Price, Kaufman & Kammholz	**Auditors:**	KPMG Peat Marwick LLP
Patent Counsel:	Wallenstein & Wagner, Ltd.	**Traded (Symbol):**	AMEX, CSE (BIN)
Investor Relations:	Doran J. Unschuld, Pres.	**Stockholders:**	1,114
Human Resources:	James Lindquist	**Employees:**	1,750
Mgt. Info. Svcs.:	Robert Haugh	**Annual Meeting:**	In April

Bio-logic Systems Corp.

One Bio-logic Plaza, Mundelein, Illinois 60060-3700
Telephone: (847) 949-5200

Bio-logic Systems Corp. designs, develops, assembles, and markets computerized systems for use by medical practitioners, hospitals, and clinics to perform various electro-diagnostic tests and brain mapping. Electro-diagnostic tests done by the company's systems are typically used by physicians, primarily neurologists, otolaryngologists, anesthesiologists, audiologists, and psychiatrists, as an aid in diagnosis of neurological and sensory disorders, brain disorders, and tumors by collecting, measuring, and analyzing electrical signals generated by the brain. Incorporated in Delaware in 1981.

Directors   (In addition to indicated officers)

Irving Kupferberg
Albert Milstein

Craig Moore
Charles Z. Weingarten

Officers   (Directors*)

*Gabriel Raviv, Pres. & C.E.O.
Thomas S. Lacy, V.P.—Sales & Mktg.

*Gil Raviv, Secy.
William K. Roenitz, Cont. & Treas.

Consolidated Balance Sheet   As of February 28, 1997 (000 omitted)

Assets		Liabilities & Stockholders' Equity	
Current assets	$ 9,469	Current liabilities	$ 1,824
Net property, plant & equipment	1,828	Long-term debt	563
Other assets	2,627	Deferred items	338
		*Stockholders' equity	11,199
Total	$13,924	Total	$13,924

*4,229,119 shares common stock outstanding.

Consolidated Income Statement

Years Ended Abt. Feb. 28	Thousands — — — —		Per Share — — —		Common Stock Price Range Fiscal Year
	Revenue	Net Income	Earnings	Cash Dividends	
1997	$14,857	$684	$ .17	$ .00	4-1/2 — 2-1/2
1996	14,602	892	.21	.00	5-5/8 — 2-1/8
1995	12,073	740	.18	.00	3-3/4 — 1-3/4
1994	10,749	540	.13	.00	5 — 2-3/4
1993	10,985	100	.02	.00	5-7/8 — 2-3/4

Transfer Agent & Registrar: American Stock Transfer & Trust Co.

General Counsel:
  Bachner, Tally, Polevoy & Misher LLP

Investor Relations: Gabriel Raviv, Pres.

Human Resources: Faith I. Curtis, Mgr.

Mgt. Info. Svcs.:   William K. Roenitz, Cont.

Auditors: Grant Thornton LLP

Traded (Symbol):   NASDAQ (BLSC)

Stockholders: 277

Employees: 89

Annual Meeting: In August

Boise Cascade Office Products Corporation

800 West Bryn Mawr Road, Itasca, Illinois 60143
Telephone: (630) 773-5000

Boise Cascade Office Products Corporation is a leading direct supplier of office products to businesses in the United States and, beginning in 1996, in Australia, Canada, and the United Kingdom. The company distributes a broad line of branded and private label products for use in the office, including consumable supplies, furniture, computer-related items, and other products. The company's product line is offered through its annual full-line catalog and a variety of specialized catalogs, and sold by the company's direct sales force. Boise Cascade Corporation owns 81 percent of the company's outstanding common stock. Principal subsidiaries include The Reliable Corp. and Grand & Toy, Ltd. In November 1996, the company acquired Oregon Wholesale Novelty Company, Inc., an advertising specialties company based in Portland, Oregon. Incorporated in Delaware in 1995.

Directors (In addition to indicated officers)

George J. Harad, Chm.
John B. Carley
James G. Connelly III

Theodore Crumley
A. William Reynolds

Officers (Directors*)

*Peter G. Danis, Jr., Pres. & C.E.O.
Christopher C. Milliken, Sr. V.P.—Oper.
Carol B. Moerdyk, Sr. V.P. & C.F.O.
Lawrence E. Beeson, V.P.—Mktg.
Kenneth W. Cupp, V.P. & Region Mgr.
Darrell R. Elfeldt, V.P. & Cont.
David A. Goudge, V.P.—Prod. Mktg.

John A. Love, V.P.—Hum. Res.
Michael F. Meehan, V.P. & Region Mgr.
Stephen M. Thompson, V.P. & Region Mgr.
Peter D. Vanexan, V.P. & Managing Dir.—Grand & Toy
A. James Balkins III, Secy.
Richard L. Black, Pres.—The Reliable Corp.

Consolidated Balance Sheet   As of December 31, 1996 (000 omitted)

Assets		Liabilities & Stockholders' Equity	
Current assets	$499,188	Current liabilities	$330,547
Net property, plant & equipment	132,562	Long-term debt	140,024
Goodwill, net	261,706	Deferred items	4,470
Other assets	11,906	Other liabilities	25,536
		*Stockholders' equity	404,785
Total	$905,362	Total	$905,362

*62,750,318 shares common stock outstanding.

Consolidated Income Statement

Years Ended Dec. 31	Thousands — — — —		Per Share[a] — — — —		Common Stock Price Range[ab] Calendar Year
	Net Sales	Net Income	Earnings	Cash Dividends	
1996	$1,985,564	$55,349	$ .89	$ .00	49-1/2 — 16-1/2
1995	1,315,953	43,179	.70	.00	21-3/8 — 10-7/8
1994	908,520	26,465	.43		
1993	682,819	18,046			
1992	625,860	6,321[c]			

[a]Adjusted to reflect a 2-for-1 stock split in May 1996.
[b]Initial public offering in April 1995.
[c]Includes a charge to reflect FAS 106, resulting in a cumulative effect of $2,444,000.

Transfer Agent & Registrar: ChaseMellon Shareholder Services, L.L.C.; Boise Cascade Shareholder Svcs.; West One Bank

General Counsel:	John W. Holleran	Traded (Symbol):	NYSE (BOP)
Investor Relations:	Wayne M. Rancourt, Dir.	Stockholders:	1,900
Human Resources:	John A. Love, V.P.	Employees:	8,500
Mgt. Info. Svcs.:	Carol B. Moerdyk, Sr. V.P.	Annual Meeting:	In April
Auditors:	Arthur Andersen LLP	Internet:	www.bcop.com

Borg-Warner Automotive, Inc.

200 South Michigan Avenue, Chicago, Illinois 60604
Telephone: (312) 322-8500

Borg-Warner Automotive, Inc. develops, manufactures, and markets highly engineered components primarily for automotive powertrain applications. These products are produced and sold worldwide, primarily to original equipment manufacturers of passenger cars, light trucks, and sport-utility vehicles. The company's principal subsidiaries include: Powertrain Systems Corporation; Automatic Transmissions Systems Corporation; Morse TEC Corporation; and Air/Fluid Systems Corporation. Incorporated in Delaware in 1987.

Directors (In addition to indicated officers)

Dr. Andrew F. Brimmer
Jere A. Drummond
Albert J. Fitzgibbons III
Paul E. Glaske

Ivan W. Gorr
James J. Kerley
Alexis P. Michas

Officers (Directors*)

*John F. Fiedler, Chm. & C.E.O.
Gary P. Fukayama, Grp. Pres.
Fred M. Kovalik, Exec. V.P.
Ronald M. Ruzic, Exec. V.P.
Robin J. Adams, V.P. & Treas.

William C. Cline, V.P. & Cont.
Christopher A. Gebelein, V.P.—Bus. Dev.
Laurene H. Horiszny, V.P., Gen. Coun. & Secy.
Geraldine Kinsella, V.P.—Hum. Res.
Robert D. Welding, V.P.

Consolidated Balance Sheet   As of December 31, 1996 (000 omitted)

Assets		Liabilities & Stockholders' Equity	
Current assets	$ 253,100	Current liabilities	$ 337,900
Net property, plant & equipment	534,200	Long-term debt	279,300
Other assets	836,300	Deferred items	370,600
		Other liabilities	7,000
		*Stockholders' equity	628,800
Total	$1,623,600	Total	$1,623,600

*23,644,840 shares common stock outstanding.

Consolidated Income Statement[a]

Years Ended Dec. 31	Thousands — — — — Net Sales	Net Income	Per Share — — — Earnings	Cash Dividends	Common Stock Price Range[b] Calendar Year
1996	$1,540,100	$ 41,800[c]	$ 1.77[c]	$ .60	40-7/8 — 28-3/8
1995	1,329,100	74,200	3.15	.60	33-7/8 — 22-3/8
1994	1,223,400	64,400	2.75	.60	34 — 21-5/8
1993	985,400	(98,000)[d]	(4.21)[d]	.00	28 — 20-1/2
1992	926,000	(12,100)	(.53)		

[a]For periods prior to 1993, the financial statements reflect the company as a subsidiary of Borg-Warner Security Corporation, subject to certain allocations.
[b]Initial public offering in August 1993.
[c]Includes an after-tax loss of $35,000,000 ($1.49 per share) on the company's sale of its North American manual transmission business.
[d]Includes a charge to reflect FAS 106, resulting in a cumulative effect of $130,800,000 ($5.62 per share).

Transfer Agent & Registrar: ChaseMellon Shareholder Services, L.L.C.

General Counsel:	Laurene H. Horiszny, V.P.	Auditors:	Deloitte & Touche LLP
Investor Relations:	Mary E. Brevard, Dir.	Traded (Symbol):	NYSE (BWA)
		Stockholders:	137
Human Resources:	Geraldine Kinsella, V.P.	Employees:	9,800
Mgt. Info. Svcs.:	Leonard Murrell, Mgr.	Annual Meeting:	In April

Borg-Warner Security Corporation

200 South Michigan Avenue, Chicago, Illinois 60604
Telephone: (312) 322-8500

Borg-Warner Security Corporation provides a broad line of protective services, including guard, alarm, armored transport, and courier services. The company entered the protective services industry in 1977 through the acquisition of Baker Industries, Inc. Borg-Warner's guard services units provide a variety of guard and related security services to more than 14,000 government and business customers throughout the United States, Canada, and the United Kingdom under the Wells Fargo®, Burns®, and Globe names. The company's alarm services unit designs, installs, monitors, and services electronic detection systems located at the premises of approximately 146,000 commercial and residential customers in the U.S. and Canada under the Wells Fargo® and Pony Express® names. The company's armored transport services unit is a security-related cash service business that provides armored transport services, automated teller machine servicing, and cash management services in the U.S. under the Wells Fargo® name. Borg-Warner's courier services unit transports time-sensitive, non-negotiable financial documents and small packages for Federal Reserve banks, financial institutions, and commercial business entities under the Pony Express® name. Principal subsidiaries are: Borg-Warner Protective Services Corporation; Wells Fargo Alarm Services, Inc.; and Pony Express Courier Corp. The company also owns a 49 percent equity interest in Loomis, Fargo & Co., a company created in January 1997 through the merger of Houston-based Loomis Armored Inc. and the company's Wells Fargo Armored Service Corp. subsidiary. Incorporated in Delaware in 1987.

Directors (In addition to indicated officers)

James J. Burke, Jr.	Dale W. Lang	Alexis P. Michas
Albert J. Fitzgibbons III	Robert A. McCabe	H. Norman Schwarzkopf
Arthur F. Golden	Andrew McNally IV	Donald C. Trauscht

Officers (Directors*)

*J. Joe Adorjan, Chm., Pres. & C.E.O.
John D. O'Brien, Sr. V.P.
Craig J. Bollinger, V.P.—Risk Mgt.

Robert T. Lackey, V.P., Gen. Coun. & Corp. Secy.
Timothy M. Wood, V.P.—Fin. & C.F.O.
Brian S. Cooper, Treas.

Consolidated Balance Sheet As of December 31, 1996 (000 omitted)

Assets		Liabilities & Stockholders' Equity	
Current assets	$167,100	Current liabilities	$178,100
Net property, plant & equipment	203,100	Long-term debt	438,200
Other assets	390,600	Other liabilities	103,300
		*Stockholders' equity	41,200
Total	$760,800	Total	$760,800

*22,446,100 shares common stock outstanding.

Consolidated Income Statement[a]

Years Ended Dec. 31	Thousands — — — — Net Revenues	Net Income	Per Share — — — — Earnings	Cash Dividends	Common Stock Price Range Calendar Year
1996	$1,711,200	$ 13,900	$ .59	$ .00	13-1/8 — 8-1/4
1995	1,708,500	8,400	.36	.00	13 — 5-1/2
1994	1,626,800	13,800	.59	.00	22 — 8-1/4
1993	1,592,100	(218,200)	(9.54)	.00	22-7/8 — 18[b]
1992	1,457,900	52,900	2.69		

[a]From continuing operations.
[b]Initial public offering in January 1993.

Transfer Agent & Registrar: The Bank of New York

General Counsel:	Robert T. Lackey, V.P.	Auditors:	Deloitte & Touche LLP
Investor Relations:	Jeffrey S. Cartwright, Dir.	Traded (Symbol):	NYSE (BOR)
Human Resources:	John D. O'Brien, Sr. V.P.	Stockholders:	250
		Employees:	75,250
Mgt. Info. Svcs.:	Steve Derry	Annual Meeting:	In April

Brookdale Living Communities, Inc.

77 West Wacker Drive, Suite 3900, Chicago, Illinois 60601
Telephone: (312) 456-0239

Brookdale Living Communities, Inc. provides senior and assisted living services to the elderly through its facilities located in urban and suburban areas of major metropolitan markets. The company operates 10 senior and assisted living facilities containing a total of 2,168 units. The company's facilities are designed for middle- to upper-income residents who desire an upscale residential environment providing the highest level of quality, care, and value. In addition to studio, one-bedroom, and two-bedroom units, Brookdale provides all residents with basic services, such as meal service, 24-hour emergency response, housekeeping, concierge services, transportation, and recreational services. In addition, the company provides assistance with activities of daily living to its more frail residents. In the Chicago area, the company owns and/or operates The Devonshire in Lisle, The Hallmark in Chicago at 2960 North Lake Shore Drive, and The Heritage in Des Plaines. Brookdale is also developing a facility in Glen Ellyn, Illinois. In May 1997, the company completed an initial public offering of 5,175,000 shares of common stock. The Prime Group, Inc. owns approximately 58.6 percent of the company's stock. Incorporated in Delaware in 1996.

Directors   (In addition to indicated officers)

Wayne D. Boberg
Bruce L. Gewertz, M.D.

Darryl W. Hartley-Leonard
Daniel J. Hennessy

Officers   (Directors*)

*Michael W. Reschke, Chm.
*Mark J. Schulte, Pres. & C.E.O.
*Darryl W. Copeland, Jr., Exec. V.P.
 Stephan T. Beck, V.P.—Oper.
 Timothy W. Getty, V.P.—Mktg.
 Mark J. Iuppenlatz, V.P.—Dev.

Margaret B. Shontz, V.P.—Hum. Res.
Craig G. Walczyk, V.P. & C.F.O.
Matthew F. Whitlock, V.P.—Acquis.
Robert J. Rudnick, Secy. & Gen. Coun.
Sheryl A. Wolf, Cont.

Consolidated Balance Sheet[a]   As of December 31, 1996 (000 omitted)

Assets		Liabilities & Stockholders' Equity	
Current assets	$ 17,339	Current liabilities	$ 7,566
Real estate, net	115,403	Long-term debt	96,167
Other assets	13,756	Deferred gain	17,728
		*Stockholders' equity	25,037
Total	$146,498	Total	$146,498

[a]Pro forma.
*7,175,000 shares common stock outstanding.

Consolidated Income Statement

Year Ended Dec. 31	Thousands — — — — Revenues	Net Income	Per Share — — — Earnings	Cash Dividends	Common Stock Price Range Calendar Year
1996[a]	$41,463	$(1,313)	$ (.18)		

[a]Unaudited pro forma. Initial public offering in May 1997.

Transfer Agent & Registrar:	LaSalle National Bank		
General Counsel:	Robert J. Rudnick, Secy.	Auditors:	Ernst & Young LLP
Investor Relations: Darryl W. Copeland, Jr., Exec. V.P.		Traded (Symbol):	NASDAQ (BLCI)
Human Resources:	Margaret B. Shontz, V.P.	Employees:	885
Mgt. Info. Svcs.:	Craig G. Walczyk, V.P.	Annual Meeting:	As set by Directors

Brunswick Corporation

1 North Field Court, Lake Forest, Illinois 60045-4811
Telephone: (847) 735-4700

Brunswick Corporation serves worldwide active recreation markets with leading consumer brands in fishing, camping, biking, bowling, and pleasure boating. The company has five operating divisions. The Mercury Marine Division produces Mercury, Mariner, and Force outboard motors, and MerCruiser stern drives and inboard engines. The US Marine Division produces Bayliner and Maxum pleasure boats, and Trophy and Robalo offshore fishing boats. The Sea Ray Division manufactures Sea Ray pleasure boats, Baja high-performance boats, and Boston Whaler offshore fishing boats. The Brunswick Outdoor Recreation Group produces Zebco fishing reels, reel/rod combinations, American Camper and Remington camping equipment, Mongoose and Roadmaster bicycles, Igloo ice coolers, and Motor-Guide trolling motors. The Brunswick Indoor Recreation Group produces bowling capital equipment, consumer products, and billiard tables, and operates a chain of 126 bowling centers in North America and Europe. Incorporated in Delaware in 1907.

Directors (In addition to indicated officers)

Nolan D. Archibald	George D. Kennedy	Jack F. Reichert
Michael J. Callahan	Jay W. Lorsch	Kenneth Roman
Manuel A. Fernandez	Rebecca P. Mark	Roger W. Schipke
Peter Harf	Bettye Martin Musham	

Officers (Directors*)

*Peter N. Larson, Chm. & C.E.O.
Peter B. Hamilton, Sr. V.P. & C.F.O.
Mary D. Allen, V.P. & Gen. Coun.
Kathryn J. Chieger, V.P.—Corp. & Inv. Rel.
Jim W. Dawson, V.P.
Frederick J. Florjancic, Jr., V.P.
David D. Jones, V.P.
James Knox, V.P.

Richard S. O'Brien, V.P. & Treas.
Victoria J. Reich, V.P. & Cont.
Kenneth B. Zeigler, V.P. & Chf. Hum. Rel. Off.
Jervis B. Perkins, Staff V.P.
James A. Schenk, Staff V.P.
Judith P. Zelisko, Staff V.P.
Michael D. Schmitz, Asst. Secy.

Consolidated Balance Sheet As of December 31, 1996 (000 omitted)

Assets		Liabilities & Stockholders' Equity	
Current assets	$1,241,800	Current liabilities	$ 831,100
Net property, plant & equipment	685,400	Long-term debt	455,400
Other assets	875,200	Deferred items	318,200
		*Stockholders' equity	1,197,700
Total	$2,802,400	Total	$2,802,400

*98,466,048 shares common stock outstanding.

Consolidated Income Statement

Years Ended Dec. 31	Thousands — — — —		Per Share — — — —		Common Stock
	Net Sales	Net Income	Earnings	Cash Dividends	Price Range Calendar Year
1996	$3,160,300	$185,800	$1.88	$ .50	25-3/4 — 18-1/8
1995	2,906,300	158,000[a]	1.64[a]	.50	24 — 16-3/8
1994	2,592,000	127,100[a]	1.33[a]	.44	25-1/8 — 17
1993[b]	2,125,000	34,600[a]	.36[a]	.44	18-1/2 — 12-1/2
1992[c]	1,980,500	1,800[a]	.02[a]	.44	17-3/4 — 12-1/4

[a]Excludes non-recurring charges and discontinued operations.
[b]Includes FAS 112, resulting in an after-tax provision of $14,600,000. The company also recorded an after-tax provision of $4,600,000 for redemption of $100,000,000 in sinking fund debentures.
[c]Includes FAS 106, resulting in after-tax provisions of $2,800,000 in 1992 and $38,300,000 for the cumulative prior years' effect.

Transfer Agent & Registrar:	Brunswick Corporation		
Corporate Counsel:	Mayer, Brown & Platt		
Investor Relations:	Kathryn J. Chieger, V.P.	**Traded (Symbol):**	NYSE, CSE, PSE, London (BC)
Human Resources:		**Stockholders:**	18,400
	Kenneth B. Zeigler, V.P. & Chf. Hum. Rel. Off.	**Employees:**	22,800
Mgt. Info. Svcs.:	Joseph Wolke, Dir.	**Annual Meeting:**	Last Wednesday in April
Auditors:	Arthur Andersen LLP	**Internet:**	www.enw.com/brunswick/

BT Office Products International, Inc.

2150 East Lake Cook Road, Suite 590, Buffalo Grove, Illinois 60089-1877
Telephone: (847) 793-7500

BT Office Products International, Inc. is a leading full-service distributor of office products, serving primarily medium- and large-sized businesses and institutions in major markets, both in the United States and Europe. The company offers its customers a full range of office products, including traditional office supplies, office furniture, computer supplies and accessories, copiers and office equipment, business forms, and advertising specialty and promotional products. Kelly Paper provides wholesale printing supplies for small commercial printers in the western U.S. In July 1995, the company completed an initial public offering of 10,000,000 shares of common stock. In 1996, BT Office Products entered new markets and expanded current operations through the acquisition of 16 office products distributors in the United States, five in Germany, one in Sweden, and one in the Netherlands. Incorporated in Delaware in 1984.

Directors (In addition to indicated officers)

Frank J. de Wit, Chm.
Philip E. Beekman
Rob W.J.M. Bonnier

Lorrence T. Kellar
Frans H.J. Koffrie

Officers (Directors*)

*Rudolf A.J. Huyzer, Pres. & C.E.O.
Thomas F. Cullen, V.P., Gen. Coun. & Corp. Secy.
Richard C. Dubin, V.P. & Reg. Pres.—Midwest-West
David Kirshner, V.P. & Reg. Pres.—Great Lakes

Frank J. Leonard, V.P.—Fin. & C.F.O.
Michael J. Miller, Sr. V.P.—Strategic Systems
Janhein H. Pieterse, V.P. & Pres.—BT Office Products-Europe

Consolidated Balance Sheet As of December 31, 1996 (000 omitted)

Assets		Liabilities & Stockholders' Equity	
Current assets	$392,006	Current liabilities	$238,061
Net property, plant & equipment	78,415	Long-term debt	219,702
Other assets	272,398	Other liabilities	16,404
		*Stockholders' equity	268,652
Total	$742,819	Total	$742,819

*33,471,000 shares common stock outstanding.

Consolidated Income Statement

Years Ended Dec. 31	Thousands — — — — Net Sales	Net Income	Per Share[a] — — — Earnings[b]	Cash Dividends	Common Stock Price Range[a] Calendar Year
1996	$1,412,514	$ 14,701	$ .44	$ .00	23-7/8 — 8-1/8
1995	1,132,370	6,690	.24	.00	16 — 11-1/4
1994	789,541	(159)	(.01)		
1993	586,854	(4,892)[c]	(.21)[c]		
1992	475,311	(3,491)	(.15)		

[a]Initial public offering in July 1995.
[b]Per share data from 1992 to 1994 reflects a stock split that occurred in connection with the 1995 reorganization which resulted in 23,400,000 shares outstanding.
[c]Reflects a charge of $692,000 ($.03 per share) for adoption of FAS No. 106.

Transfer Agent & Registrar:	LaSalle National Trust, N.A.		
General Counsel:	Thomas F. Cullen, V.P.	Traded (Symbol):	NYSE (BTF)
Investor Relations:	Frank J. Leonard, V.P.	Stockholders:	3,300
Human Resources:	Edward R. Youngman, V.P.	Employees:	6,600
Mgt. Info. Svcs.:	Michael J. Miller, Sr. V.P.	Annual Meeting:	In May
Auditors:	Coopers & Lybrand LLP	Internet:	www.btopi.com

Calumet Bancorp, Inc.

1350 East Sibley Boulevard, Dolton, Illinois 60419
Telephone: (708) 841-9010

Calumet Bancorp, Inc. is the holding company for Calumet Federal Savings and Loan Association ("Association") of Chicago, a federally chartered stock savings and loan association. The Association attracts retail deposits from the Chicago area with its greatest emphasis on the south Chicago suburban communities and the northwest Indiana communities that it serves. The Association's home office is located in Chicago, its main administrative office is in Dolton, Illinois, and its four full-service branch offices are located in Chicago, Dolton, Lansing, and Sauk Village, Illinois. It also operates through several service corporation subsidiaries, including Calumet Savings Service Corporation, Calumet Residential Corporation, and Calumet Mortgage Corporation of Idaho. Incorporated in Delaware in 1991.

Directors (In addition to indicated officers)

Tytus R. Bulicz
Louise Czarobski
Darryl Erlandson

William A. McCann
Henry J. Urban, D.D.S.

Officers (Directors*)

*Thaddeus Walczak, Chm. & C.E.O.
*Carole J. Lewis, Pres.
 John L. Garlanger, Sr. V.P. & Treas.

Jean A. Adams, V.P.
Susan M. Linkus, V.P. & Secy.

Consolidated Balance Sheet As of December 31, 1996 (000 omitted)

Assets		Liabilities & Stockholders' Equity	
Cash & cash equivalents	$ 9,175	Deposits	$360,978
Loans receivable, net	383,770	Borrowings	59,850
Investment securities	85,332	Other liabilities	7,625
Other assets	31,940	*Stockholders' equity	81,764
Total	$510,217	Total	$510,217

*2,377,028 shares common stock outstanding.

Consolidated Income Statement

Years Ended Dec. 31	Thousands — — — — Total Income	Net Income	Per Share[a] — — — — Earnings	Cash Dividends	Common Stock Price Range[ab] Calendar Year
1996	$41,911	$ 5,399	$2.05	$ .00	34 — 27-1/2
1995	39,733	5,965	2.06	.00	28-1/2 — 21
1994	39,202	7,419	2.47	.00	25-1/2 — 19-1/2
1993	40,571	10,532[c]	3.22[c]	.00	24 — 15-5/8
1992	39,143	6,697	1.91	.00	16-3/8 — 10-3/8

[a]Adjusted to reflect a 3-for-2 stock split in the form of a 50% common stock dividend in November 1994.
[b]Initial public offering on February 20, 1992.
[c]Includes a gain to reflect FAS 109, resulting in a cumulative effect of $1,500,000 ($.46 per share).

Transfer Agent & Registrar: Harris Trust and Savings Bank

General Counsel:
 Kemp, Grzelakowski & Lorenzini, Ltd.

Investor Relations: John L. Garlanger, Sr. V.P.

Human Resources: Debbie Cattoni, V.P.

Auditors: Crowe, Chizek & Co. LLP

Traded (Symbol): NASDAQ (CBCI)
Stockholders: 1,278
Employees: 150
Annual Meeting: In April
Internet: www.calumetbancorp.com

Capsure Holdings Corp.

Two North Riverside Plaza, Suite 600, Chicago, Illinois 60606
Telephone: (312) 879-1900

Capsure Holdings Corp. is a holding company whose principal subsidiaries are Western Surety Company and Universal Surety of America. Through Western Surety Company and Universal Surety of America, the company provides surety and fidelity bonds in all 50 states through a combined network of 120,000 independent agents. In May 1996, the company completed the sale of its United Capitol Insurance Company and its subsidiaries, to a subsidiary of Frontier Insurance Group, Inc. In December 1996, Capsure announced that it would merge with a division of CNA Financial Corporation to form a new company, CNA Surety Corporation, pending shareholder approval in the summer of 1997. Incorporated in Delaware in 1988; present name adopted in 1993.

Directors   (In addition to indicated officers)

Rod F. Dammeyer
Herbert A. Denton
Bradbury Dyer III
Talton R. Embry
Dan L. Kirby

Joe P. Kirby
Donald W. Phillips
L.G. Schafran
Richard I. Weingarten

Officers   (Directors*)

*Samuel Zell, Chm. & C.E.O.
*Bruce A. Esselborn, Pres.
Arthur A. Greenberg, Sr. V.P. & Treas.
Mary Jane Robertson, Sr. V.P. & C.F.O.
Ronald D. Bobman, V.P.—M&A

John S. Heneghan, V.P. & Cont.
*Sheli Z. Rosenberg, V.P. & Asst. Secy.
Kelly L. Stonebraker, V.P. & Gen. Coun.
John M. Zoeller, V.P.—Taxes
Susan S. Obuchowski, Secy.

Consolidated Balance Sheet   As of December 31, 1996 (000 omitted)

Assets		Liabilities & Stockholders' Equity	
Current assets	$ 5,642	Reserves	$108,444
Invested assets & cash	165,268	Long-term debt	60,000
Other assets	142,229	Other liabilities	22,112
		*Stockholders' equity	122,583
Total	$313,139	Total	$313,139

*15,804,749 shares common stock outstanding.

Consolidated Income Statement

Years Ended Dec. 31	Thousands — — — — — Total Revenues	Net Income	Per Share — — — — Earnings[a]	Cash Dividends	Common Stock Price Range[b] Calendar Year
1996	$110,650	$13,379	$ .82	$10.00[c]	18-7/8 — 8
1995	117,510	20,530	1.33	.00	17-7/8 — 12-3/8
1994[d]	112,555	14,378	.95	.00	16 — 12-1/8
1993	107,915	16,284	1.08	.00	19-3/8 — 12-1/4
1992[ef]	57,133	10,695	.88	.00	14-3/8 — 6-7/8

[a]Fully diluted.
[b]Traded on NASDAQ prior to June 16, 1993.
[c]The company paid a special cash dividend on October 4, 1996, to all holders of record on September 25, 1996.
[d]Includes the results of Universal Surety of America since the date of acquisition in September 1994.
[e]Includes the results of Surewest Financial Corp. since the date of acquisition in August 1992.
[f]Restated to reflect FAS 109.

Transfer Agent & Registrar: Bank of Boston
General Counsel: Kelly L. Stonebraker, V.P.
Investor Relations: Susan S. Obuchowski, Secy.
Auditors: Coopers & Lybrand L.L.P.

Traded (Symbol):   NYSE (CSH)
Stockholders: 2,300
Employees: 550
Annual Meeting: In May

A.M. Castle & Co.

3400 North Wolf Road, Franklin Park, Illinois 60131
Telephone: (847) 455-7111

A.M. Castle & Co. is a North American industrial distributor of specialty metals such as carbon, alloy, and stainless steels; aluminum; nickel alloys; titanium; and copper and brass. The metals that A.M. Castle distributes are used by more than 30,000 customers in a highly diversified range of end-use industries. These include: pollution control equipment and machine tools; agricultural, construction, and mining machinery; electric and power generation equipment; oil and oil field services; chemical and petroleum refineries; and the space shuttle and commercial aircraft. Domestically, the company maintains a coast-to-coast metals service center network consisting of 26 locations with more than two million square feet of capacity. In Canada, A.M. Castle serves customers from three service centers in the provinces of Manitoba, Ontario, and Quebec. Principal subsidiaries include Total Plastics, Inc. In April 1997, the company agreed to acquire Chicago-based Keystone Tube Co., a distributor of tubular products. Incorporated in Illinois in 1904; reincorporated in Delaware in 1967.

Directors   (In addition to indicated officers)

Daniel T. Carroll
William K. Hall
Robert S. Hamada
Patrick Herbert

John P. Keller
John W. McCarter, Jr.
John W. Puth
Richard A. Virzi

Officers   (Directors*)

*Michael Simpson, Chm.
*Richard G. Mork, Pres. & C.E.O.
*Edward F. Culliton, V.P. & C.F.O.
Sven G. Ericsson, V.P.—Intl.
M. Bruce Herron, V.P.—West Region
Stephen V. Hooks, V.P.—Midwest Region
Fritz Oppenlander, V.P.—Oper.

Richard G. Phifer, V.P.—East Region
Alan D. Raney, V.P.—Advanced Materials Grp.
Robert A. Rosenow, V.P.—Plate & Carbon Grp.
Gise Van Baren, V.P.—Alloy Prod. Grp.
Paul J. Winsauer, V.P.—Hum. Res.
Jerry M. Aufox, Secy. & Legal Coun.
James A. Podojil, Treas. & Cont.

Consolidated Balance Sheet   As of December 31, 1996 (000 omitted)

Assets		Liabilities & Stockholders' Equity	
Current assets	$163,911	Current liabilities	$ 83,902
Net property, plant & equipment	62,717	Long-term debt	40,934
Other assets	34,742	Deferred items	11,427
		Other liabilities	3,181
		*Stockholders' equity	121,926
Total	$261,370	Total	$261,370

*14,009,000 shares common stock outstanding.

Consolidated Income Statement

| Years Ended Dec. 31 | Thousands — — — — | | Per Share[a] — — — | | Common Stock |
	Net Sales	Net Income	Earnings	Cash Dividends	Price Range[a] Calendar Year
1996	$672,600	$26,100	$1.86	$ .57	30-7/8 — 16-1/8
1995	627,800	26,800	1.93	.43	22-5/8 — 9-3/4
1994	536,600	15,400	1.12	.26	13-1/8 — 8-7/8
1993	474,100	6,900	.50	.22	9-3/8 — 6
1992	423,900	3,400	.25	.22	6-7/8 — 5-1/2

[a]Adjusted to reflect a 50% common stock dividend in 1994 and a 5-for-4 stock split in May 1996.

Transfer Agent & Registrar: American Stock Transfer & Trust Co.

General Counsel: Mayer, Brown & Platt

Investor Relations: Edward F. Culliton, V.P.

Human Resources: Paul J. Winsauer, V.P.

Mgt. Info. Svcs.:   Paul T. Jara, Dir.

Auditors: Arthur Andersen LLP

Traded (Symbol):   AMEX, CSE (CAS)

Stockholders: 1,613

Employees: 1,505

Annual Meeting: Fourth Thursday in April

Caterpillar Inc.
100 N.E. Adams Street, Peoria, Illinois 61629-5310
Telephone: (309) 675-1000

Caterpillar Inc., together with its consolidated subsidiaries, operates in three principal categories: the design, manufacture, and marketing of construction, mining, and agricultural machinery and equipment; the design, manufacture, and marketing of engines; and the offering of a wide range of financial services. Machinery manufactured includes: track-type tractors; bulldozers; rippers; track and wheel loaders; lift trucks; pipelayers; motor graders; wheel tractors; compactors; wheel tractor-scrapers; track and wheel excavators; skidders; automated guided vehicles; asphalt and soil compactors; backhoe loaders; log loaders; tree harvesters; off-highway trucks; asphalt and concrete paving machines; and related parts and equipment. Diesel and natural gas engines are designed for: earthmoving and construction machines; on-highway trucks; marine, petroleum, agricultural, and industrial applications; and electric power generation systems. Caterpillar Financial Services Corporation assists customers in acquiring Caterpillar and noncompetitive related equipment. In addition to 31 plants in the United States, Caterpillar maintains manufacturing facilities in Canada, England, France, Hungary, and Mexico. Incorporated in California in 1925; reincorporated in Delaware in 1986.

Directors (In addition to indicated officers)

Lilyan H. Affinito	James P. Gorter	George A. Schaefer
W. Frank Blount	Peter A. Magowan	Joshua I. Smith
John T. Dillon	Gordon R. Parker	Clayton K. Yeutter
David R. Goode		

Officers (Directors*)

*Donald V. Fites, Chm. & C.E.O.
Glen A. Barton, Grp. Pres.
Gerald S. Flaherty, Grp. Pres.
James W. Owens, Grp. Pres.
Richard L. Thompson, Grp. Pres.
R. Rennie Atterbury III, V.P., Gen.
  Coun. & Secy.
James W. Baldwin, V.P.
Vito H. Baumgartner, V.P.
James S. Beard, V.P.
Richard A. Benson, V.P.

Ronald P. Bonati, V.P.
James E. Despain, V.P.
Roger E. Fischbach, V.P.
Michael A. Flexsenhar, V.P.
Donald M. Ings, V.P.
Duane H. Livingston, V.P.
Daniel M. Murphy, V.P.
Douglas R. Oberhelman, V.P. &
  C.F.O.
Gerald Palmer, V.P.
Robert C. Petterson, V.P.

John E. Pfeffer, V.P.
Siegfried R. Ramseyer, V.P.
Alan J. Rassi, V.P.
Gerald L. Shaheen, V.P.
Gary A. Stroup, V.P.
Sherril K. West, V.P.
Donald G. Western, V.P.
Wayne M. Zimmerman, V.P.
Robert R. Gallagher, Cont.
F. Lynn McPheeters, Treas.

Consolidated Balance Sheet As of December 31, 1996 (000 omitted)

Assets		Liabilities & Stockholders' Equity	
Current assets	$ 8,783,000	Current liabilities	$ 7,013,000
Net property & equipment	3,767,000	Long-term debt	4,532,000
Other assets	6,178,000	Other liabilities	3,067,000
		*Stockholders' equity	4,116,000
Total	$18,728,000	Total	$18,728,000

*203,723,656 shares common stock outstanding.

Consolidated Income Statement

Years Ended Dec. 31	Thousands — — — —		Per Share[a] — — —		Common Stock Price Range[a] Calendar Year
	Sales	Net Income	Earnings	Cash Dividends	
1996	$15,814,000	$ 1,361,000	$ 7.07	$1.55	81 — 54
1995	15,451,000	1,136,000	5.72	1.30	75-1/4 — 48-1/4
1994	13,863,000	955,000	4.70	.63	60-3/4 — 44-1/2
1993	11,235,000	652,000[b]	3.21[b]	.30	46-1/2 — 27
1992	9,840,000	(2,435,000)[c]	(12.06)[c]	.30	31-1/8 — 20-5/8

[a]Adjusted to reflect a 2-for-1 stock split in September 1994.
[b]Includes an extraordinary loss of $29,000,000 ($.15 per share) on early retirement of debt.
[c]Includes FAS 106, FAS 109, and FAS 112, resulting in an after-tax loss of $2,217,000,000 ($10.98 per share).

Transfer Agent & Registrar: First Chicago Trust Co. of New York

General Counsel:	R. Rennie Atterbury III, V.P.	Traded (Symbol):	NYSE, CSE, BSE, PHSE, PSE, BELG, FRA, LON, GER, Swiss (CAT)
Investor Relations:	James F. Masterson, Dir.		
Human Resources:	Wayne M. Zimmerman, V.P.	Stockholders:	30,573
		Employees:	57,026
Mgt. Info. Svcs.:	Robert Hinds	Annual Meeting:	In April
Auditors:	Price Waterhouse LLP	Internet:	www.CAT.com

CCC Information Services Group Inc.

444 Merchandise Mart, Chicago, Illinois 60654-1005
Telephone: (312) 222-4636

CCC Information Services Group Inc. (CCCISG), through its operating subsidiary, CCC Information Services Inc. (CCCIS), is a leading supplier of automobile insurance claims information and processing, claims management software, and value-added communication services. The company's customers include the largest United States automobile insurance companies, most of the small- to medium-sized automobile insurance companies in the country, and more than 10,000 collision repair facilities. The company's technology-based services and products improve efficiency, manage costs, and increase consumer satisfaction in the management of automobile claims and restoration. CCCIS entered the vehicle total loss valuation market in 1980 when it introduced the first computerized vehicle valuation system based on market-specific conditions and physically inspected dealer inventories. In August 1996, CCCISG completed an initial public offering of 6,900,000 shares of common stock. Incorporated in Delaware in 1983.

Directors   (In addition to indicated officers)

John J. Byrne
Morgan W. Davis
Thomas L. Kempner

Gordon S. Macklin
Robert T. Marto
Michael R. Stanfield

Officers   (Directors*)

*David M. Phillips, Chm., Pres. & C.E.O.
J. Laurence Costin, Jr., V. Chm.
Gitesh Ramamurthy, Chf. Tech. Off. &
Pres.—Insurance Div.
John Buckner, Pres.—Automotive Svcs. Div.
Samuel B. Barash, Exec. V.P.—New Prod. Dev.,
CCCIS
Leonard L. Ciarrocchi, Exec. V.P. & C.F.O.
Blaine R. Ornburg, Exec. V.P.—New Mkt. Dev.
Stephen E. Appelbaum, Sr. V.P.—ACCLAIM
Litigation Mgt., CCCIS

Nancy T. Borghesi, Sr. V.P.—Bus. Solutions, CCCIS
William R. Geen, Sr. V.P.—Dealer Svcs., CCCIS
T. Scott Leisher, Sr. V.P.—Insurance Sales, CCCIS
Martin G. McGrath, Sr. V.P.—Mktg., CCCIS
Jack Rozint, Sr. V.P.—ACCESS Claims Svcs., CCCIS
Richard L. Rumple, Sr. V.P.—Prod. Eng., CCCIS
Michael J. D'Onofrio, V.P. & Treas.
Donald J. Hallagan, V.P., Cont. & Chf. Acct. Off.
Gerald P. Kenney, V.P., Secy. & Gen. Coun.
Kenneth McBeath, V.P.—Mgt. Info. Svcs., CCCIS
Richard W. Steel, V.P.—Hum. Res., CCCIS

Consolidated Balance Sheet   As of December 31, 1996 (000 omitted)

Assets		Liabilities & Stockholders' Equity	
Current assets	$31,383	Current liabilities	$23,290
Equipment & purchased software, net	8,088	Long-term debt	111
Goodwill, net	11,230	Deferred revenues	1,997
Deferred income taxes	6,410	Other liabilities	3,889
Other assets	1,157	Mandatorily redeemable preferred stock	4,688
		*Stockholders' equity	24,293
Total	$58,268	Total	$58,268

*23,472,355 shares common stock outstanding.

Consolidated Income Statement

Years Ended Dec. 31	Thousands — — — — Net Sales	Net Income	Per Share[a] — — — — Earnings	Cash Dividends	Common Stock Price Range[a] Calendar Year	
1996	$130,977	$ 8,150	$ .40	$ .00	24	— 12-1/2
1995	115,519	(1,717)	(.10)			
1994	91,917	(13,671)	(1.03)			
1993	51,264	(10,131)	(1.08)			
1992	45,805	(6,851)	(.74)			

[a]Initial public offering in August 1996.

Transfer Agent & Registrar: Harris Trust and Savings Bank

General Counsel:	Gerald P. Kenney, V.P.	Traded (Symbol):	NASDAQ (CCCG)
Investor Relations:	Leonard L. Ciarrocchi, Exec. V.P.	Stockholders:	140
Human Resources:	Richard W. Steel, V.P.	Employees:	950
Mgt. Info. Svcs.:	Kenneth McBeath, V.P.	Annual Meeting:	In April
Auditors:	Price Waterhouse LLP	Internet:	www.cccis.com

CDW Computer Centers, Inc.

200 North Milwaukee Avenue, Vernon Hills, Illinois 60061
Telephone: (847) 465-6000

CDW Computer Centers, Inc. is a direct marketer of more than 20,000 MS-DOS/Microsoft Windows- and Apple Macintosh-based microcomputer products at discounted prices. The company sells a broad range of microcomputer hardware and peripherals, accessories, networking products, and software through in-bound telemarketing account executives who service customers that call the company's toll-free telephone numbers. Incorporated in Illinois in 1984; reincorporated in Delaware in 1993; reincorporated again in Illinois in 1995.

Directors (In addition to indicated officers)

Michelle Collins

Joseph Levy, Jr.

Officers (Directors*)

*Michael P. Krasny, Chm., C.E.O., Secy. & Treas.
*Gregory C. Zeman, Pres.
Daniel F. Callen, V.P.—Fin., Cont. & Chf. Acct. Officer
Mary C. Gerlits, V.P.—Hum. Res.

Donald Gordon, V.P.—Adver.
Harry J. Harczak, Jr., C.F.O.
*Daniel B. Kass, V.P.—Sales
Paul A. Kozak, V.P.—Purchasing
James Shanks, V.P.—Info. Tech.

Consolidated Balance Sheet As of December 31, 1996 (000 omitted)

Assets		Liabilities & Stockholders' Equity	
Current assets	$180,822	Current liabilities	$ 57,208
Net property, plant & equipment	12,295	*Stockholders' equity	141,622
Other assets	5,713		
Total	$198,830	Total	$198,830

*21,525,000 shares common stock outstanding.

Consolidated Income Statement

Years Ended Dec. 31	Thousands — — — — — Net Sales	Net Income	Per Share[a] — — — — Earnings	Cash Dividends	Common Stock Price Range[a] Calendar Year
1996	$927,895	$34,400	$1.58	$ .00	74 — 22-1/2
1995	628,721	20,059	.95	.00	42-3/8 — 20-3/8
1994	413,270	12,113	.61	.00	23-1/8 — 9-7/8
1993	270,919	12,589[b]	.60[b]	.00	9-3/4 — 4-1/2[c]

[a]Adjusted to reflect a 2-for-1 stock split in May 1994 and a 3-for-2 stock split in July 1996.
[b]Includes a one-time tax benefit of $3,807,000 ($.20 per share).
[c]Initial public offering in May 1993.

Transfer Agent & Registrar: American Stock Transfer & Trust Co.

General Counsel: Rallo & Tepper; Saitlin, Patzik, Frank & Samotny, Ltd.		Traded (Symbol):	NASDAQ (CDWC)
Investor Relations:	Harry J. Harczak, Jr., C.F.O.	Stockholders:	2,700
Human Resources:	Mary C. Gerlits, V.P.	Employees:	735
Mgt. Info. Svcs.:	James Shanks, V.P.	Annual Meeting:	In May
Auditors:	Coopers & Lybrand L.L.P.	Internet:	www.cdw.com

Central Steel & Wire Company

3000 West 51st Street, Chicago, Illinois 60632-2198
Telephone: (773) 471-3800

Central Steel & Wire Company is an independent metals distributor that engages in the business of warehousing and distributing processed and unprocessed ferrous and nonferrous metals in forms produced generally by rolling mills. The company's principal facility is in Chicago with other warehouses in Cincinnati, Detroit, and Milwaukee. Incorporated in Illinois in 1909; reincorporated in Delaware in 1958.

Officers (Directors*)

*Frank A. Troike, Chm., C.E.O. & Treas.
*Alfred G. Jensen, Pres.
*John M. Tiernan, Exec. V.P.
 C. Daniel Blythe, V.P.
*Michael X. Cronin, V.P. & Secy.

John M. Klabacha, V.P.
*Richard L. Schroer, V.P.
Richard P. Ugolini, V.P., Compt. & Asst. Secy.
Ronald V. Kazmar, Asst. Treas.

Consolidated Balance Sheet As of December 31, 1996 (000 omitted)

Assets		Liabilities & Stockholders' Equity	
Current assets	$195,800	Current liabilities	$ 75,500
Net property, plant & equipment	33,100	Other liabilities	17,900
Other assets	7,400	*Stockholders' equity	142,900
Total	$236,300	Total	$236,300

*280,529 shares common stock outstanding.

Consolidated Income Statement

Years Ended Dec. 31	Thousands — — — — Net Sales	Net Income	Per Share — — — Earnings	Cash Dividends	Common Stock Price Range Calendar Year	
1996	$591,400	$15,100	$53.69	$42.00	634	—571
1995	626,000	17,400	61.26	40.00	596	—550
1994	595,000	14,200	49.56	40.00	605	—570
1993	503,200	5,600	19.58	22.00	625	—575
1992	459,200	2,300[a]	7.98[a]	22.00	630	—550

[a]Before cumulative effect of FAS 106, resulting in a charge of $8,600,000 ($29.84 per share).

Transfer Agent & Registrar:	First Chicago Trust Co. of New York		
General Counsel:	Schiff, Hardin & Waite	Traded:	OTC (CSTW)
Investor Relations:	Michael X. Cronin, V.P.	Stockholders:	285
Mgt. Info. Svcs.:	Richard P. Ugolini, V.P.	Employees:	1,400
		Annual Meeting:	Third Monday in April
Auditors:	KPMG Peat Marwick LLP	Internet:	www.centralsteel.com

Cerion Technologies Inc.

1401 Interstate Drive, Champaign, Illinois 61821-1090
Telephone: (217) 359-3700

Cerion Technologies Inc. manufactures precision-machined, aluminum disk substrates, which are the metallic platforms of magnetic thin film used in the hard disk drives of portable and desktop computers, network servers, add-on storage devices, and storage upgrades. The company also manufactures organic photoconductor (OPC) drum substrates which are used in the imaging drums of most laser printers and certain office copiers. The business of the company began in 1982 as Disk-Tec, Inc. and was acquired by Nashua Corporation in 1986. In May 1996, Cerion Technologies Inc. completed an initial public offering of 4,416,000 shares of common stock. Incorporated in Delaware in 1995.

Directors (In addition to indicated officers)

Gerald G. Garbacz, Chm.
Joseph A. Baute
Sheldon A. Buckler, Ph.D.

Daniel M. Junius
Ross W. Manire

Officers (Directors*)

*David A. Peterson, Pres. & C.E.O.
 Michael F. Brown, V.P.—Marketing
 Richard A. Clark, V.P.—Fin., C.F.O. & Treas.

Paul A. Harter, V.P.—Operations
William A. Hughes, V.P.—Prod. Dev.

Consolidated Balance Sheet As of December 31, 1996 (000 omitted)

Assets		Liabilities & Stockholders' Equity	
Current assets	$13,942	Current liabilities	$ 3,694
Net property, plant & equipment	9,391	Deferred items	273
		*Stockholders' equity	19,366
Total	$23,333	Total	$23,333

*7,016,184 shares common stock outstanding.

Consolidated Income Statement

Years Ended Dec. 31	Thousands — — — — Net Sales	Net Income	Per Share[a] — — — — Earnings	Cash Dividends	Common Stock Price Range[ab] Calendar Year
1996	$36,540	$ 2,505	$ .39	$ .00	19-1/2 — 2-1/4
1995[c]	28,175	2,356	.44		
1994	14,553	(183)			
1993	14,612	339			

[a]Adjusted to reflect a 1,800-for-one stock split in March 1996.
[b]Initial public offering in May 1996.
[c]Pro forma.

Transfer Agent & Registrar:	Harris Trust & Savings Bank		
General Counsel:	Sam Erwin	Traded (Symbol):	NASDAQ (CEON)
Investor Relations:	Richard A. Clark, V.P.	Stockholders:	500
Human Resources:	Rosa Li, Mgr.	Employees:	430
Mgt. Info. Svcs.:	Richard A. Clark, V.P.	Annual Meeting:	As set by Directors
Auditors:	Price Waterhouse, LLP	Internet:	www.cerion.com

CFC International, Inc.

500 State Street, Chicago Heights, Illinois 60411
Telephone: (708) 891-3456

CFC International, Inc. formulates, manufactures, and sells chemically complex multi-layered functional coatings applied to rolls of plastic film, from which its customers transfer the coatings to their own products. These coatings have five primary applications: printed wood grain for furniture; pigmented coatings used for pharmaceutical products; security products such as magnetic stripes and signature panels for credit cards; metalized coatings; and holographic products such as authentication seals. The company markets its products worldwide to more than 5,000 customers through direct sales and a network of 35 distributors. Offices, warehouses, and finishing operations are maintained in Chicago Heights; Oxnard, California; London; and Tokyo. In November 1995, the company completed an initial public offering of 1,200,000 shares of common stock. Incorporated in Delaware in 1986.

Directors   (In addition to indicated officers)

William G. Brown
Robert B. Covalt

Richard Pierce
David D. Wesselink

Officers   (Directors*)

*Roger F. Hruby, Chm. & C.E.O.
*Robert J. DuPriest, Pres. & C.O.O.
William Herring, Sr. V.P.—Oper.
David C. Beeching, V.P.—Sales &
 Mktg.-Holographics
Glenn L. Ford, V.P.—Mfg.
Robert E. Jurgens, V.P.—Sales & Mktg.

*Dennis W. Lakomy, V.P. & C.F.O.
Craig D. Newswanger, V.P.—R&D-Holographics
William Laske, Dir.—Pacific Rim Sales & Mktg.
Peter C. McGillivray, Managing Dir.—U.K. Oper.
David M. Plomin, Dir.—R&D
Jeffrey E. Norby, Cont.

Consolidated Balance Sheet   As of December 31, 1996 (000 omitted)

Assets		Liabilities & Stockholders' Equity	
Current assets	$15,267	Current liabilities	$ 4,633
Net property, plant & equipment	10,867	Long-term debt	5,564
Other assets	2,072	Deferred items	1,786
		Other liabilities	1,145
		*Stockholders' equity	15,078
Total	$28,206	Total	$28,206

*4,517,000 shares common stock outstanding.

Consolidated Income Statement

Years Ended Dec. 31	Thousands — — — —		Per Share[b] — — — —		Common Stock
	Net Sales	Net Income[a]	Earnings[a]	Cash Dividends	Price Range[c] Calendar Year
1996	$37,227	$2,983	$ .66	$ .00	18 — 8-7/8
1995	34,177	3,252	.95	.00	10-1/4 — 8-5/8
1994	27,808	1,463	.44		
1993	25,328	1,425			
1992	22,394	785			

[a]Pro forma for continuing operations.
[b]Reflects a 1.2565385-for-1 stock split in August 1995.
[c]Initial public offering in November 1995.

Transfer Agent & Registrar: Harris Trust and Savings Bank

General Counsel:	Bell, Boyd & Lloyd	Traded (Symbol):	NASDAQ (CFCI)
Investor Relations:	Aaron H. Hoffman, Mgr.	Stockholders:	14
Human Resources:	Susan Contri	Employees:	189
Mgt. Info. Svcs.:	Jeffrey E. Norby, Cont.	Annual Meeting:	In April
Auditors:	Price Waterhouse LLP	Internet:	www.cfcintl.com

Champion Parts, Inc.

751 Roosevelt Road, Building 7, Suite 110, Glen Ellyn, Illinois
60137-5904
Telephone: (630) 942-8317

Champion Parts, Inc., is a remanufacturer and marketer of automotive, truck, and farm replacement parts. Major products include carburetors, water pumps, clutches, starters, alternators, and constant velocity (CV) driveshaft assemblies for domestic and imported cars and trucks, and farm and industrial equipment. Automotive warehouse dealers and retailers are the company's primary customers, while other customers include automotive, truck, and tractor vehicle manufacturers, heavy-duty fleet specialists, and retail organizations. Domestic remanufacturing operations are conducted in plants located in Hope, Arkansas, and Beech Creek, Pennsylvania. Champion Parts (Canada) Ltd. is a foreign subsidiary. Incorporated in Illinois in 1947.

Directors (In addition to indicated officers)

John R. Gross
Raymond F. Gross
Gary S. Hopmayer

Barry L. Katz
Edward R. Kipling
Raymond G. Perelman

Officers (Directors*)

Jerry A. Bragiel, Pres. & C.E.O.
Mark Smetana, V.P.—Fin. & Secy.

Richard B. Hebert, Treas.

Consolidated Balance Sheet As of December 29, 1996 (000 omitted)

Assets		Liabilities & Stockholders' Equity	
Current assets	$13,689	Current liabilities	$23,630
Net property, plant & equipment	5,509	Long-term debt	43
Other assets	468	Deferred items	478
		*Stockholders' equity	(4,485)
Total	$19,666	Total	$19,666

*3,655,266 shares common stock outstanding.

Consolidated Income Statement

Years Ended Abt. Dec. 31	Thousands — — — — Net Sales	Net Income	Per Share — — — Earnings	Cash Dividends	Common Stock Price Range Calendar Year
1996	$ 27,556	$(1,467)	$ (.40)	$ .00	1 — 1/4
1995	52,954	(18,840)	(5.15)	.00	3-5/8 — 1/4
1994[a]	95,337	(5,839)	(1.60)	.00	5 — 2-7/8
1993	100,040	1,813	.50	.00	7-1/4 — 2-7/8
1992[a]	96,743	(7,784)	(2.13)	.00	6-1/4 — 3-1/4

[a]Includes restructuring charges of $7,700,000 in 1995, and $3,400,000 in 1994; and the reclassification of a foreign joint venture and restructuring charges of $3,223,000 in 1992.

Transfer Agent & Registrar: Harris Trust and Savings Bank

General Counsel: Lord, Bissell & Brook

Investor Relations: Mark Smetana, V.P.

Human Resources: Mark Smetana, V.P.

Mgt. Info. Svcs.:   Frank Vanek

Auditors: BDO Seidman LLP

Traded (Symbol):   OTC Bulletin

Stockholders: 823

Employees: 590

Annual Meeting: In December

Charter Financial, Inc.
114 West Broadway, Sparta, Illinois 62286-1633
Telephone: (618) 443-2166

Charter Financial, Inc. is a savings and loan holding company for Charter Bank, S.B. The bank is an Illinois chartered savings bank. Originally organized in 1894, the bank is a community-oriented savings bank that conducts business through its main office in Sparta and seven full-service branches located in Anna, Carbondale, DuQuoin, Marian, Murphysboro, and Steeleville, Illinois. The bank is principally engaged in the business of attracting retail deposits from the general public and using those funds to originate mortgage loans secured by one- to four-family residential real estate and commercial business loans. In January 1997, the company acquired Home Federal Savings Bank of Carbondale, Illinois. Incorporated in Delaware in 1995.

Directors   (In addition to indicated officers)

Truman D. Cashman
James H. Clutts
Dennis F. Doelitzsch
William A. Norton

John Petkas, Jr.
Klondis T. Pirtle
Carl S. Schlageter, M.D.
Ralph Eugene Watson

Officers   (Directors*)

*John A. Becker, Chm., Pres. & C.E.O.
*Michael R. Howell, Exec. V.P. & Treas.
*Linda M. Johnson, Sr. V.P. & Secy.
 Ronald L. Diel, V.P.

Karen P. Jacobus, V.P. & Cont.
Ronald W. Seymour, V.P.
Klay D. Tiemann, V.P.

Consolidated Balance Sheet[a]   As of September 30, 1996 (000 omitted)

Assets		Liabilities & Stockholders' Equity	
Cash and due from banks	$ 8,968	Deposits	$248,723
Investment securities	67,473	Borrowings	76,354
Mortgage backed securities	16,632	Other liabilities	6,960
Net loans	275,487	*Stockholders' equity	56,394
Net property, plant & equipment	5,990		
Other assets	13,881		
Total	$388,431	Total	$388,431

[a]Data for Charter Bank, S.B.
*4,253,459 shares common stock outstanding.

Consolidated Income Statement

Years Ended Sept. 30	Thousands — — — — Total Income	Net Income	Per Share[a] — — — Earnings	Cash Dividends	Common Stock Price Range[a] Calendar Year	
1996	$26,660	$3,058	$ .67	$ .00	13	— 10-7/8
1995[b]	21,419	2,984	.69			
1994[b]	19,677	4,097	.97			
1993[b]	19,560	3,073				
1992[b]	20,924	2,442				

[a]Initial public offering of Charter Financial, Inc. in December 1995.
[b]Data for Charter Bank, S.B.

Transfer Agent & Registrar: Registrar & Transfer Company, NJ

Investor Relations:	Linda M. Johnson, Sr. V.P.	Traded (Symbol):	NASDAQ (CBSB)
Mgt. Info. Svcs.:	Kay Morrison	Stockholders:	896
		Employees:	104
Auditors:	KPMG Peat Marwick LLP	Annual Meeting:	In January

The Cherry Corporation
3600 Sunset Avenue, Waukegan, Illinois 60087-3298
Telephone: (847) 662-9200

The Cherry Corporation designs, manufactures, and sells proprietary and custom electrical, electronic, and semiconductor components to original equipment manufacturers and distributors in three market segments: Automotive, Computer, and Consumer and Commercial. Products sold to these markets include proprietary and custom electrical switches, sensors, keyboards and related products, electronic controls and displays, and semiconductor devices. The company has facilities in the United States, Australia, the Czech Republic, England, France, Germany, Hong Kong, Japan, and Mexico. Some products are assembled in China, Malaysia, the Philippines, and South Korea. The company also participates in 50 percent joint ventures in India and Japan. Wholly owned subsidiaries are: Cherry Semiconductor Corporation; Cherry Mikroschalter, GmbH; Cherry SRO; Cherry Electrical Products Ltd.; Cherry SARL; Cherry Australia Pty., Ltd.; Cherry de Mexico, S.A. de V.C.; and Cherasia Limited. Cherry Electrical Products operates as a division of The Cherry Corporation, and the company also has a branch sales and engineering office in Japan named Cherry Automotive—Japan. The joint ventures are TVS Cherry Private Limited in India and Hirose Cherry Precision Company Limited in Japan. Incorporated in Illinois in 1953; reincorporated in Delaware in 1978.

Directors   (In addition to indicated officers)

Charles W. Denny	Robert B. McDermott
Peter A. Guglielmi	W. Ed Tyler
Thomas L. Martin, Jr.	Henry J. West

Officers   (Directors*)

*Peter B. Cherry, Chm. & Pres.	Klaus D. Lauterbach, V.P.
*Alfred S. Budnick, V.P.	Kevin G. Powers, Cont.
Dan A. King, V.P.—Fin., Treas. & Secy.	

Consolidated Balance Sheet   As of February 28, 1997 (000 omitted)

Assets		Liabilities & Stockholders' Equity	
Current assets	$124,853	Current liabilities	$ 69,633
Net property, plant & equipment	159,267	Long-term debt	37,009
Other assets	11,526	Deferred credits and taxes	20,928
		*Stockholders' equity	168,076
Total	$295,646	Total	$295,646

*7,667,119 shares Class A common and 4,750,063 shares Class B common stock outstanding.

Consolidated Income Statement

Years Ended Abt. Feb. 28	Thousands — — — —		Per Share[a] — — —		Common Stock Price Range[a] Fiscal Year
	Net Sales	Net Income	Earnings	Cash Dividends	
1997	$439,592	$15,914	$1.29	$ .00	16-3/4 — 9
1996	424,681	11,251	.92	.00	16-1/2 — 9-1/4
1995	339,237	14,823	1.36	.00	17-3/8 — 11-1/2
1994	275,269	11,033[b]	1.19[b]	.00	17 — 6-7/8
1993	266,231	10,257[c]	1.12[c]	.00	15-1/2 — 4-1/2

[a]Class A and B common stock. 1995 and prior years adjusted to reflect a 2-for-1 stock split in the form of a Class A stock dividend in July 1994.
[b]Includes a gain to reflect FAS 109, resulting in a cumulative effect of $1,542,000 ($.17 per share).
[c]Includes $2,539,000 ($.28 per share) extraordinary tax credit from utilization of operating loss carryforwards.

Transfer Agent & Registrar:	Harris Trust and Savings Bank		
General Counsel:	McDermott, Will & Emery	Traded (Symbol):	NASDAQ (CHERA; CHERB)
		Stockholders:	4,000
Investor Relations:	Dan A. King, V.P.	Employees:	4,367
Auditors:	Arthur Andersen LLP	Annual Meeting:	Third Thursday in June

Chicago Rivet & Machine Co.

901 Frontenac Road, P.O. Box 3061, Naperville, Illinois 60566
Telephone: (630) 357-8500

Chicago Rivet & Machine Co. conducts its operations in the fastener industry. Fastener operations consist of the manufacture and sale of rivets, parts and tooling, automatic rivet setting machines, and the leasing of such machines. The product lines include semi-tubular rivets, tubular and split rivets, cold-headed parts, and brake relining machines. Facilities are located in Naperville, Illinois; Tyrone, Pennsylvania; Norwell, Massachusetts; and Albia and Jefferson, Iowa. In December 1996, the company acquired H & L Tool Company, Inc., a Madison Heights, Michigan-based manufacturer of fasteners and screws for the automotive industry. Incorporated in Illinois in 1927.

Directors   (In addition to indicated officers)

Robert K. Brown	John R. Madden
Stephen L. Levy	Walter W. Morrissey

Officers   (Directors*)

*John A. Morrissey, Chm. & C.E.O.	Kimberly A. Kirhofer, Secy.
*John C. Osterman, Pres., C.O.O. & Treas.	Stephen D. Voss, Asst. Treas. & Cont.
Donald P. Long, V.P.—Sales	

Consolidated Balance Sheet   As of December 31, 1996 (000 omitted)

Assets		Liabilities & Stockholders' Equity	
Current assets	$17,330	Current liabilities	$ 5,290
Net property, plant & equipment	13,988	Long-term debt	7,200
Goodwill, net	8	Deferred items	1,060
		*Stockholders' equity	17,776
Total	$31,326	Total	$31,326

*585,748 shares common stock outstanding.

Consolidated Income Statement

Years Ended Dec. 31	Thousands — — — —		Per Share — — —		Common Stock Price Range Calendar Year
	Total Revenues[a]	Net Income	Earnings	Cash Dividends[b]	
1996[c]	$22,511	$1,948	$3.33	$1.80	36-1/2 — 29-1/4
1995	23,717	2,235	3.81	1.75	34-7/8 — 25-3/4
1994	23,013	1,909	3.25	1.55	34-3/8 — 25-7/8
1993	20,390	1,403	2.39	1.30	29-1/4 — 24
1992	15,758	952	1.62	1.20	28-3/4 — 19-5/8

[a]From continuing operations.
[b]Declared.
[c]Includes the results of H & L Tool Company, Inc. from the date of acquisition.

Transfer Agent & Registrar:	First Chicago Trust Co. of New York		
Investor Relations:	Kimberly A. Kirhofer, Secy.	**Traded (Symbol):**	AMEX (CVR)
Mgt. Info. Svcs.:	Wayne McPherson	**Stockholders:**	591
		Employees:	318
Auditors:	Price Waterhouse LLP	**Annual Meeting:**	In May

LaSalle Banks Guide

CILCORP Inc.

300 Hamilton Boulevard, Suite 300, Peoria, Illinois 61602-1238
Telephone: (309) 675-8850

CILCORP Inc. is the holding company for Central Illinois Light Company (CILCO), its principal business subsidiary, which is engaged in the generation, transmission, distribution, and sale of electric energy in an area of about 3,700 square miles, and the purchase, distribution, transportation, and sale of natural gas in an area of approximately 4,500 square miles in central and east central Illinois. CILCO's electric service area comprises 139 communities including Peoria, Illinois; the gas service area covers 129 communities including Peoria and Springfield, Illinois. CILCO owns and operates two steam-electric base load generating plants, two natural gas combustion turbine-generators, which are used for peaking service, and a 21-megawatt cogeneration plant. CILCO is interconnected with CIPSCO Inc., Commonwealth Edison Company, Illinois Power Company, and the City of Springfield (City Water, Light and Power Department) to provide for the interchange of electric energy on an emergency and mutual-help basis. Other CILCORP subsidiaries include: CILCORP Ventures Inc., which pursues investment opportunities in new ventures in energy, biotechnology, and medicine; CILCORP Investment Management Inc., which administers the company's investment policy and manages its investment portfolio comprised primarily of leveraged leases; and QST Enterprises Inc., which provides non-regulated energy and related products and services, engineering and environmental consulting and analytical services, and fiber optic and advanced Internet-based communication services and products. Incorporated in Illinois in 1985 as a holding company for CILCO, which was incorporated in Illinois in 1913.

Directors (In addition to indicated officers)

Marcus Alexis	Jerry D. Caulder	Katherine E. Smith
John R. Brazil	Homer J. Holland	Richard N. Ullman
Willard Bunn III	H. Safford Peacock	Murray M. Yeomans

Officers (Directors*)

*Robert O. Viets, Pres. & C.E.O.
William M. Shay, Exec. V.P.
John G. Sahn, V.P., Gen. Coun. & Secy.

Michael D. Austin, Treas. & Asst. Secy.
Thomas D. Hutchinson, Cont.

Consolidated Balance Sheet As of December 31, 1996 (000 omitted)

Assets		Liabilities & Stockholders' Equity	
Current assets	$ 182,207	Current liabilities	$ 157,371
Net property, plant & equipment	891,604	Long-term debt	320,666
Other assets	211,882	Deferred items	373,331
		Preferred stock of subsidiary	66,120
		*Stockholders' equity	368,205
Total	$1,285,693	Total	$1,285,693

*13,610,680 shares common stock outstanding.

Consolidated Income Statement

Years Ended Dec. 31	Thousands — — — — Operating Revenues	Net Income[a]	Per Share — — — Earnings	Cash Dividends	Common Stock Price Range Calendar Year
1996	$628,392	$27,943	$2.07	$2.46	45-1/8 — 35-1/2
1995	614,740	38,582	2.93	2.46	44-3/4 — 31-7/8
1994	605,139	32,586	2.50	2.46	37-1/2 — 28-3/4
1993	584,511	33,583	2.60	2.46	43-3/4 — 35-3/4
1992	581,225	32,097	2.48	2.46	40-5/8 — 33-5/8

[a]Available for common stockholders.

Transfer Agents: CILCORP Inc.; Continental Stock Transfer & Trust Co. of N.Y.

Registrars:
First of America Trust Co.; Continental Stock Transfer & Trust Co. of N.Y.

General Counsel: John G. Sahn, V.P.

Investor Relations: Gary A. Ebeling, Dir.

Human Resources: Todd K. Severson, V.P.

Mgt. Info. Svcs.: Joe I. Gillespie

Auditors: Arthur Andersen LLP

Traded (Symbol): NYSE, CSE (CER)

Stockholders: 12,770

Employees: 2,121

Annual Meeting: Fourth Tuesday in April

Internet: www.cilco.com

CIPSCO Incorporated

607 East Adams Street, Springfield, Illinois 62739
Telephone: (217) 523-3600

CIPSCO Incorporated is a holding company whose principal subsidiary is Central Illinois Public Service Company (CIPS), an electric and natural gas utility. Another subsidiary, CIPSCO Investment Company, manages non-utility investments and provides investment management services for affiliates. CIPS is engaged in the generation, transmission, and distribution of electricity. The utility also distributes natural gas which it purchases from pipeline suppliers and from producers. In addition, transportation service is provided for customers that purchase gas directly from suppliers. The CIPS service area is in a 20,000-square mile region of central and southern Illinois. Electric service is provided to about 322,300 customers in 557 communities. Power also is furnished to other utility systems, rural electric cooperatives, and municipal electric systems. CIPS owns and operates five interconnected electric generating stations with a combined capacity of about 2,850 megawatts. No generating facilities are under construction or planned. All generating capacity is coal fired with the exception of a small, oil-fired unit. Natural gas service is provided to about 168,700 customers in 267 communities. Maximum natural gas sendout capability is about 330,000,000 cubic feet per day. In August 1995, the company announced that CIPS would merge with Union Electric Co. and become a subsidiary of a holding company named Ameren, headquartered in St. Louis. The merger is expected to be completed in late 1997. Incorporated in Illinois in 1986.

Directors   (In addition to indicated officers)

John L. Heath
Robert W. Jackson
Gordon R. Lohman
Richard A. Lumpkin

Hanne M. Merriman
Thomas L. Shade
James W. Wogsland

Officers   (Directors*)

*Clifford L. Greenwalt, Pres. & C.E.O.
Gary L. Rainwater, Exec. V.P.
William A. Koertner, V.P., C.F.O. & Secy.
Freeman J. Kinsinger, Cont. & Asst. Treas.
R.C. Porter, Treas., Asst. Secy. & Asst. Cont.

James T. Birkett, V.P.—Generation (CIPS)
Gilbert W. Moorman, V.P.—Region Oper. (CIPS)
Graig D. Nelson, V.P.—Corp. Svc. (CIPS)
D.R. Patterson, V.P.—Region Oper. (CIPS)

Consolidated Balance Sheet   As of December 31, 1996 (000 omitted)

Assets		Liabilities & Stockholders' Equity	
Current assets	$ 206,973	Current liabilities	$ 202,262
Net property, plant & equipment	1,458,124	Long-term debt	479,227
Other assets	206,559	Deferred items	448,573
		Preferred stock of subsidiaries	80,000
		*Stockholders' equity	661,594
Total	$1,871,656	Total	$1,871,656

*34,069,542 shares common stock outstanding.

Consolidated Income Statement

Years Ended Dec. 31	Thousands — — — — — Operating Revenues	Net Income	Per Share — — — Earnings	Dividends Declared	Common Stock Price Range Calendar Year
1996	$896,715	$80,057	$2.35	$2.07	41-1/4 — 34-7/8
1995	842,262	72,015	2.11	2.03	39 — 27
1994	844,615	83,954	2.46	1.99	30-5/8 — 25-1/4
1993	844,760	85,498	2.51	1.95	33-5/8 — 29-1/4
1992	739,877	72,499	2.13	1.91	30-7/8 — 26

Transfer Agents: Illinois Stock Transfer Company; Harris Trust and Savings Bank

Registrar: Harris Trust and Savings Bank

General Counsel: Jones, Day, Reavis & Pogue

Investor Relations: Kent H. Sturhahn

Human Resources: G.B. Fritz

Auditors: Arthur Andersen LLP

Traded (Symbol):   NYSE, CSE (CIP)

Stockholders: 35,658

Employees: 2,304

Annual Meeting: Fourth Wednesday in April

Circuit Systems, Inc.

2350 East Lunt Avenue, Elk Grove Village, Illinois 60007-5699
Telephone: (847) 439-1999

Circuit Systems, Inc. manufactures single-sided, double-sided, and multilayer printed circuit boards for the electronics industry. Its customers are primarily original equipment manufacturers of computers, telecommunications equipment, and computer peripherals. Circuit boards are used in large quantities in the electronics industry to mount and interconnect microprocessors, integrated circuits, and other electronic components. The company has approximately a 20 percent interest in SigmaTron International, Inc., which is engaged in electronics contract manufacturing. Incorporated in Illinois in 1967.

Directors (In addition to indicated officers)

Richard J. Augustine   C. Joseph Incrocci
Gary R. Fairhead

Officers (Directors*)

*D.S. Patel, Chm., Pres. & C.E.O.   *Dilip S. Vyas, V.P.—Bus. Dev.
*Magan H. Patel, Exec. V.P. & Asst. Secy.   Mitchell A. Czosnyka, Treas.
Roger S. McLain, V.P.—Mktg.   *Thomas W. Rieck, Secy.
Vithal V. Patel, V.P.—Reg. Compliance &
Assets

Consolidated Balance Sheet As of April 30, 1996 (000 omitted)

Assets		Liabilities & Stockholders' Equity	
Current assets	$16,564	Current liabilities	$ 8,518
Net property, plant & equipment	24,890	Long-term debt	14,536
Investment in affiliates	2,588	Deferred items	1,560
Other assets	1,774	*Stockholders' equity	21,202
Total	$45,816	Total	$45,816

*5,321,973 shares common stock outstanding.

Consolidated Income Statement

Years Ended Apr. 30	Thousands ———— Net Sales	Net Income	Per Share ———— Earnings	Cash Dividends	Common Stock Price Range Fiscal Year
1996	$65,130	$3,084	$ .58	$ .00	7-7/8 — 3-1/8
1995	59,586	2,242	.42	.00	8-1/8 — 3
1994	60,411	4,989	.95	.00	8-7/8 — 4-3/8
1993	51,419	3,056	.59	.00	9-1/8 — 3-3/4
1992	47,234	1,785	.35	.00	5-1/4 — 1-3/8

Transfer Agent & Registrar: American Stock Transfer & Trust Co.

Legal Counsel: Rieck and Crotty, P.C.

Investor Relations: Elaine Douglas

Human Resources: Bill Blair

Mgt. Info. Svcs.: Kiran Patel

Auditors: Grant Thornton LLP

Traded (Symbol): NASDAQ (CSYI)

Stockholders: 1,450

Employees: 530

Annual Meeting: Second Friday after Labor Day

CLARCOR Inc.

2323 Sixth Street, P.O. Box 7007, Rockford, Illinois 61125
Telephone: (815) 962-8867

CLARCOR Inc. is a diversified provider of filtration and packaging products. The company is divided into two groups: the Filtration Products Group supplies filtration and purification products and systems for the over-the-road trucking, construction, farm, automotive, railroad, and industrial markets; and the Consumer Products Group develops and manufactures custom-decorated metal and plastic lithographed containers, composite containers and tubes, and plastic closures for the food, gift, arts and crafts, pharmaceutical, and household products markets. Significant wholly owned subsidiaries include: Baldwin Filters, Inc.; Hastings Filters, Inc.; J.L. Clark, Inc.; Airguard Industries, Inc.; and Clark Filter, Inc. On February 28, 1997, United Air Specialists, Inc. (UAS) became a wholly owned subsidiary of CLARCOR. CLARCOR Inc. was organized in 1904 as an Illinois corporation; reincorporated in Delaware in 1969.

Directors (In addition to indicated officers)

J. Marc Adam	Dudley J. Godfrey, Jr.
Milton R. Brown	Stanton K. Smith, Jr.
Carl J. Dargene	Don A. Wolf

Officers (Directors*)

*Lawrence E. Gloyd, Chm. & C.E.O.	Bruce A. Klein, V.P.—Fin. & C.F.O.
*Norman E. Johnson, Pres. & C.O.O.	William F. Knese, V.P. & Treas.
David J. Anderson, V.P.—Intl./Corp. Dev.	David J. Lindsay, V.P.—Admin. & C.A.O.
Marcia S. Blaylock, V.P.—Corp. Secy. & Cont.	Peter F. Nangle, V.P.—Info. Svcs.

Consolidated Balance Sheet[a]   As of November 30, 1996 (000 omitted)

Assets		Liabilities & Stockholders' Equity	
Current assets	$124,379	Current liabilities	$ 45,156
Net property, plant & equipment	78,586	Long-term debt	35,522
Other assets	40,999	Deferred items	7,798
		Other liabilities	9,429
		*Stockholders' equity	146,059
Total	$243,964	Total	$243,964

[a]The merger of UAS into CLARCOR was completed on February 28, 1997, through a pooling-of-interests. The amounts shown have not been restated for this transaction.
*14,874,969 shares common stock outstanding.

Consolidated Income Statement[a]

Years Ended Abt. Nov. 30	Thousands — — — — Net Sales	Net Income	Per Share[b] — — — Earnings	Cash Dividends	Common Stock Price Range[b] Calendar Year
1996	$333,338	$24,978	$1.68	$ .64	25-1/8 — 18-5/8
1995	290,194	21,954	1.48	.63	27 — 18-5/8
1994	270,123	21,255[c]	1.43[c]	.62	22-3/8 — 15-7/8
1993	225,319	17,251	1.16	.61	21-1/8 — 16
1992	188,625	14,139[d]	.94[d]	.60	22-1/2 — 15

[a]The merger of UAS into CLARCOR was completed on February 28, 1997, through a pooling-of-interests. The amounts shown have not been restated for this transaction.
[b]Adjusted to reflect a 3-for-2 stock split in February 1992.
[c]Includes a gain of $630,000 ($.04 per share), which is the cumulative effect of FAS 109.
[d]Includes a charge of $2,370,000 ($.16 per share), which is the cumulative effect of FAS 106.

Transfer Agent & Registrar:	First Chicago Trust Co. of New York		
General Counsel:	Sidley & Austin	**Traded (Symbol):**	NYSE (CLC)
Investor Relations:	Marcia S. Blaylock, V.P.	**Stockholders:**	7,800
Human Resources:	David J. Lindsay, V.P.	**Employees:**	2,562
Mgt. Info. Svcs.:	Peter F. Nangle, V.P.	**Annual Meeting:**	In March
Auditors:	Coopers & Lybrand L.L.P.	**Internet:**	www.clarcor.com

CNA Financial Corporation

CNA Plaza, 333 South Wabash Avenue, Chicago, Illinois 60685
Telephone: (312) 822-5000

CNA Financial Corporation is a holding company originally formed by Continental Assurance Company and Continental Casualty Company. Continental Assurance writes a complete line of individual and group life and health insurance policies. Continental Casualty and its subsidiary companies write a comprehensive line of accident, health, liability, property, and surety insurance policies. Commercial business includes such lines as workers' compensation, general liability, multiple peril, professional, and specialty insurance and reinsurance. Personal lines primarily consist of automobile and homeowners insurance. Other subsidiaries include National Fire Insurance Co. and American Casualty Company of Reading, Pennsylvania. Loews Corporation holds approximately an 84 percent ownership position in CNA Financial Corp. In May 1995, CNA Financial completed its acquisition of The Continental Corp., a New York property and casualty insurer. Incorporated in Delaware in 1967.

Directors   (In addition to indicated officers)

Antoinette Cook Bush	Joseph Rosenberg
Dennis H. Chookaszian	Richard L. Thomas
Philip L. Engel	James S. Tisch
Robert P. Gwinn	Preston R. Tisch
Walter F. Mondale	Marvin Zonis
Edward J. Noha	

Officers   (Directors*)

*Laurence A. Tisch, C.E.O.	Patricia L. Kubera, Grp. V.P. & Cont.
Peter E. Jokiel, Sr. V.P. & C.F.O.	Richard Dubberke, Asst. Secy.
Jonathan Kantor, Sr. V.P., Gen. Coun. & Secy.	Mary A. Ribikawskis, Asst. Secy.

Consolidated Balance Sheet   As of December 31, 1996 (000 omitted)

Assets		Liabilities & Stockholders' Equity	
Investments	$35,412,406	Insurance reserves	$40,415,156
Insurance receivables	12,630,359	Long-term debt	2,764,917
Property & equipment	645,389	Other liabilities	10,494,876
Other assets	12,046,578	*Stockholders' equity	7,059,783
Total	$60,734,732	Total	$60,734,732

*61,798,262 shares common stock outstanding.

Consolidated Income Statement

Years Ended Dec. 31	Thousands — — — — Revenues	Net Income	Per Share — — — Earnings	Cash Dividends	Common Stock Price Range Calendar Year
1996	$16,987,776	$ 964,840	$ 15.51	$ .00	117-1/2 — 95-3/4
1995	14,699,700	757,000	12.14	.00	123-1/4 — 64-3/4
1994	10,999,545	36,548	.51	.00	82-1/4 — 60
1993	11,010,813	267,523	4.26	.00	101 — 74-1/4
1992	10,793,442	(330,552)[a]	(5.42)[a]	.00	104-1/2 — 78-1/2

[a]Includes a gain to reflect FAS 106, FAS 109, and the discounting of certain workers' compensation and disability claim reserves, resulting in a cumulative effect of $331,892,000 ($5.37 per share).

Transfer Agent & Registrar: The First National Bank of Chicago

General Counsel: Donald M. Lowry, Sr. V.P.

Investor Relations: Roger Morris

Human Resources:
   Donna K. Weaver, Asst. V.P.

Mgt. Info. Svcs.:
   Anthony F. Saratore, Grp. V.P.

Auditors: Deloitte & Touche LLP

Traded (Symbol):   NYSE, CSE, PHSE, PSE (CNA)

Stockholders: 3,113

Employees: 24,300

Annual Meeting: First Wednesday in May

Internet: www.cna.com

LaSalle Banks Guide

Cobra Electronics Corporation

6500 West Cortland Street, Chicago, Illinois 60707
Telephone: (773) 889-8870

Cobra Electronics Corporation designs and markets consumer electronics products, including Intenna® cordless phones and answering systems, CB radios with the exclusive SoundTracker™ system, Family Radio service radios, radar/laser detection systems with the SafetyAlert™ feature in the United States and around the world, as well as Safety Alert transmitters to police, fire, and emergency vehicle markets. Subsidiaries are Cobra Electronics (Hong Kong) Limited and Dynascan Europe Ltd. In December 1995, Cobra announced that it had entered into a long-term licensing agreement with General Motors Corporation, which will allow Cobra to sell its CB radios to an estimated 8,500 General Motors and Chevrolet dealers throughout the country. Incorporated in Delaware in 1961; present name adopted in 1993.

Directors   (In addition to indicated officers)

William P. Carmichael
Samuel B. Horberg

Harold D. Schwartz

Officers   (Directors*)

*Carl Korn, Chm.
*Jerry Kalov, Pres. & C.E.O.
 James R. Bazet, Exec. V.P. & C.O.O.

Anthony A. Mirabelli, Sr. V.P.—Mktg. & Sales
*Gerald M. Laures, V.P.—Fin. & Secy.

Consolidated Balance Sheet   As of December 31, 1996 (000 omitted)

Assets		Liabilities & Stockholders' Equity	
Current assets	$31,071	Current liabilities	$23,883
Net property, plant & equipment	6,133	*Stockholders' equity	18,713
Other assets	5,392		
Total	$42,596	Total	$42,596

*6,241,648 shares common stock outstanding.

Consolidated Income Statement

Years Ended Dec. 31	Thousands — — — — Net Sales	Net Income[a]	Per Share — — — Earnings[a]	Cash Dividends	Common Stock Price Range Calendar Year
1996	$ 90,324	$ 601	$ .10	$ .00	4-1/8 — 1-1/2
1995	90,442	(1,145)	(.18)	.00	3-3/8 — 1-1/2
1994	82,131	(1,515)	(.24)	.00	3-7/8 — 1-3/4
1993	98,844	(4,392)	(.70)	.00	4-3/8 — 2-1/8
1992	117,733	(9,514)[b]	(1.52)[b]	.00	6-1/4 — 3

[a]From continuing operations.
[b]Includes FAS 109, resulting in a charge of $835,000 ($.13 per share).

Transfer Agent & Registrar: American Stock Transfer & Trust Co.

General Counsel:	Sidley & Austin	Traded (Symbol):	NASDAQ (COBR)
Investor Relations:	Gerald M. Laures, V.P.	Stockholders:	1,400
Human Resources:	Celeste Boucher-Krickl, V.P.	Employees:	126
Mgt. Info. Svcs.:	Dean Marino	Annual Meeting:	In May
Auditors:	Deloitte & Touche LLP	Internet:	www.cobraelec.com

Comdisco, Inc.

6111 North River Road, Rosemont, Illinois 60018-5159
Telephone: (847) 698-3000

Comdisco, Inc., a technology services company, is one of the world's leading providers of solutions that help organizations reduce technology cost and risk. These services include asset management; business continuity; network services; and equipment leasing and remarketing. Comdisco has more than 100 locations around the world and serves more than 8,000 customers in North and South America, Australia, Europe, and the Pacific Rim, providing a full range of solutions for reducing technology cost and risk. Incorporated in Delaware in 1971.

Directors   (In addition to indicated officers)

Alan J. Andreini
C. Keith Hartley
Rick Kash

Harry M. Jansen Kraemer, Jr.
Carolyn L. Murphy
Thomas H. Patrick

Officers   (Directors*)

* Jack F. Slevin, Chm., Pres. & C.E.O.
 Stephen W. Hamilton, Exec. V.P.—Intl.
* Nicholas K. Pontikes, Exec. V.P.
* William N. Pontikes, Exec. V.P.—Oper.
* John J. Vosicky, Exec. V.P., C.F.O. & Treas.
 Martin R. Walsh, Exec. V.P.
 James D. Duncan, Sr. V.P.—N. Amer. Sales
* Philip A. Hewes, Sr. V.P.—Legal & Secy.
 John C. Kenning, Sr. V.P.—Sales
 Hugh L. Roberts, Sr. V.P.—N. Amer. Sales
 Richard B. Zane, Sr. V.P.—N. Amer. Sales
 William O. Bray, V.P.—Tech. Integration
 Lucie A. Buford, V.P.—Hum. Res.
 Richard A. Finocchi, V.P.—Fin.
 Jeremiah M. Fitzgerald, V.P.—Legal & Gen. Coun.
 Vincent J. Fricas, V.P.—Continuity Svcs.

Allan J. Graham, V.P.—Continuity Svcs.
Thomas Huber, V.P.—Mktg.
James J. Hyland, V.P.—Inv. Rel.
David J. Keenan, V.P. & Cont.
Mary C. Moster, V.P.—Commun.
Edward A. Pacewicz, V.P.—Fin.
Gregory D. Sabatello, V.P.—Info. Svcs.
Russell S. West, V.P.—Enterprise Sys.
W. Bradford Wheatley, V.P.—Private Placements
Thomas Flohr, Pres.—Eur. Oper.
Rosemary P. Geisler, Pres.—Distributed Sys. Div.
Michael F. Herman, Pres.—Diversified Tech.
Mark Johnson, Pres.—Network Svcs.
Jeffrey P. Keohane, Pres.—Enterprise Sys.
James P. Labe, Pres.—Comdisco Ventures
David Nolan, Pres.—Continuity Svcs.

Consolidated Balance Sheet   As of September 30, 1996 (000 omitted)

Assets		Liabilities & Stockholders' Equity	
Current assets	$ 429,000	Current liabilities	$2,365,000
Net property, plant & equipment	4,759,000	Long-term debt	1,828,000
Other assets	403,000	Deferred items	274,000
		Other liabilities	325,000
		*Stockholders' equity	799,000
Total	$5,591,000	Total	$5,591,000

*49,633,000 shares common stock outstanding.

Consolidated Income Statement

Years Ended Sept. 30	Thousands — — — —		Per Share[a] — — —		Common Stock
	Total Revenue	Net Income	Earnings[b]	Cash Dividends	Price Range[a] Calendar Year
1996	$2,431,000	$ 106,000	$ 2.00	$ .28	19-7/8 — 33
1995	2,240,000	96,000	1.73	.24	21-5/8 — 12-7/8
1994	2,098,000	44,000[c]	.77[c]	.23	16-1/8 — 11-7/8
1993	2,153,000	80,000[d]	1.31[d]	.19	14 — 8-3/4
1992	2,205,000	(9,000)	(.14)	.18	15-1/2 — 8-3/8

[a]Adjusted to reflect a 3-for-2 stock split in November 1995 and a 5% stock dividend in March 1992.
[b]Based on common and common equivalent shares.
[c]Includes a one-time, after-tax charge of $42,000,000 ($.73 per share).
[d]Includes a gain to reflect FAS 109, resulting in a cumulative effect of $20,000,000 ($.33 per share).

Transfer Agent & Registrar:	Chemical Bank		
Corporate Counsel:	McBride, Baker & Coles	Traded (Symbol):	NYSE, CSE (CDO)
Investor Relations:	James J. Hyland, V.P.	Stockholders:	2,240
Human Resources:	Lucie A. Buford, V.P.	Employees:	2,100
Mgt. Info. Svcs.:	Gregory D. Sabatello, V.P.	Annual Meeting:	In January
Auditors:	KPMG Peat Marwick LLP	Internet:	www.comdisco.com

Community Financial Corp.

240 East Chestnut Street, Olney, Illinois 62450-2295
Telephone: (618) 395-8676

Community Financial Corp. is the holding company for Community Bank & Trust, N.A., which operates through five offices in southeastern Illinois. The bank was originally chartered in 1883 as Olney Building and Loan Association. The principal business of the bank historically has consisted of attracting deposits from the general public and investing those deposits in loans secured by first mortgages on one- to four-family residences in the bank's market area. To an increasing extent, however, the bank originates agricultural loans because of the economic base of the surrounding communities. The bank also originates automobile and commercial business loans. In May 1997, the company completed its acquisition of American Bancshares, Inc., the holding company for American Bank of Illinois in Highland, Illinois. Incorporated in Illinois in 1994.

Directors   (In addition to indicated officers)

Michael F. Bauman
William O. Cantwell
Roger A. Charleston

Brad A. Jones
Clyde R. King
Allen D. Welker

Officers   (Directors*)

*Charles M. DiCiro, Chm.
*Shirley B. Kessler, Pres. & C.E.O.

Wayne H. Benson, Exec. V.P.
Douglas W. Tompson, C.F.O.

Consolidated Balance Sheet   As of December 31, 1996 (000 omitted)

Assets		Liabilities & Stockholders' Equity	
Cash and cash equivalents	$ 12,618	Deposits	$139,100
Investment securities	17,352	Borrowings	10,621
Mortgage backed securities	28,319	Other liabilities	1,996
Net loans	122,307	*Stockholders' equity	34,082
Other assets	5,203		
Total	$185,799	Total	$185,799

*2,387,612 shares common stock outstanding.

Consolidated Income Statement

Years Ended Dec. 31	Thousands — — — — —		Per Share[a] — — — —		Common Stock Price Range[a] Calendar Year
	Total Income	Net Income	Earnings	Cash Dividends	
1996	$14,652	$ 773	$ .35	$ .25	13-3/4 — 11-3/4
1995	14,437	2,033	.42[b]	.00	13-3/8 — 10-3/4
1994[c]	12,729	710[d]			
1993[c]	12,928	1,725			
1992[c]	14,212	1,753			

[a]Initial public offering in June 1995.
[b]Reflects net earnings after June 29, 1995, conversion of Community Bank & Trust to a National Association.
[c]Reclassified to conform to 1995 presentation.
[d]Includes an extraordinary item of $701,000.

Transfer Agent & Registrar: Registrar and Transfer Co.

General Counsel: Ray W. Vaughn

Investor Relations: Douglas W. Tompson, C.F.O.

Human Resources: Deborah Waxler, Asst. V.P.

Auditors:
  Larsson, Woodyard & Henson, LLP

Traded (Symbol):   NASDAQ (CFIC)

Stockholders: 746

Employees: 66

Annual Meeting: In May

Continental Materials Corporation

225 West Wacker Drive, Suite 1800, Chicago, Illinois 60606-1229
Telephone: (312) 541-7200

Continental Materials Corporation is a holding company that operates in two business segments: Heating and Air Conditioning and Construction Materials. In the Heating and Air Conditioning segment, Williams Furnace Co. manufactures and sells heating and cooling equipment including wall furnaces, console heaters, and fan coil units. Phoenix Manufacturing, Inc. manufactures and sells evaporative air coolers. In the Construction Materials segment, both Transit Mix Concrete Co. and Transit Mix of Pueblo, Inc. produce and distribute ready mix concrete, sand, gravel, and other building materials. Castle Concrete Company produces limestone, sand, and gravel. The sales of the Construction Materials segment are confined to the Front Range area in south central Colorado. Sales of heating and cooling equipment are nationwide. Through Continental Catalina, Inc., the company holds a 30 percent interest in Oracle Ridge Mining Partners, a partnership which owns a copper property near Tuscon, Arizona. Incorporated in Delaware in 1954.

Directors (In addition to indicated officers)

Thomas H. Carmody
Betsy R. Gidwitz
Ralph W. Gidwitz
Ronald J. Gidwitz

William G. Shoemaker
Theodore R. Tetzlaff
Darrell M. Trent

Officers (Directors*)

*James G. Gidwitz, Chm. & C.E.O.
*Joseph J. Sum, V.P. & Treas.

Mark S. Nichter, Secy. & Cont.

Consolidated Balance Sheet As of December 28, 1996 (000 omitted)

Assets		Liabilities & Stockholders' Equity	
Current assets	$32,834	Current liabilities	$16,213
Net property, plant & equipment	18,818	Long-term debt	6,500
Other assets	2,241	Deferred items	1,830
		*Stockholders' equity	29,350
Total	$53,893	Total	$53,893

*1,104,221 shares common stock outstanding.

Consolidated Income Statement[ab]

Years Ended Abt. Dec. 31	Thousands — — — — — Net Sales	Net Income	Per Share — — — — Earnings	Cash Dividends	Common Stock Price Range Calendar Year
1996	$92,768	$2,355	$2.13	$ .00	21-1/2 — 11-3/4
1995	75,560	681	.60	.00	13-3/8 — 10-7/8
1994	75,294	1,385	1.21	.00	13-7/8 — 7-7/8
1993	62,495	40[c]	.03[c]	.00	9-3/4 — 6-3/4
1992	60,982	137	.12	.00	10-1/8 — 6-1/8

[a]Imeco, Inc., was sold June 30, 1993. As such, net sales do not include Imeco for any year shown. Net income and earnings per share, however, include the effects of the discontinued operation.
[b]Certain prior years' amounts have been reclassified to conform with the current presentation.
[c]Includes an extraordinary charge of $1,335,000 ($1.15 per share).

Transfer Agent & Registrar: LaSalle National Trust, N.A.

Corporate Counsel:
  Wildman, Harrold, Allen & Dixon

Investor Relations: Mark S. Nichter, Secy.

Human Resources:
  Annemarie Bruckner, Office Mgr.

Mgt. Info. Svcs.: Mark S. Nichter, Secy.

Auditors: Coopers & Lybrand L.L.P.

Traded (Symbol): AMEX (CUO)

Stockholders: 3,000

Employees: 748

Annual Meeting: Fourth Wednesday in May

Corcom, Inc.

844 East Rockland Road, Libertyville, Illinois 60048
Telephone: (847) 680-7400

Corcom, Inc. is a supplier of radio frequency interference filters and power entry products. The company's catalog of approximately 500 designs offers a complete variety of sizes, configurations, power ratings, and environmental capabilities to the commercial and industrial electronics industries. Domestically, Corcom filters are sold by 28 independent distributors, and by 31 distributors in 24 foreign countries. In addition to English, the catalog is available in German and Japanese. Company subsidiaries include: Corcom S.A. de C.V.; Corcom Far East Ltd.; and Corcom GmbH. Facilities are located in Illinois, Germany, Hong Kong, and Mexico. Incorporated in Illinois in 1955.

Directors   (In addition to indicated officers)

Carolyn A. Berry
David B. Pivan
Herbert L. Roth

James A. Steinback
Gene F. Straube
Renato Tagiuri

Officers   (Directors*)

*Werner E. Neuman, Pres.
Thomas J. Buns, V.P.—Fin. & Treas.
Fernando Peña, V.P.—Mfg.

Michael P. Raleigh, V.P.—Eng. & Qual. Assur.
Walter Roth, Secy.

Consolidated Balance Sheet   As of December 31, 1996 (000 omitted)

Assets		Liabilities & Stockholders' Equity	
Current assets	$18,850	Current liabilities	$ 3,155
Net property, plant & equipment	4,377	Long-term debt	102
		*Stockholders' equity	19,970
Total	$23,227	Total	$23,227

*3,815,543 shares common stock outstanding.

Consolidated Income Statement

Years Ended Dec. 31	Thousands — — — — Net Sales	Net Income	Per Share — — — Earnings	Cash Dividends	Common Stock Price Range Calendar Year
1996	$33,166	$ 5,472	$ 1.38	$ .00	12-3/4 — 5
1995	30,660	2,786	.72	.00	8-1/4 — 2-3/4
1994	26,726	1,243	.33	.00	5 — 1-1/2
1993	25,854	(2,047)	(.58)	.00	2-1/4 — 1
1992ᵃ	26,990	(305)	(.09)	.00	1-1/2 — 1

ᵃNet income and earnings per share restated.

Transfer Agent & Registrar: American Stock Transfer & Trust Co.

General Counsel: D'Ancona & Pflaum

Investor Relations: Thomas J. Buns, V.P.

Human Resources: Sherril W. Bishop

Auditors: Coopers & Lybrand L.L.P.

Traded (Symbol):   NASDAQ (CORC)
Stockholders: 500
Employees: 710
Annual Meeting: In May
Internet: www.cor.com

CORUS BANKSHARES, INC.

3959 North Lincoln Avenue, Chicago, Illinois 60613
Telephone: (773) 549-7100

CORUS BANKSHARES, INC. (formerly River Forest Bancorp, Inc.) is a bank holding company in the business of providing financial services to customers in the Chicago metropolitan area. In June 1996, the company announced that it had merged four of its subsidiaries—River Forest State Bank and Trust, Commercial National Bank, Lincoln National Bank, and Aetna Bank, NA—into CORUS BANK, NA. It also announced that later in 1996, it would consolidate its remaining three subsidiaries—First National Bank of Calumet City, First National Bank of Wheeling, and Madison Bank NA—into CORUS BANK. The bank offers general banking services such as checking, savings, and time deposit accounts; commercial, mortgage, home equity, student, and personal loans; safe deposit boxes; and a variety of additional services. The company also operates CORUS FINANCIAL, INC., which specializes in medical financing plans for patients of hospitals and other healthcare providers. Incorporated in Minnesota in 1958; present name adopted in 1996.

Directors   (In addition to indicated officers)

Karl H. Horn
Michael Levitt
Rodney D. Lubeznik

Michael Tang
William H. Wendt III

Officers   (Directors*)

*Joseph C. Glickman, Chm.
*Robert J. Glickman, Pres. & C.E.O.
David H. Johnson III, Exec. V.P.
Michael Stein, Exec. V.P.
Terence W. Keenan, Sr. V.P.

Timothy H. Taylor, Sr. V.P. & C.F.O.
Michael J. McClure, First V.P. & Chf. Acct. Off.
James Kolovos, V.P.—Taxes
Lawrence P. Wyrobek, Secy.

Consolidated Balance Sheet   As of December 31, 1996 (000 omitted)

Assets		Liabilities & Stockholders' Equity	
Cash & due from banks	$ 57,508	Total deposits	$1,900,679
Federal funds sold	98,500	Short term borrowings	6,317
Securities	390,283	Other liabilities	35,942
Net loans, net of allowance	1,590,477	Long-term debt	40,000
Net property, plant & equipment	28,650	*Stockholders' equity	235,590
Other assets	53,110		
Total	$2,218,528	Total	$2,218,528

*14,820,242 shares common stock outstanding.

Consolidated Income Statement

Years Ended Dec. 31	Thousands — — — —		Per Share — — —		Common Stock Price Range Calendar Year
	Total Income[a]	Net Income	Earnings	Cash Dividends	
1996	$213,702	$43,905	$2.93	$ .48	33 — 24-3/4
1995	185,225	35,770	2.35	.36	25-1/2 — 16-3/8
1994	127,776	24,016	1.57	.29	22-7/8 — 17-3/4
1993	113,864	25,322	1.66	.27	19-1/4 — 16-3/8
1992	120,110	23,278	1.53	.23	21 — 16-1/8

[a]Certain prior-year amounts have been reclassified to conform with the 1995 presentation.

Transfer Agent & Registrar: Mellon Securities Transfer Services

Investor Relations: Timothy H. Taylor, Sr. V.P.

Human Resources: Thomas Grace, First V.P.

Mgt. Info Svcs.:
David H. Johnson III, Exec. V.P.

Auditors: Arthur Andersen LLP

Traded (Symbol):   NASDAQ (CORS)

Stockholders: 516

Employees: 704

Annual Meeting: In May

Internet: www.financial-net.com/corus

Culligan Water Technologies, Inc.

One Culligan Parkway, Northbrook, Illinois 60062
Telephone: (847) 205-6000

Culligan Water Technologies, Inc. is a leading manufacturer and distributor of water purification and treatment products for household, commercial, and industrial applications. Products and services include filters for tap water and household water softeners, highly sophisticated equipment and services designed for complex commercial and industrial applications, and bottled water. Brand names include Culligan® and Everpure®. The company's products are sold and serviced in more than 90 countries through a worldwide network of more than 1,400 sales and service centers. The company was spun off from Samsonite Corporation in September 1995. Incorporated in Delaware in 1945 to succeed a company established in 1936.

Directors (In addition to indicated officers)

R. Theodore Ammon
Bernard Attal
Leon D. Black
Robert H. Falk

Mark H. Rachesky
Robert L. Rosen
Marc J. Rowan
Stephen J. Solarz

Officers (Directors*)

*Douglas A. Pertz, Pres. & C.E.O.
Edward A. Christensen, V.P., Gen. Coun. & Secy.
Michael E. Salvati, V.P.—Fin. & C.F.O.

Kenneth I. Wellings, V.P.—Intl.
Michael A. Siri, Treas.
Ron M. Pertl, Asst. Treas.
William F. White, Asst. Secy. & Asst. Treas.

Consolidated Balance Sheet As of January 31, 1997 (000 omitted)

Assets		Liabilities & Stockholders' Equity	
Current assets	$152,654	Current liabilities	$ 73,231
Net property, plant & equipment	78,740	Long-term debt	36,231
Intangible assets, net	76,883	Deferred items	29,805
Other assets	29,085	Other liabilities	24,455
		*Stockholders' equity	173,640
Total	$337,362	Total	$337,362

*21,342,957 shares common stock outstanding.

Consolidated Income Statement

Years Ended Jan. 31	Thousands — — — — Net Sales	Net Income[a]	Per Share[b] — — — — Earnings	Cash Dividends	Common Stock Price Range[b] Calendar Year
1997	$371,018	$30,232[c]	$1.41	$ .00	
1996	304,502	20,383[d]	.98	.00	40-3/4 — 23-3/8
1995	280,051	34,683			
1994	264,100	31,800			

[a]Adjusted income before interest and taxes.
[b]Spun off from Samsonite Corporation in September 1995. In December 1995, the company completed a public offering of 4,025,000 shares.
[c]Excludes the amortization of reorganization value in excess of identifiable assets, and includes the pro forma impact of the refinancing and offering as of January 31, 1997.
[d]Excludes the amortization of reorganization value in excess of identifiable assets, and includes a gain on an insurance settlement related to a fire at the company's Belgian facility in July 1996.

Transfer Agent & Registrar:	The First National Bank of Boston		
General Counsel:	Edward A. Christensen, V.P.	Traded (Symbol):	NYSE (CUL)
Investor Relations:	Katie Whalen	Stockholders:	97
Human Resources:	David Horslev	Employees:	2,700
Mgt. Info. Svcs.:	Mark Wall	Annual Meeting:	In June
Auditors:	KPMG Peat Marwick LLP	Internet:	www.culligan-man.com

Damen Financial Corporation

200 West Higgins Road, Schaumburg, Illinois 60195-3788
Telephone: (847) 882-5320

Damen Financial Corporation is the holding company for Damen National Bank (formerly known as Damen Federal Bank for Savings). The bank currently serves the financial needs of communities in its market area through its main office in Schaumburg and branch offices located in Chicago and Burbank, Illinois. In September 1995, Damen Federal Bank for Savings, which was founded in 1916, converted from a federally chartered mutual savings bank to a federally chartered stock savings bank. In September 1995, the company completed an initial public offering of 3,967,500 shares of common stock. Incorporated in Delaware in 1995.

Directors (In addition to indicated officers)

Charles J. Caputo
Carol A. Diver

Nicholas J. Raino
Edward R. Tybor

Officers (Directors*)

*Mary Beth Poronsky Stull, Chm., Pres. & C.E.O.
Kenneth D. Vanek, Sr. V.P.

*Janine M. Poronsky, V.P. & Secy.
Gerald J. Gartner, C.F.O. & Treas.

Consolidated Balance Sheet As of September 30, 1996 (000 omitted)

Assets		Liabilities & Stockholders' Equity	
Cash & cash equivalents	$ 1,181	Deposits	$118,973
Total investment securities	48,231	Borrowings	59,600
Total mortgage-backed securities	88,098	Other liabilities	3,112
Loans receivable	91,146	*Stockholders' equity	52,870
Net property, plant & equipment	3,503		
Other assets	2,396		
Total	$234,555	Total	$234,555

*3,770,117 shares common stock outstanding.

Consolidated Income Statement

Years Ended Sept. 30	Thousands — — — — Operating Income	Net Income	Per Share[a] — — — — Earnings	Cash Dividends	Common Stock Price Range[a] Calendar Year	
1996	$16,843	$1,780[b]	$ .49[b]	$ .12	13	— 10-3/4
1995[c]	11,989	1,812	.50	.00	12-1/4 — 10	
1994[d]	11,395	559				
1993[d]	14,331	2,304				
1992[d]	15,308	1,875				

[a]Initial public offering in September 1995.
[b]Excludes a special SAIF assessment, net of tax, of $2,300,000 ($.63 per share).
[c]10 months.
[d]Fiscal years ended November 30. In 1995, the fiscal year end was changed to September 30.

Transfer Agent & Registrar:	Registrar and Transfer Company, NJ		
General Counsel:	Wheeler, Wheeler & Wheeler	Traded (Symbol):	NASDAQ (DFIN)
Investor Relations:	Janine M. Poronsky, V.P.	Stockholders:	316
Human Resources:	Janine M. Poronsky, V.P.	Employees:	30
Auditors: Cobitz, Vandenberg & Fennessy		Annual Meeting:	In February

LaSalle Banks Guide

Dean Foods Company

3600 North River Road, Franklin Park, Illinois 60131-2185
Telephone: (847) 678-1680

Dean Foods Company purchases, processes and distributes dairy and specialty food products. Primarily a dairy company until the early 1960s, Dean Foods has achieved product diversification through internal development and acquisition. Its dairy products include fluid milk and related products, ice cream, and frozen novelties. Specialty food products include processed vegetables, pickles, relishes, dips, puddings, sauces, and powdered products. In addition to its own and acquired brand names, the company processes and distributes private-label products to supermarkets, food service outlets, various food service distributors, and other food processors. Dean Foods operates 61 manufacturing facilities and a number of distribution warehouses in 21 states, Mexico, and the Caribbean. Subsidiaries include: Dean Foods Vegetable Company; Dean Pickle and Specialty Products; Mayfield Dairy Farms; and Reiter Dairy. In March 1997, the company acquired Meadows Distributing Co., the largest distributor of ice cream and other frozen desserts in the Chicago area. Incorporated in Illinois in 1929; reincorporated in Delaware in 1968.

Directors (In addition to indicated officers)

Edward A. Brennan	John P. Frazee, Jr.	Richard P. Mayer
Lewis M. Collens	Bert A. Getz	Andrew J. McKenna
Paula H. Crown	John S. Llewellyn, Jr.	Alexander J. Vogl

Officers (Directors*)

*Howard M. Dean, Chm. & C.E.O.
*Philip A. Marineau, Pres. & C.O.O.
*Thomas L. Rose, V. Chm.
Daniel E. Green, Grp. V.P.—Specialty Dairy Div.
James R. Greisinger, Grp. V.P. & Pres.—Dean Pickle and Specialty Prod.
Dennis J. Purcell, Grp. V.P.
Roger A. Ragland, Grp. V.P.—Intl.
Jeffrey P. Shaw, Grp. V.P. & Pres.—Dean Foods Vegetable Co.
*Thomas A. Ravencroft, Sr. V.P. & Pres.—Dairy Div.

Eric A. Blanchard, V.P., Secy. & Gen. Coun.
Jenny L. Carpenter, V.P.—Sales & Mktg. Specialty Food Prod.
Gary A. Corbett, V.P.—Govt. & Dairy Industry Rel.
Gary D. Flickinger, V.P.—Prod.
William R. McManaman, V.P.—Finance & C.F.O.
George A. Muck, V.P.—Res. and Dev.
Douglas A. Parr, V.P.—Dairy Sales & Mktg.
Cameron C. Hitchcock, Treas.
William M. Luegers, Cont.
Gary P. Reitz, C.I.O.

Consolidated Balance Sheet   As of May 26, 1996 (000 omitted)

Assets		Liabilities & Stockholders' Equity	
Current assets	$ 584,399	Current liabilities	$ 398,457
Net property, plant & equipment	525,667	Long-term debt	221,653
Other assets	112,174	Deferred items	94,438
		*Stockholders' equity	507,692
Total	$1,222,240	Total	$1,222,240

*40,133,019 shares common stock outstanding.

Consolidated Income Statement

Years Ended Abt. May 30	Thousands — — — — Net Sales	Net Income[a]	Per Share[b] — — — Earnings[a]	Cash Dividends	Common Stock Price Range[b] Calendar Year
1996	$2,814,268	$(49,688)[c]	$(1.24)[c]	$ .72	32-3/4 — 21-3/4
1995	2,630,182	80,059	2.01	.68	31-7/8 — 27-3/4
1994	2,431,203	71,941	1.81	.64	33-1/2 — 25-1/4
1993	2,274,340	68,409	1.73	.60	32-7/8 — 23-1/8
1992	2,289,441	62,016	1.53	.56	31-1/2 — 22-3/4

[a]Includes an aftertax net gain of $1,179,000 ($.03 per share) related to changes in accounting principles in 1994 and a net charge of $9,100,000 ($.14 per share) for an unusual item in 1992.
[b]Adjusted to reflect a 3-for-2 stock split in August 1991.
[c]Includes an after-tax charge of $97,720 ($2.44 per share) related to the adoption of a plan to reduce costs, rationalize production capacity, and provide for severance and environmental costs.

Transfer Agent & Registrar: Harris Trust and Savings Bank

General Counsel:	Eric A. Blanchard, V.P.	Auditors:	Price Waterhouse LLP
Investor Relations:	Lu Ann Lilja, Dir.—Corp. Comm.	Traded (Symbol):	NYSE (DF)
Human Resources:	Neil Finnerty, Dir.	Stockholders:	9,481
		Employees:	11,500
Mgt. Info. Svcs.:	Gary Rietz, C.I.O.	Annual Meeting:	In October

Deere & Company

John Deere Road, Moline, Illinois 61265-8098
Telephone: (309) 765-8000

Deere & Company and its subsidiaries manufacture, distribute, and finance the sale and leasing of mobile power machinery, and provide credit, insurance, and health care products. The company's machine products are divided into three industry segments: agricultural equipment, industrial equipment, and lawn and grounds-care equipment. Agricultural equipment includes: tractors, tillage, soil preparation, planting and harvesting equipment, and crop handling equipment. The products in the industrial equipment segment consist of: utility tractors and smaller earthmoving equipment, medium capacity construction and earthmoving equipment, and forestry machines. This segment also includes the manufacture and distribution of engines and drivetrain components for the original equipment manufacturer (OEM) market. The products in the lawn and grounds-care equipment segment are manufactured and distributed for commercial and residential uses, including small tractors for lawn, garden, and utility purposes; riding and walk-behind mowers; golf course equipment; utility transport vehicles; snow blowers; and other outdoor power products. Company subsidiaries include: John Deere Credit Company; John Deere Finance Limited; John Deere Insurance Group; John Deere Insurance Company of Canada; and John Deere Health Care, Inc. Deere & Company operates factories in the United States, Argentina, Canada, France, Germany, South Africa, and Spain. Foreign sales branches are located in Argentina, Australia, Canada, England, France, Germany, Italy, South Africa, and Spain. Incorporated in Delaware in 1958.

Directors (In addition to indicated officers)

John R. Block	Samuel C. Johnson	William A. Schreyer	John R. Walter
Leonard A. Hadley	Arthur L. Kelly	John R. Stafford	Arnold R. Weber
Regina E. Herzlinger	Agustin Santamarina V	David H. Stowe, Jr.	

Officers (Directors*)

* Hans W. Becherer, Chm. & C.E.O.
Joseph W. England, Sr. V.P.
Robert W. Lane, Sr. V.P. & C.F.O.
John K. Lawson, Sr. V.P.
Michael S. Plunkett, Sr. V.P.
G. Bart Bontems, V.P.
Wade P. Clark, V.P.
Robert J. Combs, V.P.
Frank S. Cottrell, V.P., Gen. Coun. & Secy.
Mertroe B. Hornbuckle, V.P.
John J. Jenkins, V.P. & Compt.
Nathan J. Jones, V.P. & Treas.
Richard G. Kleine, V.P.
Robert D. Wismer, V.P.
Bernard L. Hardiek, Pres.—AG Equip. Div.

Michael Frank, Sr. V.P.—AG Equip. Div.
Robert W. Porter, Sr. V.P.—AG Equip. Div.
Adel A. Zakaria, Sr. V.P.—A.G. Equip. Div.
Pierre E. Leroy, Pres.—IND Equip. Div.
H.J. Markley, Sr. V.P.—IND Equip. Div.
Jeffrey H. Peterson, Sr. V.P.—IND Equip. Div.
James D. White, Sr. V.P.—IND Equip. Div.
Ferdinand F. Korndorf, Pres.—C&CE Div.
Ronald R. McDermott, Sr. V.P.—Deere Power Systems Grp.
Mark C. Rostvold, Sr. V.P.—C&CE Div.
Eugene L. Schotanus, Exec. V.P.—Fin. Svc.
Dennis E. Hoffmann, Pres.—J.D. Ins. Grp.
Michael P. Orr, Pres.—J.D. Credit Co.
Richard J. VanBell, Pres.—J.D. Health Care Inc.

Consolidated Balance Sheet As of October 31, 1996 (000 omitted)

*Assets		*Liabilities & Stockholders' Equity	
Net property, plant & equipment	$ 1,351,704	Liabilities	$11,095,516
Other assets	13,300,981	**Stockholders' equity	3,557,169
Total	$14,652,685	Total	$14,652,685

*Balance sheet no longer categorized due to adoption of FAS 94.
**257,266,092 shares common stock outstanding, less treasury.

Consolidated Income Statement[a]

Years Ended Oct. 31	Thousands — — — —		Per Share — — — —		Common Stock
	Total Revenues	Net Income	Earnings	Cash Dividends	Price Range[b] Calendar Year
1996	$11,229,393	$ 817,286	$ 3.14	$ .80	47-1/8 — 33
1995	10,291,000	706,105	2.71	.75	36 — 21-5/8
1994	8,977,000	603,563	2.34	.68	30-1/4 — 20-3/8
1993	7,696,000	(920,860)[c]	(3.97)[c]	.67	26-1/8 — 14-1/8
1992	6,930,000	37,426	.16	.67	18 — 12-1/4

[a]Conforms with the requirements of FAS 94.
[b]Restated to reflect a 3-for-1 stock split in November 1995.
[c]Includes a one-time charge adopted November 1, 1992, to reflect FAS 106 and FAS 112, resulting in a cumulative effect of $1,105,300,000 ($4.77 per share); and restructuring costs of $80,000,000 ($.34 per share).

Transfer Agent & Registrar: ChaseMellon Shareholder Services, L.L.C.

General Counsel:	Frank S. Cottrell, Sr. V.P.	Traded (Symbol):	NYSE, CSE, Frankfurt (DE)
Investor Relations:	Marie Z. Ziegler, Dir.	Stockholders:	29,304
Human Resources:	Michael S. Plunkett, Sr. V.P.	Employees:	33,919
Mgt. Info. Svcs.:	John K. Lawson, Sr. V.P.	Annual Meeting:	In February
Auditors:	Deloitte & Touche LLP	Internet:	www.deere.com

DEKALB Genetics Corporation

3100 Sycamore Road, DeKalb, Illinois 60115-9600
Telephone: (815) 758-3461

DEKALB Genetics Corporation, through its subsidiaries, engages in the development and continual improvement of important products to two segments of agriculture: seed (primarily corn, soybeans, sorghum, and sunflower), and hybrid swine-breeding stock. The company operates its business segments through its seed division, and through its wholly owned subsidiaries, which include DEKALB Swine Breeders, Inc. Other subsidiaries include: DEKALB Argentina, S.A.; DEKALB Canada, Inc.; DEKALB Europa GmbH; and DEKALB Italia, S.P.A. In March 1996, DEKALB announced that it had completed a sale of equity to Monsanto Company as part of a long-term research and development collaboration. In February 1996, the company announced that it had received a United States patent covering prediction of corn yield using inherited genetic markers. In January 1996, the company announced that it had also received the first U.S. patent covering insect-resistant corn plants. Incorporated in Delaware in 1988.

Directors (In addition to indicated officers)

Charles J. Arntzen, Ph.D.	Virginia Roberts Holt
Allan Aves	Douglas C. Roberts
Robert T. Fraley	John T. Roberts
Tod R. Hamachek	H. Blair White
Paul H. Hatfield	William M. Ziegler

Officers (Directors*)

*Bruce P. Bickner, Chm. & C.E.O.
*Richard O. Ryan, Pres. & C.O.O.
 Richard T. Crowder, Sr. V.P.—Intl. Seed Oper.
 John H. Witmer, Jr., Sr. V.P., Gen. Coun. & Secy.
 Janis M. Felver, V.P. & C.A.O.
 Catherine Mackey, V.P.—Research

John Pfund, V.P.—Research
Thomas R. Rauman, V.P.—Fin. & C.F.O.
Debra J. Shecterle, V.P.—Hum. Res.
David R. Wagley, V.P. & Treas.
Robert W. Donaldson, Asst. Treas.
Roy L. Poage, Pres.—DEKALB Swine Breeders, Inc.

Consolidated Balance Sheet   As of August 31, 1996 (000 omitted)

Assets		Liabilities & Stockholders' Equity	
Current assets	$190,000	Current liabilities	$ 87,300
Net property, plant & equipment	119,500	Long-term debt	85,000
Other assets	53,800	Deferred items	22,400
		*Stockholders' equity	168,600
Total	$363,300	Total	$363,300

*2,403,580 shares Class A common and 14,647,937 shares Class B common stock outstanding.

Consolidated Income Statement[a]

Years Ended Aug. 31	Thousands — — — — Operating Revenues	Net Income	Per Share — — — Earnings	Cash Dividends	Common Stock Price Range[bc] Calendar Year
1996	$387,500	$17,000	$1.03	$ .27	53-1/4 — 15
1995	319,400	10,700	.69	.27	15 — 8-1/8
1994	300,200	10,600	.68	.27	12 — 8-1/8
1993	277,400	1,700	.11	.27	11-3/8 — 7-1/2
1992	285,900	10,300	.67	.27	11-1/2 — 7-3/4

[a]Restated to reflect discontinued operations 1994-1992 (revenues only).
[b]Class B common stock only.
[c]Adjusted to reflect a 3-for-1 stock split in May 1996.

Transfer Agent & Registrar:	American Stock Transfer & Trust Co.		
General Counsel:	John H. Witmer, Jr., Sr. V.P.	Traded (Symbol):	NYSE (DKB)
Investor Relations:	Thomas R. Rauman, V.P.	Stockholders:	2,098
Human Resources:	Debra J. Shecterle, V.P.	Employees:	1,882
Mgt. Info. Svcs.:	Jim Nesmith, V.P.	Annual Meeting:	In January
Auditors:	Arthur Andersen LLP	Internet:	www.dekalb.com

Delphi Information Systems, Inc.

3501 Algonquin Road, Suite 500, Rolling Meadows, Illinois 60008
Telephone: (847) 506-3100

Delphi Information Systems, Inc. is a leading provider of management information and automation systems to independent property and casualty agencies and brokerages in North America. The company develops, markets, and supports computer application software systems, which enhance the efficiency and profitability of agencies, brokerages, and insurance carriers. The systems automate the areas of sales management, policy and claims administration, accounting, financial reporting, rating and electronic interface. Delphi also markets and supports computer hardware to operate its software systems. Incorporated in Delaware in 1976.

Directors (In addition to indicated officers)

Yuval Almog
Bill Baumel
Larry G. Gerdes

Richard R. Janssen
Donald L. Lucas

Officers (Directors*)

John W. Trustman, Pres. & C.E.O.

*James Harsch, V.P.—Admin. & C.F.O.

Consolidated Balance Sheet As of March 31, 1997 (000 omitted)

Assets		Liabilities & Stockholders' Equity	
Current assets	$11,964	Current liabilities	$14,092
Net property, plant & equipment	2,242	Other liabilities	37
Other assets	8,371	*Stockholders' equity	8,448
Total	$22,577	Total	$22,577

*36,351,168 shares common stock outstanding.

Consolidated Income Statement

Years Ended March 31	Thousands — — — —		Per Share — — —		Common Stock Price Range Fiscal Year
	Revenues	Net Income	Earnings	Cash Dividends	
1997	$27,714	$(5,884)[a]	$ (.19)	$ .00	2-1/8 — 3/4
1996	44,081	(11,833)[b]	(1.37)	.00	3-1/4 — 3/4
1995	53,040	(1,681)	(.23)	.00	4 — 1/2
1994	53,605	(8,922)[c]	(1.34)	.00	7-1/4 — 3-1/2
1993	51,607	531	.07	.00	7-3/4 — 5-3/4

[a]Includes pretax charges of $1,297,000 related to restructuring.
[b]Includes pretax charges of $5,724,000 related to restructuring.
[c]Includes pretax charges of $6,490,000 related to restructuring.

Transfer Agent & Registrar: Chemical Trust Co. of California

General Counsel:	Schiff, Harden & Waite	Traded (Symbol):	NASDAQ (DLPH)
Investor Relations:	Sharon Wells, Asst. Cont.	Stockholders:	412
Human Resources:	James Harsch, V.P.	Employees:	194
Mgt. Info. Svcs.:	Art Regalado, Dir.	Annual Meeting:	In September
Auditors:	Arthur Andersen LLP	Internet:	www.dlph.com

LaSalle Banks Guide

DeVRY INC.

One Tower Lane, Oakbrook Terrace, Illinois 60181-4624
Telephone: (630) 571-7700

DeVRY INC. is a holding company which, through its wholly owned subsidiary, Keller Graduate School of Management, Inc., owns and operates the DeVRY Institutes of Technology, the Keller Graduate School of Management (KGSM), Corporate Educational Services (CES), and Becker CPA Review. The DeVRY Institutes and KGSM collectively form a leading private degree-granting higher education system in North America. The DeVRY Institutes were founded in 1931 and for more than 60 years have provided career-oriented technical education to high school graduates in the United States and Canada. KGSM, founded in 1973, employs a faculty of practicing business professionals to teach master's degree programs in business administration, project management, telecommunications management, and human resource management to working adults at multiple sites in the U.S. The DeVRY Institutes and KGSM are each accredited by the Commission on Institutions of Higher Education of the North Central Association of Colleges and Schools. The DeVRY Institutes are located on 10 campuses in the U.S. and four campuses in Canada. KGSM operates 20 campuses in Illinois, Arizona, California, Georgia, Missouri, Virginia, and Wisconsin. CES offers on-site training and educational programs tailored to specific client needs. Becker CPA Review offers test preparation for CPA and CMA examinations in the U.S. and internationally. Incorporated in Delaware in 1987.

Directors (In addition to indicated officers)

Ewen Akin	Frederick A. Krehbiel
Charles Bowsher	Thurston E. Manning
David S. Brown	Robert C. McCormack
Sister Ann Ida Gannon, B.V.M.	Julie A. McGee
Robert E. King	Hugo J. Melvoin

Officers (Directors*)

*Dennis J. Keller, Chm. & C.E.O.	Norman M. Levine, V.P.—Cont. & C.F.O.
*Ronald L. Taylor, Pres. & C.O.O.	Patrick L. Mayers, V.P.—Academic Affairs, KGSM
Marilynn J. Cason, Sr. V.P.—Admin., Gen. Coun. & Corp. Secy.	Gerald A. Murphy, V.P.—Reg. Oper.
Norman C. Metz, Sr. V.P.	James Otten, V.P.—Reg. Oper.
O. John Skubiak, Sr. V.P.	Kenneth Rutkowski, V.P.—Oper. Svcs. & Admin.
George W. Fisher, V.P.—Reg. Oper.	Vijay Shah, V.P.—Admissions
Michael J. LaForte, Jr., V.P.—Oper.	Edward J. Steffes, V.P.—Mktg.
	Sharon Thomas-Parrott, V.P.—Govt. Rel.

Consolidated Balance Sheet   As of June 30, 1996 (000 omitted)

Assets		Liabilities & Stockholders' Equity	
Current assets	$ 61,567	Current liabilities	$ 52,460
Net property, plant & equipment	71,441	Long-term debt	61,500
Other assets	45,081	Deferred items	2,207
		Other liabilities	4,635
		*Stockholders' equity	57,287
Total	$178,089	Total	$178,089

*16,621,852 shares common stock outstanding (as of balance sheet date).

Consolidated Income Statement

Years Ended June 30	Thousands — — — — Net Sales	Net Income	Per Share[a] — — — Earnings	Cash Dividends	Common Stock Price Range[a] Calendar Year
1996	$260,007	$19,245	$1.14	$ .00	25-3/8 — 12-7/8
1995	228,593	14,896	.89	.00	14-1/8 — 7-5/8
1994	211,437	12,225	.73	.00	16-3/4 — 11-3/4
1993	191,915	9,431	.57	.00	14-7/8 — 9-3/4
1992	179,196	21,687[b]	1.36[b]	.00	10-7/8 — 6-5/8

[a]Adjusted to reflect a 2-for-1 stock split in June 1995.
[b]Includes a gain to reflect FAS 109, resulting in a cumulative effect of $15,798,000 ($.99 per share).

Transfer Agent & Registrar: Harris Trust and Savings Bank

General Counsel:	Marilynn J. Cason, Sr. V.P.	Traded (Symbol):	NYSE, CSE (DV)
Investor Relations:	Norman M. Levine, V.P.	Stockholders:	3,300
Human Resources:	Marilynn J. Cason, Sr. V.P.	Employees:	2,193
Mgt. Info. Svcs.:	Richard E. Lermer	Annual Meeting:	In November
Auditors:	Price Waterhouse LLP	Internet:	www.devry.com

Diamond Home Services, Inc.

222 Church Street, Diamond Plaza, Woodstock, Illinois 60098
Telephone: (815) 334-1414

Diamond Home Services, Inc. is a national marketer and contractor of installed home improvement products, including roofing, gutters, doors, and fencing. The company markets its products directly to residential customers in 44 states through a combination of national and local advertising. Approximately 750 sales associates in 75 sales offices located in major cities across the U.S. provide a presence in markets covering approximately 80 percent of the owner-occupied households in the U.S. Diamond Home Services installs its products through a network of more than 1,300 qualified independent contractors and purchases its products through local and regional independent distributors. In November 1995, the company formed Marquise Financial, a wholly owned subsidiary, to provide an additional financing alternative for the company's products. In June 1996, the company completed an initial public offering of 3,420,000 shares. Incorporated in Delaware in 1993.

Directors (In addition to indicated officers)

James F. Beré, Jr.   George A. Stinson
Jacob Pollock

Officers (Directors*)

*C. Stephen Clegg, Chm., Pres. & C.E.O.   Ann Crowley Patterson, V.P.—Admin.
 Frank Cianciosi, V.P.—Natl. Sales   Richard G. Reece, V.P., C.F.O. & Treas.
 Jerome Cooper, V.P.—Installations   Joseph U. Schorer, V.P., Gen. Coun. & Secy.
*James M. Gillespie, V.P.—Bus. Dev.

Consolidated Balance Sheet As of December 31, 1996 (000 omitted)

Assets		Liabilities & Stockholders' Equity	
Current assets	$36,811	Current liabilities	$14,321
Net property, plant & equipment	1,607	Long-term liabilities	8,236
Other assets	20,375	*Stockholders' equity	36,236
Total	$58,793	Total	$58,793

*9,075,425 shares common stock outstanding.

Consolidated Income Statement

Years Ended Dec. 31	Thousands — — — — Net Sales	Net Income	Per Share — — — Earnings	Cash Dividends	Common Stock Price Range[a] Calendar Year
1996	$157,068	$ 6,815	$ .88	$ .00	34-1/2 — 13
1995	124,848	3,735	.60		
1994	94,186	1,995			
1993	20,548	(1,179)			

[a]Initial public offering in June 1996.

Transfer Agent & Registrar: Harris Trust and Savings Bank

General Counsel:	Joseph U. Schorer, V.P.	Auditors:	Ernst & Young LLP
Investor Relations:	Richard G. Reece, V.P.	Traded (Symbol):	NASDAQ (DHMS)
		Stockholders:	500
Human Resources:	Wayne Tompkins, V.P.	Employees:	1,300
Mgt. Info. Svcs.:	Stuart Davidson, V.P.	Annual Meeting:	As set by Directors

Diamond Technology Partners Incorporated

875 North Michigan Avenue, Suite 3000, Chicago, Illinois 60611
Telephone: (312) 255-5000

Diamond Technology Partners Incorporated is a management consulting firm that devises business strategies enabled by information technology (IT), and manages the implementation of those strategies. The company leads its clients through a process which broadens their understanding of the ways that IT can be incorporated into their businesses to gain competitive advantages in their markets. Diamond's professionals, working closely with client personnel, perform thorough analyses of the client's current business with a focus on alternative IT-driven business strategies. The company was founded in January 1994, and now serves clients in a variety of industries ranging in size from Fortune 500 companies to smaller, private companies. In February 1997, the company was spun off from Safeguard Scientifics, Inc., which continues to own approximately eight percent of the company's common stock. Incorporated in Illinois in 1994; reincorporated in Delaware in 1996.

Directors (In addition to indicated officers)

Edward R. Anderson
Donald R. Caldwell

Alan Kay
John D. Loewenberg

Officers (Directors*)

*Melvyn E. Bergstein, Chm., Pres. & C.E.O.
*Michael E. Mikolajczyk, Sr. V.P., C.F.O., Chf. Admin. Off. & Treas.

*Christopher J. Moffitt, Sr. V.P. & Secy.
*James C. Spira, Sr. V.P.

Consolidated Balance Sheet As of March 31, 1997 (000 omitted)

Assets		Liabilities & Stockholders' Equity	
Current assets	$22,919	Current liabilities	$ 7,194
Net property, plant & equipment	1,989	*Stockholders' equity	18,300
Other assets	586		
Total	$25,494	Total	$25,494

*11,316,000 shares common stock outstanding.

Consolidated Income Statement

Years Ended Mar. 31	Thousands — — — — Net Revenues	Net Income	Per Share[a] — — — — Earnings	Cash Dividends	Common Stock Price Range[a] Calendar Year
1997	$37,557	$ 633	$ .06		
1996	26,339	1,236	.13		
1995	12,843	(377)	(.05)		
1994[b]	261	(886)	(.35)		

[a]Spun off from Safeguard Scientifics, Inc. in February 1997.
[b]From company's inception on January 28, 1994, to March 31, 1994.

Transfer Agent & Registrar: ChaseMellon Shareholder Services, L.L.C.

General Counsel:	Gordon & Glickson P.C.	Traded (Symbol):	NASDAQ (DTPI)
Investor Relations:	Julia S. Wallace, Dir.	Employees:	177
Human Resources:	Phil Garrison	Annual Meeting:	To be determined
Auditors:	KPMG Peat Marwick LLP	Internet:	www.diamtech.com

LaSalle Banks Guide

Dominick's Supermarkets, Inc.

505 Railroad Avenue, Northlake, Illinois 60164
Telephone: (708) 562-1000

Dominick's Supermarkets, Inc. is the second largest supermarket operator in the greater Chicago metropolitan area. The company operates 85 full-service supermarkets under the Dominick's® name, including 27 Fresh Stores, and 17 price impact supermarkets under the Omni name. The company's principal operating subsidiary is Dominick's Finer Foods, Inc. In October 1996, the company completed an initial public offering of 9,200,000 shares of common stock. Incorporated in Delaware in 1995.

Directors (In addition to indicated officers)

Linda McLoughlin Figel
Patrick L. Graham
David B. Kaplan

Antony P. Ressler
Ira L. Tochner

Officers (Directors*)

*Ronald W. Burkle, Chm.
*Robert A. Mariano, Pres. & C.E.O.
*Darren W. Karst, Exec. V.P.—Fin. & Admin., C.F.O. & Secy.
Robert E. McCoy, Exec. V.P.—Oper.
John W. Boyle, Grp. V.P.—Info. Planning & Store Dev.

Robert R. DiPiazza, Grp. V.P.—Perishable Merch.
Donald G. Fitzgerald, Grp. V.P.—Non-Perishable Merch. & Logistics
Donald S. Rosanova, Grp. V.P.—Omni Div.
Alice F. Smedstad, Grp. V.P.—Hum. Res.
Herbert R. Young, Grp. V.P.—Sales, Mktg. & Adv.

Consolidated Balance Sheet   As of November 2, 1996 (000 omitted)

Assets		Liabilities & Stockholders' Equity	
Current assets	$ 325,509	Current liabilities	$ 308,434
Net property, plant & equipment	368,224	Long-term debt	400,644
Other assets	459,252	Other liabilities	264,836
		*Stockholders' equity	179,071
Total	$1,152,985	Total	$1,152,985

*21,359,036 shares common stock outstanding.

Consolidated Income Statement

Years Ended Abt. Oct. 31	Thousands — — — — Total Sales	Net Income	Per Share[a] — — — Earnings	Cash Dividends	Common Stock Price Range[ab] Calendar Year
1996	$2,511,962	$(6,932)[c]	$ (.96)[c]	$ .00	22-1/2 — 18
1995[d]	2,433,800	(10,600)[e]	(1.10)[e]		
1994[f]	2,409,911	7,517[g]			
1993[f]	2,330,231	7,593			
1992[f]	2,285,700	7,600			

[a] Adjusted to reflect a 14.638-for-1 stock split in October 1996.
[b] Initial public offering in October 1996.
[c] Includes an extraordinary loss (after-tax) of $6,360,000 ($.41 per share) for the early retirement of debt.
[d] Pro forma.
[e] Includes an extraordinary loss (after-tax) of $4,585,000 ($.30 per share) for the early retirement of debt.
[f] Predecessor company.
[g] Includes an extraordinary loss (after-tax) of $6,324,000 for the early retirement of debt.

Transfer Agent & Registrar: First Chicago Trust Co. of New York

General Counsel:	Thomas D. Roti	Traded (Symbol):	NYSE, CSE (DFF)
Investor Relations:	C. Mark Hussey	Stockholders:	199
Human Resources:	Alice Smedstad, Grp. V.P.	Employees:	17,982
Auditors:	Ernst & Young LLP	Annual Meeting:	In March

R.R. Donnelley & Sons Company

77 West Wacker Drive, Chicago, Illinois 60601-1696
Telephone: (312) 326-8000

R.R. Donnelley & Sons Company is a leading participant in the information industry, providing a broad range of services in print and digital media. The company is a leading supplier of commercial, print, and print-related services in the United States. It is a major supplier in the United Kingdom, and also provides services in other locations in Europe, Latin America, and Asia. Primary services provided to customers include presswork and binding, including on-demand customized publications; conventional and digital pre-press operations, including desktop publishing and filmless color imaging necessary to create a printed image; software replication, translation, and localization; design and related creative services (provided through Mobium); electronic communication networks for simultaneous worldwide product releases; and digital services to publishers. The company provides these services to more than 5,000 customers. In June 1996, the company spun off Metromail Corporation, its wholly owned subsidiary, through an initial public offering of 13,800,000 shares of common stock. In November 1996, Donnelley also spun off its Donnelley Enterprise Solutions Incorporated subsidiary in an initial public offering of 2,900,000 shares of common stock. Incorporated in Delaware in 1956.

Directors (In addition to indicated officers)

Martha Layne Collins	George A. Lorch	Bide L. Thomas
Charles C. Haffner III	M. Bernard Puckett	H. Blair White
Judith H. Hamilton	John M. Richman	Stephen M. Wolf
Thomas S. Johnson	William D. Sanders	

Officers (Directors*)

*William L. Davis, Chm. & C.E.O.
*James R. Donnelley, V. Chm.
Steven J. Baumgartner, Exec. V.P. & Sect.
   Pres.—Global Commer. Print
Cheryl A. Francis, Exec. V.P. & C.F.O.
W. Ed Tyler, Exec. V.P. & Sect. Pres.—Info. Mgt.
Jonathan P. Ward, Exec. V.P. & Sect.
   Pres.—Commer. Print
Michael B. Allen, Pres.—Info. Svcs.
Ronald E. Daly, Pres.—Telecomm.
Joseph C. Lawler, Pres.—Merchandise Media

Robert E. Logan, Pres.—Latin Amer.
Rhonda S. MacQueen, Pres.—Fin. Svcs.
James T. Mauck, Pres.—Eur.
Grant McGuire, Pres.—Book Publishing Svcs.
Robert S. Pyzdrowski, Pres.—Mag. Publishing Svcs.
James G. Turner, Pres.—Asia
Steven B. Bono, Sr. V.P.—Corp. Aff.
John C. Campanelli, Sr. V.P.—Tech., Info. Sys. & Env. Aff.
Steven L. Grupe, Sr. V.P.—Worldwide Procurement
Ann E. Weiser, Sr. V.P.—Hum. Res.

Consolidated Balance Sheet As of December 31, 1996 (000 omitted)

Assets		Liabilities & Stockholders' Equity	
Current assets	$1,752,857	Current liabilities	$1,147,547
Net property, plant & equipment	1,944,727	Long-term debt	1,430,671
Goodwill	610,101	Deferred items	253,850
Other assets	541,319	Other liabilities	385,655
		*Stockholders' equity	1,631,281
Total	$4,849,004	Total	$4,849,004

*145,553,795 shares common stock outstanding.

Consolidated Income Statement

Years Ended Dec. 31	Thousands — — — — Net Sales	Net Income	Per Share[a] — — — — Earnings	Cash Dividends	Common Stock Price Range[a] Calendar Year
1996	$6,598,958	$(157,623)	$(1.04)	$ .74	35-7/8 — 28-7/8
1995	6,511,786	298,793	1.95	.68	41-1/4 — 28-7/8
1994	4,888,786	268,603	1.75	.60	32-1/2 — 26-7/8
1993	4,387,761	109,420[b]	.71[b]	.54	32-3/4 — 26-1/8
1992	4,193,072	234,659	1.51	.51	33-3/4 — 23-3/4

[a]Adjusted to reflect a 2-for-1 stock split in September 1992.
[b]Includes a charge to reflect FAS 106 and FAS 109, resulting in a cumulative effect of $69,500,000 ($.45 per share); a restructuring charge of $60,800,000 ($.39 per share); and a deferred income tax charge of $6,200,000 ($.04 per share) related to a federal income tax rate increase.

Transfer Agent & Registrar: First Chicago Trust Co. of New York

Investor Relations:	Jonathan M. Singer, Dir.	Traded (Symbol):	NYSE, CSE, PSE (DNY)
Human Resources:	Ann E. Weiser, Sr. V.P.	Stockholders:	11,500
Mgt. Info. Svcs.:	W. Ed Tyler, Exec. V.P.	Employees:	38,000
		Annual Meeting:	In March
Auditors:	Arthur Andersen LLP	Internet:	www.rrd.com

Donnelley Enterprise Solutions Incorporated

161 North Clark Street, Suite 2400, Chicago, Illinois 60601
Telephone: (312) 419-7600

Donnelley Enterprise Solutions Incorporated is a single-source provider of integrated information management services to professional service organizations, large law firms, investment banks, and accounting firms. The company offers its clients the opportunity to focus on their core businesses by outsourcing a variety of functions, including business services and information technology services. In November 1996, the company was spun off from R.R. Donnelley & Sons Company, which currently holds approximately 42.8 percent of the company's common stock. Incorporated in Delaware in 1989 as a successor to a business started in 1983; present name adopted in 1996.

Directors (In addition to indicated officers)

Daniel I. Malina
Charles F. Moran

W. Ed Tyler

Officers (Directors*)

*Rhonda I. Kochlefl, Chm., Pres. & C.E.O.
 Luke F. Botica, Sr. V.P. & C.F.O.
*Leo S. Spiegel, Sr. V.P. & Chf. Tech. Off.

Linda A. Finkel, Pres.—Donnelley Bus. Svcs. Div.
Robert A. Lento, Pres.—LANSystems Div.
David J. Shea, Pres.—Sys. Mgt. Div.

Consolidated Balance Sheet   As of December 31, 1996 (000 omitted)

Assets		Liabilities & Stockholders' Equity	
Current assets	$43,257	Current liabilities	$25,108
Net property, plant & equipment	12,646	Deferred items	311
Goodwill, net	20,213	Other liabilities	1,305
Other assets	60	*Stockholders' equity	49,452
Total	$76,176	Total	$76,176

*5,005,000 shares common stock outstanding.

Consolidated Income Statement

Years Ended Dec. 31	Thousands — — — —		Per Share[a] — — — —		Common Stock Price Range[a] Calendar Year
	Revenues	Net Income	Earnings	Cash Dividends	
1996[b]	$96,464	$ 625	$ .12	$ .00	26-1/4 — 19-1/4
1995[b]	65,944	303			
1994	34,745	1,735			
1993	23,527	861			
1992	17,985	270			

[a]Spun off from R.R. Donnelley & Sons Company in November 1996.
[b]Includes the results of LANSystems, Inc. which the company acquired in June 1995.

Transfer Agent & Registrar: American Stock Transfer & Trust Co.

Investor Relations:	Rhonda I. Kochlefl, Chm.	**Traded (Symbol):**	NASDAQ (DEZI)
Human Resources:	Kenneth M. Goldstein	**Stockholders:**	1,000
		Employees:	932
Mgt. Info. Svcs.:	Lon Spooner	**Annual Meeting:**	In May
Auditors:	Arthur Andersen LLP	**Internet:**	www.desi.net

LaSalle Banks Guide

Duff & Phelps Credit Rating Co.

55 East Monroe Street, 35th Floor, Chicago, Illinois 60603
Telephone: (312) 368-3100

Duff & Phelps Credit Rating Co. is an international agency providing credit ratings on bonds, debentures, preferred stocks, commercial paper, certificates of deposit, and other fixed income securities, as well as structured financings and insurance company claims-paying ability. The credit rating business was established in 1980 and currently has offices in Chicago, New York, and London; joint ventures in North and South America, Europe, Asia, and Africa; and a designated rating agency in Japan. Principal subsidiary is Duff & Phelps Credit Rating Co. of Europe. Incorporated in Illinois in 1987.

Directors (In addition to indicated officers)

Donald J. Herdrich
Jonathan Ingham

Milton L. Meigs

Officers (Directors*)

*Paul J. McCarthy, Jr., Chm., C.E.O. & C.F.O.
*Philip T. Maffei, Pres. & C.O.O.
Larry A. Brossman, Exec. V.P.

Ernest T. Elsner, Exec. V.P.
Peter J. Stahl, Exec. V.P.—Mktg.
Marie C. Becker, V.P., Secy. & Cont.

Consolidated Balance Sheet As of December 31, 1996 (000 omitted)

Assets		Liabilities & Stockholders' Equity	
Current assets	$10,940	Current liabilities	$10,854
Net property, plant & equipment	4,540	Long-term debt	5,500
Other assets	26,646	Other liabilities	717
		*Stockholders' equity	25,055
Total	$42,126	Total	$42,126

*5,152,000 shares common stock outstanding.

Consolidated Income Statement

Years Ended Dec. 31	Thousands — — — —		Per Share[a] — — —		Common Stock Price Range[a] Calendar Year
	Revenues	Net Income	Earnings	Cash Dividends	
1996	$53,083	$8,975	$1.54	$ .12	24-1/8 — 14
1995	45,983	7,632	1.28	.12	16 — 8-5/8
1994	40,409	6,466	1.12	.03	12-1/2 — 7-7/8
1993	32,635	6,497[b]	1.10		
1992	24,697	3,400[b]	.59		

[a]Spun off from Duff & Phelps Corporation in October 1994.
[b]Unaudited pro forma.

Transfer Agent & Registrar: Harris Trust and Savings Bank

General Counsel: Ernest T. Elsner, Exec. V.P.

Investor Relations: Marie C. Becker, V.P.

Human Resources: Jim Jenik, Mgr.

Mgt. Info. Svcs.: James Stewart, V.P.

Auditors: Arthur Andersen LLP

Traded (Symbol): NYSE (DCR)

Stockholders: 124

Employees: 250

Annual Meeting: In May

Eagle Finance Corp.

1425 Tri-State Parkway, Gurnee, Illinois 60031-4060
Telephone: (847) 855-7150

Eagle Finance Corp. is a specialized financial services company engaged primarily in acquiring and servicing automobile retail installment sale contracts for purchases of late model used automobiles (cars and light trucks) by "non-prime" consumers, who typically have limited access to traditional credit sources. The company also makes direct consumer loans, finances leases, purchases other retail installment sale contracts, and offers, as agent, insurance and other products related to consumer finance transactions. Incorporated in Delaware in 1961.

Directors (In addition to indicated officers)

Robert H. Arnold
Ronald B. Clonts, V. Chm.
E. Bruce Fredrikson

Robert L. Jooss
Walter J. O'Brien

Officers (Directors*)

*Charles F. Wonderlic, Chm. & C.E.O.
Robert J. Braasch, Pres. & C.F.O.
Samuel M. Keith, C.O.O.

*Richard E. Wonderlic, Exec. V.P.
Howard J. Adamski, V.P. & Treas.
Melida Torres, V.P. & Cont.

Consolidated Balance Sheet As of December 31, 1996 (000 omitted)

Assets		Liabilities & Stockholders' Equity	
Current assets	$61,591	Current liabilities	$32,828
Other assets	2,177	Long-term debt	17,978
		Other liabilities	2,654
		*Stockholders' equity	10,308
Total	$63,768	Total	$63,768

*4,189,100 shares common stock outstanding.

Consolidated Income Statement

Years Ended Dec. 31	Thousands — — — — —		Per Share[a] — — —		Common Stock
	Total Income	Net Income	Earnings[b]	Cash Dividends	Price Range[ac] Calendar Year
1996	$32,438	$(5,349)	$(1.28)	$ .00	14-1/4 — 5
1995	29,475	325	.08	.00	25-1/4 — 12-1/2
1994	13,711	3,951	.93	.00	16-3/4 — 9
1993	6,168	1,686	.37		
1992	5,757	1,070	.23		

[a]Adjusted to reflect an 11,666.667-for-1 stock split in April 1994.
[b]Pro forma.
[c]Initial public offering in July 1994.

Transfer Agent & Registrar: Harris Trust and Savings Bank

General Counsel:
  Barack, Ferrazzano, Kirschbaum,
  Perlman & Nagelberg

Investor Relations: Robert J. Braasch, Pres.

Human Resources: Charles F. Wonderlic, Jr., V.P.

Mgt. Info. Svcs.: Thomas Shouf

Auditors: KPMG Pear Marwick LLP
Traded (Symbol): NASDAQ (EFCW)
Stockholders: 2,000
Employees: 258
Annual Meeting: In May

Eagle Food Centers, Inc.

Route 67 and Knoxville Road, Milan, Illinois 61264
Telephone: (309) 787-7700

Eagle Food Centers, Inc., operates a regional supermarket chain with 92 stores under the trade names "Eagle Food Centers" and "Eagle Country Markets®," "Eagle Country Warehouse," and "BOGO's." The stores operate in the Quad Cities area of Illinois and Iowa; north, central, and eastern Illinois; eastern Iowa; and the Chicago/Fox Valley and northwestern Indiana areas. Eagle supermarkets offer a full line of groceries, meats, fresh produce, dairy products, delicatessen and bakery products, health and beauty aids, and other general merchandise, as well as video rental and floral service. Subsidiaries include Milan Distributing Co., Eagle Country Markets, Inc., and Eagle Pharmacy Co. Incorporated in Delaware in 1987.

Directors (In addition to indicated officers)

Peter B. Foreman
Steven M. Friedman
Michael J. Knilans
Alain M. Oberrotman

Marc C. Particelli
Pasquale V. Petitti
William J. Snyder

Officers (Directors*)

*Martin J. Rabinowitz, Chm.
*Robert J. Kelly, Pres. & C.E.O.

*Herbert T. Dotterer, Sr. V.P.—Fin., C.F.O. & Secy.
David S. Norton, Sr. V.P.—Retail

Consolidated Balance Sheet As of February 1, 1996 (000 omitted)

Assets		Liabilities & Stockholders' Equity	
Current assets	$108,922	Current liabilities	$ 97,192
Net property, plant & equipment	118,473	Long-term debt	112,083
Other assets	27,353	Other liabilities	18,785
		*Stockholders' equity	26,688
Total	$254,748	Total	$254,748

*11,051,994 shares common stock outstanding.

Consolidated Income Statement

Years Ended Abt. Jan. 31	Thousands — — — — Net Sales	Net Income	Per Share — — — Earnings	Cash Dividends	Common Stock Price Range Fiscal Year
1997	$1,014,889	$ 3,248	$ .29	$ .00	
1996[a]	1,023,664	(18,692)	(1.68)	.00	6-7/8 — 1-5/8
1995	1,015,063	(18,874)	(1.71)	.00	8-1/2 — 1-1/8
1994	1,062,348	(10,132)[b]	(.91)	.00	8-1/4 — 5
1993	1,081,538	8,222[c]	.74[c]	.00	8-3/4 — 6

[a]53 weeks.
[b]Includes a pretax store-closing charge of $17,000,000 and an extraordinary charge (after-tax) of $4,000,000 for the early retirement of debt.
[c]Includes a non-recurring charge of $744,000 ($.06 per share) related to the solicitation of the holders of the 13-1/2% subordinated notes to waive a restrictive covenant to allow the company to repurchase up to $20,000,000 of its common stock.

Transfer Agent & Registrar: First Chicago Trust Co. of New York

General Counsel:
  Davis, Brown, Koehn, Shors & Roberts, P.C.

Investor Relations: Herbert T. Dotterer, Sr. V.P.

Auditors: Deloitte & Touche LLP

Traded (Symbol): NASDAQ (EGLE)
Stockholders: 3,400
Employees: 7,500
Annual Meeting: In June

ELEK-TEK, Inc.

7350 North Linder Avenue, Skokie, Illinois 60077-3217
Telephone: (847) 677-7660

ELEK-TEK, Inc. is a full-line, regional marketer of microcomputer products, including hardware, software, related accessories, and supplies. Since its origin in the Chicago area in 1979, ELEK-TEK has steadily expanded its base of operations. Its multi-channel distribution system comprises eight retail superstores (five in the Chicago metropolitan area and one each in Denver, Indianapolis, and Kansas City); a national catalog operation; and direct sales divisions in all locations which are geared to corporate, educational, and government buyers. ELEK-TEK carries all major brands, including IBM, Apple, COMPAQ, Hewlett-Packard, Lotus, Microsoft, and Novell. Incorporated in Illinois in 1979; reincorporated in Delaware in 1993.

Directors   (In addition to indicated officers)

Robert J. Lipsig, Chm.
Dennis G. Flanagan
Susan J. Kaiser

Harvey Kinzelberg
Alvin Richer

Officers   (Directors*)

*Richard Rodriguez, Pres. & C.E.O.
Scott Koerner, Sr. V.P.—Sales
Karim Hadchiti, V.P.—Oper.

Miguel A. Martinez, V.P. & C.F.O.
Jane M. McCarthy, V.P.—Hum. Res.
Dave Zasada, V.P.—Mktg. & Merch.

Consolidated Balance Sheet   As of December 31, 1996 (000 omitted)

Assets		Liabilities & Stockholders' Equity	
Current assets	$65,328	Current liabilities	$67,491
Net property, plant & equipment	15,587	Other liabilities	2,286
Other assets	126	*Stockholders' equity	11,264
Total	$81,041	Total	$81,041

*6,300,000 shares common stock outstanding.

Consolidated Income Statement

Years Ended Dec. 31	Thousands — — — — Net Sales	Net Income	Per Share[a] — — — Earnings	Cash Dividends	Common Stock Price Range[ab] Calendar Year
1996	$333,498	$(10,563)	$(1.68)	$ .00	5-1/4 — 1-7/8
1995	338,025	(299)	(.05)	.00	5-1/8 — 2-3/4
1994	305,602	3,461	.55	.00	19 — 7
1993	222,194	4,451[c]	.78[c]	.00	17-3/4 — 9-1/4
1992	176,824	2,721[c]	.51[c]		

[a]Adjusted to reflect a 48-for-1 stock split in June 1993.
[b]Initial public offering in August 1993.
[c]Pro forma.

Transfer Agent & Registrar: LaSalle National Trust, N.A.

General Counsel:	Lord, Bissell & Brook	Traded (Symbol):	NASDAQ (ELEK)
Investor Relations:	Miguel A. Martinez, V.P.	Stockholders:	2,200
Human Resources:	Jane M. McCarthy, V.P.	Employees:	720
Mgt. Info. Svcs.:	Keith Nitahara	Annual Meeting:	In June
Auditors:	Coopers & Lybrand L.L.P.	Internet:	www.elektek.com

Enterprise Systems, Inc.

1400 South Wolf Road, Wheeling, Illinois 60090-6524
Telephone: (847) 537-4800

Enterprise Systems, Inc. is a healthcare information services company that develops, markets, installs, and services an integrated suite of application software products that assist healthcare providers in managing their operations. These resource management systems focus on cost containment and address a broad range of non-clinical management needs, including materials management, operating room logistics, and patient scheduling. In October 1995, the company completed an initial public offering of 2,425,000 shares of common stock. In March 1997, Enterprise Systems announced that it had signed a definitive agreement to be acquired by HBO & Company, an Atlanta-based supplier of medical information software. The transaction, subject to stockholder approval, is expected to close late in the second quarter of 1997. Incorporated in Illinois in 1981; reincorporated in Delaware in 1995.

Directors (In addition to indicated officers)

Robert A. Compton
Bernard Goldstein

M. Fazle Husain

Officers (Directors*)

*Thomas R. Hutchinson, Chm.
*Glen E. Tullman, C.E.O.
Joseph E. Carey, Pres. & Secy.
David A. Carlson, Exec. V.P.—Bus. Dev.

Robert W. Rook, Jr., Exec. V.P.—Hum. Res.
Stanley A. Crane, Chf. Tech. Off.
Steven M. Katz, C.O.O.
David B. Mullen, C.F.O.

Consolidated Balance Sheet As of December 31, 1996 (000 omitted)

Assets		Liabilities & Stockholders' Equity	
Current assets	$48,905	Current liabilities	$ 9,420
Net property, plant & equipment	4,108	Deferred items	1,985
Other assets	13,218	*Stockholders' equity	54,826
Total	$66,231	Total	$66,231

*8,131,248 shares common stock outstanding.

Consolidated Income Statement

Years Ended Dec. 31	Thousands — — — —		Per Share[a] — — —		Common Stock Price Range[a] Calendar Year
	Revenues	Net Income	Earnings	Cash Dividends	
1996	$52,316	$(939)	$ (.12)	$ .00	39-5/8 — 13-1/2
1995	33,248	800	.13	.00	37-3/4 — 17-3/4
1994	24,712	28	.01		
1993	20,427	749	.15		
1992	17,024	759	.16		

[a]Initial public offering in October 1995.

Transfer Agent & Registrar:	Harris Trust and Savings Bank			
General Counsel:	Sachnoff & Weaver, Ltd.		Traded (Symbol):	NASDAQ (ESIX)
Investor Relations:	Kathy Sharro		Stockholders:	1,831
Human Resources:	Robert W. Rook, Jr., Exec. V.P.		Employees:	500
Mgt. Info. Svcs.:	Tim Belec		Annual Meeting:	In May
Auditors:	KPMG Peat Marwick LLP		Internet:	www.esicorp.com

Envirodyne Industries, Inc.

701 Harger Road, Suite 190, Oak Brook, Illinois 60521
Telephone: (630) 571-8800

Envirodyne Industries, Inc., through Viskase Corporation, is a producer of cellulosic casings used in preparing and packaging processed meat products, and is a major producer of specialty films for packaging and preserving poultry, fresh meat products, and processed meats and cheeses. Viskase Corporation is also a leading domestic and international manufacturer of plasticized polyvinyl chloride films. The company, through Clear Shield National, Inc. and Sandusky Plastics, Inc., produces thermoformed and injection molded plastic containers and disposable plastic cutlery, drinking straws, custom dining kits, and related products. Incorporated in Delaware in 1970.

Directors   (In addition to indicated officers)

Robert N. Dangremond
Michael E. Heisley

Gregory R. Page
Mark D. Senkpiel

Officers   (Directors*)

*F. Edward Gustafson, Chm., Pres., C.E.O. & C.O.O.
Gordon S. Donovan, V.P., C.F.O. & Treas.

Stephen M. Schuster, V.P., Gen. Coun. & Secy.

Consolidated Balance Sheet   As of December 26, 1996 (000 omitted)

Assets		Liabilities & Stockholders' Equity	
Current assets	$238,121	Current liabilities	$130,415
Net property, plant & equipment	461,808	Long-term debt	521,179
Other assets	173,818	Deferred taxes	64,811
		Other liabilities	53,697
		*Stockholders' equity	103,645
Total	$873,747	Total	$873,747

*14,545,107 shares common stock outstanding.

Consolidated Income Statement

Years Ended Abt. Dec. 31	Thousands — — — — Net Sales	Net Income	Per Share — — — — Earnings	Cash Dividends	Common Stock Price Range Calendar Year
1996	$651,356	$(13,682)	$ (.96)	$ .00	5-7/8 — 2-7/8
1995	650,212	(21,519)[a]	(1.59)[a]	.00	4-7/8 — 2-7/8
1994	599,029	(3,612)	(.27)	.00	10-7/8 — 3-3/8
1993	587,385	85,589[b]			
1992[c]	575,705	(36,996)			

[a]Includes an extraordinary loss of $4,196,000 ($.31 per share) reflecting the write-off of deferred fees relating to a June 1995 refinancing.
[b]Includes an extraordinary gain of $183,784,000 from the implementation of the plan of reorganization.
[c]Due to the implementation of the plan of reorganization and fresh start reporting, financial statements for the new restructured company (effective December 31, 1993) are not comparable to those of prior years.

Transfer Agent & Registrar:	Fleet National Bank of Connecticut, N.A.		
General Counsel:	Stephen M. Schuster, V.P.	Traded (Symbol):	NASDAQ (EDYN)
		Stockholders:	243
Investor Relations:	Gordon S. Donovan, V.P.	Employees:	4,900
Auditors:	Coopers & Lybrand L.L.P.	Annual Meeting:	In May

Evans, Inc.

36 South State Street, Chicago, Illinois 60603
Telephone: (312) 855-2000

Evans, Inc. is a retailer of quality fur apparel in the United States. The company also wholesales fur apparel to retailers, distributes furs through various catalogs, provides certain related fur services, and in the Chicago area only, retails women's ready-to-wear apparel in 10 stores. The company has 15 stores in the metropolitan areas of Chicago, Austin and Dallas, Texas, and Washington, D.C., and operates leased departments in 41 locations of major retailers throughout the U.S., including Marshall Field and Co., Filene's Basement, Lazarus, Strawbridge & Clothier, Dayton's, Hudson's, Rich's, and others. Some of the fur apparel offered is specially made according to designs and specifications furnished to manufacturers. Incorporated in Delaware in 1963.

Directors (In addition to indicated officers)

Dennis S. Bookshester
Edmond D. Cicala
Gwendolyn L. Stanback

Harold Sussman
Ernest R. Wish

Officers (Directors*)

*David B. Meltzer, Chm.
*Patrick J. Regan, Pres. & C.E.O.
*Robert K. Meltzer, Exec. V.P.—Gen. Mdse.
  Mgr.

Samuel B. Garber, V.P., Secy. & Gen. Coun.
William E. Koziel, V.P. & C.F.O.
Dean Obrecht, V.P.—Hum. Res.
John Sarama, V.P.—Oper.

Consolidated Balance Sheet As of March 1, 1997 (000 omitted)

Assets		Liabilities & Stockholders' Equity	
Current assets	$35,597	Current liabilities	$24,301
Net property, plant & equipment	3,918	Long-term debt	1,224
Other assets	3,107	Other liabilities	43
		*Stockholders' equity	17,054
Total	$42,622	Total	$42,622

*4,918,301 shares common stock outstanding.

Consolidated Income Statement

Years Ended Abt. Feb. 28	Thousands — — — —		Per Share — — —		Common Stock Price Range Calendar Year
	Total Revenues	Net Income	Earnings	Cash Dividends	
1997	$ 82,704	$(4,724)	$ (.96)	$ .00	
1996	96,566	234	.05	.00	1-7/8 — 1
1995	86,817	(12,064)	(2.40)	.00	2-3/8 — 1
1994	96,785	1,960[a]	.39[a]	.00	3-7/8 — 1-3/4
1993	107,072	1,620	.33	.00	4-1/2 — 2-5/8

[a]Includes a gain to reflect FAS 109, resulting in a cumulative effect of $1,500,000 ($.30 per share).

Transfer Agent & Registrar:	Harris Trust and Savings Bank		
General Counsel:	Samuel B. Garber, V.P.	**Traded (Symbol):**	NASDAQ (EVAN)
Investor Relations:	Patrick J. Regan, Pres.	**Stockholders:**	750
Human Resources:	Dean Obrecht, V.P.	**Employees:**	800
Auditors:	Coopers & Lybrand L.L.P.	**Annual Meeting:**	In July

EVEREN Capital Corporation
77 West Wacker Drive, Chicago, Illinois 60601
Telephone: (312) 574-6000

EVEREN Capital Corporation is the parent company of EVEREN Securities, Inc. and EVEREN Clearing Corp. EVEREN Securities is a full-service, nationwide super-regional brokerage firm with appoximately 140 offices in 27 states. EVEREN Clearing provides securities execution and clearing services and commodities clearing services for EVEREN Securities and other broker-dealers. EVEREN Securities and EVEREN Clearing are members of the Securities Investor Protection Corporation and the New York Stock Exchange. In October 1996, EVEREN Capital completed an initial public offering of 4,600,000 shares of common stock. Incorporated in Delaware in 1995.

Directors   (In addition to indicated officers)

William T. Esrey
Jack Kemp

Homer J. Livingston, Jr
William C. Springer

Officers   (Directors*)

*James R. Boris, Chm. & C.E.O.
*Stephen G. McConahey, Pres. & C.O.O.
Stanley R. Fallis, Sr. Exec. V.P. &
  Dir.—Admin. & Oper.
David M. Greene, Sr. Exec. V.P. &
  Dir.—Client Svcs.
Arthur J. McGivern, Sr. Exec. V.P. &
  Dir.—Corp. Dev.

Janet L. Reali, Sr. Exec. V.P., Gen. Coun. & Secy.
Thomas R. Reedy, Sr. Exec. V.P. & Dir.—Capital
  Mkts.
John G. Sullivan, Sr. Exec. V.P. & Dir.—Mktg. &
  Invest. Svcs.
Daniel D. Williams, Sr. Exec. V.P., C.F.O. & Treas.
Thomas M. Mansheim, Exec. V.P., Cont. & Chf.
  Acct. Off.

Consolidated Balance Sheet   As of December 31, 1996 (000 omitted)

Assets		Liabilities & Stockholders' Equity	
Cash & cash equivalents	$ 46,592	Bank loans & loans payable	$ 277,699
Receivables	918,703	Securities	555,975
Securities	785,215	Deferred income taxes	13,491
Fixed assets, net	36,136	Other liabilities	688,145
Other assets	37,699	*Stockholders' equity	289,035
Total	$1,824,345	Total	$1,824,345

*16,611,889 shares common stock outstanding.

Consolidated Income Statement

Years Ended Dec. 31	Thousands — — — —		Per Share[a] — — —		Common Stock Price Range[a] Calendar Year
	Revenues	Net Income	Earnings	Cash Dividends	
1996	$570,555	$ 62,498[b]	$4.94[c]	$ .09	23-3/8 — 17-1/8
1995	543,169	(15,854)[d]			
1994	529,970	(2,238)			
1993	673,732	(3,640)[e]			
1992	677,464	38,433			

[a]Initial public offering in October 1996.
[b]Includes a pretax gain of $50,200,000 ($30,200,000 after-tax) on the sale of a subsidiary.
[c]Earnings (loss) per common share are not presented for prior periods as such historical per-share information is not indicative of the company's continuing capital structure.
[d]Includes non-recurring charges of $22,000,000 after-tax in connection with the employee buyout of EVEREN from Kemper Corporation.
[e]Includes an extraordinary loss of $5,458,000 for a change in accounting principles.

Transfer Agent & Registrar:	Harris Trust and Savings Bank		
General Counsel:	Janet L. Reali, Sr. Exec. V.P.	Auditors:	Deloitte & Touche, LLP
Investor Relations:	Caron L. Schreiber, Sr. V.P.	Traded (Symbol):	NYSE (EVR)
		Stockholders:	618
Human Resources:	Jennifer DiBiase, Asst. V.P.	Employees:	3,200
Mgt. Info. Svcs.:	William G. Kieffer, V.P.	Annual Meeting:	In May

Factory Card Outlet Corp.

745 Birginal Drive, Bensenville, Illinois 60106-1212
Telephone: (630) 238-0010

Factory Card Outlet Corp. operates a chain of company-owned superstores offering a large assortment of party supplies, greeting cards, gift wrap, and other special occasion merchandise. The company operates 122 stores in 14 states, primarily in the Midwest and mid-Atlantic regions of the United States. Factory Card's superstores provide customers with a value-oriented, "one-stop" shopping destination for party and special occasion merchandise for all major holidays and celebratory events, including birthdays, graduations, weddings, baby showers, and other family, religious, and special occasions. The company's wholly owned operating subsidiary is Factory Card Outlet of America Ltd. Incorporated in Delaware in 1989.

Directors (In addition to indicated officers)

Stewart M. Kasen, Chm.	Richard A. Doppelt
Michael I. Barach	William E. Freeman
Dr. Robert C. Blattberg	J. Bayard Kelly
Bart A. Brown, Jr.	James L. Nouss, Jr.

Officers (Directors*)

*Charles R. Cumello, Pres. & C.E.O.
Glen J. Franchi, Exec. V.P. & Treas.
Vincent G. Brown, V.P.—Real Estate
Joseph M. Cabon, V.P.—Distr.
Matthew F. Ellis, V.P.—Hum. Res.
Robert J. Kendzior, V.P.—Mktg.

Robert Krentzman, V.P.—Mgt. Info. Svcs.
Martin J. Merksamer, V.P. & Gen. Merch. Mgr.
Leoonard F. Rucker, V.P.—Retail Store Oper.
Thomas W. Stoltz, V.P.—Fin.
Carol A. Travis, V.P. & Secy.

Consolidated Balance Sheet As of June 29, 1996 (000 omitted)

Assets		Liabilities & Stockholders' Equity	
Current assets	$43,349	Current liabilities	$19,744
Net fixed assets	14,924	Revolving credit note payable	13,127
Deferred financing costs	244	Long-term debt	664
Deferred income taxes	312	Other liabilities	8,421
Other assets	251	*Stockholders' equity	17,124
Total	$59,080	Total	$59,080

*933,720 shares common stock outstanding.

Consolidated Income Statement

Years Ended Abt. Jun. 30	Thousands — — — — Net Sales	Net Income	Per Share[a] — — — Earnings	Cash Dividends	Common Stock Price Range[a] Calendar Year
1996	$94,589	$ 70	$ .01	$ .00	9-1/2 — 9
1995	63,174	368	.08		
1994	37,341	449	.13		
1993	24,333	865	.26		
1992	17,330	368	.11		

[a]Initial public offering in December 1996.

Transfer Agent & Registrar: Registrar & Transfer Co. of Cranford, New Jersey

General Counsel:
  Sonnenschein Nath & Rosenthal

Investor Relations: Carol A. Travis, V.P.

Human Resources: Matthew F. Ellis, V.P.

Mgt. Info. Svcs.: Robert Krentzman, V.P.

Auditors: KPMG Peat Marwick LLP

Traded (Symbol): NASDAQ (FCPY)

Stockholders: 66

Employees: 1,983

Annual Meeting: In October

Fansteel Inc.

Number One Tantalum Place, North Chicago, Illinois 60064-3388
Telephone: (847) 689-4900

Fansteel Inc. is a specialty metals manufacturer of components used in the aircraft/aerospace, weapon systems, metalworking, energy, and automotive industries. Its principal products include tungsten carbide cutting tools; coal mining tools and accessories; toolholding devices; wear parts; titanium, nickel base, and high alloy steel forgings; sand mold aluminum and magnesium castings; special wire forms; and investment castings. The company classifies its products into two business segments: industrial tools and metal fabrications. Sales of the company's products are made through a direct sales organization and through distributors, representatives, and agents. In the industrial tools segment, distributors and agents account for the majority of sales. In July 1996, the company acquired American Sintered Technologies, Inc., a manufacturer of ferrous and nonferrous powdered metal components. Established in 1907; incorporated in Delaware in 1917.

Directors   (In addition to indicated officers)

Betty B. Evans
Robert S. Evans
Thomas M. Evans, Jr.

Peter J. Kalis
Jack S. Petrik

Officers   (Directors*)

*William D. Jarosz, Chm., Pres. & C.E.O.
R. Michael McEntee, V.P. & C.F.O.

Michael J. Mocniak, V.P., Gen. Coun. & Secy.

Consolidated Balance Sheet   As of December 31, 1996 (000 omitted)

Assets		Liabilities & Stockholders' Equity	
Current assets	$48,031	Current liabilities	$19,489
Net property, plant & equipment	14,306	Long-term debt	1,779
Other assets	19,790	Other liabilities	5,575
		*Stockholders' equity	55,284
Total	$82,127	Total	$82,127

*8,598,858 shares common stock outstanding.

Consolidated Income Statement

Years Ended Dec. 31	Thousands ————— Net Sales	Net Income	Per Share ——— Earnings	Cash Dividends	Common Stock Price Range Calendar Year
1996	$120,834	$4,277	$ .50	$ .00	8-1/4 — 5-5/8
1995	102,598	3,333	.39	.30	8-1/4 — 5-3/4
1994	89,287	3,609	.42	.40	8 — 6-1/8
1993	89,387	906[a]	.11[a]	.40	8-7/8 — 6-3/4
1992	127,145	5,232	.61	.50	9-3/8 — 6-3/8

[a]Includes a net loss from previously discontinued operations of $1,676,000 ($.19 per share).

Transfer Agent & Registrar: ChaseMellon Shareholder Services, L.L.C.

General Counsel:	Michael J. Mocniak, V.P.	Auditors:	Ernst & Young LLP
Investor Relations:	William D. Jarosz, Chm.	Traded (Symbol):	NYSE, CSE (FNL)
		Stockholders:	812
Human Resources:	Michael J. Mocniak, V.P.	Employees:	1,031
Mgt. Info. Svcs.:	Daniel K. Garrity	Annual Meeting:	In April

Federal Signal Corporation

1415 West 22nd Street, Oak Brook, Illinois 60521-9945
Telephone: (630) 954-2000

Federal Signal Corporation manufactures and supplies products through its four groups: Safety Products, Sign, Tool, and Vehicle. The Safety Products Group manufactures a variety of visual and audible warning and signaling devices, safety containment products for handling and storing hazardous materials, and parking, revenue, and access control systems. The Sign Group designs, engineers, manufactures, and installs illuminated and non-illuminated advertising sign displays. The Tool Group manufactures a variety of die components for metal stamping, precision cutting, and deep grooving tools. The Vehicle Group manufactures custom-designed fire trucks, aerial access platforms, rescue vehicles, and self-propelled street sweeping, vacuum loader, and catch basin cleaning vehicles. Major subsidiaries include: Dayton Progress Corporation; Elgin Sweeper Company; Emergency One, Inc.; Federal APD, Inc.; Ravo International; Superior Emergency Vehicles, Ltd.; Guzzler Manufacturing, Inc.; Vactor Manufacturing, Inc.; Justrite Manufacturing, Inc.; and Manchester Tool Company. Federal Signal has 60 manufacturing facilities and offices throughout North America. Internationally, the company has plants and offices located throughout Europe and the Far East. In August 1995, the company acquired Bronto Skylift oy Ab, a Tampere, Finland-based manufacturer of access platforms for both the fire rescue and heavy-duty truck-mounted industrial markets. In June 1996, the company acquired Victor Industries Ltd., a manufacturer of hazardous-area lighting products, of Newcastle, England. Incorporated in Illinois in 1901; reincorporated in Delaware in 1969.

Directors (In addition to indicated officers)

J. Patrick Lannan, Jr.	Thomas N. McGowen, Jr.	Richard R. Thomas
James A. Lovell, Jr.	Walter R. Peirson	

Officers (Directors*)

*Joseph J. Ross, Chm., Pres. & C.E.O.
John A. DeLeonardis, V.P.—Taxes
Henry L. Dykema, V.P. & C.F.O.
Robert W. Racic, V.P. & Treas.

Richard L. Ritz, V.P. & Cont.
Kim A. Wehrenberg, V.P., Gen. Coun. & Secy.
Anna M. Bourne, Asst. Cont.
Jennifer L. Sherman, Asst. Secy. & Corp. Atty.

Consolidated Balance Sheet As of December 31, 1996 (000 omitted)

Assets		Liabilities & Stockholders' Equity	
Current assets	$267,006	Current liabilities	$226,413
Lease financing receivables (Fin. Svcs.)	170,988	Short-term borrowings (Fin. Svcs.)	148,205
Net property, plant & equipment	82,825	Long-term debt	34,311
Other assets & intangibles	183,082	Deferred taxes	22,183
		*Stockholders' equity	272,789
Total	$703,901	Total	$703,901

*45,952,000 shares common stock outstanding.

Consolidated Income Statement

Years Ended Dec. 31	Thousands — — — —		Per Share[b] — — — —		Common Stock
	Sales	Net Income[a]	Earnings[a]	Cash Dividends	Price Range[b] Calendar Year
1996	$896,357	$62,033[c]	$1.35[c]	$ .58	28-1/4 — 20-7/8
1995	816,127	51,610[d]	1.13[d]	.50	25-7/8 — 19-5/8
1994	677,228	46,770	1.02	.42	21-3/8 — 16-7/8
1993	565,163	39,780	.86	.36	21 — 15-3/4
1992	518,223	34,460	.75	.31	17-5/8 — 12-3/8

[a]From continuing operations.
[b]Adjusted to reflect a 4-for-3 stock split in March 1994 and 3-for-2 stock splits distributed in April 1992 and March 1991.
[c]Includes an aftertax gain of $4,700,000 ($.06 per share) for the sale of a subsidiary.
[d]Includes a nonrecurring aftertax charge of $4,200,000 ($.09 per share) for a litigation settlement.

Transfer Agent & Registrar:	Harris Trust and Savings Bank		
General Counsel:	Kim A. Wehrenberg, V.P.	Stockholders:	16,000
Investor Relations:	Henry L. Dykema, V.P.	Employees:	6,233
Auditors:	Ernst & Young LLP	Annual Meeting:	In April
Traded (Symbol):	NYSE (FSS)	Internet:	www.federalsignal.com

Fidelity Bancorp, Inc.
5455 West Belmont Avenue, Chicago, Illinois 60641
Telephone: (773) 736-4414

Fidelity Bancorp, Inc. is the holding company for Fidelity Federal Savings Bank. Originally organized in 1906, Fidelity Federal conducts its business through its main office and four full-service branch offices, located in Chicago, Franklin Park, and Schaumburg, Illinois. In addition to traditional mortgage loans, consumer loans, and retail banking products, the bank generates non-interest income from its full-service securities brokerage services offered through INVEST Financial Corporation, as well as insurance and annuity products. Incorporated in Delaware in 1993.

Directors   (In addition to indicated officers)

Paul J. Bielat	Raymond J. Horvat
Patrick J. Flynn	Bonnie J. Stolarczyk

Officers   (Directors*)

*Raymond S. Stolarczyk, Chm. & C.E.O.	Grant M. Berntson, Sr. V.P. & Secy.
*Thomas E. Bentel, Pres. & C.O.O.	James R. Kinney, Sr. V.P. & C.F.O.

Consolidated Balance Sheet   As of September 30, 1996 (000 omitted)

Assets		Liabilities & Stockholders' Equity	
Loans receivable	$266,735	Deposits	$275,993
Mortgage-backed securities	26,484	Other liabilities	63,879
Assets available for sale	84,579	*Stockholders' equity	53,792
Premises & equipment	3,988		
Other assets	11,878		
Total	$393,664	Total	$393,664

*3,278,894 shares common stock outstanding.

Consolidated Income Statement

Years Ended Sept. 30	Thousands — — — —		Per Share[a] — — — —		Common Stock Price Range[a] Fiscal Year
	Total Income	Net Income	Earnings	Cash Dividends	
1996	$32,511	$2,142[b]	$ .72	$ .24	14 — 17-1/8
1995	27,398	3,084	.94	.12	16 — 10
1994	22,354	2,680[c]	.71[c]	.00	13 — 10-1/4
1993	23,683	3,616			
1992	25,088	2,754			

[a]Initial public offering in December 1993.
[b]Includes an extraordinary pretax charge of $1,600,000 for SAIF.
[c]Pro forma.

Transfer Agent & Registrar: Harris Trust and Savings Bank			
General Counsel:		Auditors:	KPMG Peat Marwick LLP
Barack Ferrazzano Kirschbaum Perlman & Nagelberg		Traded (Symbol):	NASDAQ (FBCI)
		Stockholders:	643
Investor Relations:	Judi Leaf	Employees:	117
Human Resources:	Lindalee Hansen	Annual Meeting:	In January

LaSalle Banks Guide   95

First Alert, Inc.

3901 Liberty Street Road, Aurora, Illinois 60504-8122
Telephone: (630) 851-7330

First Alert, Inc., through its subsidiaries, is a manufacturer and marketer of a broad range of residential safety products, anchored by its leadership position in the United States residential smoke and carbon monoxide detector market through retail distribution channels. Additional products include fire extinguishers, rechargeable flashlights and lanterns, electronic and electromechanical timers, night lights, fire security safes and chests, fire escape ladders, and passive infrared motion sensors. All of the company's manufacturing occurs in its two facilities in Juarez, Mexico, except fire extinguisher manufacturing which occurs in the company's Aurora, Illinois, facility. The company's principal subsidiary is BRK Brands, Inc. Incorporated in Delaware in 1992.

Directors   (In addition to indicated officers)

John R. Albers
Anthony J. DiNovi
David V. Harkins

Albert L. Prillaman
Scott A. Schoen

Officers   (Directors*)

*Malcolm Candlish, Chm.
*B. Joseph Messner, Pres. & C.E.O.
William K. Brouse, V.P.—Sales
Mark A. Devine, V.P.—Eng.
Douglas H. Kellam, V.P.—Mktg.

*Michael A. Rohl, V.P. & C.F.O.
Wally G. Schell, Jr., V.P.—Bus. Tech.
Edward J. Tyranski, V.P.—Oper.
Paul Bors, Treas.

Consolidated Balance Sheet   As of December 31, 1996 (000 omitted)

Assets		Liabilities & Stockholders' Equity	
Current assets	$127,947	Current liabilities	$ 54,199
Net property, plant & equipment	29,803	Long-term debt	40,000
Other assets	28,741	Deferred items	3,369
		Other liabilities	71
		*Stockholders' equity	88,852
Total	$186,491	Total	$186,491

*24,183,000 shares common stock outstanding.

Consolidated Income Statement

Years Ended Dec. 31	Thousands — — — —		Per Share[a] — — —		Common Stock Price Range[ab] Calendar Year
	Net Sales	Net Income	Earnings	Cash Dividends	
1996	$205,607	$(18,702)	$ (.76)	$ .00	11-3/8 — 3
1995	246,266	11,437	.46	.00	18-1/2 — 8-1/4
1994	248,404	17,625	.78	.00	22-1/2 — 8-3/4
1993	157,625	5,042	.25		
1992	131,061	1,237	.08		

[a]Adjusted to reflect a 2-for-1 stock split in October 1994 and a 3.1-for-1 stock split in March 1994.
[b]Initial public offering in March 1994.

Transfer Agent & Registrar:	The First National Bank of Boston		
General Counsel:	Hutchins, Wheeler & Dittmar	**Auditors:**	Price Waterhouse LLP
Investor Relations:	Michael A. Rohl, V.P.	**Traded (Symbol):**	NASDAQ (ALRT)
		Stockholders:	5,000
Human Resources:	Karoline K. Keeley	**Employees:**	2,125
Mgt. Info. Svcs.:	James Champion	**Annual Meeting:**	In May

First Bankers Trustshares, Inc.

1201 Broadway, P.O. Box 3566, Quincy, Illinois 62305-3566
Telephone: (217) 228-8000

First Bankers Trustshares, Inc. is the holding company for First Bankers Trust Company, N.A. The bank provides comprehensive financial products and services to retail, institutional, and corporate customers in the tri-state area of west central Illinois, northeast Missouri, and southeast Iowa. A community-oriented financial institution, First Bankers Trust Company, which traces its beginnings to 1946, operates three banking facilities located in Quincy, Illinois, and one facility in Mendon, Illinois (in northern Adams County). Incorporated in Delaware in 1988.

Directors   (In addition to indicated officers)

David E. Connor, Chm.
William D. Daniels

Donald E. Mitchell
Dennis R. Williams

Officers   (Directors*)

*Donald K. Gnuse, Pres. & C.E.O.
*George H. Pfister, V.P.

*Steven E. Siebers, Secy. & Treas.
Joe J. Leenerts, Asst. Secy.

Consolidated Balance Sheet   As of December 31, 1996 (000 omitted)

Assets		Liabilities & Stockholders' Equity	
Cash & due from banks	$ 10,849	Total deposits	$140,104
Investment securities	52,053	Long-term debt	4,980
Net loans	109,283	Funds & securities under	20,721
Other assets	6,459	agreement to repurchase	
		Other liabilities	1,901
		*Stockholders' equity	10,938
Total	$178,644	Total	$178,644

*316,722 shares common stock outstanding.

Consolidated Income Statement

Years Ended Dec. 31	Thousands — — — — Net Sales	Net Income	Per Share — — — Earnings	Cash Dividends	Common Stock Price Range Calendar Year
1996	$13,412	$1,797	$5.34	$ .51	32-1/2 — 26-1/4
1995	12,367	1,347	3.77	.47	26-3/4 — 25
1994	11,198	1,010	2.68	.43	25 — 20-1/2
1993	10,744	1,153	3.14	.30	20-1/2 — 11
1992	11,772	886	2.29	.00	14 — 12

Transfer Agent & Registrar: First Bankers Trust Company

General Counsel:	Hinshaw & Culbertson	Traded (Symbol):	OTC
Investor Relations:	Joe J. Leenerts	Stockholders:	213
Human Resources:	Joe J. Leenerts	Employees:	73
Auditors:	McGladrey & Pullen, LLP	Annual Meeting:	Second Tuesday in May

First Busey Corporation

P.O. Box 123, 201 West Main Street, Urbana, Illinois 61801
Telephone: (217) 365-4556

First Busey Corporation is a bank holding company that owns one community bank subsidiary, a trust company subsidiary, and a securities broker-dealer subsidiary. Through its subsidiaries, the company engages in retail, commercial, and correspondent banking, and provides trust and investment services. The company's bank subsidiary is Busey Bank. Non-banking subsidiaries are First Busey Trust & Investment Co., a full-service investment company offering professional financial planning, and First Busey Securities, Inc., a full-service brokerage firm. Incorporated in Delaware in 1978; reincorporated in Nevada in 1993.

Directors (In addition to indicated officers)

Joseph M. Ambrose	V.B. Leister
Samuel P. Banks	Linda M. Mills
Thomas O. Dawson	Robert C. Parker
Victor F. Feldman	John W. Pollard, M.D.
Kenneth M. Hendren	Edwin A. Scharlau II
Judith L. Ikenberry	Benjamin Snyder
E. Phillips Knox	David C. Thies
P. David Kuhl	Arthur R. Wyatt

Officers (Directors*)

*Douglas C. Mills, Chm., Pres. & C.E.O.
 Barbara J. Kuhl, Exec. V.P., Secy. & Treas.

Robert E. Beskow, Sr. V.P.—Acct. & Auditing
Scott L. Hendrie, Sr. V.P. & C.F.O.

Consolidated Balance Sheet As of December 31, 1996 (000 omitted)

Assets		Liabilities & Stockholders' Equity	
Current assets	$260,088	Deposits	$766,927
Net loans	563,369	Long-term debt	5,000
Net property, plant & equipment	21,588	Short-term debt	14,405
Other assets	19,873	Other liabilities	5,169
		*Stockholders' equity	73,417
Total	$864,918	Total	$864,918

*6,846,712 shares common stock outstanding.

Consolidated Income Statement

Years Ended Dec. 31	Thousands — — — — Total Income	Net Income	Per Share[a] — — — Earnings	Cash Dividends[b]	Common Stock Price Range[ab] Calendar Year
1996	$69,966	$9,306	$1.34	$ .65	23-3/4 — 18
1995	63,053	8,775	1.27	.59	18-1/2 — 16
1994	55,132	8,238	1.19	.53	16-7/8 — 14-3/8
1993	54,527	7,364	1.07	.53	14-5/8 — 11-7/8
1992	54,376	5,938	.96	.46	10-7/8 — 10

[a]Adjusted to reflect 3-for-2 stock splits in May 1993 and May 1996.
[b]Class A common stock.

Transfer Agent & Registrar: First Busey Corporation

General Counsel:	Chapman & Cutler	Traded (Symbol):	OTC (FBSYA)
Investor Relations:	Elizabeth N. Brunk	Stockholders:	978
Human Resources:	Lisa A. Davis	Employees:	383
Mgt. Info. Svcs.:	Jeffrey Gaines	Annual Meeting:	In April
Auditors:	McGladrey & Pullen, LLP	Internet:	www.busey.com

First Chicago NBD Corporation

One First National Plaza, Chicago, Illinois 60670
Telephone: (312) 732-4000

First Chicago NBD Corporation (the corporation) is a multi-bank holding company engaged primarily in three lines of business: credit card; regional banking, which includes retail banking and middle-market banking; and corporate and institutional banking and corporate investments. Through its bank subsidiaries, the corporation provides consumer and corporate banking products and services. The corporation's lead bank subsidiary is The First National Bank of Chicago. The corporation is also the parent corporation of NBD Bank (Michigan); American National Bank and Trust Company of Chicago; FCC National Bank; NBD Bank, N.A. (Indiana); NBD Bank (Florida); and several other bank subsidiaries. In addition, the corporation directly or indirectly owns the stock of various nonbank companies engaged in businesses related to banking and finance. Incorporated in Delaware in 1972.

Directors (In addition to indicated officers)

Terence E. Adderley	Richard A. Manoogian
James K. Baker	William T. McCormick, Jr.
John H. Bryan	Andrew J. McKenna
Siegfried Buschmann	Earl L. Neal
James S. Crown	James J. O'Connor
Maureen A. Fay, O.P.	Thomas E. Reilly, Jr.
Charles T. Fisher III	Adele Simmons
William G. Lowrie	Richard L. Thomas

Officers (Directors*)

*Verne G. Istock, Chm., Pres. & C.E.O.
*Thomas H. Jeffs II, V. Chm.
*Scott P. Marks, Jr., V. Chm.
*David J. Vitale, V. Chm.
Frederick M. Adams, Jr., Exec. V.P.
John W. Ballantine, Exec. V.P.
David P. Bolger, Exec. V.P.
William H. Elliott III, Exec. V.P.
Sherman I. Goldberg, Exec. V.P., Gen. Coun. & Secy.

Philip S. Jones, Exec. V.P.
W. G. Jurgensen, Exec. V.P.
Thomas J. McDowell, Exec. V.P.
Timothy P. Moen, Exec. V.P.
Susan S. Moody, Exec. V.P.
Andrew J. Paine, Jr., Exec. V.P.
Robert A. Rosholt, Exec. V.P. & C.F.O.
Willard A. Valpey, Exec. V.P.

Consolidated Balance Sheet As of December 31, 1996 (000 omitted)

Assets		Liabilities & Stockholders' Equity	
Cash & due from banks	$ 13,297,000	Deposits	$ 63,669,000
Securities	11,990,000	Funds borrowed	15,431,000
Other short-term investments	4,197,000	Long-term debt	8,454,000
Net loans & lease financing	65,007,000	Other liabilities	8,058,000
Properties & equipment	1,415,000	*Stockholders' equity	9,007,000
Other assets	8,713,000		
Total	$104,619,000	Total	$104,619,000

*313,473,520 shares common stock outstanding.

Consolidated Income Statement

Year Ended Dec. 31	Thousands — — — —		Per Share — — —		Common Stock Price Range Calendar Year
	Operating Income	Net Income	Earnings	Cash Dividends	
1996	$10,117,000	$1,436,000	$4.39	$1.48	58-7/8 — 34-3/4
1995	10,681,000	1,150,000	3.45	1.35	42-1/2 — 27-3/8

Transfer Agent & Registrar: First Chicago Trust Co. of New York

General Counsel:	Sherman I. Goldberg, Exec. V.P.	Traded (Symbol):	NYSE, CSE, PSE (FCN)
Investor Relations:	Caroline S. Grace	Stockholders:	39,438
		Employees:	33,414
Human Resources:	Timothy P. Moen, Exec. V.P.	Annual Meeting:	In May
Auditors:	Arthur Andersen LLP	Internet:	www.fcnbd.com

First Commonwealth, Inc.

444 North Wells Street, Suite 600, Chicago, Illinois 60610
Telephone: (312) 644-1800

First Commonwealth, Inc. is a leading provider of managed dental care benefits in the Midwest, with more than 500,000 current members in Chicago, Detroit, Indianapolis, Milwaukee, and St. Louis. The company's dental HMO product has the largest market share and provider network in its core Chicago market, and is growing in its expanding regional markets. First Commonwealth has broadened its spectrum of products from dental HMOs to include traditional indemnity coverage and a PPO network, creating a full-service solution that is distributed through over 1,400 independent brokers and a direct sales force. In December 1996, the company acquired Champion Dental Services Inc., a St. Louis-based managed dental care company. Incorporated in Delaware in 1986.

Directors   (In addition to indicated officers)

Richard M. Burdge, Sr.	Jackson W. Smart, Jr.
William J. McBride	

Officers   (Directors*)

*Christopher C. Multhauf, Chm. & C.E.O.	Mark R. Lundberg, V.P.—Sales
*David W. Mulligan, Pres., C.O.O. & Secy.	Scott B. Sanders, C.F.O. & Treas.
Gregory D. Stobbe, Sr. V.P.—Opers.	

Consolidated Balance Sheet   As of December 31, 1996 (000 omitted)

Assets		Liabilities & Stockholders' Equity	
Current assets	$21,023	Current liabilities	$14,331
Net property, plant & equipment	1,622	Deferred items	167
Other assets	11,809	*Stockholders' equity	19,956
Total	$34,454	Total	$34,454

*3,600,996 shares common stock outstanding.

Consolidated Income Statement

Years Ended Dec. 31	Thousands — — — — Total Revenue	Net Income	Per Share — — — Earnings	Cash Dividends	Common Stock Price Range[a] Calendar Year
1996	$44,099	$2,732	$ .76	$ .00	29 — 16-1/2
1995	33,315	2,004	.67	.00	27-1/4 — 19-3/4
1994	22,077	1,348[b]	.47[b]		
1993	17,337	1,005[b]	.36[b]		
1992	11,265	1,142[b]	.41[b]		

[a]Initial public offering in November 1995.
[b]Pro forma.

Transfer Agent & Registrar:	First Chicago Trust Co. of New York		
General Counsel:	Sidley & Austin	Traded (Symbol):	NASDAQ (FCWI)
Investor Relations:	Scott B. Sanders, C.F.O.	Stockholders:	150
		Employees:	120
Auditors:	Arthur Andersen LLP	Annual Meeting:	In April

First Enterprise Financial Group, Inc.

500 Davis Street, Suite 1005, Evanston, Illinois 60201
Telephone: (847) 866-8665

First Enterprise Financial Group, Inc., which operates under the name First Enterpise Acceptance Company (FEAC), is a specialty finance company engaged primarily in purchasing and servicing installment sales contracts originated by automobile dealers for financing the sale of used automobiles, vans, and light trucks. The company provides financing for customers who have limited access to traditional sources of credit, due to limited credit histories, low incomes, or past credit problems. First Enterprise also offers various insurance, warranty, and other products in conjunction with its purchases of installmant contracts. The company operates 35 branch offices in eight southeastern states: Alabama, Florida, Georgia, Mississippi, North Carolina, South Carolina, Tennessee, and Virginia. The company's corporate headquarters are located in Evanston with operations headquarters in Enterprise, Alabama. In July 1996, the company completed an initial public offering of 2,169,636 shares of common stock. Incorporated in Illinois in 1990.

Directors   (In addition to indicated officers)

Louis J. Glunz, Ph.D.
M. William Isbell

Joseph H. Stegmayer

Officers   (Directors*)

*Michael P. Harrington, Chm., Pres. & C.E.O.
*Thomas G. Parker, Pres. & C.O.O.—FEAC
Jan W. Erfert, V.P. & Treas.

*Paul A. Stinneford, V.P., Secy. & Gen. Coun.
*Kenneth L. Stucky, V.P. & Chf. Adm. Off.—FEAC

Consolidated Balance Sheet   As of December 31, 1996 (000 omitted)

Assets		Liabilities & Stockholders' Equity	
Cash & restricted cash	$ 5,910	Senior debt	$ 61,153
Finance receivables, net	107,188	Notes payable—securitized pool	36,733
Net property, plant & equipment	1,256	Accounts payable & accrued	5,229
Other assets	5,402	expenses	
		Other liabilities	325
		*Stockholders' equity	16,316
Total	$119,756	Total	$119,756

*5,285,955 shares common stock outstanding.

Consolidated Income Statement[a]

Years Ended Dec. 31	Thousands — — — —		Per Share[b] — — — —		Common Stock
	Total Income	Net Income	Earnings	Cash Dividends	Price Range[b] Calendar Year
1996	$28,000	$ 3,578[cd]	$ .63[c]	$ .00	11-1/8 — 7
1995	14,645	2,285[c]	.46[c]		
1994	7,335	661	.42		
1993	4,684	1,032			
1992	2,161	(85)			

[a]For all periods prior to 1996, the company was an S corporation and not subject to income taxes.
[b]Initial public offering in July 1996.
[c]Pro forma.
[d]Includes a gain to reflect the conversion to C-corporation status, resulting in a tax benefit of $267,000. Also includes an extraordinary charge of $150,000 in aftertax expense resulting from the early extinguishment of debt.

Transfer Agent & Registrar: LaSalle National Trust, N.A.

General Counsel:	Paul A. Stinneford, V.P.	Traded (Symbol):	NASDAQ (FENT)
Investor Relations:	Jan W. Erfert, V.P.	Stockholders:	1,100
Human Resources:	Cynthia McDuffie	Employees:	228
Mgt. Info. Svcs.:	Nielt Ash	Annual Meeting:	In May
Auditors:	Grant Thornton LLP	Internet:	www.fent.com

First Evergreen Corporation

3101 West 95th Street, Evergreen Park, Illinois 60805
Telephone: (708) 422-6700

First Evergreen Corporation is the holding company for First National Bank of Evergreen Park. The bank offers full-service banking, including transaction services, investment services, trust services, and depository and transfer services. The bank also offers individual retirement and Keogh accounts, and assists customers in the purchase and sale of corporate stocks and bonds, municipal bonds, and United States Treasury bills, notes, and bonds. Incorporated in 1978.

Directors   (In addition to indicated officers)

Alfred E. Bleeker
Jerome J. Cismoski

Martin F. Ozinga

Officers   (Directors*)

*Kenneth J. Ozinga, Chm. & Pres.
Robert C. Wall, V.P.

*Stephen M. Hallenbeck, Treas. & Secy.

Consolidated Balance Sheet   As of December 31, 1996 (000 omitted)

Assets		Liabilities & Stockholders' Equity	
Current assets	$ 217,424	Current liabilities	$ 388,339
Net property, plant & equipment	29,647	Other liabilities	1,335,234
Other assets	1,662,942	*Stockholders' equity	186,440
Total	$1,910,013	Total	$1,910,013

*401,637 shares common stock outstanding.

Consolidated Income Statement

Years Ended Dec. 31	Thousands — — — — Operating Income	Net Income	Per Share — — — Earnings	Cash Dividends	Common Stock Price Range Calendar Year
1996	$133,160	$20,692	$51.42	$15.00	467-1/4 — 382-1/2
1995	131,440	20,230	50.11	13.00	433-1/4 — 382-1/2
1994	121,539	20,415	50.29	13.00	391-1/2 — 344-3/4
1993	126,706	21,970	53.77	9.00	357-3/4 — 309-1/4
1992	126,484	18,959	45.95	8.00	315-1/4 — 269-5/8

Transfer Agent & Registrar: First Evergreen Corporation

General Counsel:
  Barry N. Voorn—FNB of Ever. Pk.

Investor Relations: Kenneth J. Ozinga, Chm.

Human Resources:
  John A. Camphouse, V.P.-FNB of Ever. Pk.

Mgt. Info. Svcs.:
  Barbara L. Heidegger, Sr. V.P.-FNB of Ever. Pk.

Auditors: Ernst & Young LLP

Traded: OTC (When-issued basis)

Stockholders: 494

Employees: 3

Annual Meeting: In April

First Financial Bancorp, Inc.

121 East Locust Street, Belvidere, Illinois 61008
Telephone: (815) 544-3167

First Financial Bancorp, Inc. is the holding company for First Federal Savings Bank. First Federal is a federally chartered savings institution engaged primarily in the business of originating one- to four-family residential mortgage loans in its primary market area. As a community-oriented savings bank, it offers traditional deposit and loan products through its two full-service offices in Belvidere, Illinois, and its loan origination office in Rockford, Illinois. The bank has a wholly owned subsidiary, First Financial Services of Belvidere, Illinois, Inc., which offers annuities and insurance products on an agency basis at the bank's full-service locations. Incorporated in Delaware in 1993.

Directors (In addition to indicated officers)

Jack R. Manley
Charles G. Popp
Nancy Sylvester

James V. Twyning
Richard E. Winkelman

Officers (Directors*)

*Steven C. Derr, Pres. & C.E.O.
 Donald J. Kucera, V.P.

Robert Opperman, V.P.
Keith D. Hill, C.F.O. & Treas.

Consolidated Balance Sheet As of December 31, 1996 (000 omitted)

Assets		Liabilities & Stockholders' Equity	
Cash & cash equivalents	$ 1,652	Deposits	$65,838
Investment securities	4,857	FHLB advances	20,450
Loans receivable	73,815	Advance payments by borrowers	339
Mortgage-backed securities	10,193	Other liabilities	563
Other assets	3,998	*Stockholders' equity	7,325
Total	$94,515	Total	$94,515

*424,876 shares common stock outstanding.

Consolidated Income Statement

Years Ended Dec. 31	Thousands — — — — Total Income	Net Income	Per Share — — — Earnings	Cash Dividends	Common Stock Price Range Calendar Year
1996	$6,495[a]	$(158)	$ (.35)	$ .00	16-1/4 — 15
1995	6,025	648	1.37	.00	16-1/4 — 12
1994	5,079	572	1.23	.00	13-1/2 — 9-1/4
1993	5,513	496		.00	10 — 8[b]
1992	6,222	740			

[a]Includes operating and non-operating income.
[b]Initial public offering in October 1993.

Transfer Agent & Registrar:	Registrar and Transfer Company		
General Counsel:	Strom Sewell Larson & Popp	Traded (Symbol):	NASDAQ (FFBI)
Investor Relations:	Keith D. Hill, C.F.O. & Treas.	Stockholders:	323
Human Resources	Pat McCoy, Oper. Mgr.	Employees:	38
Auditors:	Crowe, Chizek & Co.	Annual Meeting:	In April

First Merchants Acceptance Corporation

570 Lake Cook Road, Suite 126, Deerfield, Illinois 60015
Telephone: (847) 948-9300

First Merchants Acceptance Corporation is a specialty consumer finance company engaged in financing the purchase of used automobiles through the acquisition of dealer-originated retail install-ment contracts. Such contracts are entered into by automobile dealers with borrowers who do not have access to credit from traditional lending sources. Commencing operations in June 1991, the company currently operates 14 regional dealer service centers serving 37 states. The company's principal subsidiary is First Merchants Automobile Receivable Corporation. Incorporated in Delaware in 1991.

Directors (In addition to indicated officers)

Thomas A. Hiatt
Marcy H. Shockey

Solomon A. Weisgal
Stowe W. Wyant

Officers (Directors*)

*William N. Plamondon, Co-Pres. & Co-C.E.O.
*Richard J. Uhl, Co-Pres. & Co-C.E.O.
John R. Griggs, Exec. V.P. & C.O.O.
Alan J. Appelman, Sr. V.P.
Norman Smagley, Sr. V.P. & C.F.O.

Craig A. Adams, V.P.
Mark Floyd, V.P.
Brian W. Hausmann, V.P.
Allen D. Rice, V.P.
Richard P. Vogelman, Gen. Coun. & Secy.

Consolidated Balance Sheet[a]   As of December 31, 1995 (000 omitted)

Assets		Liabilities & Stockholders' Equity	
Net receivables	$237,608	Senior revolving credit facility	$104,000
Finance receivables held for sale, net	32,265	Notes payable-securitized pools, net	70,379
Restricted cash	6,318	Subordinated notes, net	9,720
Other assets, including cash	6,083	Other liabilities	13,896
		*Stockholders' equity	84,279
Total	$282,274	Total	$282,274

[a]Financial data for the year ending December 31, 1996, unavailable at this publication's press time.
*6,525,519 shares common stock outstanding.

Consolidated Income Statement

Years Ended Dec. 31	Thousands — — — — Total Revenues	Net Income	Per Share[a] — — — — Earnings	Cash Dividends	Common Stock Price Range[a] Fiscal Year
1996[b]					27 — 14-1/4
1995	$39,548	$6,701	$1.35	$.00	27-1/4 — 10
1994	16,023	1,621	.85	.00	12-1/2 — 9[c]
1993	6,755	938	.32		
1992	2,038	327	.17		

[a]Adjusted to reflect a 23.184-for-1 stock split in September 1994.
[b]Financial data for the year ending December 31, 1996, unavailable at this publication's press time.
[c]Initial public offering in September 1994.

Transfer Agent & Registrar: Harris Trust and Savings Bank

Securities Counsel:
  Sonnenschein, Nath & Rosenthal

Investor Relations: Norman Smagley, Sr. V.P.

Human Resources: Anne Kazelak, Mgr.

Auditors: Deloitte & Touche LLP

Traded (Symbol): NASDAQ (FMAC)

Stockholders: 3,700

Employees: 700

Annual Meeting: In May

First Midwest Bancorp, Inc.

300 Park Boulevard, Suite 405, Itasca, Illinois 60143-2636
Telephone: (630) 875-7450

First Midwest Bancorp, Inc. is a leading bank holding company engaged in the business of commercial banking, investment management, trust, mortgage, and related services through its bank affiliate, First Midwest Bank, N.A. and two other affiliates. First Midwest Bank has assets of $3.1 billion; its trust-investment management affiliate, First Midwest Trust Company manages $1.4 billion in customers' assets. Its mortgage affiliate, First Midwest Mortgage Company, originates mortgages and services a portfolio of $900 million. Through these affiliates, First Midwest provides banking and related financial services to both business and individual customers in northern Illinois and eastern Iowa markets. Approximately 80 percent of First Midwest's business is centered around the metropolitan Chicago area. On June 20, 1997, First Midwest Bancorp announced that it had entered into a definitive agreement to acquire SparBank, Incorporated, the holding company of the $445 million McHenry State Bank, located in McHenry, Illinois. With the acquisition, First Midwest's assets increase to approximately $3.5 billion, continuing it as the third largest bank holding company headquarters in Illinois. Incorporated in Delaware in 1982.

Directors (In addition to indicated officers)

Bruce S. Chelberg	Joseph W. England	Sister Norma Janssen, O.S.F.
O. Ralph Edwards	Thomas M. Garvin	J. Stephen Vanderwoude

Officers (Directors*)

*C.D. Oberwortmann, Chm.
*Robert P. O'Meara, Pres. & C.E.O.
*Andrew B. Barber, V. Chm.
*John M. O'Meara, Exec. V.P. & C.O.O.

Donald J. Swistowicz, Exec. V.P.—Corp. Admin. & C.F.O.
Alan R. Milasius, Sr. V.P. & Secy.

Consolidated Statement of Condition As of December 31, 1996 (000 omitted)

Assets		Liabilities & Stockholders' Equity	
Cash & cash equivalents	$ 107,595	Total deposits	$2,260,667
Federal funds sold & short-term investments	36,568	Short-term borrowings	493,142
		Other liabilities	103,289
Investment securities	21,336	*Stockholders' equity	262,140
Securities available for sale	770,256		
Net loans	2,055,129		
Net property, plant & equipment	49,354		
Other assets	79,000		
Total	$3,119,238	Total	$3,119,238

*16,906,540 shares common stock outstanding.

Consolidated Income Statement[a]

Years Ended Dec. 31	Thousands — — — — Total Oper. Income	Net Income	Per Share[b] — — — Earnings	Cash Dividends	Common Stock Price Range[b] Calendar Year
1996	$268,604	$33,716[c]	$1.97[c]	$ .70	33 — 21-3/8
1995	276,022	25,685[d]	1.51[d]	.61	23-7/8 — 18-5/8
1994	233,560	23,158[e]	1.37[e]	.54	23 — 17-5/8
1993	214,870	24,228	1.41	.48	22-5/8 — 15-3/8
1992	219,418	19,902	1.14	.42	16-1/4 — 11-3/8

[a]All results have been restated to include the 1995 acquisition of CF Bancorp, Inc., accounted for as a pooling-of-interets.
[b]Adjusted to reflect a 5-for-4 stock split in December 1996.
[c]Includes an after-tax acquisition credit of $228,000 ($.01 per share) net of a one-time SAIF assessment.
[d]Includes an after-tax acquisition charge of $3,670,000 ($.22 per share) net of an after-tax restructuring credit of $494,000 ($.03 per share).
[e]Includes an after-tax restructuring charge of $2,379,000 ($.14 per share).

Transfer Agent & Registrar:	American Stock Transfer & Trust Co.		
General Counsel:	Hinshaw & Culbertson	Auditors:	Ernst & Young LLP
Investor Relations:	James M. Roolf, Sr. V.P.	Traded (Symbol):	NASDAQ (FMBI)
		Stockholders:	3,007
Human Resources:	Phillip E. Glotfelty	Employees:	1,217
Mgt. Info. Svcs.:	Kent S. Belasco	Annual Meeting:	In April

LaSalle Banks Guide

First National Bancorp, Inc.

78 North Chicago Street, Joliet, Illinois 60431
Telephone: (815) 726-4371

First National Bancorp, Inc. is a multi-bank holding company providing financial and other banking services to customers located primarily in suburban Will, Grundy, and Kendall Counties, Illinois. First National Bancorp was established in 1986 as a one-bank holding company for the First National Bank of Joliet. Expansion has continued through the acquisition in 1989 of Southwestern Suburban Bank, Bolingbrook; the Bank of Lockport in 1990; and Plano Bancshares, Inc., the parent of Community Bank of Plano, in 1994. The subsidiary banks make loans to both individuals and commercial entities. Incorporated in Illinois in 1986.

Directors (In addition to indicated officers)

Sheldon C. Bell
George H. Buck
Watson A. Healy
Paul A. Lambrecht
Harvey J. Lewis

Walter F. Nolan
Charles R. Peyla
Louis R. Peyla
Howard E. Reeves

Officers (Directors*)

*Kevin T. Reardon, Chm. & C.E.O.

*Albert G. D'Ottavio, Pres., C.O.O., Treas. & Secy.

Consolidated Balance Sheet As of December 31, 1996 (000 omitted)

Assets		Liabilities & Stockholders' Equity	
Current assets	$788,226	Current liabilities	$739,749
Net property, plant & equipment	17,880	Long-term debt	6,951
Other assets	18,464	Other liabilities	6,479
		*Stockholders' equity	71,391
Total	$824,570	Total	$824,570

*1,215,902 shares common stock outstanding.

Consolidated Income Statement

Years Ended Dec. 31	Thousands — — — —		Per Share[a] — — — —		Common Stock Price Range[a] Calendar Year	
	Total Income	Net Income	Earnings	Cash Dividends		
1996	$60,203	$8,521	$7.01	$3.00	90	—77
1995	57,689	8,211	6.75	2.75	77	—64
1994	45,908	7,507	6.17	2.68	64	—57
1993	43,637	7,366	6.06	2.50	57-1/8	—51-3/8
1992	45,232	6,826	5.61	2.50	51-3/8	—44-1/4

[a]Adjusted to reflect a 7-for-5 stock split in 1994.

Transfer Agent & Registrar: First National Bancorp, Inc.

General Counsel:
Herschbach, Tracy, Johnson, Bertani & Wilson

Investor Relations: James Limacher, Sr. V.P.

Human Resources: Betty J. McTee, V.P.

Mgt. Info. Svcs.: Olivier May, Dir.

Auditors: Crowe, Chizek & Co. LLP

Traded (Symbol): OTC

Stockholders: 1,674

Employees: 357

Annual Meeting: In March

First Oak Brook Bancshares, Inc.

1400 Sixteenth Street, Oak Brook, Illinois 60521
Telephone: (630) 571-1050

First Oak Brook Bancshares, Inc. is a bank holding company formed under the Bank Holding Company Act of 1956, as amended. The company owns all of the outstanding capital stock of Oak Brook Bank, an Illinois state-chartered bank. The bank has seven locations in Du Page County and two in Cook County. The business of First Oak Brook Bancshares consists primarily of the ownership, supervision, and control of its subsidiary. The company provides its subsidiary with advice, counsel, and specialized services in various fields of financial, legal, and banking policy and operations. First Oak Brook Bancshares also engages in negotiations designed to lead to the acquisition of other banks and closely related businesses. Oak Brook Bank is engaged in the general retail and commercial banking business. The services offered include demand and savings deposits, corporate cash management services, commercial lending products such as commercial loans, mortgages, and letters of credit, and personal lending products such as residential mortgages, home equity lines, and Gold and Silver MasterCard. In addition, private banking products and services are offered, including discount brokerage, mutual funds, and precious metal sales. Oak Brook Bank has a full-service trust and land trust department. In June 1997, the company announced that Oak Brook Bank had entered into an agreement to sell its credit card portfolio. The transaction is expected to close in July 1997. Incorporated in Delaware in 1983.

Directors (In addition to indicated officers)

Miriam Lutwak Fitzgerald, M.D.
Geoffrey R. Stone

Alton M. Withers
Robert M. Wrobel

Officers (Directors*)

*Eugene P. Heytow, Chm. & C.E.O.
*Frank M. Paris, V. Chm.
*Richard M. Rieser, Jr., Pres.
Rosemarie Bouman, V.P., C.F.O. & Treas.
Mary C. Carnevale, V.P. & Chf. Hum. Res.
　Officer

George C. Clam, V.P. & Chf. Banking Officer
William E. Navolio, V.P., Gen. Coun. & Secy.
Susanne Griffith, Auditor
Joseph Garro, Assoc. Gen. Coun.
Lola Donofrio, Asst. Treas.

Consolidated Balance Sheet As of December 31, 1996 (000 omitted)

Assets		Liabilities & Stockholders' Equity	
Current assets	$743,264	Current liabilities	$703,490
Net property, plant & equipment	17,470	Other liabilities	5,612
Other assets	7,921	*Stockholders' equity	59,553
Total	$768,655	Total	$768,655

*1,518,611 shares common and 1,854,482 shares Class A common stock outstanding.

Consolidated Income Statement

Years Ended Dec. 31	Thousands — — — —		Per Share[ab] — — —		Common Stock Price Range[ab] Calendar Year
	Total Income	Net Income	Earnings	Cash Dividends	
1996	$57,197	$7,107	$2.06	$ .38	25-1/2 — 20-1/2
1995	52,528	6,692	1.95	.32	21-1/2 — 16-1/2
1994	45,305	6,194	1.81	.28	20-1/2 — 14-1/2
1993	42,001	5,533	1.62	.24	15-1/2 — 10-1/8
1992	39,733	4,313	1.27	.22	11-3/4 — 8-5/8

[a]Class A common stock; common stock dividends for the years 1996-1992 were $.32, $.26, $.22, $.19, and $.18 per share, respectively.
[b]Adjusted for 50% stock dividends paid in September 1994 and November 1992, and a 25% stock dividend paid in December 1993.

Transfer Agent & Registrar:	Oak Brook Bank		
General Counsel:	William E. Navolio, V.P.	Traded (Symbol):	NASDAQ (FOBBA, Class A)
Investor Relations:	Rosemarie Bouman, V.P.	Stockholders:	393
Human Resources:	Mary C. Carnevale, V.P.	Employees:	284
Mgt. Info. Svcs.:	Edward Berkheimer	Annual Meeting:	In May
Auditors:	Ernst & Young LLP	Internet:	www.obb.com

Firstbank of Illinois Co.

205 South Fifth Street, Springfield, Illinois 62701
Telephone: (217) 753-7543

Firstbank of Illinois Co. is the largest bank holding company headquartered in downstate Illinois, currently operating 39 offices in 13 Illinois counties and six offices in Missouri. The majority of business is commercial and retail banking, trust and investment management, business lending, agriculture credit, and management services, provided through the company's subsidiaries in central and southern Illinois and in the St. Louis metropolitan area. Company subsidiaries in Illinois include: Central Bank (Fairview Heights); Elliott State Bank (Jacksonville); Farmers and Merchants Bank of Carlinville; The First National Bank of Central Illinois (Springfield); First Trust and Savings Bank of Taylorville; FFG Trust Inc. (Springfield); and FFG Investments Inc. (Springfield). Subsidiaries in Missouri include: Colonial Bank (Des Peres); Duchesne Bank (St. Peters); and Zemenick & Walker, Inc. (St. Louis). Zemenick & Walker, Inc. was acquired in January 1997 as a part of Firstbank's newly formed asset management group, providing fee-only investment-advisory services to Firstbank clients. Incorporated in Delaware in 1974.

Directors   (In addition to indicated officers)

Leo J. Dondanville, Jr.
William R. Enlow
William T. Grant, Jr.
Robert W. Jackson

William R. Schnirring
Robert L. Sweney
P. Richard Ware
Richard E. Zemenick

Officers   (Directors*)

*Mark H. Ferguson, Chm., Pres. & C.E.O.
*William B. Hopper, V. Chm.
Larry A. Burton, Exec. V.P.—Fin. Svcs.
Sandra L. Stolte, Exec. V.P.
David W. Waggoner, Exec. V.P.
Chris R. Zettek, Exec. V.P., C.F.O. & Treas.

Duane L. Gerlach, Sr. V.P. & C.L.O.
Daniel R. Davis, V.P. & Cont.
Jack Griggs, V.P.—Mktg.
William V. Peterman, V.P. & Corp. Auditor
Steven Schweizer, V.P. & Oper. Center Mgr.
John R. Smith, V.P. & Chf. Invest. Officer

Consolidated Balance Sheet   As of December 31, 1996 (000 omitted)

Assets		Liabilities & Stockholders' Equity	
Cash & due from banks	$ 110,686	Deposits	$1,738,263
Securities	478,184	Borrowed funds	39,585
Other short-term investments	45,815	Long-term debt	3
Net loans	1,278,303	Other liabilities	19,717
Properties & equipment	43,463	*Stockholders' equity	207,636
Other assets	48,753		
Total	$2,005,204	Total	$2,005,204

*10,335,475 shares common stock outstanding.

Consolidated Income Statement

Years Ended Dec. 31	Thousands — — — —		Per Share[a] — — — —		Common Stock Price Range[a] Calendar Year
	Total Revenue	Net Income	Earnings	Cash Dividends	
1996	$162,409	$27,873	$2.66	$ .96	34-3/4 — 29-1/2
1995	154,569	25,742	2.46	.88	31-1/2 — 25-1/2
1994	138,813	23,454	2.37	.80	25-7/8 — 22-5/8
1993	139,258	20,643	2.20	.72	26-1/8 — 23-3/8
1992	153,651	17,067	1.83	.64	25-3/8 — 18-1/2

[a]Adjusted to reflect a 3-for-2 stock split in March 1995.

Transfer Agent & Registrar: Firstbank of Illinois Co.

General Counsel: Brown, Hay & Stephens

Investor Relations: Chris R. Zettek, Exec. V.P.

Human Resources: Diane Schwab, Coordinator

Mgt. Info. Svcs.:   Steven Schweizer, V.P.

Auditors: KPMG Peat Marwick LLP

Traded (Symbol):   NASDAQ (FBIC)

Stockholders: 2,144

Employees: 927

Annual Meeting: In April

Florsheim Group Inc.

200 North LaSalle Street, Chicago, Illinois 60601-1014
Telephone: (312) 458-2500

Florsheim Group Inc. designs, manufactures, and sources a diverse and extensive range of products in the middle- to upper-price range of the men's quality footwear market. Florsheim distributes its products to more than 6,000 department and specialty store locations worldwide and through approximately 350 company-owned specialty and outlet stores. Incorporated in Delaware in 1987.

Directors (In addition to indicated officers)

Bernard Attal
Robert H. Falk
Michael S. Gross
John J. Hannan
Joshua J. Harris

John H. Kissick
Richard B. Loynd
Ronald J. Mueller
Michael D. Weiner

Officers (Directors*)

*Charles J. Campbell, Chm., Pres. & C.E.O.
L. David Sanguinetti, Exec. V.P.—Mktg.,
C.O.O. & Pres.—Retail Div.
Karen Nyman Latham, V.P. & C.F.O.

Gregory J. Van Gasse, V.P.—Mktg. & Dir.—New Prod. Div.
Thomas W. Joseph, Pres.—Intl. Div.

Consolidated Balance Sheet As of December 30, 1996 (000 omitted)

Assets		Liabilities & Stockholders' Equity	
Current assets	$130,719	Current liabilities	$ 35,603
Net property, plant & equipment	24,974	Long-term debt	69,450
Other assets	29,545	Deferred items	20,614
		Other liabilities	1,916
		*Stockholders' equity	57,655
Total	$185,238	Total	$185,238

*8,379,287 shares common stock outstanding.

Consolidated Income Statement

Years Ended Abt. Dec. 31	Thousands — — — —		Per Share[a] — — —		Common Stock Price Range[a] Calendar Year	
	Net Sales	Net Income	Earnings	Cash Dividends		
1996	$244,855	$ 1,964	$ .23	$ .00	6	—3-1/2
1995	285,307	(4,846)	(.58)	.00	6	—3-1/2
1994[b]	302,001	1,573	.19	.00	9-1/4	—5-5/8
1993[b]	299,625	7,221	.87			
1992[c]	311,888					

[a]Spun off from INTERCO INCORPORATED in November 1994.
[b]Pro forma.
[c]Due to fresh start reporting, net income figure is not meaningful.

Transfer Agent & Registrar: Harris Trust and Savings Bank

Investor Relations:
    Karen Nyman Latham & Thomas E. Poggensee

Auditors: KPMG Peat Marwick LLP

Traded (Symbol):   NASDAQ (FLSC)

Stockholders: 1,900
Employees: 2,100
Annual Meeting: In May
Internet: www.florsheim.com

FMC Corporation

200 East Randolph Drive, Chicago, Illinois 60601
Telephone: (312) 861-6000

FMC Corporation participates on a worldwide basis in four broad markets: Performance Chemicals, Industrial Chemicals, Machinery and Equipment, and Defense Systems. Chemical products include industrial and agricultural chemicals and food additives. Machinery manufactured includes equipment for defense, energy and transportation, as well as food and agricultural machinery. The company, through its subsidiaries, operates 117 manufacturing facilities and mines in 27 states and 28 countries, and two research facilities. In 1994, the company and Harsco Corp. completed the formation of a joint venture, United Defense L.P., which combined their defense operations. Incorporated in Delaware in 1928.

Directors (In addition to indicated officers)

B.A. Bridgewater, Jr.
Patricia A. Buffler, Ph.D.
Albert J. Costello
Paul L. Davies, Jr.
Jean A. François-Poncet

Pehr G. Gyllenhammar
Edward C. Meyer
William F. Reilly
James R. Thompson
Clayton K. Yeutter

Officers (Directors*)

*Robert N. Burt, Chm. & C.E.O.
*Larry D. Brady, Pres.
William F. Beck, Exec. V.P.
Michael J. Callahan, Exec. V.P. & C.F.O.
William J. Kirby, Sr. V.P.—Admin.
J. Paul McGrath, Sr. V.P. & Gen. Coun.
Alfredo Bernad, V.P. & Pres.—FMC Europe
Patricia D. Brozowski, V.P.—Comm.
Charles H. Cannon, Jr., V.P. & Gen. Mgr.—Food Mach.
Robert J. Fields, V.P.—Envir., Health, Safety & Toxicology
W. Reginald Hall, V.P. & Gen. Mgr.—Specialty Chem.
Robert I. Harries, V.P. & Gen. Mgr.—Chem. Prod.

Patrick J. Head, V.P.
Henry Kahn, V.P. & Treas.
Ronald D. Mambu, V.P. & Cont.
James A. McClung, V.P.—Worldwide Mktg.
Michael W. Murray, V.P.—Hum. Res.
Joseph H. Netherland, V.P. & Gen. Mgr.—Energy & Trans. Equip.
Thomas W. Rabaut, V.P. & Pres./C.E.O.—United Defense, L.P.
Harold S. Russell, V.P.—Govt. Aff.
William H. Schumann, V.P. & Gen. Mgr.—Ag. Prod.
Peter E. Weber, V.P. & Pres.—Latin Amer./Middle East/Africa
William J. Wheeler, V.P.—Chem. Dev.

Consolidated Balance Sheet As of December 31, 1996 (000 omitted)

Assets		Liabilities & Stockholders' Equity	
Current assets	$2,193,100	Current liabilities	$2,021,400
Net property, plant & equipment	1,959,300	Long-term debt	1,268,400
Other assets	837,400	Other liabilities	844,200
		*Stockholders' equity	855,800
Total	$4,989,800	Total	$4,989,800

*37,480,854 shares common stock outstanding.

Consolidated Income Statement

Years Ended Dec. 31	Thousands — — — —		Per Share — — —		Common Stock Price Range Calendar Year
	Total Revenue[a]	Net Income	Earnings	Cash Dividends	
1996	$5,080,600	$ 210,700	$ 5.54	$ .00	77-3/4 — 62-1/4
1995	4,507,700	215,600	5.72	.00	79-1/2 — 57-3/8
1994	3,989,300	173,400	4.66	.00	65 — 45-1/2
1993	3,663,200	36,300[b]	.98[b]	.00	53 — 41-1/2
1992	3,832,900	(75,700)[c]	(2.06)[c]	.00	53 — 42-5/8

[a]From continuing operations.
[b]Includes extraordinary items, net of taxes, of $4,683,000 ($.13 per share).
[c]Includes extraordinary items, net of taxes, of $11,417,000 ($.31 per share); FAS 106, net of taxes, of $183,730,000 ($4.99 per share); and provision for discontinued operations, net of taxes, of $49,200,000 ($1.34 per share).

Transfer Agent & Registrar: Harris Trust and Savings Bank

General Counsel:	J. Paul McGrath, Sr. V.P.	Traded (Symbol):	NYSE, CSE, PSE (FMC)
Investor Relations:	Randall Woods, Dir.	Stockholders:	11,339
		Employees:	22,048
Human Resources:	Michael W. Murray, V.P.	Annual Meeting:	In April
Auditors:	KPMG Peat Marwick LLP	Internet:	www.fmc.com

Fruit of the Loom, Inc.

5000 Sears Tower, 233 South Wacker Drive, Chicago, Illinois 60606
Telephone: (312) 876-1724

Fruit of the Loom, Inc. is a marketing-oriented, vertically integrated, international basic apparel company, emphasizing branded products for consumers ranging from infants to senior citizens. The company manufactures and markets men's and boy's underwear, women's and girls' underwear, printable activewear, outerwear, casualwear, sportswear, and childrenswear. Through over 60 locations world-wide, the company manufactures products under such brands names as Fruit of the Loom®, BVD®, Gitano®, Best®, Cumberland Bay®, and Screen Stars®. Licensed brands include Munsingwear®, Wilson®, Botany 500®, and John Henry®. Licensed apparel bearing the logos or insignia of the major sports leagues and their teams and the names of certain popular players, as well as the logos of most major colleges and universities, are marketed under the Pro Player® and Fans Gear® brands. Incorporated in Delaware in 1985.

Directors (In addition to indicated officers)

Omar Z. Al Askari	Henry A. Johnson
Dennis S. Bookshester	A. Lorne Weil
Lee W. Jennings	Sir Brian G. Wolfson

Officers (Directors*)

*William F. Farley, Chm. & C.E.O.	J. Gary Raley, Sr. V.P.—Sales
*Richard C. Lappin, Pres. & C.O.O.	Burgess D. Ridge, Sr. V.P.—Admin. & Secy.
*Larry K. Switzer, Sr. Exec. V.P. & C.F.O.	Joyce M. Russell, Sr. V.P.—Legal
Richard D. Davis, Sr. V.P. & Gen. Mgr.—Activewear	John D. Wendler, Sr. V.P.—Mktg.
Brian J. Hanigan, Sr. V.P. & Treas.	Gary D. Wood, Sr. V.P.—Mfg.
G. William Newton, Sr. V.P.—Fin.	Walter J. Sluzas, V.P.—Tax
	Mark A. Steinkrauss, V.P.—Corp. Rel.

Consolidated Balance Sheet As of December 31, 1996 (000 omitted)

Assets		Liabilities & Stockholders' Equity	
Current assets	$ 842,100	Current liabilities	$ 326,700
Net property, plant & equipment	899,900	Long-term debt	867,400
Other assets	805,000	Deferred items	16,900
		Other liabilities	271,200
		*Stockholders' equity	1,064,800
Total	$2,547,000	Total	$2,547,000

*69,937,600 shares Class A and 6,690,976 shares Class B common stock outstanding.

Consolidated Income Statement

Years Ended Abt. Dec. 31	Thousands — — — — — Net Sales	Net Income[a]	Per Share — — — — Earnings[a]	Cash Dividends	Common Stock Price Range[b] Calendar Year	
1996	$2,447,400	$ 152,200	$ 1.98	$ .00	39	— 22-1/2
1995	2,403,100	(227,300)[c]	(2.99)	.00	27-3/4	— 16-1/2
1994	2,297,800	60,300[d]	.79	.00	33	— 23
1993	1,884,400	212,800[e]	2.80[e]	.00	49-1/4	— 22-7/8
1992	1,855,100	188,500	2.48	.00	49-5/8	— 26-5/8

[a]From continuing operations before extraordinary items and cumulative effect of change in accounting principles.
[b]Class A common stock.
[c]Includes charges of $372,900,000 related to the write-down of goodwill, costs associated with closing or realigning manufacturing facilities, personnel reduction costs, and other various items.
[d]Includes pretax charges of approximately $40,000,000 to write down inventories to net realizable value and a pretax charge of $18,000,000 related to the write-off of Artex intangibles.
[e]Includes a pretax gain of $67,300,000 ($.55 per share) from the company's investment in Acme Boot Co., Inc.

Transfer Agent & Registrar:	ChaseMellon Shareholder Services, L.L.C.		
Legal Counsel:	Joyce M. Russell, Sr. V.P.	Traded (Symbol):	NYSE (FTL)
Investor Relations:	Mark A. Steinkrauss, V.P.	Stockholders:	30,000
		Employees:	34,000
Human Resources:	Marett Cobb, V.P.	Annual Meeting:	In May
Auditors:	Ernst & Young LLP	Internet:	www.fruit.com

Arthur J. Gallagher & Co.

The Gallagher Centre, Two Pierce Place, Itasca, Illinois 60143-3141
Telephone: (630) 773-3800

Arthur J. Gallagher & Co. and its subsidiaries are engaged in providing insurance brokerage, risk management, and related services to clients in the United States and abroad. The company's principal activity is the negotiation and placement of insurance for its clients. The company services and places insurance for commercial, industrial, institutional, governmental, religious, and personal accounts. Arthur J. Gallagher also specializes in furnishing risk management services. Risk management involves assisting clients in analyzing risks and in determining whether proper protection is best obtained through the purchase of insurance or through retention of all or a portion of those risks and the adoption of corporate risk management policies and cost-effective loss control and prevention programs. Risk management services also include claims management, loss control consulting, and property appraisals. Gallagher Bassett Services, Inc., the company's principal subsidiary, is a provider of risk management services dedicated to serving the needs of corporations and institutions worldwide. Services include claims management, risk management consulting, information management, property appraisals, and other specialized services. Other major subsidiaries and divisions include: The Brokerage Services Division; Gallagher Benefit Services; Gallagher Benefit Administrators; Gallagher Bassett International Ltd.; Arthur J. Gallagher International, Inc.; Arthur J. Gallagher (UK) Limited; Arthur J. Gallagher & Co. (Bermuda) Limited; International Special Risk Services, Inc.; and Corporate Information Services. Arthur J. Gallagher operates through a network of approximately 150 offices located throughout the U.S. and five abroad. Founded in 1927; reincorporated in Delaware in 1972.

Directors   (In addition to indicated officers)

T. Kimball Brooker
Jack M. Greenberg

Philip A. Marineau
James R. Wimmer

Officers   (Directors*)

*Robert E. Gallagher, Chm.
*J. Patrick Gallagher, Jr., Pres. & C.E.O.
*Michael J. Cloherty, Exec. V.P.—Fin.
Bill G. Jensen, Sr. V.P.
*Walter F. McClure, Sr. V.P.
James J. Braniff III, V.P.
Bette J. Brinkerhoff, V.P.
*John G. Campbell, V.P.
Peter J. Durkalski, V.P.

James W. Durkin, Jr., V.P.
Nicholas M. Elsberg, V.P.
James S. Gault, V.P.
*Frank M. Heffernan, Jr., V.P.
Clark W. Johnson, V.P.
Jack H. Lazzaro, V.P.
David R. Long, V.P.
James G. McFarlane, V.P.
David E. McGurn, Jr., V.P.
Richard J. McKenna, V.P.

John C. Rosengren, V.P. & Gen. Coun.
Richard R. Rothman, V.P.
John D. Stancik, V.P.
Gary M. Van der Voort, V.P.
Warren G. Van der Voort, Jr., V.P.
Carl E. Fasig, Secy.
David B. Hoch, Cont.
Mark P. Strauch, Treas.
Christine D. Greb, Asst. Secy.
Robert F. Mason, Asst. Cont.

Consolidated Balance Sheet   As of December 31, 1996 (000 omitted)

Assets		Liabilities & Stockholders' Equity	
Current assets	$463,940	Current liabilities	$444,742
Net property, plant & equipment	26,001	Other liabilities	11,152
Marketable securities	36,881	*Stockholders' equity	134,530
Non-current assets	52,509		
Other assets	11,093		
Total	$590,424	Total	$590,424

*16,293,000 shares common stock outstanding.

Consolidated Income Statement[a]

Years Ended Dec. 31	Thousands — — — —		Per Share — — — —		Common Stock Price Range Calendar Year
	Revenues	Net Income	Earnings	Cash Dividends	
1996	$456,679	$45,803	$2.63	$1.16	39-1/2 — 29-1/8
1995	439,530	42,545	2.47	1.00	38 — 30-1/8
1994	393,972	37,166	2.16	.88	36-3/8 — 28-1/8
1993	363,359	31,186	1.75	.72	37-3/8 — 25-1/2
1992	327,825	25,029	1.45	.64	29-1/4 — 21

[a]The financial information for all periods prior to 1996 has been restated for significant acquisitions accounted for using the pooling-of-interests method.

Transfer Agent & Registrar:	Harris Trust and Savings Bank		
Outside Counsel:	Lord, Bissell & Brook	Traded (Symbol):	NYSE (AJG)
Investor Relations:	Michael J. Cloherty, Exec. V.P.	Stockholders:	700
Human Resources:	Bette J. Brinkerhoff, V.P.	Employees:	3,939
Mgt. Info. Svcs.:	Nicholas M. Elsberg, V.P.	Annual Meeting:	In May
Auditors:	Ernst & Young LLP	Internet:	www.ajg.com

GATX Corporation

500 West Monroe Street, Chicago, Illinois 60661-3676
Telephone: (312) 621-6200

GATX Corporation is a holding company whose subsidiaries engage in the leasing and management of railroad tank cars and specialized freight cars; provide equipment and capital asset financing and related services; own and operate tank storage terminals, pipelines, and related facilities; engage in Great Lakes shipping; and provide distribution and logistics support services and warehousing facilities. Major subsidiaries include: General American Transportation Corporation, a tank car and specialized railcar lessor; GATX Terminals Corporation, an independent bulk liquid storage and pipeline company; GATX Financial Services, Inc. which, through its principal subsidiary, GATX Capital Corp., is a leading non-bank financial services company; American Steamship Company, which competes with other Great Lakes commercial fleets and with steel companies that operate captive fleets; and GATX Logistics, Inc., a leading full-service third-party provider of warehousing, distribution, and logistics support services. Incorporated in New York in 1916.

Directors (In addition to indicated officers)

James M. Denny
Richard M. Fairbanks
William C. Foote
Deborah M. Fretz

Richard A. Giesen
Miles L. Marsh
Charles Marshall
Michael E. Murphy

Officers (Directors*)

*Ronald H. Zech, Chm., Pres. & C.E.O
David B. Anderson, V.P.—Corp. Dev., Gen. Coun. & Secy.
William L. Chambers, V.P.—Hum. Res.
Gail L. Duddy, V.P.—Compensation & Benefits

David M. Edwards, V.P.—Fin. & C.F.O.
Brian A. Kenney, V.P. & Treas.
Ralph L. O'Hara, Cont.

Consolidated Balance Sheet As of December 31, 1996 (000 omitted)

Assets		Liabilities & Stockholders' Equity	
Cash & receivables	$1,039,100	Accounts payable & accrued expenses	$ 364,300
Net operating lease assets & facilities	2,846,400	Total debt	2,907,900
Other assets	864,700	Deferred items	703,100
		*Stockholders' equity	774,900
Total	$4,750,200	Total	$4,750,200

*20,274,735 shares common stock outstanding.

Consolidated Income Statement

Years Ended Dec. 31	Thousands — — — —		Per Share — — —		Common Stock Price Range Calendar Year
	Gross Income	Net Income	Earnings	Cash Dividends	
1996	$1,414,400	$ 102,700	$ 4.37	$1.72	51-1/4 — 43
1995	1,246,400	100,800	4.30	1.60	54-1/4 — 40-3/8
1994	1,155,000	91,500	3.88	1.50	44-5/8 — 38-1/4
1993	1,086,900	72,700	2.99	1.40	42-1/4 — 31-3/8
1992	1,019,100	(16,500)[a]	(1.53)[a]	1.30	33-3/4 — 24-1/4

[a]Includes a charge to reflect FAS 106 and FAS 109, resulting in a cumulative effect of $45,800,000 ($2.35 per share).

Transfer Agent & Registrar:	ChaseMellon Shareholder Services, L.L.C.			
General Counsel:	David B. Anderson, V.P.	Traded (Symbol):	NYSE, CSE, London (GMT)
Investor Relations:	George S. Lowman, Dir.	Stockholders:	3,774
Human Resources:	William L. Chambers, V.P.	Employees:	6,000
Mgt. Info. Svcs.:	Robert A. Kane, Dir.	Annual Meeting:	In April
Auditors:	Ernst & Young LLP	Internet:	www.gatx.com

Gaylord Container Corporation

500 Lake Cook Road, Suite 400, Deerfield, Illinois 60015-4921
Telephone: (847) 405-5500

Gaylord Container Corporation manufactures and markets corrugated containers, corrugated sheets, containerboard, unbleached kraft paper, and multiwall bags. Facilities include three containerboard and unbleached kraft paper mills, 14 corrugated container plants, three sheet feeder plants, two multiwall bag facilities, one preprint linerboard plant, and marketing operations throughout the United States. Gaylord serves customers in the industrial, agricultural, commercial, and consumer markets. The company's three paper mills use both virgin and recycled fiber to produce linerboard and unbleached kraft paper in a wide variety of grades and weights. Gaylord's corrugated container plants manufacture corrugated shipping containers, and such specialty products as label-laminated and precision die-cut boxes, point-of-purchase and display containers, solid fiber products, and bulk boxes. Gaylord's multiwall bag plants service the agricultural, food, pet supply, pet food, and plastics industries. Incorporated in Delaware in 1986.

Directors (In addition to indicated officers)

Mary Sue Coleman
Harve A. Ferrill
John E. Goodenow
David B. Hawkins
John Hawkinson

Warren J. Hayford
Richard S. Levitt
Ralph L. MacDonald, Jr.
Thomas H. Stoner

Officers (Directors*)

*Marvin A. Pomerantz, Chm. & C.E.O.
Dale E. Stahl, Pres. & C.O.O.
Daniel P. Casey, Exec. V.P. & C.F.O.
Lawrence G. Rogna, Sr. V.P.

Ray C. Dillon, V.P.—Primary Prod. Oper.
Michael J. Keough, V.P.—Container Oper.
Jeffrey B. Park, V.P.—Cont.
David F. Tanaka, V.P., Gen. Coun. & Secy.

Consolidated Balance Sheet As of September 30, 1996 (000 omitted)

Assets		Liabilities & Stockholders' Equity	
Current assets	$236,100	Current liabilities	$166,300
Net property	612,300	Long-term debt	623,100
Other assets	66,000	Other liabilities	29,100
Deferred charges	18,600	*Stockholders' equity	114,500
Total	$933,000	Total	$933,000

*52,688,233 shares common stock outstanding.

Consolidated Income Statement

Years Ended Sept. 30	Thousands — — — — Net Sales	Net Income	Per Share — — — — Earnings	Cash Dividends	Common Stock Price Range[a] Calendar Year
1996	$ 922,000	$ 8,600	$ .16	$ .00	11-1/2 — 5-3/8
1995	1,051,400	134,200	2.44	.00	15-1/2 — 7-1/8
1994	784,400	(84,000)	(1.57)	.00	9-3/4 — 4-3/8
1993	733,500	130,200[b]	2.61[b]	.00	4-3/4 — 1-7/8
1992	722,800	(132,500)	(8.54)	.00	4-7/8 — 2-3/8

[a]Class A common stock.
[b]Includes an extraordinary gain of $201,500,000 ($4.04 per share) on the retirement of subordinated debt in connection with a financial restructuring.

Transfer Agent & Registrar: Harris Trust and Savings Bank

General Counsel:	Kirkland & Ellis	Traded (Symbol):	AMEX (GCR)
Human Resources:	Lawrence G. Rogna, Sr. V.P.	Stockholders:	725
Mgt. Info. Svcs.:	Paul Gross, Dir.	Employees:	3,900
Auditors:	Deloitte & Touche LLP	Annual Meeting:	In February

General Binding Corporation
One GBC Plaza, Northbrook, Illinois 60062-4195
Telephone: (847) 272-3700

General Binding Corporation (GBC) designs, manufactures, and distributes a broad line of business machines and related supplies. Products manufactured include binding and laminating machines, paper shredders, visual communication products, and photo identification systems. GBC also manufactures consumable supply items, including: plastic bindings, customized binders, laminating films, standard and specialty metal looseleaf elements, and plastic sheeting for covers and binders. GBC products are marketed under the GBC, Quartet, Shredmaster, U.S. RingBinder, Bates, Sickinger, GBC Pro-Tech, Fordigraph, and VeloBind names. International operations are located in Australia, Austria, Belgium, Canada, France, Germany, India, Italy, Japan, Mexico, the Netherlands, New Zealand, Spain, Switzerland, and the United Kingdom. Subsidiaries include U.S. RingBinder Corp. In January 1997, the company purchased the assets and business of Quartet Manufacturing Company, located in Skokie, Illinois. In April 1997, GBC completed its acquisition of Baker School Specialty Co., Inc., an Orange, Massachusetts-based manufacturer and distributor of office and school supplies. Incorporated in Delaware in 1947.

Directors   (In addition to indicated officers)

Harry J. Bruce	Thomas V. Kalebic
Richard U. De Schutter	Arthur C. Nielsen, Jr.
Theodore Dimitriou	Warren R. Rothwell
Rudolph Grua	Robert J. Stucker

Officers   (Directors*)

*William N. Lane III, Chm.
*Govi C. Reddy, Pres. & C.E.O.
Walter M. Hebb, Sr. V.P.—Asia & Pacific Oper.
Elliott L. Smith, Sr. V.P.—Americas
Eugene J. Angel, V.P. & Pres.—U.S. RingBinder Corp.
Govind K. Arora, V.P.—Document Lamin. Div.
Stephen Firth, V.P.—European Oper.
William P. Heffernan, V.P.—Mergers & Acquis.
Joseph J. LaPorte, V.P.—Corp. Rel.
Edward J. McNulty, V.P. & C.F.O.

Steven Rubin, V.P., Secy. & Gen. Coun.
Thomas F. Gueth, V.P.—Auto. Finishing Div.
James E. Guither, V.P.—GBC Pro-Tech
Richard A. McCallion, V.P.—Desktop Bind. Div.
Robert F. Neuschel, V.P.—Custom Supplies
Robert C. O'Connor, V.P.—Film Prod. Div.
Wally G. Schnell, Jr., V.P.—Bus. Tech.
Charles K. Shattuck, V.P.—Bus. Dev.
Robert Zanchelli, V.P.—N. Amer. Sales
Richard R. Gilbert, Pres.—Quartet Mfg. Co.
Howard B. Green, Grp. Pres.—Off. Prod.

Consolidated Balance Sheet   As of December 31, 1996 (000 omitted)

Assets		Liabilities & Stockholders' Equity	
Current assets	$237,214	Current liabilities	$112,129
Net property, plant & equipment	69,011	Long-term debt	87,029
Other assets	87,481	Deferred items	12,187
		Other liabilities	10,229
		*Stockholders' equity	172,132
Total	$393,706	Total	$393,706

*15,749,879 shares common and 2,398,275 shares Class B common stock outstanding.

Consolidated Income Statement

Years Ended Dec. 31	Thousands — — — — Net Sales	Net Income[a]	Per Share — — — Earnings[a]	Cash Dividends	Common Stock Price Range Calendar Year
1996	$536,836	$25,213	$1.60	$ .43	30-3/4 — 19-1/4
1995	458,391	21,500	1.37	.42	23 — 14-1/4
1994	420,449	15,703	1.00	.41	22 — 14-3/8
1993	376,138	14,994	.95	.40	19-1/4 — 11-1/2
1992	368,643	16,380	1.04	.37	21-1/2 — 14-1/2

[a]From continuing operations.

Transfer Agent & Registrar:	Harris Trust and Savings Bank		
Corporate Counsel:	Steven Rubin, V.P.	Traded (Symbol):	NASDAQ (GBND)
Investor Relations:	Joseph J. LaPorte, V.P.	Stockholders:	796
Human Resources:	Perry Zukowski, Asst. V.P.	Employees:	3,226
Mgt. Info. Svcs.:	Wally G. Schnell, Jr., V.P.	Annual Meeting:	In May
Auditors:	Arthur Andersen LLP	Internet:	www.generalbinding.com

General Employment Enterprises, Inc.

Oakbrook Terrace Tower, One Tower Lane, Suite 2100, Oakbrook Terrace, Illinois 60181-4600
Telephone: (630) 954-0400

General Employment Enterprises, Inc. provides contract temporary staffing and permanent placement services for business and industry. Its 34 branch offices are located strategically in major metropolitan and suburban business centers in 13 states. The company's wholly owned subsidiary, Triad Personnel Services, Inc., provides clients with information systems employees and technical personnel for contract temporary assignments. Operating under the trade styles General Employment, Business Management Personnel, and Omni One, the company also specializes in the placement of regular, full-time computer, engineering, technical, and accounting personnel. These placements range from entry-level trainee to senior-level management positions. Incorporated in Illinois in 1962.

Directors (In addition to indicated officers)

Sheldon Brottman
Leonard Chavin
Delain G. Danehey

Walter T. Kerwin, Jr.
Howard S. Wilcox

Officers (Directors*)

*Herbert F. Imhoff, Chm. & C.E.O.
*Herbert F. Imhoff, Jr., Pres., C.O.O. & Gen. Coun.
Gregory Chrisos, V.P.—Triad Personnel Services, Inc.

Nancy C. Frohnmaier, V.P. & Corp. Secy.
Marilyn L. White, V.P.—Perm. Placement Oper.
Kent M. Yauch, C.F.O. & Treas.

Consolidated Balance Sheet   As of September 30, 1996 (000 omitted)

Assets		Liabilities & Stockholders' Equity	
Current assets	$8,810	Current liabilities	$4,400
Net property & equipment	361	Other liabilities	375
Other assets	410	*Stockholders' equity	4,806
Total	$9,581	Total	$9,581

*2,652,000 shares common stock outstanding.

Consolidated Income Statement

Years Ended Sept. 30	Thousands — — — — Net Revenues	Net Income	Per Share[a] — — — — Earnings	Cash Dividends	Common Stock Price Range[a] Fiscal Year
1996	$23,241	$ 1,641	$ .63	$ .04	16-1/4 — 4-1/4
1995	16,744	1,068	.42	.00	8-3/4 — 3-7/8
1994	14,196	663	.26	.00	3-7/8 — 1-1/4
1993	10,851	61	.03	.00	3 — 1-7/8
1992	10,189	(605)	(.25)	.00	1-3/4 — 7/8

[a]Adjusted to reflect 15% stock dividends paid in November 1996, 1995, and 1994.

Transfer Agent & Registrar: Continental Stock Transfer & Trust Co.

General Counsel: Herbert F. Imhoff, Jr., Pres.

Investor Relations: Doris A. Cooper, Comm. Mgr.

Human Resources: Sherry L. Hubacek

Mgt. Info. Svcs.:   Alex J. Mitre

Auditors: Ernst & Young LLP
Traded (Symbol):   AMEX (JOB)
Stockholders: 1,064
Employees: 360
Annual Meeting: In February

General Instrument Corporation

8770 West Bryn Mawr Avenue, Suite 1300, Chicago, Illinois 60631
Telephone: (773) 695-1000

General Instrument Corporation (GI) is a leading developer of technology, systems, and product solutions for the interactive delivery of video, voice, and data. On January 7, 1997, the company announced that it will restructure into three separate companies, each a leader in its distinct global growth markets. NextLevel Systems, Inc., to be headquartered at GI's current address in Chicago, will emerge as a leading worldwide supplier of systems and components for high-performance networks delivering video, voice, and Internet/data services in the cable, satellite, and telephony markets. CommScope, Inc., based in Hickory, North Carolina, is the world's leading supplier of coaxial cable and high-performance electronic cables. General Semiconductor, Inc., currently GI's Power Semiconductor Division, is headquartered in Melville, New York. It is the world's leading supplier of low-to-medium power rectifiers and transient surge suppressors. The restructuring will give the management of each business the ability to focus on its own markets, customer requirements, and growth opportunities. The restructuring is expected to be completed in the summer of 1997. Incorporated in Delaware in 1990.

Directors   (In addition to indicated officers)

John Seely Brown	Theodore J. Forstmann	J. Tracy O'Rourke
Lynn Forester	Steven B. Klinsky	Felix G. Rohatyn
Nicholas C. Forstmann	Alex J. Mandl	

Officers   (Directors*)

*Richard S. Friedland, Chm. & C.E.O.
Richard D. Badler, V.P.—Commun.
Michael R. Bernique, V.P. & Pres.—Satellite Data
Paul J. Berzenski, V.P. & Cont.
Edward D. Breen, V.P. & Pres.—Broadband Networks
Gardham W. Comb, V.P.—Internal Audit
Charles T. Dickson, V.P. & C.F.O.
Thomas A. Dumit, V.P., Gen. Coun. & C.A.O.

Susan M. Meyer, V.P. & Secy.
Ronald A. Ostertag, V.P. & Pres.—Power Semiconductor Div.
Kenneth R. Pelowski, V.P.—Corp. Dev.
Quincy Rodgers, V.P.—Govt. Aff.
Geoffrey S. Roman, V.P.
Richard C. Smith, V.P.—Taxes & Treas.
Clark E. Tucker, V.P.—Hum. Res.
*Frank M. Drendel, Pres. & C.E.O.—CommScope Div.

Consolidated Balance Sheet   As of December 31, 1996 (000 omitted)

Assets		Liabilities & Stockholders' Equity	
Current assets	$1,083,085	Current liabilities	$ 534,720
Net property, plant & equipment	571,051	Long-term debt	698,825
Other assets	1,052,715	Deferred items	21,457
		Other liabilities	278,696
		*Stockholders' equity	1,173,153
Total	$2,706,851	Total	$2,706,851

*136,912,885 shares common stock outstanding.

Consolidated Income Statement

Years Ended Dec. 31	Thousands Net Sales	Thousands Net Income	Per Share[a] Earnings	Per Share[a] Cash Dividends	Common Stock Price Range[a] Calendar Year
1996	$2,689,688	$ 148,936[b]	$ 1.09[b]	$ .00	34-3/8 — 18-1/8
1995	2,432,024	213,782[c]	1.72[c]	.00	41-5/8 — 18-1/4
1994	2,036,323	216,535[d]	1.76[d]	.00	34-5/8 — 21-1/4
1993	1,392,522	90,583	.74	.00	30-1/8 — 11-5/8
1992	1,074,695	(41,395)[e]	(.42)[e]	.00	13 — 5-3/4[f]

[a]Adjusted to reflect a 2-for-1 stock split in August 1994.
[b]Excludes charges totaling $150,800,000 ($1.14 per share) due to the company's plan to separate into three independent companies; Next Level litigation costs; and other charges primarily related to the transition to the company's next-generation digital products and the writedown of certain assets.
[c]Excludes a net one-time charge of $90,000,000 ($.72 per share) for purchased in-process technology related to the acquisition of Next Level Communications.
[d]Excludes an income tax benefit of $30,000,000 ($.24 per share) as a result of a reduction in a valuation allowance related to deferred income tax assets.
[e]Excludes an extraordinary charge of $11,598,000 ($.12 per share) related to the early extinguishment of debt.
[f]Initial public offering in June 1992.

Transfer Agent & Registrar: Chase Mellon Shareholder Services, L.L.C.

Outside Counsel:
  Fried, Frank, Harris, Shriver & Jacobson

Investor Relations: Charles T. Dickson, V.P.

Human Resources: Clark E. Tucker, V.P.

Auditors: Deloitte & Touche LLP

Traded (Symbol):	NYSE (GIC)
Stockholders:	899
Employees:	14,200
Annual Meeting:	In July
Internet:	www.gi.com

LaSalle Banks Guide

The Goodheart-Willcox Company, Inc.

18604 West Creek Drive, Tinley Park, Illinois 60477
Telephone: (708) 687-5000

The Goodheart-Willcox Company, Inc. publishes textbooks and workbooks for junior and senior high schools; vocational, technical and private trade schools; and colleges and universities. Its books are also used for apprentice training, adult education, home study, and do-it-yourselfers. Current catalogs list approximately 375 texts, workbooks, computer software supplements, and instructor's guides published by the company. Publishing activities encompass the search for and development of authors in the preparation of their product, editing manuscripts, designing textbooks, arranging for art work and illustrations, typesetting the manuscript, contracting for printing and binding, and marketing its textbooks. The company's subsidiary is G/W Investment Company, Inc. Incorporated in Delaware in 1972.

Directors (In addition to indicated officers)

Walter C. Brown, Ed.D.
Robert C. DeBolt
Wilma Pitts Griffin, Ph.D.

Clois E. Kicklighter, Ed.D.
Loraine J. Mix

Officers (Directors*)

*John F. Flanagan, Pres. & C.E.O.
Donald A. Massucci, V.P.—Admin. & Treas.

Dick G. Snyder, V.P.—Sales & Secy.

Consolidated Balance Sheet As of April 30, 1997 (000 omitted)

Assets		Liabilities & Stockholders' Equity	
Current assets	$ 7,679	Current liabilities	$ 2,718
Net property, plant & equipment	4,769	Deferred items	169
Other assets	1,617	Long-term debt	2,605
		*Stockholders' equity	8,573
Total	$14,065	Total	$14,065

*584,700 shares common stock outstanding.

Consolidated Income Statement

Years Ended April 30	Thousands — — — — Net Sales	Net Income	Per Share — — — Earnings	Cash Dividends	Common Stock Price Range Fiscal Year
1997	$16,631	$2,775	$3.75	$ .90	45-3/4 — 26
1996	14,645	1,596	2.13	.80	27 — 21
1995	14,708	2,017	2.70	.80	22 — 17
1994	12,641	1,357	1.81	.70	20 — 16
1993	11,873	1,220	1.63	.60	26 — 18

Transfer Agent & Registrar: The First National Bank of Chicago

General Counsel:
Hedberg, Tobin, Flaherty & Whalen

Investor Relations: John F. Flanagan, Pres.

Human Resources: John F. Flanagan, Pres.

Mgt. Info. Svcs.:   Donald A. Massucci, V.P.

Auditors: Grant Thornton LLP

Traded (Symbol):   NASDAQ (GWOX)

Stockholders: 150

Employees: 50

Annual Meeting: In July

W.W. Grainger, Inc.
455 Knightsbridge Parkway, Lincolnshire, Illinois 60069-3620
Telephone: (847) 793-9030

W.W. Grainger, Inc. is a leader in the distribution of maintenance, repair, and operating supplies, and related information to the commercial, industrial, contractor, and institutional markets in North America. The company's core business, Grainger, distributes air compressors, air-conditioning and refrigeration equipment and components, air tools, and paint spraying equipment. Other products include blowers, electric motors, fans, gas engine-driven power plants, gearmotors, heating equipment, and controls. Additional products are hydraulic equipment, janitorial supplies, lighting fixtures and components, liquid pumps, material handling and storage equipment, motor controls, office equipment, outdoor equipment, and plant and office maintenance equipment. An important selling tool, the General Catalog, contains more than 78,000 items. Grainger is also an important resource for both product and procurement process information. The company operates a national distribution center in Niles, Illinois, and regional distribution centers in Kansas City, Missouri, and Greenville County, South Carolina. The company also operates zone distribution centers in Carol Stream, Illinois; Ontario, California; Atlanta, Georgia; Arlington, Texas; Cranbury, New Jersey; and Macedonia, Ohio, and a network of 349 branches in all 50 states, Puerto Rico, and Mexico. The company's other businesses include Acklands - Grainger Inc., Canada's largest nationwide distributor of broad line industrial supplies; Lab Safety Supply, Inc., a leader in business-to-business direct marketing of safety products; and Parts Company of America, a distributor of repair and replacement parts. Incorporated in Illinois in 1928.

Directors   (In addition to indicated officers)

George R. Baker	Wilbur H. Gantz	James D. Slavik	Fred L. Turner
Robert E. Elberson	John W. McCarter, Jr.	Harold B. Smith	Janiece S. Webb

Officers   (Directors*)

* David W. Grainger, Chm.
* Richard L. Keyser, Pres. & C.E.O.
* Jere D. Fluno, V. Chm.
James M. Baisley, Sr. V.P., Gen. Coun. & Secy.
Donald E. Bielinski, Sr. V.P.—Mktg. & Sales
Wesley M. Clark, Sr. V.P.—Oper. & Qual.
P. Ogden Loux, Sr. V.P.—Fin. & C.F.O.
John W. Slayton, Jr., Sr. V.P.—Prod. Mgmt.
Rick L. Adams, V.P. & Pres.—Parts Co. of Amer.
Yang C. Chen, V.P.—Asia Pacific
Barbara M. Chilson, V.P. & Gen. Mgr.—Elect. Commerce
Timothy M. Ferrarell, V.P.—Mktg.
Gary J. Goberville, V.P.—Hum. Res.
Dennis G. Jensen, V.P.—Field Oper.
Michael R. Kight, V.P. & Gen. Mgr.—Dir. Sales

Fred E. Loepp, V.P.—Prod. Line Oper.
Larry J. Loizzo, V.P. & Pres.—Lab Safety Supply, Inc.
Micheal G. Murray, V.P.—Adm. Svcs.
Robert D. Pappano, V.P.—Fin. Rept./Inv. Rel.
Richard D. Quast, V.P.—Real Estate
John J. Rozwat, V.P.
James T. Ryan, V.P.—Info. Svcs.
John A. Schweig, V.P. & Gen. Mgr.—Bus. Dev./Intl.
James M. Tenzillo, V.P. & Gen. Mgr.—Dir. Mktg.
Robert A. Thrush, V.P.—Prod. Line Dev.
Peter J. Torrenti, V.P. & Gen. Mgr.—Integ. Supply
Paul J. Wallace, V.P.—Fin. Svcs.
Douglas E. Witt, V.P.—Natl. Accts.
Philip M. West, Treas.
Douglas C. Cummings, Pres.—Acklands - Granger Inc.

Consolidated Balance Sheet   As of December 31, 1996 (000 omitted)

Assets		Liabilities & Stockholders' Equity	
Current assets	$1,320,243	Current liabilities	$ 616,068
Net property, plant & equipment	550,984	Long-term debt	6,152
Other assets	247,794	Deferred items	2,207
		Other liabilities	31,932
		* Stockholders' equity	1,462,662
Total	$2,119,021	Total	$2,119,021

*52,928,426 shares common stock outstanding.

Consolidated Income Statement

Years Ended Dec. 31	Thousands — — — — Net Sales	Net Income	Per Share — — — Earnings	Cash Dividends	Common Stock Price Range Calendar Year
1996	$3,537,207	$208,526	$4.04	$ .98	81-1/2 — 62-5/8
1995	3,276,910	186,665	3.64	.89	67-5/8 — 55-1/2
1994	3,023,076	127,874[a]	2.50[a]	.78	69-1/8 — 51-1/2
1993	2,628,398	148,447[b]	2.86[b]	.71	66-3/4 — 51-5/8
1992	2,364,421	137,242	2.58	.65	61 — 39

[a]Includes restructuring charges of $49,779,000 ($.97 per share).
[b]Includes a charge to reflect FAS 106, FAS 109 and FAS 112, with a cumulative effect of $820,000 ($.02 per share).

Transfer Agent & Registrar:	The First National Bank of Boston		
Corporate Counsel:	Lord, Bissell & Brook	Traded (Symbol):	NYSE, CSE (GWW)
Investor Relations:	Robert D. Pappano, V.P.	Stockholders:	2,000
Human Resources:	Gary J. Goberville, V.P.	Employees:	14,601
Mgt. Info. Svcs.:	James T. Ryan, V.P.	Annual Meeting:	Last Wednesday in April
Auditors:	Grant Thornton LLP	Internet:	www.grainger.com

Grand Premier Financial, Inc.

486 West Liberty Street, Wauconda, Illinois 60084-2489
Telephone: (847) 487-1818

Grand Premier Financial, Inc. is a registered bank holding company whose operations consist primarily of financial activities common to the commercial banking industry, including trust and investment services, data processing, electronic banking services, and insurance. The primary function of the company is to coordinate the operations and policies of its subsidiaries: Grand National Bank; Grand Premier Trust and Investment, Inc. N.A.; Grand Premier Insurance, Inc.; and Grand Premier Operating Systems, Inc. The company operates 34 general sales offices in northern Illinois under its banking charter. These offices provide a full array of financial services and products to individuals, businesses, local governmental units, and institutional customers. Grand Premier Operating Systems, Inc. provides data processing and operational services to the company and its subsidiaries. Grand Premier Insurance Services, Inc. is a full line casualty and life insurance agency. Grand Premier Trust and Investment, Inc. N.A. provides a full line of fiduciary and investment services throughout the company's general market area. Incorporated in Delaware in 1976; reincorporated in Delaware in 1996; present name adopted in 1996.

Directors   (In addition to indicated officers)

Jean M. Barry	Thomas D. Flanagan	H. Barry Musgrove
Frank J. Callero	R. Gerald Fox	Joseph C. Piland
Brenton J. Emerick	Edward G. Maris	Stephen J. Schostok
James Esposito	Howard A. McKee	John Simcic

Officers   (Directors*)

*Richard L. Geach, Chm. & C.E.O.
*Robert W. Hinman, Pres. & C.O.O.
*David L. Murray, Sr. Exec. V.P. & C.F.O.
*Alan J. Emerick, Exec. V.P. & Chf. Adm. Off.
 William T. Theobald, Exec. V.P. & Chf. Credit Off.
 Larry W. O'Hara, Sr. V.P. & Dir.—Mktg.

Kenneth A. Urban, Pres.—Grand Premier Trust & Invest., Inc. N.A.
Scott Dixon, Reg. Pres.
Jack J. Emerick, Reg. Pres.
Joseph E. Esposito, Reg. Pres.
Reid L. French, Reg. Pres.
Ralph M. Zicco, Reg. Pres.

Consolidated Balance Sheet   As of December 31, 1996 (000 omitted)

Assets		Liabilities & Stockholders' Equity	
Cash & cash equivalents	$ 65,955	Deposits	$1,417,394
Investment securities	540,092	Short-term borrowings	23,486
Net loans	955,366	Long-term borrowings	30,000
Bank premises & equipment	33,321	Other liabilities	13,569
Other assets	47,804	*Stockholders' equity	158,089
Total	$1,642,538	Total	$1,642,538

*19,983,679 shares common stock outstanding.

Consolidated Income Statement

Years Ended Dec. 31	Thousands — — — — Interest Income	Net Income	Per Share[a] — — — — Earnings	Cash Dividends	Common Stock Price Range[a] Calendar Year
1996	$114,370	$13,317	$ .62	$ .27	13 — 8-1/4
1995	108,782	17,029	.79	.19	9-3/4 — 6-1/2
1994	92,166	13,344	.60	.18	8-1/4 — 5-7/8
1993	84,801	12,296	.59	.16	7-7/8 — 6-1/8
1992	86,422	10,600	.53	.15	8-3/8 — 4-3/8

[a]Adjusted to reflect a 200 percent stock dividend declared in May 1994 and a 10 percent stock dividend declared in 1992.

Transfer Agent & Registrar: Grand Premier Trust and Investment, Inc. N.A.

General Counsel: Schiff, Hardin & Waite

Investor Relations:
 David L. Murray, Sr. Exec. V.P.

Auditors: KPMG Peat Marwick LLP

Traded (Symbol):   NASDAQ (GPFI)

Stockholders: 1,231

Employees: 690

Annual Meeting: In May

Great American Bancorp, Inc.
1311 South Neil Street, Champaign, Illinois 61820
Telephone: (217) 356-2265

Great American Bancorp, Inc. is the holding company for First Federal Savings Bank of Champaign-Urbana, which conducts business from its administrative and branch office located in Champaign, Illinois, and its two branch offices. The bank is a community-oriented savings institution whose business consists primarily of accepting deposits from customers within its market area, and investing those funds in mortgage loans secured by one- to four-family residences. In June 1995, the company completed an initial public offering of 2,052,750 shares of common stock. Incorporated in Delaware in 1995.

Directors   (In addition to indicated officers)

Dr. Morgan C. Powell, Chm.
James S. Acheson

Clinton C. Atkins
Ronald Kiddoo

Officers   (Directors*)

*George R. Rouse, Pres. & C.E.O.

Jane F. Adams, C.F.O., Secy. & Treas.

Consolidated Balance Sheet   As of December 31, 1996 (000 omitted)

Assets		Liabilities & Stockholders' Equity	
Cash & equivalents	$ 26,410	Deposits	$100,714
Investment securities	3,400	Other liabilities	1,193
Net loans	91,443	*Stockholders' equity	30,462
Net property, plant & equipment	7,306		
Other assets	3,810		
Total	$132,369	Total	$132,369

*1,671,691 shares common stock outstanding.

Consolidated Income Statement

Years Ended Dec. 31	Thousands — — — —		Per Share[a] — — —		Common Stock Price Range[a] Calendar Year
	Total Income	Net Income	Earnings[b]	Cash Dividends	
1996[c]	$11,448	$ 534	$ .27	$ .58	15-1/4 — 13
1995[d]	8,487	753	.37	.00	14-3/4 — 11-3/4
1994[d]	7,665	729			
1993[d]	8,602	1,065			
1992[d]	9,760	688			

[a]Initial public offering in June 1995.
[b]Fully diluted.
[c]Fifteen months ended December 31. In November 1995, the company changed to calendar year reporting.
[d]Twelve months ended September 30.

Transfer Agent & Registrar:	American Securities Transfer and Trust, Inc.		
General Counsel:	Muldoon, Murphy & Faucette	Traded (Symbol):	NASDAQ (GTPS)
		Stockholders:	473
Investor Relations:	Jane F. Adams, C.F.O.	Employees:	67
Auditors:	Geo. S. Olive & Co., LLC	Annual Meeting:	In April

Grubb & Ellis Company

2215 Sanders Road, Suite 400, Northbrook, Illinois 60062
Telephone: (847) 753-9010

Grubb & Ellis Company is one of the nation's largest full-service commercial real estate firms, with offices in 65 markets nationwide. The company's wholly owned subsidiary, Axiom Real Estate Management, Inc., provides property and facility management services, and is one of the largest property management firms in the United States, with over 90 million square feet of property under management. The company also has its own representative office in London. In January 1997, the company relocated to Northbrook from San Francisco, California. Incorporated in Delaware in 1980 as successor to a firm established in 1958.

Directors (In addition to indicated officers)

R. David Anacker
Lawrence S. Bacow
Joe F. Hanauer
C. Michael Kojaian
Sidney Lapidus

Reuben S. Leibowitz
Robert J. McLaughlin
John D. Santoleri
Todd A. Williams

Officers (Directors*)

*Neil Young, Chm., Pres. & C.E.O.
Brian Parker, Sr. V.P. & C.F.O.
Phillip D. Royster, Sr. V.P.
Robert J. Walner, Sr. V.P., Gen. Coun. & Secy.

Michael P. McKiernan, Pres.—Commer. Brokerage Oper., Eastern U.S.
Donald D. Morrow, Pres.—Commer. Brokerage Oper., Western U.S.
Steven F. Pope, Pres.—Grubb & Ellis Affiliates
Steven D. Scruggs, Pres.—Corp. & Inst. Svcs.

Consolidated Balance Sheet   As of June 30, 1996 (000 omitted)

Assets		Liabilities & Stockholders' Equity	
Current assets	$22,735	Current liabilities	$ 16,450
Net equipment and leasehold improvements	5,194	Long-term debt	27,850
		Other liabilities	12,833
Other assets	1,729	*Stockholders' equity	(27,475)
Total	$29,658	Total	$ 29,658

*8,916,415 shares common stock outstanding.

Consolidated Income Statement

Years Ended June 30	Thousands — — — — Net Sales	Net Income[a]	Per Share[b] — — — Earnings	Cash Dividends	Common Stock Price Range[b] Calendar Year
1996	$193,728	$ (910)[c]	$ (.10)	$ .00	5-1/4 — 1-7/8
1995	185,784	(1,183)[c]	(.16)	.00	2-3/4 — 1-7/8
1994	185,182	(20,034)[d]	(4.92)	.00	4-1/4 — 1-5/8
1993[e]	207,410	(59,184)[d]	(15.66)	.00	8 — 1-7/8
1992[e]	240,323	(49,317)[d]	(14.54)	.00	12-1/2 — 4-3/8

[a]After the accrual of dividends applicable to preferred stockholders in the amounts of $3,012,000 in 1996, $2,739,000 in 1995, $2,494,000 in 1994, and $998,000 in 1993.
[b]Adjusted to reflect a 1-for-5 reverse stock split in January 1993.
[c]Includes favorable adjustments relating to special charges and unusual items in the amounts of $462,000 in 1996 and $2,600,000 in 1995.
[d]Includes expenses related to special charges and unusual items in the amounts of $13,200,000 in 1994, $44,900,000 in 1993, and $37,000,000 in 1992.
[e]Unaudited.

Transfer Agent & Registrar: Harris Trust Company of California

General Counsel:	Robert J. Walner, Sr. V.P.	Traded (Symbol):	NYSE, PSE (GBE)
Investor Relations:	Mark R. Friedlander, Dir.	Stockholders:	2,367
Human Resources:	Vince Ristucci, V.P.	Employees:	3,700
Mgt. Info. Svcs.:	Arthur Przbyl, Dir.—Info. Tech.	Annual Meeting:	In November
Auditors:	Ernst & Young LLP	Internet:	www.grubb-ellis.com

HA-LO Industries, Inc.

5980 Touhy Avenue, Niles, Illinois 60714
Telephone: (847) 647-2300

HA-LO Industries, Inc. is a distributor in the specialty and premium advertising products industry. The company's revenue base largely comprises Fortune 500 companies, professional sports teams, and other organizations with high name recognition. Specialty and premium advertising products are generally articles of merchandise imprinted or otherwise customized with an advertiser's name, logo, or message, and used by the advertiser for marketing, sales incentives and awards, and development of goodwill for a targeted audience. Because such products are designed to be useful to the recipient, messages imprinted on these products enjoy repeated exposure. Examples of these products include jackets, hats, T-shirts, calendars, pens, coffee mugs, key chains, and more upscale items such as crystalware and desk accessories. The company functions as a single source to meet its customers' needs for specialty and premium advertising products. HA-LO utilizes its in-house art and production departments to assist its customers in creating innovative programs. Major divisions include Ha-Lo Sports, Events by HA-LO, Market USA, and Duncan & Hill. In January 1997, the company completed its acquisition of Creative Concepts in Advertising, Inc., a Beverly Hills, Michigan-based specialty advertising products distributor. Incorporated in Illinois in 1986.

Directors   (In addition to indicated officers)

David Hermelin
Thomas Herskovits
Jordan R. Katz

Marshall J. Katz
Seymour N. Okner
Neil A. Ramo

Officers   (Directors*)

*Lou Weisbach, Chm., Pres. & C.E.O.
*Linden Nelson, V. Chm.
*David C. Robbins, Exec. V.P.
Barbara G. Berman, V.P.—Retail Accts. & Secy.
David Blumenthal, V.P.—Info. Sys.
Gene Eherenfeldt, V.P.—Sales

Sabina Filipovic, V.P.—Hum. Rel. & Asst. Secy.
Barry Margolin, V.P.—Fin., Cont. & Asst. Secy.
Michael P. Nemlich, V.P.—Corp. Dev. & Fin. Rel.
Gregory J. Kilrea, C.F.O.
*Richard A. Magid, C.O.O.

Consolidated Balance Sheet   As of December 31, 1996 (000 omitted)

Assets		Liabilities & Stockholders' Equity	
Current assets	$68,215	Current liabilities	$25,730
Net property, plant & equipment	9,682	Deferred items	4,657
Other assets	9,737	*Stockholders' equity	57,247
Total	$87,634	Total	$87,634

*16,756,109 shares common stock outstanding.

Consolidated Income Statement

Years Ended Dec. 31	Thousands — — — — Net Sales	Net Income	Per Share[a] — — — Earnings	Cash Dividends	Common Stock Price Range[a] Calendar Year
1996	$254,888	$9,369[b]	$ .53[b]	$ .00	32-1/4 — 10-3/4
1995	211,266	4,673[c]	.33[c]	.00	16-3/8 — 3-1/4
1994	145,821	3,924[c]	.32[c]	.00	4-1/8 — 2-5/8
1993	104,954	1,867[c]	.16[c]	.00	3-3/4 — 2
1992	99,755	3,007[c]	.31[c]	.00	4 — 3

[a]Adjusted to reflect a 2,776.428-for-1 stock split in September 1992, a 3-for-2 stock split in June 1996, and a 25 percent stock dividend in December 1996.
[b]Includes a non-recurring after-tax charge of $1,016,000 ($.05 per share) related to the Market USA acquisition in September 1996.
[c]Pro forma. HA-LO elected to be treated as an S corporation for federal income tax purposes through the initial public offering completed on November 4, 1992. Accordingly, the company was not subject to federal income taxes for such periods. Additionally, acquisitions completed in September 1996 and December 1995, and accounted for as pooling-of-interests, also had to be treated as S corporations. Pro forma net income and earnings per share include an unaudited provision for federal and state taxes at an effective rate of 38 percent in 1992 and 40 percent thereafter.

Transfer Agent & Registrar: Harris Trust and Savings Bank

General Counsel:	Neal Gerber & Eisenberg	Traded (Symbol):	NASDAQ (HALO)
Investor Relations:	Michael P. Nemlich, V.P.	Stockholders:	680
Human Resources:	Sabina Filipovic, V.P.	Employees:	2,300
Mgt. Info. Svcs.:	David Blumenthal, V.P.	Annual Meeting:	In June
Auditors:	Arthur Andersen LLP	Internet:	www.ha-lo.com

Hartmarx Corporation

101 North Wacker Drive, Chicago, Illinois 60606-7389
Telephone: (312) 372-6300

Hartmarx Corporation is the holding company for Hart Schaffner & Marx and other subsidiaries. Hartmarx manufactures and markets quality clothing, including men's suits, sportcoats and slacks, men's and women's sportswear and golfwear, and women's career apparel. In addition to Hart Schaffner & Marx, men's apparel is sold under the following labels: Hickey-Freeman, Graham & Gunn, Pierre Cardin, Society Brand Ltd., Tommy Hilfiger, Austin Reed, Palm Beach, Evan Picone, Burberry's, Henry Grethel, Jack Nicklaus, Bobby Jones, Gieves & Hawkes, Perry Ellis, Daniel Hechter, Nicklaus, Fumagalli's, Nino Cerruti, KM by Krizia, Confezioni Riserva, Wimbledon by Racquet Club, Allyn St. George, Sansabelt, John Alexander, and J.G. Hook. Women's apparel is sold under the following labels: Barrie Pace, Austin Reed, Hawksley & Wight, Suburbans, Nicklaus for Women, and Bobby Jones for Women. Hartmarx subsidiaries operate 23 apparel manufacturing and distribution facilities in 11 states and two countries (Costa Rica and Mexico). In November 1996, Hartmarx completed the acquisition of Plaid Clothing Group Inc. of New York. Incorporated in Delaware in 1983.

Directors (In addition to indicated officers)

A. Robert Abboud
Samawal A. Bakhsh
Jeffrey A. Cole
Raymond F. Farley

Donald P. Jacobs
Charles Marshall
Michael B. Rohlfs
Stuart L. Scott

Officers (Directors*)

*Elbert O. Hand, Chm. & C.E.O.
*Homi B. Patel, Pres. & C.O.O.
Glenn R. Morgan, Exec. V.P. & C.F.O.
Frederick G. Wohlschlaeger, Sr. V.P., Gen. Coun. & Secy.

Frank A. Brenner, V.P.—Mkt. Services
James E. Condon, V.P. & Treas.
Linda J. Valentine, V.P.—Comp. & Ben.
Andrew A. Zahr, Cont.

Consolidated Balance Sheet As of November 30, 1996 (000 omitted)

Assets		Liabilities & Stockholders' Equity	
Current assets	$320,466	Current liabilities	$119,845
Net property, plant & equipment	43,909	Long-term debt	148,428
Deferred income taxes	43,285	*Stockholders' equity	161,966
Other assets	22,579		
Total	$430,239	Total	$430,239

*33,365,317 shares common stock outstanding.

Consolidated Income Statement

Years Ended Nov. 30	Thousands — — — — Net Sales[a]	Net Income[b]	Per Share — — — Earnings[b]	Cash Dividends	Common Stock Price Range Calendar Year
1996	$610,180 ·	$ 24,555	$ .74	$ .00	6-1/2 — 3-3/4
1995	595,272	3,147	.10	.00	6-7/8 — 4-1/4
1994	621,847	16,148	.50	.00	7-3/8 — 5
1993	606,148	6,220	.20	.00	8-1/4 — 5-1/8
1992	684,171	(220,245)	(8.59)	.00	8-5/8 — 3

[a]1994 and prior years restated to reflect the company's former retail businesses (Kuppenheimer, HSSI Inc., and Country Miss retail) as discontinued operations.
[b]1994 includes an extraordinary charge, net of tax benefit, of $3,862,000 ($.12 per share); 1992 includes an after-tax restructuring charge of $190,800,000 ($7.44 per share); 1991 includes an after-tax retail consolidation charge of $8,900,000 ($.40 per share).

Transfer Agent & Registrar: The First National Bank of Chicago; First Chicago Trust Co. of New York

General Counsel:
Frederick G. Wohlschlaeger, Sr. V.P.

Investor Relations: James E. Condon, V.P.

Human Resources: Linda J. Valentine, V.P.

Auditors: Price Waterhouse LLP

Traded (Symbol): NYSE, CSE (HMX)
Stockholders: 6,400
Employees: 8,600
Annual Meeting: In April

HealthCare COMPARE Corp.

3200 Highland Avenue, Downers Grove, Illinois 60515-1223
Telephone: (630) 241-7900

HealthCare COMPARE Corp. is an independent provider of health care utilization review and cost management services. These services control a client's health care costs by reducing unnecessary hospital admissions and lengths of stay, and by monitoring the medical necessity and appropriateness of other health care services. AFFORDABLE Health Care Concepts, a wholly owned subsidiary, negotiates medical provider prices in order to develop and maintain preferred provider networks for the exclusive use of its clients. In addition, AFFORDABLE collects and analyzes health care cost data. The company's current clients include corporate employers, group health insurance carriers, third party administrators, government employee groups, unions and trusts, health maintenance organizations, and worker's compensation carriers. In February 1996, the company announced the acquisition of American Life and Health Insurance Company and its subsidiary insurance company. Incorporated in Delaware in 1982.

Directors   (In addition to indicated officers)

Robert J. Becker, M.D.
Michael J. Boskin, Ph.D.
Robert S. Colman
Harold S. Handelsman

Burton W. Kanter
Don Logan
David E. Simon

Officers   (Directors*)

*Thomas J. Pritzker, Chm.
*James C. Smith, Pres. & C.E.O.
*Daniel S. Brunner, Exec. V.P.—Govt. Aff.
Mary Anne Carpenter, Exec. V.P.—Svc. Products
Patrick G. Dills, Exec. V.P.—Managed Care Sales

*Ronald H. Galowich, Exec. V.P. & Secy.
Edward L. Wristen, Exec. V.P.—Risk Products
Joseph E. Whitters, V.P.—Fin. & C.F.O.
Susan Smith, Asst. Secy. & Gen. Coun.

Consolidated Balance Sheet   As of December 31, 1996 (000 omitted)

Assets		Liabilities & Stockholders' Equity	
Cash & investments	$265,897	Claims reserves	$ 8,750
Accounts receivable	24,515	Other liabilities	21,382
Net property, plant & equipment	46,656	*Stockholders' equity	323,206
Other assets	16,270		
Total	$353,338	Total	$353,338

*35,244,000 shares common stock outstanding.

Consolidated Income Statement[a]

Years Ended Dec. 31	Thousands — — — — Revenues	Net Income	Per Share — — — — Earnings	Cash Dividends	Common Stock Price Range Calendar Year
1996	$247,804	$78,995	$2.24	$ .00	53 — 36-3/4
1995	214,338	66,537	1.89	.00	47-7/8 — 27-5/8
1994	186,606	50,669	1.45	.00	34-3/8 — 15-1/2
1993	157,650	38,471	1.08	.00	31-7/8 — 10-1/2
1992	133,501	18,116	.51	.00	43-1/4 — 25

[a]A wholly owned subsidiary of the company merged with Occupational-Urgent Care Health Systems, Inc. in February 1992. The transaction was accounted for as a pooling of interests. Therefore, financial statements have been restated to include the accounts of OUCH. In connection with the merger, the company recorded in 1992 a one-time charge of $16,000,000 for costs and expenses incurred by the company and OUCH. As a result of this charge, the company's net income in 1992 was reduced by $11,500,000 ($.33 per share).

Transfer Agent & Registrar:	LaSalle National Bank		
Corporate Counsel:	Neal Gerber & Eisenberg	Auditors:	Deloitte & Touche LLP
Investor Relations:	Joseph E. Whitters, V.P.	Traded (Symbol):	NASDAQ (HCCC)
		Stockholders:	15,000
Human Resources:	Nancy Zambon, V.P.	Employees:	1,500
Mgt. Info. Svcs.:	Ron Boeving, V.P.	Annual Meeting:	In May

Help At Home, Inc.

223 West Jackson, Suite 500, Chicago, Illinois 60606
Telephone: (312) 663-4244

Help At Home, Inc. and its wholly owned subsidiaries, Lakeside Home Health Agency, Inc., Oxford Healthcare, and Rosewood Home Health, Inc. provides homemaker and other custodial care services, as well as in-home skilled nursing services, in Alabama, Illinois, Indiana, Mississippi, and Missouri. In January 1996, the company announced that it was undertaking a pilot project with the U.S. Department of the Navy to provide in-home respite care services to servicemen and their families. In December 1995, the company completed an initial public offering of 813,375 units of common stock and warrants. Incorporated in Delaware in 1995.

Directors (In addition to indicated officers)

Dr. Michael Morgenstern
Robert Rubin

Steven L. Venit

Officers (Directors*)

*Louis Goldstein, Chm., C.E.O. & Treas.
*Joel Davis, C.O.O., Gen. Couns. & Secy.

Sharon S. Harder, C.F.O.

Consolidated Balance Sheet As of June 30, 1996 (000 omitted)

Assets		Liabilities & Stockholders' Equity	
Current assets	$5,871	Current liabilities	$2,414
Net property, plant & equipment	309	Long-term debt	389
Other assets	2,992	Deferred taxes	383
		*Stockholders' equity	5,986
Total	$9,172	Total	$9,172

*1,869,375 shares common stock outstanding.

Consolidated Income Statement

Years Ended June 30	Thousands — — — —		Per Share[ab] — — —		Common Stock Price Range[a] Calendar Year	
	Revenues	Net Income	Earnings[c]	Cash Dividends		
1996	$11,885	$718	$ .41	$ .00	8-3/8	— 4-3/4
1995	7,929	547	.52	.00	6	— 5-1/2
1994	3,609	134	.13			
1993[d]	2,956	61	.06			

[a]Initial public offering in December 1995.
[b]Reflects 1-for-2 reverse stock split in November 1995.
[c]Fully diluted.
[d]Unaudited.

Transfer Agent & Registrar:	Illinois Stock Transfer Company		
General Counsel:	Joel Davis, C.O.O.	Traded (Symbol):	NASDAQ (HAHI)
Investor Relations:	Joel Davis, C.O.O.	Stockholders:	300
		Employees:	6,500
Auditors:	Coopers & Lybrand L.L.P.	Annual Meeting:	As set by Directors

Hemlock Federal Financial Corporation

5700 West 159th Street, Oak Forest, Illinois 60452-3198
Telephone: (708) 687-9400

Hemlock Federal Financial Corporation is a savings and loan holding company that owns all of the outstanding capital stock of Hemlock Federal Bank for Savings. The bank, originally chartered in 1904, converted from a federally chartered mutual savings bank to a federally chartered stock savings bank in 1997. As a community-oriented financial institution, the bank serves the financial needs of communities in its market area. It attracts deposits from the general public and uses these deposits and other funds to originate one- to four-family residential mortgage loans, and also multi-family, consumer, and other loans. The bank's main office is in Oak Forest, with two branch offices in Chicago and Oak Lawn. In April 1997, in conjunction with the bank's conversion to a federally chartered stock savings bank, the company completed an initial public offering of 1,805,000 shares of common stock. Incorporated in Delaware in 1997.

Directors   (In addition to indicated officers)

Kenneth J. Bazarnik
Frank A. Bucz

Charles Gjondla
G. Gerald Schiera

Officers   (Directors*)

*Maureen G. Partynski, Chm. & C.E.O.
*Michael R. Stevens, Pres.

*Rosanne Pastorek-Belczak, V.P. & Secy.
Jean M. Thornton, V.P., Cont. & Treas.

Consolidated Balance Sheet   As of December 31, 1996 (000 omitted)

Assets		Liabilities & Stockholders' Equity	
Cash & cash equivalents	$ 17,410	Deposits	$131,243
Securities	72,157	Other liabilities	3,048
Loans receivable, net	53,536	*Stockholders' equity	12,115
Premises & equipment	1,043		
Other assets	2,260		
Total	$146,406	Total	$146,406

*1,800,000 shares common stock outstanding.

Consolidated Income Statement

Years Ended Dec. 31	Thousands — — — — Total Income	Net Income	Per Share[a] — — — — Earnings	Cash Dividends	Common Stock Price Range[a] Calendar Year
1996	$10,524	$162			
1995	10,272	952			
1994	8,884	539			
1993	9,542	977			
1992	10,956	764			

[a]Initial public offering in April 1997.

Transfer Agent & Registrar: Registrar & Transfer Co.

General Counsel: Silver, Freedman & Taff

Investor Relations: Rosanne Pastorek-Belczak, V.P.

Human Resources:
   Rosanne Pastorek-Belczak, V.P.

Auditors: Crowe, Chizek & Co. LLP

Traded (Symbol):   NASDAQ (HMLK)

Employees: 59

Annual Meeting: In April

Heritage Financial Services, Inc.

17500 South Oak Park Avenue, Tinley Park, Illinois 60477
Telephone: (708) 532-8000

Heritage Financial Services, Inc. is a multi-bank holding company which owns Heritage Bank in Blue Island, Illinois, the First National Bank of Lockport, in Lockport, Illinois, and Heritage Trust Company, in Tinley Park, Illinois. Through its bank subsidiaries, the company operates 15 banking locations in the southwest metropolitan Chicago market. Heritage Bank, the company's principal subsidiary, offers a complete range of financial products and services to individuals, businesses and municipal customers. Reincorporated in Illinois in 1984 as the successor to County Bankshares, Inc.

Directors (In addition to indicated officers)

John J. Gallagher
Lael W. Mathis
Jack Payan
Arthur E. Sieloff

John L. Sterling
Chester Stranczek
Arthur G. Tichenor
Dominick J. Velo

Officers (Directors*)

*Richard T. Wojcik, Chm. & C.E.O.
*Frederick J. Sampias, Pres.

*Ronald P. Groebe, Sr. Exec. V.P. & Secy.
Paul A. Eckroth, Exec. V.P. & Treas.

Consolidated Balance Sheet As of December 31, 1996 (000 omitted)

Assets		Liabilities & Stockholders' Equity	
Net loans	$ 629,597	Total deposits	$1,053,303
Cash & due from banks	43,830	Securities sold under agree-	40,706
Securities, held to maturity	115,913	ments to repurchase	
Securities, available for sale	392,754	Federal funds purchased	13,000
Securities, trading	262	Note payable	7,000
Net property, plant & equipment	18,786	Other liabilities	9,324
Other assets	27,878	*Stockholders' equity	105,687
Total	$1,229,020	Total	$1,229,020

*7,881,007 shares common stock outstanding.

Consolidated Income Statement

| Years Ended Dec. 31 | Thousands — — — — | | Per Share[a] — — — — | | Common Stock |
	Total Income	Net Income	Earnings	Cash Dividends	Price Range[a] Calendar Year
1996	$91,548	$14,838	$1.78	$ .52	22 — 18-1/4
1995	80,831	13,294	1.60	.44	19-1/2 — 15-3/4
1994	66,645	12,417	1.50	.36	19-3/4 — 15-3/4
1993	61,360	11,025	1.34	.32	17-1/2 — 12-3/4
1992	60,697	9,618	1.18	.30	14 — 10-1/4

[a]Adjusted to reflect a 2-for-1 stock split in April 1992.

Transfer Agent & Registrar: Harris Trust and Savings Bank

Corporate Counsel: Joel S. Corwin

Investor Relations:
Paul A. Eckroth, Exec. V.P. & Treas.

Human Resources: Karen Myers, Dir.

Mgt. Info. Svcs.: Linda Duggan, Dir.

Auditors: Arthur Andersen LLP

Traded (Symbol): NASDAQ (HERS)

Stockholders: 770

Employees: 490

Annual Meeting: In April

Hollinger International Inc.

401 N. Wabash Ave., Suite 740, Chicago, Illinois 60611
Telephone: (312) 321-3000

Hollinger International Inc. (formerly American Publishing Company) is the leading newspaper publishing group in the United States (based on paid daily newspapers owned and operated), where it publishes a total of 410 newspapers and related publications. Internationally, the company publishes *The Jerusalem Post* and *The Daily Telegraph*. Major subsidiaries are Hollinger International Publishing Inc., American Publishing Company, The Sun-Times Company, and The Telegraph Group Limited. Incorporated in Delaware in 1991; present name adopted in 1995.

Directors (In addition to indicated officers)

Dwayne O. Andreas
Richard Burt
Raymond G. Chambers
Daniel W. Colson
Henry A. Kissinger
Marie-Josee Kravis, O.C.
Shmuel Meitar

Richard N. Perle
Robert S. Strauss
A. Alfred Taubman
James R. Thompson
Lord Weidenfeld
Leslie H. Wexner

Officers (Directors*)

*Conrad M. Black, Chm. & C.E.O.
*F. David Radler, Pres. & C.O.O.
J.A. Boultbee, Exec. V.P. & C.F.O.
Peter Y. Atkinson, V.P.
*Barbara Amiel Black, V.P.—Editorial

Paul B. Healy, V.P.—Corp. Dev. & Inv. Rel.
Kenneth L. Serota, V.P.—Law & Fin.; Secy.
F.A. Creasey, Cont.
Linda Loye, Asst. Secy.

Consolidated Balance Sheet As of December 31, 1996 (000 omitted)

Assets		Liabilities & Stockholders' Equity	
Current assets	$ 487,560	Current liabilities	$ 919,971
Net property, plant & equipment	505,902	Long-term debt	675,263
Intangible assets, net of accum.	1,497,019	Deferred income taxes	70,705
depreciation		Other liabilities	917,570
Other assets	698,607	*Stockholders' equity	605,579
Total	$3,189,088	Total	$3,189,088

*69,565,754 shares Class A common and 14,990,000 shares Class B common stock outstanding.

Consolidated Income Statement

Years Ended Dec. 31	Thousands — — — — Net Sales	Net Income	Per Share[a] — — — — Earnings	Cash Dividends	Common Stock Price Range[ab] Calendar Year
1996	$1,862,714	$ 31,663	$ .37	$ .40	13-7/8 — 9-1/8
1995	964,251	6,202	.11	.10	13 — 9-1/4
1994[c]	808,310	102,772	1.90	.05	14-1/2 — 10

[a]Initial public offering in May 1994.
[b]Class A common stock.
[c]Includes the results of Chicago Sun-Times since March 31, 1994, the date of acquisition.

Transfer Agent & Registrar:	First Chicago Trust Co. of New York		
General Counsel:	Kirkpatrick & Lockhart	Traded (Symbol):	NYSE (HLR)
		Stockholders:	4,700
Investor Relations:	Paul B. Healy, V.P.	Employees:	8,820
Auditors:	KPMG Peat Marwick LLP	Annual Meeting:	In May

Home Products International, Inc.

4501 West 47th Street, Chicago, Illinois 60632
Telephone: (773) 890-1010

Home Products International, Inc. (formerly Selfix, Inc.) designs, manufactures, and markets a broad range of consumer home products, including more than 300 houseware products and a line of plastic exterior shutters. The company markets in a number of categories: home bathwares and hooks, home/closet organization products, juvenile products, home improvement products, and storage containers. The company's houseware products are designed to satisfy everyday household storage and organizational needs, and its shutters are designed for easy assembly from standard components into custom lengths. Houseware products are sold in the United States and other countries, principally to mass merchandisers, drug and hardware store chains, variety outlets, and supermarkets. Shutters are sold primarily in the eastern U.S. and Canada through building products distributors. Subsidiaries are Selfix, Inc.; Shutters, Inc.; and Tamor Corporation. Effective January 1, 1997, the company acquired Tamor, a Leominster, Massachusetts-based designer, manufacturer, and marketer of quality plastic houseware products. Incorporated in Illinois in 1962; reincorporated in Delaware in 1987; present name adopted in 1997.

Directors   (In addition to indicated officers)

Charles R. Campbell
Marshall Ragir
Jeffrey C. Rubenstein

Daniel B. Shure
Joel D. Spungin

Officers   (Directors*)

*James R. Tennant, Chm. & C.E.O.;
  C.E.O.—Selfix
James E. Winslow, Exec. V.P., C.F.O. &
  Secy.; Exec. V.P.—Selfix
Dennis M. Gerrard, Pres.—Tamor
Leonard J. Tocci, C.E.O.—Tamor

Jeffrey R. Dolan, Sr. V.P.—Sales, Selfix
Peter L. Graves, V.P.—Prod. Mktg., Selfix
Robert Holz, V.P.—Intl. Sales, Selfix
David E. Limanni, V.P.—Mfg., Tamor
Michael J. Ricard, V.P. & Gen. Mgr., Shutters
Richard M. Tocci, V.P.—Oper., Tamor

Consolidated Balance Sheet[a]   As of March 29, 1997 (000 omitted)

Assets		Liabilities & Stockholders' Equity	
Current assets	$36,608	Current liabilities	$25,407
Net property, plant & equipment	23,880	Long-term debt	51,141
Other assets	31,643	*Stockholders' equity	15,583
Total	$92,131	Total	$92,131

[a]Unaudited.
*4,381,684 shares common stock outstanding.

Consolidated Income Statement

Years Ended Abt. Dec. 31	Thousands — — — — Net Sales	Net Income	Per Share — — — Earnings	Cash Dividends	Common Stock Price Range Calendar Year
1996	$38,200	$ 806	$ .21	$ .00	9-1/4 — 4-1/8
1995	41,039	(4,010)[a]	(1.11)[a]	.00	5-7/8 — 4
1994	40,985	(6,003)[b]	(1.70)[b]	.00	9-1/4 — 4
1993	39,711	1,515	.43	.00	7-1/2 — 2-3/4
1992	35,209	(781)	(.23)	.00	7 — 2-7/8

[a]Includes restructuring charges of $2,051,000.
[b]Includes restructuring charges of $1,701,000.

Transfer Agent & Registrar: ChaseMellon Shareholder Services, L.L.C.

General Counsel:
  Much Shelist Freed Denenberg Ament
  Bell & Rubenstein, P.C.

Investor Relations: James E. Winslow, Exec. V.P.

Human Resources: Robert Anderson

Mgt. Info. Svcs.:   James E. Winslow, Exec. V.P.

Auditors: Arthur Andersen LLP

Traded (Symbol):   NASDAQ (HPII)

Stockholders: 747

Employees: 493

Annual Meeting: In May

HomeCorp, Inc.

1107 East State Street, P.O. Box 4779, Rockford, Illinois 61110-4779
Telephone: (815) 987-2200

HomeCorp, Inc. is the holding company for HomeBanc, a federal savings bank, one of northern Illinois' oldest financial institutions. HomeCorp was formed in 1989 as part of the conversion from mutual to stock ownership of HomeBanc. The bank operates 10 full-service offices in northern Illinois, including six in Rockford and two each in Freeport and Dixon. HomeBanc serves its customers with a wide range of contemporary retail banking products. Mortgage and consumer installment lending are emphasized, as well as financing and investment services for small business. Stock, bond, and annuity sales are promoted through a relationship with INVEST Financial Corporation. Incorporated in Delaware in 1989.

Directors   (In addition to indicated officers)

Karl H. Erickson, Chm.
Robert C. Hauser
Adam A. Jahns

Larry U. Larson
Richard W. Malmgren
David R. Rydell

Officers   (Directors*)

*C. Steven Sjogren, Pres. & C.E.O.
*John R. Perkins, Exec. V.P. & C.F.O.

*Wesley E. Lindberg, Secy.
Dirk J. Meminger, Treas. & Chf. Acct. Officer

Consolidated Balance Sheet   As of December 31, 1996 (000 omitted)

Assets		Liabilities & Stockholders' Equity	
Current assets	$ 14,141	Current liabilities	$ 87,816
Net property, plant & equipment	3,869	Long-term debt	223,938
Investments	38,937	Other liabilities	3,212
Loans	261,012	*Stockholders' equity	20,858
Other assets	17,865		
Total	$335,824	Total	$335,824

*1,128,779 shares common stock outstanding.

Consolidated Income Statement

Years Ended Dec. 31	Thousands — — — — Net Sales	Net Income	Per Share[a] — — — Earnings	Cash Dividends	Common Stock Price Range[a] Calendar Year
1996	$28,512	$ 359	$ .30	$ .00	19-7/8 — 16-1/2
1995	26,380	1,207	1.03	.00	15-1/2 — 10-3/8
1994	23,601	(3,712)[b]	(3.21)[b]	.00	18-1/2 — 9-3/4
1993	24,406	1,606[c]	1.39[c]	.00	15-1/2 — 10-3/8
1992	28,330	1,641	1.43	.00	10-1/2 — 5-3/8

[a]Adjusted to reflect a 3-for-2 stock split in March 1993.
[b]Includes a charge to reflect FAS 72, resulting in a cumulative effect of $4,340,424 ($3.75 per share).
[c]Includes a gain to reflect FAS 109, resulting in a cumulative effect of $440,000 ($.38 per share).

Transfer Agent & Registrar: Firstar Trust Co.

General Counsel:
  Reno, Zahm, Folgate, Lindberg & Powell

Investor Relations: C. Steven Sjogren, Pres.

Human Resources: Kathleen S.J. Bergstrom

Mgt. Info. Svcs.:   Marsha A. Abramson

Auditors: Ernst & Young LLP

Traded (Symbol):   NASDAQ (HMCI)

Stockholders: 1,350

Employees: 182

Annual Meeting: In April

LaSalle Banks Guide

Horace Mann Educators Corporation

1 Horace Mann Plaza, Springfield, Illinois 62715-0001
Telephone: (217) 789-2500

Horace Mann Educators Corporation is an insurance holding company which, through its subsidiaries, markets and underwrites personal lines of property/casualty and life insurance, and retirement annuities. The company also underwrites and markets a limited line of group life and health insurance products. Horace Mann markets its products primarily to educators and other employees of public schools and their families. The company sells and services its products through its own sales force. Subsidiaries are Horace Mann Insurance Company, Teachers Insurance Company, Allegiance Insurance Company, and Horace Mann Life Insurance Company. In December 1996, the company announced that it planned to withdraw from the group medical insurance business over the following two years. Founded in 1945 in Springfield, Illinois; incorporated in Delaware in 1968.

Directors (In addition to indicated officers)

William W. Abbott
Leonard I. Green
Donald G. Heth
Dr. Emita B. Hill

Jeffrey L. Morby
Shaun F. O'Malley
William J. Schoen

Officers (Directors*)

*Ralph S. Saul, Chm.
*Paul J. Kardos, Pres. & C.E.O.
Larry K. Becker, Exec. V.P. & C.F.O.
Edward L. Najim, Exec. V.P.
Walter E. Stooksbury, Exec. V.P.
Gerard F. Bonnett, Sr. V.P.

Valerie A. Chrisman, Sr. V.P.
H. Albert Inkel, Sr. V.P.
George J. Zock, Sr. V.P. & Treas.
Ann M. Caparrós, V.P., Gen. Coun. & Secy.
Roger W. Fisher, V.P. & Cont.
Frank L. Purcell, V.P.

Consolidated Balance Sheet As of December 31, 1996 (000 omitted)

Assets		Liabilities & Stockholders' Equity	
Investments	$2,784,336	Policy liabilities	$2,310,030
Other assets	1,076,690	Long-term debt	99,564
		Other liabilities	967,037
		*Stockholders' equity	484,395
Total	$3,861,026	Total	$3,861,026

*29,213,398 shares common stock outstanding.

Consolidated Income Statement

Years Ended Dec. 31	Thousands — — — — Total Revenues[a]	Net Income	Per Share — — — Earnings	Cash Dividends	Common Stock Price Range Calendar Year
1996	$703,800	$64,600	$2.75	$ .44	40-3/4 — 28
1995	692,400	74,000	2.95	.36	31-1/4 — 20-1/8
1994	656,800	62,900	2.17[b]	.29	28-3/4 — 19-1/8
1993	648,900	77,200	2.67	.24	32-1/2 — 22-1/4
1992	645,100	58,100	2.01[b]	.20	29 — 18-3/8

[a]From continuing operations.
[b]Includes an extraordinary charge of $.06 per share in 1994 and $.47 per share in 1992 due to retirement of debt.

Transfer Agent & Registrar:	American Stock Transfer & Trust Co.		
General Counsel:	Ann M. Caparrós, V.P.	Traded (Symbol):	NYSE (HMN)
Investor Relations:	George J. Zock, Sr. V.P.	Stockholders:	4,500
Human Resources:	Jay Qualls, V.P.	Employees:	2,700
Mgt. Info. Svcs.:	Frank Purcell, V.P.	Annual Meeting:	In June
Auditors:	KPMG Peat Marwick LLP	Internet:	www.horacemann.com

Household International, Inc.

2700 Sanders Road, Prospect Heights, Illinois 60070
Telephone: (847) 564-5000

Household International, Inc. is a leading provider of consumer finance and credit card services in the United States, Canada, and the United Kingdom. Through its subsidiaries, the company is the oldest and one of the largest finance companies, and sixth largest Visa/MasterCard issuer in the United States. Major subsidiaries include: Household Finance Corporation; Household Credit Services; Household Retail Services; HFC Auto Credit; HFC Bank, plc (UK); and Household Financial Corp., Ltd. (Canada). In June 1997, the company completed its acquisition of the consumer finance business of San Francisco based Transamerica Corp. Incorporated in Delaware in 1925; reincorporated in Delaware in 1981.

Directors (In addition to indicated officers)

Robert J. Darnall
Gary G. Dillon
John A. Edwardson
Mary Johnston Evans
Dudley Fishburn, M.P.
Cyrus F. Freidheim, Jr.

Louis E. Levy
George A. Lorch
John D. Nichols
James B. Pitblado
S. Jay Stewart
Louis W. Sullivan, M.D.

Officers (Directors*)

*William F. Aldinger, Chm. & C.E.O.
Lawrence N. Bangs, Grp. Exec.
Robert F. Elliott, Grp. Exec.
Joseph W. Saunders, Grp. Exec.
David A. Schoenholz, Exec. V.P. & C.F.O.
David B. Barany, Sr. V.P.—C.I.O.
Colin P. Kelly, Sr. V.P.—Hum. Res.
Kenneth H. Robin, Sr. V.P.—Gen. Coun.
Charles A. Albright, V.P.—Chf. Credit Off.

John W. Blenke, V.P.—Corp. Law & Asst. Secy.
Richard J. Kolb, V.P.—Mgt. Reporting & Analysis
Steven L. McDonald, V.P.—Corp. Cont.
Craig A. Streem, V.P.—Inv. Rel.
Paul R. Shay, Asst. Gen. Couns. & Secy.
Edgar D. Ancona, Managing Dir. & Treas.
Michael A. DeLuca, Managing Dir.—Taxes
Randall L. Raup, Managing Dir.—Strat. & Dev.

Consolidated Balance Sheet As of December 31, 1996 (000 omitted)

Assets		Liabilities & Stockholders' Equity	
Receivables	$24,244,800	Short-term debt	$ 8,793,200
Net property, plant & equipment	353,100	Long-term debt	14,802,000
Other assets	4,996,600	Other liabilities	2,678,100
		*Stockholders' equity	3,321,200
Total	$29,594,500	Total	$29,594,500

*97,065,254 shares common stock outstanding.

Consolidated Income Statement

Years Ended Dec. 31	Thousands — — — — Net Revenues	Net Income	Per Share[a] — — — Earnings[b]	Cash Dividends	Common Stock Price Range[a] Calendar Year
1996	$3,538,200	$538,600	$5.30	$1.46	98-1/8 — 52
1995	3,587,300	453,200	4.30	1.31	68-3/8 — 35-7/8
1994	3,360,600	367,600	3.50	1.23	39-3/4 — 28-1/2
1993	3,305,000	298,700	2.85	1.18	40-3/8 — 27
1992	2,760,400	190,900	1.93	1.15	30-1/4 — 20-3/4

[a]Adjusted to reflect a 2-for-1 stock split in October 1993.
[b]Fully diluted.

Transfer Agent & Registrar: Harris Trust and Savings Bank

General Counsel:	Kenneth H. Robin, Sr. V.P.	Traded (Symbol):	
Investor Relations:	Craig A. Streem, V.P.	NYSE, CSE, PHSE, BSE, PSE (HI)	
Human Resources:	Colin P. Kelly, Sr. V.P.	Stockholders:	12,535
Mgt. Info. Svcs.:	David B. Barany, Sr. V.P.	Employees:	13,066
Auditors:	Arthur Andersen LLP	Annual Meeting:	Second Wednesday in May

Hub Group, Inc.

377 East Butterfield Road, Suite 700, Lombard, Illinois 60148
Telephone: (630) 271-3600

Hub Group, Inc. is North America's largest intermodal marketing company and a leader in knowledge-based logistics solutions. The company operates through a nationwide network of 34 offices, or Hubs, that are strategically located in markets with significant concentrations of shipping customers and one or more railheads. Through this network, the company serves more than 10,000 customers with comprehensive intermodal, truckload, less-than-truckload, air freight, international, and logistics services. In May 1996, Hub Group, Inc. completed the purchase of the domestic distribution services segment of American President Companies, Ltd. Incorporated in Delaware in 1995, as successor to a business founded in 1971.

Directors (In addition to indicated officers)

Gary D. Eppen
Charles R. Reaves

Martin P. Slark

Officers (Directors*)

*Phillip C. Yeager, Chm.
*David P. Yeager, V. Chm. & C.E.O.
*Thomas L. Hardin, Pres. & C.O.O.
John T. Donnell, Exec. V.P.—Marketing
William L. Crowder, V.P.—Fin., C.F.O. &
Treas.

Robert L. Maro, V.P.—Info. Svcs.
Mark A. Yeager, V.P., Gen. Coun. & Secy.
Daniel F. Hardman, Pres.—Chicago Region
Robert J. Jensen, Pres.—Hub Group Oper. Mgt.

Consolidated Balance Sheet   As of December 31, 1996 (000 omitted)

Assets		Liabilities & Stockholders' Equity	
Current assets	$131,550	Current liabilities	$115,673
Net property, plant & equipment	14,058	Long-term debt	28,714
Other assets	55,617	Other liabilities	10,714
		*Stockholders' equity	46,124
Total	$201,225	Total	$201,225

*5,261,250 shares Class A common stock and 662,296 shares Class B common stock outstanding.

Consolidated Income Statement

Years Ended Dec. 31	Thousands — — — — Net Revenues	Net Income	Per Share[a] — — — — Earnings	Cash Dividends	Common Stock Price Range[a] Calendar Year
1996	$754,243	$6,803	$1.35	$ .00	27 - 3/8 — 14
1995[b]	710,820	5,331	1.02		

[a]Initial public offering in March 1996.
[b]Unaudited pro forma.

Transfer Agent & Registrar: Harris Trust and Savings Bank

General Counsel:	Mark A. Yeager, V.P.	Auditors:	Arthur Andersen LLP
Investor Relations:	William L. Crowder, V.P.	Traded (Symbol):	NASDAQ (HUBG)
		Stockholders:	3,325
Human Resources:	Carol Troop, Dir.	Employees:	1,050
Mgt. Info. Svcs.	Robert L. Maro, V.P.	Annual Meeting:	As set by Directors

IDEX Corporation

630 Dundee Road, Northbrook, Illinois 60062
Telephone: (847) 498-7070

IDEX Corporation, through its subsidiaries, designs, manufactures, and markets a broad range of fluid handling and industrial products which include: industrial pumps; dispensing and mixing equipment for color formation; firefighting pumps and rescue tools; lubrication systems; low-horsepower compressors; tooling and sheet metal fabricating equipment; stainless steel banding and clamping devices; sign-mounting systems; and vibration control devices. Subsidiaries are organized into two segments: Fluid Handling and Industrial Products. The Fluid Handling Group consists of Corken, a producer of vane and turbine pumps, compressors, and valves for the LP gas industry; Fluid Management manufactures dispensing and mixing equipment for paints, colorants, inks, dyes, and other liquids and pastes; Hale, a manufacturer of truck-mounted and portable fire pumps and products which form the Hurst Jaws of Life® and Lukas rescue tool systems; Lubriquip, a producer of automatic lubrication systems for use in machinery, compressors, and vehicles; Micropump, a manufacturer of small precision-engineered, magnetically driven pumps used in industrial, medical, and electronic applications; Pulsafeeder, a manufacturer of specialty metering pumps, controls, and systems for the process industries; Viking Pump, a producer of positive displacement rotary gear pumps and spur gear pumps sold to process industries; and Warren Rupp, a manufacturer of air-operated and motor-driven double diaphragm pumps used in industrial applications. The Industrial Products Group consists of Band-It, a producer of stainless steel bands, buckles, and preformed clamps and related installation tools for industrial, automotive, energy, and maintenance applications; Signfix, a United Kingdom-based manufacturer of sign-mounting systems and related equipment; Strippit, a manufacturer of tooling and computer-controlled turret punching machinery sold to the precision metal fabrication industry; and Vibratech, a producer of mechanical energy absorption and vibration control devices for use in transportation equipment and machinery. Incorporated in Delaware in 1987.

Directors (In addition to indicated officers)

Richard E. Heath
Henry R. Kravis
William H. Luers
Paul E. Raether

Clifton S. Robbins
George R. Roberts
Neil A. Springer
Michael T. Tokarz

Officers (Directors*)

*Donald N. Boyce, Chm., Pres. & C.E.O.
Frank J. Hansen, Sr. V.P.—Oper. & C.O.O.
Wayne P. Sayatovic, Sr. V.P.—Fin., C.F.O. & Secy.
Mark W. Baker, V.P.—Grp. Exec.
Jerry N. Derck, V.P.—Hum. Res.
James R. Fluharty, V.P.—Corp. Mktg.

P. Peter Merkel, Jr., V.P.—Grp. Exec.
Dennis L. Metcalf, V.P.—Bus. Dev.
Wade H. Roberts, Jr., V.P.—Grp. Exec.
Clinton L. Kooman, Cont.
Douglas C. Lennox, Treas.

Consolidated Balance Sheet   As of December 31, 1996 (000 omitted)

Assets		Liabilities & Stockholders' Equity	
Current assets	$201,170	Current liabilities	$ 92,857
Net property, plant & equipment	102,383	Long-term debt	271,709
Intangible assets	274,511	Other liabilities	23,698
Other assets	5,709	*Shareholders' equity	195,509
Total	$583,773	Total	$583,773

*28,925,867 shares common stock outstanding.

Consolidated Income Statement

Years Ended Dec. 31	Thousands — — — — —		Per Share[b] — — — —		Common Stock Price Range[b] Calendar Year
	Net Sales	Net Income[a]	Earnings[a]	Cash Dividends	
1996	$562,561	$50,198	$1.69	$ .43	27-5/8 — 19-7/8
1995	487,336	45,325	1.53	.37	29-1/2 — 18-3/8
1994	399,502	33,610	1.15	.00	19-1/2 — 15-1/8
1993	308,638	25,326	.87	.00	16 — 9-3/4
1992	277,129	20,146	.71	.00	10-5/8 — 7-3/8

[a]Before extraordinary items.
[b]Adjusted to reflect 3-for-2 stock splits effected in the form of 50 percent stock dividends in January 1995 and January 1997.

Transfer Agent & Registrar:	Harris Trust and Savings Bank		
Investor Relations:	Wayne P. Sayatovic, Sr. V.P.	Traded (Symbol):	NYSE, CSE (IEX)
Human Resources:	Jerry N. Derck, V.P.	Shareholders:	1,305
Mgt. Info. Svcs.:	Douglas C. Lennox, Treas.	Employees:	3,598
Auditors:	Deloitte & Touche LLP	Annual Meeting:	In March

Illinois Central Corporation

455 North Cityfront Plaza Drive, Chicago, Illinois 60611-5504
Telephone: (312) 755-7500

Illinois Central Corporation is a holding company with three principal subsidiaries: Illinois Central Railroad (ICRR); CCP Holdings, Inc. (CCPH); and IC Financial Services Corporation (ICF). ICRR, formed in 1851 as the first U.S. land-grant railroad, operates a 2,700-mile freight railroad in six states between Chicago and the Gulf of Mexico, primarily transporting chemicals, grain and milled grain, coal, paper, and intermodal commodities. CCPH, whose principal subsidiaries are the Chicago, Central and Pacific Railroad and the Cedar River Railroad, operates an 850-mile system between Chicago and Omaha, Nebraska, with connecting lines to Cedar Rapids and Sioux City, Iowa. ICF finances the acquisition of locomotives and freight cars which are leased to ICRR. Incorporated in Delaware in 1989; present name adopted in 1989.

Directors (In addition to indicated officers)

Gilbert H. Lamphere, Chm.
George D. Gould
William B. Johnson
Alexander P. Lynch

Samuel F. Pryor IV
F. Jay Taylor
John V. Tunney
Alan H. Washkowitz

Officers (Directors*)

*E. Hunter Harrison, Pres. & C.E.O.
John D. McPherson, Sr. V.P.—Oper.
Donald H. Skelton, Sr. V.P.—Mktg. & Sales
James M. Harrell, V.P.—Hum. Res.

David C. Kelly, V.P.—Maint.
Ronald A. Lane, V.P., Gen. Coun. & Secy.
Dale W. Phillips, V.P. & C.F.O.
John V. Mulvaney, Cont.

Consolidated Balance Sheet As of December 31, 1996 (000 omitted)

Assets		Liabilities & Stockholders' Equity	
Current assets	$ 248,600	Current liabilities	$ 232,000
Net property, plant & equipment	1,624,100	Long-term debt	633,700
Other assets	38,700	Deferred taxes	356,600
		Other liabilities	133,600
		*Stockholders' equity	555,500
Total	$1,911,400	Total	$1,911,400

*61,406,831 shares common stock outstanding.

Consolidated Income Statement

Years Ended Dec. 31	Thousands — — — — Net Revenues	Net Income	Per Share[a] — — — Earnings	Cash Dividends	Common Stock Price Range[a] Calendar Year
1996[b]	$657,500	$136,600	$2.21	$ .80	34-3/8 — 23-5/8
1995	645,300	118,400[c]	1.88[c]	.68	28-3/4 — 20-1/2
1994	595,300	113,900	1.78	.56	25-3/4 — 19
1993	564,700	91,700[d]	1.43[d]	.43	24 — 15-3/4
1992	547,400	72,500[e]	1.13[e]	.23	17 — 11

[a]Adjusted for 3-for-2 stock splits in February 1992 and March 1996.
[b]Includes the results of CCP Holdings, Inc. from June 13 (the date of acquisition) to December 31.
[c]Includes an extraordinary charge after-tax of $11,400,000 ($.18 per share) for early retirement of debt.
[d]Before an extraordinary charge of $23,400,000 ($.55 per share) and the cumulative effect of FAS 106 and FAS 112.
[e]Before FAS 109, which resulted in a cumulative effect of $23,400,000 ($.55 per share).

Transfer Agent & Registar: The First National Bank of Boston

General Counsel:	Ronald A. Lane, V.P.	Auditors:	Arthur Andersen LLP
Investor Relations:	Ann G. Thoma	Traded (Symbol):	NYSE (IC)
Human Resources:	James M. Harrell, V.P.	Stockholders:	25,000
		Employees:	3,617
Mgt. Info. Svcs.:	Dale W. Phillips, V.P.	Annual Meeting:	In May

Illinois Tool Works Inc.
3600 West Lake Avenue, Glenview, Illinois 60025-5811
Telephone: (847) 724-7500

Illinois Tool Works Inc. manufactures and markets a variety of highly engineered products and systems that provide specific, problem-solving solutions for a diverse customer base worldwide. The company's products include Engineered Components—plastic and metal components, fasteners and assemblies; industrial fluids and adhesives; fastening tools and accessories; and welding products and Industrial Systems and Consumables—systems and related consumables for consumer and industrial packaging; industrial spray coating equipment and systems; and quality assurance equipment and systems. The company has 345 flexible operating units located in 34 countries. Incorporated in Delaware in 1961.

Directors (In addition to indicated officers)

Julius W. Becton, Jr.	Richard M. Jones
Michael J. Birck	George D. Kennedy
Marvin D. Brailsford	Richard H. Leet
Susan Crown	Robert C. McCormack
H. Richard Crowther	Phillip B. Rooney
L. Richard Flury	Ormand J. Wade

Officers (Directors*)

*W. James Farrell, Chm. & C.E.O.
*Harold B. Smith, Chm. of the Exec. Committee
Frank S. Ptak, V. Chm.—Global Auto. & Indus. Components
Russell M. Flaum, Exec. V.P.—Signode Packaging Systems
Dennis J. Martin, Exec. V.P.—Welding Prods.
F. Ronald Seager, Exec. V.P.—Cons. Pack. Prod. & Syst.
David B. Speer, Exec. V.P.—Const. Prods. & Finishing Sys.

Hugh J. Zentmyer, Exec. V.P.—Spec. Indus. Pack. & Qual. Meas. Sys.
Michael W. Gregg, Sr. V.P. & Cont.—Acct.
Stewart S. Hudnut, Sr. V.P., Gen. Coun. & Secy.
John Karpan, Sr. V.P.—Hum. Res.
Jon Kinney, Sr. V.P. & Cont.—Oper.
Gary F. Anton, V.P.—Internal Audit
Thomas W. Buckman, V.P.—Patents & Tech.
Robert V. McGrath, V.P.—Tax
Michael J. Robinson, V.P. & Treas.
Allan C. Sutherland, V.P.—Leasing & Invest.
Donald L. Van Erden, V.P.—Res. & Adv. Devel.

Consolidated Balance Sheet As of December 31, 1996 (000 omitted)

Assets		Liabilities & Stockholders' Equity	
Current assets	$1,701,092	Current liabilities	$1,219,325
Net property, plant & equipment	808,340	Long-term debt	818,947
Other assets	2,296,730	Other liabilities	371,865
		*Stockholders' equity	2,396,025
Total	$4,806,162	Total	$4,806,162

*123,886,000 shares common stock outstanding.

Consolidated Income Statement

Years Ended Dec. 31	Thousands — — — — Operating Revenues	Net Income	Per Share[a] — — — Earnings	Cash Dividends	Common Stock Price Range[a] Calendar Year
1996	$4,996,681	$486,315	$3.93	$ .70	87-1/4 — 51-7/8
1995	4,178,080	387,608	3.29	.62	65-1/2 — 39-3/4
1994	3,461,315	277,783	2.45	.54	45-1/2 — 36-3/4
1993	3,159,181	206,570	1.83	.49	40-1/2 — 32-1/2
1992	2,811,645	192,080	1.72	.45	34-3/8 — 28-1/2

[a]Adjusted to reflect a 2-for-1 stock split in June 1993.

Transfer Agent & Registrar: Harris Trust and Savings Bank

General Counsel:	Stewart S. Hudnut, Sr. V.P.	Traded (Symbol):	NYSE, CSE (ITW)
Investor Relations:	Linda Williams, Dir.	Stockholders:	4,511
Human Resources:	John Karpan, Sr. V.P.	Employees:	24,400
Auditors:	Arthur Andersen LLP	Annual Meeting:	In May

Illinova Corporation

500 South 27th Street, Decatur, Illinois 62525-1805
Telephone: (217) 424-6600

Illinova Corporation is an energy services holding company. Through its subsidiaries, the company is engaged principally in the generation, transmission, distribution, and sale of electric energy, and the distribution, transportation, and sale of natural gas in parts of northern, central, and southern Illinois. Illinois Power Company (IP), a wholly owned subsidiary, serves Belleville, Bloomington, Champaign, Danville, Decatur, East St. Louis, Galesburg, Granite City, Normal, and Urbana. The company's territory spans about 15,000 square miles, and it serves more than one-half million people. IP operates five major electric generating stations and one nuclear generating station. It also owns eight gas storage fields, predominantly in southern Illinois. Illinova Generating Company, another wholly owned subsidiary, invests in, develops, and operates independent power projects worldwide. A third subsidiary, Illinova Power Marketing, Inc., markets energy and energy-related services to various customers outside the Illinois Power franchise territory. In April 1996, Illinova announced the formation of a new subsidiary, Illinova Energy Partners, which will offer a wide range of customized energy services nationwide. Incorporated in Illinois in 1994; present name adopted in 1994.

Directors (In addition to indicated officers)

Richard R. Berry	Sheli Z. Rosenberg	Walter M. Vannoy
C. Steven McMillan	Walter D. Scott	Marilou M. von Ferstel
Robert M. Powers	Ronald L. Thompson	John D. Zeglis

Officers (Directors*)

*Larry D. Haab, Chm., Pres. & C.E.O.
Larry F. Altenbaumer, C.F.O., Treas. & Cont.
Leah Manning Stetzner, Gen. Coun. & Secy.
Alec G. Dryer, Pres.—Illinova Generating Company
Robert A. Schultz, Pres.—Illinova Energy Partners & Illinova Power M
David W. Butts, Sr. V.P.—Illinois Power

John G. Cook, Sr. V.P.—Illinois Power
Paul L. Lang, Sr. V.P.—Illinois Power
Ralph F. Tschantz, Sr. V.P.—Illinova Energy Partners
Wilfred Connell, V.P.—Illinois Power
Richard W. Eimer, V.P.—Illinois Power
Cynthia G. Steward, Cont.—Illinois Power
Eric B. Weekes, Treas.—Illinois Power

Consolidated Balance Sheet As of December 31, 1996 (000 omitted)

Assets		Liabilities & Stockholders' Equity	
Current assets	$ 468,700	Current liabilities	$ 748,000
Deferred charges	434,400	Long-term debt	1,636,400
Other assets & investments	4,809,700	Deferred items	1,399,000
		Other liabilities	293,200
		*Stockholders' equity	1,636,200
Total	$5,712,800	Total	$5,712,800

*75,700,000 shares common stock outstanding.

Consolidated Income Statement

Years Ended Dec. 31	Thousands — — — —		Per Share — — — —		Common Stock
	Operating Revs.	Net Income[a]	Earnings	Cash Dividends	Price Range Calendar Year
1996	$1,688,700	$ 190,300	$ 2.51	$1.12	30-3/8 — 24-5/8
1995	1,641,400	148,100	1.96	1.00	30　— 21-1/4
1994	1,589,500	158,200	2.09	.80	22-5/8 — 18-1/8
1993	1,581,200	(81,900)	(1.08)	.80	25-7/8 — 20-1/8
1992	1,479,500	93,200	1.23	.80	25-1/8 — 19-1/4

[a]Applicable to common stock.

Transfer Agent & Registrar:	Illinois Power Company		
General Counsel:	Leah Manning Stetzner	Traded (Symbol):	NYSE, CSE (ILN)
Investor Relations:	Paul G. Blair, Dir.	Stockholders:	35,000
Human Resources:	David W. Butts, Sr. V.P.	Employees:	3,635
Mgt. Info. Svcs.:	David W. Butts, Sr. V.P.	Annual Meeting:	Second Wednesday in April
Auditors:	Price Waterhouse LLP	Internet:	www.illinova.com

IMC Global Inc.
2100 Sanders Road, Northbrook, Illinois 60062-6146
Telephone: (847) 272-9200

IMC Global Inc. is a leading producer of crop nutrients for agriculture. It mines and processes potash in the U.S. and Canada; and is a joint venture partner in IMC-Agrico Company, a leading producer, marketer, and distributor of phosphate crop nutrients and animal feed ingredients. The company is also a major distributor of crop nutrients and related products in the United States through its Rainbow® and FARMARKET® distribution networks. IMC also markets potash and other products to industrial users and produces sulphur and oil through joint venture operations. The company's North America customers include wholesale and retail crop nutrient producers and regional agricultural cooperatives. Internationally, IMC Global's products are sold through one Canadian and three domestic export associations, mainly to Brazil, India, Japan, Pakistan, the People's Republic of China, Turkey, and several European countries. In March 1996, IMC Global merged with The Vigoro Corporation, a Chicago-based producer and distributor of potash, nitrogen-based fertilizers, and related products. The name IMC Global was retained. Incorporated in Delaware in 1987; present name adopted in 1994.

Directors (In addition to indicated officers)

Raymond F. Bentele
Rod F. Dammeyer
James M. Davidson

Harold H. MacKay, Q.C.
David B. Mathis
Thomas H. Roberts, Jr.
Joseph P. Sullivan

Richard L. Thomas
Billie B. Turner
Clayton Yeutter

Officers (Directors*)

*Wendell F. Bueche, Chm.
*Robert E. Fowler, Jr., Pres. & C.E.O.
Brian J. Smith, Exec. V.P. & C.F.O.
C. Steven Hoffman, Sr. V.P.
John U. Huber, Sr. V.P. & Pres.—IMC Kalium
B. Russell Lockridge, Sr. V.P.—Hum. Res.

Marschall I. Smith, Sr. V.P. & Gen. Coun.
Robert M. VanPatten, Sr. V.P. & Pres.—IMC AgriBusiness
Eileen A. Kamerick, V.P. & Treas.
Eugene M. McCluskey, Dir.—Taxes & Asst. Secy.
Anne M. Scavone, Cont.
Rose Marie Williams, Secy.

Consolidated Balance Sheet As of June 30, 1996 (000 omitted)

Assets		Liabilities & Stockholders' Equity	
Current assets	$ 918,200	Current liabilities	$ 366,400
Net property, plant & equipment	2,351,300	Long-term debt	736,700
Other assets	167,300	Deferred items	315,700
		Other liabilities	352,000
		Minority interest	509,700
		*Stockholders' equity	1,156,300
Total	$3,436,800	Total	$3,436,800

*92,317,900 shares common stock outstanding.

Consolidated Income Statement[a]

Years Ended June 30	Thousands — — — — Net Sales	Net Income	Per Share[b] — — — — Earnings	Cash Dividends	Common Stock Price Range[b] Calendar Year
1996	$2,981,000	$ 144,300[c]	$ 1.56[c]	$ .33	44-1/2 — 32-1/4
1995	2,736,100	180,900[d]	1.99[d]	.26	40-7/8 — 20-5/8
1994	2,125,300	19,200[e]	.23[e]	.15	24-5/8 — 15-3/8
1993	1,438,100	(127,000)[f]	(1.67)[f]	.32	23-5/8 — 12-1/8
1992	1,621,100	(66,100)[g]	(.87)[g]	.37	34 — 18-5/8

[a]Reflects merger with The Vigoro Corporation, which was accounted for as a pooling-of-interests.
[b]Adjusted to reflect a 2-for-1 stock split in November 1995.
[c]Includes special one-time charges of $69,600,000 ($.75 per share) for costs related to the merger with The Vigoro Corporation.
[d]Includes an extraordinary loss of $6,500,000 ($.07 per share) for debt retirement, and a one-time charge of $5,900,000 ($.07 per share) for the cumulative effect of an accounting change.
[e]Includes a one-time charge of $25,200,000 ($.31 per share) related to the early extinguishment of debt.
[f]Includes a one-time charge of $47,100,000 ($.62 per share) for the cumulative effect on prior years of FAS 106 as of July 1, 1992.
[g]Includes a one-time charge of $197,500,000 ($2.60 per share) for the cumulative effect on prior years of FAS 109 as of July 1, 1991.

Transfer Agent & Registrar: American Stock Transfer & Trust Co.

General Counsel:	Marschall I. Smith, Sr. V.P.	Auditors:	Ernst & Young LLP
Investor Relations:	David A. Prichard, V.P.	Traded (Symbol):	NYSE, CSE (IGL)
		Stockholders:	600
Human Resources:	B. Russell Lockridge, Sr. V.P.	Employees:	9,200
Mgt. Info. Svcs.:	Catherine J. Liebl, V.P.	Annual Meeting:	In October

LaSalle Banks Guide

Information Resources, Inc.

150 North Clinton Street, Chicago, Illinois 60661-1416
Telephone: (312) 726-1221

Information Resources, Inc. (IRI) provides a variety of information, software, and consulting services to clients in the consumer packaged goods industry. IRI's services include proprietary databases, advanced analytical consulting, and software application products which assist clients in testing, executing, monitoring, and evaluating their marketing, sales, and distribution programs. IRI's services are available in the United States, Europe, and other international markets. Incorporated in Delaware in 1982.

Directors (In addition to indicated officers)

James G. Andress
Edwin E. Epstein
Gerald J. Eskin, Ph.D.
John D.C. Little, Ph.D.
Leonard M. Lodish, Ph.D.

Edward E. Lucente
Edith W. Martin, Ph.D.
Jeffrey P. Stamen
Glen L. Urban, Ph.D.

Officers (Directors*)

*Thomas W. Wilson, Jr., Chm.
*Gian M. Fulgoni, C.E.O.
 Edward S. Berger, Secy. & Gen. Coun.

Gary M. Hill, C.F.O.
Randall S. Smith, Grp. Pres.—Oper. & Intl.

Consolidated Balance Sheet As of December 31, 1996 (000 omitted)

Assets		Liabilities & Stockholders' Equity	
Current assets	$118,183	Current liabilities	$ 83,603
Net property, plant & equipment	54,592	Long-term debt	5,500
Other assets	161,718	Deferred items	16,670
		Other liabilities	2,392
		*Stockholders' equity	226,328
Total	$334,493	Total	$334,493

*27,886,406 shares common stock outstanding.

Consolidated Income Statement

Years Ended Dec. 31	Thousands — — — —		Per Share — — —		Common Stock Price Range Calendar Year
	Revenues	Net Income	Earnings	Cash Dividends	
1996	$405,603	$(7,558)	$ (.26)	$ .00	16-1/4 — 11
1995	399,916	(11,678)	(.43)	.00	17-7/8 — 10-1/8
1994	376,570	(15,515)[a]	(.60)[a]	.00	39-1/4 — 11-1/4
1993	334,544	24,079[b]	.89[b]	.00	44 — 27
1992	276,362	19,247	.78	.00	35-3/4 — 18-1/2

[a]Includes a charge to reflect a change in accounting method to recognize revenue, resulting in a cumulative effect of $6,594,000 ($.26 per share).
[b]Includes a gain to reflect FAS 109, resulting in a cumulative effect of $1,864,000 ($.07 per share).

Transfer Agent & Registrar:	Harris Trust and Savings Bank		
General Counsel:	Freeborn & Peters	Traded (Symbol):	NASDAQ (IRIC)
Investor Relations:	Robert Bregenzer, Sr. V.P.	Stockholders:	3,293
Human Resources:	Gary Newman, Exec. V.P.	Employees:	4,000
Auditors:	Ernst & Young LLP	Annual Meeting:	In May

Inland Steel Industries, Inc.

30 West Monroe Street, Chicago, Illinois 60603
Telephone: (312) 346-0300

Inland Steel Industries, Inc. has three primary business units. Inland Steel Company, an integrated steel producer, mines iron ore, makes iron, and produces carbon and high-strength, low-alloy steels. Its sole steelmaking facility is the 1,900-acre Indiana Harbor Works at East Chicago, Indiana, with an annual raw steelmaking capacity of six million tons. Ryerson Tull, Inc., which is 87 percent-owned by the company, is the nation's largest metal distributor, with 60 centers in the U.S. and Mexico that process and distribute carbon, stainless and alloy steels, aluminum, nickel, brass, copper, and industrial plastics to 60,000 customers. Inland International, Inc. is the company's international marketing, trading, and distribution arm. Inland International was formed in January 1994. Inland Steel Industries, Inc., also is involved in several joint ventures through its business units. Incorporated in Delaware in 1986.

Directors   (In addition to indicated officers)

A. Robert Abboud
James A. Henderson
Robert B. McKersie
Leo F. Mullin

Jean-Pierre Rosso
Joshua I. Smith
Nancy H. Teeters
Arnold R. Weber

Officers   (Directors*)

*Robert J. Darnall, Chm., Pres. & C.E.O.
Dale E. Wiersbe, Sr. V.P. & C.O.O.
Judd R. Cool, V.P.—Hum. Res.
Jay M. Gratz, V.P. & C.F.O.
H. William Howard, V.P.—Info. Tech.

George A. Ranney, Jr., V.P. & Gen. Coun.
Vicki L. Avril, Treas.
James M. Hemphill, Cont.
Charles B. Salowitz, Secy.

Consolidated Balance Sheet   As of December 31, 1996 (000 omitted)

Assets		Liabilities & Stockholders' Equity	
Current assets	$1,227,800	Current liabilities	$ 536,800
Net property, plant & equipment	1,637,000	Long-term debt	773,200
Other assets	676,800	Deferred items	1,312,700
		Other liabilities	129,900
		*Stockholders' equity	789,000
Total	$3,541,600	Total	$3,541,600

*50,556,350 shares common stock outstanding.

Consolidated Income Statement

Years Ended Dec. 31	Thousands — — — — Net Sales	Net Income	Per Share — — — — Earnings	Cash Dividends	Common Stock Price Range Calendar Year	
1996	$4,584,100	$ 95,700	$ 1.23	$ .20	29	— 16
1995	4,781,500	146,800	2.69	.20	36-3/4	— 21-1/4
1994	4,497,000	107,400	1.81	.00	42	— 29-3/8
1993	3,888,200	(37,600)[a]	(1.96)[a]	.00	35	— 20
1992	3,494,300	(815,600)[b]	(25.82)[b]	.00	27	— 16-1/4

[a]Includes facility shutdown provision of $14,700,000 ($.41 per share) after tax.
[b]Includes a charge to reflect FAS 106, resulting in a cumulative after-tax effect of $656,200,000 ($19.99 per share).

Transfer Agent & Registrar:	Harris Trust and Savings Bank		
Corporate Counsel:	Mayer, Brown & Platt	Traded (Symbol):	NYSE, CSE (IAD)
Investor Relations:	Ann K. Zastrow, Mgr.	Stockholders:	15,000
Human Resources:	Judd R. Cool, V.P.	Employees:	15,410
Mgt. Info. Svcs.:	H. William Howard, V.P.	Annual Meeting:	In May
Auditors:	Price Waterhouse LLP	Internet:	www.inland.com

Insurance Auto Auctions, Inc.

850 East Algonquin Road, Suite 100, Schaumburg, Illinois 60173
Telephone: (847) 705-9550

Insurance Auto Auctions, Inc. and its subsidiaries offer insurance companies and other vehicle suppliers cost-effective salvage processing solutions. The company provides a complete solution to the cost recovery of vehicles that have been damaged in accidents or stolen and recovered. In an accident, theft, or other claims adjustment process, insurance companies typically take possession of a vehicle. Insurance Auto Auctions sells these vehicles at live or closed bid auctions on a competitive basis at one of the company's 46 facilities across the United States. In May 1996, the company relocated to Illinois from North Hollywood, California. Incorporated in 1982 in California; present name adopted in 1991.

Directors (In addition to indicated officers)

Maurice A. Cocca
Susan B. Gould
Christopher G. Knowles

Melvin R. Martin
Thomas J. O'Malia
Glen E. Tullman

Officers (Directors*)

*Bradley S. Scott, Chm.
*James P. Alampi, Pres. & C.E.O.
Kevin J. Code, V.P.—Sales & Mktg.
Donald J. Comis, V.P.—Central Div.
Gerald C. Comis, V.P.—Cust Svc. & Indust. Rel.
Peter B. Doder, V.P.—Western Div.

Stephen L. Green, V.P. & Cont.
Linda C. Larrabee, Sr. V.P.—Fin., C.F.O. & Secy.
Marcia C. McAllister, V.P.—Pub. Affairs
Charles E. Rice, V.P.—Info. Sys.
Patrick T. Walsh, V.P.—Eastern Div.

Consolidated Balance Sheet As of December 31, 1996 (000 omitted)

Assets		Liabilities & Stockholders' Equity	
Current assets	$ 54,051	Current liabilities	$ 34,372
Net property, plant & equipment	21,596	Long-term debt	26,670
Other assets	136,157	Other liabilities	4,173
		*Stockholders' equity	146,589
Total	$211,804	Total	$211,804

*11,282,838 shares common stock outstanding.

Consolidated Income Statement

Years Ended Dec. 31	Thousands — — — — Net Sales	Net Income	Per Share — — — Earnings	Cash Dividends	Common Stock Price Range Calendar Year
1996	$281,893	$ 3,102[a]	$ .27	$ .00	13-3/8 — 7-3/4
1995	257,996	3,136[a]	.27	.00	36 — 6-1/2
1994	172,125	10,985	.98	.00	38-5/8 — 24-1/2
1993	104,086	6,618	.74	.00	45-1/2 — 17-1/2
1992	60,535	4,379	.61	.00	23 — 12-1/8

[a]Includes special charges of $1,395,000 in 1996 and $4,226,000 in 1995 related to the company's repositioning to achieve its strategic objectives.

Transfer Agent & Registrar: Bank of Boston

General Counsel:
  Gunderson Dettmer Stough Villeneuve Franklin & Hachigian, LLP

Investor Relations: Linda C. Larrabee, Sr. V.P.

Human Resources: David Rogers, Dir.

Mgt. Info. Svcs.: Charles E. Rice, V.P.

Auditors: KPMG Peat Marwick LLP
Traded (Symbol): NASDAQ (IAAI)
Stockholders: 1,700
Employees: 630
Annual Meeting: In June
Internet: www.iaaspecialty.com

Intercargo Corporation

1450 East American Lane, 20th Floor, Schaumburg, Illinois 60173-6090
Telephone: (847) 517-2990

Intercargo Corporation is a holding company that serves as a management and administrative organization for its insurance company subsidiaries, which mainly provide specialized insurance coverages for companies involved in international trade. The primary coverages underwritten by the subsidiaries are U.S. Customs bonds, marine insurance, errors and omissions insurance, and other property and casualty coverages. Intercargo's market consists primarily of importers and exporters, custom brokers and freight forwarders (service firms engaged in the movement of international cargo for their clients), and other global traders. Intercargo serves customers in all major trading centers across the United States and has established a presence in Canada, the United Kingdom, and Hong Kong. The company's primary subsidiaries are Intercargo Insurance Company; International Advisory Services, Inc.; Intercargo International Limited; TRM Insurance Services, Inc.; and Intercargo Insurance Company H.K. Limited (wholly owned by Intercargo Insurance Company). Incorporated in Delaware in 1985.

Directors   (In addition to indicated officers)

Kenneth A. Bodenstein
Arthur J. Fritz, Jr.
Albert J. Gallegos

Arthur L. Litman
Robert B. Sanborn
Michael L. Sklar

Officers   (Directors*)

*James R. Zuhlke, Chm.
Stanley A. Galansky, Pres. & C.E.O.
Gary C. Bhojwani, V.P.—Mktg.

Michael L. Rybak, V.P. & C.F.O.
Dean T. Bruner, Cont.
Robert S. Kielbas, Dir.—Intl. Bus. Dev.

Consolidated Balance Sheet   As of December 31, 1996 (000 omitted)

Assets		Liabilities & Stockholders' Equity	
Cash & cash equivalents	$ 18,492	Losses & loss adj. expense	$ 47,037
Investments	66,643	Unearned premiums	17,617
Premiums receivable	16,231	Notes payable	9,735
Equipment	2,277	Other liabilities	11,309
Other assets	30,067	*Stockholders' equity	48,012
Total	$133,710	Total	$133,710

*7,659,981 shares common stock outstanding.

Consolidated Income Statement

Years Ended Dec. 31	Thousands — — — — Total Revenues	Net Income	Per Share — — — Earnings[a]	Cash Dividends	Common Stock Price Range Calendar Year
1996	$68,241	$6,404	$ .84	$ .18	11-1/2 — 7-1/2
1995	94,186	2,139	.28	.18	14-3/4 — 8
1994	80,885	4,981	.65	.18	12-1/4 — 7-1/4
1993	50,712	2,138	.30	.17	14-1/2 — 10
1992	46,376	4,379	.68	.08	17 — 10

[a]From continuing operations.

Transfer Agent & Registrar: Harris Trust and Savings Bank

Human Resources: Lauren Nessler

Mgt. Info. Svcs.:   Jose Davila

Auditors: Ernst & Young LLP

Traded (Symbol):   NASDAQ (ICAR)
Stockholders: 2,144
Employees: 222
Annual Meeting: Third Friday in May

The Interlake Corporation

550 Warrenville Road, Lisle, Illinois 60532-4387
Telephone: (630) 852-8800

The Interlake Corporation is a diversified multinational company operating in two business segments. The Engineered Materials segment includes Special Materials (ferrous metal powder used to manufacture precision parts) and Aerospace Components (precision jet engine components and jet engine fan blade repair). The Handling segment includes automated systems, hardware, and supplies used to convey, store, retrieve, and sort. Interlake's sales offices, warehouses and manufacturing plants are located in the United States, Australia, Belgium, England, and Germany. Major subsidiaries include: Chem-tronics, Inc.; Dexion (Australia) Pty. Ltd.; Dexion Group plc; Hoeganaes Corporation; and Interlake Material Handling. In October 1996, Interlake sold its packaging businesses to Samuel Manu-Tech Inc. of Etobicoke, Ontario, Canada. Incorporated in New York in 1905; reincorporated in Delaware in 1986.

Directors (In addition to indicated officer)

John A. Canning, Jr.
James C. Cotting
John E. Jones
Frederick C. Langenberg

Quentin C. McKenna
William G. Mitchell
Erwin E. Schulze

Officers (Directors*)

*W. Robert Reum, Chm., Pres. & C.E.O.
Craig A. Grant, V.P.—Hum. Res.
Stephen Gregory, V.P.—Fin. & C.F.O.

Stephen R. Smith, V.P., Gen. Coun. & Secy.
John P. Miller, Cont.
Donn A. York, Treas.

Consolidated Balance Sheet As of December 29, 1996 (000 omitted)

Assets		Liabilities & Stockholders' Equity	
Current assets	$272,097	Current liabilities	$ 159,136
Net property, plant & equipment	145,099	Long-term debt	395,060
Other assets	40,527	Deferred items	9,346
		Other liabilities	122,315
		*Stockholders' equity	(228,134)
Total	$457,723	Total	$ 457,723

*23,112,999 shares common stock outstanding.

Consolidated Income Statement

Years Ended Abt. Dec. 31	Thousands — — — — Net Sales[a]	Net Income	Per Share — — — Earnings	Cash Dividends	Common Stock Price Range Calendar Year
1996	$709,585	$ 55,244[b]	$ 1.74[b]	$ .00	4-1/2 — 1-3/4
1995	689,913	765[c]	.03[c]	.00	3-1/4 — 1-5/8
1994	622,400	(40,751)[d]	(1.85)	.00	3-7/8 — 1-1/2
1993	559,192	(25,962)[e]	(1.18)	.00	4-3/4 — 2-1/2
1992	585,270	(27,698)[f]	(1.67)[f]	.00	9-3/8 — 3-1/4

[a]From continuing operations.
[b]Includes income from discontinued operations, net of applicable income taxes, of $46,376,000; an extraordinary loss on early retirement of debt of $267,000 ($.01 per share); and a cumulative effect of changes in accounting principles of $1,876,000.
[c]Includes an extraordinary loss on early retirement of debt of $3,448,000 ($.15 per share).
[d]Includes goodwill writedown of $34,174,000.
[e]Includes a restructuring charge of $5,611,000 and a non-operating charge of $4,750,000 for environmental matters.
[f]Includes an extraordinary loss on early retirement of debt of $7,567,000 ($.46 per share) and the cumulative effect of FAS 106 and FAS 109 of $6,141,000 ($.37 per share).

Transfer Agent & Registrar:	First Chicago Trust Co. of New York		
General Counsel:	Jones, Day, Reavis & Pogue	Traded (Symbol):	NYSE, CSE (IK)
Investor Relations:	Stephen R. Smith, V.P.	Stockholders:	6,595
Human Resources:	Craig A. Grant, V.P.	Employees:	3,839
Mgt. Info. Svcs.:	Bruce E. Steimle, Dir.	Annual Meeting:	In April
Auditors:	Price Waterhouse LLP	Internet:	www.interlake.com

IWI Holding Limited

Oakmont Centre, 1010 Executive Court, Suite 300, Westmont, Illinois 60559

Telephone: (630) 887-8288

IWI Holding Limited and its U.S. subsidary, Imperial World, Inc., are engaged in the design, assembly, merchandising, and wholesale distribution of fine jewelry. The majority of the company's sales are under the trade name *World Pacific Jewelry*. IWI distributes its products to department stores, mass merchandisers, and specialty stores. In December 1994, the company completed an initial public offering of 1,700,000 shares of common stock. In February 1995, IWI Holding purchased the corporate name, all trade names, customer lists, other intangibles, and active dies and molds of Ullenberg Corp., a distributor of jewelry in the U.S. In July 1995, Imperial World acquired the Daco Group of Companies in Toronto. Incorporated in the British Virgin Islands in 1993.

Directors (In addition to indicated officers)

David F. Chui, Chm.
Michael Kaplan
James B. McCarthy

James W. Pierpont
Jack Reiff

Officers (Directors*)

*Bruce W. Anderson, Pres. & C.E.O.
*Joseph K. Lau, Sr. V.P., C.O.O. & Secy.

Richard J. Mick, V.P.—Sales
*Richard W. Sigman, V.P.—Fin. & C.F.O.

Consolidated Balance Sheet As of December 31, 1996 (000 omitted)

Assets		Liabilities & Stockholders' Equity	
Current assets	$27,315	Current liabilities	$15,277
Net property, plant & equipment	2,453	Long-term debt	204
		*Stockholders' equity	14,287
Total	$29,768	Total	$29,768

*2,582,900 shares common stock outstanding.

Consolidated Income Statement

Years Ended Dec. 31	Thousands — — — — Net Sales	Net Income	Per Share[a] — — — Earnings	Cash Dividends	Common Stock Price Range[a] Calendar Year
1996	$30,840	$(5,936)	$(2.25)	$ .00	3-1/4 — 1/2
1995	41,710	(1,384)	(.53)	.00	10-1/4 — 1-7/8
1994	41,902	2,291	.87	.00	8-5/8 — 8-1/2
1993	35,616	1,760[b]	.57[b]		
1992	33,402	1,209[b]	.87[b]		

[a]Initial public offering in December 1994.
[b]Pro forma.

Transfer Agent & Registrar:	Continental Stock Transfer & Trust Co., NY		
General Counsel:	Vander Kam & Sanders	Traded (Symbol):	NASDAQ (JEWLF)
		Stockholders:	1,400
Investor Relations:	Richard W. Sigman, V.P.	Employees:	100
Auditors:	Ernst & Young LLP	Annual Meeting:	As set by Directors

JG Industries, Inc.

5630 West Belmont Avenue, Chicago, Illinois 60634
Telephone: (773) 481-5400

JG Industries, Inc., is a Chicago-based retailing concern that operates 10 Goldblatt's department stores with nine locations in the Chicago area and one in Indiana. Goldblatt's stores offer a broad range of fashion-wearing apparel for the entire family. The department stores also sell hard-line merchandise, including toys, sporting goods, cosmetics, luggage, housewares, textiles, and domestics. Incorporated in Illinois in 1928.

Directors (In addition to indicated officers)

Sheldon C. Collen
Sheldon Harris

Wallace W. Schroeder

Officers (Directors*)

*William Hellman, Chm. & C.E.O.
*Clarence Farrar, Pres. & C.O.O.
*Lionel H. Goldblatt, V.P.

*Philip Rootberg, V.P.
Evelyn P. Egan, Treas. & Secy.

Consolidated Balance Sheet As of January 25, 1997 (000 omitted)

Assets		Liabilities & Stockholders' Equity	
Current assets	$ 8,533	Current liabilities	$ 5,091
Net property, plant & equipment	5,513	Long-term debt, less current portion	1,164
Other assets	1,629	Other long-term liabilities	867
		Minority interest	1,262
		*Stockholders' equity	7,291
Total	$15,675	Total	$15,675

*2,405,770 shares common stock outstanding.

Consolidated Income Statement

Years Ended Abt. Jan. 31	Thousands — — — — Net Sales[a]	Net Income	Per Share[b] — — — — Earnings	Cash Dividends	Common Stock Price Range[b] Calendar Year
1997	$60,198	$(2,150)	$(1.17)	$ .00	
1996	72,964	2,753	1.05	.00	4-7/8 — 1-1/4
1995	77,106	487	.11	.00	6-3/4 — 3
1994	76,900	(1,346)	(.70)	.00	6-3/4 — 3
1993	77,482	(7,149)	(4.22)	.00	10-1/2 — 3-3/8

[a]From continuing operations.
[b]Adjusted to reflect a 1-for-3 reverse stock split in December 1996.

Transfer Agent & Registrar:	First Chicago Trust Co. of New York		
Investor Relations:	Evelyn P. Egan, Treas.	Stockholders:	2,464
Auditors:	Coopers & Lybrand L.L.P.	Employees:	696
Traded (Symbol):	NASDAQ, CSE (JGICD)	Annual Meeting:	In June

Johnstown America Industries, Inc.

980 North Michigan Avenue, Suite 1000, Chicago, Illinois 60611
Telephone: (312) 280-8844

Johnstown America Industries, Inc. has five operating units: Johnstown America Corporation, Johnstown, Pennsylvania, a leading manufacturer of railroad freight cars that are used principally for hauling coal, intermodal containers, highway trailers, and agricultural and mining products; JAIX Leasing Company, Chicago, Illinois, a lessor of new and remanufactured freight cars; Freight Car Services, Inc., Danville, Illinois, a rebuilder and repairer of freight cars; Truck Components, Inc., Rockford, Illinois, a leading supplier of wheel-end components for the medium and heavy-duty truck industry and a leading producer of complex iron castings for a wide range of industries; and Bostrom Seating, Inc., Piedmont, Alabama, a leading manufacturer of suspension and static seating for the heavy-duty truck market. Incorporated in Delaware in 1991.

Directors (In addition to indicated officers)

Camillo Santomero
R. Philip Silver

Francis A. Stroble

Officers (Directors*)

*Thomas M. Begel, Chm., Pres. & C.E.O.
*Andrew M. Weller, Exec. V.P. & C.F.O.
David W. Riesmeyer, V.P. & Treas.
Kenneth Tallering, V.P., Secy. & Gen. Coun.
James D. Cirar, Pres.—Johnstown America Corp.

Edward J. Whalen, Pres.—JAIX Leasing Co./Freight Car Svcs. Inc.
Thomas Cook, Pres. & C.E.O.—Truck Components, Inc.
Timothy Masek, Pres.—Bostrom Seating, Inc.

Consolidated Balance Sheet   As of December 31, 1996 (000 omitted)

Assets		Liabilities & Stockholders' Equity	
Current assets	$142,830	Current liabilities	$115,611
Net property, plant & equipment	123,859	Long-term debt	186,939
Other assets	288,594	Senior subordinated debt	100,000
		Other liabilities	89,196
		*Stockholders' equity	63,537
Total	$555,283	Total	$555,283

*9,754,000 shares common stock outstanding.

Consolidated Income Statement

Years Ended Dec. 31	Thousands — — — — Net Sales	Net Income	Per Share[a] — — — Earnings	Cash Dividends	Common Stock Price Range[ab] Calendar Year
1996	$559,972	$(5,371)	$ (.55)	$ .00	5-5/8 — 2-1/2
1995[c]	668,601	5,585	.57	.00	16-3/4 — 4-1/4
1994	468,525	5,697	.58	.00	30-1/4 — 10-1/2
1993	329,122	2,463[d]	.30[d]	.00	26-1/4 — 14
1992	204,500	(731)	(.13)		

[a]Adjusted to reflect a 2-for-5 reverse stock split in July 1993.
[b]Initial public offering in July 1993.
[c]Reflects the acquisition of Truck Components, Inc. (August 1995) and Bostrom Seating, Inc. (January 1995).
[d]Includes an extraordinary charge of $2,918,000 ($.36 per share) from the repayment of debt.

Transfer Agent & Registrar: The First National Bank of Boston

Investor Relations:	Andrew M. Weller, Exec. V.P.	Stockholders:	2,500
Auditors:	Arthur Andersen LLP	Employees:	3,800
Traded (Symbol):	NASDAQ (JAII)	Annual Meeting:	In May

Juno Lighting, Inc.

2001 South Mt. Prospect Road, P.O. Box 5065, Des Plaines, Illinois 60017-5065
Telephone: (847) 827-9880

Juno Lighting, Inc. manufactures and markets a full line of recessed and track lighting fixtures for use in new construction and remodeling of commercial, institutional, and residential buildings. The company produces more than 300 styles of fixtures and related equipment of both contemporary and traditional design with a variety of finishes. Principal products use both incandescent and fluorescent light sources. The company also produces a line of exit and emergency lighting products that are electronically powered and protected. This product line uses LED (light emitting diode) technology as its light source. More than 94 percent of the company's sales are to electrical distributors and wholesale lighting outlets in the United States. Warehouse facilities are located in the metropolitan areas of Atlanta, Dallas, Indianapolis, Los Angeles, Philadelphia, and Toronto. Subsidiaries are Juno Lighting, Ltd. and Indy Lighting, Inc. Incorporated in Illinois in 1976; reincorporated in Delaware in 1983.

Directors (In addition to indicated officers)

George M. Ball

Allan Coleman

Officers (Directors*)

*Robert S. Fremont, Chm. & C.E.O.
*Ronel W. Giedt, Pres. & C.O.O.
George J. Bilek, V.P.—Fin. & Treas.
Glenn R. Bordfeld, V.P.—Sales

Charles F. Huber, V.P.—Corp. Dev.
*Thomas W. Tomsovic, V.P.—Oper.
*Julius Lewis, Secy.

Consolidated Balance Sheet As of November 30, 1996 (000 omitted)

Assets		Liabilities & Stockholders' Equity	
Current assets	$120,441	Current liabilities	$ 15,976
Net property, plant & equipment	42,805	Long-term debt	4,433
Other assets	14,935	Deferred items	2,111
		*Stockholders' equity	155,661
Total	$178,181	Total	$178,181

*18,513,012 shares common stock outstanding.

Consolidated Income Statement

Years Ended Nov. 30	Thousands — — — — Net Sales	Net Income	Per Share[a] — — — — Earnings	Cash Dividends	Common Stock Price Range[a] Calendar Year
1996	$131,479	$19,897	$1.08	$ .32	18-1/2 — 13
1995	126,364	19,974	1.08	.30	21 — 14
1994	126,777	22,907	1.23	.26	21 — 16-1/4
1993	109,098	18,213	.98	.22	21 — 15-1/2
1992	96,633	15,321	.83	.17	18-1/4 — 10

[a]Adjusted to reflect a 2-for-1 stock split in April 1992.

Transfer Agent & Registrar: First Chicago Trust Co. of New York

General Counsel:
Sonnenschein Nath & Rosenthal

Investor Relations: George J. Bilek, V.P.

Human Resources: George J. Bilek, V.P.

Mgt. Info. Svcs.: George J. Bilek, V.P.

Auditors: Price Waterhouse LLP

Traded (Symbol): NASDAQ (JUNO)

Stockholders: 316

Employees: 1,025

Annual Meeting: In April

Landauer, Inc.
2 Science Road, Glenwood, Illinois 60425-1586
Telephone: (708) 755-7000

Landauer, Inc. engages in the detection of personal exposure to occupational and environmental hazards in the workplace and at home. The company specializes in providing complete radiation dosimetry programs, which include the manufacture of various types of personal radiation exposure detection monitors, the distribution and collection of the monitors to and from clients, and the analysis and reporting of exposure findings. Services are used by hospitals, universities, national laboratories, nuclear power plants, medical and dental offices, and other industries in which radiation poses a potential threat to employees. Landauer also offers assessment of the concentration of radon gas in homes and other buildings through its long-term alpha-track radon gas detectors. The company operates a 50 percent owned subsidiary in Japan, Nagase-Landauer, Ltd., which is involved in radiation monitoring in that country. Landauer branch offices are located in California, New Jersey, Texas and the United Kingdom. Incorporated in Delaware in 1987.

Directors (In addition to indicated officers)

Robert J. Cronin
Gary D. Eppen, Ph.D.
Richard R. Risk

Paul B. Rosenberg
Herbert Roth, Jr.
Michael D. Winfield

Officers (Directors*)

*Marvin G. Schorr, Chm.
*Thomas M. Fulton, Pres. & C.E.O.
Brent A. Latta, Exec. V.P.
James M. O'Connell, V.P., C.F.O., Treas. & Secy.

R. Craig Yoder, V.P.—Oper.
Larry A. Barden, Gen. Coun.
Lester A. Core, Asst. Secy.

Consolidated Balance Sheet As of September 30, 1996 (000 omitted)

Assets		Liabilities & Stockholders' Equity	
Current assets	$21,319	Current liabilities	$16,744
Net property, plant & equipment	7,725	*Stockholders' equity	24,859
Other assets	12,559		
Total	$41,603	Total	$41,603

*8,477,285 shares common stock outstanding.

Consolidated Income Statement

Years Ended Sept. 30	Thousands — — — — Net Revenue	Net Income	Per Share[a] — — — — Earnings	Cash Dividends	Common Stock Price Range[a] Calendar Year
1996	$36,516	$10,899	$1.29	$1.10	24-7/8 — 19-1/4
1995	34,032	10,061	1.19	1.00	22-1/8 — 16-1/4
1994	31,653	8,903	1.05	.88	17 — 13-1/8
1993	29,406	8,023	.95	.80	17-1/4 — 14-5/8
1992	27,823	7,882	.93	1.15	21-3/8 — 14-1/2

[a]Adjusted to reflect a 2-for-1 stock split in January 1992.

Transfer Agent & Registrar: American Stock Transfer & Trust Co.

Investor Relations: James M. O'Connell, V.P.

Corporate Counsel: Sidley & Austin

Human Resources: James M. O'Connell, V.P.

Mgt. Info. Svcs.: Emil A. Plecko

Auditors: Arthur Andersen LLP

Traded (Symbol): AMEX, CSE (LDR)

Stockholders: 600

Employees: 260

Annual Meeting: In February

Lawson Products, Inc.

1666 East Touhy Avenue, Des Plaines, Illinois 60018
Telephone: (847) 827-9666

Lawson Products, Inc. is an international distributor of approximately 33,000 expendable maintenance, repair and replacement fasteners, parts, chemical specialties, welding rods, and supplies. These products are used for the repair and maintenance of capital equipment of all types in the industrial, heavy duty equipment, buildings and grounds maintenance, and transportation fields. Additionally, the company distributes 12,000 production components to the original equipment manufacturer marketplace. Sales are made to a wide variety of industrial, mining, institutional, governmental, agricultural, automotive, and apartment building maintenance customers through approximately 1,800 agents in the United States, Canada, England, Mexico, and Puerto Rico. Distribution centers for maintenance items are located in Georgia, Illinois, Nevada, New Jersey, North Carolina, Texas, Canada, and England. Production components are distributed through the company's subsidiary, Assembley Component Systems, Inc., with distribution systems located in Alabama, Arkansas, Illinois, Mississippi, and Tennessee. Specialized subsidiaries include Cronatron Welding Systems, Inc. and Drummond American Corporation. Incorporated in Illinois in 1952; reincorporated in Delaware in 1982.

Directors   (In addition to indicated officers)

James T. Brophy   Ronald B. Port, M.D.   Robert G. Rettig

Officers   (Directors*)

*Bernard Kalish, Chm. & C.E.O.
*Sidney L. Port, Chm. of the Exec. Comm.
*Peter G. Smith, Sr., Pres. & C.O.O.
*Hugh L. Allen, Exec. V.P.—Sales & Mktg.
Jeffrey B. Belford, Exec. V.P.—Oper.
Roger F. Cannon, Exec. V.P.—Sales & Mktg.
Walter L. Anderson, V.P.—Eng.
George H. Buckingham, V.P.—East. Field Sales
James N. Buckingham, V.P.—Mexico & Latin Amer. Dev.

John M. Del Sasso, V.P.—Dist.
Daniel Luber, V.P.—Corp. Planning & Dev.
James H. Mann, V.P.—Info. Svcs.
Joseph L. Pawlick, V.P. & Cont.
James L. Schmidt, V.P.—Admin.
Donald A. Schneider, V.P.—Res. & Dev.
*Jerome Shaffer, V.P. & Treas.
James J. Smith, V.P.—Hum. Res.
Robert J. Spedale, V.P.—Purch. & Prod. Dev.
Robert J. Washlow, Secy.

Consolidated Balance Sheet   As of December 31, 1996 (000 omitted)

Assets		Liabilities & Stockholders' Equity	
Current assets	$103,100	Current liabilities	$ 24,350
Net property, plant & equipment	40,053	Other liabilities	22,066
Other assets	32,009	*Stockholders' equity	128,746
Total	$175,162	Total	$175,162

*11,311,464 shares common stock outstanding.

Consolidated Income Statement

Years Ended Dec. 31	Thousands — — — —		Per Share — — —		Common Stock Price Range Calendar Year
	Net Sales	Net Income	Earnings	Cash Dividends	
1996	$250,289	$19,995	$1.73	$ .52	26-1/4 — 21
1995	223,537	21,120	1.75	.51	28-1/2 — 23-1/2
1994	213,097	20,524	1.55	.48	31 — 21-3/4
1993	195,735	18,117	1.34	.44	30-3/4 — 23-1/4
1992	186,709	15,343	1.13	.40	31-1/4 — 22

Transfer Agent & Registrar: The First National Bank of Chicago

General Counsel:
  McDermott, Will & Emery; Vedder, Price, Kaufman & Kammholz

Investor Relations: Bernard Kalish, Chm.

Human Resources: James J. Smith, V.P.

Mgt. Info. Svcs.:   James H. Mann, V.P.

Auditors: Ernst & Young LLP
Traded (Symbol):   NASDAQ (LAWS)
Stockholders: 1,185
Employees: 1,050
Annual Meeting: In May

Lawter International, Inc.

990 Skokie Boulevard, Northbrook, Illinois 60062
Telephone: (847) 498-4700

Lawter International, Inc. manufactures and markets specialty chemicals. Products include: printing ink vehicles and components, which enable printing inks to carry color onto a variety of printing surfaces; synthetic and hydrocarbon resins for the production of printing inks, varnishes and other coatings, adhesives, rubber compounds, and plastics; and coatings used in the production of paint, printing ink, paper coatings, plastic products, and rubber compounds. The company's domestic plants are located in Illinois, Alabama, California, New Jersey, Tennessee, and Wisconsin. Plants outside the United States are located in Belgium, Canada, Denmark, England, Germany, Ireland, Italy, the People's Republic of China, Singapore, and Spain. In November 1996, the company announced that it would move its corporate headquarters to southern Wisconsin in the fall of 1997. Incorporated in Delaware in 1958 to succeed a company established in 1940.

Directors   (In addition to indicated officers)

William P. Clark
Arthur A. Hartman
Leonard P. Judy

Richard D. Nordman
Fred G. Steingraber

Officers   (Directors*)

* John O'Mahoney, Chm. & C.E.O.
* John P. Jilek, Pres. & C.O.O.
  Ludwig P. Horn, V.P.

Mark W. Joslin, C.F.O. & Treas.
Victoria J. Patrick, Asst. Secy.

Consolidated Balance Sheet   As of December 31, 1996 (000 omitted)

Assets		Liabilities & Stockholders' Equity	
Current assets	$156,587	Current liabilities	$ 82,177
Net property, plant & equipment	92,117	Long-term debt	29,050
Equity investment	24,833	Deferred items	36,281
Other assets	19,586	*Stockholders' equity	145,615
Total	$293,123	Total	$293,123

*45,348,535 shares common stock outstanding.

Consolidated Income Statement

Years Ended Dec. 31	Thousands — — — — Net Sales	Net Income	Per Share — — — Earnings	Cash Dividends	Common Stock Price Range Calendar Year
1996	$193,814	$28,775	$ .64	$ .40	13 — 10-3/8
1995	204,835	16,278[a]	.36[a]	.40	14-3/8 — 10-1/4
1994	191,056	29,405	.66	.40	13-3/4 — 10-3/4
1993	172,249	5,027[b]	.11[b]	.40	15-1/2 — 12-1/8
1992	167,568	27,015	.62	.40	14-7/8 — 11-7/8

[a]Includes an aftertax charge of $11,300,000 ($.25 per share) relating to consolidation of manufacturing facilities, primarily in Europe; reduction of personnel; disposal of certain assets; and other various charges.
[b]Includes adjustments of $21,600,000 ($.48 per share) for taxes on foreign earnings; $6,400,000 ($.14 per share) for other charges; and a credit of $4,025,000 ($.09 per share) for FAS 109.

Transfer Agent & Registrar:	Harris Trust and Savings Bank		
General Counsel:	Bell, Boyd & Lloyd	Traded (Symbol):	NYSE (LAW)
Investor Relations:	John O'Mahoney, Chm.	Stockholders:	3,000
Human Resources:	Sue Vollmer	Employees:	502
Auditors:	Arthur Andersen LLP	Annual Meeting:	In April

LaSalle Banks Guide

The Leap Group, Inc.

22 West Hubbard Street, Chicago, Illinois 60610
Telephone: (312) 494-0300

The Leap Group, Inc. is a strategic and creative communications company that develops and implements integrated brand marketing campaigns using traditional and new media, primarily for market-leading clients. Traditional marketing services provided by the company include television, print, radio, and outdoor advertising in addition to promotions, direct mail, and package and logo design. New media services include digital interactive applications such as World Wide Web sites and CD-ROMs. Headquartered in Chicago, the company also maintains offices in Los Angeles, New York, San Francisco, and Moscow. The company's wholly owned operating subsidiaries are: The Leap Partnership, Inc.; Lilypad Services, Inc.; Quantum Leap Communications, Inc.; Tadpole Productions, Inc.; and YAR Communications, Inc., a New York City-based advertising and marketing agency acquired by the company in April 1997. In September 1996, The Leap Group completed an initial public offering of 4,000,000 shares of common stock. Incorporated in Delaware in 1996.

Directors   (In addition to indicated officers)

Guy B. Day
John G. Keane

Thomas McElligott

Officers   (Directors*)

*R. Steven Lutterbach, Chm. & C.E.O.
*Thomas R. Sharbaugh, Pres.
*Frederick R. Smith, V. Chm. & C.O.O.
*George Gier, Exec. V.P. & Chf. Mktg./Info. Off.
 Joseph A. Sciarotta, Exec. V.P. & Chf. Creative Off.

Robert C. Bramlette, Chf. Legal/Strat. Off. & Secy.
Peter Vezmar, C.F.O. & Treas.
*Yuri Radzievsky, Pres. & C.E.O.—YAR Communications, Inc.

Consolidated Balance Sheet   As of January 31, 1997 (000 omitted)

Assets		Liabilities & Stockholders' Equity	
Current assets	$37,605	Current liabilities	$ 2,911
Net property, plant & equipment	1,190	Long-term debt	366
Other assets	1,065	*Stockholders' equity	36,583
Total	$39,860	Total	$39,860

*13,600,000 shares common stock outstanding.

Consolidated Income Statement

Years Ended Jan. 31	Thousands — — — —		Per Share[a] — — —		Common Stock
	Net Sales	Net Income	Earnings	Cash Dividends	Price Range[a] Calendar Year
1997	$16,088	$ 1,306	$ .12	$ .00	
1996	8,210	700	.07	.00	10-1/2 — 5-1/4
1995	4,679	(1,065)	(.11)	.00	
1994[b]	373	(76)	(.01)	.00	

[a]Initial public offering in September 1996.
[b]From the company's inception on September 20, 1993, to January 31, 1994.

Transfer Agent & Registrar:	First Chicago Trust Co. of New York		
General Counsel:	Robert C. Bramlette	Traded (Symbol):	NASDAQ (LEAP)
Investor Relations:	Beth Pastor	Stockholders:	150
Human Resources:	Diane Jozefowicz	Employees:	282
Mgt. Info. Svcs.:	George Gier, Exec. V.P.	Annual Meeting:	In June
Auditors:	Arthur Andersen LLP	Internet:	www.leapgroup.com

Lifeway Foods, Inc.
7625 North Austin Street, Skokie, Illinois 60077
Telephone: (847) 967-1010

Lifeway Foods, Inc. produces and distributes a variety of specialty dairy products. The company's products include Kefir, a drinkable product similar to but distinct from yogurt, in several flavors sold under the name "Lifeway's Kefir"; a plain farmer's cheese sold under the name "Lifeway's Farmer's Cheese"; and a fruit sugar-flavored product similar in consistency to cream cheese sold under the name of "Sweet Kiss." In 1995, the company began marketing a vegetable-based seasoning under the name "Golden Zesta." The company currently distributes its products throughout the Chicago metropolitan area through local food stores. In addition, the products are sold throughout the United States and Ontario, Canada. The company has also expanded the distribution of some of its products internationally by exporting to Eastern Europe through its wholly owned subsidiary, Lifeway International, Inc. Incorporated in Illinois in 1986.

Directors   (In addition to indicated officers)

Renzo Bernardi   Pol Sikar
Rick D. Salm

Officers   (Directors*)

*Michael Smolyansky, Pres., C.E.O., C.F.O. &   Valeriy Nikolenko, V.P.—Prod. & Secy.
   Treas.

Consolidated Balance Sheet   As of December 31, 1996 (000 omitted)

Assets		Liabilities & Stockholders' Equity	
Current assets	$2,316	Current liabilities	$ 620
Net property, plant & equipment	2,877	Long-term debt	1,469
Other assets	67	Deferred items	37
		*Stockholders' equity	3,134
Total	$5,260	Total	$5,260

*3,785,377 shares common stock outstanding.

Consolidated Income Statement

Years Ended Dec. 31	Thousands — — — — Net Sales	Net Income	Per Share — — — — Earnings	Cash Dividends	Common Stock Price Range Calendar Year
1996	$5,295	$618	$ .16	$ .00	3-7/8 — 1-3/8
1995	4,498	441	.12	.00	4-1/4 — 1-1/8
1994	3,542	216	.06	.00	2-1/4 — 1-1/8
1993	3,004	101	.03	.00	2-7/8 — 2-1/2
1992	2,446	98	.03	.00	3-3/8 — 2

Transfer Agent & Registrar: Affiliated Stock Transfer Co.

General Counsel: Futro & Associates

Auditors:
   Gleeson, Sklar, Sawyers & Cumpata LLP

Traded (Symbol):   NASDAQ (LWAY)

Stockholders: 347

Employees: 38

Annual Meeting: In June

Internet: www.lifeway.net & www.kefir.com

Lindberg Corporation

6133 North River Road, Suite 700, Rosemont, Illinois 60018
Telephone: (847) 823-2021

Lindberg Corporation provides heat treating services and produces a variety of metal parts. The company serves many markets, including the automotive, truck, construction equipment, consumer durables, defense and aerospace, and tool and die industries. Commercial heat treating services are provided from 18 manufacturing facilities offering a variety of thermal processes. These include hardening and tempering; carburizing; nitriding; selective hardening; solution treating and aging; stress relieving; normalizing; and other specialty or proprietary processes. Aluminum and zinc die castings and assemblies are produced at Impact Industries and Arrow-Acme. Harris Metals provides precision aluminum castings. Impact Industries, Inc. is a principal subsidiary. Incorporated in Illinois in 1924; reincorporated in Delaware in 1976.

Directors (In addition to indicated officers)

Raymond F. Decker
Raymond A. Jean

John W. Puth
J. Thomas Schanck

Officers (Directors*)

*George H. Bodeen, Chm.
*Leo G. Thompson, Pres. & C.E.O.
Michael W. Nelson, Sr. V.P. &
  Pres.—Lindberg Heat Treating Co.
Stephen S. Penley, Sr. V.P. & C.F.O.
Terrence D. Brown, V.P.

Geoffrey S. Calhoun, V.P.
Roger J. Fabian, V.P.
Paul J. McCarren, V.P.
Jerome R. Sullivan, V.P. & Mgr.—Hum. Res.
Brian J. McInerney, Treas.

Consolidated Balance Sheet As of December 31, 1996 (000 omitted)

Assets		Liabilities & Stockholders' Equity	
Current assets	$26,029	Current liabilities	$12,613
Net property, plant & equipment	44,963	Long-term debt	20,759
Other assets	7,103	Deferred items	6,848
		Other liabilities	4,828
		*Stockholders' equity	33,047
Total	$78,095	Total	$78,095

*4,779,141 shares common stock outstanding.

Consolidated Income Statement

Years Ended Dec. 31	Thousands — — — —		Per Share — — — —		Common Stock Price Range Calendar Year
	Revenues	Net Income	Earnings	Cash Dividends	
1996	$114,020	$ 5,016	$ 1.03	$ .29	11-1/8 — 6-3/8
1995	122,004	5,635	1.18	.25	7-1/2 — 5-1/4
1994	99,858	4,374	.92	.21	8-3/4 — 4-1/8
1993[a]	69,619	(1,318)	(.28)	.20	5-3/4 — 3-1/2
1992	71,039	942	.20	.24	5-1/2 — 3

[a]Includes a charge of $8,261,000 ($5,122,000 after-tax) for the restructuring of the company's heat treat operations and a gain of $1,500,000 ($.32 per share) reflecting an accounting change. Excluding these items, net income for 1993 was $2,304,473 ($.49 per share).

Transfer Agent & Registrar:	Harris Trust and Savings Bank		
General Counsel:	Bell, Boyd & Lloyd	**Traded (Symbol):**	NASDAQ (LIND)
Investor Relations:	Stephen S. Penley, Sr. V.P.	**Stockholders:**	1,300
Human Resources:	Jerome R. Sullivan, V.P.	**Employees:**	1,071
Auditors:	Arthur Andersen LLP	**Annual Meeting:**	In April

Littelfuse, Inc.

800 East Northwest Highway, Des Plaines, Illinois 60016
Telephone: (847) 824-1188

Littelfuse, Inc. is a leading designer, manufacturer, and marketer of fuses and other circuit protection devices for use in the electronic, automotive, and general industrial markets. The company manufactures its products on fully integrated manufacturing and assembly equipment, much of which is designed and built by its own engineers. Littelfuse conducts a majority of its own fabrication and maintains product quality through a rigorous quality assurance program. In addition to its Des Plaines world headquarters, the company has manufacturing facilities in Arcola, Centralia, and Watseka, Illinois, and also in China, England, Korea, Mexico, and Switzerland. In addition to Illinois, Littelfuse also has sales, engineering, and distribution facilities in Brazil, England, Hong Kong, Japan, the Netherlands, and Singapore. Littelfuse, Inc. is the successor to the corporation bearing the same name which was originally formed in 1927 and subsequently acquired by Tracor, Inc. in 1968. Incorporated in Delaware in 1991.

Directors (In addition to indicated officers)

Anthony Grillo
Bruce A. Karsh

John E. Major
John J. Nevin

Officers (Directors*)

*Howard B. Witt, Chm., Pres. & C.E.O.
Jon B. Anderson, V.P.—Hum. Res.
Kenneth R. Audino, V.P.—Quality Assurance
 & Reliability
William S. Barron, V.P.—Sales & Mktg.

James F. Brace, V.P., Treas. & C.F.O.
David J. Krueger, V.P.—Eng.
Hans Ouwehand, V.P.—Eur. Oper.
Lloyd J. Turner, V.P.—Oper.
Mary S. Muchoney, Secy.

Consolidated Balance Sheet As of December 28, 1996 (000 omitted)

Assets		Liabilities & Stockholders' Equity	
Current assets	$ 73,809	Current liabilities	$ 51,044
Net property, plant & equipment	63,889	Long-term debt	44,556
Other assets	72,253	Deferred items	5,417
		Other liabilities	312
		*Stockholders' equity	108,622
Total	$209,951	Total	$209,951

*9,888,000 shares common stock outstanding.

Consolidated Income Statement

Years Ended Abt. Dec. 31	Thousands — — — — Net Sales	Net Income	Per Share — — — — Earnings	Cash Dividends	Common Stock Price Range Calendar Year
1996	$241,446	$21,735	$1.81	$ .00	48-5/8 — 32-3/4
1995	219,535	19,272	1.55	.00	38-1/2 — 25-3/4
1994	194,454	15,227	1.25	.00	31 — 20
1993	160,712	9,987	.83	.00	27-1/2 — 17
1992	149,832	654	.06	.00	19-1/4 — 7a

aBegan trading in September 1992.

Transfer Agent & Registrar: LaSalle National Bank

General Counsel: Chapman & Cutler

Investor Relations: Art Skwerski, Dir.

Human Resources: Jon B. Anderson, V.P.

Mgt. Info. Svcs.: Lisa Finch, Dir.

Auditors: Ernst & Young LLP

Traded (Symbol): NASDAQ (LFUS)

Stockholders: 1,900

Employees: 2,550

Annual Meeting: In April

M~Wave, Inc.

216 Evergreen Street, Bensenville, Illinois 60106
Telephone: (630) 860-9542

M~Wave, Inc., through its wholly owned subsidiary, Poly Circuits, Inc., manufactures microwave frequency components (MFC) and high frequency circuit boards (HFCB) on Teflon-based laminates. The company's MFC and HFCB are used in wireless communication systems and other devices and equipment operating in the microwave frequency spectrum of 800 Mhz and above, such as cellular telephone, direct broadcast satellite television, global positioning satellite systems, personal communication networks, and military smart weapons and antenna systems. Another subsidiary is PC Dynamics Corp. Incorporated in Delaware in 1992.

Directors   (In addition to indicated officers)

Timothy A. Dugan
Lavern D. Kramer

Eric C. Larson

Officers   (Directors*)

*Joseph A. Turek, Chm. & C.E.O.
Michael Bayles, Pres. & C.O.O.

Paul H. Schmitt, C.F.O., Secy. & Treas.

Consolidated Balance Sheet   As of December 31, 1996 (000 omitted)

Assets		Liabilities & Stockholders' Equity	
Current assets	$ 7,714	Current liabilities	$ 3,112
Net property, plant & equipment	12,463	Long-term debt	2,605
Other assets	1,659	Deferred items	1,107
		*Stockholders' equity	15,012
Total	$21,836	Total	$21,836

*3,021,000 shares common stock outstanding.

Consolidated Income Statement

Years Ended Dec. 31	Thousands — — — — Net Sales	Net Income	Per Share[a] — — — — Earnings	Cash Dividends	Common Stock Price Range[a] Calendar Year
1996	$22,644	$(4,357)	$(1.44)	$ .00	8-3/4 — 1-3/4
1995	29,512	1,263[b]	.41	.00	18-3/4 — 5-3/4
1994	28,009	3,746[c]	1.25	.00	17-3/4 — 9-3/4
1993	19,606	3,534	1.20	.00	27 — 3-3/4
1992	10,658	1,050	.40	.00	7-3/4 — 2-1/4[d]

[a]Adjusted to reflect a 100-for-1 share exchange with the former stockholders of Poly Circuits, Inc., in January 1992.
[b]Includes a litigation settlement of $561,000.
[c]Includes a $425,000 non-recurring gain.
[d]Initial public offering in April 1992.

Transfer Agent & Registrar: Harris Trust and Savings Bank

General Counsel:
  Sonnenschein Nath & Rosenthal

Investor Relations: Paul H. Schmitt, C.F.O.

Human Resources: Paul H. Schmitt, C.F.O.

Mgt. Info. Svcs.:   Paul H. Schmitt, C.F.O.

Auditors: Deloitte & Touche LLP

Traded (Symbol):   NASDAQ (MWAV)

Stockholders: 2,200

Employees: 187

Annual Meeting: In June

MAF Bancorp, Inc.
55th Street and Holmes Avenue, Clarendon Hills, Illinois 60514-1596
Telephone: (630) 325-7300

MAF Bancorp, Inc. is a registered savings and loan holding company and is engaged in the savings and loan business through its wholly owned subsidiary, Mid America Federal Savings Bank. The bank is a community-oriented financial institution offering various financial services to its customers through 20 retail banking offices. The bank's market area is generally defined as the city of Chicago and its western suburbs. It is principally engaged in the business of attracting deposits from the general public and using such deposits, along with other borrowings, to make loans secured by real estate, primarily single-family residential and, to a lesser extent, various types of consumer loans. Through wholly owned subsidiaries, the holding company and the bank are engaged in real estate development activities. Additionally, the bank operates an insurance agency which provides general insurance services. As a federally chartered savings bank, deposits are insured by the Federal Deposit Insurance Corporation. In May 1996, the company completed a merger with N.S. Bancorp. Incorporated in Delaware in 1989.

Directors (In addition to indicated officers)

Robert J. Bowles, M.D.	Joe F. Hanauer	Lois B. Vasto
Nicholas J. DiLorenzo, Sr.	Henry Smogolski	Andrew J. Zych
Terry Ekl	F. William Trescott	

Officers (Directors*)

*Allen H. Koranda, Chm. & C.E.O.	Kenneth B. Rusdal, Sr. V.P.
*Kenneth Koranda, Pres.	Sharon Wheeler, Sr. V.P.
Jerry A. Weberling, Exec. V.P. & C.F.O.	Gail Brzostek, First V.P.
Gerard J. Buccino, Sr. V.P. & Cont.	Carolyn Pihera, First V.P. & Corp. Secy.
Michael J. Janssen, Sr. V.P.	Alan Schatz, First V.P.
David W. Kohlsaat, Sr. V.P.	Diane Stutte, First V.P.
Tom Miers, Sr. V.P.	William Haider, Pres.—MAF Dev. Inc. & Mid Amer. Dev. Svcs. Inc.

Consolidated Balance Sheet   As of December 31, 1996 (000 omitted)

Assets		Liabilities & Stockholders' Equity	
Cash & due from banks	$ 45,732	Total deposits	$2,262,226
Interest-bearing deposits	55,285	Other liabilities	717,490
Federal funds sold	24,700	*Stockholders' equity	250,625
Investment securities	171,818		
Mortgage-backed securities	359,587		
Loans receivable, net	2,430,113		
Net property & equipment	32,302		
Goodwill	26,347		
Other assets	84,457		
Total	$3,230,341	Total	$3,230,341

*10,490,133 shares common stock outstanding.

Consolidated Income Statement

Years Ended Dec. 31	Thousands — — — — Total Income	Net Income	Per Share[a] — — — — Earnings	Cash Dividends	Common Stock Price Range[ab] Calendar Year	
1996[b]	$124,786	$ 8,775	$ .81	$ .18	36	— 22-1/4
1996[c]	160,195	17,209	2.76	.32	27	— 20-5/8
1995[c]	131,613	15,043	2.54	.29	21-3/4 — 16-3/8	
1994[c]	123,426	13,450	2.22	.00	22-1/4 — 16	
1993[c]	127,167	13,946	2.26	.00	17-7/8 — 8-1/4	
1992[c]	138,391	9,796	1.63	.00	9 — 4-1/8	

[a]Adjusted to reflect a 10% stock dividend in August 1995 and a 3-for-2 stock split in August 1993.
[b]Six months ended December 31, 1996. Company changed to calendar year reporting in 1996. Stock price represents calendar year.
[c]Twelve months ended June 30. Stock prices represent fiscal years.

Transfer Agent & Registrar:	Harris Trust and Savings Bank		
General Counsel:	Muldoon, Murphy & Faucette	Auditors:	KPMG Peat Marwick LLP
Investor Relations:	Michael J. Janssen, Sr. V.P.	Traded (Symbol):	NASDAQ (MAFB)
		Stockholders:	4,700
Human Resources:	David W. Kohlsaat, Sr. V.P.	Employees:	808
Mgt. Info. Svcs.:	Kenneth B. Rusdal, Sr. V.P.	Annual Meeting:	In April

Market Facts, Inc.

3040 West Salt Creek Lane, Arlington Heights, Illinois 60005
Telephone: (847) 590-7000

Market Facts, Inc. gathers and analyzes information to help private companies and other organizations make better decisions. This objective is accomplished through consumer and industrial surveys and other forms of marketing research. Most of Market Facts' revenues are derived from sales of custom marketing research services to major consumer goods manufacturers. Company clients also include medium- and smaller-sized marketers of products and services, as well as public agencies, trade associations, and other institutions. Market Facts has established a wide array of data collection facilities and information processing systems, and is a leading organization in its industry. Offices are located in Illinois, California, Massachusetts, New Jersey, Ohio, and Virginia. Major subsidiaries include: Market Facts—New York, Inc. and Market Facts of Canada, Ltd. Incorporated in Illinois in 1946; reincorporated in Delaware in 1966.

Directors   (In addition to indicated officers)

William W. Boyd	Karen E. Predow	Jack R. Wentworth
Henrik Falktoft	Ned L. Sherwood	

Officers   (Directors*)

*Verne B. Churchill, Chm.	Lawrence R. Levin, Sr. V.P.
*Thomas H. Payne, Pres. & C.E.O.	Gregory J. McMahon, Sr. V.P.
*Glenn W. Schmidt, Exec. V.P.	Donald J. Morrison, Sr. V.P.
*Sanford M. Schwartz, Exec. V.P. &	Timothy Q. Rounds, Sr. V.P.
Pres.—Market Facts—New York, Inc.	William E. Seymour III, Sr. V.P.
Ronald P. Duda, Sr. V.P.	Timothy J. Sullivan, Sr. V.P. & Treas.
Michael H. Freehill, Sr. V.P.	Stephen J. Weber, Sr. V.P.
Janith P. Fuller, Sr. V.P.	John C. Robertson, Chm.—Market Facts of
Peter L. Greensmith, Sr. V.P.	Canada, Ltd.
*Lawrence W. Labash, Sr. V.P.	Richard W. Bennett, Pres.—Market Facts of
Peter J. LaSalle, Sr. V.P.	Canada, Ltd.
	Wesley S. Walton, Secy.

Consolidated Balance Sheet   As of December 31, 1996 (000 omitted)

Assets		Liabilities & Stockholders' Equity	
Current assets	$20,158	Current liabilities	$17,053
Net property, plant & equipment	17,481	Long-term debt	10,296
Other assets	746	Deferred items	64
		Other liabilities	447
		*Stockholders' equity	10,525
Total	$38,385	Total	$38,385

*3,461,854 shares common stock outstanding.

Consolidated Income Statement

Years Ended Dec. 31	Thousands —————		Per Share[a] ————		Common Stock
	Revenues	Net Income	Earnings	Cash Dividends	Price Range[a] Calendar Year
1996	$83,796	$ 4,278	$ 1.14	$ .20	21-3/8 — 5
1995	64,609	2,226	.57	.19	7-1/2 — 3-5/8
1994	55,483	1,434	.38	.15	5-1/2 — 3-1/4
1993	45,609	1,074	.30	.11	3-5/8 — 1-7/8
1992	40,718	(437)	(.13)	.10	3-1/2 — 1-3/4

[a]Adjusted to reflect a 2-for-1 stock split in December 1996.

Transfer Agent & Registrar:	First Chicago Trust Co. of New York		
General Counsel:	Keck, Mahin & Cate	Traded (Symbol):	NASDAQ (MFAC)
Investor Relations:	Timothy J. Sullivan, Sr. V.P.	Stockholders:	771
Human Resources:	Charise D. Davis, V.P.	Employees:	1,300
Mgt. Info. Svcs.:	Peter J. LaSalle, Sr. V.P.	Annual Meeting:	In April
Auditors:	KPMG Peat Marwick LLP	Internet:	www.marketfacts.com

Marks Bros. Jewelers, Inc.

155 North Wacker Drive, Suite 500, Chicago, Illinois 60606
Telephone: (312) 782-6800

Marks Bros. Jewelers, Inc. is a leading, national specialty retailer of fine jewelry, operating 176 stores in 24 states as of April 1997. Founded in 1895, the company operates stores in regional and super-regional shopping malls under the names Whitehall Co. Jewellers® (129 stores), Lundstrom Jewelers® (42 stores), and Marks Bros. Jewelers℠ (5 stores). In May 1996, the company completed an initial public offering of 3,269,500 shares of common stock. Incorporated in Delaware in 1947 as the successor to a business dating back to 1895.

Directors (In addition to indicated officers)

Rodney L. Goldstein
Daniel H. Levy

Norman J. Patinkin
Jack A. Smith

Officers (Directors*)

*Hugh M. Patinkin, Chm., Pres. & C.E.O.
*John R. Desjardins, Exec. V.P.—Fin. &
  Admin., Treas. & Secy.

Lynn D. Eisenheim, Exec. V.P.—Merch.
*Matthew M. Patinkin, Exec. V.P.—Store Oper.

Consolidated Balance Sheet   As of January 31, 1997 (000 omitted)

Assets		Liabilities & Stockholders' Equity	
Current assets	$70,133	Current liabilities	$44,309
Net property, plant & equipment	16,305	Long-term debt	10,520
Other assets	7,095	Other liabilities	1,197
		*Stockholders' equity	37,507
Total	$93,533	Total	$93,533

*10,061,142 shares common stock outstanding.

Consolidated Income Statement

Years Ended Jan. 31	Thousands — — — — Net Sales	Net Income	Per Share[a] — — — Earnings	Cash Dividends	Common Stock Price Range[ab] Calendar Year
1997	$155,474	$ 17,400[c]	$2.05[c]	$ .00	
1996	131,022	16,972[d]	3.16[d]	.00	28-1/4 — 11-1/2
1995	106,683	571	.11		
1994	91,106	(7,002)[e]			
1993	88,141	(3,557)[f]			

[a]Adjusted to reflect a 35.4-for-1 stock split in April 1996.
[b]Initial public offering in May 1996.
[c]Includes an extraordinary gain of $10,057,000 ($.31 per share) from the early extinguishment of debt.
[d]Includes an income tax benefit of $14,924,000 from the reversal of the company's valuation allowance and the corresponding recognition of a deferred tax asset.
[e]Includes a charge of $8,526,000 for the cumulative effect of an accounting change.
[f]Includes a gain of $2,700,000 for receipt of deferred proceeds from the sale of discontinued operations in fiscal 1992.

Transfer Agent & Registrar: Boston EquiServe

General Counsel:	Sidley & Austin	Auditors:	Coopers & Lybrand L.L.P.
Investor Relations:	John R. Desjardins, Exec. V.P.	Traded (Symbol):	NASDAQ (MBJI)
		Stockholders:	170
Human Resources:	Matthew M. Patinkin, Exec. V.P.	Employees:	1,100
Mgt. Info. Svcs.:	John R. Desjardins, Exec. V.P.	Annual Meeting:	In June

LaSalle Banks Guide

Material Sciences Corporation

2200 East Pratt Boulevard, Elk Grove Village, Illinois 60007-5995
Telephone: (847) 439-8270

Material Sciences Corporation is a diversified coated-materials company with operations in laminates, coil coatings, structural composites, metallizing, and electrogalvanizing. Coated and electroplated sheet-metal coils, structural composites, and laminate materials are used by other manufacturers in motor vehicles, industrial and commercial building products, appliances, office equipment, furniture, lighting fixtures, containers, and a wide range of other products. Metallized materials are used in the manufacture of energy-control films, high-efficiency reflectors, and electronic displays, as well as in food packaging and data storage applications. Subsidiaries include Pre Finish Metals Incorporated and Deposition Technologies, Inc. Incorporated in Delaware in 1983.

Directors (In addition to indicated officers)

Jerome B. Cohen
Roxanne J. Decyk
Eugene W. Emmerich
E.F. Heizer, Jr.

J. Frank Leach
Irwin P. Pochter
Howard B. Witt

Officers (Directors*)

*G. Robert Evans, Chm.
*Gerald G. Nadig, Pres. & C.E.O.
Thomas E. Moore, Exec. V.P. & C.O.O.
Frank D. Graziano, Sr. V.P.—Tech.
Anton F. Vitzthum, Sr. V.P.—Mfg.

Frank J. Lazowski, Jr., V.P.—Human Res.
Robert J. Mataya, V.P.—Bus. Plan. & Dev.
James J. Waclawik, Sr., V.P., C.F.O. & Secy.
David J. DeNeve, Cont.

Consolidated Balance Sheet   As of February 28, 1997 (000 omitted)

Assets		Liabilities & Stockholders' Equity	
Current assets	$ 75,005	Current liabilities	$ 43,851
Net property, plant & equipment	154,386	Long-term liabilities	76,865
Other assets	24,698	*Stockholders' equity	133,373
Total	$254,089	Total	$254,089

*15,339,384 shares common stock outstanding.

Consolidated Income Statement

Years Ended Abt. Feb. 28	Thousands — — — —		Per Share[a] — — — —		Common Stock Price Range[a] Fiscal Year
	Net Sales	Net Income	Earnings	Cash Dividends	
1997	$278,017	$16,236	$1.04	$ .00	21 — 14-1/2
1996[b]	236,150	8,497	.55	.00	22-3/8 — 12-1/8
1995	227,658	16,740	1.10	.00	17-3/4 — 13-3/4
1994	187,701	11,802	.78	.00	17-5/8 — 10-5/8
1993	156,230	7,617[c]	.56[c]	.00	12 — 7-7/8

[a]Adjusted to reflect a 3-for-2 stock split in June 1994.
[b]Restated.
[c]Includes FAS 106 and 109, resulting in a cumulative charge to net earnings of $1,283,000 ($.11 per share).

Transfer Agent & Registrar:	Mellon Securities Transfer Services		
General Counsel:	Kirkland & Ellis	Traded (Symbol):	NYSE (MSC)
Investor Relations:	Robert J. Mataya, V.P.	Stockholders:	999
Human Resources:	Frank J. Lazowski, Jr., V.P.	Employees:	988
		Annual Meeting:	In June
Auditors:	Arthur Andersen LLP	Internet:	www.matsci.com

May & Speh, Inc.

1501 Opus Place, Downers Grove, Illinois 60515-5713
Telephone: (630) 964-1501

May & Speh, Inc. provides computer-based information management services to clients with significant database marketing requirements. The company provides direct marketing services, including database creation, data warehousing, modeling and analysis, list processing, and data enhancement to clients in a range of industries, including financial services, consumer products, insurance, and retail. Additionally, the company designs and builds user-friendly relational databases, and it provides high-speed data processing and outsourcing services. In March 1996, the company completed an initial public offering of 6,700,000 shares of common stock. In July 1996, the company acquired GIS Information Systems, Inc., a provider of data processing outsourcing services, from Boston-based Faneuil, Inc. Incorporated in Delaware in 1995, as successor to a company founded in 1947.

Directors (In addition to indicated officers)

Deborah A. Bricker
Casey G. Cowell

Paul Yovovich

Officers (Directors*)

*Albert J. Speh, Jr., Chm.
*Lawrence J. Speh, V. Chm. & C.E.O.
*Peter I. Mason, Pres. & C.O.O.
Terrance C. Cieslak, Exec. V.P. & Chf. Tech. Off.
*Robert C. Early, Exec. V.P.—Corp. Dev.
Michael J. Loeffler, Exec. V.P.—Sales/Dir. Mktg. Svcs.

Eric M. Loughmiller, Exec. V.P. & C.F.O.
Claudia J. Colalillo, Sr. V.P.—Org. Dev.
John Jazwiec, Sr. V.P. & C.I.O.
Willard E. Engel, Jr., V.P., Chf. Acct. Off. & Treas.
Joseph C. Grossestreuer, V.P.— Sales/Outsourcing Svcs.

Consolidated Balance Sheet As of September 30, 1996 (000 omitted)

Assets		Liabilities & Stockholders' Equity	
Current assets	$ 59,930	Current liabilities	$ 13,781
Net property, plant & equipment	32,290	Long-term debt	22,251
Goodwill	16,864	Deferred income taxes	3,455
Other assets	6,134	*Stockholders' equity	75,731
Total	$115,218	Total	$115,218

*24,934,154 shares common stock outstanding.

Consolidated Income Statement

Years Ended Sept. 30	Thousands — — — —		Per Share[a] — — —		Common Stock
	Net Revenues	Net Income	Earnings	Cash Dividends	Price Range[ab] Calendar Year
1996	$77,223	$10,224	$ .42	$ .00	21-1/2 — 10-7/8
1995	61,641	7,861	.39		
1994	51,667	5,838	.26		
1993	41,792	3,406	.15		
1992	32,231	1,652	.07		

[a]Adjusted to reflect 12-for-1 stock split in December 1995.
[b]Initial public offering in March 1996.

Transfer Agent & Registrar: Harris Trust and Savings Bank

General Counsel:	Peter I. Mason, Pres.	Auditors:	Price Waterhouse LLP
Investor Relations:	Robert C. Early, Exec. V.P.	Traded (Symbol):	NASDAQ (SPEH)
		Stockholders:	165
Human Resources:	Claudia J. Colalillo, Sr. V.P.	Employees:	496
Mgt. Info. Svcs.:	John Jazwiec, Sr. V.P.	Annual Meeting:	In March

McDonald's Corporation

McDonald's Plaza, Oak Brook, Illinois 60521
Telephone: (630) 623-3000

McDonald's Corporation is the world's largest foodservice retailer, with more than 21,000 McDonald's restaurants in 101 countries. McDonald's has pioneered food quality specifications, equipment technology, marketing, training programs, and standard-setting operational and supply systems. Approximately 85 percent of McDonald's restaurants are locally owned and operated by independent entrepreneurs who provide capital and management skills. McDonald's restaurants outside of the United States accounted for nearly 60 percent of the company's operating income in 1996. Reincorporated in Delaware in 1965 to continue a business established in 1955.

Directors   (In addition to indicated officers)

Hall Adams, Jr.	Donald G. Lubin	Roger W. Stone
Gordon C. Gray	Andrew J. McKenna	Robert N. Thurston
Enrique Hernandez, Jr.	Edward H. Rensi	B. Blair Vedder, Jr.
Donald R. Keough	Terry L. Savage	

Officers   (Directors*)

*Fred L. Turner, Sr. Chm.
*Michael R. Quinlan, Chm. & C.E.O.
*James R. Cantalupo, Pres. & C.E.O.—Intl.
*Jack M. Greenberg, V. Chm. & Chm./C.E.O.—U.S.A.
Paul D. Schrage, Sr. Exec. V.P. & Chf. Mktg. Off.
Winston B. Christiansen, Exec. V.P.
Michael L. Conley, Exec. V.P. & C.F.O.
Robert J. Doran, Exec. V.P.
Patrick J. Flynn, Exec. V.P.
Jeffrey B. Kindler, Exec. V.P. & Gen. Coun.
James A. Skinner, Exec. V.P.—Intl.
Stanley R. Stein, Exec. V.P.
Shelby Yastrow, Exec. V.P.
O. Thomas Albrecht, Sr. V.P. & Chf. Purch. Off.
Claire Babrowski, Sr. V.P.—Restaurant Sys.
Brad Ball, Sr. V.P.
*Robert M. Beavers, Jr., Sr. V.P.
Joe Beckwith, Sr. V.P.
Burton D. Cohen, Sr. V.P.
Carl F. Dill, Jr., Sr. V.P.
Henry Gonzalez, Sr. V.P.

David B. Green, Sr. V.P.
Robbin L. Hedges, Sr. V.P. & Intl. Rel. Ptnr.—Eur.
William Hockett, Sr. V.P.
Noel Kaplan, Sr. V.P.—Alliance Relationships
Raymond C. Mines, Jr., Sr. V.P.—Franchisee Relationships
Carleton Day Pearl, Sr. V.P. & Treas.
Christopher Pieszko, Sr. V.P. & Cont.
Paul S. Preston, Sr. V.P. & Intl. Rel. Ptnr.—Eur.
Lynal A. Root, Sr. V.P. & Chm.—Purch. Div.
Eduardo Sanchez, Sr. V.P. & Intl. Rel. Ptnr.—Latin Amer.
W. Robert Sanders, Sr. V.P.
Richard G. Starmann, Sr. V.P.
Delbert H. Wilson, Sr. V.P.
Peter D. Ritchie, Chm.—Australia & Intl. Rel. Ptnr.—Pacific
John S. Charlesworth, Pres.—Midwest Div.
Kevin Dunn, Pres.—Great Lakes Div.
Alan Feldman, Pres.—Northeast Div.
Debra A. Koenig, Pres.—Southeast Div.
Michael Roberts, Pres.—Western Div.

Consolidated Balance Sheet   As of December 31, 1996 (000 omitted)

Assets		Liabilities & Stockholders' Equity	
Current assets	$ 1,102,500	Current liabilities	$ 2,135,300
Net property and equipment	14,352,100	Long-term debt	5,556,600
Intangible assets	747,000	Deferred items	975,900
Other assets	1,184,400	*Stockholders' equity	8,718,200
Total	$17,386,000	Total	$17,386,000

*694,600,000 shares common stock outstanding.

Consolidated Income Statement

Years Ended Dec. 31	Thousands — — — —		Per Share[a] — — — —		Common Stock
	Total Revenues	Net Income	Earnings	Cash Dividends[b]	Price Range[a] Calendar Year
1996	$10,687,000	$1,573,000	$2.21	$ .29	54-1/4 — 41
1995	9,795,000	1,427,000	1.97	.26	45-1/8 — 28-5/8
1994	8,321,800	1,224,400	1.68	.23	31-3/8 — 25-5/8
1993	7,408,100	1,082,500	1.45	.21	29-5/8 — 22-3/4
1992	7,133,300	958,600	1.30	.20	25-1/4 — 19-1/4

[a]Adjusted to reflect a 2-for-1 stock split in June 1994.
[b]Declared.

Transfer Agent & Registrar:	First Chicago Trust Co. of New York		
Corporate Counsel:	Sonnenschein Nath & Rosenthal	Traded (Symbol):	NYSE, CSE, FRA, Tokyo, 2 GER, 3 Swiss (MCD)
Investor Relations:	Mary Healy, Asst. V.P.		
Human Resources:	Stanley R. Stein, Exec. V.P.	Stockholders:	925,000
		Employees:	183,000
Mgt. Info. Svcs.:	Carl F. Dill, Jr., Sr. V.P.	Annual Meeting:	In May
Auditors:	Ernst & Young LLP	Internet:	www.mcdonalds.com

McWhorter Technologies, Inc.
400 East Cottage Place, Carpentersville, Illinois 60110
Telephone: (847) 428-2657

McWhorter Technologies, Inc. is a leading manufacturer of resins used in the domestic paint and coatings industry, and is a manufacturer of resins used in the reinforced fiberglass plastics industry. These resins are a primary component of paint and coatings used in a variety of protective and decorative applications. Resins used for reinforced fiberglass plastics are a primary component for a variety of fiberglass products. Incorporated in Delaware in 1994.

Directors (In addition to indicated officers)

Michelle L. Collins
Edward M. Giles
D. George Harris

John G. Johnson, Jr.
Heinn F. Tomfohrde III

Officers (Directors*)

*John R. Stevenson, Chm. & C.E.O.
*Jeffrey M. Nodland, Pres. & C.O.O.
 Patrick T. Heffernan, Sr. V.P.—Liquid Coating
  Resins

Kevin W. Brolsma, V.P.—Powder Coating
  Resins/Envir., Hlth. & Safety
Douglas B. Rahrig, V.P.—Tech.
Louise Tonozzi-Frederick, V.P. & C.F.O.

Consolidated Balance Sheet As of October 31, 1996 (000 omitted)

Assets		Liabilities & Stockholders' Equity	
Current assets	$ 71,396	Current liabilities	$ 46,862
Net property, plant & equipment	73,630	Long-term debt	13,145
Other assets	8,228	Deferred items	10,486
		Other liabilities	3,037
		*Stockholders' equity	79,724
Total	$153,254	Total	$153,254

*10,465,940 shares common stock outstanding.

Consolidated Income Statement

Years Ended Abt. Oct. 31	Thousands — — — — Net Sales	Net Income	Per Share[a] — — — — Earnings	Cash Dividends	Common Stock Price Range[a] Calendar Year
1996	$315,925	$13,833	$1.32	$ .00	22-7/8 — 12-7/8
1995	311,398	11,070	1.02	.00	18-1/8 — 14-1/8
1994[b]	281,340	10,010[c]	.92[c]	.00	19-1/4 — 13-1/4
1993[b]	272,432	10,125	.93		
1992	103,545	4,748			

[a]Spun off from The Valspar Corporation in April 1994.
[b]Pro forma combined, McWhorter Technologies, Inc. and the Resin Products Division of Cargill, Incorporated.
[c]Includes an after-tax charge of $1,497,000 ($.14 per share) for the writedown of a Los Angeles resin facility.

Transfer Agent & Registrar: Wachovia Bank of North Carolina, N.A.

General Counsel:	McDermott, Will & Emery	Auditors:	Ernst & Young LLP
Investor Relations:	Louise Tonozzi-Frederick, V.P.	Traded (Symbol):	NYSE (MWT)
		Stockholders:	1,800
Human Resources:	Mia Igyarto	Employees:	550
Mgt. Info. Svcs.:	Robin Mechelke	Annual Meeting:	In February

Medicus Systems Corporation

One Rotary Center, Suite 1111, Evanston, Illinois 60201-4802
Telephone: (847) 570-7500

Medicus Systems Corporation is a developer and provider of specialized decision support systems and services that address information needs across the entire spectrum of healthcare delivery. The company's comprehensive, integrated products and services are used by diverse heathcare organizations to optimize reimbursement and manage resources to improve the financial and clinical outcomes of patient care and the health of enrolled populations. In February 1996, Medicus Systems Corporation completed a spin-off of its managed care business. Incorporated in Delaware in 1984.

Directors (In addition to indicated officers)

William G. Brown
Jon E.M. Jacoby
Richard C. Jelinek, Ph.D.

John P. Kunz
Risa Lavizzo-Mourey, M.D.
Gail L. Warden

Officers (Directors*)

*Patrick C. Sommers, Chm., Pres. & C.E.O.
Angus Carroll, Sr. V.P.
Lon Gruen, Sr. V.P.
Robert C. Steffel, Sr. V.P.
Daniel P. DiCaro, V.P. & C.F.O.

Susan Doctors, V.P.
Lynda Hernandez, V.P.
Timothy K. Rutledge, V.P.
*William G. Brown, Secy.

Consolidated Balance Sheet   As of May 31, 1996 (000 omitted)

Assets		Liabilities & Stockholders' Equity	
Current assets	$22,151	Current liabilities	$ 9,579
Net property, plant & equipment	1,951	*Stockholders' equity	18,201
Other assets	3,678		
Total	$27,780	Total	$27,780

*6,432,015 shares common stock outstanding.

Consolidated Income Statement[a]

Years Ended May 31	Thousands — — — — Total Revenues	Net Income	Per Share — — — Earnings	Cash Dividends	Common Stock Price Range Calendar Year
1996	$31,065	$(3,726)	$ (.57)	$ .12	4-1/4 — 9
1995	33,829	3,024	.45	.12	
1994	29,153	3,225	.51	.00	
1993	19,817	2,116	.39	.00	
1992	18,331	1,997	.37	.00	

[a]Restated to reflect continuing operations subsequent to the spin-off of the managed care business in February 1996 and a restructuring charge incurred in May 1996.

Transfer Agent & Registrar:	Harris Trust and Savings Bank		
General Counsel:	Bell, Boyd & Lloyd	Traded (Symbol):	NASDAQ (MECS)
Investor Relations:	Daniel P. DiCaro, V.P.	Stockholders:	2,200
Human Resources:	Susan Doctors, V.P.	Employees:	200
Auditors:	Price Waterhouse LLP	Annual Meeting:	In March

Merchants Bancorp, Inc.

34 South Broadway Avenue, Aurora, Illinois 60507
Telephone: (630) 896-9000

Merchants Bancorp, Inc., is the holding company for The Merchants National Bank in Aurora, Illinois; the Fox Valley Bank in St. Charles, Illinois; and the Hinckley State Bank in Hinckley, Illinois. Merchants National Bank conducts a full-service community banking and trust business. Along with four locations and its main office in Aurora, the bank also has locations in Oswego and Geneva, Illinois. The Fox Valley Bank and Hinckley State Bank both offer full-service banking in their respective communities. Fox Valley has an additional office in Geneva, Illinois, and Hinckley has another in Sugar Grove, Illinois. Incorporated in Delaware in 1981.

Directors   (In addition to indicated officers)

C. Tell Coffey	Frank A. Sarnecki
William C. Glenn	John J. Swalec
William F. Hejna, M.D.	Norman L. Titiner
John M. Lies	William S. Wake
James D. Pearson	

Officers   (Directors*)

*Calvin R. Myers, Chm., Pres. & C.E.O.
 J. Douglas Cheatham, V.P. & C.F.O.

Frank K. Voris, V.P.
Dana K. Hopp, Treas. & Secy.

Consolidated Balance Sheet   As of December 31, 1996 (000 omitted)

Assets		Liabilities & Stockholders' Equity	
Cash & due from banks	$ 42,455	Deposits	$600,970
Federal funds sold	2,613	Federal funds purchased	44,525
Total securities	194,780	Notes payable	14,000
Loans held for sale	4,149	Other liabilities	6,716
Net loans	449,528	*Stockholders' equity	58,198
Net property, plant & equipment	12,100		
Other assets	18,784		
Total	$724,409	Total	$724,409

*2,606,690 shares common stock outstanding.

Consolidated Income Statement

Years Ended Dec. 31	Thousands — — — —		Per Share[a] — — —		Common Stock
	Total Income	Net Income	Earnings	Cash Dividends	Price Range[ab] Calendar Year
1996	$60,001	$6,528	$2.53	$ .56	27-3/4 — 33-1/2
1995	46,793	6,196	2.41	.48	28-1/2 — 21-1/2
1994	39,797	5,459	2.13	.37	27 — 21
1993	36,152	4,734[c]	2.25[c]	.34	22-1/2 — 15
1992	34,117	4,050	2.03	.28	15 — 11-3/8

[a]Adjusted to reflect a 3-for-1 stock split in April 1993.
[b]Initial public offering in October 1993. The company's common stock previously did not trade on any national or regional exchange, but certain brokerage firms did make a market in the common stock.
[c]Includes a gain to reflect FAS 109, resulting in a cumulative effect of $300,000 ($.14 per share).

Transfer Agent & Registrar: Harris Trust and Savings Bank

General Counsel:
  Barack, Ferrazzano, Kirschbaum & Perlman

Investor Relations: J. Douglas Cheatham, V.P.

Human Resources: Susan M. Anderson, V.P.

Mgt. Info. Svcs: Allen R. Klokow, Mgr.

Auditors: Crowe, Chizek & Co. LLP

Traded (Symbol): NASDAQ (MBIA)

Stockholders: 785

Employees: 265

Annual Meeting: In April

Internet: www.bnt.com/mnb

Mercury Finance Company

100 Field Drive, Suite 340, Lake Forest, Illinois 60045
Telephone: (847) 295-8600

Mercury Finance Company specializes in financing the sale of previously owned automobiles for new and used car dealers. The company makes direct cash loans and sells credit insurance to its customers through its 247 branch offices in 25 states. In June 1997, Mercury completed the sale of Lyndon Insurance Group subsidiary to Frontier Insurance Group, Inc. Incorporated in Delaware in 1988.

Directors (In addition to indicated officers)

John N. Brincat
Dennis H. Chookaszian
William C. Croft
Clifford R. Johnson

Andrew McNally IV
Bruce I. McPhee
Fred G. Steingraber
Philip J. Wicklander

Officers (Directors*)

*William A. Brandt, Pres. & C.E.O.
Richard P. Bosson, V.P.—Oper.
Jeffrey R. Brincat, V.P.—Adm.
John N. Brincat, Jr., V.P.—Oper.
George R. Carey, V.P.—Oper.
Steven G. Gould, V.P.—Oper.

Al H. Green, V.P.—Portfolio Mgt. & Insurance
Charles H. Lam, V.P.—Oper.
Gerald M. Mizel, V.P.—Oper.
Edward G. Stautzenbach, V.P.—Mktg.
Sheila M. Tilson, V.P. & Asst. Secy.
Bradley S. Vallem, Asst. V.P. & Treas.

Consolidated Balance Sheet[a]   As of December 31, 1995 (000 omitted)

Assets		Liabilities & Stockholders' Equity	
Finance receivables, net	$1,105,993	Short-term debt	$ 489,990
Net property, plant & equipment	7,022	Long-term debt	468,250
Other assets	533,903	Income taxes	22,640
		Other liabilities	369,773
		*Stockholders' equity	296,265
Total	$1,646,918	Total	$1,646,918

[a]Financial data for the year ending December 31, 1996, unavailable at this publication's press time.
*176,477,520 shares common stock outstanding.

Consolidated Income Statement

Years Ended Dec. 31	Thousands — — — —		Per Share[a] — — — —		Common Stock Price Range[a] Calendar Year
	Interest Income	Net Income	Earnings	Cash Dividends	
1996[b]					15-3/8 — 9-3/4
1995	$270,416	$110,907	$.64	$.25	16-5/8 — 8-1/4
1994	211,565	86,545	.49	.19	19-1/8 — 11-1/8
1993	165,054	64,927	.37	.14	20-3/8 — 11-1/4
1992	121,531	45,723	.26	.09	12-5/8 — 7-3/4

[a]Adjusted to reflect a 3-for-2 stock split in October 1995, a 4-for-3 stock split in June 1993, a 2-for-1 stock split in May 1992, and 4-for-3 stock splits in December 1991 and April 1991.
[b]Financial data for the year ending December 31, 1996, and prior years' restated financials unavailable at this publication's press time.

Transfer Agent & Registrar: Harris Trust Company of New York

Investor Relations: Bradley S. Vallem, Treas.

Human Resources: Robert Lutgen, V.P.

Auditors: Arthur Andersen LLP

Traded (Symbol):   NYSE, CSE (MFN)
Stockholders: 12,000
Employees: 1,500
Annual Meeting: In April

Metal Management, Inc.

500 North Dearborn Street, Suite 405, Chicago, Illinois 60610
Telephone: (312) 645-0700

Metal Management, Inc. and its wholly owned subsidiaries are engaged in the business of dismantling, processing, marketing, brokering, and recycling of ferrous and non-ferrous metals. In April 1996, the company adopted the name Metal Management, Inc. and acquired EMCO Recycling Corporation of Phoenix, Arizona. Since that time, the company has completed mergers with or acquired a number of companies including Cozzi Iron & Metal, Inc.; the Isaac Group; HouTex Metals Company; the MacLeod Group of Companies; Proler Southwest Inc.; Proler Steelworks LLC; and Reserve Iron & Metal L.P. The company's EMCO Recycling Corporation subsidiary is Arizona's largest recycling company. In April 1996, the company relocated from Berkeley, California, to Chicago. Incorporated in Delaware in 1986; present name adopted in 1996.

Directors (In addition to indicated officers)

Donald F. Moorehead, Jr.   Harold Rubenstein

Officers (Directors*)

*T. Benjamin Jennings, Chm. & Chf. Dev. Off.
*Gerard M. Jacobs, C.E.O.
*Albert Cozzi, Pres. & C.O.O.
*George A. Isaac III, Exec. V.P. &
  Pres.—Isaac Group
*George O. Moorehead, Exec. V.P. &
  Pres—EMCO Recycling

*Frank Cozzi, V.P. & Pres.—Cozzi Iron & Metal Co.
 Robert C. Larry, V.P. & C.F.O.
*Xavier Hermosillo, Secy.
*Paul D. Joseph, Pres.—Reserve Iron & Metal
*Ian MacLeod, C.E.O.—MacLeod Group
*Michael Melnik, Pres.—HouTex Metals

Consolidated Balance Sheet   As of March 31, 1997 (000 omitted)

Assets		Liabilities & Stockholders' Equity	
Current assets	$25,708	Current liabilities	$39,263
Net property, plant & equipment	20,208	Long-term debt	5,170
Other assets	24,209	Other liabilities	2,544
		*Stockholders' equity	23,148
Total	$70,125	Total	$70,125

*10,154,740 shares common stock outstanding.

Consolidated Income Statement

| Years Ended Mar. 31 | Thousands — — — — | | Per Share — — — | | Common Stock Price Range Calendar Year |
	Net Sales[a]	Net Income[a]	Earnings[a]	Cash Dividends	
1997[b]	$65,196	$(2,010)	$ (.22)	$ .00	5-5/8 — 3-1/8

[a]From continuing operations.
[b]Because of changes to the company's operations and financial structures, prior years are not comparable to 1997.

Transfer Agent & Registrar: ChaseMellon Shareholder Services, L.L.C.

General Counsel: Erhard Chorlé

Investor Relations: Xavier Hermosillo, Secy.

Auditors: Price Waterhouse LLP

Traded (Symbol): NASDAQ (MTLM)

Stockholders: 2,500

Employees: 600

Annual Meeting: In July

Methode Electronics, Inc.

7444 West Wilson Avenue, Chicago, Illinois 60656-4549
Telephone: (708) 867-9600

Methode Electronics, Inc. and its wholly owned subsidiaries are engaged principally in the development and manufacture of component devices that connect, convey, and control electrical energy, pulse, and signal. Production is centered around space-saving circuitry under the general headings of controls, connectors, power distribution systems, fiber optic components, printed circuits, and cables. These products are basic components used in the production of electrical and electronic apparatus, instruments, and systems. Principal customers include equipment manufacturers in the computer, automotive, communications, industrial, military, and aerospace industries. Methode serves the component needs of more than 2,000 businesses in North America and overseas. The company has 19 manufacturing and two testing facilities. Subsidiaries include: Duel Systems Inc.; Graphic Research, Inc.; Technical Components, Inc.; Methode of California; Methode Electronics Far East P.T.E. Ltd.; Methode Electronics Europe Ltd.; Merit Malta Methode; Intertrace Technology; Methode Development Co.; Methode Mikon Ltd.; Methode New England Co. Inc.; and Methode Electronics Ireland Ltd. Incorporated in Illinois in 1946; reincorporated in Delaware in 1966.

Directors   (In addition to indicated officers)

William C. Croft   George C. Wright
Raymond J. Roberts

Officers   (Directors*)

*William J. McGinley, Chm. & Pres.   Robert J. Kuehnau, V.P. & Treas.
*Michael G. Andre, Sr. Exec. V.P.   * James W. Ashley, Secy.
*Kevin J. Hayes, C.F.O.   * James W. McGinley, Pres.—ElectroOptics Grp.

Consolidated Balance Sheet   As of October 31, 1996 (000 omitted) Unaudited

Assets		Liabilities & Stockholders' Equity	
Current assets	$142,873	Current liabilities	$ 40,542
Net property, plant & equipment	71,771	Deferred items	10,409
Other assets	19,002	Other liabilities	1,918
		*Stockholders' equity	180,777
Total	$233,646	Total	$233,646

*33,925,049 shares Class A common and 1,237,866 shares Class B common stock outstanding.

Consolidated Income Statement

Years Ended Apr. 30	Thousands — — — — Net Sales	Net Income	Per Share[a] — — — Earnings	Cash Dividends[b]	Common Stock Price Range[ac] Fiscal Year
1997	$343,092	$37,219	$1.06	$ .20	23 — 12-3/4
1996	307,538	32,373	.93	.16	16-3/4 — 11
1995	270,748	26,121	.75	.08	13-5/8 — 8-5/8
1994	213,298	20,976	.61	.03	11-1/2 — 7
1993	172,038	14,748[d]	.43[d]	.03	9-1/8 — 3-7/8

[a]Adjusted to reflect a 3-for-2 stock split in October 1995 and a 100% stock dividend paid January 15, 1993, in Class A stock for each share of Class A and Class B outstanding.
[b]Represents dividends paid on Class A common stock. The cash dividend on the Class A and Class B common stock was increased to $.20 per share for fiscal 1997.
[c]Class A common stock.
[d]From continuing operations.

Transfer Agent & Registrar: ChaseMellon Shareholder Services, L.L.C.

General Counsel:	Keck, Mahin & Cate	Traded (Symbol):	NASDAQ (METH)
Investor Relations:	William J. McGinley, Chm.	Stockholders:	1,820
Human Resources:	Robert J. Kuehnau, V.P.	Employees:	3,250
Mgt. Info. Svcs.:	Ronald Duffy	Annual Meeting:	In September
Auditors:	Ernst & Young LLP	Internet:	www.methode.com

Metromail Corporation

360 East 22nd Street, Lombard, Illinois 60148
Telephone: (630) 620-3300

Metromail Corporation is a leading provider of database marketing, direct marketing, and reference products and services in the United States and the United Kingdom. Metromail helps its customers identify and reach targeted audiences utilizing its comprehensive, proprietary consumer database encompassing more than 90 percent of the households in the U.S. The company also provides customers with database marketing software and related services. Metromail provides its information, information services, and software services to a wide variety of organizations engaged in direct mail, telephone, and target marketing; as well as to clients who desire specific reference and information services. The company's clients include Fortune 500 companies, as well as numerous small- and mid-size businesses. In June 1996, Metromail was spun off from R.R. Donnelley & Sons Company, which currently holds approximately 38.4 percent of the company's common stock. Incorporated in Delaware in 1979, as successor to a business formed in 1946.

Directors (In addition to indicated officers)

Robert C. McCormack
Peter F. Murphy

Jonathan P. Ward

Officers (Directors*)

*Barton L. Faber, Chm.
*Susan L. Henricks, Pres. & C.E.O.
Philip H. Bonello, Sr. V.P. & Gen.
Mgr.—On-Line Svcs.
Ronald G. Eidell, Sr. V.P. & C.F.O.

Thomas J. Quarles, Sr. V.P., Gen. Coun., C.A.O.
& Secy.
Mac E. Rodgers, Sr. V.P. & Gen. Mgr.—Info. Svcs.
Tery R. Larrew, Pres.—Customer Insight Co. &
Database Mktg. Svcs.

Consolidated Balance Sheet As of December 31, 1996 (000 omitted)

Assets		Liabilities & Stockholders' Equity	
Current assets	$133,816	Current liabilities	$ 52,758
Net property, plant & equipment	45,313	Other liabilities	30,100
Goodwill	255,799	*Stockholders' equity	360,548
Other assets	8,478		
Total	$443,406	Total	$443,406

*22,427,600 shares common stock outstanding.

Consolidated Income Statement

Years Ended Dec. 31	Thousands — — — — Net Sales	Operating Earnings	Per Share[a] — — — — Earnings	Cash Dividends	Common Stock Price Range[a] Calendar Year
1996	$281,445	$ 13,862	$ .62	$ .00	23-3/8 — 16
1995	237,187	2,735	.12		
1994	195,471	1,987	.09		
1993	163,715	(8,854)[b]			
1992	153,681	(3,153)			

[a]Spun off from R.R. Donnelley & Sons Company in June 1996.
[b]Includes an cumulative after-tax charge of $4,388,000 for a change in accounting for post retirement benefits other than pensions.

Transfer Agent & Registrar: American Stock Transfer & Trust Company

General Counsel: Thomas J. Quarles, Sr. V.P.

Investor Relations:
Ronald G. Eidell, Sr. V.P. & C.F.O.

Human Resources: J.E. Treadway

Mgt. Info. Svcs. Phillip Neeson

Auditors: Arthur Andersen LLP

Traded (Symbol): NYSE (ML)
Stockholders: 117
Employees: 3,155
Annual Meeting: In April
Internet: www.metromail.com

The Metzler Group, Inc.

520 Lake Cook Road, Suite 500, Deerfield, Illinois 60015
Telephone: (847) 914-9100

The Metzler Group, Inc. is a leading nationwide provider of consulting services to electric utilities and other energy-related businesses. The company offers a wide range of consulting services related to information technology, process/operations management, strategy, and marketing and sales designed to assist its clients in succeeding in a business environment of changing regulation, increasing competition, and evolving technology. In October 1996, the company completed an initial public offering of 3,500,000 shares of common stock. Incorporated in Delaware in 1996.

Directors (In addition to indicated officers)

Peter B. Pond
James T. Ruprecht

Mitchell H. Saranow

Officers (Directors*)

*Robert P. Maher, Chm., Pres. & C.E.O.
*Gerald R. Lanz, C.O.O.

James F. Hillman, C.F.O. & Treas.

Consolidated Balance Sheet As of December 31, 1996 (000 omitted)

Assets		Liabilities & Stockholders' Equity	
Current assets	$37,222	Current liabilities	$ 3,350
Net property, plant & equipment	359	Deferred income tax	125
		Other liabilities	14
		*Stockholders' equity	34,092
Total	$37,581	Total	$37,581

*10,585,000 shares common stock outstanding.

Consolidated Income Statement

Years Ended Dec. 31	Thousands — — — —		Per Share[a] — — —		Common Stock
	Revenues	Net Income	Earnings	Cash Dividends	Price Range[a] Calendar Year
1996[b]	$22,093	$ 4,035[cde]	$ .40[c]	$ .00	36-3/4 — 16
1995[b]	13,460	1,192[cdf]	.12[c]		
1994	10,420	(184)			
1993	10,380	154			
1992	9,216	(265)			

[a]Initial public offering in October 1996.
[b]From January 1, 1996, to the initial public offering on October 4, 1996, the company operated as an S corporation and was not subject to income taxes.
[c]Pro forma.
[d]Includes federal and state income taxes of $1,799,403 in 1996 and $1,110,117 in 1995 that would have been required had the company been not been an S corporation.
[e]Reflects an increase in selling, general, and administrative expense of $1,019,460 that would have been paid under a compensation plan adopted July 1, 1996.
[f]Reflects a decrease in selling, general, and administrative expense of $2,775,293 had the compensation plan been in effect in 1995.

Transfer Agent & Registrar: Harris Trust and Savings Bank

General Counsel: Sachnoff & Weaver

Investor Relations: Thomas Stenson

Auditors: KPMG Peat Marwick LLP

Traded (Symbol): NASDAQ (METZ)
Stockholders: 1,400
Employees: 67
Annual Meeting: In May

MFRI, Inc.

7720 Lehigh Avenue, Niles, Illinois 60714-3491
Telephone: (847) 966-1000

MFRI, Inc. is engaged in the manufacture and sale of filter bags for use in industrial air pollution control systems known as "baghouses." The company also engineers, designs, and manufactures specialty piping systems, and leak detection and location systems. MFRI is the successor corporation to Midwesco Filter Resources, Inc. Midwesco Filter, a wholly owned subsidiary, manufactures and sells a wide variety of filter bags for baghouse air pollution control and particulate collection systems. Baghouses are used in a wide variety of domestic and foreign industries to limit particulate emissions, primarily to comply with environmental regulations. The company manufactures bags in standard industry sizes, shapes, and fabrics, and to custom specifications, maintaining manufacturing standards for more than 8,000 styles of filter bags. Midwesco Filter manufactures substantially all of the seamless tube filter bags sold in the United States. Products manufactured by Perma-Pipe, Inc., another wholly owned subsidiary, include secondary containment piping systems for transporting hazardous fluids and petroleum products; and insulated and jacketed district heating and cooling piping systems for efficient energy distribution to multiple locations from central energy plants. Perma-Pipe's leak detection and location systems are sold as part of its piping system products, and on a stand-alone basis, to monitor areas where fluid intrusion may contaminate the environment, endanger personal safety, cause a fire hazard, or damage equipment or property. Thermal Care, acquired near the end of 1996, manufactures a full line of industrial process cooling equipment, primarily chillers, cooling towers, mold temperature controllers, and plant circulating systems. Most of its products are used in the plastic molding industry. Other applications include metalizing lasers, welders, and reaction injection equipment. These products are sold throughout the U.S., Canada, and Latin America. Incorporated in Delaware in 1993; present name adopted in 1994.

Directors (In addition to indicated officers)

Arnold F. Brookstone
Bradley E. Mautner

Eugene Miller
Stephen B. Schwartz

Officers (Directors*)

*David Unger, Chm., Pres. & C.E.O.
*Henry M. Mautner, V. Chm.
 Michael D. Bennett, V.P., Secy. & Treas.
 Thomas A. Benson, V.P.
*Fati A. Elgendy, V.P.
 Bill Ervin, V.P.
 Joseph P. Findley, V.P.

*Don Gruenberg, V.P.
 J. Tyler Headley, V.P.
 Robert Maffei, V.P.
*Gene K. Ogilvie, V.P.
 Stephen P. Russell, V.P.
 Herbert J. Sturm, V.P.

Consolidated Balance Sheet   As of January 31, 1997 (000 omitted)

Assets		Liabilities & Stockholders' Equity	
Current assets	$45,249	Current liabilities	$17,405
Restricted cash from bond proceeds	3,880	Long-term debt	23,921
Net property, plant & equipment	15,054	Deferred items	1,148
Other assets	11,145	*Stockholders' equity	32,854
Total	$75,328	Total	$75,328

*4,962,000 shares common stock outstanding.

Consolidated Income Statement

Years Ended Abt. Jan. 31	Thousands — — — — Net Sales	Net Income	Per Share — — — Earnings	Cash Dividends	Common Stock Price Range Calendar Year
1997	$93,573	$3,230	$ .70	$ .00	
1996	85,838	2,373	.52	.00	8-1/8 — 5-3/4
1995	75,495	1,203	.27	.00	7-1/2 — 4
1994[a]	62,390	2,569	.60	.00	9-1/4 — 4-3/4
1993[a]	51,490	1,132	.26	.00	8-3/4 — 6-3/8

[a]Pro forma results as if the acquisition of Perma-Pipe had taken place at the beginning of fiscal 1993.

Transfer Agent & Registrar: Harris Trust and Savings Bank

Legal Counsel:	Rudnick & Wolfe	Auditors:	Deloitte & Touche LLP
Investor Relations:	Michael D. Bennett, V.P.	Traded (Symbol):	NASDAQ (MFRI)
		Stockholders:	1,350
Human Resources:	Michael D. Bennett, V.P.	Employees:	558
Mgt. Info. Svcs.:	Steve Harbaugh	Annual Meeting:	In June

The Middleby Corporation

1400 Toastmaster Drive, Elgin, Illinois 60120
Telephone: (847) 741-3300

The Middleby Corporation is engaged in the manufacture and sale of commercial foodservice equipment. It designs, develops, manufactures, and markets a broad line of equipment used for the preparation and cooking of food in commercial and institutional kitchens and restaurants in the United States and internationally. Founded in 1888 as The Middleby Marshall Oven Company, its principal business units today include: Middleby Marshall, which produces automated conveyor cooking systems and processing equipment; Toastmaster, which produces cooking and warming equipment for commercial use; Southbend, which specializes in heavy-duty cooking and steam equipment; Asbury Associates, which is an export management and distribution company; and Middleby Phillipines Company, which designs, fabricates, and installs semi-custom kitchen equipment units in Asian markets. In early 1997, Middleby sold its Victory Refrigeration Company subsidiary to an investor group led by local management at Victory. Incorporated in Delaware in 1985.

Directors   (In addition to indicated officers)

Robert R. Henry
A. Don Lummus
John R. Miller III
Philip G. Putnam

Sabin C. Streeter
Joseph G. Tompkins
Laura B. Whitman
Robert L. Yohe

Officers   (Directors*)

*William F. Whitman, Jr., Chm.
*David P. Riley, Pres. & C.E.O.

John J. Hastings, Exec. V.P., C.F.O., Secy. & Treas.

Consolidated Balance Sheet   As of December 28, 1996 (000 omitted)

Assets		Liabilities & Stockholders' Equity	
Current assets	$49,332	Current liabilities	$24,286
Net property, plant & equipment	18,843	Long-term debt	37,352
Other assets	17,793	Other liabilities	1,880
		*Stockholders' equity	22,450
Total	$85,968	Total	$85,968

*8,470,938 shares common stock outstanding.

Consolidated Income Statement

Years Ended Abt. Dec. 31	Thousands — — — — Net Sales[a]	Net Income[a]	Per Share — — — Earnings	Cash Dividends	Common Stock Price Range Calendar Year
1996	$124,765	$ 473[b]	$ .05[b]	$ .00	14 — 4-3/4
1995	139,188	3,474	.40	.00	9-3/4 — 3-7/8
1994	129,967	3,050	.36	.00	4-7/8 — 2-5/8
1993	119,355	3,432[c]	.41[c]	.00	4-1/8 — 1-3/4
1992	109,219	(1,894)	(.23)	.00	3-3/8 — 1-1/8

[a]Certain amounts in the 1995-1992 data have been reclassified to be consistent with the fiscal 1996 presentation and reflect the elimination of a subsidiary sold in early 1997.
[b]Includes a loss from discontinued operations of $2,610,000 ($.30 per share).
[c]Includes unusual income item of $14,800,000 ($1.77 per share) related to the settlement of a legal dispute.

Transfer Agent & Registrar:	Continental Stock Transfer & Trust Co.		
General Counsel:	D'Ancona & Pflaum	**Traded (Symbol):**	NASDAQ (MIDD)
Investor Relations:	John J. Hastings, Exec. V.P.	**Stockholders:**	2,500
Human Resources:	John J. Hastings, Exec. V.P.	**Employees:**	965
Mgt. Info. Svcs.:	John J. Hastings, Exec. V.P.	**Annual Meeting:**	In May
Auditors:	Arthur Andersen LLP	**Internet:**	www.middleby.com

Midway Games Inc.

3401 North California Avenue, Chicago, Illinois 60618
Telephone: (773) 961-2222

Midway Games Inc. is a leading designer, publisher, and marketer of interactive entertainment software played in both the coin-operated and home markets. The company's games are available for play on all major dedicated home video game platforms, including Nintendo®, Sony, and Sega®, and for personal computers. Since the late 1970s, Midway has released many of the industry's leading games including Mortal Kombat, Cruis'n USA, NBA Jam, Joust, Defender, Pac-Man, and Space Invaders. The company's principal subsidiaries are Midway Home Entertainment Inc. and Atari Games Corporation. In March 1996, Midway acquired Atari from Warner Communications Inc. In October 1996, Midway completed an initial public offering of 5,100,000 shares of common stock. WMS Industries Inc. currently holds 33,400,000 shares (86.8 percent) of the company's common stock. Incorporated in Delaware in 1988.

Directors   (In addition to indicated officers)

William C. Bartholomay
William E. McKenna
Norman J. Menell
Louis J. Nicastro

Harvey Reich
Ira S. Sheinfeld
Gerald O. Sweeney
Richard D. White

Officers   (Directors*)

*Neil D. Nicastro, Chm., Pres. & C.E.O.
*Harold H. Bach, Jr., Exec. V.P.—Fin., C.F.O. & Treas.

*Byron C. Cook, Exec. V.P.—Home Video
*Kenneth J. Fedesna, Exec. V.P.—Coin-Op Video
Barbara M. Norman, V.P., Gen. Coun. & Secy.

Consolidated Balance Sheet   As of June 30, 1996 (000 omitted)

Assets		Liabilities & Stockholders' Equity	
Current assets	$ 88,579	Current liabilities	$100,197
Net property, plant & equipment	5,927	Long-term debt	7,863
Excess of purchase cost over net assets acquired	22,765	Deferred income taxes	2,794
		Other liabilities	1,920
Other assets	991	*Stockholders' equity	5,488
Total	$118,262	Total	$118,262

*38,500,000 shares common stock outstanding at October 30, 1996.

Consolidated Income Statement

Years Ended June 30	Thousands — — — — Total Revenue	Net Income	Per Share[a] — — — Earnings	Cash Dividends	Common Stock Price Range[b] Calendar Year
1996	$245,423	$25,229	$ .76	$ .00	25-1/2 — 18-3/4
1995	180,479	29,139	.87		
1994	121,882	28,023	.84		
1993[c]	85,631	15,839	.47		
1992[c]	38,330	6,237	.19		

[a]Per share earnings based on 33,400,000 pro forma shares outstanding.
[b]Initial public offering in October 1996. Price from November 1 through December 31, 1996.
[c]Unaudited.

Transfer Agent & Registrar:	The Bank of New York		
General Counsel:	Shack & Siegel, P.C.	Stockholders:	2,000
Investor Relations:	Howard H. Bach, Jr., Exec. V.P.	Employees:	326
Auditors:	Ernst & Young LLP	Annual Meeting:	In January
Traded (Symbol):	NYSE (MWY)	Internet:	www.midwaygames.com

LaSalle Banks Guide

Minuteman International, Inc.

111 South Rohlwing, Addison, Illinois 60101
Telephone: (630) 627-6900

Minuteman International, Inc. manufactures and distributes commercial and industrial vacuums, floor, carpet and lawn care equipment, and chemical cleaning and coating products. The company's products include vacuums, floor maintenance machines, carpet maintenance machines, sweepers and automatic scrubbers, chemical cleaning and coating products, and complementary accessories. The company's products are distributed throughout the United States and Canada by more than 550 independent distributors and are also sold in many foreign markets. The company's products generally are not sold to consumers for home use. Subsidiaries include: Minuteman Canada Inc.; Multi-Clean and Parker Sweeper Divisions of Minuteman International, Inc.; and Minuteman International Foreign Sales Corp. Incorporated in Illinois in 1951 as Hako Minuteman, Inc.; present name adopted in 1994.

Directors (In addition to indicated officers)

Frederick W. Hohage
Tyll Necker

Frank R. Reynolds, Jr.
James C. Schrader, Jr.

Officers (Directors*)

*Jerome E. Rau, Pres. & C.E.O.
Gary E. Palmer, V.P.—Eng.
Gregory J. Rau, V.P.—Sales

Michael A. Rau, V.P.—Multi-Clean
Thomas J. Nolan, C.F.O., Secy. & Treas.
Michael Gravelle, Pres.—Minuteman Canada Inc.

Consolidated Balance Sheet As of December 31, 1996 (000 omitted)

Assets		Liabilities & Stockholders' Equity	
Current assets	$22,098	Current liabilities	$ 2,914
Net property, plant & equipment	8,648	Deferred items	200
Other assets	222	*Stockholders' equity	27,854
Total	$30,968	Total	$30,968

*3,568,385 shares common stock outstanding.

Consolidated Income Statement

Years Ended Dec. 31	Thousands — — — —		Per Share — — —		Common Stock Price Range Calendar Year	
	Net Sales	Net Income	Earnings	Cash Dividends		
1996	$49,120	$3,161	$ .89	$ .40	10	— 7-1/4
1995	46,300	2,824	.79	.40	11	— 9
1994	41,518	3,203	.90	.34	13	— 9-1/2
1993	38,237	2,349	.66	.28	11-1/2	— 6-1/4
1992	32,659	1,611	.45	.28	10	— 5-1/2

Transfer Agent & Registrar: Chase Mellon Shareholder Services, L.L.C.

General Counsel: Frank R. Reynolds, Jr.

Investor Relations: Thomas J. Nolan, C.F.O.

Human Resources: Thomas J. Nolan, C.F.O.

Mgt. Info. Svcs.: Thomas J. Nolan, C.F.O.

Auditors: Ernst & Young LLP

Traded (Symbol): NASDAQ (MMAN)

Stockholders: 1,100

Employees: 275

Annual Meeting: In April

MMI Companies, Inc.

540 Lake Cook Road, Deerfield, Illinois 60015-5290
Telephone: (847) 940-7550

MMI Companies, Inc. is an international health care risk management company providing liability insurance, clinical risk management services, managed care, and strategic planning consultation to healthcare organizations, physicians, and allied healthcare professionals nationwide. Principal subsidiaries include: American Continental Insurance Co.; American Continental Life Insurance Co.; Health Providers Insurance Co.; Management Science Associates, Inc.; McManis Associates, Inc.; and MMI Risk Management Resources, Inc. Through these subsidiaries, the company offers products and services that enable its clients to manage insurance, clinical, and business risks associated with providing healthcare. In April 1996, MMI acquired substantially all the assets of Management Science Associates, Inc. Incorporated in Delaware in 1983.

Directors (In addition to indicated officers)

Richard R. Barr
George B. Caldwell
K. James Ehlen, M.D.
F. Laird Facey, M.D.
William M. Kelley
Andrew David Kennedy

Timothy R. McCormick
Gerald L. McManis
Scott S. Parker
Edward C. Peddie
Joseph D. Sargent

Officers (Directors*)

*B. Frederick Becker, Chm. & C.E.O.
Anna Marie Hajek, Exec. V.P. & Pres.—MMI Healthcare Services Group
Paul M. Orzech, Exec. V.P., C.F.O. & Treas.
Steve A. Schleisman, Exec. V.P. & Pres.—MMI Ins. Grp.
Merrilee Hepler, Sr. V.P.—Hum. Res.
Richard A. Linden, Sr. V.P. & C.I.O.
Wayne A. Sinclair, Sr. V.P., Gen. Coun. & Secy.

Carl R. Follo, V.P.
Joseph R. Herman, V.P. & Cont.
Michael S. LaSala, V.P.—Structured Settlement Oper.
M. Elizabeth Sassano, V.P. & Asst. Gen. Coun.
Scott T. Veech, V.P.—Fin.
Sally Benjamin Young, V.P.—Corp. Commun.

Consolidated Balance Sheet   As of December 31, 1996 (000 omitted)

Assets		Liabilities & Stockholders' Equity	
Investments	$ 788,451	Policy liabilities	$ 695,830
Other assets	269,567	Other liabilities	110,222
		*Stockholders' equity	251,966
Total	$1,058,018	Total	$1,058,018

*11,625,000 shares common stock outstanding.

Consolidated Income Statement

| Years Ended Dec. 31 | Thousands — — — — | | Per Share[a] — — — — | | Common Stock |
	Total Revenues	Net Income	Earnings	Cash Dividends	Price Range[a] Calendar Year
1996	$243,178	$21,015[b]	$1.96[b]	$ .24	33-1/4 — 22
1995	218,744	22,695	2.42	.20	25-1/2 — 14-7/8
1994	177,205	15,051	1.73	.16	15-7/8 — 12-1/8
1993	154,864	14,181	1.90	.12	16-3/8 — 13-1/8
1992	142,074	5,078[cd]	.77[cd]	.11	

[a]Adjusted to reflect a 1.375-for-1 stock split in March 1993. Initial public offering in June 1993.
[b]Includes a loss from discontinued operations of $5,100,000 ($.48 per share).
[c]Includes a gain to reflect FAS 109, resulting in a cumulative effect of $5,419,000 ($.82 per share).
[d]Includes a loss from discontinued operations of $7,024,000 ($1.06 per share).

Transfer Agent & Registrar:	ChaseMellon Shareholder Services, L.L.C.		
General Counsel:	Wayne A. Sinclair, Sr. V.P.	Traded (Symbol):	NYSE (MMI)
Investor Relations:	Paul M. Orzech, Exec. V.P.	Annual Meeting:	In April
Human Resources:	Merrilee Hepler, Sr. V.P.	Stockholders:	407
Mgt. Info. Svcs.:	Richard A. Linden, Sr. V.P.	Employees:	725
Auditors:	Ernst & Young LLP	Internet:	www.mmicompanies.com

Molex Incorporated

2222 Wellington Court, Lisle, Illinois 60532-1682
Telephone: (630) 969-4550

Molex Incorporated is a worldwide designer, manufacturer, marketer, and distributor for the high technology electronics industry. Molex supplies connectors, conductor cable, terminals, interconnection systems (including fiberoptic), associated application equipment, and switches to manufacturers of business machines, telecommunications equipment, video tape recorders, computers and computer peripheral equipment, home entertainment products, medical electronics, testing apparatus, home appliances, premise wiring systems, and automobiles. Molex's 30,000 products are sold through direct sales offices and representatives in 20 countries. Manufacturing facilities include over 40 plants on six continents. Incorporated in Delaware in 1972 as the successor to an Illinois corporation of the same name formed in 1957.

Directors (In addition to indicated officers)

Michael J. Birck
Douglas K. Carnahan
Edgar D. Jannotta
Fred L. Krehbiel

Donald G. Lubin
Masahisa Naitoh
Robert J. Potter

Officers (Directors*)

*Frederick A. Krehbiel, Chm. & C.E.O.
*John H. Krehbiel, Jr., Pres.
 Werner W. Fichtner, V.P.
 James E. Fleischhacker, V.P.
 J. Joseph King, V.P.—Intl. Oper.
 Robert B. Mahoney, V.P. & Treas.

Kathi M. Regas, V.P.
Ronald L. Schubel, V.P.
Martin P. Slark, V.P.
Goro Tokuyama, V.P.
Raymond C. Wieser, V.P.
Louis A. Hecht, Corp. Secy. & Gen. Coun.

Consolidated Balance Sheet   As of June 30, 1996 (000 omitted)

Assets		Liabilities & Stockholders' Equity	
Current assets	$ 734,589	Current liabilities	$ 275,182
Net property, plant & equipment	613,125	Long-term debt	7,450
Other assets	113,285	Deferred items	13,977
		Other liabilities	33,119
		*Stockholders' equity	1,131,271
Total	$1,460,999	Total	$1,460,999

*116,510,000 shares common stock outstanding (Classes A and B).

Consolidated Income Statement

Years Ended June 30	Thousands — — — — Net Revenue	Net Income	Per Share[a] — — — — Earnings	Cash Dividends	Common Stock Price Range[a] Calendar Year
1996	$1,382,673	$145,586	$1.45	$ .06	39-3/4 — 27-1/4
1995	1,197,747	124,035	1.24	.03	37 — 24-3/4
1994	964,108	94,852	.96	.02	28-3/4 — 19-3/8
1993	859,283	71,055	.72	.02	24-1/2 — 16-1/2
1992	776,192	67,464	.69	.01	20-1/4 — 15-1/8

[a]Adjusted to reflect 25% stock dividends in September 1995, November 1994, and November 1992.

Transfer Agent & Registrar: Harris Trust and Savings Bank

General Counsel: Louis A. Hecht, Corp. Secy.

Investor Relations: Neil Lefort, Dir.

Human Resources: Kathi Regas, V.P.

Mgt. Info. Svcs.:   Richard R. Haugen

Auditors: Deloitte & Touche LLP

Traded (Symbol):
NASDAQ, London SE (MOLX, Common stock; MOLXA-Class A)

Stockholders: 6,062
Employees: 9,500
Annual Meeting: In October
Internet: www.molex.com

Morton International, Inc.

100 North Riverside Plaza, Chicago, Illinois 60606-1596
Telephone: (312) 807-2000

Morton International, Inc. operates two commercial businesses consisting of specialty chemicals and salt. The specialty chemicals segment manufactures high technology chemical products for a wide variety of customer applications. The salt segment produces and sells salt principally in the United States and Canada, under the MORTON and WINDSOR trademarks, for human and animal consumption, water conditioning, highway ice melting, and for industrial and chemical uses. In January 1997, Morton announced that it would acquire Compagnie des Salins du Midi et des Salines de l'Est, a French salt producer. In May 1997, Morton spun off its inflatable restraint systems segment, which merged with Autoliv AB of Stockholm, Sweden, to form a new company, Autoliv, Inc. Incorporated in Indiana in 1989; reincorporated in 1997.

Directors   (In addition to indicated officers)

Ralph M. Barford	Richard L. Keyser
James R. Cantalupo	Frank W. Luerssen
William T. Creson	Edward J. Mooney, Jr.
W. James Farrell	George A. Schaefer
Dennis C. Fill	Roger W. Stone

Officers   (Directors*)

*S. Jay Stewart, Chm. & C.E.O.
*William E. Johnston, Jr., Pres. & C.O.O.
Walter W. Becky II, Grp. V.P.—Salt
Daniel D. Feinberg, Grp. V.P.—Electronic Mat.
James J. Fuerholzer, Grp. V.P.—Adhesives and Chem. Spec.
Stephen A. Gerow, Grp. V.P.—Coatings

Raymond P. Buschmann, V.P.—Legal Affs. and Gen. Coun.
Albert E. Greene, V.P.—Health, Safety & Envir.
Nancy A. Hobor, V.P.—Comm. & Inv. Rel.
Christopher K. Julsrud, V.P.—Hum. Res.
Thomas F. McDevitt, V.P.—Fin. & C.F.O.
P. Michael Phelps, V.P. & Corp. Secy.
Lewis N. Liszt, Cont.
Bruce G. Wolfe, Treas.

Consolidated Balance Sheet   As of June 30, 1996 (000 omitted)

Assets		Liabilities & Stockholders' Equity	
Current assets	$1,196,200	Current liabilities	$ 557,300
Net property, plant & equipment	1,145,800	Long-term debt	218,500
Other assets	429,500	Deferred items	53,400
		Other liabilities	269,500
		*Stockholders' equity	1,672,800
Total	$2,771,500	Total	$2,771,500

*142,414,016 shares common stock outstanding.

Consolidated Income Statement

Years Ended June 30	Thousands — — — —		Per Share[a] — — — —		Common Stock Price Range[a] Calendar Year
	Net Sales	Net Income	Earnings	Cash Dividends	
1996	$3,612,500	$334,200	$2.24	$ .52	43 — 33-1/4
1995	3,325,900	294,100	1.96	.44	32 — 25-3/4
1994	2,849,600	226,500	1.51	.37	37-1/4 — 25-3/4
1993	2,309,800	32,500[b]	.22[b]	.32	33-1/2 — 19-1/4
1992	2,043,900	144,500	.98	.32	21-5/8 — 16-7/8

[a]Adjusted to reflect a 3-for-1 stock split in August 1994.
[b]Includes a charge to reflect FAS 106 and FAS 112, resulting in a cumulative effect of $94,400,000 ($.64 per share).

Transfer Agent & Registrar:	First Chicago Trust Co. of New York		
General Counsel:	Raymond P. Buschmann, V.P.	Traded (Symbol):	NYSE, CSE (MII)
Investor Relations:	Nancy A. Hobor, V.P.	Stockholders:	10,625
Human Resources:	Christopher K. Julsrud, V.P.	Employees:	10,160
Mgt. Info. Svcs.:	Carl S. Utley, V.P.	Annual Meeting:	In October
Auditors:	Ernst & Young LLP	Internet:	www.morton.com

Motorola, Inc.

1303 East Algonquin Road, Schaumburg, Illinois 60196-1065
Telephone: (847) 576-5000

Motorola, Inc. is a leading provider of electronic equipment, systems, components, and services produced for both domestic and international markets. The Land Mobile Products Sector is a principal supplier of mobile and portable FM two-way radio and radio data communications systems. The Messaging, Information and Media Sector designs, manufactures, and distributes products for paging and radio data systems worldwide. Products include modems, multiplexers, and integrated network management systems. The Semiconductor Products Sector manufactures discrete semiconductors and integrated circuits, including microprocessors, memories, logic, analog, and application specific ICs. The Cellular Subscriber Sector manufactures cellular mobile and portable telephones. The Cellular Networks and Space Sector manufactures cellular systems, advanced electronics systems, and satellite communications for commercial and government customers. The Automotive, Energy and Components Sector manufactures electronic engine controls, sensors, and power conversion equipment as well as electronic components such as batteries, crystals, and ceramics. Incorporated in Illinois in 1928; reincorporated in Delaware in 1973.

Directors   (In addition to indicated officers)

H. Laurance Fuller	Donald R. Jones	John F. Mitchell	John E. Pepper, Jr.
Robert W. Galvin	Judy C. Lewent	Thomas J. Murrin	Samuel C. Scott III
Anne P. Jones	Walter E. Massey	Nicholas Negroponte	B. Kenneth West
			John A. White

Officers   (Directors*)

* Gary L. Tooker, Chm.
* Christopher B. Galvin, C.E.O.
* Robert L. Growney, Pres. & C.O.O.
  Keith J. Bane, Exec. V.P. & Chf. Corp. Staff Officer
  Arnold S. Brenner, Exec. V.P. & Gen. Mgr.—Japan Group
  Thomas D. George, Exec. V.P. & Pres./Gen. Mgr.—Semicond. Prod.
  Glenn A. Gienko, Exec. V.P. & Dir.—Hum. Res.
  Merle L. Gilmore, Exec. V.P. & Pres./Gen. Mgr.—Land Mobile Prod.
  Carl F. Koenemann, Exec. V.P. & C.F.O.
  James A. Norling, Exec. V.P. & Pres./Gen Mgr.—Mess. Info. & Media

Hector de J. Ruiz, Exec. V.P., Office of the Pres., Semicond. Prod.
Jack M. Scanlon, Exec. V.P. & Pres./Gen. Mgr.—Cellular Networks
Frederick T. Tucker, Exec. V.P. & Gen. Mgr.—Auto., Energy & Control
Robert N. Weisshappel, Exec. V.P. & Pres./Gen. Mgr.—Cellular Subscriber
Richard W. Younts, Exec. V.P. & Dir.—Int'l.
William V. Braun, Sr. V.P. & Dir.—R&D
Peter Lawson, Sr. V.P., Gen. Coun. & Secy.
Garth L. Milne, Sr. V.P. & Treas.

Consolidated Balance Sheet   As of December 31, 1996 (000 omitted)

Assets		Liabilities & Stockholders' Equity	
Current assets	$11,319,000	Current liabilities	$ 7,995,000
Net property, plant & equipment	9,768,000	Long-term debt	1,931,000
Other assets	2,989,000	Deferred items	1,108,000
		Other liabilities	1,247,000
		* Stockholders' equity	11,795,000
Total	$24,076,000	Total	$24,076,000

*593,400,000 shares common stock outstanding.

Consolidated Income Statement

Years Ended Dec. 31	Thousands — — — —		Per Share[b] — — —		Common Stock Price Range[b] Calendar Year
	Sales[a]	Net Income	Earnings[c]	Cash Dividends[d]	
1996	$27,973,000	$1,154,000	$1.90	$ .44	68-1/2 — 44-1/8
1995[e]	27,037,000	2,048,000	3.37	.40	82-1/2 — 51-1/2
1994	22,245,000	1,560,000	2.65	.31	61-1/8 — 42-1/8
1993	16,963,000	1,022,000	1.78	.22	53-3/4 — 24-3/8
1992	13,303,000	576,000[f]	1.05[f]	.20	26-5/8 — 16-1/8

[a]Includes FAS 94, consolidation of majority-owned subsidiaries.
[b]Adjusted to reflect 2-for-1 stock splits in February 1994 and November 1992.
[c]Fully diluted.
[d]Declared.
[e]Restated.
[f]Before a charge to reflect FAS 106, resulting in a cumulative effect of $123,000,000 ($.22 per share).

Transfer Agent & Registrar: Harris Trust and Savings Bank

General Counsel:	Peter Lawson, Sr. V.P.	Traded (Symbol):	NYSE, CSE, LONDON, TOKYO (MOT)
Investor Relations:	Edward Gams, V.P.	Stockholders:	1,055,000
Human Resources:	Glenn A. Gienko, Exec. V.P.	Employees:	139,000
Mgt. Info. Svcs.:	John Major, Sr. V.P.	Annual Meeting:	In May
Auditors:	KPMG Peat Marwick LLP	Internet:	www.mot.com

Multigraphics, Inc.

431 Lakeview Court, Mt. Prospect, Illinois 60056
Telephone: (847) 375-1700

Multigraphics, Inc. (formerly AM International, Inc.) provides equipment, supplies, and services to the graphics market. The company distributes a broad product line of equipment and supplies, and provides services through its own direct sales and services organizations in the United States. Products include small offset printing equipment and automated copy/duplicating machines, as well as pre- and post-press products and supplies. In May 1993, the company filed for Chapter 11 bankruptcy relief. It was discharged from bankruptcy in October 1993, and since that time has divested all of its Multigraphics-International operations. In August 1996, the company sold its Sheridan Systems division to Heidelberger Druckmaschinen AG of Germany. Incorporated in Delaware in 1924 as Addressograph Securities Corporation, an outgrowth of a business originally started in 1893; present name adopted in 1997.

Directors   (In addition to indicated officers)

Robert E. Anderson III
Jeffrey D. Benjamin

Robert N. Dangremond
Jeff M. Moore

Officers   (Directors*)

*Thomas D. Rooney, Pres. & C.E.O.
 Steven R. Andrews, V.P., Gen. Coun. & Secy.

Gregory T. Knipp, V.P. & C.F.O.

Consolidated Balance Sheet   As of July 31, 1996 (000 omitted) Unaudited

Assets		Liabilities & Stockholders' Equity	
Current assets	$85,643	Current liabilities	$73,923
Net property, plant & equipment	10,867	Long-term debt	8,527
Other assets	1,452	Other liabilities	13,216
		*Stockholders' equity	2,296
Total	$97,962	Total	$97,962

*7,010,000 shares common stock outstanding.

Consolidated Income Statement

Years Ended July 31	Thousands — — — —		Per Share[b] — — —		Common Stock Price Range[b] Calendar Year
	Net Sales[a]	Net Income	Earnings	Cash Dividends	
1996	$168,052	$(45,499)[c]	$(6.49)	$ .00	5-7/8 — 1-1/4
1995	191,485	4,613[d]	.66	.00	9-3/8 — 5-3/4
1994[e]	163,816	6,652[d]	.95	.00	12-1/4 — 8-1/2

[a]From continuing operations.
[b]Not adjusted to reflect a 1-for-2.5 reverse stock split approved by the company's stockholders on May 28, 1997.
[c]Includes a net loss of $25,342,000 from discontinued operations.
[d]Includes net income of $8,764,000 in 1995 and $4,570,000 in 1994 from discontinued operations.
[e]From September 30, 1993, through July 31, 1994. Due to reorganization and fresh start reporting, financial statements for the new reorganized company are not comparable to those of predecessor.

Transfer Agent & Registrar: First Chicago Trust Co. of New York

General Counsel:	Steven R. Andrews, V.P.	Traded (Symbol):	AMEX (MTI)
Investor Relations:	Thomas D. Rooney, Pres.	Stockholders:	6,000
		Employees:	650
Human Resources:	Joyce Huston	Annual Meeting:	In December
Auditors:	Arthur Andersen LLP	Internet:	www.am-multi.com

LaSalle Banks Guide   **179**

MYR Group Inc.

1701 West Golf Road, Suite 1012, Rolling Meadows, Illinois 60008-4007
Telephone: (847) 290-1891

MYR Group Inc. (formerly The L.E. Myers Co. Group) is a holding company whose principal assets consist of all of the outstanding shares of capital stock of The L.E. Myers Co., Harlan Electric Co., and Hawkeye Construction, Inc. The Group's principal business is electric utility line construction, commercial and industrial electrical construction, telecommunications construction services, and mechanical construction. The company also installs and maintains municipal street lighting and traffic control systems. The company generally serves the electric utility industry as a prime construction contractor, the commercial and industrial construction marketplace and telecommunications industry as a subcontractor, and the mechanical marketplace as both prime contractor and subcontractor. Incorporated in Delaware in 1982; present name adopted in 1995.

Directors   (In addition to indicated officers)

William G. Brown
Allen E. Bulley, Jr.

John M. Harlan
Bide L. Thomas

Officers   (Directors*)

*Charles M. Brennan III, Chm. & C.E.O.
 William S. Skibitsky, Pres. & C.O.O.
 Byron D. Nelson, Sr. V.P., Secy. & Gen.
  Coun.

Elliott C. Robbins, Sr. V.P., Treas. & C.F.O.
Betty R. Johnson, Cont.

Consolidated Balance Sheet   As of December 31, 1996 (000 omitted)

Assets		Liabilities & Stockholders' Equity	
Current assets	$70,646	Current liabilities	$56,475
Net property, plant & equipment	22,239	Long-term debt	8,874
Intangible assets	2,466	Deferred items	3,446
Other assets	3,135	Other liabilities	121
		*Stockholders' equity	29,570
Total	$98,486	Total	$98,486

*3,237,000 shares common stock outstanding.

Consolidated Income Statement[a]

Years Ended Dec. 31	Thousands — — — — Contract Revenues[b]	Net Income[b]	Per Share — — — Earnings[b]	Cash Dividends	Common Stock Price Range Calendar Year
1996	$310,577	$3,968	$1.15	$ .20	12-7/8 — 10
1995[c]	266,965	3,429	1.01	.18	11-7/8 — 8
1994	86,842	2,329	.70	.17	10-1/4 — 7-1/4
1993	108,515	1,633	.48	.16	13-3/8 — 6-3/8
1992	110,251	3,584	1.03	.14	19 — 11-3/8

[a]Includes FAS 109, resulting in a charge to net income of $867,000 ($.33 per share) in 1992 and $1,302,000 ($.50 per share) in 1991.
[b]From continuing operations.
[c]Includes Harlan Electric Co. since January 1995 (effective date of acquisition).

Transfer Agent & Registrar: Harris Trust and Savings Bank

General Counsel:	Byron D. Nelson, Sr. V.P.	Traded (Symbol):	NYSE (MYR)
Investor Relations:	Charles M. Brennan III, Chm.	Stockholders:	820
Human Resources:	James Urbas	Employees:	3,000
Mgt. Info. Svcs.:	Richard Beemster	Annual Meeting:	In May
Auditors:	Deloitte & Touche LLP	Internet:	www.myrgroup.com

Nalco Chemical Company

One Nalco Center, Naperville, Illinois 60563-1198
Telephone: (630) 305-1000

Nalco Chemical Company is a leading manufacturer and marketer of water treatment and process chemicals and services. The company serves many industries, including steelmaking, pulp and papermaking, mining and mineral processing, automotive, metalworking, oil refining and petroleum, power generation, food and beverage, light industrial, hospitals, and office buildings in more than 120 countries. Diversey Water Technologies is a principal subsidiary. Incorporated in Delaware in 1928.

Directors (In addition to indicated officers)

Jose Luis Ballesteros
Harold G. Bernthal
Harry Corless
Howard M. Dean
John P. Frazee, Jr.

Arthur L. Kelly
Frederick A. Krehbiel
William A. Pogue
John J. Shea

Officers (Directors*)

*Edward J. Mooney, Chm. & C.E.O.
Milford B. Harp, Exec. V.P.—Oper.
W. Steven Weeber, Exec. V.P.—Oper. Staff
George M. Brannon, Grp. V.P. & Pres.—Nalco Pacific
Peter Dabringhausen, Grp. V.P. & Pres.—Process Chem. Div.
Stephen D. Newlin, Grp. V.P. & Pres.—Nalco Europe

Gilberto Pinzon, Grp. V.P. & Pres.—Nalco Latin Amer.
J. David Tinsley, Grp. V.P. & Pres.—Water & Waste Treat. Div.
Ronald J. Allain, Sr. V.P.—R&D
David R. Bertran, Sr. V.P.—Mfg. & Logistics
William E. Buchholz, Sr. V.P. & C.F.O.
James F. Lambe, Sr. V.P.—Hum. Res.
William E. Parry, V.P. & Gen. Coun.

Consolidated Balance Sheet As of December 31, 1996 (000 omitted)

Assets		Liabilities & Stockholders' Equity	
Current assets	$ 385,200	Current liabilities	$ 289,700
Net property, plant & equipment	522,000	Long-term debt	252,600
Other assets	487,300	Deferred items	42,900
		Other liabilities	154,800
		*Stockholders' equity	654,500
Total	$1,394,500	Total	$1,394,500

*67,024,000 shares common stock outstanding.

Consolidated Income Statement

Years Ended Dec. 31	Thousands — — — —		Per Share — — — —		Common Stock Price Range Calendar Year
	Net Sales[a]	Net Income	Earnings	Cash Dividends	
1996	$1,303,500	$154,500	$1.97	$1.00	39 — 28-1/8
1995	1,214,500	153,700	1.95	.99	38-5/8 — 28-1/8
1994	1,246,800	97,100[b]	1.19[b]	.95	37-7/8 — 29-3/4
1993	1,291,600	85,600[c]	1.02[c]	.89	37-7/8 — 30-1/4
1992	1,286,900	145,000	1.79	.84	40-7/8 — 30-3/8

[a]Amounts for 1994-1992 include the company's petroleum chemicals operations, which were transferred to the Nalco/Exxon joint venture in September 1994.
[b]Includes a $54,000,000 after-tax charge for formation and consolidation expenses.
[c]Includes a $10,600,000 net charge for extraordinary loss from retirement of debt, and a $56,500,000 net charge for cumulative effect of change in accounting for post-retirement benefits other than pensions.

Transfer Agent & Registrar:	First Chicago Trust Co. of New York		
Corporate Counsel:	Mayer, Brown & Platt	Traded (Symbol):	NYSE (NLC)
Investor Relations:	Joseph R. Esterman, Div. V.P.	Stockholders:	5,349
Human Resources:	James F. Lambe, Sr. V.P.	Employees:	6,502
Mgt. Info. Svcs.:	Mark A. Lega, Div. V.P.	Annual Meeting:	In April
Auditors:	Price Waterhouse LLP	Internet:	www.nalco.com

National Surgery Centers, Inc.

30 South Wacker Drive, Suite 2302, Chicago, Illinois 60606
Telephone: (312) 655-1400

National Surgery Centers, Inc. owns and operates freestanding ambulatory surgery centers that provide the medical and administrative support necessary for physicians to perform non-emergency surgical procedures. The company operates a network of 32 outpatient centers in 12 states. National Surgery Centers provides high-quality surgical services in a cost-effective setting, focusing primarily on secondary and other selected markets. In November 1995, the company completed an initial public offering of 3,450,000 shares of common stock. In October 1996, the company completed a secondary offering of 2,415,511 shares of common stock. Incorporated in Illinois in 1987; reincorporated in Delaware in 1995.

Directors (In addition to indicated officers)

John K. Carlyle	Donald E. Linder, M.D.
Russell L. Carson	Rocco A. Ortenzio
John T. Henley, Jr., M.D.	

Officers (Directors*)

*E. Timothy Geary, Chm., Pres. & C.E.O.	Dennis D. Solheim, V.P.—Dev.
Bryan S. Fisher, V.P., C.F.O., Treas. & Secy.	Dennis J. Zamojski, V.P.—Oper.
Richard D. Pence, V.P.—Oper.	

Consolidated Balance Sheet As of December 31, 1996 (000 omitted)

Assets		Liabilities & Stockholders' Equity	
Current assets	$ 70,213	Current liabilities	$ 10,245
Net property, plant & equipment	33,362	Long-term debt	6,990
Other assets	38,677	Other liabilities	7,348
		*Stockholders' equity	117,669
Total	$142,252	Total	$142,252

*11,933,308 shares common stock outstanding.

Consolidated Income Statement

Years Ended Dec. 31	Thousands — — — — Net Revenues	Net Income	Per Share[a] — — — Earnings	Cash Dividends	Common Stock Price Range[ab] Calendar Year
1996	$77,359	$ 6,914	$ .70	$ .00	38-1/4 — 14-3/8
1995	53,165	2,846	.52	.00	15-3/8 — 12-1/8
1994	41,707	1,120	.26		
1993[c]	35,230	(43,236)	(11.35)		
1992	18,894	2	.00		

[a]Adjusted to reflect a 3-for-1 stock exchange in September 1995 and a 3-for-2 stock split effected as a 50 percent stock dividend in May 1996.
[b]Initial public offering in November 1995.
[c]Includes a non-recurring charge of approximately $50,900,000 ($43,800,000 after-tax benefit), principally incurred in connection with the writedown of goodwill.

Transfer Agent & Registrar:	Harris Trust and Savings Bank		
General Counsel:	Bell, Boyd & Lloyd	Traded (Symbol):	NASDAQ (NSCI)
Investor Relations:	Bryan S. Fisher, V.P.	Stockholders:	900
		Employees:	519
Auditors:	Ernst & Young LLP	Annual Meeting:	In May

Navistar International Corporation
455 North Cityfront Plaza Drive, Chicago, Illinois 60611
Telephone: (312) 836-2000

Navistar International Corporation is a holding company whose principal operating subsidiary, Navistar International Transportation Corp., manufactures and markets medium and heavy diesel trucks, school buses, mid-range diesel engines, and replacement parts in North America. Navistar also distributes these products in selected export markets. Products are sold worldwide through nearly 1,000 independent dealers and distribution outlets. Navistar International's brand of trucks include: diesel-powered truck/tractors used for local and long-distance hauling of freight; cab and chassis units used for medium hauling and for hauling heavy loads over rugged terrain and highways; and school buses. Navistar International also provides wholesale and retail financing, product leasing, and casualty insurance coverage services through wholly owned finance subsidiaries. Other major subsidiaries include Navistar Financial Corporation and Navistar International Corporation Canada. Incorporated in Delaware in 1965.

Directors   (In addition to indicated officers)

William F. Andrews
Andrew F. Brimmer
Richard F. Celeste
John D. Correnti
William C. Craig
Jerry E. Dempsey

John F. Fiedler
Mary Garst
Michael N. Hammes
Walter J. Laskowski
William F. Patient

Officers   (Directors*)

*John R. Horne, Chm., Pres. & C.E.O.
 Donald DeFosset, Jr., Exec. V.P. &
   Pres.—Truck Group
*Robert C. Lannert, Exec. V.P. & C.F.O.

Robert A. Boardman, Sr. V.P. & Gen. Coun.
Thomas M. Hough, V.P. & Treas.
J. Steven Keate, V.P. & Cont.
Steven K. Covey, Secy.

Consolidated Balance Sheet   As of October 31, 1996 (000 omitted)

Assets		Liabilities & Stockholders' Equity	
Cash & cash equivalents	$ 487,000	Current liabilities	$ 820,000
Property and equipment, net	770,000	Long-term debt	1,420,000
Other assets	4,069,000	Other liabilities	2,170,000
		*Stockholders' equity	916,000
Total	$5,326,000	Total	$5,326,000

*49,400,000 shares common and 24,293,000 shares Class B common stock outstanding.

Consolidated Income Statement

Years Ended Oct. 31	Thousands — — — —		Per Share[a] — — —		Common Stock
	Sales & Revenues	Net Income	Earnings	Cash Dividends	Price Range[a] Calendar Year
1996	$5,754,000	$ 65,000	$ .49	$ .00	12-1/8 — 8-3/8
1995	6,342,000	164,000	1.83	.00	17-1/2 — 9-1/4
1994	5,337,000	82,000	.72	.00	26-5/8 — 12-1/4
1993	4,721,000	(501,000)[b]	(15.19)[b]	.00	33-3/4 — 19-1/4
1992	3,897,000	(212,000)[c]	(9.55)[c]	.00	40 — 17-1/2

[a]Adjusted to reflect a 1-for-10 reverse stock split in August 1993.
[b]Includes a charge of $513,000,000 for the issuance of Class B common stock to a retiree supplemental trust in settlement of a reduction in retiree health and life insurance benefits, and a charge to reflect FAS 106 and FAS 109, resulting in a cumulative effect of $228,000,000 ($6.56 per share).
[c]Includes a $65,000,000 ($2.58 per share) charge to discontinued operations for the settlement of two lawsuits brought by the Pension Benefit Guaranty Corporation.

Transfer Agent & Registrar:	Harris Trust and Savings Bank		
General Counsel:	Robert A. Boardman, Sr. V.P.	Traded (Symbol):	NYSE, CSE, PSE (NAV)
Investor Relations:	Carmen Corbett, Asst. to Treas.	Stockholders:	124,284
Human Resources:	Joseph V. Thompson	Employees:	14,187
Mgt. Info. Svcs.:	Arthur Data	Annual Meeting:	In March
Auditors:	Deloitte & Touche LLP	Internet:	wwwext.navistar.com

NeoMedia Technologies, Inc.

2150 Western Court, Suite 230, Lisle, Illinois 60532
Telephone: (630) 435-9200

NeoMedia Technologies, Inc. provides computer software and consulting services to all sizes and types of organizations, from small, privately owned companies to large, multi-national organizations. The company offers its services and products through three principal business units: intelligent document solutions, document system solutions, and systems transition solutions. As part of the services provided in connection with these units, the company often recommends, specifies, supplies, and installs hardware equipment and software products from third-party suppliers, many of whom have associations with the company. In November 1996, NeoMedia completed an initial public offering of 1,700,000 shares of common stock. Incorporated in Delaware in 1996 as successor to a business founded in 1989; present name adopted in 1996.

Directors (In addition to indicated officers)

A. Hayes Barclay
James J. Keil

Paul Reece

Officers (Directors*)

*Charles W. Fritz, Chm., Pres. & C.E.O.
Dan Trampel, Sr. V.P.—Sales
*Robert T. Durst, Jr., V.P.—Tech. & Bus. Dev.,
  Chf. Tech. Off.

Rick D. Hollingsworth, V.P.—Tech. Oper.
*Charles T. Jensen, V.P., C.F.O. & Treas.
*William E. Fritz, Secy.

Consolidated Balance Sheet As of December 31, 1996 (000 omitted)

Assets		Liabilities & Stockholders' Equity	
Current assets	$10,331	Current liabilities	$ 5,350
Net property, plant & equipment	278	Long-term debt	1,589
Other assets	657	*Stockholders' equity	4,327
Total	$11,266	Total	$11,266

*5,114,316 shares common stock outstanding.

Consolidated Income Statement

Years Ended Dec. 31	Thousands — — — — Net Sales	Net Income	Per Share[ab] — — — Earnings	Cash Dividends	Common Stock Price Range[a] Calendar Year
1996	$17,518	$(3,075)	$ (.72)	$ .00	7-1/2 — 5-1/8
1995	12,801	(1,131)	(.26)		
1994	15,528	(192)	(.05)		

[a]Initial public offering in November 1996.
[b]Reflects a 15,555.60975-for-1 stock split in March 1996 and a .90386-for-1 reverse stock split in November 1996.

Transfer Agent & Registrar: American Stock Transfer & Trust Co.

General Counsel:	Fishman & Merrick, PC	Traded (Symbol):	NASDAQ (NEOM)
Investor Relations:	Charles T. Jensen, V.P.	Stockholders:	63
		Employees:	59
Human Resources:	John Mantica	Annual Meeting:	In July
Auditors:	Coopers & Lybrand, L.L.P.	Internet:	www.neomedia-tech.com

Newell Co.

Newell Center, 29 East Stephenson Street, Freeport, Illinois 61032
Telephone: (815) 235-4171

Newell Co. is a manufacturer and marketer of consumer products for the volume purchaser. Newell's multi-product offering includes: Mirro and WearEver cookware and bakeware; Amerock cabinet hardware; Anchor Hocking glassware and plasticware; EZ Paintr paint applicators; Goody Hair Accessories; Intercraft and Barnes picture frames; Levolor and Newell window treatments; Lee Rowan and System Works home storage products; Bulldog home hardware; BernzOmatic torches; Stuart Hall stationery; Rolodex desktop accessories; and Sanford, Eberhard Faber, and Berol markers and writing instruments. These consumer products are sold through a variety of retail and wholesale distribution channels. Incorporated in Delaware in 1903.

Directors (In addition to indicated officers)

Daniel C. Ferguson, Chm.
Alton F. Doody
Gary H. Driggs
Robert L. Katz
John J. McDonough

Elizabeth C. Millett
Cynthia A. Montgomery
Allan P. Newell
Henry B. Pearsall

Officers (Directors*)

*William P. Sovey, V. Chm. & C.E.O.
*Thomas A. Ferguson, Jr., Pres. & C.O.O.
Richard C. Dell, Grp. Pres.
William J. Denton, Grp. Pres.
James E. Gillies, Sr. V.P.—Canadian Mktg. Dev.
Donald L. Krause, Sr. V.P.—Cont.
Byron H. Stebbins, Sr. V.P.—Mktg. Dev.
William T. Alldredge, V.P.—Fin.
John M. Avampato, V.P.—Corp. Info. Svcs.

Thomas H. Beyer, V.P. & Grp. Cont.
Clarence R. Davenport, V.P., Treas. & C.I.O.
William K. Doppstadt, V.P.—Pers. Rel.
Brett E. Gries, V.P.—Acct. & Tax
Kenneth E. Hankins, V.P.—Oper. Svcs.
Peter J. Martin, V.P. & Grp. Cont.
Dale L. Matschullat, V.P. & Gen. Coun.
Richard H. Wolff, Assoc. Gen. Coun. & Secy.
Ronn L. Claussen, Asst. Treas.
Shirley K. Martin, Asst. Secy.

Consolidated Balance Sheet As of December 31, 1996 (000 omitted)

Assets		Liabilities & Stockholders' Equity	
Current assets	$1,108,114	Current liabilities	$ 637,013
Net property, plant & equipment	555,434	Long-term debt	672,033
Other assets	1,341,506	Deferred income taxes	47,477
		Other liabilities	156,691
		* Stockholders' equity	1,491,840
Total	$3,005,054	Total	$3,005,054

*158,900,000 shares common stock outstanding.

Consolidated Income Statement

Years Ended Dec. 31	Thousands — — — — Net Sales	Net Income	Per Share[a] — — — — Earnings	Cash Dividends	Common Stock Price Range[a] Calendar Year
1996	$2,872,817	$256,479	$1.62	$ .56	33-3/4 — 25
1995	2,498,400	222,500	1.41	.46	27-1/4 — 20-5/8
1994	2,074,934	195,575	1.24	.39	23-7/8 — 19
1993	1,645,036	165,334	1.05	.35	21-1/2 — 15-3/8
1992	1,451,656	119,137[b]	.77[b]	.30	26-1/2 — 16-1/2

[a]Adjusted to reflect a 2-for-1 stock split in September 1994.
[b]Includes FAS 106, resulting in a cumulative charge of $44,134,000 ($.29 per share).

Transfer Agent & Registrar: First Chicago Trust Co. of New York

General Counsel: Dale L. Matschullat, V.P.

Investor Relations: Ross A. Porter, Jr., Dir.

Human Resources: William K. Doppstadt, V.P.

Mgt. Info. Svcs.: Clarence R. Davenport, V.P.

Auditors: Arthur Andersen LLP
Traded (Symbol): NYSE, CSE (NWL)
Stockholders: 15,500
Employees: 22,000
Annual Meeting: In May

NICOR Inc.

1844 Ferry Road, P.O. Box 3014, Naperville, Illinois 60566-7014
Telephone: (630) 305-9500

NICOR Inc. is a holding company whose principal business is Northern Illinois Gas, one of the nation's largest gas distribution companies. Northern Illinois Gas delivers natural gas to about 1.9 million customers, including transportation service, and gas storage and supply backup to approximately 21,000 commercial and industrial customers who purchase their own gas supplies. NICOR also owns Tropical Shipping, which transports containerized freight between Florida and 26 ports in the Caribbean region. NICOR has also developed a number of unregulated businesses that relate to the company's strengths and talents in gas distribution. Incorporated in Illinois in 1976.

Directors   (In addition to indicated officers)

Robert M. Beavers, Jr.	Dennis J. Keller
Bruce P. Bickner	Charles S. Locke
John H. Birdsall III	Sidney R. Petersen
W.H. Clark	Daniel R. Toll
John E. Jones	Patricia A. Wier

Officers   (Directors*)

*Thomas L. Fisher, Chm., Pres. & C.E.O.
 David L. Cyranoski, Sr. V.P., Secy. & Cont.
 Thomas A. Nardi, Sr. V.P.—Nonutility Oper. & Bus. Dev.

Edwin M. Werneke, V.P.—Supply Ventures
Donald W. Lohrentz, Treas.

Consolidated Balance Sheet   As of December 31, 1996 (000 omitted)

Assets		Liabilities & Stockholders' Equity	
Current assets	$ 573,400	Current liabilities	$ 699,800
Net property, plant & equipment	1,771,900	Long-term debt	518,000
Other assets	93,300	Deferred items	343,800
		Other liabilities	139,900
		*Stockholders' equity	737,100
Total	$2,438,600	Total	$2,438,600

*49,492,000 shares common stock outstanding.

Consolidated Income Statement

Years Ended Dec. 31	Thousands — — — — Operating Revenues	Net Income	Per Share — — — Earnings	Cash Dividends[a]	Common Stock Price Range Calendar Year
1996	$1,850,700	$136,200[b]	$2.72[b]	$1.32	37-1/8 — 25-3/8
1995	1,480,100	99,800	1.96	1.28	28-1/2 — 21-3/4
1994	1,609,400	109,500	2.07	1.26	29-1/4 — 21-7/8
1993	1,673,900	111,700[b]	2.01[b]	1.22	31-5/8 — 24-1/8
1992	1,546,500	108,300[b]	1.91[b]	1.18	25-3/4 — 19

[a]Declared.
[b]Includes income from discontinued operations of $15,000,000 ($.30 per share) in 1996; $2,300,000 ($.04 per share) in 1993; and $13,300,000 ($.24 per share) in 1992.

Transfer Agent & Registrar:	Harris Trust and Savings Bank		
General Counsel:	Mayer, Brown & Platt	Traded (Symbol):	NYSE, CSE (GAS)
Investor Relations:	Randall S. Horn, Dir.	Stockholders:	39,300
Human Resources:	Rebecca C. Bacidore, Mgr.	Employees:	3,300
Mgt. Info. Svcs.:	Kathleen L. Halloran, Sr. V.P.	Annual Meeting:	In April
Auditors:	Arthur Andersen LLP	Internet:	www.nicorinc.com

NIPSCO Industries, Inc.

5265 Hohman Avenue, Hammond, Indiana 46320-1775
Telephone: (219) 853-5200

NIPSCO Industries, Inc. (Industries), serves as the holding company for a number of subsidiaries, including four regulated companies: Northern Indiana Public Service Company (Northern Indiana); Kokomo Gas and Fuel Company (Kokomo Gas); Northern Indiana Fuel and Light Company, Inc. (NIFL); and Crossroads Pipeline Company (Crossroads). Industries' major non-utility subsidiaries include NIPSCO Development Company, Inc. (Development); NIPSCO Energy Services, Inc. (Services); Primary Energy, Inc. (Primary); and NIPSCO Capital Markets, Inc. (Capital Markets). NIPSCO Industries Management Services Company, a subsidiary of Industries, provides executive, financial, gas supply, sales and marketing, and administrative and general services to Northern Indiana and other subsidiaries of Industries. Northern Indiana supplies natural gas and electric energy to the public, operating in 30 counties in northern Indiana, serving an area of about 12,000 square miles with a population of approximately 2,188,000. Kokomo Gas supplies natural gas to the public, operating in Kokomo and the surrounding six-county area with a population of approximately 100,000. NIFL supplies natural gas to the public in the northeast corner of Indiana having a population of approximately 66,700. Crossroads is an interstate natural gas pipeline. Development makes various investments, including real estate and venture capital investments. Services coordinates the energy-related diversification ventures of Industries. Primary arranges energy-related projects with large industrial customers. Capital Markets handles financing for ventures of Industries and its subsidiaries other than Northern Indiana. In March 1997, Industries completed its acquisition of IWC Resources Corp., the parent of Indianapolis Water Co. Incorporated in Indiana in 1987.

Directors (In addition to indicated officers)

Steven C. Beering	Ian M. Rolland
Arthur J. Decio	Edmund A. Schroer
Ernestine M. Raclin	John W. Thompson
Denis E. Ribordy	Robert J. Welsh, Jr.

Officers (Directors*)

*Gary L. Neale, Chm., Pres. & C.E.O.
 Stephen P. Adik, Exec. V.P., C.F.O. & Treas.
 Patrick J. Mulchay, Exec. V.P. & C.O.O.—Northern
   Ind. Public Svc. Co.
 Jeffrey W. Yundt, Exec. V.P. & C.O.O.—Energy
   Svcs.

Joseph L. Turner, Jr., Sr. V.P.—Major Accts.
Nina M. Rausch, Secy.
Jerry M. Springer, Cont. & Asst. Secy.
Dennis E. Senchak, Asst. Treas.

Consolidated Balance Sheet As of December 31, 1996 (000 omitted)

Assets		Liabilities & Stockholders' Equity	
Current assets	$ 511,079	Current liabilities	$1,022,199
Net property, plant & equipment	3,194,788	Long-term debt	1,127,106
Other assets	568,476	Deferred items	759,435
		Other liabilities	265,102
		*Stockholders' equity	1,100,501
Total	$4,274,343	Total	$4,274,343

*59,805,661 shares common stock outstanding.

Consolidated Income Statement

Years Ended Dec. 31	Thousands — — — — Operating Revenues	Net Income	Per Share — — — — Earnings	Cash Div. Paid	Common Stock Price Range Calendar Year
1996	$1,821,626	$176,734	$2.88	$1.68	40-1/4 — 35-1/4
1995	1,722,325	175,465	2.72	1.56	38-1/2 — 29-1/4
1994	1,676,401	163,987	2.48	1.44	33 — 26-1/8
1993	1,677,872	156,140	2.31	1.32	34-7/8 — 26-1/8
1992	1,582,356	136,648	2.00	1.24	26-5/8 — 22-1/2

Transfer Agent & Registrar: Harris Trust and Savings Bank

General Counsel: Schiff, Hardin & Waite

Investor Relations: Dennis E. Senchak, Asst. Treas.

Human Resources:
  Owen C. Johnson, Jr., V.P.—NIPSCO Indust. Mgt. Svcs. Co.

Mgt. Info. Svcs.:
  Dorothy M. Hawkins, Dir.—NIPSCO Indust. Mgt. Svcs. Co.

Auditors: Arthur Andersen LLP

Traded (Symbol):   NYSE, CSE, PSE (NI)

Stockholders: 35,339

Employees: 4,168

Annual Meeting: In April

Internet: www.nipsco.com

North Bancshares, Inc.
100 West North Avenue, Chicago, Illinois 60610-1399
Telephone: (312) 664-4320

North Bancshares, Inc. is the holding company organized for North Federal Savings Bank, a federally chartered stock savings bank. The bank primarily serves the Old Town, Lincoln Park, Gold Coast, and Lake View areas of Chicago. Originally organized in 1886, the bank converted to a federal mutual savings bank in 1986. It changed to a stock savings bank in connection with its initial public offering in 1993. The bank attracts retail deposits from the general public and invests those funds primarily in first mortgages on owner-occupied and non-owner occupied, one- to four-family residences and mortgage-backed and investment securities. Incorporated in Delaware in 1993.

Directors   (In addition to indicated officers)

James L. Ferstel	Michael J. Perri
Elmer L. Hass	Robert H. Rusher

Officers   (Directors*)

*Mary Ann Hass, Chm. & C.E.O.	Victor E. Caputo, Exec. V.P. & Secy.
*Joseph A. Graber, Pres. & C.O.O.	Martin W. Trofimuk, V.P. & Treas.

Consolidated Balance Sheet   As of December 31, 1996 (000 omitted)

Assets		Liabilities & Stockholders' Equity	
Current assets	$116,412	Current liabilities	$ 86,775
Net property, plant & equipment	1,061	Long-term debt	12,000
		Other liabilities	928
		*Stockholders' equity	17,770
Total	$117,473	Total	$117,473

*1,057,950 shares common stock outstanding.

Consolidated Income Statement

Years Ended Dec. 31	Thousands — — — — Total Income	Net Income	Per Share — — — Earnings	Cash Dividends	Common Stock Price Range[a] Calendar Year
1996	$8,769	$492[b]	$ .44[b]	$ .40	16-1/2 — 13-3/8
1995	7,909	696	.56	.25	14-1/4 — 11
1994	6,060	45	.03	.25	14 — 11
1993	6,691	622			13 — 10-1/2
1992	7,559	988[c]			

[a]Initial public offering in December 1993.
[b]Includes a one-time FDIC assessment of $285,000 ($.78 per share).
[c]Includes a charge to reflect FAS 109, resulting in a cumulative effect of $96,000.

Transfer Agent & Registrar:	Harris Trust and Savings Bank		
General Counsel:	Silver, Freedman & Taff, L.L.P.	Traded (Symbol):	NASDAQ (NBSI)
Investor Relations:	Joseph A. Graber, Pres.	Stockholders:	650
Human Resources:	Victor E. Caputo, Exec. V.P.	Employees:	36
Mgt. Info. Svcs.:	Joseph A. Graber, Pres.	Annual Meeting:	In April
Auditors:	KPMG Peat Marwick LLP	Internet:	www.northfederal.com

Northern States Financial Corporation

1601 North Lewis Avenue, Waukegan, Illinois 60085
Telephone: (847) 244-6000

Northern States Financial Corporation is a holding company for Bank of Waukegan and First Federal Bank, Fsb. The principal business of the company consists of attracting deposits from the general public, making commercial loans and loans secured by residential and commercial real estate, making consumer loans, and operating a trust business. Bank of Waukegan is an Illinois-chartered bank with two banking offices in Waukegan and one in Antioch, Illinois. First Federal Bank primarily offers traditional deposit services and mortgage loans. Incorporated in Delaware in 1984.

Directors   (In addition to indicated officers)

Jack H. Blumberg
Frank Furlan
Harry S. Gaples
Laurence A. Guthrie
James A. Hollensteiner

Raymond Mota
Frank Ryskiewicz
Henry G. Tewes
Arthur J. Wagner

Officers   (Directors*)

*Fred Abdula, Chm. & C.E.O.
*Kenneth W. Balza, V.P. & Treas.
 Joseph F. Tomasello, V.P.

Thomas M. Nemeth, Asst. V.P.
*Helen Rumsa, Secy.

Consolidated Balance Sheet   As of December 31, 1996 (000 omitted)

Assets		Liabilities & Stockholders' Equity	
Cash & due from banks	$ 31,982	Deposits	$328,795
Investments	149,850	Other borrowings	36,758
Loans, net	227,814	Other liabilities	6,176
Other assets	16,918	*Stockholders' equity	54,835
Total	$426,564	Total	$426,564

*889,273 shares common stock outstanding.

Consolidated Income Statement

Years Ended Dec. 31	Thousands — — — — Total Income	Net Income	Per Share — — — Earnings	Cash Dividends[a]	Common Stock Price Range Calendar Year	
1996	$34,910	$6,011	$6.76	$2.00	87	— 69
1995	33,595	4,937	5.57	1.65	71	— 63
1994	30,139	4,475	5.05	1.45	67-1/2	— 55
1993	30,376	4,434	5.01	1.30	55	— 42
1992	33,029	4,170	4.71	1.15	47	— 38

[a]Declared.

Transfer Agent & Registrar: Firstar Trust Co.

General Counsel: Chapman & Cutler

Investor Relations:
  Thomas M. Nemeth, Asst. V.P.

Human Resources: Kerry J. Biegay, V.P.

Mgt. Info. Svcs.:   Kerry J. Biegay, V.P.

Auditors: Crowe, Chizek & Co. LLP

Traded (Symbol): NASDAQ (NSFC)

Stockholders: 463

Employees: 127

Annual Meeting: In April

LaSalle Banks Guide

Northern Trust Corporation

50 South LaSalle Street, Chicago, Illinois 60675
Telephone: (312) 630-6000

Northern Trust Corporation is a multi-bank holding company with subsidiaries in Illinois, Arizona, California, Connecticut, Florida, Georgia, New York, and Texas. Its principal subsidiary, The Northern Trust Company, was established in 1889. Northern Trust Corporation is also the parent company of: Northern Trust Bank of Arizona N.A.; Northern Trust Bank of Florida N.A., Miami, Florida; Northern Trust Bank of California N.A.; Northern Trust Bank of Texas N.A.; The Northern Trust Company of New York; Northern Securities Services, Canada, Ltd.; Northern Futures Corporation; Northern Trust Securities, Inc.; Northern Trust Retirement Consulting, Inc.; Berry, Hartell, Evers & Osborne, Inc.; Northern Trust Global Advisors, Inc.; and Northern Trust Services, Inc. The Northern Trust Company offers a full range of banking, trust, savings, bond, and international services to individuals and corporations. All Illinois, Arizona, California, Florida, and Texas affiliate banks are full-service commercial banks. Northern Trust Securities, Inc. is a securities distribution unit for individual investors, correspondent banks, and corporations. Incorporated in Delaware in 1971.

Directors (In addition to indicated officers)

Duane L. Burnham	Robert A. Helman	Edward J. "Ted" Mooney
Dolores E. Cross	Arthur L. Kelly	Harold B. Smith
Susan Crown	Frederick A. Krehbiel	William D. Smithburg
Robert S. Hamada	William G. Mitchell	Bide L. Thomas

Officers (Directors*)

*William A. Osborn, Chm. & C.E.O.
*Barry G. Hastings, Pres. & C.O.O.
Perry R. Pero, Sr. Exec. V.P. & C.F.O.
James J. Mitchell, Exec. V.P.
Sheila A. Penrose, Exec. V.P.
Peter L. Rossiter, Exec. V.P., Gen. Coun. & Secy.
James M. Snyder, Exec. V.P.
Mark Stevens, Exec. V.P.

William S. Trukenbrod, Exec. V.P.
William R. Dodds, Jr., Sr. V.P.
David L. Eddy, Sr. V.P. & Treas.
Laurie K. McMahon, Sr. V.P.
William H. Miller, Sr. V.P.
Daniel S. O'Keefe, Sr. V.P.
Dan E. Phelps, Sr. V.P. & Gen. Auditor
Harry W. Short, Sr. V.P. & Cont.

Statement of Condition As of December 31, 1996 (000 omitted)

Assets		Liabilities & Stockholders' Equity	
Cash & due from banks	$ 1,292,500	Deposits	$13,796,200
Securities	4,814,900	Funds borrowed	4,910,200
Other short-term investments	3,196,900	Senior notes	305,000
Net loans & lease financing	10,789,100	Notes payable	427,800
Properties & equipment	291,500	Other liabilities	625,000
Other assets	1,223,400	*Stockholders' equity	1,544,100
Total	$21,608,300	Total	$21,608,300

*111,247,732 shares common stock outstanding.

Consolidated Income Statement

Years Ended Dec. 31	Thousands — — — —		Per Share[a] — — —		Common Stock Price Range[a] Calendar Year
	Operating Income	Net Income	Earnings	Cash Dividends	
1996	$1,929,400	$258,800	$2.20	$ .65	37-3/4 — 24-5/8
1995	1,782,100	220,000	1.85	.55	28 — 15-7/8
1994	1,482,100	182,200	1.58	.46	21-5/8 — 16-1/8
1993	1,260,200	167,900	1.48	.39	25-1/4 — 18-1/2
1992	1,232,200	149,500	1.32	.33	21-5/8 — 16-3/8

[a]Adjusted to reflect a 3-for-2 stock split in December 1992 and a 2-for-1 stock split in December 1996.

Transfer Agent & Registrar: Harris Trust and Savings Bank

General Counsel: Peter L. Rossiter, Exec. V.P.

Investor Relations: Laurie K. McMahon, Sr. V.P.

Human Resources: William N. Setterstrom, Sr. V.P.

Auditors: Arthur Andersen LLP

Traded (Symbol): NASDAQ (NTRS)
Stockholders: 3,335
Employees: 6,933
Annual Meeting: Third Tuesday in April
Internet: www.northerntrust.com

LaSalle Banks Guide

Northwestern Steel and Wire Company

121 Wallace Street, Sterling, Illinois 61081-3558
Telephone: (815) 625-2500

Northwestern Steel and Wire Company is a major mini-mill producer of structural steel, rod, and fabricated wire products. The company's structural steel products include wide flange beams, light structural shapes, and merchant bars, which are sold nationwide for use in the construction and manufacturing industries. The company's rod and wire products include nails, concrete reinforcing mesh, residential and agricultural fencing, and a wide range of other wire products. Incorporated in Illinois in 1879.

Directors   (In addition to indicated officers)

William F. Andrews
Warner C. Frazier
Darius W. Gaskins, Jr.
James A. Kohlberg

Christopher Lacovara
Michael E. Lubbs
Albert G. Pastino
George W. Peck IV

Officers   (Directors*)

*Thomas A. Gildehaus, Chm. & C.E.O.
Richard D. Way, Pres. & C.O.O.
Timothy J. Bondy, V.P., C.F.O., Secy. & Treas.
Kenneth J. Burnett, V.P.—Oper., Houston

William H. Hillpot, V.P.—Wire Oper. & Materials Mgt.
Andrew R. Moore, V.P.—Hum. Res.
Michael S. Venie, V.P.—Sales & Mktg.
David C. Oberbillig, V.P.—Sales, Wire Prods. Div.

Consolidated Balance Sheet   As of July 31, 1996 (000 omitted)

Assets		Liabilities & Stockholders' Equity	
Current assets	$190,279	Current liabilities	$105,742
Net property, plant & equipment	241,189	Long-term debt	153,646
Other assets	11,050	Other liabilities	77,114
		*Stockholders' equity	106,016
Total	$442,518	Total	$442,518

*24,438,698 shares common stock outstanding.

Consolidated Income Statement

Years Ended July 31	Thousands — — — — Net Sales	Net Income	Per Share — — — — Earnings	Cash Dividends	Common Stock Price Range Calendar Year
1996	$661,069	$ 20,670	$ .83	$ .00	9-1/8 — 4-1/2
1995	638,420	26,978	1.07	.00	10 — 5-7/8
1994	603,609	10,010	.40	.00	12-1/4 — 8-7/8
1993	539,210	(47,695)[a]	(2.62)[a]	.00	9-1/8 — 7-1/4[b]
1992	470,049	(22,372)	(1.72)		

[a]Includes an extraordinary loss related to early retirement of debt and a charge to reflect FAS 106, resulting in a cumulative effect of $46,173,000 ($2.54 per share).
[b]Initial public offering in June 1993.

Transfer Agent & Registrar:	Fleet National Bank		
General Counsel:	Katten Muchin & Zavis	Auditors:	Coopers & Lybrand L.L.P.
Investor Relations:	Timothy J. Bondy, V.P.	Traded (Symbol):	NASDAQ (NWSW)
		Stockholders:	1,387
Human Resources:	Andrew R. Moore, V.P.	Employees:	2,500
Mgt. Info. Svcs.:	Larry See	Annual Meeting:	In January

LaSalle Banks Guide

The John Nuveen Company

333 West Wacker Drive, Chicago, Illinois 60606
Telephone: (312) 917-7700

The John Nuveen Company, through its wholly owned subsidiaries, John Nuveen & Co. Incorporated, Nuveen Advisory Corp., and Nuveen Institutional Advisory Corp., specializes in asset management and investment banking. Originally organized as an underwriter of municipal bonds, the company now specializes in the sponsorship, marketing, and management of a variety of investment products for individual investors. Nuveen began to develop and market investment products in 1961 with the introduction of its first tax-free unit investment trust (UIT). Currently, the company sponsors more than 100 investment products, including UITs, short-term money market funds, long-term mutual funds, and closed-end funds that issue common stock that is traded on domestic stock exchanges and, in some cases, also issue preferred stock. The John Nuveen Company is 78 percent owned by St. Paul Cos. Incorporated in Delaware in 1992 as a successor to the business formed in 1898 by John Nuveen.

Directors   (In addition to indicated officers)

Willard L. Boyd	Douglas W. Leatherdale
W. John Driscoll	Paul J. Liska
Duane R. Kullberg	Patrick A. Thiele

Officers   (Directors*)

*Timothy R. Schwertfeger, Chm. & C.E.O.	Bruce P. Bedford, Exec. V.P.
*Anthony T. Dean, Pres. & C.O.O.	O. Walter Renfftlen, V.P. & Cont.
John Amboian, Exec. V.P., C.F.O. & Secy.	H. William Stabenow, V.P. & Treas.

Consolidated Balance Sheet   As of December 31, 1996 (000 omitted)

Assets		Liabilities & Stockholders' Equity	
Current assets	$267,282	Current liabilities	$ 51,507
Net property, plant & equipment	14,073	Deferred items	23,414
Other assets	73,896	Other liabilities	8,436
		*Stockholders' equity	271,894
Total	$355,251	Total	$355,251

*33,119,234 shares common stock outstanding.

Consolidated Income Statement

Years Ended Dec. 31	Thousands — — — — Total Revenues	Net Income	Per Share — — — Earnings	Cash Dividends	Common Stock Price Range[a] Calendar Year
1996	$232,347	$72,529	$1.98	$ .78	28-3/4 — 23-3/4
1995	236,230	70,620	1.87	.68	27 — 20-3/4
1994	220,301	58,211	1.52	.64	27-1/8 — 19-1/8
1993	245,732	70,444	1.76	.56	41-5/8 — 23-7/8
1992	221,212	59,440[b]	1.58[b]	.24	30-3/8 — 15-1/8

[a]Initial public offering in May 1992.
[b]Includes two one-time accounting charges.

Transfer Agent & Registrar:	The Bank of New York		
General Counsel:	Sidley & Austin	Traded (Symbol):	NYSE (JNC)
Investor Relations:	Jeffrey Kratz	Stockholders:	3,700
Human Resources:	Michael G. Gaffney	Employees:	525
Auditors:	KPMG Peat Marwick LLP	Annual Meeting:	In May

Oil-Dri Corporation of America

410 North Michigan Avenue, Suite 400, Chicago, Illinois 60611
Telephone: (312) 321-1515

Oil-Dri Corporation of America is a leading developer, manufacturer, and marketer of sorbent products for consumer, industrial, environmental, agricultural, and specialty markets. Consumer products include Cat's Pride® and Lasting Pride™ brand cat litters as well as premium private label products. These products are marketed by food brokers to the grocery products industry and by inside sales to major mass merchandisers. Floor absorbents under the Oil-Dri® name are sold to factories, automotive service establishments, and industrial distributors. Environmental clean-up materials include Oil-Dri Lite® sorbents. These non-clay products are light weight, very absorbent, and offer recycling and incineration options to end users. The Agrisorbents™ Product Group markets Agsorb® carriers for crop protection chemicals, Pel-Unite® and ConditionAde® feed binders, and other agriculturally related products. The Fluids Purification Group provides sorbent technologies under the names Pure-Flo® and Ultra-Clear® for the bleaching, filtration, and clarifying of all processed edible oils and oleo chemicals. Oil-Dri also manufactures Fresh Step® and Control® for The Clorox Company. Corporate headquarters are located in Chicago; research & development is in Vernon Hills, Illinois; and domestic mining and processing facilities are located in Georgia, Mississippi, and Oregon. Foreign offices and facilities are located in Canada, the United Kingdom, and Switzerland. Incorporated in Delaware in 1969 as successor to a company founded in 1941.

Directors (In addition to indicated officers)

J. Steven Cole	Paul J. Miller
Ronald B. Gordon	Haydn H. Murray
Robert D. Jaffee	Allan H. Selig
Edgar D. Jannotta	

Officers (Directors*)

*Richard M. Jaffee, Chm. & C.E.O.	James T. Davis, V.P.—Mfg.
*Joseph C. Miller, V. Chm.	Donald J. Deegan, V.P.—Strat. Planning
*Daniel S. Jaffee, Pres. & C.O.O.	Norman B. Gershon, V.P.—Intl.
Richard V. Hardin, Grp. V.P.—Tech.	Michael L. Goldberg, V.P. & C.F.O.
Louis T. Bland, V.P.—Hum. Res.	Richard L. Pietrowski, Treas.
Thomas F. Cofsky, V.P.—Logistics, Quality & Service	

Consolidated Balance Sheet   As of July 31, 1996 (000 omitted)

Assets		Liabilities & Stockholders' Equity	
Current assets	$ 48,210	Current liabilities	$ 17,811
Net property, plant & equipment	58,212	Long-term debt	22,652
Other assets	11,270	*Stockholders' equity	77,229
Total	$117,692	Total	$117,692

*6,806,891 shares common stock outstanding.

Consolidated Income Statement

Years Ended July 31	Thousands — — — — Net Sales	Net Income	Per Share — — — — Earnings	Cash Dividends	Common Stock Price Range Calendar Year
1996	$153,787	$3,374	$ .50	$ .32	16-3/8 — 11-7/8
1995	153,899	8,002	1.15	.31	20 — 14-1/8
1994	147,147	9,852	1.41	.28	25 — 17-7/8
1993	140,866	9,419	1.34	.25	25 — 18-1/2
1992	124,585	7,100	1.01	.24	22-1/2 — 15

Transfer Agent & Registrar: Harris Trust and Savings Bank

Legal Counsel: Sonnenschein Nath & Rosenthal	Auditors:	Blackman Kallick Bartelstein, LLP
	Traded (Symbol):	NYSE (ODC)
Investor Relations: Kelly McGrail, Mgr.	Stockholders:	1,281
Human Resources: Karen Jaffee-Cofsky, Dir.	Employees:	650
Mgt. Info. Svcs.: Sam Colello	Annual Meeting:	In December

Old Republic International Corporation

307 North Michigan Avenue, Chicago, Illinois 60601-5382
Telephone: (312) 346-8100

Old Republic International Corporation is an insurance holding company whose principal subsidiaries underwrite and market specialty insurance lines in the property, liability, mortgage guaranty, title, life, and disability insurance fields. Old Republic is a leading issuer of workers' compensation insurance by virtue of the company's 40 years of experience and service to the coal and other industries. Since 1978, the company has been engaged in the title insurance business, following the acquisition of Minnesota Title Financial Corporation and its subsidiaries. In early 1980, the company entered the mortgage guaranty insurance business through its acquisition of Republic Mortgage Insurance Company. In early 1985, the company expanded its property and liability insurance with the acquisition of Bitco Corporation and its insurance subsidiaries. Principal subsidiaries include: Old Republic Insurance Company; Old Republic Life Insurance Company; Bituminous Casualty Corporation; Great West Casualty Company; Old Republic National Title Insurance Company; Old Republic General Title Insurance Corporation; Republic Mortgage Insurance Company; and International Business and Mercantile REassurance Co. Incorporated in Delaware in 1969.

Directors (In addition to indicated officers)

Harrington Bischof	John W. Popp
Jimmy A. Dew	Arnold L. Steiner
Kurt W. Kreyling	David Sursa
Peter Lardner	William G. White, Jr.
Wilbur S. Legg	

Officers (Directors*)

*A.C. Zucaro, Chm., Pres. & C.E.O.	Spencer LeRoy III, Sr. V.P., Gen. Coun. & Secy.
Paul D. Adams, Sr. V.P., C.F.O. & Treas.	William F. Schumann, Sr. V.P.
*Anthony F. Colao, Sr. V.P.	*William A. Simpson, Sr. V.P.

Consolidated Balance Sheet   As of December 31, 1996 (000 omitted)

Assets		Liabilities and Stockholders' Equity	
Investments and cash	$4,521,800	Policy liabilities	$ 635,700
Reinsurance reserves	1,396,200	Benefit & claim reserves	3,541,800
recoverable		Debt & debt equivalents	154,000
Sundry assets	738,200	Sundry liabilities	404,100
		Preferred stock	20,600
		*Stockholders' equity	1,900,000
Total	$6,656,200	Total	$6,656,200

*86,938,763 shares common stock outstanding.

Consolidated Income Statement

Years Ended Dec. 31	Thousands — — — —		Per Share[a] — — —		Common Stock
	Total Revenue	Net Income	Earnings	Cash Dividends	Price Range[a] Calendar Year
1996	$1,803,900	$230,300	$2.41	$ .41	27-3/4 — 20
1995	1,695,900	212,700	2.42	.34	23-5/8 — 14-1/8
1994	1,679,000	151,000	1.70	.31	16-1/4 — 12-1/2
1993	1,736,300	175,100	1.99	.29	18-1/4 — 14-1/2
1992	1,617,000	174,700	2.06	.26	17-5/8 — 11-5/8

[a]Adjusted for a 100 percent stock dividend in March 1992 and a 50 percent stock dividend declared in March 1996.

Transfer Agent & Registrar:	First Chicago Trust Co. of New York		
General Counsel:	Spencer LeRoy III, Sr. V.P.	Traded (Symbol):	NYSE (ORI)
Investor Relations:	A.C. Zucaro, Pres.	Stockholders:	3,950
Human Resources:	Charles Strizak, Dir.	Employees:	5,650
Auditors:	Coopers & Lybrand L.L.P.	Annual Meeting:	In May

OPTION CARE, Inc.

100 Corporate North, Suite 212, Bannockburn, Illinois 60015
Telephone: (847) 615-1690

OPTION CARE, Inc. is a full service home health care company with 183 locations in 37 states, including 28 company-owned locations. OPTION CARE provides home infusion therapy, nursing services, respiratory services, and home medical equipment through its owned locations and home infusion therapy through its supporting franchise network. The company also serves as a network manager of home health care providers for managed care payors. Home infusion therapy, which constitutes the largest portion of patient care revenue, consists of the following therapies: total parenteral nutrition, anti-infective therapy, pain management, enteral nutrition, and chemotherapy. Subsidiaries are Option Care Enterprises, Inc.; Option Care Capital Services, Inc.; Women's Health of Option Care, Inc.; Management By Information, Inc.; and Option Care, Inc. (California). Incorporated in Delaware in 1991.

Directors (In addition to indicated officers)

James G. Andress
Jerome F. Sheldon

Roger W. Stone

Officers (Directors*)

*John N. Kapoor, Ph.D., Chm.
*Erick "Rick" Hanson, Pres. & C.E.O.
Cathy Bellehumeur, Sr. V.P., Gen. Coun. & Secy.

James W. Duncan, Sr. V.P.
Paul S. Jurewicz, Sr. V.P. & C.F.O.

Consolidated Balance Sheet As of December 31, 1996 (000 omitted)

Assets		Liabilities & Stockholders' Equity	
Current assets	$28,816	Current liabilities	$ 7,358
Net property, plant & equipment	4,322	Long-term debt	12,461
Other assets	10,903	Deferred items	637
		Other liabilities	45
		*Stockholders' equity	23,540
Total	$44,041	Total	$44,041

*10,527,000 shares common stock outstanding.

Consolidated Income Statement[a]

Years Ended Dec. 31	Thousands — — — — Total Revenues	Net Income	Per Share[b] — — — — Earnings	Cash Dividends	Common Stock Price Range[b] Calendar Year
1996	$70,521	$(20,256)[c]	$(1.93)	$ .00	8-3/8 — 3-1/8
1995	65,503	2,988	.29	.00	5-1/4 — 1-3/4
1994	62,019	(1,978)[d]	(.19)	.00	4-1/4 — 1-7/8
1993	52,843	272[e]	.03	.00	12-1/4 — 3-1/4
1992	43,599	3,689	.36	.00	12 — 6-1/4[f]

[a]Restated to reflect acquisition accounted for as pooling-of-interests.
[b]Adjusted to reflect a 6-for-5 stock split effected in the form of a common stock dividend on February 13, 1992.
[c]Includes a write-off for goodwill of $24,200,000.
[d]Includes $6,536,000 charge for asset write-offs and other unusual expenses.
[e]Includes charges of $4,250,000 for restructuring expenses.
[f]Initial public offering in April 1992.

Transfer Agent & Registrar:	U.S. Stock Transfer Corp.		
General Counsel:	Cathy Bellehumeur, Sr. V.P.	**Traded (Symbol):**	NASDAQ (OPTN)
Investor Relations:	Paul S. Jurewicz, Sr. V.P.	**Stockholders:**	308
Human Resources:	Pam Dietmeyer, V.P.	**Employees:**	532
Mgt. Info. Svcs.:	James F. Pierce, V.P.	**Annual Meeting:**	In May
Auditors:	KPMG Peat Marwick LLP	**Internet:**	www.optioncare.com

Outboard Marine Corporation

100 Sea Horse Drive, Waukegan, Illinois 60085-2195
Telephone: (847) 689-6200

Outboard Marine Corporation (OMC) is a leading global manufacturer of marine engines, boats, and accessories, primarily for recreational use. OMC is a leading manufacturer of outboard motors, with its Johnson® and Evinrude® brands. OMC, a leading boat builder in the United States, also manufactures and distributes boats internationally. Its boat brands, such as Chris-Craft®, are among the best known brands in the world. OMC also markets a full line of marine parts and accessories. Its products are sold through a comprehensive network of dealers and distributors. In 1996, approximately 74 percent of sales came from the U.S., which represents the world's largest market for recreational marine products. In the marine services area, the company distributes various marine parts and accessories under the Genuine Parts® brand through its dealer network. All of OMC's products are sold in the U.S. and Canada, and most of its principal products are sold throughout the world. Major subsidiaries include: Outboard Marine Corp. of Canada, Ltd.; OMC Europe V.O.F.; Outboard Marine Asia Limited; Outboard Marine Corp. Australia; Outboard Marine Latin America/Carribean; OMC Aluminum Boat Group; OMC Fishing Group Inc.; and OMC Recreational Boat Group Limited Partnership. In July 1997, OMC signed a definitive agreement to be acquired by Detroit Diesel Corporation. The transaction, subject to regulatory approval, is expected to close within 90 days. Incorporated in Delaware in 1936.

Directors   (In addition to indicated officers)

Frank Borman	Richard T. Lindgren	Richard J. Stegemeier
William C. France	J. Willard Marriott, Jr.	Richard F. Teerlink
Ilene S. Gordon	Donald L. Runkle	

Officers   (Directors*)

*Harry W. Bowman, Chm., Pres. & C.E.O.	Miles E. Dean, V.P. & Cont.
George L. Schueppert, Exec. V.P. & C.F.O.	John D. Flaig, V.P.—Prod. Integrity
Carlisle R. Davis, Sr. V.P.—Oper., MPPG	Edgar M. Frandle, V.P.—Info. Syst. & Tech. & C.I.O.
Richard H. Medland, Sr. V.P. & Chf. Admin. Off.	Thomas G. Goodman, Treas.
Clark J. Vitulli, Sr. V.P. & Pres.—OMC Boat Group	Robert J. Moerchen, Asst. Treas.
D. Jeffrey Baddeley, V.P., Secy. & Gen. Coun.	Robert S. Romano, Asst. Secy. & Asst. Gen. Coun.

Consolidated Balance Sheet   As of September 30, 1996 (000 omitted)

Assets		Liabilities & Stockholders' Equity	
Current assets	$467,500	Current liabilities	$253,300
Net property, plant & equipment	218,900	Long-term debt	177,600
Other assets	187,300	Deferred items	100,700
		Other liabilities	104,500
		*Stockholders' equity	237,600
Total	$873,700	Total	$873,700

*20,000,000 shares common stock outstanding.

Consolidated Income Statement

Years Ended Sept. 30	Thousands — — — — Net Sales	Net Income	Per Share — — — Earnings	Cash Dividends	Common Stock Price Range Calendar Year
1996	$1,121,500	$ (7,300)	$ (.36)	$ .40	21-7/8 — 14-3/8
1995	1,229,200	51,400	2.56	.40	24-7/8 — 17-1/2
1994	1,078,400	48,500	2.42	.40	25-7/8 — 17-3/8
1993	1,034,600	(282,500)a	(14.42)a	.40	25-1/4 — 15-1/4
1992	1,064,600	1,900	.10	.40	26-5/8 — 15-1/8

aIncludes restructuring charges and FAS 106 and FAS 109, resulting in a cumulative effect of $117,500,000 ($6.00 per share).

Transfer Agent & Registrar:	First Chicago Trust Co. of New York		
General Counsel:	D. Jeffrey Baddeley, V.P.	Traded (Symbol):	NYSE, BSE, CSE, PHSE, PSE (OM)
Investor Relations:	Stanley R. Main, Dir.	Stockholders:	4,505
Human Resources:	Richard H. Medland, Sr. V.P.	Employees:	8,283
Mgt. Info. Svcs.:	Edgar M. Frandle, V.P.	Annual Meeting:	Third Thursday in January
Auditors:	Arthur Andersen LLP	Internet:	www.omc-online.com

PC Quote, Inc.

300 South Wacker Drive, Suite 300, Chicago, Illinois 60606-6688
Telephone: (312) 913-2800

PC Quote, Inc. is a software developer and vendor of last-sale and bid and ask information for the Consolidated Tape Associations, the Option Price Reporting Authority, the National Association of Security Dealers, and all major U.S. commodities exchanges. The company subscribes to the high-speed vendor lines provided by each of the above authorities and maintains a real-time database which provides last-sale, bid and ask, and theoretical values to various application programs developed by the company and available to customers. Its principal product and service is PC QUOTE. The primary users of the company's products and services are professional investors, such as securities brokers and dealers, traders, and portfolio managers. PC Quote maintains sales offices in Chicago, Los Angeles, New York, and San Diego. Incorporated in Illinois in 1980; reincorporated in Delaware in 1987.

Directors (In addition to indicated officers)

Ronald Langley

Officers (Directors*)

*Louis J. Morgan, Chm. & Treas.
Howard C. Meltzer, Pres.
Jim R. Porter, C.E.O.
Michael J. Kreutzjans, Sr. V.P.—Sys. Dev.

Frederick L. McEnany, V.P.—Sales
Kristen J. Mologousis, V.P.—Internet Sales
Michael A. Press, V.P.—Fin.
Darlene E. Czaja, Corp. Secy.

Consolidated Balance Sheet As of December 31, 1996 (000 omitted)

Assets		Liabilities & Stockholders' Equity	
Current assets	$ 2,647	Current liabilities	$ 4,138
Net property, plant & equipment	2,764	Other liabilities	2,085
Software development costs	5,790	*Stockholders' equity	5,331
Other assets	353		
Total	$11,554	Total	$11,554

*7,251,463 shares common stock outstanding.

Consolidated Income Statement

Years Ended Dec. 31	Thousands — — — — Operating Revenues	Net Income	Per Share — — — — Earnings	Cash Dividends	Common Stock Price Range Calendar Year
1996	$17,032	$(3,256)	$ (.45)	$ .00	16 — 2-1/4
1995	13,392	1,512	.21	.00	27-1/2 — 1-1/8
1994	12,904	305	.04	.00	3-1/8 — 1
1993	12,206	185	.03	.00	3-3/4 — 3/4
1992	10,951	118	.02	.00	1-3/4 — 5/8

Transfer Agent & Registrar:	American Securities Transfer, Inc.		
General Counsel:	Wildman, Harrold, Allen & Dixon	Traded (Symbol):	AMEX (PQT)
Investor Relations:	Darlene E. Czaja, Corp. Secy.	Stockholders:	319
Human Resources:	Darlene E. Czaja, Corp. Secy.	Employees:	75
Mgt. Info. Svcs.:	Michael J. Kreutzjans, Sr. V.P.	Annual Meeting:	In June
Auditors:	McGladrey & Pullen L.L.P.	Internet:	www.pcquote.com

Peapod, Inc.

9933 Woods Drive, Skokie, Illinois 60077
Telephone: (847) 583-9400

Peapod, Inc. is the leading interactive, online grocery shopping and delivery company, and a provider of targeted media and research services. Founded in 1989, the company provides an integrated, comprehensive service designed to address the distinct needs of online consumers, grocery retailers, and consumer goods companies. The company provides consumers a user-friendly, highly functional virtual supermarket and personalized shopping, delivery or pick-up, and customer services. Consumers access the company's service through a proprietary dial-up network or the Internet. Peapod's systems link with those of the retailer to allow the company to create multiple, customized online stores that conform to local merchandising, pricing, and promotional strategies. The company also provides a forum for interactive advertising and promotion as well as extensive product research. As of March 31, 1997, Peapod had 43,200 members in seven metropolitan markets: Chicago, SanFrancisco/San Jose, Columbus, Boston, Houston, Atlanta, and Dallas. In June 1997, the company completed an initial public offering of 4,000,000 shares of common stock. Incorporated in Delaware in 1996 as successor to an entity organized in 1989.

Directors (In addition to indicated officers)

Tasso H. Coin
Steven M. Friedman

Trygve E. Myhren
Seth L. Pierrepont

Officers (Directors*)

*Andrew B. Parkinson, Chm., Pres. & C.E.O.
Timothy M. Dorgan, Exec. V.P.—Interactive Mktg. Svcs.
*Thomas L. Parkinson, Exec. V.P.—Chf. Tech. Off.

John C. Walden, Exec. V.P.—Fin. & Bus. Dev.
John A. Furton, Sr. V.P.—Field Support & Retailer Svcs.

Consolidated Balance Sheet[a]   As of March 31, 1996 (000 omitted)

Assets		Liabilities & Stockholders' Equity	
Current assets	$11,290	Current liabilities	$ 6,918
Net property and equipment	2,183	Deferred items	607
Other assets	446	Other liabilities	360
		*Stockholders' equity	6,034
Total	$13,919	Total	$13,919

[a]Pro forma.
*100 shares common stock outstanding.

Consolidated Income Statement[a]

Years Ended Dec. 31	Thousands — — — —		Per Share[b] — — — —		Common Stock
	Total Revenues	Net Income	Earnings	Cash Dividends	Price Range[b] Calendar Year
1996	$29,172	$(9,566)	$ (.75)[c]		
1995	15,943	(6,592)			
1994	8,346	(4,347)			
1993	3,705	(1,676)			
1992	1,493	(1,042)			

[a]For predecessor company, Peapod LP.
[b]Initial public offering in June 1997.
[c]Pro forma.

Transfer Agent & Registrar: First Chicago Trust Co. of New York

General Counsel: Sidley & Austin

Auditors: KPMG Peat Marwick LLP

Traded (Symbol):   NASDAQ (PPOD)

Stockholders: N/A
Employees: 1,300
Annual Meeting: As set by Directors
Internet: www.peapod.com

Peoples Energy Corporation

130 East Randolph Drive, Chicago, Illinois 60601-6207

Telephone: (312) 240-4000

Peoples Energy Corporation (Peoples) operates solely as a holding company, with its principal business centered in the distribution of natural gas. Peoples is the parent company of The Peoples Gas Light and Coke Company, as well as North Shore Gas Company. Both public utility subsidiaries are engaged primarily in the purchase, storage, distribution, sale, and transportation of natural gas. Peoples Gas also owns and operates an underground gas storage reservoir and a liquefied natural gas plant at Manlove Field near Champaign, Illinois. Peoples Gas serves approximately 839,000 residential, commercial, and industrial retail sales and transportation customers within the City of Chicago. North Shore Gas, headquartered in Waukegan, Illinois, serves nearly 137,000 residential, commercial, and industrial retail sales and transportation customers within its 275 square-mile service area in northeastern Illinois. Peoples District Energy Corporation, a wholly owned subsidiary of Peoples formed in May 1992, is a 50 percent participant in a partnership that provides heating and cooling services to the McCormick Place Exposition and Convention Center in Chicago. Neither the partnership nor its partners are regulated as a public utility. Three other wholly owned subsidiaries of Peoples are: Peoples Energy Services Corporation, a provider of natural gas and energy management related services; Peoples NGV Corp., a participant in a partnership to develop on-site fueling services for natural gas-powered fleet vehicles; and Peoples Energy Resources Corp., which pursue energy-related ventures. Neither the three subsidiaries nor any of their partners are regulated as public utilities. Incorporated in Illinois in 1967.

Directors   (In addition to indicated officers)

William J. Brodsky
Pastora San Juan Cafferty
Frederick C. Langenberg
Homer J. Livingston, Jr.

William G. Mitchell
Earl L. Neal
Richard P. Toft
Arthur R. Velasquez

Officers   (Directors*)

*Richard E. Terry, Chm. & C.E.O.
*J. Bruce Hasch, Pres. & C.O.O.
 Thomas M. Patrick, Exec. V.P.
*Michael S. Reeves, Exec. V.P.

James Hinchliff, Sr. V.P. & Gen. Coun.
Kenneth S. Balaskovits, V.P., C.F.O. & Cont.
Emmet P. Cassidy, Secy. & Treas.

Consolidated Balance Sheet   As of September 30, 1996 (000 omitted)

Assets		Liabilities & Stockholders' Equity	
Current assets	$ 282,895	Current liabilities	$ 266,607
Net property, plant & equipment	1,381,079	Long-term debt	527,064
Other assets	119,776	Deferred items	308,894
		*Stockholders' equity	681,185
Total	$1,783,750	Total	$1,783,750

*34,960,399 shares common stock outstanding.

Consolidated Income Statement

Years Ended Sept. 30	Thousands — — — — Operating Revenues	Net Income	Per Share — — — Earnings	Cash Dividends[a]	Common Stock Price Range Calendar Year
1996	$1,198,657	$103,438	$2.96	$1.83	29-5/8 — 37-3/8
1995	1,033,401	62,154	1.78	1.80	31-3/4 — 24-1/4
1994	1,279,488	74,399	2.13	1.80	32-1/8 — 23-1/4
1993	1,258,941	73,375	2.11	1.78	35 — 27-1/2
1992	1,096,752	70,384	2.06	1.75	31-5/8 — 24-3/8

[a]Declared.

Transfer Agent & Registrar:	Harris Trust and Savings Bank		
General Counsel:	James Hinchliff, Sr. V.P.	Traded (Symbol):	NYSE, CSE, PSE (PGL)
Investor Relations:	Emmet P. Cassidy, Secy.	Stockholders:	27,756
Human Resources:	John C. Ibach, V.P.	Employees:	3,049
Mgt. Info. Svcs.:	Willard S. Evans, Jr., V.P.	Annual Meeting:	Fourth Friday in February
Auditors:	Arthur Andersen LLP	Internet:	www.PECorp.com

Pinnacle Banc Group, Inc.

2215 York Road, Suite 208, Oak Brook, Illinois 60521
Telephone: (630) 574-3550

Pinnacle Banc Group, Inc. is a multi-bank holding company registered under the Bank Holding Company Act of 1956, as amended, and is engaged in the business of banking through the ownership of subsidiary banks. Subsidiaries are Pinnacle Bank and Pinnacle Bank of the Quad-Cities, each organized as state banking corporations, with a total of 14 banking locations. Pinnacle Banc Group is a legal entity separate and distinct from its subsidiary banks. The major source of the corporation's revenues is dividends from its subsidiary banks. Each of the subsidiary banks is a full-service bank encompassing most of the standard functions of commercial and savings banking including commercial, consumer, and real estate lending; installment credit lending; collections; safe deposit operations; and other services tailored for individual customer needs. The banks also offer a full range of deposit services, which include demand, savings and time deposits. Pinnacle Bank and Pinnacle Bank of the Quad-Cities also provide trust services to their clients. Lending activities of the subsidiary banks include term loans, lines and letters of credit, revolving credits, participations, indirect automobile financing, personal loans, student loans, and residential and commercial mortgages. Incorporated in Illinois in 1979.

Directors (In addition to indicated officers)

Mark P. Burns	James L. Greene	William C. Nickels
William J. Finn, Jr.	Donald G. King	John E. O'Neill
Samuel M. Gilman	James A. Maddock	James R. Phillip, Jr.
Albert Giusfredi	James J. McDonough	

Officers (Directors*)

*John J. Gleason, Sr., Chm.
*John J. Gleason, Jr., V. Chm. & C.E.O.
*William P. Gleason, Pres.
*Kenneth C. Whitener, Jr., Exec. V.P. & Chf. Investment Off.

*Richard W. Burke, Secy.
Glenn M. Mazade, Chf. Credit Off.
Sara J. Mikuta, C.F.O.

Consolidated Balance Sheet As of December 31, 1996 (000 omitted)

Assets		Liabilities & Stockholders' Equity	
Current assets	$ 23,095	Total deposits	$ 877,552
Interest bearing deposits	3,424	Long-term debt	32,800
Securities	434,558	Other liabilities	37,200
Net loans	516,705	*Stockholders' equity	100,824
Net property, plant & equipment	17,301		
Other assets	53,293		
Total	$1,048,376	Total	$1,048,376

*7,619,487 shares common stock outstanding.

Consolidated Income Statement

Years Ended Dec. 31	Thousands — — — — Total Income	Net Income	Per Share[a] — — — Earnings	Cash Dividends	Common Stock Price Range[a] Calendar Year
1996	$63,995	$ 7,127	$1.05	$ .83	23 — 17-7/8
1995	65,254	12,493	1.89	.77	22-5/8 — 17-7/8
1994	38,537	2,255	.34	.72	24-3/8 — 17-5/8
1993	55,136	12,993[b]	1.91[b]	.64	24-1/2 — 20
1992	58,418	12,914	1.87	.59	20-5/8 — 12

[a]Adjusted to reflect a 3-for-2 stock split in February 1997.
[b]Includes a gain to reflect FAS 109, resulting in a cumulative effect of $1,700,000 ($.25 per share).

Transfer Agent & Registrar: Harris Trust and Savings Bank

General Counsel:
  Burke, Warren & MacKay, P.C.

Investor Relations: John J. Gleason, Jr., V. Chm.

Human Resources: Denise Medema, Dir.

Mgt. Info. Svcs.: Keith J. Gottschalk, Dir.

Auditors: Arthur Andersen LLP
Traded (Symbol): NASDAQ (PINN)
Stockholders: 1,350
Employees: 369
Annual Meeting: In April

Pioneer Railcorp

1318 South Johanson Road, Peoria, Illinois 61607
Telephone: (309) 697-1400

Pioneer Railcorp is a shortline railroad holding company operating in one business segment, railroad transportation. The company currently operates 14 shortline railroads. Pioneer's rail system provides shipping links for customers along its routes, and interchanges with six major railroads and four smaller railroads. The company's rail system is devoted to carrying freight. Wholly owned subsidiaries include: Pioneer Railroad Equipment Co., Ltd., which leases equipment to the company's subsidiary railroads, and also purchases and sells equipment to and from unrelated parties; and Pioneer Railroad Services, Inc., which provides accounting, management, and agency services to the company's subsidiary railroads, and also sells computer technical services and equipment to unrelated parties. In 1996, Pioneer acquired four shortline railroads. Incorporated in Iowa in 1986.

Directors (In addition to indicated officers)

John S. Fulton

Officers (Directors*)

*Guy L. Brenkman, Chm., Pres. & C.E.O.
*J. Michael Carr, C.F.O. & Asst. Treas.
 Daniel A. LaKemper, Secy.

*John P. Wolk, Treas.
 Kevin L. Williams, Asst. Secy.

Consolidated Balance Sheet As of December 31, 1996 (000 omitted)

Assets		Liabilities & Stockholders' Equity	
Current assets	$ 3,630	Current liabilities	$ 6,066
Net property, plant & equipment	20,131	Long-term debt	12,564
Other assets	1,247	Deferred items	1,968
		Other liabilities	1,188
		*Stockholders' equity	3,222
Total	$25,008	Total	$25,008

*4,573,343 shares common stock outstanding.

Consolidated Income Statement

Years Ended Dec. 31	Thousands — — — — Operating Revenue	Net Income	Per Share[a] — — — Earnings	Cash Dividends	Common Stock Price Range[a] Calendar Year
1996	$10,979	$102	$ .02	$ .00	4-1/8 — 1-7/8
1995	8,557	462	.11	.00	4-1/2 — 2
1994	6,367	391	.08	.00	3 — 2
1993	4,947	244[b]	.04[b]	.00	2-1/8 — 1
1992	3,200	180	.04	.00	

[a]Adjusted to reflect a 2-for-1 stock split in July 1995. No established trading market before July 28, 1993.
[b]Includes a charge to reflect FAS 109, resulting in a cumulative effect of $155,000 ($.04 per share).

Transfer Agent & Registrar:	Pioneer Railcorp		
General Counsel:	Daniel A. LaKemper	Stockholders:	1,994
Investor Relations:	Kevin L. Williams, Mgr.	Employees:	100
Auditors:	McGladrey & Pullen, LLP	Annual Meeting:	In June
Traded (Symbol):	NASDAQ (PRRR); CSE (PRR)	Internet:	www.pioneer-railcorp.com

LaSalle Banks Guide

Pittway Corporation

200 South Wacker Drive, Suite 700, Chicago, Illinois 60606-5802
Telephone: (312) 831-1070

Pittway Corporation and its subsidiaries manufacture professional fire and burglar alarm equipment and systems, and other security products; publish technical journals and directories; produce trade shows and conferences; and operate mail marketing services. Pittway and its subsidiaries also develop real estate and participate in joint ventures with Metco Properties in real estate development. The company's security products divisions operate manufacturing facilities in St. Charles, Illinois; Northford, Connecticut; and Syosset, New York. Internationally, plants are located in Xi'an, China; Burgess Hill, England; Milan and Trieste, Italy; and Juarez, Mexico. Publishing divisions are headquartered in Cleveland, Ohio, with a division in New York City. Real estate operations are located in Chicago, Illinois, and Wesley Chapel, Florida. Major subsidiaries and divisions include: Ademco Security Group; Ademco Distribution, Inc.; Pittway Systems Technology Group; Pittway Real Estate; and Penton Publishing, Inc. Incorporated in Delaware in 1925.

Directors (In addition to indicated officers)

Eugene L. Barnett
E. David Coolidge III

Anthony Downs
William W. Harris

Jerome Kahn, Jr.
Leo F. Mullin

Officers (Directors*)

*Neison Harris, Chm.
*Irving B. Harris, Chm. Exec. Comm.
*King Harris, Pres. & C.E.O.
*Sidney Barrows, V. Chm.
*Leo A. Guthart, V. Chm.
*Fred J. Conforti, V.P.

Paul R. Gauvreau, V.P.—Fin., Treas. & Asst. Secy.
Thomas L. Kemp, V.P.
Daniel J. Ramella, V.P.
Edward J. Schwartz, V.P.
Philip McCanna, Cont.
James F. Vondrak, Secy.

Consolidated Balance Sheet As of December 31, 1996 (000 omitted)

Assets		Liabilities & Stockholders' Equity	
Current assets	$499,516	Current liabilities	$224,201
Net property, plant & equipment	137,601	Long-term debt	87,916
Investments	127,754	Deferred liabilities	80,104
Other assets	74,222	*Stockholders' equity	446,872
Total	$839,093	Total	$839,093

*3,938,832 shares common and 16,987,622 shares Class A common stock outstanding.

Consolidated Income Statement

| Years Ended Dec. 31 | Thousands — — — — | | Per Share — — — — | | Common Stock |
	Net Sales[a]	Net Income[a]	Earnings[a]	Cash Dividends[b]	Price Range[b] Calendar Year
1996	$1,111,575	$50,480[c]	$2.41[c]	$ .33	53-3/4 — 38-1/4
1995	945,669	40,372	1.93	.33	46 — 25
1994	778,026	33,060[d]	1.58[d]	.33	27-1/8 — 20-7/8
1993	650,105	21,240	1.02	.37	26-1/8 — 11-7/8
1992	568,301	12,460	.60	.73	23-1/8 — 17-1/8

[a]From continuing operations.
[b]Class A common stock. Dividends paid on common stock in 1996 were $.27 per share. Price range of common stock in 1996 was 53-1/2 — 39.
[c]Excludes a gain of $8,149,000 ($.39 per share) on sale of investments and a gain of $14,413,000 ($.69 per share) on stock offering.
[d]Excludes a gain of $11,800,000 ($.57 per share) on sale of investments.

Transfer Agent & Registrar:	Harris Trust and Savings Bank		
General Counsel:	Kirkland & Ellis	Stockholders:	1,800
Investor Relations:	Edward J. Schwartz, V.P.		
Auditors:	Price Waterhouse LLP	Employees:	6,800
Traded (Symbol):	NYSE (PRY, Common; PRYA, Class A)		
		Annual Meeting:	In May

Platinum Entertainment, Inc.

2001 Butterfield Road, Suite 1400, Downers Grove, Illinois 60515
Telephone: (630) 769-0033

Platinum Entertainment, Inc. produces, licenses, acquires, markets, and distributes high quality recorded music for a variety of music formats. The company and its wholly owned subsidiaries currently produce for the Gospel, Adult Contemporary, Country, Blues, Urban, Dance, Classical, and Themed Music formats, primarily under the CGI Records, Light Records, River North Records, Intersound, and House of Blues labels. Platinum's products include new releases, typically by artists established in a particular format, as well as compilations and repackagings of previously recorded music, that enable the company to exploit its catalog of master recordings. In March 1996, the company completed an initial public offering of 2,650,000 shares of common stock. Platinum completed the acquisition of Intersound, Inc., a Rosewell, Georgia, record firm, in January 1997, and announced that it had agreed to purchase the domestic music business, including the international music business excluding Europe and the former Soviet Union, of K-tel International, Inc. in March 1997. Incorporated in Delaware in 1991.

Directors (In addition to indicated officers)

Michael P. Cullinane
Craig J. Duchossois
Andrew J. Filipowski
Rodney L. Goldstein

Paul L. Humenansky
Thomas Salentine
Isaac Tigrett

Officers (Directors*)

*Steven D. Devick, Chm., C.E.O. & Pres.
*Douglas C. Laux, C.F.O. & Secy.

Thomas R. Leavens, C.O.O. & Gen. Coun.

Consolidated Balance Sheet As of February 28, 1997 (000 omitted) Unaudited

Assets		Liabilities & Stockholders' Equity	
Current assets	$23,387	Current liabilities	$42,305
Net property, plant & equipment	1,249	Convertible debentures	5,000
Other assets	37,455	*Stockholders' equity	14,786
Total	$62,091	Total	$62,091

*5,171,439 shares common stock outstanding.

Consolidated Income Statement

Years Ended May 31	Thousands — — — — Gross Revenues	Net Income[a]	Per Share[b] — — — Earnings	Cash Dividends	Common Stock Price Range[b] Calendar Year
1996	25,488	(4,401)	(1.79)	.00	19-1/2 — 7-1/4
1995	15,866	(4,840)	(4.17)		
1994[c]	8,929	(1,454)			
1993	5,489	(1,799)			

[a]From continuing operations.
[b]Initial public offering in March 1996.
[c]Pro forma to reflect a 12-month period.

Transfer Agent & Registrar:	American Stock Transfer & Trust Co.		
General Counsel:	Katten Muchin & Zavis	Traded (Symbol):	NASDAQ (PTET)
Investor Relations:	Douglas C. Laux, C.F.O.	Stockholders:	48
		Employees:	161
Human Resources:	Jayme Delong	Annual Meeting:	In October
Auditors:	Ernst & Young LLP	Internet:	www.platinument.com

PLATINUM technology, inc.

1815 S. Meyers Road, Oakbrook Terrace, Illinois 60181
Telephone: (630) 620-5000

PLATINUM technology, inc. provides software solutions for managing the open enterprise environment. By leveraging its expertise in relational technology, PLATINUM offers open enterprise systems management products and integrated solutions that help information services organizations manage the prevailing complex, multi-platform, multi-operating system, and multi-vendor computing environment. PLATINUM's products and services increase the efficiency of individual computing systems and databases as well as the interoperability of these systems and databases in distributed environments. PLATINUM has sales offices across the United States, in Canada, and in Japan, with wholly owned subsidiaries in 17 countries and international affiliates in 33 countries. Incorporated in Delaware in 1987.

Directors   (In addition to indicated officers)

James E. Cowie
Steven D. Devick

Arthur P. Frigo
Gian M. Fulgoni

Officers   (Directors*)

*Andrew J. Filipowski, Chm., Pres. & C.E.O.
*Michael P. Cullinane, Exec. V.P. & C.F.O.
*Paul L. Humenansky, Exec. V.P. & C.O.O.

Michael Matthews, Exec. V.P.—Worldwide Mktg.
Thomas A. Slowey, Exec. V.P.—Domestic Sales
Paul A. Tatro, Exec. V.P.—Intl. Oper.

Consolidated Balance Sheet   As of December 31, 1996 (000 omitted)

Assets		Liabilities & Stockholders' Equity	
Current assets	$366,093	Current liabilities	$156,472
Property, plant & equipment	72,343	Long-term debt	115,800
Goodwill	37,352	Deferred items	43,537
Other assets	134,753	Other liabilities	2,502
		*Stockholders' equity	292,230
Total	$610,541	Total	$610,541

*59,000,000 shares common stock outstanding.

Consolidated Income Statement[a]

Years Ended Dec. 31	Thousands — — — —		Per Share — — —		Common Stock Price Range Calendar Year
	Revenues	Net Income	Earnings	Cash Dividends	
1996[b]	$468,065	$(64,922)[c]	$(1.14)	$ .00	18-3/8 — 9-3/4
1995[b]	326,411	(111,567)[d]	(2.50)	.00	25-3/4 — 15
1994[b]	243,607	(1,562)[e]	(.04)	.00	23-1/4 — 10
1993	175,380	625[f]	.02	.00	25 — 7-1/4
1992	141,964	(2,433)[g]	(.06)	.00	25-1/4 — 11-1/4

[a]Results for 1992-1995 give retroactive effect to acquisitions which have been accounted for under the pooling-of-interests method.
[b]Unaudited pro forma 1994-96. Total revenues and net income are given as if the transactions had occurred on December 31, 1996.
[c]Reflects pretax charges of $48,456,000 for acquired in-process technology and $5,782,000 for merger costs.
[d]Reflects pretax charges of $88,493,000 for acquired in-process technology and $30,819,000 for merger costs.
[e]Reflects a pretax charge of $24,594,000 for acquired in-process technology.
[f]Reflects pretax charges of $8,735,000 for acquired in-process technology and $4,659,000 for restructuring costs.
[g]Reflects a pretax charge of $7,873,000 for restructuring costs.

Transfer Agent & Registrar: Harris Trust and Savings Bank

General Counsel:	Michael Wyatt, V.P.	Traded (Symbol):	NASDAQ (PLAT)
Investor Relations:	Maria Dalesandro	Stockholders:	1,195
Human Resources:	Marc Ugol, Sr. V.P.	Employees:	4,000
Mgt. Info. Svcs.:	Lynn Wilson, Chf. Info. Off.	Annual Meeting:	In May
Auditors:	KPMG Peat Marwick LLP	Internet:	www.platinum.com

Playboy Enterprises, Inc.

680 North Lake Shore Drive, Chicago, Illinois 60611

Telephone: (312) 751-8000

Playboy Enterprises, Inc. is an international publishing and entertainment company that publishes *Playboy* magazine and related media, including newsstand specials and calendars; operates a direct marketing business, including the *Playboy*, *Collectors' Choice Music*, and *Critics' Choice Video* catalogs; creates and distributes programming for Playboy's domestic pay television network, worldwide home video, and international television; licenses Playboy trademarks for use on apparel, accessories, and products for consumers around the world; produces and markets CD-ROM products; and maintains a site on the Internet. Foreign editions of *Playboy* magazine are published in the following countries: Argentina, Australia, Brazil, Czech Republic, Germany, Greece, Italy, Japan, Mexico, the Netherlands, Poland, South Africa, Spain, and Taiwan. The company's publishing interests include a 20 percent stake in the *duPont Registry*, a monthly guide to classical and luxury automobiles. Major subsidiaries of the company include: Lifestyle Brands, Ltd.; Playboy Preferred, Inc.; Playboy Models, Inc.; Playboy Products and Services International, B.V.; Playboy Entertainment Group, Inc.; Alta Loma Productions, Inc.; Critics' Choice Video, Inc.; Special Editions, Ltd.; Lake Shore Press, Inc.; Impulse Productions, Inc.; Playboy Clubs International, Inc.; After Dark Video, Inc.; Playboy Records, Inc.; and Playboy Shows, Inc. Incorporated in Illinois in 1953; merged into a wholly owned Delaware subsidiary in 1964; present name adopted in 1971.

Directors (In addition to indicated officers)

Dennis S. Bookshester
David I. Chemerow

Donald G. Drapkin
Sol Rosenthal

Sir Brian G. Wolfson

Officers (Directors*)

*Christie Hefner, Chm. & C.E.O.
Hugh M. Hefner, Chm. Emer. & Ed.-in-Chf.
Linda G. Havard, Exec. V.P.—Fin./Oper. & C.F.O.
Marianne Howatson, Exec. V.P. & Pres.—Publishing Grp.
Anthony J. Lynn, Exec. V.P. & Pres.—Enter. Grp.
Robert J. Perkins, Exec. V.P.—Mktg. & Corp. Dev.
*Richard S. Rosenzweig, Exec. V.P.
Howard Shapiro, Exec. V.P.—Law/Admin., Gen. Coun. & Secy.

Herbert M. Laney, Sr. V.P. & Pres.—Catalog Grp.
Rebecca S. Maskey, Sr. V.P.—Fin.
Denise Bindelglass, V.P.—Hum. Res.
Martha O. Lindeman, V.P.—Corp. Commun. & Inv. Rel.
Cindy Rakowitz, V.P.—Public Rel.
John A. Ullrick, V.P.—Mgmt. Info. Svcs.
Robert D. Campbell, Treas.
Michael Dannhauser, Asst. Cont.
John A. McDonald, Asst. Cont.

Consolidated Balance Sheet   As of June 30, 1996 (000 omitted)

Assets		Liabilities & Stockholders' Equity	
Current assets	$108,909	Current liabilities	$ 90,021
Net property & equipment	11,894	Long-term debt	347
Other assets	30,066	Other liabilities	8,218
		*Stockholders' equity	52,283
Total	$150,869	Total	$150,869

*5,042,381 shares Class A common and 16,477,143 shares Class B common stock outstanding.

Consolidated Income Statement

Years Ended June 30	Thousands — — — — Net Revenues[a]	Net Income	Per Share — — — — Earnings	Cash Dividends	Common Stock Price Range[b] Calendar Year
1996	$276,587	$ 4,252	$ .21	$ .00	15-3/4 — 8-3/8
1995	247,249	629	.03	.00	9-5/8 — 7-5/8
1994	218,987	(9,484)[c]	(.48)[c]	.00	11 — 6
1993	214,875	365	.02	.00	11 — 6-5/8
1992	193,749	3,510[d]	.19[d]	.00	9-1/2 — 5-7/8

[a]From continuing operations.
[b]Class A common stock.
[c]Includes restructuring expenses, unusual items, nonrecurring expenses, and a gain to reflect FAS 109, which resulted in a cumulative gain of $2,887,000 ($.14 per share).
[d]Includes extraordinary credits of $1,688,000 ($.09 per share).

Transfer Agent & Registrar: Harris Trust and Savings Bank

General Counsel:	Howard Shapiro, Exec. V.P.	Traded (Symbol):	NYSE, PSE (PLA A, Class A; PLA, Class B)
Investor Relations:	Martha O. Lindeman, V.P.	Stockholders:	8,445 Class A; 9,004 Class B
Human Resources:	Denise Bindelglass, V.P.	Employees:	636
Mgt. Info. Svcs.:	John A. Ullrick, V.P.	Annual Meeting:	In November
Auditors:	Coopers & Lybrand L.L.P.	Internet:	www.playboy.com

PORTEC, Inc.

One Hundred Field Drive, Suite 120, Lake Forest, Illinois 60045-2597
Telephone: (847) 735-2800

PORTEC, Inc. is a diversified manufacturer and marketer of engineered products for the construction equipment, materials handling, and railroad industries. The Construction Equipment segment manufactures and markets the Kolberg, Pioneer, and Innovator product lines. The Kolberg and Pioneer lines include machinery and systems used in the construction, mining, and road-building industries. The Innovator product line consists of grinders and screens for the processing of green yard waste, waste wood, and demolition debris. The Materials Handling segment, consisting of the Flomaster Division, Pathfinder Division, and Countec Recycling Systems Division, manufactures and markets materials handling equipment, such as electronic wire guidance lift-truck controls and systems, specialty conveyor products, and conveyor systems for solid waste recycling. The Railroad segment manufactures and markets a variety of railroad products. The Railway Maintenance Products Division manufactures and markets track components, including rail joints, rail anchors and lubricators, and jacking systems for railroad car repair facilities. The Shipping Systems Division is a major supplier of railroad load securement systems and devices for shipping containers, building products, automobiles, military vehicles, farm implements, and heavy construction equipment. Portec, Ltd., the company's Canadian subsidiary, engineers and markets a broad range of railway track products in Canada. Portec (U.K.) Ltd., the company's British subsidiary, manufactures and markets railway track products and materials handling equipment. Incorporated in Delaware in 1928.

Directors   (In addition to indicated officers)

J. Grant Beadle	John F. McKeon
Frank T. MacInnis	Arthur McSorley, Jr.
Frederick J. Mancheski	L.L. White, Jr.

Officers   (Directors*)

*Albert Fried, Jr., Chm.	Nancy A. Kindl, V.P., C.F.O., Treas. & Secy.
*Michael T. Yonker, Pres. & C.E.O.	Kevin C. Rorke, V.P.
John S. Cooper, Sr. V.P. & Grp. Mgr.—Railway	

Consolidated Balance Sheet   As of December 31, 1996 (000 omitted)

Assets		Liabilities & Stockholders' Equity	
Current assets	$42,100	Current liabilities	$16,119
Net property, plant & equipment	14,543	Long-term debt	10,768
Other assets	9,307	Deferred items	4,077
		*Stockholders' equity	34,986
Total	$65,950	Total	$65,950

*4,373,596 shares common stock outstanding.

Consolidated Income Statement

Years Ended Dec. 31	Thousands — — — —		Per Share[a] — — — —		Common Stock Price Range Calendar Year
	Net Sales	Net Income	Earnings	Cash Dividends	
1996	$97,338	$6,891	$1.50	$ .08	11-1/8 — 8-7/8
1995	97,072	2,898	.63	.00	14 — 9-1/2
1994	96,474	6,825	1.49	.00	16-7/8 — 10-1/4
1993	76,324	4,696	1.05	.00	15-1/8 — 6-5/8
1992	68,638	5,513	1.37	.00	7-5/8 — 3-5/8

[a]Adjusted to reflect 10% stock dividends paid in December 1994, 1993, and 1992.

Transfer Agent & Registrar: Harris Trust and Savings Bank

General Counsel:	Schiff, Hardin & Waite	Traded (Symbol):	NYSE, CSE (POR)
Investor Relations:	Nancy A. Kindl, V.P.	Stockholders:	1,168
Human Resources: Patricia A. Riccio, Emp. Ben. Mgr.		Employees:	671
Auditors:	Price Waterhouse LLP	Annual Meeting:	In April

Premark International, Inc.

1717 Deerfield Road, Deerfield, Illinois 60015-3900
Telephone: (847) 405-6000

Premark International, Inc. was formed in 1986 when it was spun off from Dart & Kraft, Inc. It owns and markets brand names such as Hobart®, Wilsonart®, West Bend®, Florida Tile®, and Precor®. Premark is comprised of three segments: the Food Equipment Group; the Decorative Products Group; and the Consumer Products Group. Premark's largest segment, the Food Equipment Group, is the largest supplier of commercial food equipment and service to the foodservice and food retail markets. This group manufacturers and sells products for food preparation, warewashing, weighing and wrapping, cooking, baking, and refrigeration, under leading brand names such as Hobart®, Vulcan®, and Foster®. Premark's largest business in the Decorative Products Group is Wilsonart International. Wilsonart® laminate is used in countertops, cabinets, furniture, and fixtures. Also included in this group is Florida Tile®, a manufacturer and distributor of ceramic floor and wall tile. West Bend® small electric appliances and direct-to-the-home premium cookware, and Precor® high-end aerobic fitness equipment comprise the Consumer Products Group. In May 1996, Premark spun-off Tupperware in a distribution to shareholders. In June 1996, the company sold its Hartco subsidiary to Triangle Pacific Corporation. Incorporated in Delaware in 1986.

Directors   (In addition to indicated officers)

William O. Bourke	W. James Farrell	David R. Parker
Harry W. Bowman	Richard S. Friedland	Janice D. Stoney
Ruth M. Davis, Ph.D.	Joseph E. Luecke	
Lloyd C. Elam, M.D.	John B. McKinnon	

Officers   (Directors*)

*Warren L. Batts, Chm.
*James M. Ringler, Pres. & C.E.O.
Joseph W. Deering, Grp. V.P. & Pres.—Food Eqmt.
Thomas W. Kieckhafer, Corp. V.P. & Pres.—West Bend
William R. Reeb, Corp. V.P. & Pres.—Wilsonart Intl.
James C. Coleman, Sr. V.P.—Hum. Res.

John M. Costigan, Sr. V.P., Gen. Coun. & Secy.
Lawrence B. Skatoff, Sr. V.P. & C.F.O.
Raymond Barbosa, V.P.—Taxes & Tax Coun.
L. John Fletcher, V.P., Asst. Gen. Coun. & Asst. Secy.
Isabelle C. Goossen, V.P. & Treas.
Robert W. Hoaglund, V.P. & Cont.
Anthony C. Scolaro, V.P.—Planning & Bus. Dev.

Consolidated Balance Sheet   As of December 28, 1996 (000 omitted)

Assets		Liabilities & Stockholders' Equity	
Current assets	$1,054,000	Current liabilities	$ 459,600
Net property, plant & equipment	416,400	Long-term debt	115,900
Other assets	190,400	Deferred items	120,800
		Other liabilities	88,600
		*Stockholders' equity	875,900
Total	$1,660,800	Total	$1,660,800

*62,727,064 shares common stock outstanding.

Consolidated Income Statement[a]

Years Ended Abt. Dec. 31	Thousands — — — — Net Sales	Net Income	Per Share[b] — — — Earnings	Dividends Declared	Common Stock Price Range[b] Calendar Year
1996	$2,267,600	$95,400[c]	$1.47[c]	$ .73	55-1/8 — 15-1/4
1995	2,213,400	78,900	1.24	1.01	54-3/4 — 38-1/2
1994	2,118,300	70,800	1.06	.74	48 — 33-5/8
1993	1,867,600	50,500	.75	.55	41-7/8 — 19-1/8
1992	1,833,700	44,600[d]	.68	.48	25-5/8 — 14-7/8

[a]From continuing operations.
[b]Adjusted to reflect a 2-for-1 stock split in June 1994.
[c]Excludes an after-tax loss of $38,100,000 ($.60 per share) for the sale of Hartco.
[d]Excludes an after-tax loss of $98,900,000 for adoption of FAS 106 and a $15,000,000 gain for adoption of FAS 109.

Transfer Agent & Registrar:	Norwest Bank Minnesota		
General Counsel:	John M. Costigan, Sr. V.P.	Traded (Symbol):	NYSE, PSE, London (PMI)
		Stockholders:	21,700
Investor Relations:	Isabelle C. Goossen, V.P. & Treas.	Employees:	16,300
Human Resources:	Kirk Mueller, Dir.	Annual Meeting:	In May
		Internet:	www.premarkintl.com
Auditors:	Ernst & Young LLP		

LaSalle Banks Guide

Prime Capital Corporation

10275 West Higgins Road, Suite 200, Rosemont, Illinois 60018
Telephone: (847) 294-6000

Prime Capital Corporation is a provider of merchant banking and financial services. Prime has provided a variety of services since its inception in 1977, including: equipment leasing and rentals, financial consulting, private placement of long-term debt, tax-exempt financing, joint ventures, project development, diagnostic imaging center development, and healthcare equipment remarketing. Incorporated in 1977; reincorporated in Delaware in 1986.

Directors (In addition to indicated officers)

Mark P. Bischoff
Lee W. Jennings

William D. Smithburg
Robert R. Youngquist, D.D.S.

Officers (Directors*)

*James A. Friedman, Chm., Pres. & C.E.O.
John W. Altergott, Sr. V.P.

Robert C. Benson, Sr. V.P. & C.F.O.
Joseph Rinehart, Sr. V.P.

Consolidated Balance Sheet   As of December 31, 1996 (000 omitted)

Assets		Liabilities & Stockholders' Equity	
Cash & cash equivalents	$14,504	Current liabilities	$54,200
Net property plant & equipment	364	Long-term debt	5,000
Leased equipment, net	1,370	Deferred items	8,414
Net invest. in direct fin. leases	56,004	Other liabilities	4,341
Other assets	8,770	*Stockholders' equity	9,057
Total	$81,012	Total	$81,012

*4,290,000 shares common stock outstanding.

Consolidated Income Statement

Years Ended Dec. 31	Thousands — — — —		Per Share — — — —		Common Stock Price Range Calendar Year
	Revenues	Net Income	Earnings	Cash Dividends	
1996	$17,482	$ 4,026	$ .85	$ .00	6-1/4 — 1-5/8
1995	7,038	(1,836)	(.43)	.00	2-1/4 — 5/8
1994	4,678	(1,998)	(.47)	.00	1-3/8 — 3/4
1993	7,559	2,008	.47	.00	1-1/2 — 1/2
1992	10,695	1,808	.42	.00	1-1/2 — 1/2

Transfer Agent & Registrar: Lake Forest Bank & Trust

General Counsel:
  Bischoff, Maurides & Swabowski, Ltd.

Investor Relations: Trish DiBenardi

Human Resources: Teri A. Folisi

Mgt. Info. Svcs.   Kathy Locke

Auditors: KPMG Peat Marwick LLP
Traded (Symbol):   NASDAQ (PMCP)
Stockholders: 413
Employees: 52
Annual Meeting: In July

Princeton National Bancorp, Inc.

606 South Main Street, Princeton, Illinois 61356-2080
Telephone: (815) 875-4444

Princeton National Bancorp, Inc., a bank holding company, is a commercial banking and trust institution in north central Illinois (Bureau, DeKalb, Grundy, Kane, Kendall, LaSalle, and Marshall counties). The company conducts a full-service community banking and trust business through its subsidiary, Citizens First National Bank, which was organized in 1865. Incorporated in Delaware in 1981.

Directors (In addition to indicated officers)

Thomas R. Lasier, Chm.
Don S. Browning
John Ernat
Donald E. Grubb
Harold C. Hutchinson, Jr.

Thomas M. Longman
Ervin I. Pietsch
Stephen W. Samet
Craig O. Wesner

Officers (Directors*)

*Tony J. Sorcic, Pres. & C.E.O.
James B. Miller, Exec. V.P.
Lou Ann Birkey, Asst. V.P. & Corp. Secy.

Todd D. Fanning, C.F.O.
Dennis B. Guthrie, Treas.
Patricia L. Boesch, Auditor

Consolidated Balance Sheet As of December 31, 1996 (000 omitted)

Assets		Liabilities & Stockholders' Equity	
Cash & due from banks	$ 18,033	Total deposits	$358,701
Federal funds sold	3,100	Short-term borrowings	13,537
Investment securities	117,028	Long-term borrowings	4,350
Net loans	259,150	Other liabilities	3,622
Premises & equipment	9,147	*Stockholders' equity	40,197
Other assets	13,949		
Total	$420,407	Total	$420,407

*2,723,966 shares common stock outstanding.

Consolidated Income Statement

Years Ended Dec. 31	Thousands — — — — Total Income	Net Income	Per Share[a] — — — — Earnings	Cash Dividends[b]	Common Stock Price Range[a] Calendar Year
1996	$31,974	$3,427	$1.26	$ .38	19-1/2 — 16-1/2
1995	30,198	358	.13	.36	17-1/4 — 12-1/4
1994	28,339	3,758	1.39	.33	16 — 12-3/4
1993	24,785	3,750	1.38	.32	17 — 11
1992	25,180	3,240	1.32	.30	11-5/8 — 9-7/8

[a]Adjusted to reflect a 3-for-2 stock split in December 1994.
[b]Declared.

Transfer Agent & Registrar: Princeton National Bancorp, Inc.

General Counsel: Schiff, Hardin & Waite

Investor Relations: Lou Ann Birkey, Asst. V.P.

Human Resources: Betty Walters

Mgt. Info. Svcs.:   Tony J. Sorcic, Pres.

Auditors: KPMG Peat Marwick LLP
Traded (Symbol):   NASDAQ (PNBC)
Stockholders: 574
Employees: 196
Annual Meeting: In April

The Quaker Oats Company

321 North Clark Street, Chicago, Illinois 60610-4714
Telephone: (312) 222-7111

The Quaker Oats Company is an international marketer of consumer grocery products. The Grocery Products Group includes Quaker Oats and Quaker 100% Natural, Cap'n Crunch, Quaker Life, and Quaker Toasted Oatmeal cereals. Other products are Quaker Chewy Granola Bars, Quaker Rice Cakes, Gatorade thirst quencher, and Rice-A-Roni and Noodle Roni. Major subsidiaries are The Gatorade Company; Continental Coffee Products Co.; Golden Grain Co.; Stokely-Van Camp, Inc.; Quaker Oats Limited, UK; and The Quaker Oats Company of Canada Limited. In May 1997, the company completed the sale of its Snapple iced teas and fruit juice drinks business to the New York-based Triarc Companies. Incorporated in New Jersey in 1901.

Directors (In addition to indicated officers)

Frank C. Carlucci
Silas S. Cathcart
Kenneth I. Chenault

John H. Costello
Judy C. Lewent
Vernon R. Loucks, Jr.

Thomas C. MacAvoy
Walter J. Salmon
William L. Weiss

Officers (Directors*)

*William D. Smithburg, Chm., Pres. & C.E.O.
*Luther C. McKinney, Sr. V.P.—Law & Corp. Aff.
Douglas J. Ralston, Sr. V.P.—Hum. Res.
Robert S. Thomason, Sr. V.P.—Fin. & C.F.O.
John A. Boynton, V.P. & Chf. Cust. Officer
John H. Calhoun, V.P.—Intl. Law
Penelope C. Cate, V.P.—Govt. Rel.
Michael L. Cohen, V.P.—Hum. Res.
Janet K. Cooper, V.P. & Treas.

Margaret M. Eichman, V.P.—Inv. Rel.
Scott Gantwerker, V.P.—Qual. Worldwide
Thomas L. Gettings, V.P. & Cont.
John G. Jartz, V.P. & Gen. Coun.
James E. LeGere, V.P.—Mgt. Info. Svcs.
I. Charles Mathews, V.P.—Diver. Mgmt.
Mart C. Matthews, V.P. & Assoc. Gen. Coun.
Kenneth W. Murray, V.P.—Internal Audit

Consolidated Balance Sheet As of December 31, 1996 (000 omitted)

Assets		Liabilities & Stockholders' Equity	
Current assets	$ 889,700	Current liabilities	$1,354,700
Net property, plant & equipment	1,200,700	Long-term debt	993,500
Other assets	2,304,000	Deferred items	238,400
		Other liabilities	558,900
		*Stockholders' equity	1,248,900
Total	$4,394,400	Total	$4,394,400

*135,466,000 shares common stock outstanding.

Consolidated Income Statement

Years Ended Dec. 31	Thousands — — — —		Per Share[b] — — —		Common Stock
	Net Sales[a]	Net Income	Earnings	Cash Dividends[c]	Price Range[b] Calendar Year
1996	$5,199,000	$247,900[d]	$1.80[d]	$1.14	39-1/2 — 30-3/8
1995[e]	2,733,100	13,700	.09	.57	
1995[f]	6,365,200	802,000[g]	5.97[g]	1.14	37-1/2 — 30-3/8
1994[f]	5,955,000	231,500[h]	1.68[h]	1.06	42-1/2 — 29-3/4
1993[f]	5,730,600	171,300[i]	1.17[i]	.96	38-1/2 — 30-1/4
1992[f]	5,576,400	247,600	1.63	.86	37-1/8 — 25-1/8

[a]Excludes discontinued operations.
[b]Adjusted to reflect a 2-for-1 stock split in November 1994.
[c]Declared.
[d]Includes a pretax gain of $136,400,000 ($.60 per share) on divestiture of U.S. and Canadian frozen food and Italian products businesses and a charge of $23,000,000 ($.14 per share) for restructuring.
[e]Six months ended December 31. In 1995, the company changed to calendar year reporting.
[f]Twelve months ended June 30.
[g]Includes a pretax gain of $1,170,000 ($5.20 per share) related to divestitures and restructuring charges of $76,500,000 ($.35 per share) for cost reduction and realignment activities.
[h]Includes restructuring charges and gains on divestitures, which together net to a pretax charge of $108,600,000 ($.48 per share).
[i]Includes a charge to reflect FAS 106 and FAS 109, resulting in a cumulative effect of $115,500,000 ($.79 per share); and restructuring charges and gains on divestitures, which together net to a pretax charge of $20,500,000 ($.09 per share).

Transfer Agent & Registrar:	Harris Trust and Savings Bank		
General Counsel:	John G. Jartz, V.P.	Traded (Symbol):	NYSE, CSE, PSE, LONDON, (OAT)
Investor Relations:	Margaret M. Eichman, V.P.	Stockholders:	29,690
Human Resources:	Douglas J. Ralston, Sr. V.P.	Employees:	14,800
Mgt. Info. Svcs.:	James E. LeGere, V.P.	Annual Meeting:	In May
Auditors:	Arthur Andersen LLP	Internet:	www.quakeroats.com

Quixote Corporation

One East Wacker Drive, Chicago, Illinois 60601
Telephone: (312) 467-6755

Quixote Corporation, through its wholly owned subsidiary, Energy Absorption Systems, Inc., develops, manufactures, and markets energy-absorbing highway crash cushions and related highway safety products for the protection of motorists and highway workers. Facilities are located in Chicago, Illinois; Pell City, Alabama; Hayward and Rocklin, California; and South Bend, Indiana. In March 1997, Quixote completed the sale of its Disc Manufacturing, Inc. subsidiary to Cinram Ltd. of Toronto, Canada. Incorporated in Delaware in 1969.

Directors   (In addition to indicated officers)

William G. Fowler
Lawrence C. McQuade

Robert D. van Roijen, Jr.

Officers   (Directors*)

*Philip E. Rollhaus, Jr., Chm. & C.E.O.
*Leslie J. Jezuit, Pres. & C.O.O.
*James H. DeVries, Exec. V.P. & Secy.

Myron R. Shain, Exec. V.P.—Fin. & Treas.
Daniel P. Gorey, V.P., C.F.O. & Treas.
Joan R. Riley, Asst. Gen. Coun. & Asst. Secy.

Consolidated Balance Sheet   As of June 30, 1996 (000 omitted)

Assets		Liabilities & Stockholders' Equity	
Current assets	$ 18,411	Current liabilities	$ 12,313
Net property, plant & equipment	13,113	Long-term debt	58,000
Other assets	3,158	Deferred items	53
Net assets of discontinued oper.	83,303	*Stockholders' equity	47,619
Total	$117,985	Total	$117,985

*7,952,180 shares common stock outstanding.

Consolidated Income Statement[a]

Years Ended June 30	Thousands — — — — Net Sales	Net Income	Per Share — — — Earnings	Cash Dividends	Common Stock Price Range Calendar Year
1996	$46,750	$(9,892)	$(1.24)	$ .24	10-7/8 — 5-1/2
1995	46,522	5,950	.73	.22	13-1/4 — 7-3/4
1994	43,433	11,644	1.44	.21	22-3/4 — 10-3/4
1993	35,648	9,441	1.20	.20	18 — 11-3/4
1992	32,757	7,967	1.03	.00	15-3/4 — 9-1/2

[a]Restated to reflect the businesses of the Disc Manufacturing, Inc. and Legal Technologies segments as discontinued operations.

Transfer Agent & Registrar:	Bank of Boston		
Outside Counsel:	McBride Baker & Coles	Traded (Symbol):	NASDAQ (QUIX)
Investor Relations:	Joan R. Riley, Dir.	Stockholders:	2,124
		Employees:	350
Human Resources:	Dorothy French	Annual Meeting:	In November
Auditors:	Coopers & Lybrand L.L.P.	Internet:	www.energyabsorption.com

Racing Champions Corporation

800 Roosevelt Road, Buiding C, Suite 320, Glen Ellyn, Illinois 60137
Telephone: (630) 790-3507

Racing Champions Corporation is a leading producer and marketer of collectible scaled die-cast vehicle replicas. The company is best known for its extensive line of officially licensed, high quality collectible replicas of actual race cars and related vehicles from the five most popular U.S. professional racing series, including NASCAR. Beginning in 1996, the company began to expand into non-racing collectibles by introducing the Racing Chapions Mint® line of high quality die cast replicas of classic and late-model vehicles. In 1997, the company began producing two lines of collectible pewter figures, Comic Book Champions®, a series of pewter comic book figures set in action poses, and Sports Champions®, a line of pewter replicas of popular athletes. In order to produce its wide variety of vehicle replicas, the company has entered into over 450 different licensing agreements with racing teams, drivers and sponsors, vehicle manufacturers, and major racing series sanctioning sponsors. Products are manufactured by six independently owned factories in China. In June 1996, the company completed an initial public offering of 5,750,000 shares of common stock. Incorporated in Delaware in 1996.

Directors (In addition to indicated officers)

Daniel M. Gill
Samuel B. Guren

Avy H. Stein

Officers (Directors*)

*Robert E. Dods, Pres.
*Boyd L. Meyer, Exec. V.P.
 M. Kevin Camp, V.P.—Licensing & Asst.
 Secy.

Peter J. Henseler, V.P.—Mktg.
John F. Olsen, V.P.—Sales
Curtis W. Stoelting, V.P.—Fin./Oper. & Secy.
*Peter K.K. Chung, Pres.—Racing Champions Ltd.

Consolidated Balance Sheet   As of December 31, 1996 (000 omitted)

Assets		Liabilities & Stockholders' Equity	
Current assets	$ 14,241	Current liabilities	$ 24,591
Net property, plant & equipment	7,228	Long-term debt	70,141
Excess purch. price over net	87,140	Deferred items	2,935
assets acquired, net		*Stockholders' equity	11,413
Other assets	471		
Total	$109,080	Total	$109,080

*3,571,415 pro forma shares common stock outstanding.

Consolidated Income Statement[a]

Years Ended Dec. 31	Thousands — — — —		Per Share[b] — — — —		Common Stock
	Net Sales	Net Income	Earnings	Cash Dividends	Price Range[b] Calendar Year
1996	$65,999	$ 4,744[c]	$ .36		
1995	48,592	12,182[d]			
1994	43,268	10,563[d]			
1993	31,047	6,938[d]			

[a]Pro forma.
[b]Initial public offering in June 1997.
[c]Includes a non-recurring incentive bonus expense of $2,389,000 and a purchase accounting inventory write-up adjustment of $1,367,000, both in connection the company's recapitalization in April 1996.
[d]Does not include a provision for income taxes for entities structured as S corporations.

Transfer Agent & Registrar: The First National Bank of Boston

General Counsel:
  Reinhart, Boerner, Van Deuren, Norris
  & Rieselbach

Investor Relations: Curtis W. Stoelting, V.P.

Human Resources: Barbara Gilbertsen

Mgt. Info. Svcs.:   Michael A. Midtgaard, Mgr.

Auditors: Arthur Andersen LLP
Traded (Symbol):   NASDAQ (RACN)
Employees: 78
Annual Meeting: To be determined
Internet: www.racingchamps.com

Richardson Electronics, Ltd.

40W267 Keslinger Road, P.O. Box 393, LaFox, Illinois 60147-0393
Telephone: (630) 208-2200

Richardson Electronics, Ltd. is an international distributor and manufacturer of electron tubes and power semiconductors used primarily to control electrical power or as display devices in a variety of industrial, communication, and scientific applications. The company also distributes a variety of closed-circuit television equipment. Richardson distributes more than 100,000 products including small power tubes, traveling wave tubes, klystrons, thyratrons, rectifiers, RF power transistors, ignitrons, planar triodes, magnetrons, and cathode ray tubes. Richardson sells electron tubes primarily to the replacement market. Sales offices are located in Illinois, California, Georgia, Massachusetts, New York, and Texas; and in the following foreign countries: Australia, Brazil, Canada, France, Germany, Italy, Japan, Korea, Mexico, the Netherlands (European headquarters), Singapore, Spain, Taiwan, Thailand, and the United Kingdom. Major subsidiaries are Richardson International and Richardson Electronics (Europe) Ltd. Richardson has a manufacturing facility located in LaFox, Illinois. In August 1996, the company acquired Tubemaster Inc. of Grand Prarie, Texas. In March 1997, Richardson acquired Burtek Systems Inc. of Vancouver, Canada. Incorporated in Illinois in 1947; reincorporated in Delaware in 1986.

Directors (In addition to indicated officers)

Arnold R. Allen	Ad Ketelaars
Jacques Bouyer	Harold L. Purkey
Kenneth J. Douglas	Samuel Rubinovitz
Scott Hodes, Asst. Secy.	

Officers (Directors*)

* Edward J. Richardson, Chm. & C.E.O.
* Bruce Johnson, Pres. & C.O.O.
  Flint Cooper, Exec. V.P.—Security Sys.
* Joel Levine, Sr. V.P.—Solid State Components
  William G. Seils, Sr. V.P., Secy. & Gen. Coun.
  Charles J. Acurio, V.P.—Display Prods.
  Page Chiang, V.P.—Oper. & Security Sys. Div.
* William J. Garry, V.P.—Fin. & C.F.O.

Joseph C. Grill, V.P.—Hum. Res.
Kathleen M. McNally, V.P.—Mktg. Oper.
James R. Patterson, V.P.—Sales, Solid State & Components
Bart F. Petrini, V.P.—Electron Device Grp.
* Robert L. Prince, V.P.—Worldwide Sales Admin.
  Kevin F. Reilly, V.P.—Info. Sys. & C.I.O.
  Ronald G. Ware, Treas.

Consolidated Balance Sheet As of May 31, 1996 (000 omitted)

Assets		Liabilities & Stockholders' Equity	
Current assets	$157,405	Current liabilities	$ 24,254
Net property, plant & equipment	16,054	Long-term debt	92,025
Investments	2,190	Deferred taxes	1,087
Other assets	4,509	* Stockholders' equity	62,792
Total	$180,158	Total	$180,158

*8,569,895 shares common and 3,243,788 shares Class B common stock outstanding.

Consolidated Income Statement

Years Ended May 31	Thousands — — — — Net Sales	Net Income	Per Share — — — Earnings	Cash Dividends	Common Stock Price Range Calendar Year
1996	$239,667	$ 8,111	$ .68	$ .16	11-7/8 — 7
1995ab	208,118	3,008	.26	.16	11-3/4 — 6-3/4
1994c	172,094	(19,809)	(1.75)	.16	9 — 3-3/4
1993	159,215	2,802	.25	.16	10-1/2 — 5-1/2
1992	158,789	1,707	.15	.16	10-1/4 — 6-3/4

aIncludes a charge of $4,700,000 for the settlement of a U.S. government claim related to a 1989 contract.
bIncludes an extraordinary gain of $527,000 ($.05 per share) resulting from the repurchase of $4,910,000 of its 7-1/4% convertible debentures.
cThe company established a $26,500,000 provision, which included $21,400,000 for the estimated costs of a plan to dispose of its manufacturing operations in Brive, France, and $5,100,000 for incremental costs related to the phasedown of its LaFox, Illinois, manufacturing facility.

Transfer Agent & Registrar: Harris Trust and Savings Bank

General Counsel:	William G. Seils, Sr. V.P.	Traded (Symbol):	NASDAQ (RELL)
Investor Relations:	William J. Garry, V.P.	Stockholders:	740
Human Resources:	Joseph C. Grill, V.P.	Employees:	582
Mgt. Info. Svcs.:	Kevin F. Reilly, V.P.	Annual Meeting:	In October
Auditors:	Ernst & Young LLP	Internet:	www.rell.com

RLI Corp.

9025 North Lindbergh Drive, Peoria, Illinois 61615-1499
Telephone: (309) 692-1000

RLI Corp. is a holding company which, through its subsidiaries, underwrites selected property and casualty insurance. The principal specialty insurance coverages written by the company are commercial property, general liability, personal and commercial umbrella, and directors' and officers' liability. In addition, the company writes errors and omissions liability, professional liability, primary and excess employer's indemnity, in-home business owners coverage, and contract and miscellaneous surety bonds. Major subsidiaries include: RLI Insurance Company and Mt. Hawley Insurance Company. Incorporated in Delaware in 1984 as the successor to an Illinois corporation incorporated in 1965; reincorporated in Illinois in 1993.

Directors (In addition to indicated officers)

Bernard J. Daenzer, J.D., CPCU
Richard J. Haayen
William R. Keane
Gerald I. Lenrow, Esq.

John S. McGuinness, Ph.D., CPCU
Edwin S. Overman, Ph.D., CPCU
Edward F. Sutkowski, Esq.
Robert O. Viets

Officers (Directors*)

*Gerald D. Stephens, Pres.
Joseph E. Dondanville, V.P. & C.F.O.
Mary Beth Nebel, V.P. & Gen. Coun.
Kim J. Hensey, Secy.
Michael A. Price, Treas.
Jonathan E. Michael, Pres. & C.O.O., RLI Ins. Grp.

Gregory J. Tiemeier, Sr. V.P.—Oper. & Tech., RLI Ins. Grp.
Roger M. Buss, V.P.—Mgt. Info. Svcs., RLI Ins. Grp.
Michael E. Quine, V.P.—Admin., RLI Ins. Grp.
Michael J. Stone, V.P.—Claims, RLI Ins. Grp.
Thomas V. Warthen, V.P.—Actuarial Svcs., RLI Ins. Grp.

Consolidated Balance Sheet As of December 31, 1996 (000 omitted)

Assets		Liabilities & Stockholders' Equity	
Cash and investments	$537,946	Unearned premiums	$129,782
Ceded unearned premiums	53,705	Unpaid losses & settlement exp.	405,801
Reins. balances recov. on unpaid losses/sett. exp.	165,017	Reinsurance balances payable	23,700
		Long-term debt	46,000
Net property, plant & equipment	12,127	Other liabilities	40,152
Premiums & reinsurance balances received	37,167	*Stockholders' equity	200,039
Other assets	39,512		
Total	$845,474	Total	$845,474

*7,821,730 shares common stock outstanding.

Consolidated Income Statement

Years Ended Dec. 31	Thousands — — — —		Per Share[a] — — — —		Common Stock
	Revenues	Net Income	Earnings	Cash Dividends	Price Range[a] Calendar Year
1996	$155,354	$ 25,696	$ 3.25	$ .55	33-1/2 — 22-3/8
1995[b]	155,954	7,950[c]	1.01[c]	.51	25 — 16-1/4
1994[b]	156,722	(4,776)[c]	(.61)[c]	.45	22-1/4 — 16-1/2
1993[b]	143,100	15,948	2.10	.42	22-7/8 — 19-1/4
1992[b]	117,582	16,207	2.26	.40	20-5/8 — 12-3/4

[a]Adjusted to reflect a 5-for-4 stock split in June 1995.
[b]Restated to include the effect of the change to the equity method of accounting for the company's former subsidiary, RLI Vision Corp., renamed Maui Jim, Inc. The financial retstatement represents a change in presentation only and does not have a dilutive effect on historical periods.
[c]Reflects losses incurred as a result of the Northridge, California, earthquake which occurred on January 17, 1994, reducing net income and earnings per share by $18,600,000 ($2.37 per share) in 1995 and $25,000,000 ($3.21 per share) in 1994.

Transfer Agent & Registrar: Norwest Bank Minnesota, N.A.

Outside Counsel:	Sutkowski & Washkuhn Ltd.	Traded (Symbol):	NYSE (RLI)
Investor Relations:	Michael A. Price, Treas.	Stockholders:	826
Human Resources:	Michael E. Quine, V.P.	Employees:	357
Mgt. Info. Svcs.:	Roger M. Buss, V.P.	Annual Meeting:	In May
Auditors:	KPMG Peat Marwick LLP	Internet:	www.rlicorp.com

Rodman & Renshaw Capital Group, Inc.

233 South Wacker Drive, Suite 4500, Chicago, Illinois 60606
Telephone: (312) 526-2000

Rodman & Renshaw Capital Group, Inc., is a holding company which, through its principal subsidiary, Rodman & Renshaw, Inc., is a full-service securities broker-dealer and commodities futures commission merchant with memberships on the New York Stock Exchange and other principal stock exchanges. The company offers investment banking, research, and investor services to business organizations, tax-exempt entities, financial institutions and fiduciaries, other securities and commodities dealers, and individual investors. In addition to Chicago, the company has offices in New York, San Francisco, Dallas, and Boston. In 1993, Abaco Casa de Bolsa, S.A. de C.V., Abaco Grupo Financiero acquired a majority of the company. Incorporated in Delaware in 1980.

Directors (In addition to indicated officers)

Jorge Lankenau Rocha, Chm.
Alexander C. Anderson

Ernesto Arechavala
Eduardo Camarena Legaspi

Officers (Directors*)

*Joseph P. Shanahan, Pres. & C.E.O.
Gilbert R. Ott, Jr., Exec. V.P., Gen. Coun. & Secy.

Thomas G. Pinou, Exec. V.P. & C.F.O.
*Francis L. Kirby, Sr. Managing Dir.—Retail Fin. Svcs.

Consolidated Balance Sheet As of December 31, 1996 (000 omitted)

Assets		Liabilities & Stockholders' Equity	
Current assets	$25,047	Current liabilities	$51,631
Net property, plant & equipment	7,431	*Stockholders' equity	(7,848)
Other assets	11,305		
Total	$43,783	Total	$43,783

*6,646,000 shares common stock outstanding.

Consolidated Income Statement

Years Ended Dec. 31	Thousands — — — —		Per Share — — — —		Common Stock Price Range Calendar Year
	Revenues	Net Income	Earnings	Cash Dividends	
1996	$60,574	$(21,791)	$(3.28)	$ .00	2-1/2 — 7/8
1995	72,525	(29,982)	(4.63)	.00	5 — 1-3/8
1994[a]	32,194	(4,164)	(.91)	.00	7-7/8 — 3-5/8
1993[b]	87,309	256	.06	.00	9-3/4 — 5
1992[b]	84,378	1,989	.46	.00	5-3/4 — 4

[a]The company's fiscal year has been changed to December 31. Financial results are from June 25 through December 31, 1994.
[b]Fiscal year ended about June 30.

Transfer Agent & Registrar: Continental Stock Transfer & Trust Co.

General Counsel:	Gilbert R. Ott, Jr., Exec. V.P.	Auditors:	Coopers & Lybrand LLP
Investor Relations:	William J. Bakker, V.P.	Traded (Symbol):	NYSE (RR)
		Stockholders:	183
Human Resources:	Jan Williams, V.P.	Employees:	267
Mgt. Info. Svcs.:	Roberto Alamanza, V.P.	Annual Meeting:	In September

Ryerson Tull, Inc.

2621 West 15th Place, Chicago, Illinois 60608
Telephone: (773) 762-2121

Ryerson Tull, Inc., through its wholly owned operating subsidiaries Ryerson and Tull, is a general line metals distributor and processor. The company has facilities throughout the continental U.S. and Mexico and is among the largest purchasers of steel in the U.S. With over 70 interconnected facilities that place it within several hundred miles of most of its customers, Ryerson Tull is generally able to make deliveries of stock items within 24 hours of receipt of a customer order. Ryerson, the predecessor of the company, was founded in 1842. The company acquired Tull, AFCO Metals, Inc., and Southern Metals Corporation in 1986, 1988, and 1989, respectively, establishing the company's presence in the southeastern U.S. In 1989, the company acquired Processed Metals, Inc., adding facilities in Minnesota and Iowa. In 1990, the company acquired the Metra division of Schnitzer Steel, Inc., with facilities in Portland, Oregon; Phoenix, Arizona; and Salt Lake City, Utah. The company also owns a 50 percent interest in Ryerson de Mexico, a general line metals service center and processor with 12 facilities in Mexico. In June 1996, the company completed an initial public offering of 5,220,000 shares of common stock. Incorporated in Delaware in 1986; present name adopted in May 1996.

Directors (In addition to indicated officers)

Richard G. Cline
James A. Henderson
Jerry K. Pearlman

Donald S. Perkins
Jean-Pierre Rosso
Ronald L. Thompson

Officers (Directors*)

*Robert J. Darnall, Chm.
*Neil S. Novich, Pres. & C.E.O.
Jay M. Gratz, V.P.—Fin. & C.F.O.
William Korda, V.P.—Hum. Res.
Darell R. Zerbe, V.P.—Info. Tech.
Lily L. May, Cont.
Vicki L. Avril, Treas.

Charles B. Salowitz, Secy.
Stephen E. Makarewicz, Pres.—Tull
Carl G. Lusted, Pres.—Ryerson Central
Gary J. Niederpruem, Pres.—Ryerson East
Thomas S. Cygan, Pres.—Ryerson West
Timothy L. LaPerre, Pres.—Ryerson Coil

Consolidated Balance Sheet As of December 31, 1996 (000 omitted)

Assets		Liabilities & Stockholders' Equity	
Current assets	$586,200	Current liabilities	$160,600
Net property, plant & equipment	251,000	Long-term debt	263,200
Other assets	95,000	Other liabilities	144,000
		*Stockholders' equity	364,400
Total	$932,200	Total	$932,200

*39,300,000 shares common stock outstanding.

Consolidated Income Statement

Years Ended Dec. 31	Thousands — — — —		Per Share[a] — — — —		Common Stock
	Net Sales	Net Income	Earnings	Cash Dividends	Price Range[ab] Calendar Year
1996	$2,394,000	$ 63,300	$1.61	$ .00	16-1/8 — 12-1/2
1995	2,450,100	88,500			
1994	2,197,500	53,300			
1993	1,893,300	26,700			
1992	1,716,600	(80,800)[c]			

[a]Adjusted to reflect a 17,000,000-for-1 stock split in June 1996.
[b]Initial public offering in June 1996.
[c]Reflects cumulative effect of adoption of FAS No. 106 of $72,300,000 and cumulative effect of adoption of FAS No. 109 of $11,800,000.

Transfer Agent & Registrar:	Harris Trust and Savings Bank		
General Counsel:	Mayer, Brown & Platt	Auditors:	Price Waterhouse LLP
Investor Relations:	Timothy J. McIntyre	Traded (Symbol):	NYSE (RT)
Human Resources:	William Korda, V.P.	Stockholders:	109
		Employees:	4,823
Mgt. Info. Svcs.:	Darell R. Zerbe, V.P.	Annual Meeting:	As set by Directors

Rymer Foods Inc.

4600 South Packers Avenue, Suite 400, Chicago, Illinois 60609
Telephone: (773) 927-7777

Rymer Foods Inc. is engaged in the production of frozen, pre-seasoned, portion-controlled entrees for restaurants, foodservice and retail customers. The company's principal subsidiary is Rymer Meat Inc. which processes beef into ready-to-cook, portion-controlled seasoned steaks and other beef products. The operating company engages in the development and production of proprietary "signature" recipes for chain restaurant customers. Rymer operates a manufacturing facility in Illinois. On August 28, 1996, the company completed the sale of its Rymer International Seafood Inc. subsidiary to BGL I, Inc., an entity formed by the former president of the seafood subsidiary. Incorporated in Delaware in 1969.

Directors (In addition to indicated officers)

Samuel I. Bailin
Joseph Colonnetta

David E. Jackson
Hannah H. Strasser

Officers (Directors*)

*P. Edward Schenk, Chm., Pres. & C.E.O.
 Edward M. Hebert, Sr. V.P.—Fin., Treas. &
 C.F.O.

Barbara A. McNicholas, Secy.

Consolidated Balance Sheet As of October 26, 1996 (000 omitted)

Assets		Liabilities & Stockholders' Equity	
Current assets	$21,566	Current liabilities	$32,090
Net property, plant & equipment	1,988	Long-term debt	70
Plant held for sale	1,600	Deferred items	772
Other assets	920	*Stockholders' equity	(6,858)
Total	$26,074	Total	$26,074

*10,753,934 shares common stock outstanding.

Consolidated Income Statement

Years Ended Abt. Oct. 31	Thousands — — — — Net Salesª	Net Income	Per Share — — — — Earnings	Cash Dividends	Common Stock Price Range Calendar Year	
1996	$ 44,329	$(9,164)	$ (.85)	$ .00	1-1/2 —	1/4
1995	79,920	(29,330)	(2.69)	.00	3-1/4 —	5/8
1994	106,252	6,478ᵇ	.18	.00	4-1/2 — 1-5/8	
1993	99,644	(11,441)ᶜ	(3.50)ᶜ	.00	3-3/8 —	7/8
1992	92,665	(9,423)	(2.20)	.00	4-7/8 — 1	

ªRestated to reclassify the results of Rymer Chicken Inc. and Rymer International Seafood Inc. as discontinued operations.
ᵇIncludes gain on dispositions (primarily Rymer Chicken) of $4,474,000.
ᶜIncludes an extraordinary gain from restructuring of subordinated debentures of $11,388,000 ($1.67 per share); a restructuring charge of $2,020,000; and restructuring expense resulting from goodwill writedown of $20,828,000.

Transfer Agent & Registrar:	ChaseMellon Shareholder Services, L.L.C.
General Counsel:	Rudnick & Wolfe
Investor Relations:	Edward M. Hebert, Sr. V.P.
Auditors:	Coopers & Lybrand L.L.P.

Traded (Symbol):	NYSE (RYR)
Stockholders:	750
Employees:	257
Annual Meeting:	In April

Sabratek Corporation

5601 West Howard Street, Niles, Illinois 60714
Telephone: (847) 647-2760

Sabratek Corporation develops, produces, and markets technologically advanced, user-friendly, and cost effective multi-therapy infusion systems designed to meet the unique needs of the alternate-site health care market. The company's integrated infusion products incorporate advanced communications technology which is designed to reduce provider operation costs while maintaining the integrity and quality of care. Sabratek's proprietary health care information information system, MediVIEW®, provides remote programming as well as real-time diagnostic and therapeutic data capture capabilities, allowing caregivers to monitor patient compliance more effectively and allowing providers to develop outcome analyses and optional clinical protocols. In June 1996, the company completed an initial public offering of 2,875,000 shares of common stock. Incorporated in Illinois in 1989; reincorporated in Delaware in 1991.

Directors (In addition to indicated officers)

Scott Hodes	Marvin Samson
Mark Lampert	L. Peter Smith
William D. Lautman	Edison W. Spencer, Jr.
William H. Lomicka	

Officers (Directors*)

*K. Shan Padda, Chm., C.E.O. & Treas.
Anil K. Rastogi, Ph.D., Pres. & C.O.O.
*Doron C. Levitas, V. Chm., V.P.—Intl. Oper. & Secy.
Stephen L. Holden, Sr. V.P. & C.F.O.

Alan E. Jordan, Sr. V.P.—Sales & Mktg.
Vincent J. Capponi, V.P.—Mfg.
Joseph Moser, V.P.—Research & Dev.
Scott Skooglund, V.P.—Fin.

Consolidated Balance Sheet   As of December 31, 1996 (000 omitted)

Assets		Liabilities & Stockholders' Equity	
Current assets	$28,864	Current liabilities	$ 4,277
Net property, plant & equipment	1,775	Long-term debt	1
Other assets	2,312	Other liabilities	23
		*Stockholders' equity	28,650
Total	$32,951	Total	$32,951

*8,196,981 shares common stock outstanding.

Consolidated Income Statement

Years Ended Dec. 31	Thousands — — — — Net Sales	Net Income	Per Share[a] — — — Earnings	Cash Dividends	Common Stock Price Range[a] Calendar Year
1996	$17,696	$ (858)[b]	$ (.11)	$ .00	16-3/4 — 7-3/4
1995	4,040	(6,036)	(.90)[c]		
1994	3,315	(3,555)			
1993	1,229	(2,821)			
1992	842	(791)			

[a]Initial public offering in June 1996.
[b]Includes a non-recurring charge of $1,600,000 in connection with the initial public offering.
[c]Pro forma.

Transfer Agent & Registrar:	LaSalle National Bank		
General Counsel:	Ross & Hardies	Stockholders:	214
		Employees:	100
Auditors:	KPMG Peat Marwick LLP	Annual Meeting:	In June
Traded (Symbol):	NASDAQ (SBTK)	Internet:	www.sabratek.com

Safety-Kleen Corp.

One Brinckman Way, Elgin, Illinois 60123-7857
Telephone: (847) 697-8460

Safety-Kleen Corp. is an industrial service company focusing on the environmental needs of business through recycling and reuse of fluid waste. It is a leading provider of services to generators of spent solvents and other hazardous and non-hazardous liquid wastes and by-products, a leading provider of parts cleaner services, and a leading collector and re-refiner of used oil. The services offered are broadly grouped into the following categories: Small Quantity Generator Resource Recovery Services; Envirosystems; and Oil Recovery Services. The company's primary focus is on servicing small quantity hazardous waste generators who are typically in businesses such as auto and auto body repair, fleet operations, dry cleaning, manufacturing, and a variety of other activities. The original and largest Safety-Kleen service is the parts cleaner service, which provides equipment and solvents to customers, and also collects spent solvents for recycling and reuse. At the end of 1996, the company and its subsidiaries had 176 branch service centers in North America and 54 additional branch service centers located in seven western European countries. Major subsidiaries include Safety-Kleen Canada Inc., Safety-Kleen Parts Washer Service LTD., and Safety-Kleen Envirosystem Co. of Puerto Rico. Incorporated in Wisconsin in 1963.

Directors (In addition to indicated officers)

Richard T. Farmer
Russell A. Gwillim
Edgar D. Jannotta
Karl G. Otzen

Paul D. Schrage
Marcia E. Williams
W. Gordon Wood

Officers (Directors*)

* Donald W. Brinckman, Chm.
* John G. Johnson, Jr., Pres. & C.E.O.
  Hyman K. Bielsky, Sr. V.P.—Gen. Coun.
  Roy D. Bullinger, Sr. V.P.—Bus. Mgmt. & Mktg.
  Robert J. Burian, Sr. V.P.—Hum. Res.
  Andrew A. Campbell, Sr. V.P.—Fin. & C.F.O.
  Michael H. Carney, Sr. V.P.—Mktg. Svcs. & Cust. Care
  Joseph Chalhoub, Sr. V.P.—Oper., Oil Rec. & Envirosystems

David A. Dattilo, Sr. V.P.—Sales & Svcs.
Scott E. Fore, Sr. V.P.—Envir., Health & Safety
F. Henry Habicht II, Sr. V.P.—Corp. Dev. & Envir.
Lawrence Davenport, V.P.—Info. Svcs. & C.I.O.
Clark J. Rose, V.P.—Mfg. & Tech. Svcs.
Laurence M. Rudnick, Treas.
C. James Schulz, Cont.

Consolidated Balance Sheet As of December 28, 1996 (000 omitted)

Assets		Liabilities & Stockholders' Equity	
Current assets	$ 230,133	Current liabilities	$ 157,793
Net property, plant & equipment	646,827	Long-term debt	276,954
Intangible assets	137,209	Deferred items	49,849
Other assets	30,654	Other liabilities	79,937
		* Stockholders' equity	480,290
Total	$1,044,823	Total	$1,044,823

*58,246,939 shares common stock outstanding.

Consolidated Income Statement

Years Ended Abt. Dec. 31	Thousands — — — —		Per Share[a] — — — —		Common Stock Price Range[a] Calendar Year
	Revenues	Net Income	Earnings	Cash Dividends	
1996	$923,126	$ 61,109	$ 1.05	$ .36	18-5/8 — 13-3/8
1995	859,251	53,303	.92	.36	18-1/8 — 12-7/8
1994	791,267	50,094	.87	.36	18-1/2 — 12-3/4
1993	795,508	(101,346)[b]	(1.76)[b]	.36	24-3/4 — 13-1/8
1992[c]	794,542	45,637[d]	.79[d]	.34	32-1/4 — 22-5/8

[a]Adjusted to reflect a 3-for-2 stock split in March 1991.
[b]Includes restructuring and special charges of $136,000,000 ($2.36 per share), net of tax benefits.
[c]Fiscal year 1992 was a 53 week year. All other years presented were 52 week years.
[d]Includes a gain to reflect FAS 106 and FAS 109, resulting in a net cumulative effect of $300,000 ($.01 per share).

Transfer Agent & Registrar: First Chicago Trust Co. of New York

General Counsel:	Hyman K. Bielsky, Sr. V.P.	Traded (Symbol):	NYSE (SK)
Investor Relations:	Maureen Fisk, Dir.	Stockholders:	8,042
Human Resources:	Robert J. Burian, Sr. V.P.	Employees:	7,000
Mgt. Info. Svcs.:	Lawrence Davenport, V.P.	Annual Meeting:	In May
Auditors:	Arthur Andersen LLP	Internet:	www.safety-kleen.com

St. Paul Bancorp, Inc.

6700 West North Avenue, Chicago, Illinois 60707
Telephone: (773) 622-5000

St. Paul Bancorp, Inc. is the holding company for St. Paul Federal Bank For Savings, which is primarily engaged in attracting checking, savings, and certificates of deposit accounts from the general public, and investing those funds in a variety of mortgage and consumer loan products and high quality investment securities. Fifty-two branch offices are located in the Chicago metropolitan area. In addition, St. Paul offers its customers a variety of allied financial services through subsidiaries of the bank and holding company. St. Paul Financial Development Corp. purchases and develops real estate. SPF Insurance Agency, Inc. provides a wide range of insurance services. Investment Network, Inc., a discount brokerage firm, offers execution and clearance services for stocks, bonds, and mutual funds. Annuity Network, Inc. is engaged in sales of insurance annuity products. Incorporated in Delaware in 1987.

Directors (In addition to indicated officers)

William A. Anderson
John W. Croghan
Alan J. Fredian
Paul C. Gearen

Kenneth J. James
Jean C. Murray, O.P.
John J. Viera

Officers (Directors*)

*Joseph C. Scully, Chm. & C.E.O.
*Patrick J. Agnew, Pres. & C.O.O.
James R. Lutsch, Sr. V.P.—Info. Svcs.
Robert N. Parke, Sr. V.P.—Fin. & C.F.O.

Robert N. Pfeiffer, Sr. V.P.—Hum. Res. & Cust. Oper.
Thomas J. Rinella, Sr. V.P.—Community Lend.
Donald G. Ross, Sr. V.P.—Retail Banking
Clifford M. Sladnick, Sr. V.P., Gen. Coun. & Secy.

Consolidated Balance Sheet As of December 31, 1996 (000 omitted)

Assets		Liabilities & Stockholders' Equity	
Cash & cash equivalents	$ 190,208	Deposit accounts	$3,337,055
Marketable debt securities	49,103	FHLB advances	456,399
Mortgage-backed securities	1,162,982	Other borrowed funds	104,845
Loans receivable (net of reserves)	2,782,116	Deposits for payment of taxes & insurance	21,561
Net property, plant & equipment	47,286	Other liabilities	49,200
FHLB stock	35,211	*Stockholders' equity	388,110
Other assets	90,264		
Total	$4,357,170	Total	$4,357,170

*22,775,991 shares common stock outstanding (after 1997 split).

Consolidated Income Statement

Years Ended Dec. 31	Thousands — — — — Total Income	Net Income	Per Share[a] — — — Earnings	Cash Dividends	Common Stock Price Range[a] Calendar Year
1996	$331,976	$26,257	$1.10	$ .35	24-1/2 — 17-1/4
1995	312,471	36,394	1.49	.24	22-3/4 — 13-7/8
1994	283,033	34,512	1.36	.24	19-1/4 — 11-3/8
1993[b]	289,443	41,387	1.63	.22	16-1/2 — 10-5/8
1992	307,035	37,685	1.60	.22	12-5/8 — 6-7/8

[a]Adjusted to reflect a 3-for-2 stock split in January 1994 and a 5-for-4 stock split in January 1997.
[b]Includes the operations of Elm Financial Services as of the acquisition date, February 23, 1993.

Transfer Agent & Registrar:	The First National Bank of Boston		
General Counsel:	Clifford M. Sladnick, Sr. V.P.	Auditors:	Ernst & Young LLP
Investor Relations:	Robert E. Williams, V.P.	Traded (Symbol):	NASDAQ (SPBC)
		Stockholders:	6,591
Human Resources:	Robert N. Pfeiffer, Sr. V.P.	Employees:	1,064
Mgt. Info. Svcs.:	James R. Lutsch, Sr. V.P.	Annual Meeting:	In May

Salton/Maxim Housewares, Inc.

550 Business Center Drive, The Kensington Center, Mount Prospect,
Illinois 60056
Telephone: (847) 803-4600

Salton/Maxim Housewares, Inc. designs and markets a broad range of small kitchen appliances, and personal and beauty care appliances under the names Salton®, Maxim®, Breadman, Juiceman, Salton Time, and Salton Creations℠. The kitchen appliances currently marketed by the company include espresso-cappuccino makers, coffee makers, sandwich makers, toasters, bread makers, Hotray® warming trays, juice extractors, ice cream and yogurt makers, and a wide variety of other food preparation appliances. The company's personal and beauty care appliances include hair dryers, Wet Tunes® shower radios, curling irons and brushes, make-up mirrors, massagers, manicure systems, and facial salons. The company contracts for the manufacture of most of its products with independent manufacturers located overseas, primarily in the Far East and Europe. The company also manufactures and assembles certain appliances in its plant located in Newark, New Jersey. Incorporated in Delaware in 1991.

Directors   (In addition to indicated officers)

Frank Devine   Bert Doornmalen

Officers   (Directors*)

*David C. Sabin, Chm. & Secy.   William B. Rue, Sr. V.P. & C.O.O.
*Leonhard Dreimann, Pres. & C.E.O.

Consolidated Balance Sheet   As of June 29, 1996 (000 omitted)

Assets		Liabilities & Stockholders' Equity	
Current assets	$48,046	Current liabilities	$35,802
Net property, plant & equipment	6,232	Long-term debt	500
Non-current deferred tax assets	1,533	Other liabilities	3,254
Other assets	3,670	*Stockholders' equity	19,925
Total	$59,481	Total	$59,481

*6,508,572 shares common stock outstanding.

Consolidated Income Statement

Years Ended Abt. June 30	Thousands — — — — Net Sales	Net Income	Per Share[a] — — — Earnings	Cash Dividends	Common Stock Price Range[a] Fiscal Year
1996	$99,202	$ 4,596	$ .69	$ .00	5-1/4 — 1-5/8
1995	76,991	651	.11	.00	4-1/2 — 1-3/4
1994	48,807	(2,944)	(.58)	.00	3-1/2 — 1-1/4
1993	50,661	(3,151)	(.64)	.00	3-5/8 — 3/4
1992	48,699	(4,867)	(1.18)	.00	6-3/4 — 2

[a]Adjusted to reflect an approximately 3.16-for-1 stock split in August 1991.

Transfer Agent & Registrar:	LaSalle National Trust, N.A.			
General Counsel:	Sonnenschein Nath & Rosenthal	Traded (Symbol):	NASDAQ (SALT)
Investor Relations:	William B. Rue, Sr. V.P.	Stockholders:	1,000
Human Resources:	William B. Rue, Sr. V.P.	Employees:	122
Mgt. Info. Svcs.:	William B. Rue, Sr. V.P.	Annual Meeting:	In December
Auditors:	Deloitte & Touche LLP	Internet:	www.saltonmaxim.com

John B. Sanfilippo & Son, Inc.

2299 Busse Road, Elk Grove Village, Illinois 60007-6057
Telephone: (847) 593-2300

John B. Sanfilippo & Son, Inc. is a processor, packager, marketer, and distributor of shelled nuts, inshell nuts, and sesame sticks which are sold under a variety of private labels and under the company's Evon's®, Fisher®, Sunshine County, Flavor Tree®, and Texas Pride names. The company also markets and distributes, and in most cases, manufactures or processes a diverse product line of food and snack items including peanut butter, candy and confections, natural snacks and trail mixes, and corn snacks. The company sells its products to more than 6,000 retailers, wholesalers, and industrial, government and food service customers. Incorporated in Delaware in 1979 as the successor by merger to an Illinois corporation that was incorporated in 1959.

Directors (In addition to indicated officers)

John W.A. Buyers
William D. Fischer

J. William Petty

Officers (Directors*)

*Jasper B. Sanfilippo, Chm. & C.E.O.
*Mathias A. Valentine, Pres.
*John C. Taylor, Exec. Grp. V.P.
Gary P. Jensen, Exec. V.P.—Fin. & C.F.O.
Steven G. Taylor, Exec. V.P.

James J. Sanfilippo, V.P. & Treas.
Jasper B. Sanfilippo, Jr., V.P. & Asst. Secy.
*Michael J. Valentine, V.P. & Secy.
William R. Pokrajac, Cont.

Consolidated Balance Sheet As of December 31, 1996 (000 omitted)

Assets		Liabilities & Stockholders' Equity	
Current assets	$109,182	Current liabilities	$ 68,226
Net property, plant & equipment	80,554	Long-term debt	63,319
Other assets	15,616	Deferred items	1,187
		*Stockholders' equity	72,620
Total	$205,352	Total	$205,352

*3,687,426 shares Class A common and 5,578,140 shares common stock outstanding.

Consolidated Income Statement

Years Ended Dec. 31	Thousands — — — — Net Sales	Net Income	Per Share — — — — Earnings	Cash Dividends	Common Stock Price Range Calendar Year
1996	$294,404	$(2,991)	$ (.33)	$ .00	9-3/4— 4-3/4
1995	277,741	5,788	.63	.00	10-3/4— 5-3/8
1994	208,970	49	.00	.00	15-1/2— 4-1/2
1993	202,583	6,123	.74	.05	18 — 13-1/4
1992	191,373	6,431	.95	.05	20-3/4— 12-1/8

Transfer Agent & Registrar: American Stock Transfer & Trust Co.

General Counsel:
  Katz, Karacic, Helmin & Addis; Jenner & Block

Investor Relations: Gary P. Jensen, Exec. V.P.

Human Resources: David Meyers

Mgt. Info. Svcs.:   James A. Valentine, V.P.

Auditors: Price Waterhouse LLP
Traded (Symbol):   NASDAQ (JBSS)
Stockholders: 2,000
Employees: 1,400
Annual Meeting: In April

Sara Lee Corporation

Three First National Plaza, Chicago, Illinois 60602-4260
Telephone: (312) 726-2600

Sara Lee Corporation is a global manufacturer and marketer of packaged food and consumer products. The company markets its brand name products in more than 140 countries around the world. Sara Lee is organized into four business segments. The Packaged Meats and Bakery segment manufactures and markets frozen and fresh-baked goods, and fresh and processed meats. It also operates PYA/Monarch, the fourth-largest foodservice distributor in the U.S. The Coffee and Grocery segment produces coffee, tea, and other beverages, as well as nuts and snacks. The Household and Body care segment manufactures and markets shoe care products, toiletries, insecticides, and furniture care products. It also operates direct selling business which distributes a broad range of products through independent sales representatives. The Personal Products segment manufactures and markets hosiery, intimate apparel, knitwear, and other products. Incorporated in Maryland in 1939.

Directors (In addition to indicated officers)

Paul A. Allaire	Allen F. Jacobson	Sir Arvi H. Parbo, A.C.
Frans H.J.J. Andriessen	Vernon E. Jordan, Jr.	Rozanne L. Ridgway
Duane L. Burnham	James L. Ketelsen	Richard L. Thomas
Charles W. Coker	Joan D. Manley	Hans B. van Liemt
Willie D. Davis	Newton N. Minow	

Officers (Directors*)

*John H. Bryan, Chm. & C.E.O.	Adriaan Nühn, Sr. V.P.	Simon C. Hemus, V.P.
*Donald J. Franceschini, V. Chm.	John S. Riccitiello, Sr. V.P.	Floyd G. Hoffman, V.P.
*Michael E. Murphy, V. Chm. & C.A.O.	Judith A. Sprieser, Sr. V.P. & C.F.O.	Ronald D. Hubble, V.P.—Internal Audit
*C. Steven McMillan, Pres.	Jacques A.N. van Dijk, Sr. V.P.	Paul E. Klönhammer, V.P.
*Frank L. Meysman, Exec. V.P.	John F. Ward, Sr. V.P.	E.L. (Lee) Kramer, V.P.
George B. Bryan, Sr. V.P.	Kirk Beaudin, V.P.	Donald L. Meier, V.P.—Taxes
James R. Carlson, Sr. V.P.	Janet E. Bergman, V.P.—Inv. Rel. &	Richard Oberdorf, V.P.
Lew Frankfort, Sr. V.P.	Corp. Aff.	John A. Piazza, V.P.
Gary C. Grom, Sr. V.P.—Hum. Res.	Lee A. Chaden, V.P.	Wayne R. Szypulski, V.P. & Cont.
Janet Langford Kelly, Sr. V.P., Gen.	Charles W. Chambers, V.P.	N. Robert Utecht, V.P.
Coun. & Secy.	Maureen M. Culhane, V.P.—Fin. &	Douglas C. Volz, V.P.—Emp. Rel.
Paul J. Lustig, Sr. V.P.	Treas.	J. Randall White, V.P.
Mark J. McCarville, Sr. V.P.	L.M. deKool, V.P.	Elynor A. Williams, V.P.—Public
Lucien Nessim, Sr. V.P.	William A. Geoppinger, V.P.	Responsibility

Consolidated Balance Sheet As of June 29, 1996 (000 omitted)

Assets		Liabilities & Stockholders' Equity	
Current assets	$ 5,081,000	Current liabilities	$ 4,642,000
Net property, plant & equipment	3,007,000	Long-term debt	1,842,000
Other assets	4,514,000	Deferred income taxes	333,000
		Other liabilities	1,465,000
		*Stockholders' equity	4,320,000
Total	$12,602,000	Total	$12,602,000

*480,054,554 shares common stock outstanding.

Consolidated Income Statement

Years Ended Abt. June 30	Thousands — — — — —		Per Share[a] — — —		Common Stock Price Range[a] Calendar Year
	Net Sales	Net Income	Earnings	Cash Dividends	
1996	$18,624,000	$916,000	$1.83	$ .74	40-1/2 — 29-7/8
1995	17,719,000	804,000	1.62	.67	33-3/4 — 24-1/4
1994	15,536,000	199,000[b]	.37[b]	.63	26 — 19-3/8
1993	14,580,000	704,000	1.40	.56	31-1/8 — 21
1992	13,243,000	761,000	1.54[c]	.61[d]	32-1/2 — 23-3/8

[a]Adjusted to reflect a 2-for-1 stock split in October 1992.
[b]Includes a restructuring expense and a charge to reflect FAS 109, resulting in a cumulative effect of $530,000,000 ($1.10 per share).
[c]Includes unusual items resulting in a net gain of $.30 per share.
[d]Includes a $.12 per share special dividend.

Transfer Agent:	Sara Lee Corporation	Auditors:	Arthur Andersen LLP
Registrar:	The First National Bank of Chicago	Traded (Symbol):	
General Counsel:	Janet Langford Kelly, Sr. V.P.	NYSE, CSE, PSE, LON, AMST, FRA, 3 Swiss (SLE)	
Investor Relations:	S. Leigh Ferst, Exec. Dir.	Stockholders:	91,300
Human Resources:	Gary C. Grom, Sr. V.P.	Employees:	135,300
Mgt. Info. Svcs.:	Jerry Matsumoro	Annual Meeting:	In October

Schawk, Inc.

1695 River Road, Des Plaines, Illinois 60018-3013
Telephone: (847) 827-9494

Schawk, Inc., through its Imaging and Information Technology Group is the leading producer of color prepress imaging services for the consumer products packaging industry in the United States, particularly for food and beverage producers. The group offers a complete line of prepress services and products for the production of consumer product packaging and related marketing and advertising materials. In December 1994, the corporation previously known as Schawk, Inc., and certain affiliated corporations, were merged with and into the company's predecessor, Filtertek, Inc. Upon consummation of the merger, Filtertek changed its name to Schawk, Inc. In February 1997, the company sold its Plastics Group to ESCO Corporation of St. Louis, Missouri. Incorporated in Illinois in 1965; reincorporated in Delaware in 1972.

Directors (In addition to indicated officers)

Judith W. McCue
John T. McEnroe

Robert F. Meinken
Hollis W. Rademacher

Officers (Directors*)

*Clarence W. Schawk, Chm.
*David A. Schawk, Pres. & C.E.O.

*A. Alex Sarkisian, Exec. V.P., Secy. &
  Pres.—Imaging Grp.
*Marie Meisenbach Graul, C.F.O., Treas. & Public
  Info. Off.

Consolidated Balance Sheet As of December 31, 1996 (000 omitted)

Assets		Liabilities & Stockholders' Equity	
Current assets	$ 57,795	Current liabilities	$ 35,914
Net property, plant & equipment	27,453	Long-term debt	62,500
Other assets	75,592	Deferred items	6,998
		Other liabilities	6,502
		*Stockholders' equity	48,926
Total	$160,840	Total	$160,840

*19,915,693 shares common stock outstanding.

Consolidated Income Statement[a]

Years Ended Dec. 31	Thousands — — — — Net Sales	Net Income	Per Share — — — Earnings[b]	Cash Dividends[b]	Common Stock Price Range Calendar Year
1996	$ 90,763	$5,526	$ .22	$ .26	9-3/4 — 6-5/8
1995	87,204	6,298	.26	.26	11 — 5-7/8
1994	103,889	9,595[c]			13-3/8 — 8-1/4[d]
1993	95,809	7,608[e]			
1992	82,860	7,592[e]			

[a]From continuing operations.
[b]Because of the limited number of stockholders prior to the December 30, 1994, merger between Schawk, Inc. and Filtertek, Inc., earnings and dividends per share are not meaningful for 1992-1994.
[c]Includes a deferred tax charge of $3,000,000 for the termination of S corporation status.
[d]Stock price for Filtertek, Inc.
[e]Pro forma, based on historical net income, adjusted to reflect a provision for income taxes as if the company had been taxed as a C corporation from 1992 to 1994.

Transfer Agent & Registrar: First Chicago Trust Co. of New York

General Counsel:
  Vedder, Price, Kaufman & Kammholz

Investor Relations: Anita L. Fletcher

Human Resources: Robert Drew

Mgt. Info. Svcs.: Stephen Kaufman

Auditors: Ernst & Young LLP

Traded (Symbol): NYSE (SGK)

Stockholders: 2,100

Employees: 850

Annual Meeting: In May

Internet: www.schawk.com

Scotsman Industries, Inc.

775 Corporate Woods Parkway, Vernon Hills, Illinois 60061-3112
Telephone: (847) 215-4500

Scotsman Industries, Inc. is a worldwide supplier of refrigeration products and technologies to the foodservice, hospitality, beverage, and health care industries. Products include ice machines, refrigerators, freezers, food preparation workstations, and drink and ice dispensing equipment, and are sold internationally under the Scotsman, Crystal Tips, Booth, Tecnomac, Simag, Rapid Freeze, Delfield, Whitlenge, and Icematic brand names. The company manufactures its products through seven operations: Scotsman; Booth/Crystal Tips; Frimont; The Delfield Company; Whitlenge Drink Equipment Limited; Hartek Beverage Handling GmbH; and Castel MAC. In March 1997, the company acquired Cadillac, Michigan-based Kysor Industrial Corp., a manufacturer of refrigeration systems for supermarkets and convenience stores. Incorporated in Delaware in 1989.

Directors   (In addition to indicated officers)

Donald C. Clark
Timothy C. Collins
Frank W. Considine

Matthew O. Diggs, Jr.
George D. Kennedy
Robert G. Rettig

Officers   (Directors*)

*Richard C. Osborne, Chm., Pres. & C.E.O.
Richard M. Holden, V.P.—Hum. Res.
Donald D. Holmes, V.P.—Fin. & Secy.
Christopher D. Hughes, V.P. &
 Pres.—Booth/Crystal Tips
Randall C. Rossi, V.P. & Pres.—Scotsman Ice Sys.

William J. Rotenberry, V.P.—Bus. Dev.
Emanuele Lanzani, Exec. V.P.—Frimont & Castel MAC
Michael de St. Paer, V.P.—Whitlenge Drink Equip. Ltd.
Ludwig Klein, V.P.—Hartek Bev. Hndlg. GmbH

Consolidated Balance Sheet   As of December 29, 1996 (000 omitted)

Assets		Liabilities & Stockholders' Equity	
Current assets	$137,574	Current liabilities	$ 78,253
Net property, plant & equipment	46,659	Long-term debt	60,289
Other assets	99,031	Deferred items	3,710
		Other liabilities	9,300
		*Stockholders' equity	131,712
Total	$283,264	Total	$283,264

*10,729,513 shares common stock outstanding.

Consolidated Income Statement[a]

Years Ended Abt. Dec. 31	Thousands — — — — Net Sales	Net Income	Per Share — — — Earnings	Cash Dividends	Common Stock Price Range Calendar Year
1996[b]	$356,373	$18,568	$1.85	$ .10	24-7/8 — 17
1995[b]	324,291	15,408	1.58	.10	20 — 15-1/8
1994[c]	266,632	12,785	1.49	.10	18-1/4 — 13
1993	163,952	7,411	1.06	.10	14-1/2 — 9-1/8
1992	168,674	6,392	.90	.10	10-5/8 — 7-1/8

[a]Fiscal year ends on the Sunday nearest to December 31.
[b]Includes the results of Hartek which was acquired on December 31, 1995.
[c]Includes the results of Delfield and Whitlenge subsequent to their acquisitions on April 29, 1994.

Transfer Agent & Registrar:	Harris Trust and Savings Bank		
General Counsel:	Schiff, Hardin & Waite	Traded (Symbol):	NYSE (SCT)
Investor Relations:	Donald D. Holmes, V.P.	Stockholders:	4,800
Human Resources:	Richard M. Holden, V.P.	Employees:	4,000
Auditors:	Arthur Andersen LLP	Annual Meeting:	In May

Sears, Roebuck and Co.

3333 Beverly Road, Hoffman Estates, Illinois 60179
Telephone: (847) 286-2500

Sears, Roebuck and Co. conducts merchandising and credit operations in the United States, Canada, and Mexico. Domestic operations include: 806 department stores which sell apparel and home-related products; 1,500 off-the-mall hardware, furniture, dealer, and automotive stores; and home-related repair and installation services and credit operations. Principal subsidiaries include: Sears Canada (61.1 percent owned); Sears Roebuck de Mexico, S.A. de C.V. (15 percent owned); Western Auto Supply; Sears Logistics Services, Inc.; and Sears Roebuck Acceptance Corp. In September 1996, the company acquired California-based Orchard Supply Hardware Stores Corp. Incorporated in New York in 1906.

Directors   (In addition to indicated officers)

Hall Adams, Jr.	Richard C. Notebaert	Donald H. Rumsfeld
Warren L. Batts	Hugh B. Price	Patrick G. Ryan
Alston D. Correll, Jr.	Nancy C. Reynolds	Dorothy A. Terrell
Michael A. Miles	Clarence B. Rogers, Jr.	

Officers   (Directors*)

*Arthur C. Martinez, Chm., Pres. & C.E.O.
John H. Costello, Sr. Exec. V.P. & Gen. Mgr.—Mktg.
Alan J. Lacy, Exec. V.P. & C.F.O.
William G. Pagonis, Exec. V.P.—Logistics
Anthony J. Rucci, Exec. V.P.—Admin.
Michael D. Levin, Sr. V.P., Gen. Coun. & Secy.

Joseph A. Smialowski, Sr. V.P. & C.I.O.
Paul A. Baffico, Pres.—Auto Grp. & Tire Div.
Gary L. Crittenden, Pres.—Hardware
Steven D. Goldstein, Pres.—Credit
Robert L. Mettler, Pres.—Merchandising
William L. Salter, Pres.—Home Stores
Alan B. Stewart, Pres.—Retail Stores
Jane J. Thompson, Pres.—Home Services

Consolidated Balance Sheet   As of December 28, 1996 (000 omitted)

Assets		Liabilities & Stockholders' Equity	
Current assets	$28,447,000	Current liabilities	$14,950,000
Net property, plant & equipment	5,878,000	Long-term debt	12,170,000
Deferred income taxes	905,000	Post-retirement benefits	2,748,000
Other assets	937,000	Other liabilities	1,354,000
		Stockholders' equity	4,945,000
Total	$36,167,000	Total	$36,167,000

*391,394,000 shares common stock outstanding.

Consolidated Income Statement

Years Ended Abt. Dec. 31[a]	Thousands — — — —		Per Share — — — —		Common Stock
	Revenues[b]	Net Income[b]	Earnings[b]	Cash Dividends[c]	Price Range[c] Calendar Year
1996	$38,326,000	$ 1,271,000	$ 3.12	$ .92	53-7/8 — 38-1/4
1995	34,995,000	1,025,000	2.53	1.26	60 — 30
1994	33,110,000	857,000[d]	2.13[d]	1.60	55-1/8 — 42-1/8
1993	30,516	625,000[e]	1.56[e]	1.60	60-1/8 — 39-7/8
1992	32,943,000	(1,812,000)[f]	(4.98)[f]	2.00	48 — 37

[a]Years ended December 31 in 1994, 1993, and 1992.
[b]From continuing operations.
[c]Dividends and stock prices have not been restated to reflect the Allstate and Dean Witter, Discover distributions.
[d]Includes an extraordinary gain related to early extinguishment of debt of $195,000,000 ($.50 per share).
[e]Includes an extraordinary loss related to early extinguishment of debt of $210,800,000 ($.55 per share).
[f]Includes a charge to reflect FAS 106 and FAS 112, resulting in a cumulative effect of $1,873,400,000 ($5.07 per share).

Transfer Agent & Registrar:	First Chicago Trust Co. of New York		
General Counsel:	Michael D. Levin, Sr. V.P.	Traded (Symbol):	NYSE, CSE, PSE, London, Amsterdam, Frankfort, Tokyo, Swiss (S)
Investor Relations:	Jerome J. Leshne, Dir.		
Human Resources:	Anthony J. Rucci, Exec. V.P.	Stockholders:	242,246
Mgt. Info. Svcs.:	Joseph A. Smialowski, Sr. V.P.	Employees:	335,000
		Annual Meeting:	In May
Auditors:	Deloitte & Touche LLP	Internet:	www.sears.com

ServiceMaster Limited Partnership

One ServiceMaster Way, Downers Grove, Illinois 60515-9969
Telephone: (630) 271-1300

ServiceMaster Limited Partnership represents a portfolio of service companies with two major operating units, ServiceMaster Consumer Services and ServiceMaster Management Services. Other developing segments include ServiceMaster Diversified Health Services and International and New Business Development. ServiceMaster Consumer Services includes seven companies: ServiceMaster Residential and Commercial Services; Terminix; TruGreen-ChemLawn; Merry Maids; American Home Shield; Furniture Medic; and AmeriSpec; all of which operate through the ServiceMaster Quality Services Network of more than 5,700 company-owned and franchised businesses. ServiceMaster Management Services is a leading company serving 2,300 long-term and acute care health care customers, education customers, and industrial and commercial facilities with management of plant operations and maintenance, housekeeping, clinical equipment maintenance, food service, laundry, grounds, and energy. ServiceMaster Limited Partnership serves 6.5 million customers in the United States and in over 30 foreign countries. In February 1997, ServiceMaster completed the acquisition of Barefoot Inc., a Columbus, Ohio-based lawn-care company. Incorporated in Delaware in 1986.

Directors (In addition to indicated officers)

Paul W. Berezny, Jr.	Vincent C. Nelson
Henry O. Boswell	Kay A. Orr
Lord Griffiths of Fforestfach	Dallen W. Peterson
Sidney E. Harris	Donald G. Soderquist
Herbert P. Hess	Burton E. Sorensen
Michelle Hunt	David K. Wessner
Gunther H. Knoedler	
James D. McLennan	

Officers (Directors*)

*C. William Pollard, Chm.	Eric R. Zarnikow, V.P. & Treas.
*Carlos H. Cantu, Pres. & C.E.O.	William C. Dowdy, Pres.—Healthcare
*Phillip B. Rooney, V. Chm.	Robert D. Erickson, Pres./C.O.O.—Intl. & New Bus. Dev.
*Charles W. Stair, V. Chm.	Robert F. Keith, Pres./C.O.O.—Mgmt. Svcs.
Steven Preston, Sr. V.P. & C.F.O.	Jerry D. Mooney, Pres./C.O.O.—Healthcare New Bus.
Vernon T. Squires, Sr. V.P. & Gen. Coun.	Ernest J. Mrozek, Pres./C.O.O.—Consumer Svcs.
Deborah A. O'Connor, V.P. & Cont.	Richard Williams, Pres.—Education

Consolidated Balance Sheet   As of December 31, 1996 (000 omitted)

Assets		Liabilities & Stockholders' Equity	
Current assets	$ 499,334	Current liabilities	$ 425,552
Net property, plant & equipment	146,400	Long-term debt	482,315
Other assets	1,201,107	Other liabilities	125,299
		Minority and general partners' interest	16,908
		*Stockholders' equity	796,767
Total	$1,846,841	Total	$1,846,841

*142,398,000 shares common stock outstanding.

Consolidated Income Statement

Years Ended Dec. 31	Thousands — — — — Operating Revenues	Net Income[a]	Per Share[b] — — — — Earnings[a]	Cash Dividends	Common Stock Price Range[b] Calendar Year
1996	$3,458,328	$245,140	$1.70	$ .66	26-5/8 — 19-3/8
1995	3,202,504	172,019	1.45	.63	20-1/4 — 14-3/8
1994	2,985,207	139,883	1.20	.61	18-7/8 — 14-3/8
1993	2,758,859	115,747	1.00	.59	20-5/8 — 11-3/4
1992	2,488,854	94,394	.83	.58	13-1/4 — 9-3/4

[a]Excludes unusual items.
[b]Adjusted to reflect 3-for-2 stock splits in June 1996, June 1993, and January 1992.

Transfer Agent:	Harris Trust and Savings Bank			
General Counsel:	Vernon T. Squires, Sr. V.P.	Traded (Symbol):	NYSE (SVM)
Investor Relations:	Bruce T. Duncan, V.P.	Stockholders:	65,000
Human Resources:	William W. Hargreaves, V.P.	Employees:	50,000
Mgt. Info. Svcs.:	Douglas E. Nies, V.P.	Annual Meeting:	In May
Auditors:	Arthur Andersen LLP	Internet:	www.servicemaster.com

Shelby Williams Industries, Inc.

11-111 Merchandise Mart, Chicago, Illinois 60654
Telephone: (312) 527-3593

Shelby Williams designs, manufactures, and distributes products for the contract furniture market. The company has a significant position in the hospitality and foodservice markets through its Shelby Williams® seating line and King Arthur® line of function room furniture and Sterno® accessories. The company provides contemporary upholstered seating products under the names Preview® and Madison®. It serves health care, university, office furniture, and other institutional markets through its Thonet® division with health care and dormitory furniture, including chairs and tables, and ergonomically designed office seating products, desks, and credenzas. The company also distributes vinyl wall coverings for residential, hotel, and office use under the name Sellers & Josephson®, and markets other textile products to the architectural and design community through SW Textiles®. The company distributes floor coverings and other textile products, as well as Shelby Williams products, in Hawaii and the entire Pacific Basin through PHF®. Incorporated in Delaware in 1976.

Directors   (In addition to indicated officers)

Robert L. Haag
William B. Kaplan
Douglas A. Parker

Herbert L. Roth
Trisha Wilson

Officers   (Directors*)

*Paul N. Steinfeld, Chm. & C.E.O.
*Robert P. Coulter, Pres. & C.O.O.
*Manfred Steinfeld, Chm.—Exec. Comm.
Peter W. Barile, Exec. V.P.
Dennis E. Gurley, Sr. V.P.—Mfg.

Sam Ferrell, V.P.—Fin., Treas. & C.F.O.
William Lau, V.P.—Intl. Oper.
Michael E. Moore, V.P.—Sales
Walter Roth, Secy.

Consolidated Balance Sheet   As of December 31, 1996 (000 omitted)

Assets		Liabilities & Stockholders' Equity	
Current assets	$57,177	Current liabilities	$19,571
Net property, plant & equipment	25,961	Long-term debt	7,000
Other assets	1,540	Deferred items	2,137
		*Stockholders' equity	55,970
Total	$84,678	Total	$84,678

*8,767,000 shares common stock outstanding.

Consolidated Income Statement

Years Ended Dec. 31	Thousands — — — — Net Sales	Net Income	Per Share — — — Earnings	Cash Dividends	Common Stock Price Range Calendar Year
1996	$172,431	$8,417	$ .96	$ .30	14-3/4 — 10-1/8
1995	166,776	6,780	.76	.28	13-3/4 — 7-1/2
1994	159,072	365[a]	.04[a]	.28	14-3/8 — 7-1/2
1993	153,527	4,150	.46	.28	14-7/8 — 10-1/8
1992	140,262	3,594	.39	.24	11 — 6-3/8

[a]Reflects restructuring charges of $3,850,000 ($.43 per share).

Transfer Agent & Registrar: Wachovia Bank of North Carolina, N.A.

General Counsel:	D'Ancona & Pflaum	Auditors:	Ernst & Young LLP
Investor Relations:	Robert P. Coulter, Pres.	Traded (Symbol):	NYSE (SY)
Human Resources:	Robert P. Coulter, Pres.	Stockholders:	3,000
		Employees:	1,667
Mgt. Info. Svcs.:	Sam Ferrell, V.P.	Annual Meeting:	In May

SigmaTron International, Inc.

2201 Landmeier Road, Elk Grove Village, Illinois 60007
Telephone: (847) 956-8000

SigmaTron International, Inc. is an independent contract manufacturer of electronic components, printed circuit board assemblies, and turnkey (completely assembled) electronics products. Included among the wide range of services that the company offers its customers are manual and automatic assembly and testing of customer products; material sourcing, procurement, and control; design, manufacturing, and test engineering support; warehousing and shipment services; and assistance in obtaining product approvals from governmental and other regulatory bodies. The company provides these services through an international network of facilities located in North America and the Far East. Circuit Systems, Inc. has approximately a 20 percent interest in the company. Incorporated in Delaware in 1993.

Directors   (In addition to indicated officers)

Franklin D. Sove, Chm.
John P. Chen
William C. Mitchell
D.S. Patel

Thomas W. Rieck
Steven A. Rothstein
Dilip S. Vyas

Officers   (Directors*)

*Gary R. Fairhead, Pres. & C.E.O.
 Linda K. Blake, V.P.—Fin., C.F.O., Treas. & Secy.
 Gregory A. Fairhead, V.P.—Mexico Oper. & Asst. Secy.

John P. Sheehan, V.P.—Dir. of Mat. & Asst. Secy.
Nunzio A. Truppa, V.P.—Dom. Oper.

Consolidated Balance Sheet   As of April 30, 1996 (000 omitted)

Assets		Liabilities & Stockholders' Equity	
Current assets	$28,252	Current liabilities	$ 9,598
Net property, plant & equipment	7,230	Long-term debt	15,296
Other assets	2,833	Deferred items	652
		*Stockholders' Equity	12,769
Total	$38,315	Total	$38,315

*2,737,500 shares common stock outstanding.

Consolidated Income Statement[a]

Years Ended April 30	Thousands — — — — Net Sales	Net Income	Per Share — — — — Earnings	Cash Dividends	Common Stock Price Range[b] Calendar Year
1996	$69,600	$2,400	$ .86	$ .00	20-3/4 — 5-1/2
1995	45,345	1,891	.69	.00	9-1/4 — 6-7/8
1994	36,690	1,862[c]	.59[d]	.00	9-1/2 — 6
1993	29,764	1,383			
1992	22,123	288			

[a]In February 1991, SigmaTron, Inc., the predecessor, was restructured as a partnership. SigmaTron International, Inc. is the successor to all of the assets and liabilities of SigmaTron L.P., through a reorganization.
[b]Initial public offering in February 1994.
[c]Includes a charge to reflect FAS 109, resulting in a cumulative effect of $527,000.
[d]Unaudited pro forma.

Transfer Agent & Registrar: American Stock Transfer & Trust Co.

General Counsel:	D'Ancona & Pflaum	Traded (Symbol):	NASDAQ (SGMA)
Investor Relations:	Linda K. Blake, V.P.	Stockholders:	76
Human Resources:	Nancy Geiser	Employees:	1,500
Auditors:	Ernst & Young LLP	Annual Meeting:	In September

SoftNet Systems, Inc.
717 Forest Avenue, Lake Forest, Illinois 60045
Telephone: (847) 266-8150

SoftNet Systems, Inc. is a single-source provider for integrated imaging and telecommunications solutions. The company develops, markets, installs, and services electronic information and document management systems which allow users to request and retrieve information electronically. Products include hardware and software systems designed to capture, index, store, and retrieve information through the integration of telecommunications with magnetic disks, optical disks, microfilm, and paper. In June 1996, the company completed its acquisiton of MediaCity World, Inc., a Palo Alto, California-based Internet service provider. Incorporated in New York in 1956 as The Vader Group Inc.; present name adopted in 1993.

Directors   (In addition to indicated officers)

John G. Hamm   Ronald I. Simon

Officers   (Directors*)

*John J. McDonough, Chm. & C.E.O.   *Ian B. Aaron, C.I.O.
*A.J.R. Oosthuizen, Pres. & C.O.O.   Martin A. Koehler, V.P.—Fin. & C.F.O.

Consolidated Balance Sheet   As of September 30, 1996 (000 omitted)

Assets		Liabilities & Stockholders' Equity	
Current assets	$12,744	Current liabilities	$11,031
Net property, plant & equipment	2,314	Long-term debt	10,762
Other assets	2,427	*Stockholders' equity	3,793
Goodwill	8,101		
Total	$25,586	Total	$25,586

*6,540,000 shares common stock outstanding.

Consolidated Income Statement

Years Ended Sept. 30	Thousands — — — — Net Sales	Net Income	Per Share — — — Earnings	Cash Dividends	Common Stock Price Range Calendar Year
1996	$41,387	$(6,097)	$(1.05)	$ .00	11 — 4
1995	21,252	(9,655)	(2.22)	.00	16-3/8 — 5-3/4
1994	9,629	(1,427)	(.38)	.00	9 — 5-1/8
1993	47	(828)	(.37)	.00	7-1/8 — 2-5/8

Transfer Agent & Registrar: ChaseMellon Shareholder Services, L.L.C.

General Counsel:	McDermott, Will & Emery	Traded (Symbol):	AMEX (SOF)
Investor Relations:	Martin A. Koehler, V.P.	Stockholders:	467
		Employees:	263
Mgt. Info. Svcs.:	Ian B. Aaron, C.I.O.	Annual Meeting:	In March
Auditors:	Coopers & Lybrand L.L.P.	Internet:	www.softnet.com

Southwest Bancshares, Inc.

4062 Southwest Highway, Hometown, Illinois 60456-1134
Telephone: (708) 636-2700

Southwest Bancshares, Inc. is the holding company for Southwest Federal Savings and Loan Association of Chicago, originally organized in 1883, and Southwest Bancshares Development Corporation. Southwest Federal is a community-oriented, federally insured savings institution, focused on developing long-term deposit relationships with customers and providing residential lending, primarily in southwest Chicago and neighboring suburbs. It serves customers from six offices, the last of which was opened during 1993. It maintains one office in the Chicago Lawn community of Chicago, two offices in Oak Lawn, one in Hometown, one in Cicero, and one in Orland Park, Illinois. Southwest Bancshares Development Corporation engages in real estate development activity. Incorporated in Delaware in 1992.

Directors (In addition to indicated officers)

James W. Gee, Sr.
Joseph A. Herbert
Robert E. Lawler, D.D.S.

Frank J. Muriello
Albert Rodrigues

Officers (Directors*)

*Lawrence M. Cox, Chm.
*Richard E. Webber, Pres. & C.E.O.
 Robert J. Eckert, V.P.
 Michael J. Gembara, V.P.

Ronald D. Phares, V.P.
Mary A. McNally, Secy.
Robert C. Olson, Compt.
Noralee Goossens, Asst. Secy.

Consolidated Balance Sheet As of December 31, 1996 (000 omitted)

Assets		Liabilities & Stockholders' Equity	
Cash & cash equivalents	$ 11,680	Deposits	$280,434
Loans receivable	262,431	Borrowed funds	55,158
Mortgage-backed securities, net	32,840	Other liabilities	6,910
Other investments	61,091	*Stockholders' equity	39,859
Other assets	14,319		
Total	$382,361	Total	$382,361

*2,637,461 shares common stock outstanding.

Consolidated Income Statement

Years Ended Dec. 31	Thousands — — — — Total Income	Net Income	Per Share[ab] — — — Earnings	Cash Dividends	Common Stock Price Range[a] Calendar Year
1996	$28,537	$2,628	$ .91	$ .73	18-3/4 — 17-3/8
1995	28,137	4,532	1.31	.68	19 — 13-7/8
1994	26,125	6,067	1.61	.17	16-5/8 — 12-5/8
1993	25,948	6,402	1.59	.80[c]	14-7/8 — 10-1/8
1992	26,369	5,348	1.26	.00	11-1/2 — 7-5/8

[a]Adjusted to reflect a 3-for-2 stock split in November 1996.
[b]Initial public offering in June 1992.
[c]Special dividend.

Transfer Agent & Registrar:	Harris Trust and Savings Bank		
General Counsel:	Muldoon, Murphy & Faucette	Auditors:	Cobitz, VandenBerg and Fennessy
Investor Relations:	Ronald D. Phares, V.P.	Traded (Symbol):	NASDAQ (SWBI)
Human Resources:	Robert J. Eckert, V.P.	Stockholders:	422
		Employees:	101
Mgt. Info. Svcs.:	Michael J. Gembara, V.P.	Annual Meeting:	In April

Specialty Equipment Companies, Inc.

1245 Corporate Boulevard, Suite 401, Aurora, Illinois 60504
Telephone: (630) 585-5111

Specialty Equipment Companies, Inc. manufactures a diversified line of highly engineered commercial and institutional foodservice equipment used by a variety of quick service restaurant chains, convenience store chains, specialty chains, soft drink bottlers, and institutional foodservice operators. The company emphasizes the engineering and development of specially designed, state-of-the-art foodservice equipment, and sells a broad array of standardized foodservice equipment and related products in over 85 countries worldwide. Specialty Equipment conducts its business through four principal operating divisions: Taylor Company, Beverage-Air, Wells Manufacturing/Bloomfield Industries, and World Dryer. Incorporated in Delaware in 1984

Directors (In addition to indicated officers)

William E. Dotterweich
Avram A. Glazer
Kevin E. Glazer
Malcolm I. Glazer

Charles E. Hutchinson
Richard A. Kent
Barry L. MacLean

Officers (Directors*)

*Daniel B. Greenwood, Chm.
 Jeffrey P. Rhodenbaugh, Pres. & C.E.O.

Donald K. McKay, Exec. V.P., C.F.O., Treas. & Secy.

Consolidated Balance Sheet As of January 31, 1997 (000 omitted)

Assets		Liabilities & Stockholders' Equity	
Current assets	$132,431	Current liabilities	$ 90,303
Net property, plant & equipment	34,217	Long-term debt	155,440
Other assets	10,268	Other liabilities	2,404
		*Stockholders' equity	(71,231)
Total	$176,916	Total	$176,916

*17,985,918 shares common stock outstanding.

Consolidated Income Statement

Years Ended Jan. 31	Thousands — — — — Net Revenue	Net Income	Per Share[a] — — — Earnings	Cash Dividends	Common Stock Price Range[a] Calendar Year
1997	$401,230	$ 32,338[b]	$ 1.51[b]	$ .00	
1996	392,512	8,693[b]	.41[b]	.00	15-3/4 — 10-1/4
1995	371,730	(53,996)	(3.29)	.00	14 — 9-1/4
1994	320,873	(58,420)	(3.56)	.00	11 — 5
1993[c]	229,745	(54,198)	(3.30)	.00	7-1/4 — 4-1/2

[a]Trading commenced on December 1, 1993.
[b]Includes the recognition of tax benefits related to deferred assets of $7,200,000 ($.33 per share) in 1997 and $5,100,000 ($.24 per share) in 1996.
[c]For the period March 31, 1992, to January 31, 1993. Due to the company's emergence from Chapter 11 bankruptcy, the company adopted fresh start reporting on March 31, 1992.

Transfer Agent & Registrar: LaSalle National Trust, N.A.

General Counsel: Sonnenschein Nath & Rosenthal

Investor Relations: Donald K. McKay, Exec. V.P.

Auditors: KPMG Peat Marwick LLP

Traded (Symbol):   NASDAQ (SPEQ)

Stockholders: 1,560

Employees: 2,274

Annual Meeting: In April

Internet:
www.specialty-equipment.com

Spiegel, Inc.

3500 Lacey Road, Downers Grove, Illinois 60515-5432
Telephone: (630) 986-8800

Spiegel, Inc. is a leading international specialty retailer marketing fashionable apparel and home furnishings to customers through catalogs, innovative electronic platforms, and more than 450 specialty stores. The company features upscale American designer and brand name merchandise such as Liz Claiborne, Ralph Lauren, Calvin Klein, and Laura Ashley. Spiegel's merchandise is marketed under its own tradenames and trademarks, and under tradenames licensed from others. The company purchases all of its merchandise on the open market from about 7,600 suppliers, selling both domestically produced and imported merchandise. Customers may order merchandise either by calling a toll-free number or mailing an order form located inside the catalog. Telephone orders constitute approximately 93 percent of total orders. Eddie Bauer, Inc., a specialty retailer, sells men's and women's casual sportswear, gifts, and outdoor equipment through catalogs and 443 retail stores. Other principal subsidiaries include Newport News, Inc. and First Consumer National Bank. Spiegel Holdings, Inc. holds 99.9 percent of the company's Class B voting common stock. Spiegel and its predecessors date back to 1865, and since 1905, Spiegel has operated as a catalog merchandiser. Incorporated in Delaware in 1965.

Directors (In addition to indicated officers)

Michael Otto, Chm.	Hans-Jorg Hammer	Peer Witten
Thomas Bohlmann	Horst R. Hansen	Martin Zaepfel
Michael E. Crüsemann	Karl-August Hopmann	
Richard T. Fersch	Peter Müller	

Officers (Directors*)

*Harold S. Dahlstrand, Chm.—Off. of the Pres.; Sr. V.P.—Hum. Res.
Michael R. Moran, Off. of the Pres.; Sr. V.P., Secy. & Gen. Coun.
James W. Sievers, Off. of the Pres.; Sr. V.P.—Fin. & C.F.O.
Jon A. Coble, V.P.—Bus. Dev.
Deborah L. Koopman, V.P.—Pub. Aff. & Inv. Rel.
Jon K. Nordeen, V.P. & C.I.O.

Melissa Payner, V.P.—Merch.
John R. Steele, V.P. & Treas.
D. Skip Behm, Cont.
Gregory R. Aube, Pres.—First Consumers Natl. Bank
Richard T. Fersch, Pres.—Eddie Bauer
*John W. Irvin, Pres.—Spiegel Catalog
George D. Ittner, Pres.—Newport News
Michael L. Wilson, Pres.—Dist. Fulfillment Svcs.

Consolidated Balance Sheet As of December 31, 1996 (000 omitted)

Assets		Liabilities & Stockholders' Equity	
Current assets	$1,211,535	Current liabilities	$ 695,396
Net property, plant & equipment	399,910	Long-term debt	676,656
Other assets	334,180	Deferred items	52,024
		*Stockholders' equity	521,549
Total	$1,945,625	Total	$1,945,625

*14,618,404 shares Class A non-voting common and 93,141,654 shares Class B voting common stock outstanding.

Consolidated Income Statement

Years Ended Dec. 31	Thousands — — — — Net Sales	Net Income	Per Share[a] — — — Earnings	Cash Dividends	Common Stock Price Range[ab] Calendar Year
1996	$3,014,620	$(13,389)	$ (.12)	$ .00	13-1/4 — 6-1/2
1995	3,184,184	(9,481)	(.09)	.20	13-7/8 — 6-7/8
1994	3,015,985	25,100	.23	.20	26-3/4 — 8-3/4
1993	2,596,147	48,705	.47	.20	23-3/8 — 7-3/4
1992	2,218,732	43,224[c]	.42[c]	.18	9 — 5

[a]Adjusted to reflect a 2-for-1 stock split in October 1993.
[b]Class A non-voting common stock.
[c]Includes a gain to reflect FAS 109, resulting in a cumulative effect of $4,101,000 ($.04 per share).

Transfer Agent & Registrar:	Harris Trust and Savings Bank		
Outside Counsel:	Rooks, Pitts and Poust	Traded (Symbol):	NASDAQ (SPGLA)
Investor Relations:	Deborah L. Koopman, V.P.	Stockholders:	12,000
Human Resources:	Harold S. Dahlstrand, Sr. V.P.	Employees:	15,000
Mgt. Info. Svcs.:	Jon K. Nordeen, V.P. & C.I.O.	Annual Meeting:	In April
Auditors:	KPMG Peat Marwick LLP	Internet:	www.spiegel.com & www.ebauer.com

Sportmart, Inc.

1400 South Wolf Road, Suite 200, Wheeling, Illinois 60090
Telephone: (847) 520-0100

Sportmart, Inc. is a leading sporting goods superstore retailer. The company pioneered the sporting goods superstore concept in 1971. As of February 1997, the company operated a total of 70 stores in the following metroplitan areas: Chicago (16 stores); Los Angeles (13); San Francisco/Sacramento (11); Minneapolis (5); Seattle (3); Columbus, Ohio (3); San Diego (2); Milwaukee (2); Portland, Oregon (2); Cleveland (1); and Des Moines, Iowa (1). The company also operated 11 stores in Canada. On January 16, 1997, Sportmart announced the closing of its Canadian stores. Incorporated in Illinois in 1971; reincorporated in Delaware in 1992.

Directors (In addition to indicated officers)

Charles G. Cooper
Jerome S. Gore

Stuart C. Nathan
Lawrence J. Ring, Ph.D.

Officers (Directors*)

*Larry J. Hochberg, Chm.
*C. Mark Scott, Pres.
*Andrew S. Hochberg, C.E.O.
*John A. Lowenstein, C.O.O. & Secy.
 Thomas T. Hendrickson, Exec. V.P.—Fin. & C.F.O.
 Joseph A. DeFalco, Sr. V.P.—Hum. Res.
 Robert P. Hayes, Sr. V.P.—Merch.
 David Howard, Sr. V.P.—Mgt. Info. Svcs.
 Mitchell P. Kahn, Sr. V.P.—Corp. Dev.
 Robert M. Morrison, Sr. V.P.—Stores

John E. Smith, Jr., Sr. V.P.—Mktg.
Steven J. Boxer, V.P.—Div. Merch. & Mgr.—Footwear
Alexander R. Cameron, V.P.—Div. Merch. & Mgr.—Sports
Gregory J. Dooley, V.P. & Treas.
Gregory E. Fix, V.P., Gen. Coun. & Asst. Secy.
Frank R. Ippolito, V.P. & Cont.
Daniel D. Kester, V.P.—Planning & Allocation
David D. Southworth, V.P.—Div. Merch. & Mgr.—Fitness
John Swanstrom, V.P.—Logistics & Dist.

Consolidated Balance Sheet As of February 2, 1997 (000 omitted)

Assets		Liabilities & Stockholders' Equity	
Current assets	$193,702	Current liabilities	$184,501
Net property, plant & equipment	61,750	Other liabilities	8,177
Other assets	11,145	*Stockholders' equity	73,919
Total	$266,597	Total	$266,597

*12,843,567 shares common stock outstanding.

Consolidated Income Statement

Years Ended Abt. Jan. 31	Thousands — — — —		Per Share — — — —		Common Stock Price Range Calendar Year
	Net Sales	Net Income	Earnings	Cash Dividends	
1997	$514,611	$(27,059)	$(2.11)	$ .00	
1996	492,179	(6,444)	(.32)	.00	10-7/8 — 4-3/4
1995	424,189	8,935	.82	.00	11-1/2 — 4
1994	338,427	7,879	.77	.00	16-1/2 — 9-5/8
1993[a]	250,529	5,362[b]	.60[b]	.00	17-3/4 — 7-1/4

[a]Restated.
[b]Pro forma. Prior to the initial public offering, the company was an S corporation subject to federal (and some state) corporate income taxes. Data is adjusted to reflect a pro forma tax provision as if the company were subject to corporate income taxes for such periods.

Transfer Agent & Registrar: LaSalle National Bank

General Counsel:	Katten Muchin & Zavis	Traded (Symbol):	NASDAQ (SPMT, SPMTA)
Investor Relations: Thomas T. Hendrickson, Exec. V.P.		Annual Meeting:	In June
Human Resources:	Joseph A. DeFalco, Sr. V.P.	Stockholders:	199
Mgt. Info. Svcs.:	David Howard, Sr. V.P.	Employees:	4,246
Auditors:	Coopers & Lybrand L.L.P.	Internet:	www.sportmart.com

SPS Transaction Services, Inc.

2500 Lake Cook Road, Riverwoods, Illinois 60015
Telephone: (847) 405-0200

SPS Transaction Services, Inc. is a leading third-party provider of technology-driven operating services. Principal activities include the electronic processing of credit card transactions, as well as providing customized operating outsourcing solutions, such as private-label credit card programs, dispatch services, and on-line technical help desk support. SPS serves industries that emphasize point-of-sale and customer service operations, including specialty retail, petroleum/convenience store, office supply, electronics, health care, and airlines. The company operates its business through two wholly owned subsidiaries, SPS Payment Systems, Inc. and Hurley State Bank. SPS Transaction Services, Inc. is a 74 percent owned subsidiary of Novus Credit Services, Inc., which is a wholly owned subsidiary of Dean Witter, Discover and Co. Incorporated in Delaware in 1991.

Directors (In addition to indicated officers)

Frank T. Cary
Mitchell M. Merin
Charles F. Moran

Philip J. Purcell
Dennie M. Welsh

Officers (Directors*)

*Thomas C. Schneider, Chm. & C.F.O.
*Robert L. Wieseneck, Pres. & C.E.O.
Robert W. Archer, Sr. V.P.—Sales & Oper.
Richard F. Atkinson, Sr. V.P.—Consumer Credit Svcs.
David J. Peterson, Sr. V.P.—Comm. Tech. Svcs.
Russell J. Bonaguidi, V.P. & Cont.

Robert J. Ferkenhoff, V.P. & Chf. Info. Off.
Thomas M. Goldstein, V.P.—Fin.
Larry H. Myatt, V.P.—Mktg. & Admin.
Ruth M. O'Brien, V.P.—Teleservices
Serge Uccetta, V.P.—Comm. Acct. Svcs.
Mary Ann Warniment, V.P.—Electronic Info. Svcs.
Christine A. Edwards, Secy. & Gen. Coun.
Birendra Kumar, Treas.

Consolidated Balance Sheet As of December 31, 1996 (000 omitted)

Assets		Liabilities & Stockholders' Equity	
Current assets	$1,679,233	Current liabilities	$1,513,757
Net property, plant & equipment	25,294	Other liabilities	22,636
Other assets	56,258	*Stockholders' equity	224,392
Total	$1,760,785	Total	$1,760,785

*27,187,462 shares common stock outstanding.

Consolidated Income Statement

Years Ended Dec. 31	Thousands — — — — Operating Revenues	Net Income	Per Share[a] — — — Earnings	Cash Dividends	Common Stock Price Range[ab] Calendar Year
1996	$320,920	$23,246	$ .86	$ .00	32-1/2 — 13-1/2
1995	311,992	43,473	1.60	.00	35-1/2 — 24-3/4
1994	245,802	37,735	1.40	.00	32-3/8 — 24
1993	205,494	30,648	1.14	.00	35-5/8 — 18-1/8
1992	165,630	19,663	.76	.00	23-1/8 — 8-1/8

[a]Adjusted to reflect a 2-for-1 stock split in November 1994.
[b]Initial public offering in February 1992.

Transfer Agent & Registrar:	First Chicago Trust Co. of New York		
General Counsel:	Kirkland & Ellis	Traded (Symbol):	NYSE (PAY)
Investor Relations:	Thomas M. Goldstein, V.P.	Stockholders:	3,790
Human Resources:	Larry H. Myatt, V.P.	Employees:	3,881
Mgt. Info. Svcs.:	Robert J. Ferkenhoff, V.P.	Annual Meeting:	In April
Auditors:	Deloitte & Touche LLP	Internet:	www.spspay.com

LaSalle Banks Guide

SPSS Inc.

444 North Michigan Avenue, Chicago, Illinois 60611-3962
Telephone: (312) 329-2400

SPSS Inc. is a multi-national software products company that provides statistical product and service solutions. The company's mission is to drive the widespread use of statistics. SPSS products and services are used worldwide in corporate, academic, and government settings for all types of research and data analysis. The company's four lines of business are: business analysis, including survey research, marketing, and sales analysis and data mining; scientific research; quality improvement; and process management. Headquartered in Chicago, the company has offices and a network of distributors serving countries around the world. In September 1996, SPSS announced that it would acquire Newton, Massachusetts-based Clear Software Inc., a producer of flow-chart and process-management software. In December 1996, the company acquired Jandel Scientific Software Inc. of San Rafael, California. Incorporated in Illinois in 1975; reincorporated in Delaware in 1993.

Directors (In addition to indicated officers)

Guy de Chazal
Bernard Goldstein

Fredric Harman
Merritt Lutz

Officers (Directors*)

*Norman H. Nie, Chm.
*Jack Noonan, Pres. & C.E.O.
 Mark V. Battaglia, Exec. V.P.—Corp. Mktg.
 Ian S. Durrell, Exec. V.P.—Intl.

Edward Hamburg, Ph.D., Exec. V.P.—Corp. Oper., C.F.O. & Secy.
Susan Phelan, Exec. V.P.—Domestic Sales & Svcs.
Louise Rehling, Exec. V.P.—Prod. Dev.

Consolidated Balance Sheet As of December 31, 1996 (000 omitted)

Assets		Liabilities & Stockholders' Equity	
Current assets	$33,767	Current liabilities	$23,229
Net property, plant & equipment	5,539	Deferred items	2,245
Other assets	12,729	Other liabilities	34
		*Stockholders' equity	26,527
Total	$52,035	Total	$52,035

*8,042,426 shares common stock outstanding.

Consolidated Income Statement[a]

Years Ended Dec. 31	Thousands — — — — Net Revenues	Net Income	Per Share[b] — — — — Earnings	Cash Dividends	Common Stock Price Range[b] Calendar Year
1996	$83,989	$ 7,182	$ .85	$ .00	31-3/4 — 13-5/8
1995	73,394	3,875	.48	.00	19-5/8 — 11-3/8
1994[c]	62,594	3,956	.56	.00	14-1/4 — 8-3/8
1993	52,174	3,720	.70	.00	10-1/8 — 7[d]
1992	46,206	(4,122)[e]	(.96)		

[a]Restated to reflect FAS 109.
[b]Adjusted to reflect a 1-for-3 reverse stock split in August 1993.
[c]Includes $1,928,000 in one-time charges related to the acquisition of SYSTAT, Inc., in September 1994.
[d]Initial public offering in August 1993.
[e]Includes a pretax charge of $3,024,000 related to write-off of software.

Transfer Agent & Registrar:	Harris Trust and Savings Bank		
General Counsel:	Ross & Hardies	Traded (Symbol):	NASDAQ (SPSS)
Investor Relations:	David Pittman	Stockholders:	4,250
Human Resources:	Theresa Dear	Employees:	535
		Annual Meeting:	In June
Auditors:	KPMG Peat Marwick LLP	Internet:	www.spss.com

Spyglass, Inc.

1240 East Diehl Road, Fourth Floor, Naperville, Illinois 60563
Telephone: (630) 505-1010

Spyglass, Inc. develops, markets, and distributes World Wide Web client and server technologies for incorporation into a variety of Internet-based products and services. The company is particularly focused on the Internet device market, which consists of non-PC devices and the underlying Internet infrastructure. Spyglass markets its products to a variety of companies: Internet connectivity products to real time operating system vendors and consumer and industrial device manufacturers; and Internet infrastructure and application products to regional Bell operating companies, other telephone companies, cable companies, Internet service providers, and internetworking hardware providers. These technologies are designed to be embedded within Internet devices, software applications, and on-line services to bring Web functionality to these products and services. The company's principal technology offerings include Spyglass Mosaic, Spyglass Web Server, SurfWatch ProServer, SurfWatch, and Surfwatch for Microsoft Proxy Server. Incorporated in Illinois in 1990; reincorporated in Delaware in 1995.

Directors (In addition to indicated officers)

Brian J. Jackson
William S. Kaiser

Ray Rothrock
Steven R. Vana-Paxhia

Officers (Directors*)

*Douglas P. Colbeth, Pres. & C.E.O.
  Rich Houle, Exec. V.P.—Dev. & Svcs.
  Michael F. Tyrrell, Exec. V.P.—Bus. Dev.
  Gary Vilchick, Exec. V.P.—Fin., Admin. &
  Oper. & C.F.O.

*Tim Krauskopf, V.P. & Chf. Tech. Off.
  Randy Littleson, V.P.—Mktg.
  Thomas S. Lewicki, Cont., Treas. & Secy.

Consolidated Balance Sheet   As of September 30, 1996 (000 omitted)

Assets		Liabilities & Stockholders' Equity	
Current assets	$43,785	Current liabilities	$ 4,668
Net property, plant & equipment	3,377	Deferred items	210
Long-term accounts receivable	618	*Stockholders' equity	43,891
Other assets	989		
Total	$48,769	Total	$48,769

*11,406,645 shares common stock outstanding.

Consolidated Income Statement

Years Ended Sept. 30	Thousands — — — — — Net Revenues	Net Income	Per Share[a] — — — — Earnings	Cash Dividends	Common Stock Price Range[ab] Calendar Year	
1996	$22,307	$ 3,460	$ .27	$ .00	55	— 12-1/2
1995	12,141	1,985	.21	.00	61	— 8-1/2
1994	4,667	1,127	.15			
1993[c]	1,375	(577)	(.23)			
1992[c]	918	(645)	(.26)			

[a]Adjusted to reflect conversion of 1,724,099 shares of redeemable convertible preferred stock in June 1995, and a 2-for-1 stock split as a 100 percent stock dividend in December 1995.
[b]Initial public offering in June 1995.
[c]Does not include the results of Stonehand Inc., Surfwatch Software, Inc., or OS Technologies Corp. which were accounted for as pooling-of-interests.

Transfer Agent & Registrar:	American Stock Transfer & Trust Company		
General Counsel:	Hale & Dorr	Traded (Symbol):	NASDAQ (SPYG)
Investor Relations:	Chandler Bigelow	Stockholders:	539
Human Resources:	Lee Nelson	Employees:	145
Mgt. Info. Svcs.:	Tim Seamans	Annual Meeting:	In January
Auditors:	Price Waterhouse LLP	Internet:	www.spyglass.com

Standard Financial, Inc.

4192 South Archer Avenue, Chicago, Illinois 60632-1890
Telephone: (773) 847-1140

Standard Financial, Inc. is the holding company for Standard Federal Bank for savings, which was founded in 1909. The bank is a community-oriented thrift institution offering a variety of retail financial services to meet the needs of the communities it serves. Its deposit-gathering and retail lending markets are primarily concentrated in the communities surrounding its 14 full-service offices, located in the southwestern and western parts of the city of Chicago and neighboring suburbs in Cook and DuPage counties. Two subsidiaries, Standard Financial Mortgage, Inc., a wholesale mortgage operation, and SFB Insurance, an independent insurance agency with a consumer investment division, complete the holdings of the bank. In March 1997, Standard Financial announced that it would merge with TCF Financial Corporation of Minneapolis, Minnesota. TCF will be the surviving entity after the merger is completed in the third quarter of 1997. Incorporated in Delaware in 1994.

Directors (In addition to indicated officers)

Stasys J. Baras
Fred V. Gwyer, M.D.
Tomas A. Kisielius, M.D.
George W. Lane

Jack Levy
Albert M. Petkus
Sharon A. Reese

Officers (Directors*)

*David H. Mackiewich, Chm., Pres. & C.E.O.
*Thomas M. Ryan, Exec. V.P., C.F.O. & C.O.O.
 Kurtis D. Mackiewich, Sr. V.P.

Ruta M. Staniulis, Sr. V.P.
Leonard A. Metheny, V.P. & Secy.
Randall R. Schwartz, V.P. & Gen. Coun.

Consolidated Balance Sheet   As of December 31, 1996 (000 omitted)

Assets		Liabilities & Stockholders' Equity	
Cash & cash equivalents	$ 43,298	Total deposits	$1,719,300
Investment securities	153,501	Advances from FHLB	385,000
Mortgage-backed certificates	651,443	Advance payments by borrowers	11,470
Loans receivable	1,485,459	for taxes & ins.	
Other assets	71,520	Other liabilities	21,373
		*Stockholders' equity	268,078
Total	$2,405,221	Total	$2,405,221

*16,173,235 shares common stock outstanding.

Consolidated Income Statement

Years Ended Dec. 31	Thousands — — — —		Per Share[a] — — —		Common Stock Price Range[a] Calendar Year
	Total Income	Net Income	Earnings	Cash Dividends	
1996	$166,376	$11,912	$ .76	$ .32	21-1/4 — 14-1/8
1995	137,279	16,717	.98	.00	14-7/8 — 9-1/2
1994	104,682	11,055	.37	.00	11-3/4 — 9
1993[b]	97,189	3,868			
1992[b]	114,820	10,007			

[a]Initial public offering in July 1994.
[b]Information is for Standard Federal Bank for savings.

Transfer Agent & Registrar: Harris Trust and Savings Bank

General Counsel:	Randall R. Schwartz, V.P.	Auditors:	Ernst & Young LLP
Investor Relations:	Thomas M. Ryan, Exec. V.P.	Traded (Symbol):	NASDAQ (STND)
Human Resources:	Patricia Barrera	Stockholders:	4,463
		Employees:	466
Mgt. Info. Svcs.:	Mark Collins, V.P.	Annual Meeting:	In April

Stepan Company

Edens Expressway and Winnetka Road, Northfield, Illinois 60093
Telephone: (847) 446-7500

Stepan Company is a major manufacturer of basic and intermediate chemicals used in a broad range of industries. Stepan produces surfactants, which are the key ingredient in consumer and industrial cleaning compounds. Manufacturers of detergents, shampoos, lotions, toothpaste, and cosmetics depend on surfactants to achieve the foaming and cleaning qualities required of their products. Stepan also produces germicidal quaternary compounds, as well as other specialty products which are often custom-made to meet individual needs. These include emulsifiers which facilitate spreading of insecticides and herbicides, and lubricant and cutting-oil ingredients. The company is also a principal supplier of phthalic anhydride, a commodity chemical intermediate which is used in polyester resins, alkyd resins, and plasticizers. Polyurethane polyols and foam systems sold by the company are used in the expanding thermal insulation market primarily by the construction and refrigeration industries. Stepan utilizes a network of modern production facilities located in North and South America, Europe, and the Philippines. Incorporated in Illinois in 1940; reincorporated in Delaware in 1959.

Directors (In addition to indicated officers)

Robert D. Cadieux
Thomas F. Grojean

Robert G. Potter
Paul H. Stepan

Officers (Directors*)

*F. Quinn Stepan, Chm., Pres. & C.E.O.
*James A. Hartlage, Ph.D., Sr. V.P.—Tech. & Oper.
Jeffrey W. Bartlett, V.P., Gen. Coun. & Corp. Secy.
Charles W. Given, V.P.—Corp. Dev.

Walter J. Klein, V.P.—Fin.
M. Mirghanbari, V.P.—Mfg. & Eng.
Ronald L. Siemon, V.P. & Gen. Mgr.—Polymers
F. Quinn Stepan, Jr., V.P. & Gen. Mgr.—Surfactants
Earl H. Wagener, Ph.D., V.P.—Res. & Dev.

Consolidated Balance Sheet As of December 31, 1996 (000 omitted)

Assets		Liabilities & Stockholders' Equity	
Current assets	$153,698	Current liabilities	$ 83,376
Net property, plant & equipment	207,159	Long-term debt	102,567
Other assets	20,155	Deferred income taxes	35,954
		Other liabilities	27,500
		*Stockholders' equity	131,615
Total	$381,012	Total	$381,012

*10,131,706 shares common stock outstanding.

Consolidated Income Statement

| Years Ended Dec. 31 | Thousands — — — — | | Per Share[a] — — — | | Common Stock |
	Net Sales	Net Income	Earnings	Cash Dividends	Price Range[a] Calendar Year
1996	$536,635	$19,067	$1.80	$ .48	20-1/2 — 15-3/4
1995	528,218	16,119	1.51	.45	20-7/8 — 14-3/4
1994	443,948	13,845	1.29	.43	17-3/4 — 12-3/8
1993	438,825	10,776	.98	.41	18-7/8 — 12-5/8
1992	435,764	15,829[b]	1.46[b]	.37	22-7/8 — 13-1/8

[a]Adjusted to reflect a 2-for-1 stock split in December 1994.
[b]Includes a gain to reflect FAS 109 and the accounting change related to investment tax credits, resulting in a cumulative effect of $5,406,000 ($.51 per share).

Transfer Agent & Registrar:	Harris Trust and Savings Bank		
General Counsel:	Mayer, Brown & Platt	Traded (Symbol):	NYSE, CSE (SCL)
Investor Relations:	Walter J. Klein, V.P.	Stockholders:	1,692
		Employees:	1,270
Human Resources:	Craig O. Gardiner, Dir.	Annual Meeting:	In May
Auditors:	Arthur Andersen LLP	Internet:	www.stepan.com

LaSalle Banks Guide

Stericycle, Inc.

1419 Lake Cook Road, Suite 410, Deerfield, Illinois 60015
Telephone: (847) 945-6550

Stericycle, Inc. is a multi-regional, integrated company employing proprietary technology to provide environmentally responsible management of regulated medical waste for the health care industry. The company's services include regulated medical waste collection, transportation, treatment, disposal, reduction, reuse, and recycling services, together with related training and education programs, consulting services, and product sales. The company operates in eight geographic service areas: (1) Arizona, California, and Utah; (2) Idaho, Oregon, Washington, and British Columbia; (3) Colorado; (4) Texas; (5) Kentucky and Tennessee; (6) Illinois, Indiana, Michigan, Ohio, and Wisconsin; (7) Connecticut, Massachusetts, Maine, New Hampshire, Rhode Island, and Vermont; and (8) Maryland, New Jersey, New York, North Carolina, South Carolina, Pennsylvania, and the District of Columbia. Stericycle acquired five registered waste management businesses in 1996, and had a total of 27,000 customers. In August 1996, the company completed an initial public offering of 3,450,000 shares of common stock. Incorporated in Delaware in December 1989.

Directors   (In addition to indicated officers)

Patrick F. Graham
John Patience

Peter Vardy
L. John Wilkerson

Officers   (Directors*)

*Jack W. Schuler, Chm.
*Mark C. Miller, Pres. & C.E.O.
Michael J. Bernert, V.P.—Eastern Region
Linda D. Lee, V.P.—Regulatory Aff. & Qual.
Assurance

James F. Polark, V.P.—Fin & C.F.O.
Richard O. Shea, V.P.—Western Region
Anthony J. Tomasello, V.P.—Oper.

Consolidated Balance Sheet   As of December 31, 1996 (000 omitted)

Assets		Liabilities & Stockholders' Equity	
Current assets	$23,781	Current liabilities	$ 9,164
Net property, plant & equipment	12,007	Long-term debt	4,591
Other assets	19,367	Other liabilities	1,386
		*Stockholders' equity	40,014
Total	$55,155	Total	$55,155

*10,000,264 shares common stock outstanding.

Consolidated Income Statement

Years Ended Dec. 31	Thousands — — — —		Per Share[a] — — —		Common Stock Price Range[a] Calendar Year
	Revenues	Net Income	Earnings	Cash Dividends	
1996	$24,542	$(2,389)	$ (.30)	$ .00	11-3/4 — 7
1995	21,339	(4,544)	(.65)		
1994	16,141	(10,293)	(4.88)		
1993	9,141	(9,761)	(4.63)		
1992	5,010	(14,377)[b]	(6.81)		

[a]Initial public offering in August 1996.
[b]Includes a nonrecurring charge of $2,747,000 for restructuring.

Transfer Agent & Registrar:	Harris Trust and Savings Bank		
General Counsel:	Johnson & Colmar	Auditors:	Ernst & Young LLP
Investor Relations:	Mark C. Miller, Pres.	Traded (Symbol):	NASDAQ (SRCL)
		Stockholders:	180
Human Resources:	Ann Shanahan	Employees:	330
Mgt. Info. Svcs.:	James F. Polark, V.P.	Annual Meeting:	In April

Stimsonite Corporation

7542 Natchez Avenue, Niles, Illinois 60714
Telephone: (847) 647-7717

Stimsonite Corporation is a manufacturer and marketer of reflective highway safety products. The company makes a range of high performance products which are designed to offer enhanced visual guidance to vehicle operators in a variety of driving conditions. These products include: highway delineation products, such as raised reflective pavement markers, thermoplastic striping materials, construction work zone markers, and roadside and other delineators; highway signing materials, such as high-performance reflective sheeting used in the construction of highway signs; and precision embossed film, which is used in internally illuminated airport runway signs, reflective truck markings, and a variety of other products that require optical grade film. Incorporated in Delaware in 1990.

Directors (In addition to indicated officers)

Lawrence S. Eagleburger
Donald H. Haider
Edward T. Harvey, Jr.

Anthony R. Ignaczak
Richard J.M. Poulson
Jay R. Taylor

Officers (Directors*)

*Terrence D. Daniels, Chm.
*Robert E. Stutz, Pres. & C.E.O.
Michael A. Cherwin, V.P.—Hum. Res.
Clifford S. Deremo, V.P.—Sales & Mktg.

Walter B. Finley, V.P.—Atlanta Oper.
Charles L. Hulsey, V.P.—Oper.
Robert M. Pricone, V.P.—Eng.
Thomas C. Ratchford, V.P.—Fin., C.F.O., Treas. & Secy.

Consolidated Balance Sheet   As of December 31, 1996 (000 omitted)

Assets		Liabilities & Stockholders' Equity	
Current assets	$34,122	Current liabilities	$18,269
Net property, plant & equipment	18,907	Long-term debt	28,300
Other assets	18,841	Other liabilities	631
		*Stockholders' equity	24,670
Total	$71,870	Total	$71,870

*8,706,150 shares common stock outstanding.

Consolidated Income Statement

Years Ended Dec. 31	Thousands — — — — Net Sales	Net Income	Per Share[a] — — — — Earnings	Cash Dividends	Common Stock Price Range[a] Calendar Year
1996	$82,712	$ (848)[b]	$ (.09)	$ .00	10 — 5-3/8
1995	68,119	2,610	.29	.00	14-1/2 — 6-7/8
1994	55,941	6,136[c]	.68[c]	.00	14-1/4 — 9-1/2
1993	45,929	(1,286)[d]	(.17)[d]	.00	11 — 9
1992	39,658	2,110[e]	.28[e]		

[a]Adjusted to reflect a 35-for-1 stock split in December 1993. Initial public offering in December 1993.
[b]Includes an after-tax restructuring charge of $2,400,000 ($.27 per share) and an extraordinary charge of $332,000 ($.04 per share).
[c]Includes an extraordinary charge of $104,000 ($.01 per share).
[d]Includes an extraordinary charge of $3,829,000 ($.50 per share).
[e]Includes a charge of $630,000 ($.08 per share) for an accounting change.

Transfer Agent & Registrar:	LaSalle National Bank		
General Counsel:	Jones, Day, Reavis & Pogue	Traded (Symbol):	NASDAQ (STIM)
Investor Relations:	Thomas C. Ratchford, V.P.	Stockholders:	500
Human Resources:	Michael A. Cherwin, V.P.	Employees:	400
Mgt. Info. Svcs.:	Thomas C. Ratchford, V.P.	Annual Meeting:	In May
Auditors:	Coopers & Lybrand L.L.P.	Internet:	www.stimsonite.com

Stone Container Corporation

150 North Michigan Avenue, Chicago, Illinois 60601-7568
Telephone: (312) 346-6600

Stone Container Corporation is a vertically integrated producer and seller of commodity paper and packaging products. Products include kraft linerboard, corrugating medium, kraft paper, newsprint, groundwood paper, market pulp, corrugated containers, folding cartons, paper bags, sacks, flexible packaging, and wood products. Subsidiaries include: Stone-Consolidated Corporation; Stone Container (Canada); Stone Europa Carton AG (Germany); Bridgewater Paper Co. (U.K.); Stone Container International Corp.; and Stone Forest Industries, Inc. The company, including its subsidiaries and affiliates, maintains manufacturing facilities in North America, Europe, Central and South America, Australia, and Asia. Incorporated in Illinois in 1945 to continue a business established in 1926; reincorporated in Delaware in 1987.

Directors (In addition to indicated officers)

William F. Aldinger III	Dionisio Garza Medina	Phillip B. Rooney
Richard A. Giesen	John D. Nichols	Alan Stone
James J. Glasser	Jerry K. Pearlman	James H. Stone
Jack M. Greenberg	Richard J. Raskin	

Officers (Directors*)

*Roger W. Stone, Chm., Pres. & C.E.O.
John D. Bence, Sr. V.P.—Euro. Pack. Oper.
Thomas P. Cutilletta, Sr. V.P.—Admin. & Cont.
Gerald M. Freeman, Sr. V.P. & Gen. Mgr.—Forest Prod. Div.
Gordon L. Jones, Sr. V.P. & Gen. Mgr.—Corrug. Container Div.
Randolph C. Read, Sr. V.P., C.F.O. & C.P.O.
John M. Riconosciuto, Sr. V.P. & Gen. Mgr.—Ind. & Specialty Pkg. Div.

*Ira N. Stone, Sr. V.P.—Corp. Mktg., Comm. & Pub. Aff.
Harold D. Wright, Sr. V.P. & Gen. Mgr.—Containerbd., Paper & Pulp
Matthew S. Kaplan, Sr. V.P.—North Amer. Oper.
William J. Klaisle, V.P.—Corp. Dev.
Leslie T. Lederer, V.P., Secy. & Counsel
Michael B. Wheeler, V.P., Treas. & Asst. Secy.
Emil Winograd, V.P. & Gen. Mgr.—Mkt. Pulp & Export sales

Consolidated Balance Sheet As of December 31, 1996 (000 omitted)

Assets		Liabilities & Stockholders' Equity	
Current assets	$1,561,200	Current liabilities	$ 889,200
Net property, plant & equipment	2,633,700	Long-term debt	3,951,100
Other assets	2,158,900	Deferred items	410,200
		Other liabilities	308,100
		*Stockholders' equity	795,200
Total	$6,353,800	Total	$6,353,800

*99,300,000 shares common stock outstanding.

Consolidated Income Statement

Years Ended Dec. 31	Thousands — — — — Net Sales	Net Income	Per Share[a] — — — — Earnings[b]	Cash Dividends	Common Stock Price Range[a] Calendar Year
1996	$5,141,800	$(126,200)	$(1.35)	$ .60	17-3/8 — 12-1/8
1995	7,351,200	255,500	2.24	.30	24-5/8 — 12-1/2
1994	5,748,700	(204,600)	(2.46)	.00	21-1/8 — 9-5/8
1993	5,059,600	(358,700)	(5.15)	.00	19-1/2 — 6-3/8
1992	5,520,700	(269,400)[c]	(3.89)[c]	.35	32-5/8 — 12-1/2

[a]Adjusted to reflect a 2% stock dividend in September 1992.
[b]Fully diluted.
[c]Restated to reflect adoption of FAS 109 retroactive to January 1, 1992.

Transfer Agent & Registrar: The First National Bank of Chicago

General Counsel:	Leslie T. Lederer, V.P.	Auditors:	Price Waterhouse LLP
Investor Relations:	Randolph C. Read, Sr. V.P.	Traded (Symbol):	NYSE (STO)
Human Resources:	Gayle M. Sparapani, Staff. V.P.	Stockholders:	6,500
		Employees:	24,200
Mgt. Info. Svcs.:	Joseph P. Thompson, Staff. V.P.	Annual Meeting:	Second Tuesday in May

SuburbFed Financial Corp.

3301 West Vollmer Road, Flossmoor, Illinois 60422-2093
Telephone: (708) 333-2200

SuburbFed Financial Corp. is the holding company for Suburban Federal Savings, a federal savings bank. Suburban Federal's offices are located throughout the southern, southwestern, and western Chicago metropolitan area and in Dyer, Indiana. Its deposits are insured by the Federal Deposit Insurance Corporation. The savings bank is principally engaged in the business of attracting deposits from the general public and using such deposits to originate residential mortgages and, to a lesser extent, consumer, construction or development, non-residential real estate, and multi-family loans. Suburban Federal also invests in mortgage-backed and investment securities and makes deposits in other financial institutions. Incorporated in Delaware in 1991.

Directors   (In addition to indicated officers)

Douglas L. Dance
Robert J. Genetski, Ph.D.
Robert L. Harris
Bruce E. Huey
Raymond J. Kalinsky

Michael L. Lowenthal
William E. Ricketts, M.D.
Alan L. Wischhover, P.C.
Paula Wolff, Ph.D.

Officers   (Directors*)

*Daniel P. Ryan, Chm., Pres. & C.E.O.
*Vernon P. Vollbrecht, V. Chm.
 Byron G. Thoren, Exec. V.P. & C.O.O.
 Peter A. Ruhl, Sr. V.P.—Lending & Savings

Steven E. Stock, Sr. V.P., C.F.O. & Treas.
Lester J. Wolf, Sr. V.P.—Hum. Res. & Mktg.
Lisa F. Morris, V.P.
Lynn M. Nevills, Secy.

Consolidated Balance Sheet   As of December 31, 1996 (000 omitted)

Assets		Liabilities & Stockholders' Equity	
Total cash & cash equivalents	$ 8,852	Deposits	$309,581
Loans receivable, net	241,815	Total borrowings	62,938
Mortgage-backed securities	133,486	Other liabilities	5,319
Investment securities	12,066	*Stockholders' equity	26,254
Other assets	7,873		
Total	$404,092	Total	$404,092

*1,254,769 shares common stock outstanding.

Consolidated Income Statement

Years Ended Dec. 31	Thousands — — — —		Per Share[a] — — —		Common Stock
	Total Income	Net Income	Earnings	Cash Dividends	Price Range[ab] Calendar Year
1996	$29,738	$1,052[c]	$ .80[c]	$ .32	20-3/4 — 16
1995	26,370	1,818	1.35	.32	27-1/4 — 16-1/4
1994	22,064	1,939	1.38	.29	17-1/8 — 13
1993	20,913	2,291	1.65	.26	15-3/8 — 11
1992	22,218	1,707	1.26	.12	11-1/2 — 6-5/8

[a]Adjusted to reflect a 3-for-2 stock split October 1995.
[b]Initial public offering in February 1992.
[c]Includes a special one-time SAIF assessment of $1.7 million ($.79 per share).

Transfer Agent & Registrar: American Stock Transfer & Trust Co.

General Counsel:		Auditors:	Cobitz, VandenBerg & Fennessy
Silver, Freedman & Taff, L.L.P.		Traded (Symbol):	NASDAQ (SFSB)
Investor Relations:	Steven E. Stock, Sr. V.P.	Stockholders:	561
Human Resources:	Lester J. Wolf, Sr. V.P.	Employees:	178
Mgt. Info. Svcs.:	Ronald H. LeClaire, V.P.	Annual Meeting:	In April

LaSalle Banks Guide

Successories, Inc.

919 Springer Drive, Lombard, Illinois 60148-6416
Telephone: (630) 953-8440

Successories, Inc. (formerly CELEX Group, Inc.) is an innovative specialty retailer and catalog company that designs, manufactures, and markets proprietary products for business and personal motivation. The products the company creates include high-quality lithographs, posters, books, cards, apparel, and awards. The company sells its products through four distribution channels: Successories® direct mail catalog; Successories® retail stores; wholesale sales; and international distributors. Incorporated in Illinois in 1990; present name adopted in 1996.

Directors   (In addition to indicated officers)

Seamas T. Coyle
Joseph C. LaBonté
Steven B. Larrick

Mervyn C. Phillips, Jr.
Michael Singletary
Guy E. Snyder

Officers   (Directors*)

*Mac Anderson, Chm.
*James M. Beltrame, Pres. & C.E.O.
John Halpin, Sr. V.P.
Raymond Mackie, Sr. V.P.—Oper.

*Michael McKee, Sr. V.P. & Creative Dir.
Peter Walts, Sr. V.P.
*Timothy C. Dillon, V.P., Gen. Coun. & Secy.
M. Andrew King, V.P., Treas. & C.F.O.

Consolidated Balance Sheet   As of April 30, 1996 (000 omitted)

Assets		Liabilities & Stockholders' Equity	
Current assets	$18,406	Current liabilities	$10,021
Net property, plant & equipment	10,615	Long-term debt	8,528
Other assets	3,145	Other liabilities	583
		*Stockholders' equity	13,034
Total	$32,166	Total	$32,166

*5,208,452 shares common stock outstanding.

Consolidated Income Statement

Years Ended April 30	Thousands — — — — Revenues	Net Income	Per Share[a] — — — Earnings	Cash Dividends	Common Stock Price Range[a] Calendar Year
1996	$35,483	$ 700	$ .13	$ .00	9-1/2 — 4-5/8
1995	44,149	(6,866)	(1.60)	.00	15 — 5-5/8
1994	29,785	2,214	.50	.00	22 — 12
1993	13,274	1,605[b]	.47[b]	.00	18 — 10-7/8
1992	5,737	102[c]	.04[c]		

[a]Adjusted to reflect a 3-for-2 stock split in March 1994.
[b]Includes a gain to reflect FAS 109, resulting in a cumulative effect of $580,000 ($.17 per share).
[c]Includes an extraordinary gain of $26,300 ($.01 per share) reflecting net operating loss carryforwards.

Transfer Agent & Registrar:	Illinois Stock Transfer Co.		
General Counsel:	Timothy C. Dillon, V.P.	Auditors:	Arthur Andersen LLP
Investor Relations:	Timothy C. Dillon, V.P.	Traded (Symbol):	NASDAQ (SCES)
		Stockholders:	600
Human Resources:	Linda Sondgeroth	Employees:	332
Mgt. Info. Svcs.:	Charles Bowen	Annual Meeting:	In August

Sundance Homes, Inc.

1375 East Woodfield Road, Suite 600, Schaumburg, Illinois 60173
Telephone: (847) 255-5555

Sundance Homes, Inc. is a builder of affordably priced, single-family homes in the Chicago metropolitan area. The company currently offers diverse product lines of single-family homes within each project, with a variety of front elevations and architectural designs that complement each other and create a sense of community within the project. The company's principal subsidiaries are Rembrandt Homes, Inc. and Chicago Urban Properties. Incorporated in Illinois in 1981.

Directors   (In addition to indicated officers)

Dennis S. Bookshester
Charles Engles

Gerald Ginsburg

Officers   (Directors*)

*Maurice Sanderman, Chm., Pres. & C.E.O.
Thomas Small, Exec. V.P.—Oper.
*Joseph Atkin, V.P. & C.F.O.

Caren Menas, V.P.—Contracts
Jon Tilkemeier, V.P.—Sales & Mktg.
David Apter, Corp. Secy.

Consolidated Balance Sheet   As of September 30, 1996 (000 omitted)

Assets		Liabilities & Stockholders' Equity	
Current assets	$81,814	Current liabilities	$30,682
Net property, plant & equipment	2,520	Notes payable	23,027
Other assets	2,072	Other liabilities	4,193
		*Stockholders' equity	28,504
Total	$86,406	Total	$86,406

*7,807,000 shares common stock outstanding.

Consolidated Income Statement

Years Ended Sept. 30	Thousands — — — — Residential Sales	Net Income	Per Share[a] — — — Earnings	Cash Dividends	Common Stock Price Range[ab] Calendar Year
1996	$120,948	$ 1,235	$ .16	$ .00	4-1/2 — 1-1/8
1995[c]	63,811	(4,216)[d]	(.54)	.00	3-7/8 — 2
1994	118,659	1,930	.25	.00	12-3/4 — 1-7/8
1993[e]	77,764	5,090	.76	.00	14-1/2 — 8
1992[e]	86,208	5,010	1.00		

[a]Adjusted to reflect a 4,700-for-1 stock split in July 1993.
[b]Initial public offering in July 1993.
[c]Nine month period. Fiscal year changed from calendar year end to September 30 in 1995.
[d]Includes a write-off adjustment of $3,657,000 to reduce the carrying value of inventories.
[e]Unaudited pro forma, based on historical net income, as adjusted to reflect a provision for income taxes as if the company had been a C corporation since inception.

Transfer Agent & Registrar: LaSalle National Trust, N.A.

General Counsel:	Katten Muchin & Zavis	Auditors:	Price Waterhouse LLP
Investor Relations:	Joseph Atkin, V.P.	Traded (Symbol):	NASDAQ (SUNH)
		Stockholders:	650
Human Resources:	Joseph Atkin, V.P.	Employees:	135
Mgt. Info. Svcs.:	Joseph Atkin, V.P.	Annual Meeting:	In March

Sundstrand Corporation

4949 Harrison Avenue, P.O. Box 7003, Rockford, Illinois 61125-7003
Telephone: (815) 226-6000

Sundstrand Corporation designs, manufactures, and sells a variety of proprietary, technology-based components and systems requiring significant research, development, engineering, and processing expertise. The company is divided into two segments: aerospace and industrial. Systems and components for aerospace applications include: electrical power generating systems; constant speed drives; variable speed constant frequency systems; engine fuel and lubricating systems; actuation systems; pneumatic systems; and turbopower systems. Products in the industrial segment include: a comprehensive line of gear drives and flexible couplings; high-speed pumps, blowers, and compressors; and rotary screw air and gas compressors. Major subsidiaries include: Falk Corporation; Sullair Corporation; Sundstrand Fluid Handling Corporation; and Milton Roy Company. Incorporated in Illinois in 1910; reincorporated in Delaware in 1966.

Directors (In addition to indicated officers)

Richard A. Abdoo
J.P. Bolduc
Gerald Grinstein

Charles Marshall
Klaus H. Murmann
Ward Smith

Berger G. Wallin

Officers (Directors*)

*Robert H. Jenkins, Chm., Pres. & C.E.O.
Paul Donovan, Exec. V.P., C.F.O. & Treas.
Ronald F. McKenna, Exec. V.P. &
  C.O.O.—Aerospace

Patrick L. Thomas, Exec. V.P. & C.O.O.—
  Industrial
DeWayne J. Fellows, V.P. & Cont.
Richard M. Schilling, V.P., Gen. Coun. & Secy.

Consolidated Balance Sheet As of December 31, 1996 (000 omitted)

Assets		Liabilities & Stockholders' Equity	
Current assets	$ 772,000	Current liabilities	$ 397,000
Net property, plant & equipment	427,000	Long-term debt	222,000
Other assets	396,000	Accrued post retirement benefits	367,000
		Other liabilities	96,000
		*Stockholders' equity	513,000
Total	$1,595,000	Total	$1,595,000

*60,362,009 shares common stock outstanding.

Consolidated Income Statement

Years Ended Dec. 31	Thousands — — — — Net Sales	Net Income	Per Share[a] — — — Earnings	Cash Dividends	Common Stock Price Range[a] Calendar Year
1996	$1,521,000	$ 114,000[b]	$ 1.87[b]	$ .68	42-3/4 — 32-1/2
1995	1,473,000	79,000[c]	1.25[c]	.60	35-3/8 — 22-1/4
1994	1,373,000	96,000[d]	1.46[d]	.60	26 — 20-1/2
1993	1,383,000	141,000[e]	1.98[e]	.60	22-3/8 — 17-1/2
1992[f]	1,479,000	(122,000)[g]	(1.68)[g]	.59	23-5/8 — 15-1/2

[a]Adjusted to reflect a 2-for-1 stock split in March 1996.
[b]Includes a charge of $23,000,000 after taxes ($.38 per share) primarily for restructuring of Sullair Europe S.A.; and a gain of $5,000,000 after taxes ($.08 per share) related to the shutdown of the Lima, Ohio, facility.
[c]Includes an after-tax restructuring charge of $40,000,000 ($.64 per share) related to the restructuring of manufacturing capacity and the divestiture of two non-core product lines.
[d]Includes a reduction of depreciation expense related to a change in depreciable lives of $6,000,000 after taxes ($.08 per share).
[e]Includes a gain of $56,000,000 after taxes ($.78 per share) on the sale of the Data Control business.
[f]Restated to reflect the Data Control business, sold in 1993, as a discontinued operation.
[g]Includes charges of $22,000,000 after taxes ($.31 per share) for restructuring of and reduction in employment in the aerospace segment; and charges of $205,000,000 after taxes ($2.84 per share) for adoption of FAS 106.

Transfer Agent & Registrar: Harris Trust and Savings Bank

General Counsel:	Richard M. Schilling, V.P.	Traded (Symbol):	NYSE, CSE, PSE (SNS)
Investor Relations:	Doug Smiley, Mgr.	Stockholders:	3,500
		Employees:	9,400
Human Resources:	Mick Roberts, Dir.	Annual Meeting:	In April
Auditors:	Ernst & Young LLP	Internet:	www.snds.com

System Software Associates, Inc.

500 West Madison Street, 32nd Floor, Chicago, Illinois 60661
Telephone: (312) 258-6000

System Software Associates, Inc. (SSA) is a leading provider of cost-effective business enterprise information systems to the industrial sector worldwide. SSA's BPCS (Business Planning and Control System) Client/Server product provides business process reengineering and integration of an enterprise's operations, including multi-mode manufacturing processes, supply chain management, and global financial solutions. The BPCS Client/Server solution delivers scaleability, interoperability, and reconfigurability in its comprehensive product suite to meet changing market demands. The distributed object computing architecture (DOCA) of the BPCS Client/Server provides the benefits of next-generation technology in conformation with industry standards. In addition to English, BPCS Client/Server products are available in nineteen other languages, including simplified and traditional Chinese, Dutch, French, German, Italian, Japanese, Korean, Portuguese, Swedish, and Spanish. The company markets, sells, and services its products to intermediate- and large-size enterprises through a worldwide network of its own sales organization and a network of approximately 90 independent software companies and major systems integrators. Incorporated in Illinois in 1981; reincorporated in Delaware in 1985.

Directors (In addition to indicated officers)

Andrew J. Filipowski
John W. Puth

William N. Weaver, Jr.

Officers (Directors*)

*Roger E. Covey, Chm., Pres. & C.E.O.
Riz Shakir, V.P.—Architecture Tech.

Joseph J. Skadra, V.P. & C.F.O.

Consolidated Balance Sheet   As of October 31, 1996 (000 omitted)

Assets		Liabilities & Stockholders' Equity	
Current assets	$241,700	Current liabilities	$171,400
Net property, plant & equipment	27,800	Long-term debt	75,100
Other assets	114,900	Deferred revenue	27,700
		*Stockholders' equity	110,200
Total	$384,400	Total	$384,400

*42,577,000 shares common stock outstanding.

Consolidated Income Statement

Years Ended Oct. 31	Thousands — — — — Total Revenues	Net Income	Per Share[a] — — — Earnings	Cash Dividends	Common Stock Price Range[a] Fiscal Year
1996	$340,800	$(32,800)	$ (.76)	$ .10	27-5/8 — 8-5/8
1995[b]	374,100	26,600	.63	.12	30 — 8-1/8
1994[b]	324,300	10,000	.25	.12	11-5/8 — 7-5/8
1993	263,400	23,400	.86	.12	16-3/4 — 7-1/8
1992	228,800	26,600	.99	.12	16-7/8 — 7-7/8

[a]Adjusted to reflect 3-for-2 stock splits in December 1995, December 1992, and December 1991.
[b]Restated.

Transfer Agent & Registrar: The First National Bank of Chicago

General Counsel: Kirk Isaacson

Investor Relations: Joseph J. Skadra, V.P.

Human Resources: Norman Maskin, Mgr.

Auditors: KPMG Peat Marwick LLP

Traded (Symbol):   NASDAQ (SSAX)
Stockholders: 404
Employees: 2,200
Annual Meeting: In May
Internet: www.ssax.com

Technology Solutions Company
205 North Michigan Avenue, Suite 1500, Chicago, Illinois 60601
Telephone: (312) 228-4500

Technology Solutions Company (TSC) is a strategic management consulting and systems integration company providing business benefits to major corporations through the application of information technology. TSC partners with clients in a wide range of industries and has earned recognition as a leader in client/server solutions for supply chain management, call center and customer service reengineering, electronic commerce, financial services, and the integration of packaged software. TSC's services include business strategic planning, market research and analysis, new venture growth services, product and distribution planning, and organizational restructuring services. TSC maintains headquarters in Chicago and major offices throughout the United States, Canada, Latin America, and Europe. In February 1997, TSC announced that it would acquire HRM Resources, Inc., a technology implementation firm based in New York. Incorporated in Delaware in 1988.

Directors (In addition to indicated officers)

Jeffrey T. Chambers
Michael J. McLaughlin
Michael J. Murray

Stephen B. Oresman
John R. Purcell

Officers (Directors*)

*William H. Waltrip, Chm.
*John T. Kohler, Pres. & C.E.O.
James S. Carluccio, Exec. V.P.
Kelly D. Conway, Exec. V.P.

Jack N. Hayden, Exec. V.P.
Michael J. McLaughlin, Exec. V.P.
Martin T. Johnson, Sr. V.P. & C.F.O.
Paul R. Peterson, Sr. V.P., Gen. Coun. & Secy.

Consolidated Balance Sheet As of May 31, 1997 (000 omitted)

Assets		Liabilities & Stockholders' Equity	
Current assets	$107,674	Current liabilities	$ 28,079
Net property, plant & equipment	6,416	*Stockholders' equity	105,787
Other assets	19,776		
Total	$133,866	Total	$133,866

* 16,488,003 shares common stock outstanding.

Consolidated Income Statement

Years Ended May 31	Thousands — — — —		Per Share[a] — — — —		Common Stock
	Total Revenues	Net Income	Earnings	Cash Dividends	Price Range[a] Calendar Year
1997	$165,088	$15,067	$.85	$.00	
1996	97,599	4,574	.30	.00	47-1/8 — 10-7/8
1995	65,817	3,367	.24	.00	15-7/8 — 4-7/8
1994	53,157	35	.00	.00	6-1/8 — 3-1/8
1993	62,474	5,706	.31	.00	10 — 4-5/8

[a]Adjusted to reflect a 3-for-2 stock split in July 1996.

Transfer Agent & Registrar:	Mellon Securities Transfer Services			
General Counsel:	Sidley & Austin	Traded (Symbol):	NASDAQ (TSCC)
Investor Relations:	Martin T. Johnson, Sr. V.P.	Stockholders:	2,500
Recruiting:	Jackie Hilt, V.P.	Employees:	950
Mgt. Info. Svcs.:	Harley Michelson, V.P.	Annual Meeting:	In September
Auditors:	Price Waterhouse LLP	Internet:	www.TechSol.com

Telephone and Data Systems, Inc.

30 North LaSalle Street, Suite 4000, Chicago, Illinois 60602-2507
Telephone: (312) 630-1900

Telephone and Data Systems, Inc. (TDS) is a diversified telecommunications company. As of December 31, 1996, United States Cellular Corporation, TDS's 80.6 percent-owned cellular telephone subsidiary, owned cellular interests representing 25.1 million population equivalents in 204 markets. United States Cellular's consolidated markets served 1,073,000 customers. TDS Telecommunications Corporation, a wholly owned telephone subsidiary, operated 105 telephone companies serving 484,500 access lines in 28 states. Aerial Communications, Inc. (previously American Portable Telecom, Inc.), the company's 82.8 percent-owned subsidiary, owns the licenses to provide PCS service in six major trading areas which encompass approximately 27.6 population equivalents. American Paging, Inc., the company's 82.3 percent-owned subsidiary, served 777,400 pagers through 51 sales and service centers. Other TDS subsidiaries include: TDS Computing Services, a systems services division; Suttle Press, Inc., a custom printing company; and Integrated Communications Services, Inc., a messaging services company. In 1996, the company acquired Deposit Telephone Co.; Tipton Telephone Company; Utelco Inc.; Nelson-Ball Ground Telephone Co.; and Myrtle Telephone Co. Incorporated in Iowa in 1968.

Directors (In addition to indicated officers)

James Barr III	Walter C.D. Carlson	Martin L. Soloman
Donald R. Brown	Donald C. Nebergall	Herbert S. Wander
Letitia G.C. Carlson, M.D.	George W. Off	

Officers (Directors*)

*LeRoy T. Carlson, Chm.	Byron A. Wertz, V.P.—Corp. Dev.
*LeRoy T. Carlson, Jr., Pres. & C.E.O.	Gregory J. Wilkinson, V.P. & Cont.
*Murray L. Swanson, Exec. V.P.—Fin. & C.F.O.	Scott H. Williamson, V.P.—Acquisitions
Michael K. Chesney, V.P.—Corp. Dev.	Michael G. Hron, Secy.
George L. Dienes, V.P.—Corp. Dev.	William S. DeCarlo, Asst. Secy.
C. Theodore Herbert, V.P.—Hum. Res.	Steven N. Fortney, Asst. Cont.—Actg. & Rptg.
*Rudolph E. Hornacek, V.P.—Eng.	Ross J. McVey, Asst. Cont. & Dir.—Tax
Karen M. Stewart, V.P.—Inv. Rel.	James W. Twesme, Asst. Treas.
Ronald D. Webster, V.P. & Treas.	Joyce M. Zeasman, Asst. Cont.—Corp. Reeng.

Consolidated Balance Sheet As of December 31, 1996 (000 omitted)

Assets		Liabilities & Stockholders' Equity	
Current assets	$ 346,070	Current liabilities	$ 509,267
Net property, plant & equipment	1,828,889	Long-term debt	982,232
Investments	1,942,604	Deferred credits	214,906
Other assets	83,406	Preferred stock & minority interests	461,623
Total	$4,200,969	*Stockholders' equity	2,032,941
		Total	$4,200,969

*54,237,180 shares common and 6,916,546 shares Series A common stock outstanding.

Consolidated Income Statement

Years Ended Dec. 31	Thousands — — — — —		Per Share — — — —		Common Stock Price Range Calendar Year
	Operating Revenues	Net Income	Earnings	Cash Dividends	
1996	$1,214,636	$128,139	$2.08	$ .40	48-7/8 — 34-3/4
1995	954,386	103,978	1.74	.38	46-3/8 — 35-5/8
1994	730,810	60,544[a]	1.07[a]	.36	51-1/2 — 35-1/2
1993	557,795	33,896	.67	.34	57 — 33-1/4
1992	432,740	38,520[a]	.91[a]	.32	41-1/4 — 30-1/8

[a]Before extraordinary charge of $769,000 ($.02 per share) in 1992; and charges of $723,000 ($.01 per share) in 1994 to reflect the cumulative effect of FAS 112; and of $6,866,000 ($.17 per share) in 1992 to reflect FAS 106.

Transfer Agent:	Harris Trust and Savings Bank		
General Counsel:	Sidley & Austin	Traded (Symbol):	AMEX (TDS)
Investor Relations:	Karen M. Stewart, V.P.	Stockholders:	4,212
		Employees:	7,718
Human Resources:	C. Theodore Herbert, V.P.	Annual Meeting:	In May
Auditors:	Arthur Andersen LLP	Internet:	www.teldta.com

Tellabs, Inc.

4951 Indiana Avenue, Lisle, Illinois 60532-1698
Telephone: (630) 378-8800

Tellabs, Inc. designs, manufactures, markets, and services voice and data transport and network access systems used in public and private communication networks worldwide. Customers include public telephone companies, long-distance carriers, government agencies, utilities, business end-users, alternate service providers, cellular and other wire service providers, cable operators, and original equipment manufacturers. The company has approximately 40 locations in the United States, Australia, Brazil, Canada, Finland, France, Germany, the United Kingdom, Hong Kong, Ireland, Korea, Mexico, New Zealand, Singapore, South Africa, Spain, Sweden, and the U.S. Virgin Islands. Major subsidiaries include: Tellabs Operations, Inc.; Telecommunications Laboratories, Inc.; Tellabs International, Inc.; Martis Oy; Tellabs Mexico, Inc.; Tellabs TG, Inc.; and Tellabs Wireless, Inc. Incorporated in Delaware in 1992.

Directors (In addition to indicated officers)

John D. Foulkes, Ph.D.	Stephanie Pace Marshall, Ph.D.	William F. Souders
Frederick A. Krehbiel	Robert P. Reuss, Emeritus	Jan H. Suwinski

Officers (Directors*)

*Michael J. Birck, Pres. & C.E.O.—Tellabs Inc.
*Peter A. Guglielmi, Exec. V.P., C.F.O. & Treas.—Tellabs Inc./Ops.
*Brian J. Jackman, Exec. V.P.—Tellabs Inc.; Pres.—Tellabs Ops.
John E. Vaughan, Exec. V.P.—Tellabs Inc.; Pres.—Tellabs Intl.
Richard T. Taylor, Sr. V.P.—Digital Sys. & Gen. Mgr.—Digital Sys.
Charles C. Cooney, V.P.—Sales & Svc.

Carol C. Gavin, Secy.—Tellabs Inc.; V.P., Gen. Coun. & Secy.—Tellabs Ops.
J. Thomas Gruenwald, V.P.—Strat. Res.
Jukka Harju, V.P.; Gen. Mgr.—Tellabs Oy; V.P.—Tellabs Intl.
J. Peter Johnson, V.P.—Fin./Treas., Asst. Secy. & Cont.
John C. Kohler, V.P.—Mfg.
Harvey R. Scull, V.P.—Advanced Bus. Dev.

Consolidated Balance Sheet As of December 27, 1996 (000 omitted)

Assets		Liabilities & Stockholders' Equity	
Current assets	$475,464	Current liabilities	$131,624
Net property, plant & equipment	162,760	Long-term debt	2,850
Goodwill, net	64,785	Deferred items	7,109
Other assets	40,814	Other liabilities	10,964
		*Stockholders' equity	591,276
Total	$743,823	Total	$743,823

*179,652,633 shares common stock outstanding.

Consolidated Income Statement

Years Ended Abt. Dec. 31	Thousands — — — — —		Per Share[a] — — —		Common Stock Price Range[a] Calendar Year
	Net Sales	Net Income	Earnings	Cash Dividends	
1996	$868,975	$117,965	$ .64	$ .00	45-1/4 — 15-1/4
1995	635,229	115,606	.63	.00	26-3/8 — 11-3/4
1994	494,153	72,389	.40	.00	14 — 5-1/2
1993	320,463	31,967	.18	.00	6-3/4 — 1-5/8
1992	258,560	16,854	.10	.00	2-1/4 — 1-3/8

[a]Adjusted to reflect 2-for-1 stock splits in the form of 100 percent stock dividends in November 1996, May 1995, and May 1994, and a 3-for-2 stock split in the form of a 50 percent stock dividend effective in November 1993.

Transfer Agent & Registrar: Harris Trust and Savings Bank

Outside Counsel:
  Vedder, Price, Kaufman & Kammholz

Investor Relations: Carol C. Gavin, V.P.

Human Resources: J. Thomas Gruenwald, V.P.

Mgt. Info. Svcs.: J. Thomas Gruenwald, V.P.

Auditors: Ernst & Young LLP

Traded (Symbol): NASDAQ (TLAB)

Stockholders: 3,035

Employees: 3,418

Annual Meeting: In April

Internet: www.tellabs.com

Teltrend Inc.
620 Stetson Avenue, St. Charles, Illinois 60174
Telephone: (630) 377-1700

Teltrend Inc. designs, manufactures, and markets a broad range of transmission products, such as channel units, repeaters, and termination units, used by telephone companies to provide voice and data services over the telephone network. Substantially all of the company's products are sold directly to the Regional Bell Operating Companies and their local affiliates for use with copper wireline in the local telephone subscriber loop. Incorporated in Delaware in 1987.

Directors (In addition to indicated officers)

Frank T. Cary
Harry Crutcher III
William R. Delk
Donald R. Hollis

Susan B. Major
Carl M. Mueller
Bernard F. Sergesketter

Officers (Directors*)

*Howard L. Kirby, Jr., Chm., Pres. & C.E.O.
Donald G. Bozeman, V.P.—Non-RBOC Sales
Michael S. Grzeskowiak, V.P.—Oper.
Douglas P. Hoffmeyer, V.P.—Fin.
Gilbert H. Hosie, V.P.—RBOC Sales
John Muntean, V.P. & Gen. Mgr.—ISDN/DDS Prod.

Jack C. Parker, V.P. & Gen. Mgr.—DLC/VF & T1/Wireless Prod.
Laurence L. Sheets, V.P. & Gen. Mgr.—HDSL Prod.
Norman C. Guenther, Asst. V.P.—Quality
Theodor A. Maxeiner, Asst. V.P.—Fin. & Cont.

Consolidated Balance Sheet As of July 27, 1996 (000 omitted)

Assets		Liabilities & Stockholders' Equity	
Current assets	$22,890	Current liabilities	$14,639
Net property, plant & equipment	5,871	*Stockholders' equity	42,645
Other assets	28,523		
Total	$57,284	Total	$57,284

*6,422,596 shares common stock outstanding.

Consolidated Income Statement

Years Ended Abt. July 31	Thousands — — — — Net Sales	Net Income	Per Share — — — — Earnings	Cash Dividends	Common Stock Price Range[a] Calendar Year
1996	$85,913	$ 12,164	$1.86	$ .00	58-1/4 — 24-1/2
1995	62,052	7,106[b]	1.19[b]	.00	47 — 16
1994	49,454	3,745[b]	.63[b]	.00	
1993	39,365	(3,307)			
1992	28,994	(54,945)			

[a]Initial public offering in June 1995.
[b]Pro forma.

Transfer Agent & Registrar:	LaSalle National Bank		
General Counsel:	Jenner & Block	Traded (Symbol):	NASDAQ (TLTN)
Investor Relations:	Carolyn Dowdell	Stockholders:	5,200
Human Resources:	Jan Lollini	Employees:	400
Mgt. Info. Svcs.:	Cindy Feldman	Annual Meeting:	As set by Directors
Auditors:	Ernst & Young LLP	Internet:	www.teltrend.com

Telular Corporation

920 Deerfield Parkway, Buffalo Grove, Illinois 60089
Telephone: (847) 465-4500

Telular Corporation is a leader in the fixed wireless telecommunications equipment industry. The company designs, develops, manufactures, and markets products based on proprietary interface technology, providing the capability to bridge wireless telecommunications customer premises equipment and wireless communications networks, whether cellular, ESMR, PCS, or satellite-based. Subsidiaries are Telular International, Inc. and Telular-Adcor Security Products, Inc. Incorporated in Delaware in 1993.

Directors   (In addition to indicated officers)

William L. DeNicolo, Chm.
John E. Berndt
Larry J. Ford

Rick Haning
David P. Mixer

Officers   (Directors*)

*Kenneth E. Millard, Pres. & C.E.O.
 Robert C. Montgomery, Exec. V.P. & C.O.O.

Thomas M. Mason, Sr. V.P., C.F.O. & Secy.
Jeffrey L. Herrmann, Corp. Cont.

Consolidated Balance Sheet   As of September 30, 1996 (000 omitted)

Assets		Liabilities & Stockholders' Equity	
Current assets	$36,226	Current liabilities	$ 9,669
Net property, plant & equipment	2,325	Long-term debt	1,500
Intangibles & other	3,388	*Stockholders' equity	30,770
Total	$41,939	Total	$41,939

*31,016,675 shares common stock outstanding.

Consolidated Income Statement

Years Ended Sept. 30	Thousands — — — — Net Sales	Net Income	Per Share[a] — — — Earnings	Cash Dividends	Common Stock Price Range[ab] Calendar Year
1996	$27,271	$(26,593)	$ (.96)	$ .00	10-1/2 — 2
1995	33,031	(19,660)	(.84)	.00	19-1/4 — 6-1/4
1994	17,734	(27,933)	(1.25)[c]	.00	24-1/2 — 6
1993[d]	6,575	(3,708)	(.18)[c]		
1992[e]	3,032	(1,552)			

[a]Adjusted to reflect a 14-for-1 stock split in January 1994.
[b]Initial public offering in January 1994.
[c]Pro forma.
[d]Nine months ending September 30. Includes results of The Telular Group L.P. for the period from January 1 to May 13, 1993, and thereafter the results of the company.
[e]Unaudited pro forma data reflecting The Telular Group L.P. and the combination of the operations of the limited partnership with the predecessor as if the limited partnership had been formed on January 1, 1992.

Transfer Agent & Registrar:	Harris Trust and Savings Bank		
Investor Relations:	Thomas M. Mason, Sr. V.P.	Stockholders:	9,000
Human Resources:	Thomas M. Mason, Sr. V.P.	Employees:	125
Auditors:	Ernst & Young LLP	Annual Meeting:	In January
Traded (Symbol):	NASDAQ (WRLS)	Internet:	www.telular.com

360° Communications Company

8725 West Higgins Road, Chicago, Illinois 60631-2702
Telephone: (773) 399-2500

360° Communications Company is a wireless communications company, serving more than 2.1 million customers in more than 104 markets covering 16 states. The company also owns minority interests in 53 additional cellular telephone markets. Its products and services are marketed through a distribution network of retail stores, local dealers, and a direct sales force. In March 1996, the company was spun-off from Sprint Corporation. On November 1, 1996, the company completed its acquisition of Independent Cellular Network, Inc., the owner and operator of cellular licenses and related systems and assets in Kentucky, Ohio, Pennsylvania, and West Virginia. Incorporated in Delaware in 1982; present name adopted in 1996.

Directors   (In addition to indicated officers)

Frank E. Reed, Chm.
Lester Crown
Michael Hooker
Robert E.R. Huntley

Valerie B. Jarrett
Alice M. Peterson
Charles H. Price II

Officers   (Directors*)

*Dennis E. Foster, Pres. & C.E.O.
 Kevin L. Beebe, Exec. V.P.—Oper.
 Michael J. Small, Exec. V.P. & C.F.O.
 Susan L. Amato, Sr. V.P.—Eng. & Network
   Oper.

Gary L. Burge, Sr. V.P.—Fin.
Kevin C. Gallagher, Sr. V.P., Gen. Coun. & Secy.
Debra L. Ferrari, V.P.—Hum. Res.

Consolidated Balance Sheet   As of December 31, 1996 (000 omitted)

Assets		Liabilities & Stockholders' Equity	
Current assets	$ 228,843	Current liabilities	$ 350,848
Net property, plant & equipment	1,083,426	Long-term debt	1,699,778
Other assets	1,499,800	Deferred income taxes	113,005
		Other liabilities	185,938
		*Stockholders' equity	462,500
Total	$2,812,069	Total	$2,812,069

*123,308,921 shares common stock outstanding.

Consolidated Income Statement

Years Ended Dec. 31	Thousands — — — — Net Revenues	Net Income	Per Share[a] — — — — Earnings	Cash Dividends	Common Stock Price Range[a] Calendar Year	
1996	$1,095,872	$ 59,519	$ .50	$ .00	27	— 21-1/2
1995	834,415	(1,695)	(.01)			
1994	626,475	(19,757)	(.17)			
1993	410,480	(51,484)	(.45)			
1992	280,119	(65,522)	(.58)			

[a]Spun-off from Sprint Corporation through a pro rata distribution to shareholders in March 1996.

Transfer Agent & Registrar:	ChaseMellon Shareholder Services, L.L.C.		
General Counsel:	Kevin C. Gallagher, Sr. V.P.	**Traded (Symbol):**	NYSE, CSE, PSE (XO)
Investor Relations:	David J. Gould	**Stockholders:**	67,766
Human Resources:	Debra L. Ferrari, V.P.	**Employees:**	4,000
Mgt. Info. Svcs.:	William C. Vail, V.P.	**Annual Meeting:**	In May
Auditors:	Ernst & Young LLP	**Internet:**	www.360.com

Titan International, Inc.

2701 Spruce Street, Quincy, Illinois 62301
Telephone: (217) 228-6011

Titan International, Inc. is a leading global manufacturer of wheel and tire assemblies for off-highway vehicles used in the agriculture, consumer, earthmoving/construction, and military markets. As a continuation of the company's focus on European expansion, recent acquisitions include Steel Wheels, Ltd., an earthmoving/construction wheel manufacturing facility in Kidderminster, England; Grasdorf Titan, GmbH, a wheel manufacturing and assembly facility in Hannover, Germany; and Titan France of Gennevilliers and St. Georges-de-Groseillers, France. The Sirmac Group of Italy, a major manufacturer of agricultural wheels was also fully acquired in 1996. Additional subsidiaries of Titan International include: Automotive Wheels, Inc. of Brea, California; Titan Wheel of Slinger, Wisconsin; Titan Tire, Inc. of Clinton, Tennessee; Nieman's Ltd. of Ventura, Iowa; TD Wheel Company of Virginia, Inc. of Saltville, Virginia; Titan Tire Corporation of Des Moines, Iowa; Titan Wheel of Greenwood, South Carolina; Titan Wheel of Merseyside, England; Titan Wheel of Quincy, Illinois; and Titan Wheel of Walcott, Iowa. Titan also operates 12 distribution centers throughout the United States. Incorporated in Illinois in 1983; present name adopted in 1997.

Directors (In addition to indicated officer)

Erwin H. Billig, Chm.
Edward J. Campbell
Richard M. Cashin, Jr.

Albert J. Febbo
Anthony L. Soave

Officers (Directors*)

*Maurice M. Taylor, Jr., Pres. & C.E.O.
Kent W. Hackamack, Treas.

Cheri T. Holley, Secy.
Michael R. Samide, C.O.O.

Consolidated Balance Sheet As of December 31, 1996 (000 omitted)

Assets		Liabilities & Stockholders' Equity	
Current assets	$284,651	Current liabilities	$103,636
Net property, plant & equipment	205,087	Long-term debt	113,096
Goodwill	41,249	Deferred income taxes	18,786
Other assets	27,605	Other liabilities	21,893
		*Stockholders' equity	301,181
Total	$558,592	Total	$558,592

*26,526,992 shares common stock outstanding.

Consolidated Income Statement

Years Ended Dec. 31	Thousands — — — — Net Sales	Net Income	Per Share[a] — — — — Earnings	Cash Dividends	Common Stock Price Range[a] Calendar Year
1996	$634,553	$35,378	$1.57	$ .06	18-1/8 — 12
1995	623,183	37,983	1.91	.05	21 — 11-5/8
1994	407,000	18,480	1.14	.03	13-5/8 — 9-5/8
1993	150,441	6,361	.46	.02	11-5/8 — 6-5/8
1992	113,170	4,072[b]	.21[b]		

[a]Adjusted to reflect 3-for-2 stock splits in March 1995 and August 1995, and a 858-for-1 stock split in March 1993. Initial public offering in May 1993.
[b]Net income before an extraordinary charge of $258,000 ($.03 per share) and for FAS 109, resulting in a charge of $275,000 ($.04 per share).

Transfer Agent & Registrar:	Harris Trust and Savings Bank		
General Counsel:	Cheri T. Holley, Secy.	Traded (Symbol):	NYSE (TWI)
Investor Relations:	Lisa Ross	Stockholders:	626
Mgt. Info. Svcs.:	Alfred Jones	Employees:	4,500
Auditors:	Price Waterhouse LLP	Annual Meeting:	In May

Tootsie Roll Industries, Inc.

7401 South Cicero Avenue, Chicago, Illinois 60629
Telephone: (773) 838-3400

Tootsie Roll Industries, Inc. has been engaged in the manufacture and sale of candy since 1896. The company's products are primarily sold under the brand names Tootsie Roll, Tootsie Roll Pops, Child's Play, Charms Blow Pop, Blue Razz, Cella's, Mason Dots, Mason Crows, Junior Mints, Charleston Chew, Sugar Daddy, and Sugar Babies. Tootsie Roll customers include wholesale distributors of candy and groceries, variety and drug store chains, discount houses, cooperative grocery associations, vending machine operators, and fundraising religious and charitable organizations. Tootsie Roll subsidiaries are located in Canada and Mexico. The company's five manufacturing facilities are located in Chicago; Cambridge, Massachusetts; New York; Covington, Tennessee; and Mexico City. The company's major subsidiaries include: The Tootsie Roll Company, Inc.; Charms Company; Cambridge Brands, Inc.; TRI Sales Co; Henry Eisen Advertising Agency, Inc.; Tootsie Roll of Canada, Ltd.; Cella's Confections, Inc.; World Trade and Marketing, Ltd.; Tri-Mass. Inc.; and Tutsi S.A. de C.V. Incorporated in Virginia in 1919.

Directors   (In addition to indicated officers)

Lana Jane Lewis-Brent

Charles W. Seibert

Officers   (Directors*)

*Melvin J. Gordon, Chm. & C.E.O.
*Ellen R. Gordon, Pres. & C.O.O.
 Thomas E. Corr, V.P.—Mktg. & Sales
 G. Howard Ember, V.P.—Fin. & Asst. Secy.
 James M. Hunt, V.P.—Phys. Distrib.

John W. Newlin, Jr., V.P.—Mfg.
Barry P. Bowen, Treas.
Daniel P. Drechney, Cont.
*William Touretz, Secy.

Consolidated Balance Sheet   As of December 31, 1996 (000 omitted)

Assets		Liabilities & Stockholders' Equity	
Current assets	$201,513	Current liabilities	$ 48,184
Net property, plant & equipment	81,687	Deferred items	9,268
Other assets	108,256	Other liabilities	21,123
		*Stockholders' equity	312,881
Total	$391,456	Total	$391,456

*15,617,000 shares common and 7,387,000 shares Class B common stock outstanding.

Consolidated Income Statement

Years Ended Dec. 31	Thousands — — — —		Per Share[a] — — —		Common Stock Price Range[a] Calendar Year
	Net Sales	Net Income	Earnings	Cash Dividends[b]	
1996	$340,909	$47,207	$2.05	$ .28	40-3/4 — 33-7/8
1995	312,660	40,368	1.75	.23	40-1/8 — 30-1/8
1994	296,932	37,931	1.65	.20	38-1/4 — 27-1/8
1993	259,593	35,442	1.54	.16	41-5/8 — 32-1/2
1992	245,424	32,032	1.39	.13	40-1/2 — 29

[a]Adjusted for a 2-for-1 stock split in July 1995 and for stock dividends.
[b]In addition to cash dividends, a 3% stock dividend is distributed each year in April.

Transfer Agent & Registrar: ChaseMellon Shareholder Services, L.L.C.

General Counsel:
  Becker Ross Stone DeStefano & Klein

Investor Relations: Barry P. Bowen, Treas.

Auditors: Price Waterhouse LLP

Traded (Symbol):   NYSE (TR)
Stockholders: 9,500
Employees: 1,750
Annual Meeting: In May

Total Control Products, Inc.

2001 North Janice Avenue, Melrose Park, Illinois 60160
Telephone: (708) 345-5500

Total Control Products, Inc. designs, develops, and markets products and technology for the control segment of the industrial automation market. The company's broad range of products are used to define, monitor, and maintain the operation, sequencing, and safety of industrial equipment and machinery on the factory floor. These products range from closed architecture programmable logic controller operator interfaces to open architecture control software and systems, and are sold primarily through an international network of independent distributors with over 200 sales locations. The company's principal product line, QuickPanel and similar products, has gained a leadership position in the operator interface market. In January 1996, the company acquired Cincinnati Dynacomp, Inc., a manufacturer of lower-end operator interface products, and in September 1996, the company acquired a controlling interest in Taylor Control Software Inc. In March 1997, Total Control completed an initial public offering of 2,000,000 shares of common stock. Incorporated in Illinois in 1983.

Directors (In addition to indicated officers)

Edward T. Hurd
Donald J. Kramer

A.B. Siemer
Julius J. Sparacino

Officers (Directors*)

*Nicholas T. Gihl, Chm., Pres. & C.E.O.
Dennis Marrano, Sr. V.P.—Oper.
Peter A. Nicholson, Sr. V.P., C.F.O., Treas. & Secy.

Kevin O'Connor, Sr. V.P.—Sales
*Neil R. Taylor, Sr. V.P.—Sofware Dev.
Frank Wood, Sr. V.P.—Prod. Dev. & Mktg.

Consolidated Balance Sheet As of March 31, 1997 (000 omitted)

Assets		Liabilities & Stockholders' Equity	
Current assets	$17,566	Current liabilities	$ 6,944
Net property, plant & equipment	2,393	Long-term debt	3,090
Other assets	11,503	Minority interest	1,521
		*Stockholders' equity	19,907
Total	$31,462	Total	$31,462

*6,916,465 shares common stock outstanding.

Consolidated Income Statement

Years Ended Mar. 31	Thousands — — — — Net Sales	Net Income[a]	Per Share[b] — — — Earnings	Cash Dividends	Common Stock Price Range[b] Calendar Year
1997	$40,821	$(1,564)	$(1.83)		
1996	25,743	997	(.11)		
1995	17,063	722	.09		
1994	11,723	(247)	(.07)		
1993	10,582	173	.04		

[a]Before non-recurring accretion to redemption value of common stock.
[b]Initial public offering in March 1997.

Transfer Agent & Registrar:	Norwest Bank Minnesota, N.A.		
General Counsel:	D'Ancona & Pflaum	Traded (Symbol):	NASDAQ (TCPS)
Investor Relations:	Peter A. Nicholson, Sr. V.P.	Stockholders:	680
Human Resources:	Peter A. Nicholson, Sr. V.P.	Employees:	238
Mgt. Info. Svcs.:	Peter A. Nicholson, Sr. V.P.	Annual Meeting:	As set by Directors
Auditors:	Arthur Andersen LLP	Internet:	www.total-control.com

Trans Leasing International, Inc.
3000 Dundee Road, Northbrook, Illinois 60062
Telephone: (847) 272-1000

Trans Leasing International, Inc. specializes in leasing medical and general office equipment to physicians and other health care and business professionals. A large portion of the equipment leased by the company is technologically advanced. The company markets its leasing services through salespeople representing various equipment suppliers with which the company does business and also through its own sales force. Trans Leasing has developed and is marketing an exclusive credit card called LeaseCard which it provides to qualified applicants for use in leasing equipment from the company. Trans Leasing Insurance Services Inc., a subsidiary selling property, casualty, and credit-life insurance to its lessees, was formed in 1982. The company maintains a separate subsidiary, Nuvotron, Inc., to handle the sale of used equipment which is returned to the company by lessees who elect not to exercise the purchase option at the end of the lease. Nuvotron, formed in 1991, also sells or disposes of repossessed equipment. The company formed T.L.I. Auto Leasing Group, Inc. (doing business as LeaseCard Auto Group) in 1991 to handle leasing services in the automobile market. Other subsidiaries include TL Lease Funding Corp. III and TL Lease Funding Corp. IV. Incorporated in Illinois in 1972; reincorporated in Delaware in 1983.

Directors   (In addition to indicated officers)

Larry Bier
Clifford V. Brokaw III

Mark C. Matthews
John W. Stodder

Officers   (Directors*)

*Larry S. Grossman, Chm. & C.E.O.
*Michael J. Heyman, Pres. & C.O.O.
 Joseph Rabito, Exec. V.P.

Kevin Dunworth, V.P.—Sales
Stephen J. Hupp, V.P.—Fin.

Consolidated Balance Sheet   As of June 30, 1996 (000 omitted)

Assets		Liabilities & Stockholders' Equity	
Current assets	$254,221	Current liabilities	$ 9,183
Net property, plant & equipment	9,520	Long-term debt	230,547
Other assets	5,686	Deferred items	3,411
		*Stockholders' equity	26,286
Total	$269,427	Total	$269,427

*4,045,375 shares common stock outstanding.

Consolidated Income Statement

Years Ended June 30	Thousands — — — — Total Revenues	Net Income	Per Share — — — — Earnings	Cash Dividends	Common Stock Price Range Fiscal Year
1996	$36,618	$1,667	$ .41	$ .12	5-7/8 — 3-1/4
1995[a]	30,529	1,567	.37	.03	4 — 3
1994	27,489	441[b]	.10[b]	.00	6 — 3-1/8
1993	24,995	2,034	.52	.00	6-3/8 — 3-3/4
1992	21,308	1,877	.64	.00	6-1/4 — 2-1/8

[a]Certain reclassifications have been made to prior years to conform with the presentation in 1995.
[b]Includes a charge to reflect FAS 109, resulting in a cumulative effect of $155,000 ($.03 per share).

Transfer Agent & Registrar: Harris Trust and Savings Bank

Corporate Counsel: Kirkland & Ellis

Investor Relations: Stephen J. Hupp, V.P.

Human Resources: Rickeia Lessig, Mgr.

Mgt. Info. Svcs.:   Martin G. Lewandowski, Dir.

Auditors: Deloitte & Touche LLP

Traded (Symbol):   NASDAQ (TLII)

Stockholders: 1,000

Employees: 160

Annual Meeting: In November

Tribune Company

435 North Michigan Avenue, Chicago, Illinois 60611-4001
Telephone: (312) 222-9100

Tribune Company is a leading media company with businesses in 19 of the nation's largest markets. Through newspapers, broadcasting, education, and new media, Tribune reaches nearly 70 percent of United States households daily. Tribune Broadcasting Co. owns 16 television stations and five radio stations, produces and syndicates television and radio programming, and owns a major league baseball team. Tribune Publishing Co. comprises four daily newspapers, electronic publishing, niche publications, and a syndication business. Tribune Education Co. provides innovative learning products and services for the school and consumer markets. In addition, Tribune has strategic investments in and alliances with emerging media and information technology businesses. Incorporated in Illinois in 1861; reincorporated as a holding company in Delaware in 1968.

Directors   (In addition to indicated officers)

Diego E. Hernandez
Robert E. La Blanc
Nancy Hicks Maynard
Andrew J. McKenna
Kristie M. Miller

James J. O'Connor
Donald H. Rumsfeld
Patrick G. Ryan
Dudley S. Taft
Arnold R. Weber

Officers   (Directors*)

*John W. Madigan, Chm., Pres. & C.E.O.
*James C. Dowdle, Exec. V.P.
Donald C. Grenesko, Sr. V.P.—Fin. & Admin.
David D. Hiller, Sr. V.P.—Dev.
Jeff R. Scherb, Sr. V.P. & Chf. Tech. Off.
David J. Granat, V.P. & Treas.
Crane H. Kenney, V.P., Gen. Coun. & Secy.

Luis E. Lewin, V.P.—Hum. Res.
R. Mark Mallory, V.P. & Cont.
Ruthellyn Musil, V.P.—Corp. Rel.
William B. Nelson, V.P.—Fin. Oper.
Andrew J. Oleszczuk, V.P.—Dev.
Shaun M. Sheehan, V.P.—Wash.

Consolidated Balance Sheet   As of December 29, 1996 (000 omitted)

Assets		Liabilities & Stockholders' Equity	
Current assets	$ 886,721	Current liabilities	$ 673,101
Net property, plant & equipment	642,708	Long-term debt	979,754
Other assets	2,171,471	Deferred items	189,673
		Other liabilities	318,866
		*Stockholders' equity	1,539,506
Total	$3,700,900	Total	$3,700,900

*122,945,000 shares common stock outstanding.

Consolidated Income Statement

Years Ended Abt. Dec. 31	Thousands — — — —		Per Share[b] — — —		Common Stock Price Range[b] Calendar Year
	Operating Revenues[a]	Net Income	Earnings	Cash Dividends	
1996	$2,405,705	$372,067	$2.88	$ .60	44-1/8 — 29
1995	2,244,674	278,165	2.00	.56	34-1/2 — 25-3/8
1994	2,112,656	242,047	1.66	.52	32-1/4 — 24-1/2
1993	1,911,538	188,606	1.28	.48	30-5/8 — 23-7/8
1992	1,820,670	119,825[c]	.78[c]	.48	34-1/2 — 19-3/8

[a]From continuing operations.
[b]Adjusted to reflect a 2-for-1 stock split in January 1997.
[c]Includes FAS 106, FAS 109 and FAS 112, resulting in a cumulative charge of $16,800,000 ($.26 per share).

Transfer Agent & Registrar:	First Chicago Trust Co. of New York			
Outside Counsel:	Sidley & Austin	Traded (Symbol):	NYSE, CSE, PSE (TRB)
Investor Relations:	Ruthellyn Musil, V.P.	Stockholders:	5,100
Human Resources:	Luis E. Lewin, V.P.	Employees:	10,700
Mgt. Info. Svcs.:	Jeff R. Scherb, Sr. V.P.	Annual Meeting:	In May
Auditors:	Price Waterhouse LLP	Internet:	www.tribune.com

TRO Learning, Inc.

Poplar Creek Office Plaza, 1721 Moon Lake Boulevard, Suite 555,
Hoffman Estates, Illinois 60194
Telephone: (847) 781-7800

TRO Learning, Inc. is a leading developer and marketer of microcomputer-based, interactive, self-paced instructional and testing systems used in a wide variety of adult settings. Offering comprehensive educational courseware specifically designed for young adult and adult learners, the company's PLATO® Learning Systems are marketed to middle schools and high schools, community colleges, job training programs, correctional institutions, government-funded programs, and corporations. The company's Aviation Training Systems are marketed to airlines worldwide for use by commercial airline pilots, maintenance crews, and cabin personnel. Incorporated in Delaware in 1989 as EduCorp; present name adopted in 1992.

Directors (In addition to indicated officers)

Jack R. Borsting, Ph.D.
Tony J. Christianson
John L. Krakauer

Maj. Gen. Vernon B. Lewis, Jr.
John Patience

Officers (Directors*)

*William R. Roach, Chm., Pres. & C.E.O.
Michael A. Hill, Sr. V.P.—PLATO Education
Andrew N. Peterson, Sr. V.P.—Fin., C.F.O.,
Treas. & Secy.
G. Thomas Ahern, V.P.—North Amer., PLATO
Education Sales
Wellesley R. Foshay, Ph.D., V.P.—
Instructional Design & Cognitive Learning

David H. LePage, V.P.—Sys. Dev., Client Sup.
& Oper.
Mary Jo Murphy, V.P.—Corp. Cont. & Chf. Acct.
Off.
John Murray, V.P.—Prod. Dev.
John Super, V.P.—Mktg.
Carl Thompson, V.P.—Custom & Aviation Training

Consolidated Balance Sheet As of October 31, 1996 (000 omitted)

Assets		Liabilities & Stockholders' Equity	
Current assets	$26,786	Current liabilities	$20,966
Net property, plant & equipment	1,368	Deferred revenue	296
Other assets	14,173	Other liabilities	253
		*Stockholders' equity	20,812
Total	$42,327	Total	$42,327

*6,167,000 shares common stock outstanding.

Consolidated Income Statement

Years Ended Oct. 31	Thousands — — — — Total Revenues	Net Income	Per Share[a] — — — — Earnings	Cash Dividends	Common Stock Price Range[a] Calendar Year
1996	$41,405	$ 982	$ .15	$ .00	22-1/4 — 7-1/2
1995	37,337	3,752	.60	.00	16-3/4 — 3-3/4
1994	28,365	3,361[b]	.53[b]	.00	10-1/2 — 3-3/4
1993[c]	26,533	4,577[d]	.76[d]	.00	17-3/4 — 5-3/4
1992[c]	22,864	3,858[d]	.86[d]	.00	14-1/4 — 10[e]

[a]Adjusted to reflect a 3.6-for-1 stock split in the form of a stock dividend in November 1992.
[b]Includes a gain to reflect FAS 109, resulting in a cumulative effect of $5,500,000 ($.87 per share).
[c]Pro forma.
[d]Includes extraordinary gains of $1,530,000 ($.25 per share) in 1993 and $1,380,000 ($.31 per share) in 1992 (tax benefits resulting from utilization of loss carryforwards).
[e]Initial public offering in December 1992.

Transfer Agent & Registrar: Harris Trust and Savings Bank

General Counsel:	Winston & Strawn	Traded (Symbol):	NASDAQ (TUTR)
Investor Relations:	Andrew N. Peterson, Sr. V.P.	Stockholders:	3,500
Human Resources:	Patricia Hawver, Dir.	Employees:	351
Mgt. Info. Svcs.:	David H. LePage, V.P.	Annual Meeting:	In March
Auditors:	Coopers & Lybrand L.L.P.	Internet:	www.tro.com

True North Communications Inc.

101 East Erie Street, Chicago, Illinois 60611-2897
Telephone: (312) 425-6500

True North Communications Inc. is a global marketing communications company whose agency brands offer advertising, direct marketing, sales promotion, and other specialized marketing services. In addition to the United States, the company has 205 offices located in 60 countries, including such regions as Asia, Canada, Europe, Latin America, and the Pacific. True North's clients represent many industries, primarily consumer goods and services. The company offers its clients yellow pages advertising through Wahlstrom & Company; direct marketing through FCB Direct; health care/pharmaceutical advertising through FCB HealthCare; sales promotion through IMPACT and Market Growth Resources; and Hispanic advertising through Siboney. Incorporated in Delaware in 1942; present name adopted in 1994.

Directors (In addition to indicated officers)

Richard S. Braddock
Laurel Cutler
Richard P. Mayer

Michael E. Murphy
Stephen T. Vehslage
Ali Wambold

Officers (Directors*)

*Bruce Mason, Chm. & C.E.O.
Theodore J. Theophilos, Exec. V.P. & Gen.
  Coun.
Dale F. Perona, Sr. V.P., Treas. & Secy.
Susan J. Geanuleas, V.P.—Corp. Comm.
John J. Rezich, V.P. & Cont.

*Gregory W. Blaine, Chm. & C.E.O.—TN
  Technologies Inc.
Mitchell T. Engel, Pres.—True North Assoc.
  Commun. Cos. & Corp. Oper
*J. Brendan Ryan, Chm. & C.E.O.—Foote, Cone &
  Belding Worldwide

Consolidated Balance Sheet   As of December 31, 1996 (000 omitted)

Assets		Liabilities & Stockholders' Equity	
Current assets	$504,246	Current liabilities	$553,191
Net property, plant & equipment	61,369	Long-term debt	31,513
Other assets	367,045	Other liabilities	106,615
		*Stockholders' equity	241,341
Total	$932,660	Total	$932,660

*23,872,000 shares common stock outstanding.

Consolidated Income Statement

Years Ended Dec. 31	Thousands — — — —		Per Share[a] — — —		Common Stock Price Range[a]
	Revenues	Net Income	Earnings	Cash Dividends	Calendar Year
1996	$493,050	$27,834	$1.20	$ .60	27-3/4 — 16-1/4
1995	439,053	19,653[b]	.87[b]	.60	21-3/4 — 15-3/4
1994	403,690	30,277	1.34	.60	24 — 19-7/8
1993	372,666	25,714	1.15	.60	24 — 14-3/4
1992	353,340	21,728[c]	1.00[c]	.60	15-3/4 — 11-7/8

[a]Adjusted to reflect a 2-for-1 stock split in the form of a 100% stock dividend in February 1995.
[b]Includes unusual items of $13,376,000 after-tax ($.60 per share), primarily due to restructuring of operations.
[c]Includes a gain to reflect FAS 109, resulting in a cumulative effect of $3,681,577 ($.17 per share).

Transfer Agent & Registrar: First Chicago Trust Co. of New York

General Counsel:
  Theodore J. Theophilos, Exec. V.P.

Investor Relations: Susan J. Geanuleas, V.P.

Human Resources: Paul Sollitto, V.P.

Mgt. Info. Svcs.:   Michael Oak

Auditors: Arthur Andersen LLP
Traded (Symbol):   NYSE (TNO)
Stockholders: 6,900
Employees: 5,022
Annual Meeting: In May

U.S. Can Corporation

900 Commerce Drive, Oak Brook, Illinois 60521
Telephone: (630) 571-2500

U.S. Can Corporation is a producer of steel and plastic containers for personal care, household, automotive, paint, and industrial products manufactured in the United States. The company conducts its principal business operations in the general packaging (non-food and non-beverage) segment of the metal container industry. The company produces aerosol, round and general line, and specialty containers, which are sold to many well-known companies. The Sherwin-Williams Company is U.S. Can's largest customer. Personal care and household products represent the primary end-use of the company's containers. The company's metal services operations provide secondary steel, as well as slitting, shearing, coating, and decorating of tin mill products for users outside the company. Many of U.S. Can's 39 manufacturing facilities, located in 12 states and five foreign countries, are strategically positioned near principal customers and suppliers. The company was formed in 1983 by an investor group led by William J. Smith, the company's chairman and chief executive officer, to acquire the container division of Sherwin-Williams. The company's principal subsidiary is U.S. Can Company. Incorporated in Delaware in 1983.

Directors (In addition to indicated officers)

Calvin W. Aurand, Jr.
Benjamin F. Bailar
Eugene B. Connolly, Jr.
Carl Ferenbach

Ricardo Poma
Francisco A. Soler
Michael J. Zimmerman

Officers (Directors*)

*William J. Smith, Chm., Pres. & C.E.O.
Frank J. Galvin, Exec. V.P.—Oper.
Timothy W. Stonich, Exec. V.P.—Fin., C.F.O. & Secy.
Charles E. Foster, Sr. V.P.—Custom & Spec. Prods.
Lawrence T. Messina, Sr. V.P.—Intl.
William S. Adams, V.P. & Grp. Exec.—Metal Svcs.
Peter J. Andres, V.P. & Treas.
Anthony F. Bonadonna, V.P.—Hum. Res.
Richard J. Krueger, V.P.—MIS

John R. McGowan, V.P. & Cont.
Larry S. Morrison, V.P.—Mfg., Custom/Spec. Prod.
Gene A. Papes, V.P.—Sales & Mktg., Aerosol Containers
Raymond J. Parker, V.P.—Eng., Eur.
David C. Schuermann, V.P. & Grp. Exec.—
  Paint/Plastic/Gen. Line
Jack J. Tunnell, V.P.—Southern & Eastern Oper.
David J. West, V.P.—Sales & Mktg., Custom/Spec. Prod.
Thomas J. Yurco, V.P.—Matl. Mgt. & Logistics

Consolidated Balance Sheet   As of December 31, 1996 (000 omitted)

Assets		Liabilities & Stockholders' Equity	
Current assets	$232,564	Current liabilities	$126,934
Net property, plant & equipment	323,114	Long-term debt	363,882
Other assets	87,938	Other liabilities	56,015
		*Stockholders' equity	96,785
Total	$643,616	Total	$643,616

*12,995,636 shares common stock outstanding.

Consolidated Income Statement

Years Ended Dec. 31	Thousands — — — — Net Sales	Net Income	Per Share[a] — — — — Earnings	Cash Dividends	Common Stock Price Range[a] Calendar Year
1996	$761,429	$ 11,751[b]	$ .90[b]	$ .00	18-1/4 — 13-1/4
1995	626,485	3,939	.31	.00	23-1/4 — 11
1994	563,153	18,570	1.73	.00	19-1/2 — 15
1993	455,127	7,522[c]	.79[c]	.00	17-1/8 — 11-1/4
1992	396,604	(12,115)[d]	(2.98)[d]		

[a] Initial public offering in March 1993.
[b] Includes an extraordinary loss, net of income taxes, of $5,250,000 ($.40 per share) on early extinguishment of debt.
[c] Includes an extraordinary loss, net of income taxes, of $3,402,000 ($.37 per share) on early extinguishment of debt.
[d] Includes FAS 106, resulting in a noncash charge, net of income taxes, of $12,537,000 ($2.83 per share).

Transfer Agent & Registrar: Harris Trust and Savings Bank

General Counsel:	Ross & Hardies	Auditors:	Arthur Andersen LLP
Investor Relations:	Timothy W. Stonich, Exec. V.P.	Traded (Symbol):	NYSE (USC)
		Stockholders:	3,500
Human Resources:	Anthony F. Bonadonna, V.P.	Employees:	4,065
Mgt. Info. Svcs.:	Richard J. Krueger, V.P.	Annual Meeting:	In April

UAL Corporation

P.O. Box 66919, Chicago, Illinois 60666
Telephone: (847) 700-4000

UAL Corporation is a holding company whose principal subsidiary is United Air Lines, Inc., a major commercial air transportation company. United has been engaged in the air transportation of persons, property, and mail since 1934, and certain predecessors began operations as early as 1926. In 1996, United served 139 airports worldwide, flew a total of 117 billion revenue passenger miles, and carried an average of 224,000 passengers a day, averaging 2,198 scheduled departures daily. United provides service to its domestic markets principally through a system of hub airports at major cities. Each hub provides United flights to a network of spoke destinations as well as flights to other United hubs. Currently, United flies from four domestic hubs: Chicago O'Hare International, Denver International, San Francisco International, and Dulles International near Washington, D.C. United is the principal carrier at each of these hubs. United also has a Pacific hub operation at Tokyo Narita Airport, and an Atlantic hub operation at London Heathrow Airport. United has developed a route system covering North America, Asia, Europe, Latin America, and the South Pacific. Incorporated in Delaware in 1968.

Directors (In addition to indicated officers)

Duane D. Fitzgerald	James J. O'Connor	Joseph V. Vittoria
Michael H. Glawe	John F. Peterpaul	Paul A. Volcker
Richard D. McCormick	Paul E. Tierney, Jr.	
John F. McGillicuddy	John K. Van de Kamp	

Officers (Directors*)

*Gerald M. Greenwald, Chm. & C.E.O.
*John A. Edwardson, Pres. & C.O.O.
 Joseph R. O'Gorman, Jr., Exec. V.P.

Stuart I. Oran, Exec. V.P.
Douglas A. Hacker, Sr. V.P. & C.F.O.
Francesca M. Maher, V.P.—Law & Corp. Secy.

Consolidated Balance Sheet As of December 31, 1996 (000 omitted)

Assets		Liabilities & Stockholders' Equity	
Current assets	$ 2,682,000	Current liabilities	$ 5,003,000
Net property, plant & equipment	8,243,000	Long-term debt & capital leases	2,986,000
Other assets	1,752,000	Other liabilities	3,693,000
		*Stockholders' equity	995,000
Total	$12,677,000	Total	$12,677,000

*58,817,480 shares common stock outstanding.

Consolidated Income Statement

Years Ended Dec. 31	Thousands — — — — Operating Revenues	Net Income	Per Share[a] — — — Earnings	Cash Dividends	Common Stock Price Range[a] Calendar Year
1996	$16,362,000	$ 533,000[b]	$ 5.04[b]	$ .00	64-3/4 — 38-5/8
1995	14,943,000	349,000[c]	4.78[c]	.00	53 — 21-7/8
1994	13,950,000	51,000[d]	(.15)[d]	.00	26-1/4 — 20-3/4[e]
1993	13,325,000	(50,000)[f]	(.85)[f]	.00	
1992	11,853,000	(956,800)[g]	(9.94)[g]	.00	

[a]Adjusted to reflect a 4-for-1 stock split in May 1996.
[b]Includes an extraordinary loss of $67,000,000 ($.78 per share) on early extinguishment of debt.
[c]Includes an extraordinary loss of $29,000,000 ($.40 per share) on early extinguishment of debt.
[d]Includes a charge to reflect FAS 112, resulting in a cumulative effect of $26,000,000 ($.34 per share).
[e]Stock price range for the period from the date of the recapitalization through year end. Comparisons of 1994 amounts to prior periods are not meaningful due to changes in the number of shares outstanding as a result of the recapitalization.
[f]Includes an extraordinary loss of $19,000,000 ($.19 per share) on early extinguishment of debt.
[g]Includes a charge to reflect FAS 106 and FAS 109, resulting in a cumulative effect of $539,600,000 ($5.60 per share).

Transfer Agent & Registrar: Harris Trust and Savings Bank

General Counsel:	Stuart I. Oran, Exec. V.P.	Traded (Symbol):	NYSE, CSE, PSE (UAL)
Investor Relations:	Cliff Hew, Mgr.	Stockholders:	17,000
Human Resources:	William P. Hobgood, Sr. V.P.—People	Employees:	86,000
Mgt. Info. Svcs.:	Andrew P. Studdert, Sr. V.P. & C.I.O.	Annual Meeting:	In April
Auditors:	Arthur Andersen LLP	Internet:	www.ual.com

Unicom Corporation

One First National Plaza, 10 S. Dearborn St., P.O. Box A-3005, Chicago, Illinois 60690-3005
Telephone: (312) 394-7399

Unicom Corporation (formerly Commonwealth Edison Company) is principally engaged in the production, purchase, transmission, distribution, and sale of electricity to a diverse base of residential, commercial, and industrial customers. The company's electric service territory has an area of about 11,500 square miles and an estimated population of eight million, including the City of Chicago, an area of about 225 square miles with an estimated population of three million. Unicom has more than 3,300,000 electric customers. Wholly owned subsidiaries are Commonwealth Edison Company and Unicom Enterprises Inc., which is the parent company of Unicom Thermal Technologies Inc. Commonwealth Edison was incorporated in Illinois in 1913; Unicom was incorporated in Illinois in 1994, when its present name was adopted.

Directors (In addition to indicated officers)

Edward A. Brennan	Sue L. Gin	Edgar D. Jannotta
James W. Compton	Donald P. Jacobs	George E. Johnson
Bruce DeMars		

Officers (Directors*)

*James J. O'Connor, Chm. & C.E.O.	William H. Dunbar, Jr., V.P.
*Leo F. Mullin, V. Chm.	J. Stanley Graves, V.P.
*Samuel K. Skinner, Pres.	Harold W. Keiser, V.P.
Thomas J. Maiman, Exec. V.P.	Emerson W. Lacey, V.P.
Robert J. Manning, Exec. V.P.	Thomas J. McCaffrey, V.P.
Donald A. Petkus, Sr. V.P.	Paul D. McCoy, V.P.
Michael J. Wallace, Sr. V.P.	J. Stephen Perry, V.P.
John C. Bukovski, V.P. & C.F.O.	James A. Small, V.P.
Frank M. Clark, V.P.	Pamela B. Strobel, V.P. & Gen. Coun.
John T. Costello, V.P.	Roger F. Kovack, Compt.
Louis O. DelGeorge, V.P.	Dennis F. O'Brien, Treas.
William H. Downey, V.P.	David A. Scholz, Secy.

Consolidated Balance Sheet   As of December 31, 1996 (000 omitted)

Assets		Liabilities & Stockholders' Equity	
Current assets	$ 1,452,810	Current liabilities	$ 1,936,086
Net utility, plant & equipment	17,226,264	Long-term debt	6,069,534
Other assets	4,708,896	Deferred items	8,352,727
		*Stockholders' equity	7,029,623
Total	$23,387,970	Total	$23,387,970

*215,954,625 shares common stock outstanding.

Consolidated Income Statement

Years Ended Dec. 31	Thousands — — — —		Per Share — — —		Common Stock Price Range Calendar Year
	Elec. Oper. Revs.	Net Income[a]	Earnings[a]	Cash Dividends[ab]	
1996	$6,937,024	$666,100	$3.09	$1.60	35-3/8 — 22-5/8
1995	6,910,045	639,511	2.98	1.60	33-7/8 — 23-1/4
1994	6,277,521	354,934	1.66	1.60	28-3/4 — 20-5/8
1993	5,260,440	46,388[c]	.22[cd]	1.60	31-5/8 — 22-7/8
1992	6,026,321	443,442	2.08	2.30	40-1/8 — 21-3/4

[a]Available for common stock.
[b]Declared.
[c]Includes a gain to reflect FAS 109, resulting in a cumulative effect of $9,738,000 ($.05 per share).
[d]Net writedown of $1.61 per share occurred during the year 1993.

Transfer Agent & Registrar: First Chicago Trust Co. of New York

General Counsel:	Pamela B. Strobel, V.P.	Traded (Symbol):	NYSE, CSE, PSE (UCM)
Investor Relations:	Kathryn Houtsma, Mgr.	Stockholders:	182,000
Human Resources:	J. Stanley Graves, V.P.	Employees:	18,460
Mgt. Info. Svcs.:	George Orlov, V.P.	Annual Meeting:	In May
Auditors:	Arthur Andersen LLP	Internet:	www.ucm.com

UNIMED Pharmaceuticals, Inc.

2150 East Lake Cook Road, Buffalo Grove, Illinois 60089-1862
Telephone: (847) 541-2525

UNIMED Pharmaceuticals, Inc. and its consolidated subsidiary develop and market prescription pharmaceutical products. Currently, the company promotes two approved drugs and is developing others targeted for the HIV/AIDS, infectious diseases, endocrinology, urology, oncology, and hematology markets. The company developed Marinol®, an appetite stimulant and antiemetic drug, and promotes it through a specialty sales force in the U.S., primarily to AIDS-treating physicians. Marinol is distributed in international markets through foreign licenses. In February 1997, the company acquired from G.D. Searle & Co. the long-term, exclusive U.S. marketing and distribution rights fo Maxaquin® (lomefloxacin), a fluoroquinolone antibiotic used in the urology and infectious disease markets. Incorporated in Delaware in 1981.

Directors   (In addition to indicated officers)

Fred Holubow
James J. Lempenau

Roland Weiser

Officers   (Directors*)

*John N. Kapoor, Ph.D., Chm.
 Robert E. Dudley, Ph.D., Pres. & C.E.O.
 David E. Riggs, Sr. V.P.—Fin./Admin. &
  C.F.O.
 John E. Lee, V.P.—Commercial Dev.

Phillip B. Donenberg, Asst. Treas. &
 Dir.—Accounting
Brian Jennings, Dir.—Natl. Sales
Donald Peckels, Dir.—Regulatory Affairs

Consolidated Balance Sheet   As of December 31, 1996 (000 omitted)

Assets		Liabilities & Stockholders' Equity	
Current assets	$27,078	Current liabilities	$ 8,177
Net property, plant & equipment	808	*Stockholders' equity	22,570
Other assets	2,861		
Total	$30,747	Total	$30,747

*8,775,499 shares common stock outstanding.

Consolidated Income Statement

Years Ended Dec. 31	Thousands — — — — Net Sales	Net Income	Per Share — — — — Earnings	Cash Dividends	Common Stock Price Range Calendar Year
1996	$7,649	$ 1,522	$ .17	$ .00	9-1/2 — 5-5/8
1995	7,320	625	.09	.00	7-5/8 — 2-3/8
1994	7,388	41	.01	.00	5-1/4 — 2
1993	6,876	(852)	(.14)	.00	11-3/4 — 3-3/4
1992[a]	3,697	(4,210)[b]	(.79)	.00	11-3/4 — 6-1/2

[a]September 30 fiscal year end.
[b]Includes a pretax charge of $2,519,000 related to restructuring.

Transfer Agent & Registrar: Harris Trust and Savings Bank

General Counsel: Katherine A. Letourneau

Securities Counsel: Rudnick & Wolfe

Investor Relations: David E. Riggs, Sr. V.P.

Human Resources:
 Phillip B. Donenberg, Asst. Treas.

Mgt. Info. Svcs.:
 Phillip B. Donenberg, Asst. Treas.

Auditors: Coopers & Lybrand L.L.P.

Traded (Symbol):   NASDAQ (UMED)

Stockholders: 3,000

Employees: 26

Annual Meeting: In April

UnionBancorp, Inc.

122 West Madison Street, Ottawa, Illinois 61350
Telephone: (815) 434-3900

UnionBancorp, Inc. is a multi-bank holding company. Through its subsidiaries, the company provides a range of commercial and retail lending services, and a variety of additional services and financial products to corporations, partnerships, and individuals in 10 Illinois counties. Principal bank subsidiaries include UnionBank, located in Streator, Illinois, and UnionBank/Sandwich, located in Sandwich, Illinois. In 1996, the company acquired Prairie Bancorp, Inc., which owned six bank subsidiaries in the Illinois communities of Carthage, Hanover, Ladd, Manlius, Tampico, and Tiskilwa. The company also acquired Country Bancshares, Inc. which owned a bank subsidiary in Macomb, Illinois. UnionBancorp's non-bank subsidiaries include UnionData Corp., which provides data processing services; Union Corporation, which serves primarily as an owner and lessor of some of the company's banks; and LaSalle County Collections, Inc., a debt collection agency located in Ottawa, Illinois. Incorporated in Delaware in 1982.

Directors (In addition to indicated officers)

Richard J. Berry
Walter E. Breipohl
L. Paul Broadus
Robert J. Doty
Lawrence J. McGrogan

I.J. Reinhardt, Jr.
H. Dean Reynolds
John A. Shinkle
Scott C. Sullivan
John A. Trainor

Officers (Directors*)

*R. Scott Grigsby, Chm., Pres. & C.E.O.
Wayne L. Bismark, Exec. V.P. & Chf. Credit Off.
Charles J. Grako, Exec. V.P., C.F.O. & Secy.

*Jimmie D. Lansford, Sr. V.P.—Org. Dev. & Planning
*John Michael Daw, Sr. Agricultural Rep.

Consolidated Balance Sheet As of December 31, 1996 (000 omitted)

Assets		Liabilities & Stockholders' Equity	
Cash and cash equivalents	$ 29,236	Total deposits	$543,744
Federal funds sold	10,267	Notes payable	13,180
Securities	223,555	Other liabilities	36,865
Net loans	343,428	Mandatory redeemable	857
Property and equipment	13,580	preferred stock	
Other assets	21,958	Minority interest in subsidiaries	795
		*Stockholders' equity	46,583
Total	$642,024	Total	$642,024

*4,386,064 shares common stock outstanding.

Consolidated Income Statement

Years Ended Dec. 31	Thousands — — — — Total Income	Net Income	Per Share[a] — — — — Earnings	Cash Dividends	Common Stock Price Range[a] Calendar Year
1996	$34,259	$2,729	$ .98	$1.36	14-1/2 — 10
1995	23,938	2,353	1.09	1.32	9 — 7-5/8
1994	20,910	2,594	1.22	1.16	7-5/8 — 6-3/4
1993	21,116	2,462	1.15		
1992	22,021	2,311	1.08		

[a]Adjusted to reflect a 3-for-1 stock split in May 1996.

Transfer Agent & Registrar: Harris Trust and Savings Bank

General Counsel:
  Barack, Ferrazano, Kirschbaum & Perlman

Investor Relations: Debra M. Tombaugh, V.P.

Human Resources: Jimmie D. Lansford, Sr. V.P.

Auditors: Crowe, Chizek & Co.

Traded (Symbol): NASDAQ (UBCD)
Stockholders: 614
Employees: 281
Annual Meeting: In April
Internet: www.ubcd.com

United States Cellular Corporation

8410 West Bryn Mawr Avenue, Suite 700, Chicago, Illinois 60631-3486
Telephone: (773) 399-8900

United States Cellular Corporation owns, operates, and invests in cellular telephone systems in metropolitan and rural areas in the United States. Through subsidiaries and joint ventures, the company has interests in systems in 204 metropolitan and rural areas in 33 states, including 73 metropolitan systems and 131 rural systems in operation as of December 1996. The company owned a majority interest in 131 of these operational cellular systems as of December 1996. The company has an agreement to acquire a majority interest in one additional system. United States Cellular coordinates sales and marketing efforts through market clusters, which offer improved operational efficiency and customer service. Telephone and Data Systems, Inc. owns over 80 percent of the outstanding common stock of the company. Incorporated in Delaware in 1983.

Directors (In addition to indicated officers)

LeRoy T. Carlson
Walter C.D. Carlson
Paul-Henri Denuit

Allan Z. Loren
Murray L. Swanson

Officers (Directors*)

*Leroy T. Carlson, Jr., Chm.
*H. Donald Nelson, Pres. & C.E.O.
Richard W. Goehring, Sr. V.P.—Eng.
Joyce V. Gab Kneeland, Sr. V.P.—Oper.
Kenneth R. Meyers, Sr. V.P.—Fin. & C.F.O.
Douglas S. Arnold, V.P.—Hum. Res.

David M. Friedman, V.P.—Mktg.
Michael A. Mutz, V.P.—Oper.
Edward W. Towers, V.P.—Mkt. & Bus. Dev.
James D. West, V.P.—Info. Svcs.
Stephen P. Fitzell, Secy.
Phillip A. Lorenzini, Cont.

Consolidated Balance Sheet As of December 31, 1996 (000 omitted)

Assets		Liabilities & Stockholders' Equity	
Current assets	$ 128,619	Current liabilities	$ 146,454
Net property, plant & equipment	650,754	Long-term debt	330,696
Investment in licenses, net	1,245,875	Deferred items	81,277
Deferred charges	60,651	Minority interest	51,270
		*Stockholders' equity	1,476,202
Total	$2,085,899	Total	$2,085,899

*53,117,313 shares common and 33,005,877 shares Series A common stock outstanding.

Consolidated Income Statement

Years Ended Dec. 31	Thousands — — — — Total Revenues	Net Income	Per Share — — — — Earnings	Cash Dividends	Common Stock Price Range Calendar Year
1996	$707,820	$ 129,929	$ 1.51	$ .00	37-3/8 — 26-7/8
1995	492,395	99,742	1.19	.00	36-1/2 — 27-3/4
1994	332,404	16,393	.21	.00	35-1/4 — 22-3/8
1993	214,310[a]	(25,441)	(.45)	.00	39-1/4 — 20-3/4
1992	139,929[a]	6,194	.11	.00	24-1/4 — 17-1/2

[a]Restated.

Transfer Agent & Registrar: Harris Trust and Savings Bank

General Counsel:	Sidley & Austin	Traded (Symbol):	AMEX (USM)
Investor Relations:	Kenneth R. Meyers, Sr. V.P.	Stockholders:	649
Human Resources:	Douglas S. Arnold, V.P.	Employees:	3,800
Mgt. Info. Svcs.:	James D. West, V.P.	Annual Meeting:	In May
Auditors:	Arthur Andersen LLP	Internet:	www.uscc.com

United Stationers Inc.

2200 East Golf Road, Des Plaines, Illinois 60016-1267
Telephone: (847) 699-5000

United Stationers Inc. is a wholesale distributor of business products. Its offerings of more than 30,000 items are available only to resellers; the company does not sell direct to end users. Through its sophisticated computer-based physical distribution network, the company provides 15,000 resellers with products from more than 500 manufacturers within 24 hours. An extensive truck fleet extends the reach of 41 regional distribution centers and 24 local distribution points. Products include office supplies, office furniture, janitorial and sanitation products, information systems supplies, microcomputers, peripherals, and retail specialty products. Comprehensive computer capabilities integrate forecasting, buying, inventory control, order entry, shipping, and invoicing. The company further supports its dealers through a variety of pricing, inventory control, catalog, and promotional program services. The company's major subsidiary is United Stationers Supply Co. In March 1995, United Stationers merged with Associated Holdings, Inc., with United Stationers being the surviving entity. Incorporated in Delaware in 1981.

Directors (In addition to indicated officers)

James T. Callier, Jr.	Jeffrey K. Hewson	Gary G. Miller
Daniel J. Good	James A. Johnson	Joel D. Spungin

Officers (Directors*)

*Frederick B. Hegi, Jr., Chm.
*Randall W. Larrimore, Pres. & C.E.O.
Daniel H. Bushell, Exec. V.P. & C.F.O.
*Michael Rowsey, Exec. V.P.
Steven R. Schwarz, Exec. V.P.

Robert H. Cornell, V.P.—Hum. Res.
Otis H. Halleen, V.P., Secy. & Gen. Coun.
Albert H. Shaw, V.P.—Oper.
Ergin Uskup, V.P.—Mgt. Info. Svcs. & C.I.O.
James A. Pribel, Treas.

Consolidated Balance Sheet As of December 31, 1996 (000 omitted)

Assets		Liabilities & Stockholders' Equity	
Current assets	$ 790,480	Current liabilities	$ 385,507
Net property, plant & equipment	173,775	Long-term obligations	552,613
Goodwill, net	115,449	Deferred items	36,828
Other assets	30,163	Other liabilities	59,099
		*Stockholders' equity	75,820
Total	$1,109,867	Total	$1,109,867

*11,446,306 shares common stock outstanding.

Consolidated Income Statement

Years Ended Dec. 31	Thousands — — — — Net Sales	Net Income	Per Share[a] — — — — Earnings	Cash Dividends	Common Stock Price Range[a] Calendar Year
1996	$2,298,170	$31,993	$2.03	$ .00	30-1/4 — 17-1/2
1995[b]	1,751,462	4,794[cd]	.22[c]	.00	27-3/4 — 8-5/8[c]
1994	470,185	6,403	.51	.00	
1993	455,731	2,962	.11	.00	
1992[f]	359,779	2,950	.19	.00	

[a]Adjusted to reflect a 100 percent stock dividend in November 1995.
[b]Reflects the results of Associated Holdings for the three months ended March 30, and the results of the merged company for the nine months ended December 31. For accounting purposes, the merger was treated as a reverse acquisiton, with Associated as the acquiring company. Prior years reflect only the results of Associated.
[c]Includes an extraordinary loss of $1,449,000 ($.11 per share) on the early retirement of debt.
[d]Includes a charge of $9,800,000 for restructuring.
[e]Due to significant changes in the company's capital structure resulting from the merger, the stock price reflects only the period from April 1 to December 31.
[f]January 31 to December 31.

Transfer Agent & Registrar:	Boston EquiServe		
General Counsel:	Otis H. Halleen, V.P.	Traded (Symbol):	NASDAQ (USTR)
Investor Relations:	Kathleen S. Dvorak, Dir.	Stockholders:	1,100
Human Resources:	Robert H. Cornell, V.P.	Employees:	5,000
Mgt. Info. Svcs.:	Ergin Uskup, V.P.	Annual Meeting:	In May
Auditors:	Ernst & Young LLP	Internet:	www.unitedstationers.com

Unitrin, Inc.

One East Wacker Drive, Chicago, Illinois 60601
Telephone: (312) 661-4600

Unitrin, Inc. is a financial services company with subsidiaries engaged in three business areas: property and casualty insurance, life and health insurance, and consumer finance. The Property and Casualty Insurance segment provides personal and commercial insurance consisting of automobile, homeowners, motorcycle, watercraft, fire, casualty, workers' compensation, and related lines. Unitrin's leading life insurance product is a traditional life insurance policy sold to individuals. Traditional life insurance products offered by Unitrin include both permanent and term insurance. The company also offers individual and group health and hospitalization insurance. Unitrin is engaged in the consumer finance business through its subsidiary, Fireside Thrift Co., which is organized under California law as an industrial loan company. Fireside's principal business is automobile financing, primarily of used automobiles, through the purchase of conditional sales contracts from automobile dealers, and direct loans. Other Unitrin subsidiaries are: United Insurance Company of America and its life and health insurance subsidiaries, Union National Life Insurance Company and The Pyramid Life Insurance Company; Trinity Universal Insurance Company and its property and casualty insurance subsidiaries, Financial Indemnity Company and Milwaukee Insurance Group and its subsidiaries; Union Automobile Indemnity Company; and other indirect subsidiaries. Incorporated in Delaware in 1990.

Directors   (In addition to indicated officers)

James E. Annable
Reuben L. Hedlund
George A. Roberts

Fayez S. Sarofim
Henry E. Singleton

Officers   (Directors*)

*Jerrold V. Jerome, Chm.
*Richard C. Vie, Pres. & C.E.O.
 David F. Bengston, V.P.
 James W. Burkett, V.P.

Thomas H. Maloney, V.P. & Gen. Coun.
Eric J. Draut, C.F.O. & Treas.
Scott Renwick, Secy.

Consolidated Balance Sheet   As of December 31, 1996 (000 omitted)

Assets		Liabilities & Stockholders' Equity	
Investments	$3,291,400	Insurance reserves	$2,053,800
Consumer loan receivables	608,600	Investment certificates &	589,900
Other receivables	376,100	passbook accounts	
Other assets	595,000	Unearned premiums	260,500
		Notes payable	59,900
		Other liabilities	426,700
		*Stockholders' equity	1,480,300
Total	$4,871,100	Total	$4,871,100

*37,340,894 shares common stock outstanding.

Consolidated Income Statement

Years Ended Dec. 31	Thousands — — — — Total Revenues	Net Income	Per Share — — — — Earnings	Cash Dividends	Common Stock Price Range Calendar Year
1996	$1,523,100	$132,500	$3.51	$2.20	56-3/8 — 44-1/4
1995	1,447,400	150,600	3.73	2.00	50-1/2 — 43
1994	1,365,500	148,400	2.96	1.50	51-1/2 — 38-1/2
1993	1,363,200	95,000	1.83	1.30	46-3/4 — 39
1992	1,362,600	123,400[a]	2.38[a]	1.10	42-3/4 — 32-3/4

[a]Includes the cumulative effect of FAS 106, resulting in a one-time after-tax charge of $39,900,000 ($.77 per share).

Transfer Agent & Registrar: First Chicago Trust Co. of New York

General Counsel:	Thomas H. Maloney, V.P.	Auditors:	KPMG Peat Marwick LLP
Investor Relations:	Scott Renwick, Secy.	Traded (Symbol):	NASDAQ (UNIT)
		Stockholders:	9,900
Human Resources:	Amy Cardella	Employees:	7,400
Mgt. Info. Svcs.:	William R. Whaley	Annual Meeting:	In May

Universal Automotive Industries, Inc.

3350 North Kedzie Avenue, Chicago, Illinois 60618-5722
Telephone: (773) 478-2323

Universal Automotive Industries, Inc. is a manufacturer and distributor of brake parts sold to the automotive aftermarket. The company specializes in the distribution of brake rotors and other brake parts, which it markets under its private label, UBP Universal Brake Parts. The company manufactures many of the brake rotors it distributes. Subsidiaries include Universal Automotive, Inc.; UBP Hungary, Inc.; and UBP Canholdings, Inc. Incorporated in Delaware in 1994.

Directors (In addition to indicated officers)

Sheldon Robinson   Sol S. Weiner

Officers (Directors*)

*Yehuda Tzur, Chm.
*Arvin Scott, Pres. & C.E.O.
*Eric Goodman, Exec. V.P.—Canadian Oper.

*Sami Israel, V.P. & Treas.
Jerome J. Hiss, C.F.O. & Secy.

Consolidated Balance Sheet As of December 31, 1996 (000 omitted)

Assets		Liabilities & Stockholders' Equity	
Current assets	$28,046	Current liabilities	$13,777
Net property, plant & equipment	8,836	Long-term debt	15,394
Other assets	1,145	*Stockholders' equity	8,856
Total	$38,027	Total	$38,027

*6,647,796 shares common stock outstanding.

Consolidated Income Statement

Years Ended Dec. 31	Thousands — — — — Net Sales	Net Income	Per Share[a] — — — Earnings	Cash Dividends	Common Stock Price Range[ab] Calendar Year
1996	$63,060	$ (493)	$ (.07)	$ .00	12 — 1-1/4
1995	46,815	64	.01	.00	12-7/8 — 9-1/2
1994	39,712	521	.11	.00	10-3/4 — 5-1/4
1993	33,170	421	.07		
1992	33,510	1,186			

[a]Adjusted to reflect a 1-for-5,200 reverse stock split in December 1994.
[b]Initial public offering in December 1994 of 1,300,000 units, each consisting of one share of common stock and one redeemable common stock purchase warrant.

Transfer Agent & Registrar: Continental Stock Transfer & Trust Co.

General Counsel:
  Shefsky Froelich & Devine, Ltd.

Investor Relations: Jerome J. Hiss, C.F.O.

Human Resources: Jerome J. Hiss, C.F.O.

Mgt. Info. Svcs.: Jerome J. Hiss, C.F.O.

Auditors:
  Altschuler, Melvoin and Glasser LLP

Traded (Symbol): CSE (UVS); NASDAQ (UVSL)

Stockholders: 900

Employees: 400

Annual Meeting: In June

Internet: www.uaiinc.com

Universal Outdoor Holdings, Inc.

321 North Clark Street, Suite 1010, Chicago, Illinois 60610
Telephone: (312) 644-8673

Universal Outdoor Holdings, Inc. is a leading outdoor advertising company operating approximately 31,049 advertising display faces in three large, regional operating areas: the Midwest, the Southeast, and the East Coast. The company is among the largest outdoor advertising companies in the metropolitan Chicago and Milwaukee markets, and has the largest presence in Indianapolis, Des Moines, and Evansville (Indiana). Universal's principal operating subsidiary is Universal Outdoor, Inc. In 1996, the company acquired five outdoor advertising companies and entered into agreements to acquire two others. In July 1996, the company completed an initial public offering of 6,200,000 shares of common stock. Incorporated in Illinois in 1975; reincorporated in Delaware in 1991.

Directors (In addition to indicated officers)

Frank K. Bynum, Jr.
Michael B. Goldberg

Michael J. Roche

Officers (Directors*)

*Daniel L. Simon, Pres. & C.E.O.
*Brian T. Clingen, V.P. & C.F.O.

Paul G. Simon, V.P., Secy. & Gen. Coun.

Consolidated Balance Sheet   As of December 31, 1996 (000 omitted)

Assets		Liabilities & Stockholders' Equity	
Current assets	$ 51,641	Current liabilities	$ 29,905
Net property, plant & equipment	382,555	Long-term debt	349,141
Goodwill & intangible assets, net	219,009	Deferred items	71,700
Other assets	25,114	Other liabilities	485
		*Stockholders' equity	227,088
Total	$678,319	Total	$678,319

*23,992,800 shares common stock outstanding.

Consolidated Income Statement

Years Ended Dec. 31	Thousands — — — — Total Revenues	Net Income	Per Share[a] — — — — Earnings	Cash Dividends	Common Stock Price Range[ab] Calendar Year
1996	$84,939	$(35,803)[c]	$(2.27)[c]	$ .00	38-1/4 — 16-1/8
1995	38,101	(3,703)	(.48)		
1994	33,180	(5,166)	(.67)		
1993	28,710	(9,321)[d]			
1992	27,896	(6,349)			

[a]Adjusted to reflect a 16-for-1 stock split in July 1996.
[b]Initial public offering in July 1996.
[c]Includes an extraordinary loss of $26,574,000 ($1.68 per share) for early extinguishment of debt.
[d]Includes an extraordinary loss of $3,260,000 for early extinguishment of debt.

Transfer Agent & Registrar:	LaSalle National Trust, N.A.		
General Counsel:	Paul G. Simon, V.P.	Traded (Symbol):	NASDAQ (UOUT)
Investor Relations:	Brian T. Clingen, V.P.	Stockholders:	2,000
Human Resources:	Belva Shinn	Employees:	1,000
Mgt. Info. Svcs.:	Peter Theodosis	Annual Meeting:	In May
Auditors:	Price Waterhouse LLP	Internet:	www.universaloutdoor.com

UNR Industries, Inc.

6718 West Plank Road, Peoria, Illinois 61604
Telephone: (309) 697-4400

UNR Industries, Inc., through its Rohn Division, manufactures towers, poles, mounts, and related accessories, used principally to support telecommunications antennae for wireless communications such as private microwave, cellular telephone, personal communications systems, commercial and amateur broadcasting, and home television. The company also produces shelters and cabinets of concrete and fiberglass to house electronic telecommunications equipment. In 1997, the company relocated its headquarters from Chicago to Peoria. Incorporated in Illinois in 1918; reincorporated in Delaware in 1970; and reincorporated in Delaware again in 1979 as UNR Industries, Inc.

Directors (In addition to indicated officers)

Gene Locks, Chm.
Charles M. Brennan III
Darius W. Gaskins, Jr.
Ruth R. McMullin

Thomas F. Meagher
Robert B. Steinberg
William J. Williams

Officers (Directors*)

*Brian B. Pemberton, Pres. & C.E.O.
Rodney B. Harrison, V.P. & Treas.

Victor E. Grimm, Secy. & Gen. Coun.
Jeffrey T. Jablonski, Dir.—Taxation

Consolidated Balance Sheet As of December 31, 1996 (000 omitted)

Assets		Liabilities & Stockholders' Equity	
Current assets	$68,888	Current liabilities	$38,670
Net property, plant & equipment	21,822	Long-term debt	12,191
Other assets	2,662	*Stockholders' equity	42,511
Total	$93,372	Total	$93,372

*52,383,000 shares common stock outstanding.

Consolidated Income Statement

Years Ended Dec. 31	Thousands — — — — Net Sales	Net Income	Per Share — — — Earnings	Cash Dividends	Common Stock Price Range Calendar Year
1996	$154,434	$ 46,041	$ .89	$2.60	10 — 5-7/8
1995	142,216	29,276	.57	2.55	9-3/4 — 5-1/4
1994[a]	107,026	31,325	.64	.20	7-1/8 — 5-1/8
1993[ab]	73,811	18,784	.40	1.20	8-1/2 — 5-7/8
1992[ab]	67,262	123,663[c]	2.74[c]	2.20	8-1/4 — 3-5/8

[a]Restated to reflect the 1995 discontinuance of UNR Leavitt, Unarco Commercial Products, UNR Home Products, and Real Time Solutions, Inc.
[b]Restated to reflect the 1994 discontinuance of Unarco Material Handling.
[c]Includes a tax benefit of $90,000,000 ($1.99 per share) as a result of tax regulations, and $8,100,000 ($.18 per share) as the result of insurance litigation settlement.

Transfer Agent & Registrar: First Chicago Trust Co. of New York

General Counsel:	Victor E. Grimm	Auditors:	Arthur Andersen LLP
Investor Relations:	Brian B. Pemberton	Traded (Symbol):	NASDAQ, CSE (UNRI)
Human Resources:	William O. Evans	Stockholders:	3,100
		Employees:	700
Mgt. Info. Svcs.:	Charles H. Wendorff	Annual Meeting:	In May

USFreightways Corporation

9700 Higgins Road, Suite 570, Rosemont, Illinois 60018
Telephone: (847) 696-0200

USFreightways Corporation operates a group of regional less-than-truckload (LTL) general commodities motor carriers, which are carriers that fill their trucks with partial loads from multiple customers. The company's regional trucking subsidiaries focus on overnight and second-day delivery and provide service throughout the United States, Puerto Rico, and Canada. The company also operates logistics subsidiaries which provide complete solutions to customers' logistics and distribution requirements. The company's largest subsidiary is USF Holland Inc., which operates throughout the central and southeastern United States. The company's other trucklines include USF Red Star Inc. in the Northeast; USF Bestway Inc. in the Southwest; USF Dugan Inc. in the Plains and southeastern states; and USF Reddaway Inc. on the West Coast. Incorporated in Delaware in 1991; present name adopted in 1996.

Directors   (In addition to indicated officers)

Morley Koffman, Chm.
Robert V. Delaney
Robert P. Neuschel

John W. Puth
Neil A. Springer
William N. Weaver, Jr.

Officers   (Directors*)

*John Campbell Carruth, Pres. & C.E.O.

Christopher L. Ellis, Sr. V.P.—Fin. & C.F.O.

Consolidated Balance Sheet   As of December 28, 1996 (000 omitted)

Assets		Liabilities & Stockholders' Equity	
Current assets	$203,577	Current liabilities	$144,348
Net property, plant & equipment	395,500	Long-term debt	178,000
Other assets	89,431	Deferred items	46,597
		Other liabilities	50,303
		*Stockholders' equity	269,260
Total	$688,508	Total	$688,508

*22,594,890 shares common stock outstanding.

Consolidated Income Statement

Years Ended Abt. Dec. 31	Thousands — — — —		Per Share[a] — — — —		Common Stock
	Operating Revenue	Net Income	Earnings	Cash Dividends	Price Range[a] Calendar Year
1996	$1,330,972	$33,807[b]	$1.51[b]	$ .37	28-1/4 — 16-3/4
1995	1,144,458	33,338	1.51	.37	28-5/8 — 16-1/4
1994	1,016,464	32,065	1.45[c]	.37	29-3/4 — 19-1/4
1993	898,920	27,348	1.20	.37	27-1/2 — 12
1992	774,678	21,092[d]	.79[d]	.28	14-3/8 — 9-3/8[e]

[a]Adjusted to reflect a 3-for-2 stock split in September 1993.
[b]Includes a charge of $2,329,000 ($.10 per share) for restructuring at USF Red Star Inc.
[c]After extraordinary charge of $.06 per share.
[d]Before cumulative effect of FAS 109.
[e]Initial public offering in February 1992.

Transfer Agent & Registrar: Harris Trust and Savings Bank

General Counsel: Sachnoff & Weaver, Ltd.

Investor Relations: Kenneth F. Ball, Dir.

Mgt. Info. Svcs.:   Tim Harvie, V.P.

Auditors: KPMG Peat Marwick LLP

Traded (Symbol):   NASDAQ (USFC)
Stockholders: 6,800
Employees: 15,400
Annual Meeting: In May
Internet: www.usfreightways.com

USG Corporation

125 South Franklin Street, Chicago, Illinois 60606-4678
Telephone: (312) 606-4000

USG Corporation is a holding company whose major subsidiaries include United States Gypsum Company; USG Interiors, Inc.; L&W Supply Corporation; and CGC Inc. These subsidiaries are diversified manufacturers, marketers, and distributors of products used primarily in the building materials industry. USG is a manufacturer of gypsum-based products, including wallboard, joint compound, and industrial gypsum. Other major product lines include ceiling suspension systems, ceiling tile, and cement board. USG's subsidiaries operate 42 manufacturing facilities in the United States, seven in Canada, and 11 in various other countries. On May 6, 1993, USG implemented a major financial restructuring. The company used the principles of fresh start accounting, resulting in excess reorganization value that is currently being amortized without cash or tax effect over a five-year period. Incorporated in Delaware in 1984.

Directors (In addition to indicated officers)

Robert L. Barnett	Lawrence M. Crutcher	Marvin E. Lesser
Keith A. Brown	W. Douglas Ford	John B. Schwemm
W.H. Clark	David W. Fox	Judith A. Sprieser
James C. Cotting	Philip C. Jackson, Jr.	

Officers (Directors*)

*William C. Foote, Chm. & C.E.O.
P. Jack O'Bryan, Pres. & C.O.O.
J. Bradford James, Exec. V.P.—Corp.
  Dev. & Distr.
Richard H. Fleming, Sr. V.P. & C.F.O.
Arthur G. Leisten, Sr. V.P. & Gen. Coun.
Harold E. Pendexter, Jr., Sr. V.P. & C.A.O.

Raymond T. Belz, V.P. & Cont.
Brian W. Burrows, V.P.—Res. & Dev.
Matthew P. Gonring, V.P.—Corp. Comm.
John E. Malone, V.P. & Treas.
Robert B. Sirgant, V.P.—Corp. Accts.
S. Gary Snodgrass, V.P.—Hum. Res. Oper.
Dean H. Goossen, Corp. Secy.

Consolidated Balance Sheet   As of December 31, 1996 (000 omitted)

Assets		Liabilities & Stockholders' Equity	
Current assets	$ 503,000	Current liabilities	$ 395,000
Net property, plant & equipment	887,000	Long-term debt	706,000
Net excess reorganization value	210,000	Deferred items	192,000
Other assets	218,000	Other liabilities	548,000
		*Stockholders' equity	(23,000)
Total	$1,818,000	Total	$1,818,000

*45,724,561 shares common stock outstanding.

Consolidated Income Statement

Years Ended Dec. 31	Thousands — — — — Net Sales	Net Income	Per Share[a] — — — — Earnings	Cash Dividends	Common Stock Price Range Calendar Year
1996	$2,590,000	$ 15,000	$ .31	$ .00	34-1/2 — 24
1995	2,444,000	(32,000)	(.71)	.00	31-3/8 — 19-1/4
1994	2,290,000	(92,000)	(2.14)	.00	36 — 17-1/4
1993[b]	1,325,000	(129,000)	(3.46)	.00	30-1/2 — 9-5/8
1993[c]	591,000	1,434,000[d]			

[a]Due to May 6, 1993, restructuring and fresh start accounting, prior period per share information is not meaningful.
[b]From May 7 to December 31. Per GAAP bankruptcy accounting rules, results for restructured company must be reported separately from predecessor company.
[c]Predecessor company from January 1 to May 6.
[d]Includes restructuring gains.

Transfer Agent & Registrar: Harris Trust and Savings Bank

General Counsel:	Arthur G. Leisten, Sr. V.P.	Traded (Symbol):	NYSE, CSE (USG)
Investor Relations:	James R. Bencomo, Dir.	Stockholders:	4,508
Human Resources:	Harold E. Pendexter, Jr., Sr. V.P.	Employees:	12,500
Mgt. Info. Svcs.:	William H. Duran, Dir.	Annual Meeting:	In May
Auditors:	Arthur Andersen LLP	Internet:	www.usgcorp.com

Varlen Corporation

55 Shuman Blvd., Suite 500, P.O. Box 3089, Naperville, Illinois
60566-7089

Telephone: (630) 420-0400

Varlen Corporation manufactures transportation products and laboratory equipment. The company supplies precision, high volume stampings to automobile manufacturers and their suppliers, and is a primary independent supplier of automatic transmission clutch plates. Varlen is a manufacturer and reconditioner of tapered roller bearings and shock control devices for freight cars and locomotives, as well as a supplier of outlet gates for covered hopper cars and locomotive components, including heating, ventilating, and air-conditioning systems, valves, toilets, and refrigerators. It is also a producer of rail anchors. The company provides aluminum castings, hubs, engineered structural foam components, and fuel water separators for the large truck and trailer market, in addition to die cast parts. Varlen produces petroleum analysis equipment for oil refineries worldwide and also performs testing services for physical property analysis of petroleum products. In addition, Varlen manufactures petroleum reference samples used to calibrate petroleum analysis equipment. Operating subsidiaries and divisions include: Aciéries de Ploermel; Chrome Crankshaft Companies; Brenco, Incorporated; Consolidated Metco, Inc.; Karl Georg; Keystone Industries, Inc.; Means Industries, Inc.; Prime Manufacturing Corporation; Unit Rail Anchor Company, Inc.; and Varlen Instruments, Inc. Incorporated in Delaware in 1969.

Directors (In addition to indicated officers)

Ernest H. Lorch, Sr. Chm.
Rudolph Grua
L. William Miles

Greg A. Rosenbaum
Joseph J. Ross
Theodore A. Ruppert

Officers (Directors*)

*Richard L. Wellek, Chm. & C.E.O.
Raymond A. Jean, Pres. & C.O.O.
George W. Hoffman, Grp. V.P.

Vicki L. Casmere, V.P., Gen. Coun. & Secy.
Richard A. Nunemaker, V.P.—Fin. & C.F.O.

Consolidated Balance Sheet As of January 31, 1997 (000 omitted)

Assets		Liabilities & Stockholders' Equity	
Current assets	$132,453	Current liabilities	$ 62,992
Net property, plant & equipment	124,580	Convertible subordinated	69,000
Other assets	136,845	debentures	
		Other long-term debt	115,353
		Deferred items	16,252
		Other liabilities	20,295
		*Stockholders' equity	109,986
Total	$393,878	Total	$393,878

*5,758,000 shares common stock outstanding.

Consolidated Income Statement

Years Ended Jan. 31	Thousands — — — — Net Sales	Net Income[a]	Per Share[b] — — — Earnings[ac]	Cash Dividends	Common Stock Price Range[b] Fiscal Year
1997	$409,475	$17,857	$2.27	$ .36	23-7/8 — 18-3/4
1996	386,987	19,609	2.43	.35	25-7/8 — 17-1/8
1995	341,521	14,762	1.92	.33	24 — 14-7/8
1994	291,908	10,766	1.57	.33	23 — 10
1993	266,054	6,317[d]	.78[d]	.33	16-5/8 — 8-3/4

[a]Includes FAS 106 and FAS 109.
[b]Restated to reflect a 10% stock dividend in 1996 and 1995, and a 3-for-2 stock split in 1993.
[c]Fully diluted.
[d]Includes cumulative effect of a change in accounting principle of $1,351,000 ($.17 per share).

Transfer Agent & Registrar: Harris Trust and Savings Bank

Investor Relations:	Richard A. Nunemaker, V.P.		
Human Resources:	John Vogel, Benefits Mgr.	Traded (Symbol):	NASDAQ (VRLN)
Mgt. Info. Svcs.:	Steven E. Obendorf, Corp. Cont.	Stockholders:	3,300
Auditors:	Deloitte & Touche LLP	Employees:	2,850
		Annual Meeting:	In May

Vita Food Products, Inc.

222 West Lake Street, Chicago, Illinois 60612
Telephone: (312) 738-4500

Vita Food Products, Inc. is one of the leading processors of herring products, and cured and smoked salmon products, in the United States. The company's products include a variety of pickled herring in cream- and wine-based sauces, and lox and nova salmon. The company markets other complementary specialty food products such as cream cheese with salmon, shrimp cocktail, hommus and horseradish products, and cocktail and tartar sauces, which it purchases from third-party food producers and markets under the Vita brand name pursuant to co-packing arrangements. In January 1997, the company completed an initial public offering of 750,000 shares of common stock. Incorporated in Illinois in 1926; reincorporated in Nevada in 1996.

Directors (In addition to indicated officers)

Sam Gorenstein
Michael Horn
Neal Jansen

Steven Rothstein
Jeffrey Rubenstein

Officers (Directors*)

*Stephen D. Rubin, Pres.
*Clark L. Feldman, Exec. V.P. & Secy.

Jay H. Dembsky, V.P., C.F.O. & Treas.

Consolidated Balance Sheet As of December 31, 1996 (000 omitted)

Assets		Liabilities & Stockholders' Equity	
Current assets	$ 8,563	Current liabilities	$ 5,335
Net property, plant & equipment	2,061	Long-term debt	5,419
Other assets	716	*Stockholders' equity	586
Total	$11,340	Total	$11,340

*2,950,000 shares common stock outstanding.

Consolidated Income Statement

Years Ended Dec. 31	Thousands — — — —		Per Share[a] — — — —		Common Stock Price Range[a] Calendar Year
	Net Sales	Net Income	Earnings	Cash Dividends	
1996	$22,688	$818	$ .28		
1995	21,410	131	.04		
1994	17,793	272	.09		

[a]Initial public offering in January 1997.

Transfer Agent & Registrar: American Stock Transfer & Trust Co.

General Counsel:
  Much Shelist Freed Denenberg Ament PC

Auditors: BDO Seidman, LLP

Traded (Symbol): AMEX, CSE (VSF)

Stockholders: 269
Employees: 118
Annual Meeting: To be announced

Vitalink Pharmacy Services, Inc.

1250 East Diehl Road, Suite 208, Naperville, Illinois 60563
Telephone: (630) 245-4800

Vitalink Pharmacy Services, Inc. is a leading institutional pharmacy company, providing pharmaceutical dispensing of individual medications, infusion therapy products and services, medical supplies, and pharmacy consulting to its customers. Vitalink's customers are nursing facilities, other institutions and their patients, and home infusion patients. Vitalink currently operates 56 institutional pharmacies and four regional infusion pharmacies. Through these operations, Vitalink provides services to 172,000 institutional beds throughout the United States. Manor Care, Inc. owns approximately 51 percent of Vitalink's common stock. In February 1997, Vitalink completed a merger with TeamCare, the pharmacy subsidiary of GranCare, Inc. Incorporated in Delaware in 1976.

Directors (In addition to indicated officers)

Stewart Bainum, Jr.
Joseph R. Buckley
Joel S. Kanter
James A. MacCutcheon

Robert L. Parker
James H. Rempe
Gary U. Rolle

Officers (Directors*)

Donna L. DeNardo, Pres. & C.O.O.
*Gene E. Burleson, C.E.O.
Arlen Reynolds, Exec. V.P.

Robert W. Horner III, Sr. V.P., Secy. & Gen. Coun.
Scott T. Macomber, Sr. V.P., C.F.O. & Treas.
Stephen A. Thompson, V.P.—Hum. Res. & Admin.

Consolidated Balance Sheet As of May 31, 1996 (000 omitted)

Assets		Liabilities & Stockholders' Equity	
Current assets	$29,876	Current liabilities	$ 7,046
Net property, plant & equipment	8,191	Other liabilities	2,578
Goodwill, net	31,194	*Stockholders' equity	86,299
Other assets	26,662		
Total	$95,923	Total	$95,923

*13,979,700 shares common stock outstanding.

Consolidated Income Statement

Years Ended May 31	Thousands — — — — Total Revenues	Net Income	Per Share — — — — Earnings	Cash Dividends	Common Stock Price Range Calendar Year	
1996	$141,115	$13,870	$ .99	$ .00	25	— 16-7/8
1995	112,257	11,680	.84	.00	25-3/8	— 11-3/4
1994	98,569	9,204	.66	.00	15-1/2	— 8-1/2
1993	65,714	7,341	.53	.00	13-1/4	— 7-1/2
1992	40,164	5,497	.46	.00	18	— 10-1/4[a]

[a]Initial public offering in March 1992.

Transfer Agent & Registrar: ChaseMellon Shareholder Services, L.L.C.

General Counsel:	Robert W. Horner III, Sr. V.P.	Traded (Symbol):	NYSE (VTK)
Investor Relations:	Scott T. Macomber, Sr. V.P.	Stockholders:	1,500
Human Resources:	Stephen A. Thompson, V.P.	Employees:	3,500
Mgt. Info. Svcs:	Chip Phillips, V.P.	Annual Meeting:	In October
Auditors:	Arthur Andersen LLP	Internet:	www.vitalink-pharmacy.com

Walgreen Co.

200 Wilmot Road, Deerfield, Illinois 60015
Telephone: (847) 940-2500

Walgreen Co. is in the retail drugstore business, selling prescription and proprietary drugs, and also carrying additional product lines such as cosmetics, toiletries, tobacco, and general merchandise. The company operates 2,193 drugstores in 34 states and Puerto Rico. Nearly 70 percent of these stores have been opened or remodeled in the last five years. Walgreen drugstores serve more than two million customers daily and are served by eight distribution centers and five photo-processing studios. Walgreens Healthcare Plus, a subsidiary, provides Walgreen's pharmacy mail service. WHP Health Initiatives provides sales and marketing services as the company's umbrella organization for managed care business. Incorporated in Illinois in 1909.

Directors (In addition to indicated officers)

William C. Foote
James J. Howard
Charles D. Hunter
Cordell Reed

John B. Schwemm
William H. Springer
Marilou M. von Ferstel

Officers (Directors*)

*Charles R. Walgreen III, Chm. & C.E.O.
*L. Daniel Jorndt, Pres. & C.O.O.
 Vernon A. Brunner, Exec. V.P.—Mktg.
 Glenn S. Kraiss, Exec. V.P.—Drug Store Oper.
 David W. Bernauer, Sr. V.P. & C.I.O.
 Roger L. Polark, Sr. V.P. & C.F.O.
 John A. Rubino, Sr. V.P.—Hum. Res.
 William A. Shiel, Sr. V.P.—Facilities Dev.
 Robert C. Atlas, V.P.—Drug Store Oper.

W. Lynn Earnest, V.P.—Drug Store Oper.
Jerome B. Karlin, V.P.—Drug Store Oper.
J. Randolph Lewis, V.P.—Distr.
Julian A. Oettinger, V.P., Gen. Coun. & Secy.
Jeffrey A. Rein, Div. V.P. & Treas.
Roger H. Clausen, Cont. & Chf. Acct. Off.
Chester G. Young, Gen. Auditor
Robert H. Halaska, Pres.—WHP Health Initiatives

Consolidated Balance Sheet   As of August 31, 1996 (000 omitted)

Assets		Liabilities & Stockholders' Equity	
Current assets	$2,019,038	Current liabilities	$1,181,955
Net property, plant & equipment	1,448,368	Deferred items	145,218
Other assets	166,240	Other liabilities	263,368
		*Stockholders' equity	2,043,105
Total	$3,633,646	Total	$3,633,646

*246,141,072 shares common stock outstanding.

Consolidated Income Statement

Years Ended Aug. 31	Thousands ———— Net Sales	Net Income	Per Share[a] ———— Earnings	Cash Dividends[b]	Common Stock Price Range[a] Calendar Year
1996	$11,778,408	$371,749	$1.50	$ .44	43-5/8 — 29-1/8
1995	10,395,096	320,791	1.30	.39	31-1/4 — 22-3/8
1994	9,234,978	281,929	1.14	.34	22-5/8 — 16-7/8
1993	8,294,840	221,666[c]	.90[c]	.30	22-3/8 — 17-5/8
1992	7,474,961	220,628	.89	.26	22-1/4 — 15-1/4

[a]Adjusted to reflect 2-for-1 stock splits in August 1995 and February 1991.
[b]Cash dividends declared.
[c]Includes a charge to reflect FAS 106 and FAS 109, resulting in a cumulative effect of $23,623,000 ($.19 per share).

Transfer Agent & Registrar: Harris Trust and Savings Bank

General Counsel:	Julian A. Oettinger, V.P.	Traded (Symbol):	NYSE, CSE (WAG)
Investor Relations:	Jeffrey A. Rein, Div. V.P.	Stockholders:	38,000
Human Resources:	John A. Rubino, Sr. V.P.	Employees:	77,000
Mgt. Info. Svcs.:	David W. Bernauer, Sr. V.P.	Annual Meeting:	Second Wednesday in January
Auditors:	Arthur Andersen LLP	Internet:	www.walgreens.com

Wallace Computer Services, Inc.

2275 Cabot Drive, Lisle, Illinois 60532
Telephone: (630) 588-5000

Wallace Computer Services, Inc. is a leading manufacturer and distributor of information management products, services, and solutions. These include forms; labeling products and supplies; electronic forms software and services; commercial printing; promotional and direct mail advertising; computer hardware, software, accessories, and supplies; printer ribbons; ATM and POS machine paper rolls; and TOPS® brand office products and stock forms. Wallace sells primarily through a direct sales force of 700 sales representatives across the United States and through the office products dealer network for TOPS products. In addition to its corporate offices in Lisle, Illinois, the company operates manufacturing and distribution facilities in 13 other states. In October 1996, Wallace acquired Post Printing Inc. of West Bend, Wisconsin. Incorporated in Illinois in 1908; reincorporated in Delaware in 1963.

Directors (In addition to indicated officers)

Richard F. Doyle	John C. Pope
Albert W. Isenman III	Robert P. Rittereiser
William N. Lane III	Neele E. Stearns, Jr

Officers (Directors*)

*Theodore Dimitriou, Chm.	Michael T. Laudizio, V.P., Secy. & Dir. of Taxes
*Robert J. Cronin, Pres. & C.E.O.	Steven F. Arpaia, V.P.—Colorform Sales Div.
Michael O. Duffield, Sr. V.P.—Oper.	Thomas G. Brooker, V.P.—Gen. Mgr., TOPS Div.
Michael T. Leatherman, Sr. V.P. & C.I.O.	Joseph J. Juszak, V.P.—Qual. & Tech. Svcs. Div.
David Bertram, V.P.	Michael D. Keim, V.P.—Mfg., Bus. Forms Div.
Bruce D'Angelo, V.P.—Corp. Sales	James E. Kersten, V.P.—Direct Sales, West
Douglas W. Fitzgerald, V.P.—Mktg.	Mark D. Mindrum, V.P.—Direct Sales, Midwest
Michael J. Halloran, V.P. & C.F.O.	Edward A. Riguardi, V.P.—Direct Sales, East
Donald J. Hoffmann, V.P.—Eng. & Res.	David M. Rousseau, V.P.—Info. Sys.
Michael M. Mulcahy, V.P. & Gen. Mgr.—Colorforms Div.	Ronald D. Seavey, V.P.—Direct Sales, Southeast
Wayne E. Richter, V.P. & Gen. Mgr.—Label Div.	

Consolidated Balance Sheet   As of July 31, 1996 (000 omitted)

Assets		Liabilities & Stockholders' Equity	
Current assets	$304,108	Current liabilities	$ 97,870
Net property, plant & equipment	288,872	Long-term debt	30,600
Other assets	102,870	Deferred items	56,937
		*Stockholders' equity	510,443
Total	$695,850	Total	$695,850

*45,587,000 shares common stock outstanding.

Consolidated Income Statement

Years Ended July 31	Thousands — — — — Net Sales	Net Income	Per Share[a] — — — — Earnings	Cash Dividends	Common Stock Price Range[a] Calendar Year
1996	$862,257	$72,999	$1.60	$ .43	30-1/2 — 26-3/8
1995	712,838	55,297	1.23	.37	30 — 12-7/8
1994	588,173	47,931	1.08	.32	18-1/8 — 12-7/8
1993	545,315	41,170	.92	.29	16-7/8 — 11-3/8
1992	511,572	39,455	.88	.27	13-7/8 — 10-7/8

[a]Adjusted to reflect a 2-for-1 stock split in July 1996.

Transfer Agent & Registrar: Boston EquiServe

Corp. Counsel:	Steven L. Carson	Traded (Symbol):	NYSE (WCS)
Investor Relations:	Bradley P. Samson	Stockholders:	3,863
Mgt. Info. Svcs.:	David M. Rousseau, V.P.	Employees:	4,131
Human Resources:	Barry White	Annual Meeting:	In November
Auditors:	Arthur Andersen LLP	Internet:	www.wallace.com

Washington National Corporation

300 Tower Parkway, Lincolnshire, Illinois 60069-3665
Telephone: (847) 793-3000

Washington National Corporation (WNC), through its subsidiaries, principally engages in the marketing and underwriting of life insurance and annuities for individuals, and specialty insurance for educators. The company's operating subsidiaries are Washington National Insurance Company (WNIC), which dates from 1911, and United Presidential Life Insurance Company (UPI). In August 1996, WNC completed the sale of its individual and small group health insurance to Schaumburg, Illinois-based Pioneer Financial Services, followed in October 1996 by the sale of the company's large group health insurance business to Trustmark Insurance Company. In November 1996, the company announced that it would merge with New York City-based PennCorp Financial Group, Inc. The merger, pending stockholder approval, is expected to close in July 1997. Incorporated in Delaware in 1968.

Directors   (In addition to indicated officers)

Frederick R. Blume	Stanley P. Hutchison
Elaine R. Bond	George P. Kendall, Jr.
Ronald L. Bornheutter	Frank L. Klapperich, Jr.
W. Francis Brennan	Lee M. Mitchell
Lee A. Ellis	Rex Reade
John R. Haire	

Officers   (Directors*)

*Robert W. Patin, Chm., Pres. & C.E.O.
Wade G. Brown, Exec. V.P. & Chf. Info. Off.
Thomas C. Scott, Exec. V.P. & C.F.O.
Joan K. Cohen, V.P., Cont. & Treas.

Craig R. Edwards, V.P., Corp. Coun. & Secy.
Kathy A. Glynn, V.P.—Internal Audit
James N. Plato, Chm./Pres./C.E.O.—UPI
Thomas Pontarelli, Chm./Pres./C.E.O.—WNIC

Consolidated Balance Sheet   As of December 31, 1996 (000 omitted)

Assets		Liabilities & Stockholders' Equity	
Invested assets	$2,379,763	Policy liabilities	$2,282,537
Deferred acquisition costs	242,488	Other liabilities	182,715
Other assets	246,945	*Stockholders' equity	403,944
Total	$2,869,196	Total	$2,869,196

*12,358,000 shares common stock outstanding.

Consolidated Income Statement

Years Ended Dec. 31	Thousands — — — —		Per Share — — — —		Common Stock Price Range Calendar Year
	Total Revenues[a]	Net Income	Earnings	Cash Dividends	
1996	$328,707	$ 6,328[b]	$ .48[b]	$1.08	30-3/4 — 25-1/8
1995	317,116	33,860	2.73	1.08	29-1/4 — 17-3/4
1994	305,320	31,301	2.53	1.08	25-1/8 — 18-5/8
1993[c]	300,174	26,666	2.45	1.08	27-7/8 — 22
1992	291,264	(5,967)[d]	(.63)[d]	1.08	23-1/2 — 16

[a]From continuing operations.
[b]Includes an after-tax loss of $25,080,000 ($2.02 per share) from the sale of the company's health business.
[c]Includes FAS 112.
[d]Includes a charge to reflect FAS 106 and FAS 109, resulting in a cumulative effect of $22,819,000 ($2.28 per share).

Transfer Agent & Registrar:	First Chicago Trust Co. of New York		
General Counsel:	Craig R. Edwards, V.P.	Traded (Symbol):	NYSE, CSE, PHSE (WNT)
Investor Relations:	Craig A. Simundza, V.P.	Stockholders:	9,207
Mgt. Info. Svcs.:	Wade G. Brown, Exec. V.P.	Employees:	454
Auditors:	Ernst & Young LLP	Annual Meeting:	In June

Waste Management, Inc.

3003 Butterfield Road, Oak Brook, Illinois 60521
Telephone: (630) 572-8800

Waste Management, Inc. (formerly WMX Technologies, Inc.) is a leading international provider of waste management services. Operations include recycling, collection, transfer, and disposal of solid and hazardous wastes, the management of low-level radioactive wastes, resource-recovery, and related waste reduction programs. The Waste Management, Inc. (WMI) subsidiary serves about 1.1 million commercial and industrial customers and approximately 12 million residential customers in the U.S. and Canada. Hazardous waste management services are provided through WMI, Chemical Waste Management, Inc. (CWM), and Advanced Environmental Technical Services, LLP, a 60 percent-owned subsidiary of CWM. Chem-Nuclear Systems, LLC, a CWM subsidiary, provides radioactive waste management services. Waste Management International plc provides waste management and related services in various countries. Wheelabrator Technologies Inc. (WTI) develops facilities for and provides services to the trash-to-energy, energy, and independent power markets. Rust International Inc., a subsidiary owned 60 percent by WMX and 40 percent by WTI, provides a variety of on-site industrial cleaning services and comprehensive hazardous, radioactive, and mixed waste management services. Incorporated in Delaware in 1968; present name adopted in 1997.

Directors (In addition to indicated officers)

H. Jesse Arnelle	James B. Edwards	Peer Pedersen
Dean L. Buntrock	Donald F. Flynn	James R. Peterson
Pastora San Juan Cafferty	Robert S. Miller	Steven G. Rothmeier
Jerry E. Dempsey	Paul M. Montrone	Alexander B. Trowbridge

Officers (Directors*)

* Ronald T. LeMay, Chm. Pres. & C.E.O.
Joseph M. Holsten, Exec. V.P. & C.O.O.
James E. Koenig, Exec. V.P.
Herbert A. Getz, Sr. V.P., Gen. Coun. & Secy.

D.P. "Pat" Payne, Sr. V.P.
John D. Sanford, Sr. V.P., C.F.O. & Treas.
Thomas C. Hau, V.P. & Cont.

Consolidated Balance Sheet   As of December 31, 1996 (000 omitted)

Assets		Liabilities & Stockholders' Equity	
Current assets	$ 3,093,224	Current liabilities	$ 3,038,708
Net property, plant & equipment	9,721,709	Long-term debt	6,971,607
*Other assets	5,551,659	Deferred items	2,197,234
		Other liabilities	1,282,744
		**Stockholders' equity	4,876,299
Total	$18,366,592	Total	$18,366,592

*Includes net assets of $214,309,000 from discontinued operations.
**483,432,549 shares common stock outstanding.

Consolidated Income Statement

Years Ended Dec. 31	Thousands — — — — Revenue[a]	Net Income[a]	Per Share — — — — Earnings[a]	Cash Dividends	Common Stock Price Range Calendar Year
1996	$9,186,970	$192,085[b]	$ .39	$ .63	36-5/8 — 27-3/4
1995	9,053,018	603,899[c]	1.24	.60	32-1/2 — 25-3/4
1994	8,482,718	784,381	1.62	.60	30-3/4 — 22-5/8
1993	7,827,280	452,776[d]	.93	.58	40-1/4 — 23
1992	8,661,027	850,036[e]	1.72	.50	46-5/8 — 32

[a]Excludes discontinued operations since 1993.
[b]Includes a charge of $277,400,000 (before minority interest) recorded by WM Intl. plc related to sale and revaluation of investments and a pretax charge of $255,000,000 for reengineering finance and administrative functions and for litigation.
[c]Includes a pretax charge of $140,600,000 recorded by CWM and a pretax charge of $194,600,000 (before minority interest) recorded by WM Intl. plc; also includes other various items.
[d]Includes a non-taxable gain of $15,109,000 (before minority interest) related to the issuance of shares by Rust, and an asset revaluation and pretax restructuring charge of $550,000,000 (before minority interest) recorded by CWM.
[e]Includes a non-taxable gain of $240,000,000 (before minority interest) from IPO of WM Intl. plc; special pretax charges of $219,900,000 (before minority interest); and one-time charges totalling $71,139,000 related to the adoption of FAS 106 and FAS 109.

Transfer Agent & Registrar: Harris Trust and Savings Bank

General Counsel:	Herbert A. Getz, Sr. V.P.	Traded (Symbol):	
Investor Relations:	John D. Sanford, Sr. V.P.	NYSE, CSE, London, Frankfurt, 3 Swiss (WMX)	
Human Resources:	Mark C. Eriks, V.P.	Stockholders:	50,000
Mgt. Info. Svcs.:	John J. Goody, V.P.	Employees:	59,700
		Annual Meeting:	In May
Auditors:	Arthur Andersen LLP	Internet:	www.wmx.com

Wells-Gardner Electronics Corporation
2701 North Kildare Avenue, Chicago, Illinois 60639
Telephone: (773) 252-8220

Wells-Gardner Electronics Corporation is an ISO 9001 video products company that designs and manufactures color video monitors for sale to the gaming, industrial, and commercial markets. The company has a domestic and international customer base. Included are makers of coin-operated video games, lottery terminals, video slot machines, video walls, and presentation monitors; and leisure and fitness, INTRANET, media, automotive, kiosk, and other display applications. The company also engages in the contract manufacturing of electronic products designed and marketed by others. Incorporated in Illinois in 1925.

Directors   (In addition to indicated officers)

John R. Blouin
William L. De Nicolo
Allan Gardner
H. Wayne Harris

Ira J. Kaufman
James J. Roberts, Jr.
Ernest R. Wish

Officers   (Directors*)

*Anthony Spier, Chm., Pres. & C.E.O.
*Randall S. Wells, Exec. V.P. & Gen. Mgr.
 Mark E. Komorowski, V.P. & Gen. Mgr.—Bus. Svcs.
 John S. Pircon, V.P.—Mktg. & Eng.

George B. Toma, V.P.—Fin., C.F.O. & Treas.
Eugene C. Ahner, Secy. & Dir.—Hum. Res.
Kathleen E. Hoppe, Dir.—M.I.S.
Larry S. Mahl, Dir.—Materials

Consolidated Balance Sheet   As of December 31, 1996 (000 omitted)

Assets		Liabilities & Stockholders' Equity	
Current assets	$11,747	Current liabilities	$ 2,730
Net property, plant & equipment	2,378	Long-term debt	1,300
		*Stockholders' equity	10,095
Total	$14,125	Total	$14,125

*4,068,426 shares common stock outstanding.

Consolidated Income Statement

Years Ended Dec. 31	Thousands — — — — Net Sales	Net Income	Per Share — — — Earnings	Cash Dividends	Common Stock Price Range Calendar Year
1996	$36,668	$ 403	$ .10	$ .00	4-7/8 — 2-1/2
1995	28,301	(1,059)a	(.26)	.00	6-1/2 — 2-1/2
1994	33,435	(1,735)	(.45)	.00	4-5/8 — 2-1/2
1993	36,011	(1,779)b	(.46)b	.00	7-1/8 — 2-7/8
1992	48,949	1,545c	.40c	.00	9-3/8 — 1-7/8

aIncludes a special charge of $886,000 and a gain of $358,000 on the sale of fixed assets.
bIncludes a gain of $102,000 ($.03 per share), the cumulative effect of a change in an accounting principle.
cIncludes an extraordinary gain of $528,000 ($.14 per share) relating to tax effect of loss carryforward.

Transfer Agent & Registrar:	Harris Trust and Savings Bank		
General Counsel:	Katten Muchin & Zavis	Traded (Symbol):	AMEX (WGA)
Investor Relations:	George B. Toma, V.P.	Stockholders:	825
Human Resources:	Eugene C. Ahner, Dir.	Employees:	178
Mgt. Info. Svcs.:	Kathleen E. Hoppe, Dir.	Annual Meeting:	Fourth Tuesday in April
Auditors:	KPMG Peat Marwick LLP	Internet:	www.wgec.com

Wesley Jessen VisionCare, Inc.

333 East Howard Avenue, Des Plaines, Illinois 60018-5903
Telephone: (847) 294-3000

Wesley Jessen VisionCare, Inc. is the leading worldwide developer, manufacturer, and marketer of specialty contact lenses, based on its share of the specialty lens market. The company's products include: cosmetic lenses, which change or enhance the wearer's eye color appearance; toric lenses, which correct vision for people with astigmatism; and premium lenses, which offer value-added features such as improved comfort for dry eyes and protection from ultraviolet light. The company offers both conventional contact lens products, which can be used typically for up to 24 months, and a broad range of disposable lenses, which are intended to be replaced every two weeks. Effective June 29, 1995, the company acquired the Wesley-Jessen contact lens business from the Schering-Plough Corporation. In October 1996, Wesley Jessen acquired the Barnes-Hind division of Pilkington plc. In February 1997, the company competed an initial public offering of 2,450,000 shares of common stock. Incorporated in Delaware in 1995 as successor to a company founded in 1946; present name adopted in 1997.

Directors (In addition to indicated officers)

John J. O'Malley

Officers (Directors*)

*Stephen G. Pagliuca, Chm.
*Kevin J. Ryan, Pres. & C.E.O.
*Adam W. Kirsch, Exec. V.P.
 Raleigh S. Althisar, Jr., V.P.—Worldwide Mfg.
 Lawrence L. Chapoy, V.P.—Res. & Dev.
 William M. Flynn, V.P.—Pan Asia

 Joseph F. Foos, V.P.—Scientific Aff.
*Edward J. Kelley, V.P.—Fin. & C.F.O.
*John W. Maki, V.P.
 George H. McCrary, V.P.—Americas
 Daniel M. Roussel, V.P.—Europe
 Thomas F. Steiner, V.P.—Mktg.

Consolidated Balance Sheet As of December 31, 1996 (000 omitted)

Assets		Liabilities & Stockholders' Equity	
Current assets	$157,386	Current liabilities	$ 79,127
Net property, plant & equipment	10,125	Long-term debt	102,975
Other assets	13,089	Negative goodwill, net	10,577
		Other liabilities	1,213
		*Stockholders' equity	(13,292)
Total	$180,600	Total	$180,600

*14,276,028 shares common stock outstanding.

Consolidated Income Statement

Years Ended Dec. 31	Thousands — — — —		Per Share[ab] — — — —		Common Stock Price Range[b] Calendar Year
	Net Sales	Net Income	Earnings	Cash Dividends	
1996	$156,752	$(2,742)[c]	$ (.19)[c]		
1995[d]	54,315	(19,715)	(1.37)		

[a]Adjusted to reflect a 3.883-for-1 stock split and the conversion of (4.549-for-1 shares of Class L common stock into common stock in February 1997.
[b]Initial public offering in February 1997.
[c]Includes an extraordinary loss of $1,671,000 ($.12 per share) from the early extinguishment of debt.
[d]From June 29 to December 31, 1995. Because of purchase method of accounting adjustments made to the predecessor's financial statements, financial data of the predecessor prior to June 29, 1995, are not comparable to those of subsequent periods.

Transfer Agent & Registrar: American Stock Transfer & Trust Co.

General Counsel:	Gerald B. Sweeney, Esq.	Traded (Symbol):	NASDAQ (WJCO)
Human Resources:	Michael Southard	Stockholders:	1,000
Mgt. Info. Svcs.:	David Weber	Employees:	2,600
Auditors:	Price Waterhouse LLP	Annual Meeting:	To be determined

Westco Bancorp, Inc.

2121 South Mannheim Road, Westchester, Illinois 60154-4363
Telephone: (708) 865-1100

Westco Bancorp, Inc. is a savings and loan holding company for First Federal Savings and Loan Association of Westchester. As a community-oriented institution, the Association offers traditional deposit and mortgage loan products to its customers. The Association currently operates out of its home office and a limited service office, both located in Westchester, Illinois, and its deposit gathering area is concentrated in the neighborhoods surrounding its offices. Westco, Inc. is another principal subsidiary. Incorporated in Delaware in 1992.

Directors (In addition to indicated officers)

James E. Dick
Rosalyn M. Lesak
Edward A. Matuga

Edward C. Moticka
Thomas J. Nowicki
Robert E. Vorel, Jr.

Officers (Directors*)

* David C. Burba, Chm. & Pres.
Richard A. Brechlin, Exec. V.P. & Treas.
Gregg P. Goossens, Exec. V.P.—Lending

Kenneth J. Kaczmarek, V.P.
Mary S. Suffi, V.P. & Secy.

Consolidated Balance Sheet As of December 31, 1996 (000 omitted)

Assets		Liabilities & Stockholders' Equity	
Total cash & cash equivalents	$ 11,389	Deposits	$255,154
Investment securities	69,564	Advance payments by borrowers	3,077
Loans receivable	223,898	Other liabilities	4,928
Other assets	6,141	*Stockholders' equity	47,833
Total	$310,992	Total	$310,992

*2,694,553 shares common stock outstanding.

Consolidated Income Statement

Years Ended Dec. 31	Thousands — — — — Total Income	Net Income	Per Share[ab] — — — — Earnings	Cash Dividends	Common Stock Price Range[a] Calendar Year
1996	$24,247	$3,288[c]	$1.16	$ .50	22-1/4 — 18-1/2
1995	23,258	4,167	1.43	.41	18-1/2 — 11-1/2
1994	21,651	3,961	1.27	.43	14 — 11
1993	22,681	4,109	1.24	.00	13-5/8 — 9-5/8
1992	23,771	2,643[d]	.76[d]	.00	10 — 7-5/8

[a]Adjusted to reflect a 3-for-2 stock split in May 1996.
[b]Initial public offering in June 1992.
[c]Reflects a special one-time assessment of SAIF insured deposits of approximately $1,600,000.
[d]Includes a charge to reflect FAS 109, resulting in a cumulative effect of $254,263 ($.07 per share).

Transfer Agent & Registrar: Harris Trust and Savings Bank

General Counsel:
 Muldoon, Murphy & Faucette, Washington, D.C.

Investor Relations: Richard A. Brechlin, Exec. V.P.

Human Resources: Mary S. Suffi, V.P.

Mgt. Info. Svcs.: Kenneth J. Kaczmarek, V.P.

Auditors:
 Cobitz, VandenBerg and Fennessy

Traded (Symbol): NASDAQ (WCBI)

Stockholders: 1,400

Employees: 55

Annual Meeting: In April

Westell Technologies, Inc.

750 North Commons Drive, Aurora, Illinois 60504
Telephone: (630) 898-2500

Westell Technologies, Inc. designs, manufactures, markets, and services a broad range of digital and analog products used by telephone companies to deliver services primarily over existing copper telephone wires. The company also markets its products and services to other telecommunications and information service providers seeking direct access to end-user customers. Westell is a leading developer and provider of telecommunications products using an emerging technology known as Asymmetric Digital Subscriber Line (ADSL). ADSL products will allow telephone companies to provide interactive multimedia services over existing copper wire, offering a more cost-effective and faster deployment alternative to fiber optic cable. The company markets its products in the U.S. principally through its domestic field sales organization and markets its products internationally in more than 40 countries with direct sales personnel and various distribution agreements. Incorporated in Delaware in 1980; present name adopted in 1995.

Directors (In addition to indicated officers)

Stefan D. Abrams
Michael A. Brunner
Paul A. Dwyer

Robert H. Gaynor, V. Chm.
Ormand J. Wade

Officers (Directors*)

*Gary F. Seamans, Chm., Pres. & C.E.O.
Robert D. Faw, C.E.O.—Westell, Inc.
J. William Nelson, Pres.—Westell, Inc.
Curtis L. Benton, Exec. V.P. & C.A.O.
Richard P. Riviere, Exec. V.P. &
    Pres.—Conference Plus

David Corey, Sr. V.P.—Global Mktg.
Marcus H. Halfner, Sr., V.P.—Bus. Dev.
Neil J. Kreitman, Sr. V.P.—Global Mfg. & Sourcing
Marc Zionts, Sr. V.P.—System Sales-U.S.
Stephen J. Hawrysz, V.P., Secy. & C.F.O.
*Melvin J. Simon, Asst. Secy. & Asst. Treas.

Consolidated Balance Sheet   As of March 31, 1997 (000 omitted)

Assets		Liabilities & Stockholders' Equity	
Current assets	$ 81,243	Current liabilities	$ 16,789
Net property, plant & equipment	14,638	Long-term debt	4,400
Other assets	12,168	Other liabilities	672
		*Stockholders' equity	86,188
Total	$108,049	Total	$108,049

*36,321,000 shares Class A & Class B common stock outstanding.

Consolidated Income Statement

Years Ended March 31	Thousands — — — — Net Revenues	Net Income	Per Share[a] — — — — Earnings	Cash Dividends	Common Stock Price Range[ab] Calendar Year
1997	$79,385	$(14,705)	$ (.41)	$ .00	
1996	83,236	(2,075)	(.07)	.00	56 —9-5/8
1995	74,029	(508)	(.02)[c]	.00	13-7/8—6-1/2
1994	51,051	213	.01[c]		
1993	43,221	1,698	.06[c]		

[a]Reflects a 29-for-1 stock split in November 1995, and a 2-for-1 stock split in the form of a 100% stock dividend in June 1996.
[b]Initial public offering in November 1995.
[c]Pro forma.

Transfer Agent & Registrar: LaSalle National Trust, N.A.

General Counsel:	McDermott, Will & Emery	Traded (Symbol):	NASDAQ (WSTL)
Investor Relations:	Stephen J. Hawrysz, V.P.	Stockholders:	114
Human Resources:	Kelly Mayoros	Employees:	822
Mgt. Info. Svcs.:	Brian Marshall	Annual Meeting:	In September
Auditors:	Arthur Andersen LLP	Internet:	www.westell.com

Whitman Corporation

3501 Algonquin Road, Rolling Meadows, Illinois 60008
Telephone: (847) 818-5000

Whitman Corporation is a consumer goods and services company which is engaged in three distinct businesses: soft drinks, automotive services, and refrigeration equipment. Pepsi-Cola General Bottlers, Inc., bottles and distributes Pepsi-Cola and other soft drinks in 12 states in the midwestern U.S. and has a joint venture in Poland. In 1996, the company signed a letter of intent with Pepsi-Cola International to distribute products in the Kaliningrad region, Belarus, and the Baltics. Midas International Corp. operates more than 2,677 automotive service shops in the U.S. and 17 other countries. Hussmann Corp. produces capital equipment to satisfy needs of supermarket, commercial refrigeration, and convenience and specialty store customers. In June 1997, the company announced that it planned to spin off its Midas and Hussmann units. Incorporated in Delaware in 1962.

Directors (In addition to indicated officer)

Herbert M. Baum	Jarobin Gilbert, Jr.
Richard G. Cline	Victoria B. Jackson
Pierre S. du Pont	Donald P. Jacobs
Archie R. Dykes	Charles S. Locke
Charles W. Gaillard	

Officers (Directors*)

*Bruce S. Chelberg, Chm. & C.E.O.
Thomas L. Bindley, Exec. V.P.
Lawrence J. Pilon, Sr. V.P.—Hum. Res.
Frank T. Westover, Sr. V.P. & Cont.
Charles H. Connolly, V.P.—Corp. Affairs &
Inv. Rel.
Louis J. Corna, V.P.—Taxes
Kathleen R. Gannon, V.P. & Treas.

William B. Moore, V.P., Secy. & Gen. Coun.
Raymond B. Werntz, V.P.—Comp. & Benefits
Robert Cushing, Pres.—Pepsi-Cola Gen. Bottlers
John R. Moore, Corp. V.P. & Pres./C.E.O.—Midas
Intl.
J. Larry Vowell, Corp. V.P. & Pres./C.E.O.—
Hussmann Corporation

Consolidated Balance Sheet   As of December 31, 1996 (000 omitted)

Assets		Liabilities & Stockholders' Equity	
Current assets	$ 855,000	Current liabilities	$ 526,000
Investments	181,300	Long-term debt	837,500
Net property, plant & equipment	734,300	Deferred items	47,100
Other assets	638,800	Other liabilities	356,600
		*Stockholders' equity	642,200
Total	$2,409,400	Total	$2,409,400

*102,587,000 shares common stock outstanding.

Consolidated Income Statement

Years Ended Dec. 31	Thousands — — — — Revenues	Net Income	Per Share — — — Earnings	Cash Dividends	Common Stock Price Range Calendar Year
1996	$3,111,300	$139,400	$1.31	$ .41	25-3/4 — 21-3/4
1995	2,946,500	133,500	1.26	.37	23-3/8 — 15-5/8
1994	2,658,800	103,200	.97	.33	18 — 14-3/4
1993	2,529,700	78,200[a]	.73[a]	.29	17 — 12-3/4
1992	2,388,000	59,800	.56	.26	16-3/8 — 12-1/4

[a]Includes a charge to reflect FAS 106, resulting in a cumulative effect of $24,000,000 ($.22 per share).

Transfer Agent & Registrar:	First Chicago Trust Co. of New York		
General Counsel:	William B. Moore, V.P.	Traded (Symbol):	NYSE, CSE, PSE (WH)
Investor Relations:	Charles H. Connolly, V.P.	Stockholders:	18,223
		Employees:	17,594
Human Resources:	Lawrence J. Pilon, Sr. V.P.	Annual Meeting:	In May
Auditors:	KPMG Peat Marwick LLP	Internet:	www.whitmancorp.com

Whittman-Hart, Inc.

311 South Wacker Drive, Suite 3500, Chicago, Illinois 60606
Telephone: (312) 922-9200

Whittman-Hart, Inc. provides strategic information technology business solutions designed to improve its clients' productivity and competitive position. Its clients consist primarily of middle market companies ranging from $50 million to $500 million in annual revenues. The company offers clients a comprehensive range of services required to successfully design, develop, and implement integrated computer systems projects in diverse computing environments. Among the services offered by the company are systems integration, strategic information technology planning, software development, packaged software implementation, business process reengineering, organizational change management, networking and connectivity, and conventional and multimedia documentation and training. Whittman-Hart sells and delivers its services through a network of nine branch offices located in Chicago, Indianapolis, Milwaukee, Denver, Cincinnati, Cleveland, Columbus, Dallas, and Peoria, as well as several client support centers. In May 1996, the company completed an initial public offering of 5,200,000 shares of common stock. Incorporated in Delaware in 1991.

Directors (In addition to indicated officers)

Paul D. Carbery   Robert F. Steel
Lawrence P. Roches

Officers (Directors*)

*Robert F. Bernard, Chm., Pres. & C.E.O.   Susan B. Reardon, Dir.—Hum. Res.
*Edward F. Szofer, V.P., C.O.O. & Secy.   Stanley F. Martin, Dir.—Mktg. & Sales
 Kevin M. Gaskey, C.F.O. & Treas.

Consolidated Balance Sheet   As of December 31, 1996 (000 omitted)

Assets		Liabilities & Stockholders' Equity	
Current assets	$84,167	Current liabilities	$10,916
Net property, plant & equipment	5,844	Deferred items	978
Notes receivable	148	*Stockholders' equity	78,719
Other assets	454		
Total	$90,613	Total	$90,613

*20,134,680 shares common stock outstanding.

Consolidated Income Statement

Years Ended Dec. 31	Thousands — — — — Revenues	Net Income	Per Share[a] — — — Earnings	Cash Dividends	Common Stock Price Range[ab] Calendar Year
1996	$87,491	$5,303	$ .30	$ .00	28-1/8 — 10-1/2
1995	49,822	1,114[c]	.08[c]		
1994	29,543	855[c]			
1993	23,422	1,073[c]			
1992	18,632	679[c]			

[a]Adjusted to reflect a 2-for-1 stock split in December 1996 and a 4-for-1 stock split in April 1996.
[b]Initial public offering in May 1996.
[c]Pro forma.

Transfer Agent & Registrar: Harris Trust and Savings Bank

General Counsel:	David P. Shelow	Traded (Symbol):	NASDAQ (WHIT)
Investor Relations:	Sara Carin	Stockholders:	100
Human Resources:	Susan B. Reardon, Dir.	Employees:	1,000
Mgt. Info. Svcs.:	Mark Gerka	Annual Meeting:	In May
Auditors:	KPMG Peat Marwick LLP	Internet:	www.whitman-hart.com

Wickes Inc.

706 North Deerpath Drive, Vernon Hills, Illinois 60061
Telephone: (847) 367-3400

Wickes Inc. (formerly Wickes Lumber Company) is a major retailer and distributor of building materials. The company sells its products and services primarily to building professionals, as well as to serious do-it-yourselfers involved in major home improvement projects. The company operates 112 lumber and building materials centers under the name "Wickes Lumber" in 24 states located in the Midwest (70 locations), the Northeast (25 locations), and the South (17 locations). Wickes also operates 11 component manufacturing facilities that produce and distribute such value-added products as pre-hung door units, roof and floor trusses, and framed wall panels. Principal subsidiaries are Lumber Trademark Company and GLC Division, Inc. Incorporated in Delaware in 1987; present name adopted in 1997.

Directors (In addition to indicated officers)

Albert Ernest, Jr.
William H. Luers
Robert E. Mulcahy III

Frederick H. Schultz
Claudia B. Slacik

Officers (Directors*)

*J. Steven Wilson, Chm. & C.E.O.
 David T. Krawczyk, Pres. & C.O.O.
*Kenneth M. Kirschner, V. Chm., Gen. Coun.
 & Secy.
 George A. Bajalia, Sr. V.P., C.F.O. & Treas.
 Gene L. Curtin, V.P.—Mgmt. Info. Svcs.

George C. Finkenstaedt, V.P.—Oper.
Jimmie J. Frank, V.P. & Sr. Mdse. Mgr.
Gene R. Logan, V.P.—Sales
Robert W. Rowatt, V.P. & Sr. Mdse. Mgr.
Robert F. Sherlock, V.P.—Mktg.
John M. Lawrence, Asst. V.P. & Cont.

Consolidated Balance Sheet   As of December 28, 1996 (000 omitted)

Assets		Liabilities & Stockholders' Equity	
Current assets	$185,061	Current liabilities	$ 68,290
Net property, plant & equipment	50,171	Long-term debt	176,376
Other assets	37,610	Other liabilities	2,677
		*Stockholders' equity	25,499
Total	$272,842	Total	$272,842

*8,159,273 shares common stock outstanding.

Consolidated Income Statement

Years Ended Abt. Dec. 31	Thousands — — — — Net Sales	Net Income	Per Share[a] — — — Earnings	Cash Dividends	Common Stock Price Range[a] Calendar Year
1996	$848,535	$ 508	$ .07	$ .00	6-5/8 — 3-1/8
1995	972,612	(15,599)[b]	(2.54)[b]	.00	16-1/4 — 5
1994	986,872	28,054[c]	4.59[c]	.00	24-3/4 — 10
1993[d]	846,842	8,183[e]	1.34[e]	.00	18-1/4 — 12-1/4
1992[d]	745,365	6,004	.98		

[a]Adjusted to reflect a 21.73-for-1 stock split in October 1993. Initial public offering in October 1993.
[b]Includes restructuring and unusual charges of $17,798,000.
[c]Includes a charge related to headquarters cost reduction program, a gain on the sale of a private label credit card portfolio, and a deferred tax benefit.
[d]Pro forma gives effect to the recapitalization plan completed on October 22, 1993, as if had occurred on December 29, 1991.
[e]Includes an extraordinary gain of $1,241,000 ($.20 per share).

Transfer Agent & Registrar: First Interstate Bank of California

General Counsel:
  Kirschner, Main, Graham, Tanner & Demont

Investor Relations:	George A. Bajalia, Sr. V.P.	Traded (Symbol):	NASDAQ (WIKS)
Human Resources:	Kenneth M. Kirschner, V. Chm.	Stockholders:	6,000
Mgt. Info. Svcs.:	Gene L. Curtin, V.P.	Employees:	3,615
Auditors:	Coopers & Lybrand L.L.P.	Annual Meeting:	In May
		Internet:	www.wickes.com

Wintrust Financial Corporation

727 North Bank Lane, Lake Forest, Illinois 60045-1951
Telephone: (847) 615-4096

Wintrust Financial Corporation is a financial services holding company consisting of five commercial banks operating in selected affluent suburban Chicago communities, and an insurance premium finance company headquartered in Deerfield, Illinois. The company provides community-oriented, personal and commercial banking services through its banking subsidiaries: North Shore Community Bank and Trust Company; Lake Forest Bank and Trust Company; Hinsdale Bank and Trust Company; Libertyville Bank and Trust Company; and Barrington Bank and Trust Company, N.A. The company provides commercial insurance premium finance loans on a national basis through its financial services subsidiary, First Premium Services, Inc. In March 1997, the company completed an offering of 1,377,512 shares of common stock. Incorporated in Illinois as North Shore Community Bancorp, Inc. in 1992; present name adopted in 1996.

Directors   (In addition to indicated officers)

Alan W. Adams	James E. Mahoney	John N. Schaper
Joseph Alaimo	James B. McCarthy	John J. Schornack
Peter Crist	Marguerite Savard McKenna	Jane R. Stein
Maurice F. Dunne, Jr.	Albin F. Moschner	Katharine V. Sylvester
Eugene Hotchkiss III	Hollis W. Rademacher	Lemuel H. Tate, Jr.
James Knollenberg	J. Christopher Reyes	Larry Wright
John S. Lillard		

Officers   (Directors*)

*Howard D. Adams, Chm. & C.E.O.
*Edward J. Wehmer, Pres. & C.O.O.
Lloyd M. Bowden, Exec. V.P.—Tech.

David A. Dykstra, Exec. V.P., C.F.O. & Treas.
Robert F. Key, Exec. V.P.—Mktg.

Consolidated Balance Sheet   As of December 31, 1996 (000 omitted)

Assets		Liabilities & Stockholders' Equity	
Cash and due from banks, non-interest bearing	$ 36,581	Total deposits	$618,029
		Short-term borrowings	7,058
Federal funds sold	38,835	Notes payable	22,057
Deposits with banks, interest-bearing	18,732	Other liabilities	16,273
		*Stockholders' equity	42,620
Securities	74,388		
Net loans	488,912		
Net property & equipment	30,277		
Other assets	18,312		
Total	$706,037	Total	$706,037

*6,603,436 shares common stock outstanding.

Consolidated Income Statement

Years Ended Dec. 31	Thousands — — — — Total Income	Net Income	Per Share[a] — — — — Earnings	Cash Dividends	Common Stock Price Range[a] Calendar Year
1996	$46,569	$ (973)	$ (.16)		
1995[b]	34,016	1,497	.24		
1994[b]	19,230	(2,236)	(.56)		
1993[b]	9,383	(3,339)	(1.14)		
1992[c]	6,602	(5,735)	(2.59)		

[a]Trading commenced in March 1997. Prior to this date there was no active market for the company's common stock.
[b]Reflects results of those banks then in operation or in organization, results of finance and leasing subsidiary operations, and results of discontinued operations.
[c]Reflects results of finance and leasing subsidiary operations, some of which have since been sold, curtailed, or discontinued, and start-up of Lake Forest Bank and Trust Co. which opened in December 1991.

Transfer Agent & Registrar:	Illinois Stock Transfer Company		
Investor Relations:	David A. Dykstra, Exec. V.P.	**Traded (Symbol):**	NASDAQ (WTFC)
Mgt. Info. Svcs.:	Lloyd M. Bowden, Exec. V.P.	**Stockholders:**	2,189
		Employees:	226
Auditors:	KPMG Peat Marwick LLP	**Annual Meeting:**	In May

Wisconsin Central Transportation Corporation

6250 North River Road, Suite 9000, Rosemont, Illinois 60018
Telephone: (847) 318-4600

Wisconsin Central Transportation Corporation (WCTC) is a leading regional railroad in the United States. In addition to Wisconsin, the company provides service to northeastern Illinois, the Upper Peninsula of Michigan, eastern Minnesota, and northern Ontario. The company's operations utilize 3,000 route miles of track and trackage rights, 235 locomotives, and 12,800 railcars. WCTC provides freight transportation to customers that ship a variety of products. Subsidiaries include: Wisconsin Central Ltd. (WCL); WCL Railcars, Inc.; Fox Valley & Western Ltd. (FVW); Wisconsin Central International, Inc. (WCI); Sault Ste. Marie Bridge Co. (SSM); Algoma Central Railway Inc. (ACRI); and WC Canada Holdings, Inc. Through WCI, the company has a 23 percent equity interest in Tranz Rail Holdings Limited, a 2,400 mile railroad providing service throughout New Zealand, and a 34 percent equity interest in British Rail's former three trainload freight companies ("TLFs") and Rail express systems Limited ("Res"), both of which were sold as part of the privatization of British Rail. The TLFs haul bulk commodities throughout Great Britain and employ a staff of 6,600, utilizing 910 locomotives and 19,300 freight cars. Res operates trains carrying the Royal Mail in Great Britain. Incorporated in Delaware in 1987.

Directors   (In addition to indicated officers)

Carl Ferenbach	A. Francis Small
Roland V. McPherson	Robert H. Wheeler
Thomas W. Rissman, Secy.	

Officers   (Directors*)

*Edward A. Burkhardt, Chm., Pres. & C.E.O.	Glenn J. Kerbs, V.P.—Eng.—WCL, FVW, ACRI, SSM
*Thomas F. Power, Jr., Exec. V.P. & C.F.O.	J. Reilly McCarren, Exec. V.P. & C.O.O.—WCL, FVW, ACRI, SSM
Earl J. Currie, V.P.—Planning	Robert F. Nadrowski, V.P.—Mechanical—WCL, FVW, ACRI, SSM
Walter C. Kelly, V.P.—Fin.	William R. Schauer, V.P.—Mktg.—WCL, FVW, ACRI, SSM
Richard P. White, V.P.—Hum. Res.	J.E. Terbell, V.P. & Gen. Mgr.—WCL, FVW, ACRI, SSM
Marty J. Mickey, Treas.	

Consolidated Balance Sheet   As of December 31, 1996 (000 omitted)

Assets		Liabilities & Stockholders' Equity	
Current assets	$111,630	Current liabilities	$139,603
Net property, plant & equipment	464,993	Long-term debt	164,303
Investment in affiliates	114,652	Deferred income taxes	73,244
		Deferred income	10,951
		Other liabilities	4,028
		*Stockholders' equity	299,146
Total	$691,275	Total	$691,275

*50,778,867 shares common stock outstanding.

Consolidated Income Statement

Years Ended Dec. 31	Thousands Operating Revenues	Net Income	Per Share[a] Earnings	Cash Dividends	Common Stock Price Range[a] Calendar Year
1996	$262,160[b]	$48,432[bc]	$ .96[bc]	$ .00	42-1/2 — 20-1/2
1995	263,427	42,509[c]	.85[c]	.00	22-7/8 — 13-1/8
1994	211,139	36,695[c]	.74[c]	.00	16-1/8 — 9-5/8
1993	151,691	15,371[cd]	.31[cd]	.00	10 — 6
1992	124,364	10,881	.28	.00	6-1/4 — 3-3/8

[a]Adjusted to reflect a 3-for-1 stock in May 1996 and a 2-for-1 stock split in July 1994.
[b]Includes a charge of $13,278,000 pretax in operating revenues and $2,493,000 pretax in interest expense for a June 1996 arbitration ruling relating to switching services from 1988 through 1993, for a cumulative loss of net income of $9,526,000 ($.19 per share).
[c]Net of extraordinary charges related to the prepayment of debt or debt restructuring net of income taxes of $1,602,000 ($.03 per share) in 1996, $2,123,000 ($.04 per share) in 1995, $1,587,000 ($.03 per share) in 1994, and $1,398,000 ($.03 per share) in 1993.
[d]Net of a cumulative effect of the adoption of FAS 109, amounting to $2,067,000 ($.04 per share).

Transfer Agent & Registrar: First National Bank of Boston

General Counsel:	Oppenheimer Wolff & Donnelly	Auditors:	KPMG Peat Marwick LLP
Investor Relations:	Thomas F. Power, Jr., Exec. V.P.	Traded (Symbol):	NASDAQ (WCLX)
		Stockholders:	5,600
Human Resources:	Richard P. White, V.P.	Employees:	2,200
Mgt. Info. Svcs.:	Samuel J. Alex, Asst. V.P.	Annual Meeting:	In May

WMS Industries Inc.

3401 North California Ave., Chicago, Illinois 60618
Telephone: (773) 961-1111

WMS Industries Inc. participates in several segments of the leisure/amusement industry. The company designs, manufactures, and sells coin-operated pinball, video, and shuffle-alley amusement games, video lottery terminals and gaming devices; and publishes home video games. The company operates through its wholly owned subsidiaries: Williams Electronics Games, Inc.; Lenc-Smith Inc.; WMS Gaming Inc.; and its 86.8 percent owned subsidiary Midway Games Inc. Games are marketed under the Williams, Bally, Atari, and Midway names. WMS Industries maintains manufacturing plants in Chicago, Cicero, and Waukegan, Illinois. Midway Games Inc. operates from facilities in California and Texas. In April 1997, the company spun off to stockholders 100 percent of its Puerto Rico-based hotel, casino, and management businesses. In October 1996, the company completed the public offering of approximately 14 percent of the common stock of Midway Games Inc. Incorporated in Delaware in 1974.

Directors (In addition to indicated officers)

Norman J. Menell, V. Chm.
George R. Baker
William C. Bartholomay
Kenneth J. Fedesna

William E. McKenna
Harvey Reich
Ira S. Sheinfeld

Officers (Directors*)

*Louis J. Nicastro, Chm.
*Neil D. Nicastro, Pres., C.E.O. & C.O.O.

Harold H. Bach, Jr., V.P.—Fin., C.F.O., Chf. Acct. Off. & Treas.
Barbara M. Norman, V.P., Secy. & Gen. Coun.

Consolidated Balance Sheet   As of June 30, 1996 (000 omitted)

Assets		Liabilities & Stockholders' Equity	
Current assets	$216,424	Current liabilities	$ 70,794
Net property, plant & equipment	38,522	Long-term debt	65,363
Discontinued operations	42,091	Deferred items	6,548
Other assets	59,408	Other liabilities	3,707
		*Stockholders' equity	210,033
Total	$356,445	Total	$356,445

*24,147,750 shares common stock outstanding.

Consolidated Income Statement

Years Ended June 30	Thousands — — — — Total Revenue[a]	Net Income[a]	Per Share[b] — — — — Earnings[a]	Cash Dividends	Common Stock Price Range[b] Calendar Year
1996	$338,625	$ 7,477[c]	$ .31[c]	$ .00	29-1/4 — 16-1/2
1995	314,494	23,012	.96	.00	24-1/4 — 16
1994	282,733	26,266	1.10	.00	29-7/8 — 15-7/8
1993	260,449	24,937	1.07	.00	34 — 17-1/8
1992	164,656	22,504[d]	1.09[d]	.00	25 — 13-3/8

[a]Restated to exclude hotels and casinos as discontinued operations.
[b]Adjusted to reflect a 2-for-1 stock split in February 1992.
[c]Includes an after-tax restructuring charge of $2,091,000 ($.09 per share).
[d]Includes tax benefits of $8,000,000 ($.39 per share).

Transfer Agent & Registrar: The Bank of New York

General Counsel: Shack & Siegel, P.C.

Investor Relations: Harold H. Bach, Jr., V.P.

Auditors: Ernst & Young LLP

Traded (Symbol):   NYSE (WMS)

Stockholders: 2,000

Employees: 4,500

Annual Meeting: In January

Woodhead Industries, Inc.

2150 East Lake Cook Road, Suite 400, Buffalo Grove, Illinois 60089
Telephone: (847) 465-8300

Woodhead Industries, Inc. engages primarily in the manufacture and sale of devices for the control and distribution of electrical power for industry. The company serves a broad range of worldwide industries with electrical specialties and mechanical motion control products. The company's products can be classified into three groups: electrical specialties, reels and power systems, and molded rubber products. Electrical specialty products include portable handlamps, low-voltage safety lights, wiring devices, weatherproof receptacles, circuit testers, portable power distribution equipment, pendant pushbutton enclosures, general purpose power and control connectors, and custom copper and fiber optic cable assemblies. Reels and power systems include such products as electric cord and cable reels, electric cable festooning systems, collector rings, static discharge reels, tool balancers, ergonomic workstations, hose reels, and multiple-cable carrier systems. To identify its electrical specialty products and for safety purposes, Woodhead makes these products in a brilliant chrome-yellow color under the name Safety Yellow®. The company distributes its products, depending on type and market, to original equipment manufacturers, directly to users, or through selected distributors worldwide. Major subsidiaries include: Daniel Woodhead Co.; Aero-Motive Co.; Aero-Motive (U.K.) Ltd.; Woodhead Canada Ltd.; AI/FOCS, Inc.; Woodhead Asia PTE. Ltd.; Woodhead Japan Corp.; AKAPP Electro Industrie, B.V.; and H.F. Vogel GmbH. Incorporated in Illinois in 1922; reincorporated in Delaware in 1977.

Directors   (In addition to indicated officers)

Daniel T. Carroll
Charles W. Denny
Dale A. Miller
Eugene P. Nesbeda

Sarilee K. Norton
Alan L. Shaffer
Robert D. Tuttle
Richard A. Virzi

Officers   (Directors*)

*C. Mark DeWinter, Chm., Pres. & C.E.O.
Robert G. Jennings, V.P.—Fin. & C.F.O.
Robert A. Moulton, V.P.—Hum. Res.

Robert J. Tortorello, V.P.—Corp. Dev., Gen. Coun. & Secy.
Joseph P. Nogal, Treas., Cont. & Asst. Secy.

Consolidated Balance Sheet   As of September 28, 1996 (000 omitted)

Assets		Liabilities & Stockholders' Equity	
Current assets	$47,050	Current liabilities	$18,729
Net property, plant & equipment	23,665	Deferred items	1,779
Other assets	7,670	*Stockholders' equity	57,877
Total	$78,385	Total	$78,385

*10,419,000 shares common stock outstanding.

Consolidated Income Statement

Years Ended Abt. Sept. 30	Thousands — — — —		Per Share[a] — — — —		Common Stock Price Range[a] Calendar Year
	Net Sales	Net Income	Earnings	Cash Dividends	
1996	$123,680	$10,671	$ .98	$ .27	15-1/2 — 10
1995	120,003	9,228	.85	.26	16-3/4 — 10-1/2
1994	105,689	7,250	.68	.23	12-1/4 — 8-7/8
1993	89,864	5,803	.55	.23	10-5/8 — 7-5/8
1992	79,518	4,755	.47	.23	8-3/4 — 5-1/8

[a]Adjusted to reflect a 3-for-2 stock split in May 1995 and a 2-for-1 stock split in January 1993.

Transfer Agent & Registrar: Harris Trust and Savings Bank

General Counsel: Robert J. Tortorello, V.P.

Investor Relations: Robert G. Jennings, V.P.

Human Resources: Robert A. Moulton, V.P.

Auditors: Arthur Andersen LLP

Traded (Symbol):   NASDAQ (WDHD)
Stockholders: 584
Employees: 1,125
Annual Meeting: In January
Internet: www.woodhead.com

Woodward Governor Company

5001 North Second Street, Rockford, Illinois 61125-7001
Telephone: (815) 877-7441

Woodward Governor Company serves prime mover control and accessory markets. Prime movers convert heat or hydraulic energy into mechanical or electrical energy. The company designs, manufactures, and services controls for prime movers including diesel engines, hydraulic turbines, steam engines, aircraft propellers, industrial gas turbines, and aircraft gas turbines. The products control the rotational speed as well as other functions of these machines. The company distributes its products by direct sale to original equipment manufacturers, service providers, and equipment users throughout the world. The company is organized into two main groups: Aircraft Controls and Industrial Controls. Plants are located in Colorado, Illinois, and New York; and Australia, Brazil, England, Germany, India, Japan, the Netherlands, and Singapore. Offices are located in Alabama, California, Illinois, Pennsylvania, Texas, and Washington; and Canada, China, Korea, Mexico, New Zealand, Poland, and the United Arab Emirates. Incorporated in Illinois in 1902 as successor to a business originally established in 1870; reincorporated in Delaware in 1976.

Directors (In addition to indicated officers)

J. Grant Beadle	Thomas W. Heenan
Vern H. Cassens	J. Peter Jeffrey
Carl J. Dargene	Mark E. Leum
Lawrence E. Gloyd	Michael T. Yonker

Officers (Directors*)

*John A. Halbrook, Chm., Pres. & C.E.O.	C. Phillip Turner, V.P.
Stephen P. Carter, V.P., C.F.O. & Treas.	Gary D. Larrew, Asst. V.P.
Ronald E. Fulkrod, V.P.	Terry A. Shetler, Asst. V.P.
Charles F. Kovac, V.P.	Carol J. Manning, Secy.

Consolidated Balance Sheet As of September 30, 1996 (000 omitted)

Assets		Liabilities & Stockholders' Equity	
Current assets	$206,098	Current liabilities	$ 84,995
Net property, plant & equipment	114,213	Long-term debt	22,696
Other assets	28,487	Other liabilities	33,112
		*Stockholders' equity	207,995
Total	$348,798	Total	$348,798

*3,040,000 shares common stock outstanding.

Consolidated Income Statement

Years Ended Sept. 30	Thousands — — — — Net Sales	Net Income	Per Share — — — Earnings	Cash Dividends	Common Stock Price Range Fiscal Year	
1996	$417,290	$ 22,178	$ 7.67	$3.72	93	— 65
1995	379,736	11,936	4.11	3.72	83	— 55
1994	333,207	(3,273)	(1.11)	3.72	87	— 65
1993	331,156	(4,028)[a]	(1.36)[a]	3.72	80	— 60
1992	374,173	20,212	7.23	3.70	113	— 70

[a]Includes a charge to reflect FAS 106, FAS 109, and FAS 112, resulting in a cumulative effect of $17,417,000 ($5.86 per share).

Transfer Agent & Registrar: Wachovia Bank and Trust Co., N.A.

Corporate Counsel:	Chapman & Cutler	Auditors:	Coopers & Lybrand L.L.P.
Intern. Counsel:	Baker & McKenzie	Traded (Symbol):	NASDAQ (WGOV)
Investor Relations:	Carol J. Manning, Secy.	Stockholders:	2,029
Human Resources:	Jerry L. Forberg, Mgr.	Employees:	3,211
Mgt. Info. Svcs.:	Tonya K. Stromquist	Annual Meeting:	In January

Wm. Wrigley Jr. Company

410 North Michigan Avenue, Chicago, Illinois 60611-4287
Telephone: (312) 644-2121

Wm. Wrigley Jr. Company is a producer of chewing gum. Products marketed under the brand names of Wrigley's Spearmint, Doublemint, Juicy Fruit, Extra, Freedent, Winterfresh, and Big Red are sold throughout the U.S. and Canada. All or some of these brands and other brands are sold in the United Kingdom, Europe, Australia, New Zealand, and more than 100 other countries. The company's main U.S. plant is in Chicago; another plant is located in Gainesville, Georgia. Foreign plants are in Australia, Austria, Canada, China, England, France, India, Kenya, the Philippines, Poland, and Taiwan. In addition, Wrigley owns four domestic associated companies: Amurol Confections Company, a manufacturer of children's confectionery products; L.A. Dreyfus Company, a manufacturer of chewing gum base; Northwestern Flavors, Inc., which processes flavorings and rectifies mint oil; and Four-Ten Corporation. Incorporated in Delaware in 1927.

Directors (In addition to indicated officers)

Charles F. Allison III	Robert P. Billingsley	Penny S. Pritzker
Lee Phillip Bell	Thomas A. Knowlton	Richard K. Smucker

Officers (Directors*)

*William Wrigley, Pres. & C.E.O.	Dennis R. Mally, V.P.—Info. Svcs.
*Douglas S. Barrie, Grp. V.P.—Intl.	Jon Orving, V.P.—Intl.
Ronald O. Cox, Grp. V.P.—Mktg.	Dushan Petrovich, V.P. & Cont.
John F. Bard, Sr. V.P.	Stefan Pfander, V.P.—Intl.
Martin J. Geraghty, Sr. V.P.—Mfg.	Wm. M. Piet, V.P.—Corp. Aff. & Corp. Secy.
Donald E. Balster, V.P.—Prod.	John A. Schafer, V.P.—Purch.
Gary R. Bebee, V.P.—Cust. Mktg.	Philip G. Schnell, V.P.—R&D
David E. Boxell, V.P.—Personnel	Christafor E. Sundstrom, V.P.—Corp. Devel.
J.E. Dy-Liacco, V.P.—Intl.	*William Wrigley, Jr., V.P.
Susan S. Fox, V.P.—Cons. Mktg.	Philip Johnson, Sr. Dir.—Benefits Comp.
Philip G. Hamilton, V.P.—Intl.	John H. Sutton, Gen. Mgr.—Converting
H.J. Kim, V.P.—Eng.	

Consolidated Balance Sheet As of December 31, 1996 (000 omitted)

Assets		Liabilities & Stockholders' Equity	
Current assets	$ 729,424	Current liabilities	$ 218,152
Net property, plant & equipment	388,149	Deferred items	24,390
Other assets	115,970	Other liabilities	93,570
		*Stockholders' equity	897,431
Total	$1,233,543	Total	$1,233,543

*92,066,000 shares common and 24,155,000 shares Class B common stock outstanding.

Consolidated Income Statement

Years Ended Dec. 31	Thousands————Net Sales	Net Income	Per Share[a]———— Earnings	Cash Dividends	Common Stock Price Range[a] Calendar Year
1996	$1,835,987	$230,272	$1.99	$1.02	62-7/8 — 48-3/8
1995	1,754,931	223,739	1.93	.96	54 — 42-7/8
1994	1,596,551	230,533[b]	1.98[b]	.90	53-7/8 — 38-1/8
1993	1,428,504	174,891	1.50	.75	46-1/8 — 29-1/2
1992	1,286,921	141,295[c]	1.21[c]	.62	39-7/8 — 22-1/8

[a]Adjusted to reflect a 3-for-1 stock split in September 1992.
[b]Includes non-recurring after-tax gain of $24,765,000 ($.21 per share).
[c]Includes a charge to reflect FAS 106 and FAS 109, resulting in a cumulative effect of $7,278,000 ($.06 per share).

Transfer Agent & Registrar: First Chicago Trust Co. of New York

General Counsel:
Howard Malovant, Asst. Corp. Secy.

Investor Relations:	Christopher J. Perille, Dir.	**Traded (Symbol):**	NYSE, CSE (WWY)
Human Resources:	David E. Boxell, V.P.	**Stockholders:**	34,950
Mgt. Info. Svcs.:	Dennis R. Mally, V.P.	**Employees:**	7,800
Auditors:	Ernst & Young LLP	**Annual Meeting:**	In March
		Internet:	www.wrigley.com

Zebra Technologies Corporation

333 Corporate Woods Parkway, Vernon Hills, Illinois 60061-3109
Telephone: (847) 634-6700

Zebra Technologies Corporation provides bar code labeling solutions principally to manufacturing and service organizations worldwide for use in automatic identification and data collection systems. The company designs, manufactures, sells, and supports a broad line of computerized label/ticket printing systems, related specialty supplies, and software. Equipment is designed to operate at the user's location to produce and dispense high quality bar coded labels in extremely time-sensitive and physically demanding environments. Zebra's solutions approach integrates its applications expertise, computerized printing systems, and specialty supplies. Applications for the company's systems include inventory control, automated warehousing, JIT (Just-In-Time) manufacturing, CIM (Computer Integrated Manufacturing), employee time and attendance records, weighing systems, tool room control, shop floor control, library systems, prescription labeling, and scientific experimentation. Major subsidiaries are: Zebra Technologies Europe, Ltd.; Zebra Technologies Preston, Ltd.; Zebra Technologies VTI, Inc.; and ZIH Corp. Incorporated in Illinois in 1969; reincorporated in Delaware in 1991.

Directors   (In addition to indicated officers)

Christopher G. Knowles
David P. Riley

Michael A. Smith

Officers   (Directors*)

*Edward L. Kaplan, Chm. & C.E.O.
 Jeffrey K. Clements, Exec. V.P.
*Gerhard Cless, Exec. V.P. & Secy.
 Jack A. LeVan, Sr. V.P.—Bus. Dev.
 Thomas C. Beusch, V.P.—Sales & Intl.

James A. Goffee, V.P.—Mfg.
Clive P. Hohberger, Ph.D., V.P.—Tech. Dev.
Charles R. Whitchurch, C.F.O. & Treas.
John H. Kindsvater, Jr., Pres.—Zebra
 Technologies VTI, Inc.

Consolidated Balance Sheet   As of December 31, 1996 (000 omitted)

Assets		Liabilities & Stockholders' Equity	
Current assets	$148,996	Current liabilities	$ 20,193
Net property, plant & equipment	11,328	Long-term debt	2,326
Deferred income taxes	147	Other liabilities	308
Other assets	2,812	*Stockholders' equity	140,456
Total	$163,283	Total	$163,283

*24,240,377 shares common stock outstanding.

Consolidated Income Statement

Years Ended Abt. Dec. 31	Thousands — — — — Net Sales	Net Income	Per Share[a] — — — Earnings	Cash Dividends	Common Stock Price Range[ab] Calendar Year
1996	$169,715	$28,915[c]	$1.19	$ .00	35-1/4 — 15-1/2
1995	148,593	22,564[d]	.94	.00	34-1/2 — 18-1/8
1994	107,103	21,073	.88	.00	28-1/8 — 11-3/4
1993	87,456	18,255	.76	.00	30-3/8 — 10-1/8
1992	58,711	11,843	.50	.00	12-3/8 — 7-1/4

[a]Adjusted to reflect a 2-for-1 stock split in December 1995 and a 93-for-1 stock split in August 1991.
[b]Class A common stock.
[c]Reflects a pretax charge of $1,117,000 for acquired in-process technology relating to the acquisition of Fenestra Computer Services.
[d]Reflects a pretax charge of $6,028,000 for acquired in-process technology relating to the acquisition of Vertical Technologies, Inc.

Transfer Agent & Registrar: Harris Trust and Savings Bank

General Counsel:	Katten Muchin & Zavis	Traded (Symbol):	NASDAQ (ZBRA)
Investor Relations:	Charles R. Whitchurch, C.F.O.	Stockholders:	2,500
Human Resources:	Bruce Beebe, Dir.	Employees:	700
Mgt. Info. Svcs.:	Dean Cochran, Dir.	Annual Meeting:	In May
Auditors:	KPMG Peat Marwick LLP	Internet:	www.zebra.com

Zeigler Coal Holding Company

50 Jerome Lane, Fairview Heights, Illinois 62208
Telephone: (618) 394-2400

Zeigler Coal Holding Company is an integrated energy company, with existing or developing businesses in coal, technology, power, environmental and engineering, asset management, and international segments. Through its subsidiaries, the company is a leading coal producer, operating nine underground and surface coal mining complexes located in Illinois, Kentucky, Ohio, West Virginia, and Wyoming. Zeigler Coal also operates import/export terminals in South Carolina and Virginia, and owns ENCOAL, a clean coal technology plant in Wyoming. In addition, a Zeigler Coal affiliate has pending a joint bid with Southern Electric International and NRG Energy to purchase out of bankruptcy the non-nuclear assets of Louisiana-based Cajun Electric Power Cooperative. Zeigler's EnerZ Corporation subsidiary, an energy trading and marketing firm, has been created to take advantage of opportunities growing out of utility deregulation. Zeigler Coal was formed in connection with a management-led buyout from Houston Natural Gas Corporation in 1985. Principal subsidiaries include: Old Ben Coal Company; Bluegrass Coal Development Co.; Mountaineer Coal Development Co.; Triton Coal Company; EnerZ Corporation; Zeigler International; Zeigler Environmental Services Company; Franklin Coal Sales Co.; Phoenix Land Company; ENCOAL; and Americoal Development Co. Incorporated in Delaware in 1985.

Directors (In addition to indicated officers)

Michael K. Reilly, Chm.
Roland E. Casati

Robert W. Ericson
John F. Manley

Officers (Directors*)

*Chand B. Vyas, Pres. & C.E.O.
W. Douglas Blackburn, Jr., Sr. V.P.—Oper.
Robert E. Mohrmann, Sr. V.P. & C.F.O.
Francis L. Barkofske, V.P.—Admin.

Brent L. Motchan, V.P., Gen. Coun. & Secy.
Sharad M. Desai, Treas.
Paul D. Femmer, Cont.

Consolidated Balance Sheet   As of December 31, 1996 (000 omitted)

Assets		Liabilities & Stockholders' Equity	
Current assets	$ 217,952	Current liabilities	$ 133,022
Net property, plant & equipment	818,870	Long-term debt	344,770
Other assets	13,803	Deferred items	380,337
		Other liabilities	59,890
		*Stockholders' equity	132,606
Total	$1,050,625	Total	$1,050,625

*28,377,000 shares common stock outstanding.

Consolidated Income Statement

Years Ended Dec. 31	Thousands — — — — Total Revenues	Net Income	Per Share[a] — — — Earnings	Cash Dividends	Common Stock Price Range[ab] Calendar Year
1996	$731,624	$ 57,964	$ 2.04	$ .25	22-1/4 — 12-1/4
1995	783,103	(11,213)[c]	(.40)	.20	14-1/4 — 9-3/4
1994	870,890	25,093[d]	1.01[d]	.05	15-3/4 — 10-1/2
1993	873,001	(146,182)[e]	(6.29)[e]	.00	
1992	503,006	74,384	3.26		

[a]Adjusted to reflect a 32-for-1 stock split in September 1994.
[b]Initial public offering in September 1994.
[c]Includes a charge of $114,662 to reflect FAS 121 (Provision for Asset Impairment).
[d]Includes an extraordinary charge of $8,400,000 ($.34 per share) for extinguishment of debt.
[e]Includes a charge to reflect FAS 106 and FAS 109, resulting in a cumulative effect of $111,946,000 ($4.82 per share).

Transfer Agent & Registrar: Harris Trust and Savings Bank

General Counsel:	Brent L. Motchan, V.P.	Traded (Symbol):	NYSE (ZEI)
Investor Relations:	Francis L. Barkofske, V.P.	Stockholders:	6,500
Human Resources:	Francis L. Barkofske, V.P.	Employees:	2,144
Mgt. Info. Svcs.:	Ronald Goss, C.I.O.	Annual Meeting:	In May
Auditors:	Deloitte & Touche LLP	Internet:	www.zeigler.com

Zenith Electronics Corporation

1000 Milwaukee Avenue, Glenview, Illinois 60025-2493
Telephone: (847) 391-7000

Zenith Electronics Corporation is a leading consumer electronics manufacturer and distributor. The company's operations are centered around one industry segment—the design, development, and manufacture of video products, including color television sets and other consumer products, and parts and accessories for such products. These products, along with video cassette recorders, are sold principally to retail dealers in the United States, and to retail dealers and wholesale distributors in foreign countries. The company also sells directly to buying groups, private label customers, and customers in the lodging, health care, and rent-to-own industries. Zenith's video products also include color picture tubes that are produced for and sold to other manufacturers, and network systems products such as cable and telecommunications set-top devices, interactive television, and data communications products, which are sold primarily to cable television operators and other commercial users of these products. In November 1995, a change in control of the company occurred, in which LG Electronics, Inc. (LGE), a Korean corporation, purchased shares of the company pursuant to a combined tender offer. LGE also purchased newly-issued shares of common stock and is now the beneficial owner of approximately 55 percent of all outstanding shares. Subsidiaries include: Zenith Electronics Corporation of Texas; Zenith Radio Canada, Ltd.; Zenith Distributing Corp. of New York; Zenco de Chihuahua, S.A. de C.V.; and Partes de Television de Reynosa, S.A. de C.V. Founded in 1918; incorporated in Illinois in 1923; reincorporated in Delaware in 1958.

Directors   (In addition to indicated officers)

T. Kimball Brooker	Robert A. Helman	Andrew McNally IV
K.S. Cho	John Koo	Yong Nam
Eugene B. Connolly	H.J. Lee	

Officers   (Directors*)

*Peter S. Willmott, Pres. & C.E.O.
Roger A. Cregg, Exec. V.P. & C.F.O.
Michael Ahn, Sr. V.P.—Oper.
Richard F. Vitkus, Sr. V.P., Gen. Coun. & Secy.
John I. Taylor, V.P.—Public Aff. & Commun.

Dennis R. Winkleman, V.P.—Hum. Res.
Ramesh G. Amin, Pres.—Consumer Elec.Div.
William G. Luehrs, Pres.—Network Sys. Div.
William J. Sims, Pres.—Zenith Sales Co.

Consolidated Balance Sheet   As of December 31, 1996 (000 omitted)

Assets		Liabilities & Stockholders' Equity	
Current assets	$475,100	Current liabilities	$450,600
Net property, plant & equipment	278,300	Other liabilities	152,700
Other assets	11,900	*Stockholders' equity	162,000
Total	$765,300	Total	$765,300

*66,458,938 shares common stock outstanding.

Consolidated Income Statement

Years Ended Dec. 31	Thousands — — — — Net Sales	Net Income	Per Share — — — — Earnings	Cash Dividends	Common Stock Price Range Calendar Year
1996	$1,287,900	$(178,000)[a]	$(2.73)	$ .00	26 — 5-7/8
1995[b]	1,273,900	(90,800)[c]	(1.85)	.00	12-1/8 — 6-5/8
1994[b]	1,469,000	(14,500)	(.35)	.00	14-1/8 — 7
1993[b]	1,228,200	(93,200)[d]	(2.89)	.00	10-1/2 — 5-7/8
1992[b]	1,243,500	(107,900)[e]	(3.66)	.00	11-1/8 — 5

[a]Includes $9,300,000 of restructuring and other charges.
[b]Restated.
[c]Includes $21,600,000 of restructuring and other charges.
[d]Includes $31,000,000 of restructuring and other charges. The company adopted FAS 112, which did not have a material effect on the financial statements.
[e]Includes $48,100,000 of restructuring and other charges. The company adopted FAS 109, which superseded FAS 96. It had no effect on the financial statements.

Transfer Agent & Registrar:	The Bank of New York		
General Counsel:	Richard F. Vitkus, Sr. V.P.	Traded (Symbol):	NYSE, CSE, 3 Swiss (ZE)
Investor Relations:	John I. Taylor, V.P.	Stockholders:	12,026
Human Resources:	Dennis R. Winkleman, V.P.	Employees:	15,900
Mgt. Info. Svcs.:	Y.K. Kim, Dir.	Annual Meeting:	In May
Auditors:	Arthur Andersen LLP	Internet:	www.zenith.com

Banks
And Savings
Institutions

_____

_____

_____

_____

_____

_____

_____

_____

_____

_____

_____

_____

_____

_____

_____

_____

_____

_____

_____

_____

American National Bank & Trust Company of Chicago

33 North LaSalle Street, Chicago, Illinois 60690
Telephone: (312) 661-5000

American National Bank and Trust Company is a wholly owned subsidiary of American National Corporation, a multi-bank holding company, which in turn is owned by First Chicago NBD Corporation. The bank offers commercial, investment, trust, real estate, international banking services, and personal financial services. The bank has 15 branch locations. An overseas branch is located in the Cayman Islands. Chartered under the National Bank Act as Straus National Bank & Trust Co. of Chicago in 1928; present name adopted in 1933.

Directors (In addition to indicated officers)

Franklin A. Cole
Lawrence I. Field
Ellis M. Goodman

Howard G. Krane
Sheila Lyne, R.S.M.
Ralph W. Muller

Jerry K. Pearlman
John W. Rogers, Jr.
Robert F. Schnoes

Officers (Directors*)

* David J. Vitale, Chm.
* David P. Bolger, Pres.
  Thomas H. Adams, Exec. V.P.
  Stephen L. Eastwood, Exec. V.P. & C.O.O.
  Robert. E. Lee, Exec. V.P.
* John Q. McKinnon, Exec. V.P.
  Alan S. Adams, Sr. V.P.
  John R. Brinkman, Sr. V.P.
  Guy W. Eisenhuth, Sr. V.P.
  Paul G. Greig, Sr. V.P.
  Richard Y. Guthrie, Sr. V.P.

Timothy C. Hadro, Sr. V.P.
Michael B. Hagen, Sr. V.P.
Dennis E. Harrison, Sr. V.P.
Kevin M. Leissring, Sr. V.P.
Nancy J. Lindsay, Sr. V.P.
John L. Losquadro, Sr. V.P.
William F. Lynch, Sr. V.P.
Douglas P. Sutton, Sr. V.P.
Thomas R. Watts, Sr. V.P.
Daniel D. Wilkening, Sr. V.P.

Consolidated Balance Sheet As of December 31, 1996 (000 omitted)

Assets		Liabilities & Stockholders' Equity	
Cash & due from banks	$ 694,079	Deposits	$6,476,985
Securities	177,080	Funds borrowed	754,838
Other short-term investments	442,150	Other liabilities	239,807
Net loans	6,656,612	Stockholders' equity	737,319
Properties & equipment	42,817		
Other assets	196,211		
Total	$8,208,949	Total	$8,208,949

Years Ended Dec. 31	Total Deposits	Demand Deposits	Time Deposits	Foreign Office Deposits	Net Loans	Capital Accounts
1996	$6,476,985	$2,391,630	$2,316,895	$1,768,460	$6,656,612	$737,319
1995	5,461,286	1,979,795	2,316,638	1,164,853	5,179,668	612,811
1994	5,159,046	2,020,140	2,080,520	1,058,386	4,627,895	562,104
1993	4,530,872	1,913,718	1,881,120	736,034	3,561,468	488,339
1992	3,880,807	1,747,326	1,623,507	509,974	3,054,730	397,942

Consolidated Income Statement

Years Ended Dec. 31	Operating Income	Operating Expenses	Net Income
1996	$629,168	$450,291	$114,390
1995	566,244	427,067	90,008
1994	467,707	337,260	84,489
1993	391,670	299,262	60,958
1992	359,305	293,169	44,796

General Counsel:	Kirkland & Ellis	Employees:	2,000
Human Resources:	Thomas H. Adams, Exec.V.P.		
Auditors:	Arthur Andersen LLP	Member:	FDIC; Federal Reserve System

Bank One, Illinois, NA

East Old State Capitol Plaza, Springfield, Illinois 62701
Telephone: (847) 866-5500

Bank One, Illinois, NA is a national banking association and a wholly owned subsidiary of Columbus, Ohio-based BANC ONE CORPORATION. As of February 15, 1997, the individual bank charters of Bank One Bloomington-Normal, Bank One Champaign-Urbana, Bank One Chicago, Bank One Peoria, Bank One Rockford, and Bank One Springfield were consolidated to create Bank One, Illinois, NA. The bank offers its customers full commercial banking services, real estate lending, consumer lending, personal banking services, and trust investment services through 52 branch offices throughout Illinois. Chartered under the National Banking Act in 1997.

Officers (Directors*)

* Thomas H. Cartwright, Chm.
* Joseph D. Barnette, Jr., Pres. & C.E.O.
* Stanley J. Calderon, Exec. V.P. & Mkt. Pres.— Chicago
* John E. Staudt, Exec V.P. & Mkt. Pres.— Springfield
* Jonathan G. Verity, Exec. V.P.

* Frank E. Walter, Exec. V.P. & Mkt. Pres.— Rockford
James Corkery, Mkt. Pres.— Peoria
Richard O'Neill, Mkt. Pres.— Champaign-Urbana
Robert Rush, Mkt. Pres.— Bloomington-Normal

Consolidated Balance Sheet[a]   As of March 31, 1997 (000 omitted)

Assets		Liabilities & Stockholders' Equity	
Cash & due from banks	$ 74,697	Deposits	$2,906,122
Securities	403,727	Fed. funds purch. & sec. sold under agreement to repurch.	256,014
Fed. funds sold & sec. purchased under agreement to resell	99,665	Other borrowings	26,632
Net loans	2,924,057	Other liabilities	49,453
Property & equipment	77,812	Stockholders' equity	409,436
Other assets	67,699		
Total	$3,647,657	Total	$3,647,657

Years Ended Dec. 31[a]	Thousands Total Deposits	Demand Deposits	Time Deposits	Net Loans	Capital Accounts

[a]Combined pro forma financial data for banks prior to the merger are unavailable for 1996 and prior years.

Consolidated Income Statement[a]

Years Ended Dec. 31	Thousands Operating Income	Operating Expenses	Net Income

[a]Combined pro forma financial data for banks prior to the merger are unavailable for 1996 and prior years.

Mgt. Info. Svcs.:	Banc One Services Corp.	Member:	FDIC; Federal Reserve System
Auditors:	Coopers & Lybrand L.L.P.	Internet:	www.bankone.com

Citibank, Federal Savings Bank

500 West Madison St., Chicago, Illinois 60661
Telephone: (312) 263-6660

Citibank, Federal Savings Bank, a wholly owned subsidiary of Citicorp Banking Corporation, operates more than 50 branches throughout the Chicagoland area. Citibank offers a full range of financial products. Twenty-four-hour banking is available at more than 200 automated teller machines within the branch network. Citiphone banking, the 24-hour telephone banking service, is another convenience available to all customers. Citibank is a member of the Cirrus and Cash Station networks. The core customer account offering is the Citibank Money Management Account, which includes checking, money market, overdraft protection, and Bankcard services. Savings products include statement savings and certificates of deposit for periods from six months to five years. Retirement accounts, IRA's, and Keoghs have additional investment options available, including brokerage and stock index accounts. Citibank also has a wide array of credit products available for its customers, including businesses, such as unsecured and secured revolving lines, fixed and variable mortgages, equity products, and traditional second mortgages.

Officers

Jean-Paul Votron, Chm. & C.E.O.
Thomas J. Tolda, V.P. & C.F.O.

Darcy Walker, V.P. & Sr. Credit Off.
David W. Young, V.P. & Treas.

Consolidated Statement of Condition   As of December 31, 1996 (000 omitted)

Assets		Liabilities & Equity Capital	
Cash, deposits & investment securities	$ 1,554,078	Deposits	$12,695,868
		Borrowings	2,287,488
Loans, net	13,981,033	Other liabilities	209,421
Other assets	1,252,250	Equity capital	1,594,584
Total	$16,787,361	Total	$16,787,361

Years Ended Dec. 31	Thousands Total Assets	Mortgage Loans	Deposits	Equity Capital
1996	$16,787,361	$11,806,312	$12,695,868	$1,594,584
1995	15,689,687	10,181,555	11,272,513	1,613,342
1994	13,523,542	9,526,295	10,302,589	1,644,142
1993	12,227,176	9,005,362	9,776,341	1,662,113
1992	10,704,302	8,832,513	8,613,018	1,504,516

Consolidated Income Statement

Years Ended Dec. 31	Thousands Net Interest Income After Loan Loss Provision	Other Income	Expenses	Net Income
1996	$525,853	$128,487	$703,182	$(35,877)
1995	465,649	101,244	612,257	(34,726)
1994	493,457	120,180	614,205	(17,627)
1993[a]	445,438	178,183	701,029	(33,811)
1992	317,255	98,870	445,414	(21,166)

[a]Citibank in Florida merged into Citibank, Federal Savings Bank on January 1, 1993; prior years were not restated.

Human Resources:	Tom Christopher, V.P.	Employees:	4,161
Mgt. Info. Svcs.:	Gerald Waldron, V.P.	Member:	FDIC
Auditors:	KPMG Peat Marwick LLP		

Cole Taylor Bank

350 East Dundee Road, Wheeling, Illinois 60090
Telephone: (847) 537-0077

Cole Taylor Bank is a wholly owned subsidiary of Taylor Capital Group, Inc. The bank provides a full range of commercial and consumer banking services to both small and mid-sized businesses, and to individuals through its ten branch offices in Chicago neighborhoods and suburban Cook and DuPage counties. Cole Taylor Bank commenced operations more than 60 years ago in Chicago as Main State Bank. On February 12, 1997, the capital stock of Cole Taylor Bank was acquired by Taylor Capital Group, Inc. from Cole Taylor Financial Group, Inc.

Directors   (In addition to indicated officers)

John S. Bubula	Elzie L. Higginbottom	Joseph Mario Moreno
Wheeler E. Chapman, Jr.	Richard Kaplan	Langdon D. Neal
Armand L. Dann	Edward T. McGowan	Barbara M. Sellstrom
Ronald D. Emanuel	Edward Meyer	Sidney J. Taylor

Officers   (Directors*)

* Jeffrey W. Taylor, Chm.
* Bruce W. Taylor, Pres. & C.E.O.
  J. Christopher Alstrin, C.F.O.
* Robert F. Corey, Sr. Exec. V.P.—Govt. Rel.
  Frank DeGradi, Exec. V.P.—Mortgage Banking
* Richard C. Keneman, Exec. V.P.—Rel. Banking
  Richard Schwartz, Exec. V.P.
  Daniel S. Bleil, Grp. Sr. V.P.

D. Fred DeRoode, Grp. Sr. V.P.—Small Bus. Banking
Thomas J. Hennessy, Grp. Sr. V.P.—Real Est. Banking
Joseph A. Kirkeeng, Grp. Sr. V.P.—Retail Banking
Daniel L. Lueken, Grp. Sr. V.P.—Sales Mgt./Oper.
Robin J. VanCastle, Grp. Sr. V.P.—Fin. Mgt.
Vicky Robertson-Mack, Grp. Sr. V.P.—Mktg.
Scott McCartan, Sr. V.P.—Trust & Chf. Invest. Off.
Roy C. Postel, Chf. Credit Off.

Consolidated Balance Sheet   As of December 31, 1996 (000 omitted)

Assets		Liabilities & Stockholders' Equity	
Cash & due from banks	$ 81,585	Total deposits	$1,406,900
Federal funds sold	5,675	Short-term borrowings	162,182
Investment securities	403,789	Long-term borrowings	86,086
Loans, net	1,200,810	Other liabilities	16,788
Property & equipment	15,247	Stockholders' equity	141,635
Other receivables	66,570		
Other assets	39,915		
Total	$1,813,591	Total	$1,813,591

Years Ended Dec. 31	Total Deposits	Interest-Bearing Deposits	Demand Deposits	Net Loans	Stockholders' Equity
1996	$1,406,900	$1,072,832	$334,068	$1,200,810	$141,635
1995	1,364,075	1,045,958	318,117	1,187,753	132,741
1994	1,293,411	974,611	318,800	1,107,344	118,997
1993	1,180,845	902,308	278,537	966,644	101,763
1992	1,130,850	869,061	261,789	890,127	94,979

Consolidated Income Statement

Years Ended Dec. 31	Total Income	Operating Expenses	Net Income
1996	$154,721	$121,750[a]	$19,693
1995	147,911	117,915[b]	18,166
1994	129,154	99,366[c]	15,902
1993	117,253	89,073[d]	12,722
1992	113,469	90,034[e]	9,962

[a]Excludes the provision for possible loan losses of $3,307,000.
[b]Excludes the provision for possible loan losses of $4,056,000.
[c]Excludes the provision for possible loan losses of $7,374,000.
[d]Excludes the provision for possible loan losses of $10,521,000.
[e]Excludes the provision for possible loan losses of $8,922,000.

Corporate Counsel:	Katten Muchin & Zavis	Auditors:	KPMG Peat Marwick LLP
Human Resources:	Robert Davis, V.P.	Employees:	613
Mgt. Info. Svcs:	Daniel L. Leuken, Grp. Sr. V.P.	Member:	FDIC; FHLB

First Bank National Association

400 North Michigan Avenue, Chicago, Illinois 60611-4181
Telephone: (312) 836-6500

First Bank National Association, a wholly owned subsidiary of First Bank System Inc., offers a complete line of personal, corporate, and trust banking services.

Officers

Kent Stone, Sr. V.P.—Retail Bank
Greg Warsek, Sr. V.P.—Comm. Real Estate
Louise Hildebrand, V.P.—Trust

Teresa McLeod, V.P.—Retail Bank
Charles Rusella, V.P.—Inst. Trust
Mark Schlagel, V.P.—Retail Bank

Consolidated Balance Sheet   As of December 31, 1996 (000 omitted)

Assets		Liabilities & Stockholders' Equity	
Cash & due from banks	$ 50,521	Deposits	$700,945
Securities	316,535	Funds borrowed	31,365
Net loans	407,692	Other liabilities	19,438
Properties & equipment	10,572	Stockholders' equity	176,462
Other assets	142,890		
Total	$ 928,210	Total	$928,210

Years Ended Dec. 31	Thousands Total Deposits	Demand Deposits	Time Deposits	Net Loans	Capital Accounts
1996	$700,945	$171,824	$529,121	$407,692	$176,462
1995	783,041	158,445	624,596	542,487	240,361
1994	887,269	188,155	699,114	552,657	283,103

Consolidated Income Statement[a]

Years Ended Dec. 31	Thousands Operating Income	Operating Expenses	Net Income
1996	$81,528	$95,234	$(13,706)
1995	99,725	84,636	5,607
1994	76,615	67,841	3,288

[a]First Bank System merged with Boulevard Bancorp, Inc. in April, 1994.

General Counsel:	Dorsey & Whitney	Employees:	195
Auditors:	Ernst & Young LLP	Member:	FDIC

First Midwest Bank, N.A.

300 Park Boulevard, Suite 400, Itasca, Illinois 60143
Telephone: (630) 875-7200

First Midwest Bank, N.A., is an affiliate of First Midwest Bancorp, Inc., a bank holding company. The bank, which operates 47 offices primarily in northern Illinois, offers full commercial banking services, consumer lending, and personal banking services. Approximately 80 percent of bank assets are situated in metropolitan Chicago. On November 30, 1996, First Midwest acquired Citizens Federal Savings Bank, F.S.B. of Davenport, Iowa, in a pooling-of-interests transaction.

Directors (In addition to indicated officers)

Brother James Gaffney
Robert P. O'Meara

Frank Waldeck

Officers (Directors*)

* John M. O'Meara, Chm. & C.E.O.
* James D. Anderson, Pres.—Central Region
* Marc R. Parise, Pres.—Western Region
* Thomas J. Schwartz, Pres.—North Metro Region
* Kent S. Belasco, Exec. V.P. & Chf. Info. Officer
* Mark M. Dietrich, Exec. V.P. & C.O.O.
* Thomas F. Franklin, Exec. V.P. & Chf. Planning Officer

* Ralph R. Leonard, Chf. Retail Credit Admin. Officer
* James M. Voss, Exec. V.P. & Chf. Comm. Credit Admin. Officer
* Judith T. Walz, Exec. V.P. & Chf. Mktg. Officer

Consolidated Balance Sheet   As of December 31, 1996 (000 omitted) Unaudited

Assets		Liabilities & Stockholder's Equity	
Cash & due from banks	$ 107,567	Deposits	$ 2,285,287
Short-term investments	22,821	Short-term borrowings	480,344
Securities	788,314	Other liabilities	86,985
Net loans	2,050,822	Stockholder's equity	216,671
Premises, furniture & equipment	46,035		
Other assets	53,728		
Total	$3,069,287	Total	$ 3,069,287

Years Ended Dec. 31	Total Assets	Interest-bearing Deposits	Noninterest-bearing Deposits	Net Loans	Capital Accounts
1996[a]	$3,069,287	$1,934,827	$350,460	$2,050,822	$216,671
1995[a]	2,938,770	1,920,604	366,537	2,051,773	205,001
1994[a]	2,764,603	1,792,583	347,624	1,866,915	187,788

Consolidated Income Statement[a]

Years Ended Dec. 31	Operating Income	Operating Expenses[b]	Net Income
1996	$253,733	$221,148	$32,585
1995	243,362	216,377	26,985
1994	212,829	182,000	30,829

[a]Restated to reflect the acquisition of Citizens Federal Savings Bank, F.S.B., accounted for as a pooling-of-interests.
[b]Includes income taxes.

General Counsel:	Hinshaw & Culbertson	Auditors:	Ernst & Young LLP
Human Resources:	Phillip E. Glotfelty, Sr. V.P.	Employees:	1,044
Mgt. Info. Svcs.:	Kent S. Belasco, Exec. V.P.	Member:	FDIC; Federal Reserve System

The First National Bank of Chicago

One First National Plaza, Chicago, Illinois 60670
Telephone: (312) 732-4000

The First National Bank of Chicago is a wholly owned subsidiary of First Chicago NBD Corporation. The bank provides a broad range of banking, fiduciary, financial, and other services on a worldwide basis to individuals, businesses, and governmental units. The bank maintains three regional offices in Houston, Los Angeles, and New York, to develop new business and to maintain closer contact with corporate and institutional banking customers. Internationally, The First National Bank of Chicago serves customers within Canada, Europe, the Middle East, Africa, and the Asia-Pacific regions.

Directors   (In addition to indicated officers)

Terence E. Adderley	Charles T. Fisher III	Earl L. Neal
James. K. Baker	Donald P. Jacobs	James J. O'Connor
John H. Bryan	William G. Lowrie	Thomas E. Reilly, Jr.
Siegfried Buschmann	Richard A. Manoogian	Adele Simmons
James S. Crown	William T. McCormick, Jr.	Richard L. Thomas
Maureen A. Fay	Andrew J. McKenna	

Officers   (Directors*)

* Verne G. Istock, Chm. & C.E.O.
* David J. Vitale, Pres.
* Thomas H. Jeffs II, V. Chm.
* Scott P. Marks, Jr., V. Chm.
 John W. Ballantine, Exec. V.P.
 David P. Bolger, Exec. V.P.
 William H. Elliott III, Exec. V.P.

Sherman I. Goldberg, Exec. V.P., Gen. Coun. & Cashier
Philip S. Jones, Exec. V.P.
W.G. Jurgensen, Exec. V.P.
Thomas J. McDowell, Exec. V.P.
Timothy P. Moen, Exec. V.P.
Susan S. Moody, Exec. V.P.
Robert A. Rosholt, Exec. V.P. & C.F.O.

Consolidated Statement of Condition   As of December 31, 1996 (000 omitted)

Assets		Liabilities & Stockholders' Equity	
Cash & due from banks	$ 9,811,237	Deposits	$32,894,653
Securities	3,335,304	Funds borrowed	11,629,921
Other short-term investments	4,253,751	Other liabilities	3,080,080
Net loans	23,029,556	Stockholders' equity	4,018,252
Other assets	11,193,058		
Total	$51,622,906	Total	$51,622,906

Years Ended Dec. 31	Total Deposits	Domestic Demand Deposits	Domestic Time Deposits	Dep. Overseas Branches & Consol. Sub.	Net Loans	Capital Accounts
1996	$32,894,653	$9,190,670	$12,842,126	$10,861,857	$23,029,556	$4,018,252
1995	29,609,746	6,217,164	8,957,079	14,435,503	16,109,349	3,048,065
1994	25,737,503	6,129,078	8,974,426	10,633,999	15,266,427	2,901,364
1993	23,124,555	7,494,138	8,376,395	7,254,022	12,968,455	2,687,686
1992	21,850,063	6,623,465	7,244,458	7,982,140	13,701,849	2,089,996

Consolidated Income Statement

Years Ended Dec. 31	Operating Income	Operating Expenses	Net Income
1996	$3,378,487	$2,815,672	$328,769
1995	3,209,042	2,948,877	156,190
1994	2,327,469	2,111,296	151,978
1993	2,512,928	2,057,837	299,336
1992	2,255,284	2,152,881	(357,466)

General Counsel:
 Sherman I. Goldberg, Exec. V.P.
Human Resources:
 Timothy P. Moen, Exec. V.P.

Auditors: Arthur Andersen LLP
Employees: 11,500
Member: FDIC; Federal Reserve System
Internet: www.fcnbd.com

First National Bank of Evergreen Park

3101 West 95th Street, Evergreen Park, Illinois 60642
Telephone: (708) 422-6700

The First National Bank of Evergreen Park is a wholly owned subsidiary of First Evergreen Corporation. The bank offers a full range of services including: transaction services, time accounts, special check services, depository and transfer services, investment securities, trust services, convenience services, international banking services, commercial loans, personal installment loans, and mortgage loans. Facilities are located in Evergreen Park, Oak Lawn, Chicago, and Orland Park. Chartered in December 1948.

Directors   (In addition to indicated officers)

Davis Boyd	Jerome J. Cismoski
Daniel Butler, Jr.	Ronald W. Ozinga
James R. Cismoski	Thomas Palmisano

Officers   (Directors*)

* Kenneth J. Ozinga, Chm. & Pres.	Barbara L. Heidegger, Sr. V.P. & Cashier
Richard H. Brown, Exec. V.P.	Russell J. Hollender, Sr. V.P.
* Stephen M. Hallenbeck, Exec. V.P.	Ronald J. Homa, Sr. V.P.
* Robert C. Wall, Exec. V.P.	* Martin F. Ozinga, Sr. V.P.
Roberta Bauer-Micetic, Sr. V.P.	Roscoe N. Rush, Sr. V.P.—Loan Div.
Terrence J. Healy, Sr. V.P.	

Statement of Condition   As of December 31, 1996 (000 omitted)

Assets		Liabilities & Stockholders' Equity	
Cash & due from banks	$ 55,654	Deposits	$1,696,632
Investment securities	1,127,833	Other liabilities	27,726
Net loans	615,653	*Stockholders' equity	185,579
Properties & equipment	31,729		
Other assets	79,068		
Total	$1,909,937	Total	$1,909,937

*716,000 shares common stock outstanding.

Years Ended Dec. 31	Thousands Total Deposits	Demand Deposits	Time Deposits	Net Loans	Capital Accounts
1996	$1,696,632	$161,028	$811,622	$615,653	$185,576
1995	1,662,445	152,986	742,808	526,703	173,229
1994	1,695,417	163,444	643,775	474,912	156,605
1993	1,718,370	146,510	471,530	412,577	146,611
1992	1,653,625	132,448	475,882	384,150	130,541

Consolidated Income Statement

Years Ended Dec. 31	Thousands Operating Income	Operating Expenses	Net Income
1996	$133,160	$104,829	$20,846
1995	131,440	104,369	20,408
1994	121,539	93,544	20,513
1993	126,706	96,299	22,156
1992	126,484	100,877	19,309

General Counsel:	Barry N. Voorn	Auditors:	Ernst & Young LLP
Human Resources:	John A. Camphouse, V.P.	Employees:	637
Mgt. Info. Svcs.:	Barbara L. Heidegger, Sr. V.P.	Member:	FDIC; Federal Reserve System

First of America Bank–Illinois, N.A.

2595 Waukegan Road, Bannockburn, Illinois 60015
Telephone: (630) 954-3100

First of America Bank–Illinois, N.A., is an affiliate bank of First of America Bank Corporation, which is headquartered in Kalamazoo, Michigan. The bank engages in commercial and retail banking, and provides trust and other financial services. First of America Bank–Illinois has 127 banking locations serving 60 distinct Illinois markets through regional banking centers located in Bloomington, Champaign, the Chicago metropolitan area, Decatur, Kankakee, Peoria, the Quad Cities, Rockford, and Springfield.

Directors   (In addition to indicated officers)

Bill Anest	Clifford L. Greenwalt	Carolyn B. Stone
John R. Brazil	Zelema Harris	William D. Sulaski
James P. Bruner	A. John Hass, Jr.	Charles F. Thomas
William F. Cellini	Jules M. Laser	Richard N. Ullman
Richard F. Chormann	John K. Lawson	Robert O. Viets
Joseph A. Feth	Charles K. Smith	Charles K. Wells

Officers   (Directors*)

* Robert K. Kinning, Chm. & C.E.O.
* Richard K. McCord, Pres. & C.O.O.
  James V. Antonacci, Sr. V.P.—Sales
  David Durak, Sr. V.P.—Trust
  Joseph A. Gregoire, Sr. V.P., Chf. Cred.
      Off., & Secy.
  Teddy I. Holden, Sr. V.P.—Audit

John R. Hunt, Sr. V.P., C.F.O., & Cashier
Linda J. Mitchell, Sr. V.P.—Human Res.
Ann Offermann, Sr. V.P.—Marketing
Eric S. Durham, V.P.
Tom Gihl, V.P.
Paul J. Stahr, V.P.
Larry Tucker, V.P.

Consolidated Statement of Condition   As of December 31, 1996 (000 omitted) Unaudited

Assets		Liabilities & Shareholders' Equity	
Cash & due from banks	$ 511,658	Deposits	$ 5,303,565
Securities	1,075,440	Fed. funds purch. & sec. sold	394,907
Federal funds sold	4,775	under agreement to repurch.	
Net loans	4,700,556	Borrowed funds	319,071
Other assets	316,974	Other liabilities	66,370
		Shareholders' equity	525,490
Total	$6,609,403	Total	$ 6,609,403

Years Ended Dec. 31	Total Assets	Total Deposits	Demand Deposits	Savings Time Deposits	Gross Loans	Capital Accounts
1996	$6,609,403	$5,303,565	$902,056	$4,401,509	$4,781,475	$525,490
1995	7,243,481	5,844,094	846,322	4,997,772	5,249,238	612,218

Consolidated Income Statement

Years Ended Dec. 31	Operating Income	Operating Expenses	Net Income
1996	$357,970	$258,467	$59,862
1995	322,654	228,426	56,962

General Counsel:	Howard & Howard	Employees:	1,930
Human Resources:	Dick Washburn	Member:	FDIC
Mgt. Info. Svcs.	Don Kenney	Internet:	www.First-of-America.com
Auditors:	KPMG Peat Marwick LLP		

Harris Trust and Savings Bank

111 West Monroe Street, P.O. Box 755, Chicago, Illinois 60690-0755
Telephone: (312) 461-2121

Harris Trust and Savings Bank, an Illinois state-chartered bank, is a wholly owned subsidiary of Harris Bankcorp, Inc. Harris Trust and Savings maintains its principal office, 58 branch offices, an international banking facility, and five automatic banking centers in the Chicago area. Additionally, Harris Trust and Savings has representative offices in Los Angeles, New York, and Tokyo; a foreign branch office in Nassau; and an Edge Act subsidiary, Harris Bank International Corporation, in New York. The bank provides a variety of banking and financial services to commercial and industrial companies, financial institutions, governmental units, not-for-profit organizations, and individuals throughout the U.S. and abroad. Services to customers include numerous types of demand and time deposit accounts; negotiable certificates of deposit; various types of loans including term, real estate, and those under lines of credit and revolving credit facilities; sales and purchases of foreign currencies; interest rate management products including swaps, forward rate agreements, and interest rate guarantees; cash management services, including lockbox and controlled disbursement processing; underwriting of municipal bonds; and financial consulting. Incorporated in Illinois in 1907.

Directors (In addition to indicated officers)

Pastora San Juan Cafferty	Wilbur H. Gantz	Charles H. Shaw
F. Anthony Comper	James J. Glasser	Richard E. Terry
Susan T. Congalton	Leo M. Henikoff	James O. Webb
Roxanne J. Decyk	Richard M. Jaffee	William J. Weisz

Officers (Directors*)

* Alan G. McNally, Chm. & C.E.O.	Edward J. Williams, Exec. V.P.
* Edward W. Lyman, Jr., V. Chm.	Michael E. Godwin, Sr. V.P.
Harry G. Ackstein, Exec. V.P.	Michael B. Lowe, Sr. V.P.
Jeffrey D. Butterfield, Exec. V.P.	Scott B. McCallum, Sr. V.P.
Charles H. Davis, Exec. V.P.	Richard J. Moreland, Sr. V.P.
Kenneth R. Keck, Exec. V.P.	Paul V. Reagan, Sr.V.P.
Louis F. Lanwermeyer, Exec. V.P.	Sohrab Zargham, Sr. V.P. & Chief Auditor
William E Thonn, Exec. V.P.	Pierre O. Greffe, C.F.O.
Charles R. Tonge, Exec. V.P.	

Consolidated Balance Sheet   As of December 31, 1996 (000 omitted)

Assets		Liabilities & Stockholders' Equity	
Cash & due from banks, incl. interest-bearing bal.	$ 1,812,800	Deposits	$ 9,726,205
Federal funds sold & sec. purch. under agreement to resell	316,275	Fed. funds borrowed & sec. sold under agreement to repurchase	1,992,067
Securities	2,759,331	Other borrowings	706,856
Trading account assets	110,355	Trading liabilities	74,165
Loans & lease financing, net of allowance	8,038,772	Other liabilities	514,807
Property & equipment	190,154	Stockholders' equity	1,192,567
Other assets	978,980		
Total	$14,206,667	Total	$14,206,667

*6,667,490 shares of common stock outstanding.

Years Ended Dec. 31	Total Deposits	Domestic Demand Deposits	Domestic Time Deposits	Foreign Office Deposits	Loans Net of Allowance	Capital Accounts
1996	$9,726,205	$3,135,907	$4,762,681	$1,827,617	$8,038,772	$1,192,567
1995	7,030,551	2,706,319	2,216,811	2,107,421	7,365,705	837,240
1994	7,015,566	2,659,945	1,869,203	2,486,418	6,280,547	729,731
1993	6,457,354	2,569,574	2,289,219	1,598,561	5,754,791	734,451
1992	6,070,590	2,534,619	2,009,542	1,526,429	5,245,690	695,134

Consolidated Income Statement

Years Ended Dec. 31	Operating Income	Expenses Including Income Taxes	Net Income
1996	$1,132,346	$1,029,266	$103,080
1995	1,094,454	985,168	109,286
1994	899,651	831,710	67,941
1993	819,250	739,793	79,457
1992	897,929	800,568	97,361

General Counsel:	Chapman & Cutler	Auditors:	KPMG Peat Marwick LLP; Coopers & Lybrand L.L.P.
Human Resources:	Michael B. Lowe, Sr. V.P.	Employees:	4,813
Mgt. Info. Svcs.:	Lloyd F. Darlington	Member:	FDIC; Federal Reserve System

Heritage Bank

12015 South Western Avenue, Blue Island, Illinois 60406
Telephone: (708) 385-2900

Heritage Bank is a wholly owned subsidiary of Heritage Financial Services, Inc. The bank operates 15 banking locations in the southwestern Chicago metropolitan market. As a commerical bank, Heritage Bank offers a complete range of finanical products and services to individuals, businesses, and municipal customers.

Directors   (In addition to indicated officers)

John J. Gallagher	John L. Sterling
Lael W. Mathis	Chester Stranczek
Jack Payan	Arthur G. Tichenor
Arthur E. Sieloff	Dominick J. Velo

Officers   (Directors*)

* Richard T. Wojcik, Chm. & C.E.O.	Susan G. Peterson, Exec. V.P.
* Frederick J. Sampias, Pres.	Albert A. Stroka, Exec. V.P. & Gen. Coun.
* Ronald P. Groebe, Sr. Exec. V.P. & Secy.	Michael J. Burke, Sr. V.P.
Ramesh L. Ajwani, Exec. V.P.	Carl D. Lindohken, Sr. V.P.
John E. Barry, Exec. V.P.	William N. Masterson, Sr. V.P.
Paul A. Eckroth, Exec. V.P.	Joseph J. Wallace, Sr. V.P.

Consolidated Balance Sheet   As of December 31, 1996 (000 omitted)

Assets		Liabilities & Stockholders' Equity	
Cash & due from banks	$ 43,780	Total deposits	$1,053,385
Federal funds sold and int.-brng. deps.	11	Fed. funds purchased &	56,383
Securities, held-to-maturity	115,639	securities sold for repur.	
Securities, available-for-sale	391,534	Other liabilities	8,587
Net loans	629,597	Stockholders' equity	103,095
Net property, plant & equipment	17,330		
Other assets	23,559		
Total	$1,221,450	Total	$1,221,450

Years Ended Dec. 31	Total Deposits	Noninterest-bearing Deposits	Net Loans	Total Capital
1996	$1,053,385	$185,786	$629,597	$103,095
1995	915,419	161,527	561,017	89,315
1994	823,835	143,623	516,095	82,024
1993	727,415	124,584	446,270	67,303
1992	670,793	116,823	425,765	56,242

Consolidated Income Statement

Years Ended Dec. 31	Interest Income	Interest Expense	Net Income
1996	$83,824	$45,669	$15,882
1995	73,785	33,217	14,049
1994	60,109	21,943	13,276
1993	55,640	21,009	11,994
1992	55,868	25,044	10,717

General Counsel:	Albert A. Stroka, Exec. V.P.	**Auditors:**	Arthur Andersen LLP
Mgt. Info. Svcs.:	Linda Duggan, Dir.	**Employees:**	482
Human Resources:	Karen Myers, Dir.	**Member:**	FDIC

LaSalle Bank

139 North Cass Avenue, Westmont, Illinois 60559
Telephone: (630) 964-1000

LaSalle Bank is a full-service commercial bank offering a full range of deposit products, mortgage loans, consumer loans, commercial loans, and alternative investment products. Through its 6 branch offices, the bank offers banking products and services to individuals and businesses. In 1995, LaSalle Bank of Lisle, LaSalle Bank Matteson, and LaSalle Bank Westmont merged to form LaSalle Bank, a wholly owned subsidiary of LaSalle National Corporation.

Directors   (In addition to indicated officers)

Scott K. Heitman

Officers   (Directors*)

* Leonard Ponte, Chm. & C.E.O.
* Richard Pearson, Pres.
* Nancy Foster, Exec. V.P. & Chf. Credit Off.
* Albert Harker, Exec. V.P.
* John Lynch, Exec. V.P.

Henry G. MacMorran, Exec. V.P.
* Michael T. McGrogan, Exec. V.P.
Steven Nowaczyk, First V.P.—Oper.
Thomas Ryan, First V.P.—Commer. Lending
A. James Dupree, V.P. & C.F.O.

Consolidated Balance Sheet   As of March 31, 1997 (000 omitted)

Assets		Liabilities & Stockholder's Equity	
Money market	$ 44,519	Deposits	$ 849,571
Securities	333,738	Purchased funds	40,749
Loans, net	533,732	Other liabilities	7,990
Other assets	46,559	Stockholder's equity	60,238
Total	$958,548	Total	$ 958,548

Years Ended Dec. 31	Thousands Total Deposits	Demand Deposits	Time Deposits	Net Loans	Capital Accounts
1996	$792,122	$121,711	$354,724	$542,323	$61,731
1995	639,241	130,475	349,749	434,419	53,547
1994	587,378	126,320	341,872	399,983	49,092

Consolidated Income Statement

Years Ended Dec. 31	Thousands Operating Income	Operating Expenses	Net Income
1996	$37,392	$24,724	$12,669
1995	34,611	24,787	9,824
1994	34,429	26,832	7,597

General Counsel:	Robert Quinn	Employees:	208
Human Resources:	John Scully	Member:	FDIC
Auditors:	Ernst & Young LLP		

LaSalle Bank FSB
135 South LaSalle Street, Chicago, Illinois 60603
Telephone: (312) 904-2000

LaSalle Bank FSB offers a full range of deposit products, mortgage loans, commercial real estate loans, construction loans, consumer loans, insurance products, and investment brokerage services. In November 1995, LaSalle Talman Bank and LaSalle Cragin Bank merged to form LaSalle Bank FSB, which operates 71 offices in the Chicago metropolitan area. Wholly owned subsidiaries include LaSalle Home Mortgage Corporation (mortgage banking), LaSalle Financial Services, Inc. (insurance agency and mutual fund sales), and Lease Plan, Illinois, Inc. LaSalle Bank FSB is a direct subsidiary of ABN AMRO North America. In June 1994, ABN AMRO North America, the parent of LaSalle National Corporation, acquired the former Cragin Federal Bank. The former Talman Home Federal Savings and Loan was acquired by ABN AMRO North America in February 1992.

Directors   (In addition to indicated officers)

Jeffrey L. Conner
Betty F. Elliot
David R. Papritz
Robert K. Quinn

Cordell Reed
Eugene A. Tracy
Joseph E. Valenti, Jr.

Officers   (Directors*)

* Scott K. Heitmann, Chm., Pres. & C.E.O.
  Jay T. Fitts, Exec. V.P.—Chf. Credit Off.
* Albert P. Harker, Jr., Exec. V.P.
* William E. Long, Exec. V.P. & Pres.—LHMC

* Henry G. MacMorran, Exec. V.P.
  Michael T. McGrogan, Exec. V.P.—
  Sr. Lending Off.
* Robert J. Taylor, Sr. V.P. & C.F.O.

Consolidated Balance Sheet   As of December 31, 1996 (000 omitted)

Assets		Liabilities & Stockholder's Equity	
Cash & securities	$ 3,417,472	Savings accounts	$ 7,728,803
Mortgage loans	6,690,820	Notes payable and other	2,051,696
Other loans	216,934	borrowings	
Properties & equipment	88,726	Other liabilities	230,139
Other assets	428,494	* Stockholder's equity	831,808
Total	$10,842,446	Total	$ 10,842,446

*101 shares common stock outstanding.

Years Ended Dec. 31	Thousands Total Assets	Mortgage Loans	Total Savings Accounts	Stockholder's Equity
1996	$10,842,446	$6,690,820	$7,728,803	$831,808
1995	10,651,884	6,537,463	7,267,394	979,446
1994[a]	10,159,833	5,906,570	7,299,867	997,674

[a]Includes 12 months of activity for LaSalle Talman Bank and seven months of activity for LaSalle Cragin Bank which was acquired June 1, 1994.

Consolidated Income Statement

Years Ended Dec. 31	Thousands Gross Income	Total Expenses	Provision for Taxes	Net Income
1996	$376,255	$326,784	$39,461	$10,010
1995	360,816	305,239	50,875	4,702
1994[a]	268,118	184,072	35,307	48,739

[a]Includes 12 months of activity for LaSalle Talman Bank and seven months of activity for LaSalle Cragin Bank which was acquired June 1, 1994.

Human Resources:	William Thornton	Employees:	2,077
Mgt. Info. Svcs.:	Michael Oberholtzer	Auditors:	Ernst & Young LLP
Depositors:	534,000	Member:	FDIC

LaSalle Banks Guide   311

LaSalle Bank N.A.
4747 West Irving Park Road, Chicago, Illinois 60641
Telephone: (773) 777-7700

LaSalle Bank N.A. provides complete consumer and commercial deposit and loan services. The bank, a subsidiary of LaSalle National Corporation, has 9 full-service branches in Chicago and the northwest suburbs, including the bank's main office in Chicago's Portage Park neighborhood. On April 28, 1997, Columbia National Bank of Chicago was merged into LaSalle Northwest National Bank. Upon consumation of the merger, the bank changed its name to LaSalle Bank N.A. Chartered under the National Bank Act in 1941; present name adopted in 1997.

Directors   (In addition to indicated officers)

Nancy DeSombre	William C. Mitchell
Fred W. Heitmann, Jr.	Herman Siegelaar
Michael R. Lutz	Joseph E. Valenti, Sr.

Officers   (Directors*)

* Norman Bobbins, Chm.	Jeffrey A. Jones, First V.P.	Russell G. Lutz, V.P.
* John J. Lynch, Jr., Pres. & C.E.O.	Steven Schultz, First V.P. & Cont.	John Matthews, V.P.
Donald V. Versen, Sr., V. Chm.	Mike Smith, First V.P.	Heather Morgenroth, V.P.
Nancy J. Foster, Exec. V.P. & C.C.O.	Monika Casey, V.P.	Robert E. Nowicki, V.P.
Lawrence G. Ryan, Exec.V.P.—Comm. Lending	Terry Collins, V.P.	Michael O'Rourke, V.P.
Richard Feller, Sr. V.P.	Tamina DeSargones, V.P.	Lucy A. Perrotti, V.P.
Deborah A. Grudzien, Sr. V.P.	Helmut Gottfert, V.P.	Elouise Russo, V.P.
Michael A. Lariviere, Sr. V.P.—Cons. Lending	Renee Hennessy, V.P.	Milos Sekulic, V.P.
Jerry Smulik, Sr. V.P.—Comm. Real Est.	Ida C. Hesotian, V.P.	Randall Slattery, V.P.
Lloyd S. Szkwarko, Sr. V.P. & C.F.O.	Thomas E. Kress, V.P.	Michael Stump, V.P.
Thomas Doherty, First V.P.	Julie Lebherz, V.P.	Linda Weber, V.P.
Jonathan Gilfillian, First V.P.		

Consolidated Balance Sheet[a]   As of December 31, 1996 (000 omitted)

Assets		Liabilities & Stockholders' Equity	
Current assets	$2,226,012	Current liabilities	$2,104,890
Net property, plant & equipment	13,707	Other liabilities	23,812
Other assets	39,615	* Stockholders' equity	150,632
Total	$2,279,334	Total	$2,279,334

[a]For LaSalle Northwest National Bank
*300,000 shares common stock outstanding.

Years Ended Dec. 31	Thousands Total Deposits	Demand Deposits	Time Deposits	Net Loans	Capital Accounts
1996	$1,797,801	$134,724	$1,663,077	$1,810,249	$150,632
1995	1,461,858	137,571	1,324,287	1,460,015	128,655
1994	1,207,447	133,103	1,074,344	1,187,792	106,468
1993	913,223	119,896	793,327	1,085,885	96,320
1992	933,958	105,287	828,671	897,257	86,570

Consolidated Income Statement[a]

Years Ended Dec. 31	Thousands Operating Income	Operating Expenses	Net Income
1996	$166,367	$141,199	$25,168
1995	137,185	116,728	20,457
1994	107,989	94,710	13,279
1993	102,960	88,410	14,550
1992	102,265	88,832	13,433

[a]For LaSalle Northwest National Bank.

Human Resources:	Russell G. Lutz, V.P.	Employees:	685
Mgt. Info. Svcs.:	Steven Schultz, First V.P.		
Auditors:	Ernst & Young LLP	Member:	FDIC; Federal Reserve System

LaSalle Bank NI

3201 North Ashland Avenue, Chicago, Illinois 60657
Telephone: (773) 525-2180

LaSalle Bank NI offers its customers a full range of commercial and personal banking services. In September 1995, LaSalle Bank Lake View and LaSalle Bank Northbrook merged to form LaSalle Bank NI. The bank is a wholly owned subsidiary of LaSalle National Corporation, which in turn is a wholly owned subsidiary of ABN AMRO Bank N.V.

Directors   (In addition to indicated officers)

Fred W. Heitmann, Jr.
Herman Siegelaar

James B. Wynsma

Officers   (Directors*)

* Norman Bobins, Chm.
* John R. Newman, Pres. & C.E.O.
* Thomas D. Roegner, Exec. V.P. & Chf. Cred. Off.
Jo Ann A. Clay, Sr. V.P.
Larry Silberman, Sr. V.P.
Gerrie Smith, Sr. V.P.
Laura Linger, First V.P. & Mgr.
Kurt Andrae, V.P.
Ken Born, V.P. & C.F.O.
Andrew Cameron, V.P.
Frank Dwojacki, V.P.
Christopher Ebert, V.P.
Carole Fiducci, V.P.
Timothy Finerty, V.P.
Tammy Gierszewicz, V.P.
Glenn Hametta, V.P.
Ann Josephson, V.P.

William M. Lloyd, V.P.
Sharon Maddex, V.P.
Mark Magnoni, V.P.
John Mangan, V.P.
Mel Marini, V.P.
Sarah McNally, V.P.
Ken Michalesko, V.P.
Debra Nadell, V.P. & Compliance Off.
Anne Nostrand, V.P.
Martin F. Quinn, V.P. & C.R.A. Off.
William T. Roberts, V.P.
John Schellinger, V.P.
Michael Smith, V.P.
Richard Snedden, V.P.
Toni Stanek, V.P.
Martin Struwing, V.P.
Beth Yura, V.P.

Consolidated Balance Sheet   As of December 31, 1996 (000 omitted)

Assets		Liabilities & Stockholders' Equity	
Current assets	$ 1,933,942	Deposits	$1,493,692
Net property, plant & equipment	21,443	Other liabilities	407,774
Other assets	62,376	Stockholders' equity	116,295
Total	$ 2,017,761	Total	$2,017,761

*425,000 shares common stock outstanding.

Years Ended Dec. 31	Thousands Total Deposits	Demand Deposits	Time Deposits	Net Loans	Capital Accounts
1996	$1,493,692	$132,902	$1,360,790	$1,162,482	$116,295
1995	1,188,219	119,413	1,068,806	818,680	101,300
1994	729,408	74,734	654,674	536,912	67,140
1993	633,863	66,229	567,634	570,407	58,285
1992	667,958	62,962	604,996	463,783	54,453

Consolidated Income Statement (Information not publicly available)

Human Resources:	Rhonda Abramson, Asst. V.P.	Employees:	327
Auditors:	Ernst & Young LLP	Member:	FDIC

LaSalle Banks Guide

LaSalle National Bank

135 South LaSalle Street, Chicago, Illinois 60603
Telephone: (312) 904-2000

LaSalle National Bank is a full-service commercial bank and wholly owned subsidiary of LaSalle National Corporation, which is a subsidiary of ABN AMRO Bank N.V. It serves businesses, institutions, and individuals throughout Chicago and the Midwest. Subsidiaries are LaSalle Business Credit, Inc. and LaSalle National Leasing Corp. LaSalle National Bank was chartered under the National Bank Act as The National Builders Bank of Chicago in 1927; present title adopted in 1940.

Directors   (In addition to indicated officers)

Eugene B. Connolly, Jr.	John Rau	Herman Siegelaar
Craig J. Duchossois	Cordell Reed	Richard A. Stein
Betty F. Elliott	Jerry M. Reinsdorf	Eugene A. Tracy
Donald H. Haider	Theodore H. Roberts	Arthur R. Velasquez
Harvey N. Medvin		

Officers   (Directors*)

* Robert K. Wilmouth, Chm.
* Norman Bobins, Pres. & C.E.O.
* Thomas C. Heagy, V. Chm.
* James B. Wynsma, V.Chm.
  M. Hill Hammock, C.O.O. & Chf. Credit Off.
  John H. Collins, Exec. V.P.—Computer & Admin. Svcs. Grp.
  Mark A. Hoppe, Exec. V.P.—Spec. Bank. Grp.
  Walter M. Macur, Exec. V.P.—Asset Based Lending & Chm.—LaSalle Bus. Credit, Inc.
  John R. Newman, Exec. V.P. & Pres.—LaSalle Bank NI
  Marty Penstien, Exec. V.P.—Invest. Port. & Int. Rt. Rsk.

Larry D. Richman, Exec. V.P.—Commer. Banking
David J. Rudis, Exec. V.P.—Commer. Banking
Mark A. Nystuen, Grp. Sr. V.P. & C.A.O.
Breck F. Hanson, Grp. Sr. V.P.—Commer. Real Est. Admin.
Michael D. Sharkey, Grp. Sr. V.P. & Pres.—LaSalle Bus. Credit, Inc.
Erick J. Peterson, Grp. Sr. V.P.—Service Prod. Admin. (Cash Mgt.)
Michael A. Piccato, Grp. Sr. V.P.—Funds Mgt.
John R. Boyaris, Sr. V.P. & C.F.O.
John E. Scully, Sr. V.P.—Hum. Res.

Consolidated Balance Sheet   As of December 31, 1996 (000 omitted)

Assets		Liabilities & Equity	
Cash & due from banks	$ 730,968	Deposits	$ 8,975,557
Fed. funds sold & sec. purch. under agreement to sell	124,512	Purchased funds and notes	3,348,562
		Other liabilities	219,238
Investment securities	3,831,362	* Equity	843,589
Loans, net	8,276,161		
Other assets	423,943		
Total	$13,386,946	Total	$13,386,946

*184,171 shares common stock outstanding.

Years Ended Dec. 31	Total Deposits	Domestic Demand Deposits	Domestic Time Deposits	Foreign Deposits	Loans, Net U/D	Capital Accounts
1996	$8,975,557	$1,710,450	$5,265,034	$2,000,073	$8,440,058	$843,589
1995	7,872,403	1,389,310	4,533,685	1,949,408	6,574,870	677,934
1994	7,065,919	1,328,045	3,895,501	1,842,373	5,490,992	602,548
1993	6,006,381	1,401,455	3,555,417	1,049,509	4,580,395	484,939
1992	4,916,231	1,131,322	3,256,227	528,682	3,747,967	411,462

Consolidated Income Statement

Years Ended Dec. 31	Gross Income	Gross Expenses	Net Income
1996	$1,013,708	$887,103	$126,605
1995	898,307	787,237	111,070
1994	719,968	630,323	89,645
1993	547,610	474,134	73,476
1992	527,871	461,473	66,398

Human Resources:	John E. Scully, Sr. V.P.	Employees:	980
Auditors:	Ernst & Young LLP	Member:	FDIC; Federal Reserve System

Liberty Federal Bank

One Grant Square, Hinsdale, Illinois 60521
Telephone: (630) 323-1776

Liberty Federal Bank (formerly Hinsdale Federal Bank for Savings) is a wholly owned subsidiary of Alliance Bancorp. The bank operates 15 retail banking offices located in Bensenville, Chicago, Clarendon Hills, Elmhurst, Forest Park, Glenview, Hinsdale, Lisle, Morton Grove, Norridge, Oak Park, West Chicago, and Westmont, Illinois. Liberty is principally engaged in the business of attracting retail deposits from the general public and investing those funds in mortgage loans and mortgage-backed securities, secured primarily by one- to four-family residential real estate loans, consumer loans, and investment securities. The bank also owns Preferred Mortgage Associates, LTD, one of the largest mortgage brokers in metropolitan Chicago. In February 1997, the bank (then operating as Hinsdale Federal Bank for Savings) completed a merger with Liberty Federal Savings Bank, with Hinsdale as the surviving bank. Upon consumation of the merger, the bank changed its name to Liberty Federal Bank.

Directors   (In addition to indicated officers)

Edward J. Burns	David D. Mill	Russel F. Stephens, Jr.
Whit G. Hughes	Edward J. Nusrala	Donald E. Sveen
Howard R. Jones	William C. O'Donnell	Vernon B. Thomas, Jr.
H. Verne Loeppert	William R. Rybak	

Officers   (Directors*)

* Fredric G. Novy, Chm.	Edward J. Munin, Sr. V.P.
* Kenne P. Bristol, Pres. & C.E.O.	Robert A. Hollis, V.P.
Richard A. Hojnicki, Exec. V.P., C.F.O. & Secy.	Gerry Murphy, V.P.
Donald A. Berg, Sr. V.P.	Tony Rosado, V.P.
Ilene M. Bock, Sr. V.P. & Cont.	Susan T. Schliep, V.P.
Richard A. Burns, Sr. V.P.	Charles Walles, V.P.
Terry W. Ekberg, Sr. V.P.	

Consolidated Balance Sheet   As of March 31, 1996 (000 omitted)

Assets		Liabilities & Stockholders' Equity	
Cash & due from banks	$ 25,525	Total deposits	$ 1,006,570
Investment securities	24,220	Repurchase agreements	52,850
Mortgage-backed securities	127,568	Other borrowings	114,340
Total loans, net	1,093,824	Other liabilities	26,186
Premises & fixed assets	6,823	Stockholders' equity	110,164
Other assets	32,150		
Total	$1,310,110	Total	$1,310,110

Quarter Ended Mar. 31	Thousands Total Deposits	Demand Deposits	Time Deposits	Net Loans	Capital Accounts
1997	$1,006,570	$28,013	$978,557	$1,093,824	$110,164

Consolidated Income Statement[a]

Year Ended Dec. 31	Thousands Operating Income	Operating Expenses	Net Income

[a]Combined pro forma financial data for banks prior to the merger are unavailable for 1996 and prior years.

General Counsel:	Rock, Fusco, Reynolds & Garvy	Auditors:	KPMG Peat Marwick LLP
Human Resources:	Susan Schliep, V.P.	Employees:	460
Mgt. Info. Svcs.:	Tony Rosado, V.P.	Internet:	www.libertyfb.com

Marquette National Bank

6316 S. Western Avenue, Chicago, Illinois 60636
Telephone: (773) 476-5100

Marquette National Bank is a wholly owned subsidiary of Marquette National Corporation. The bank has 15 facilities, which offer a full range of financial services to individuals and small businesses.

Directors (In addition to indicated officers)

Theodore J. Cachey	Thomas D. O'Reilly	John R. Thompson
James F. Capraro	Gerait Ruisard	Harold J. Tolliver, Sr.
Anthony C. Duvall	William G. Sullivan	Mark Zelisko

Officers (Directors*)

* Paul M. McCarthy, Chm.
* George S. Moncada, Pres.
* Jerome R. Martin, Exec. V.P.
* David M. Ransford, Exec. V.P.
  Robert J. Wosneski, Sr. V.P.—Leasing
  Michael J. Banky, V.P.

Donald Bonistalli, V.P.—Trust
Patrick F. Donovan, V.P. & Pers. Off..
Daniel J. Keating, V.P
Frank Mainczyk, V.P.
Daniel F. McKeown, V.P. & Cont.

Consolidated Balance Sheet   As of December 31, 1996 (000 omitted)

Assets		Liabilities & Stockholders' Equity	
Total cash & cash equivalents	$ 25,657	Total deposits	$ 911,684
Investment securities	435,243	Repurchase agreement—securities	16,936
Fed. funds sold	500	Borrowed money	50,900
Total loans, net	590,750	Other liabilities	5,492
Premises & fixed assets	14,645	Stockholders' equity	105,292
Other assets	23,509		
Total	$1,090,304	Total	$1,090,304

Years Ended Dec. 31	Total Deposits	Demand Deposits	Time & Savings Deposits	Net Loans	Stockholders' Equity
1996	$911,684	$102,916	$808,768	$590,750	$105,292
1995	734,900	65,521	669,379	305,757	83,802
1994	647,350	63,584	583,766	246,501	69,443
1993	637,029	56,110	580,919	215,191	77,667
1992	649,124	55,499	593,625	164,416	62,411

Consolidated Income Statement

Years Ended Dec. 31	Gross Income	Gross Expense	Net Income
1996	$82,873	$74,024	$8,849
1995	61,669	52,686	8,983
1994	52,359	42,370	9,629
1993	55,111	42,636	12,475
1992	57,895	47,000	10,895

General Counsel:
  McCarthy, Duffy, Neidhart & Snakard
Human Resources: Patrick F. Donovan, V.P.
Mgt. Info. Svcs.:   Jerome R. Martin, Exec. V.P.

Auditors: Bansley and Kiener
Depositors: 76,745
Employees: 385
Member: FDIC

Mid America Federal Savings Bank

55th Street and Holmes Avenue, Clarendon Hills, Illinois 60514-1596
Telephone: (630) 325-7300

Mid America Federal Savings Bank operates 21 branches located in Berwyn, Chicago, Cicero, Norridge, Riverside, LaGrange Park, Western Springs, Clarendon Hills, Downers Grove, Naperville, St. Charles, and Wheaton. Mid America Federal provides a full range of savings and financial services, including passbook, certificate, NOW and IRA/KEOGH accounts; mortgage, construction, home improvement, auto, educational, equity line of credit and consumer loans. Investment advice and brokerage services are offered through INVEST centers located in the Cicero, Clarendon Hills, Naperville, St. Charles, LaGrange, Western Springs, Riverside, and Wheaton offices. In addition, the savings bank operates two wholly owned subsidiaries: Mid America Development Services, Inc., which is involved in land acquisition and development; and Mid America Insurance Agency, Inc., which offers a variety of personal and business insurance products. Mid America is a wholly owned subsidiary of MAF Bancorp Inc.

Directors   (In addition to indicated officers)

Robert J. Bowles, M.D.
Nicholas J. DiLorenzo, Sr.
Terry A. Ekl
Joe F. Hanauer

Henry Smogolski
F. William Trescott
Lois B. Vasto
Andrew J. Zych

Officers   (Directors*)

* Allen H. Koranda, Chm. & C.E.O.
* Kenneth Koranda, Pres.
  Jerry A. Weberling, Exec. V.P. & C.F.O.
  Gerard J. Buccino, Sr. V.P. & Cont.
  William Haider, Sr. V.P.
  Michael J. Janssen, Sr. V.P.
  David W. Kohlsaat, Sr. V.P.

Tom Miers, Sr. V.P.
Kenneth B. Rusdal, Sr. V.P.
Sharon Wheeler, Sr. V.P.
Gail Brzostek, First V.P.
Alan Schatz, First V.P.
Diane Stutte, First V.P.
Carolyn Pihera, V.P. & Secy.

Consolidated Balance Sheet   As of June 30, 1996 (000 omitted)

Assets		Liabilities & Stockholder's Equity	
Cash & securities	$ 230,135	Savings accounts	$2,287,207
FHLB stock	30,729	Deposits for payment of taxes	17,056
Loans receivable, net	2,292,885	& insurance	
Mortgaged-backed securities	418,102	FHLB advances	420,500
Properties & equipment	31,245	Other borrowed funds	82,196
Other assets	98,918	Other liabilities	31,710
		Stockholder's equity	263,345
Total	$3,102,014	Total	$3,102,014

Years Ended June 30	Thousands Total Assets	Loans Receivable	Savings Accts.	Stockholder's Equity
1996	$3,102,014	$2,292,885	$2,287,207	$ 263,345
1995	1,770,946	1,574,843	1,326,159	101,539
1994	1,573,536	1,358,894	1,299,374	95,736
1993	1,539,994	1,325,852	1,297,807	92,885
1992	1,513,319	1,267,394	1,274,089	84,800

Consolidated Income Statement

Years Ended June 30	Thousands Gross Income	Interest Expense	Operating Expenses	Income To Stockholder's Equity
1996	$155,567	$90,759	$37,329	$17,244
1995	129,284	71,722	32,136	15,370
1994	122,702	67,538	30,406	14,699
1993	126,843	72,155	27,484	15,647
1992	138,373	87,264	29,707	9,807

General Counsel:	Rock, Fusco, Reynolds & Garvey	Auditors:	KPMG Peat Marwick LLP
Corporate Counsel:	Muldoon, Murphy & Faucette	Depositors:	260,000
Human Resources:	David W. Kohlsaat, Sr. V.P.	Employees:	820
Mgt. Info. Svcs.:	Kenneth B. Rusdal, Sr. V.P.	Member:	FDIC; FHLB

The Mid-City National Bank of Chicago

801 West Madison Street, Chicago, Illinois 60607

Telephone: (312) 421-7600

The Mid-City National Bank of Chicago is a wholly owned subsidiary of MidCity Financial Corporation. The bank has 10 facilities, which offer a full range of financial services to individuals and small businesses.

Directors (In addition to indicated officers)

Stanley R. Banas	Alan J. Dixon	Marshall S. Leaf
Samuel M. Budwig, Jr.	Thomas Harvey	Eugene Sawyer
Charles F. Clarke, Jr.	Patrick Henry	

Officers (Directors*)

* E.M. Bakwin, Chm.	William A. Thuma, Sr. V.P. & Trust Off.
* Kenneth A. Skopec, V. Chm. & C.E.O.	Craig M. Woods, Sr. V.P.
* Randall J. Yenerich, Pres.	Mary Ellen Braun, V.P.
* Ronald D. Santo, Exec. V.P.	B. Patrick Crowley, V.P.
John M. Blackburn, Sr. V.P.	Walter J. Koehler, Jr., V.P.
S. Frank Formica, Sr. V.P.	Richard M. Pierce, V.P.
Brian J. Griffin, Sr. V.P.	Michael R. Soehlke, V.P.
Richard M. Spielmann, Sr. V.P.	Mary Thomas, V.P.
Lawrence L. Steinert, Sr. V.P.	

Consolidated Balance Sheet   As of December 31, 1996 (000 omitted)

Assets		Liabilities & Stockholders' Equity	
Cash & due from banks	$ 35,203	Total deposits	$679,024
Investment securities	384,914	Short-term borrowed funds	13,011
Total loans, net	313,032	Other liabilities	5,513
Premises & fixed assets	13,901	*Stockholders' equity	59,242
Other assets	9,740		
Total	$756,790	Total	$756,790

* 52,000 shares common stock outstanding

Years Ended Dec. 31	Total Deposits	Demand Deposits	Time Deposits	Net Loans	Capital Accounts
1996	$679,024	$136,975	$542,049	$313,032	$59,242
1995	674,477	133,419	541,058	306,008	58,518
1994	661,390	144,741	516,649	289,514	57,030
1993	653,994	116,266	537,728	248,234	55,484
1992	653,113	99,613	553,500	246,129	53,730

Consolidated Income Statement

Years Ended Dec. 31	Gross Income	Gross Expenses[a]	Net Income
1996	$53,225	$45,780	$7,445
1995	53,288	45,569	7,719
1994	48,035	39,989	8,046
1993	48,065	40,811	7,254
1992	53,096	46,543	6,554

[a]Includes provision for income taxes.

General Counsel:	Winston & Strawn	Auditors:	KPMG Peat Marwick LLP
Human Resources:	Maryann Penczak, V.P.	Employees:	248
Mgt. Info. Svcs.:	John M. Blackburn, Sr. V.P.	Member:	FDIC

The Northern Trust Company

50 South LaSalle Street, Chicago, Illinois 60675
Telephone: (312) 630-6000

The Northern Trust Company is a wholly owned subsidiary of Northern Trust Corporation. The bank offers commercial, correspondent, cash management, corporate financial, trust, loan, personal banking and international banking services. The Northern Trust International Banking Corporation; The Northern Trust Company, Canada; Northern Global Financial Services Ltd., Hong Kong; Northern Trust Trade Services Limited, Hong Kong; Northern Trust Fund Managers (Ireland) Limited; and NorLease, Inc., are wholly owned subsidiaries. The Northern Trust Company has branches in London, Singapore, and the Cayman Islands; and a five percent-interest in Banque Rivaud, Paris. The Northern Trust Company has 16 offices in the Chicagoland area. Incorporated in Illinois in 1889.

Directors   (In addition to indicated officers)

Duane L. Burnham	Robert A. Helman	Edward J. Mooney
Dolores E. Cross	Arthur L. Kelly	Harold B. Smith
Susan Crown	Frederick A. Krehbiel	William D. Smithburg
Robert S. Hamada	William G. Mitchell	Bide L. Thomas

Officers   (Directors*)

* William A. Osborn, Chm. & C.E.O.
* Barry G. Hastings, Pres. & C.O.O.
  Perry R. Pero, Sr. Exec.V.P. & C.F.O.
  James J. Mitchell, Exec. V.P.
  Sheila A. Penrose, Exec. V.P.
  Peter L. Rossiter, Exec. V.P., Gen. Coun. & Secy.
  James M Snyder, Exec. V.P.
  Mark Stevens, Exec. V.P.

William S. Trukenbrod, Exec. V.P.
William R. Dodds, Sr. V.P.
David L. Eddy, Sr. V.P. & Treas.
Laurie K. McMahon, Sr. V.P.
William H. Miller, Sr. V.P. & C.C.O.
Daniel S. O'Keefe, Sr. V.P.
Dan E. Phelps, Sr. V.P. & Gen. Auditor
Harry W. Short, Sr. V.P. & Controller

Consolidated Balance Sheet   As of December 31, 1996 (000 omitted)

Assets		Liabilities & Stockholders' Equity	
Cash & due from banks	$ 1,090,400	Deposits	$ 11,143,300
Securities	4,400,800	Funds borrowed	4,671,900
Money market assets	3,532,600	Senior notes	305,000
Net loans & lease financing	7,865,300	Notes payable	333,900
Properties & equipment	211,300	Other liabilities	569,800
Other assets	1,026,500	Stockholders' equity	1,103,000
Total	$18,126,900	Total	$ 18,126,900

Years Ended Dec. 31	Total Deposits	Domestic Demand Deposits	Domestic Time Deposits	Foreign Office Deposits	Loans & Leases	Capital Accounts
1996	$11,143,300	$3,010,500	$4,203,100	$3,929,700	$7,986,200	$1,103,000
1995	8,841,300	2,320,500	2,792,700	3,728,100	6,660,500	865,000
1994	8,848,300	2,183,800	2,582,700	4,081,800	6,030,500	790,700
1993	7,769,400	2,039,000	2,555,400	3,175,000	5,408,300	723,800
1992	7,195,800	2,281,800	3,019,100	1,894,900	5,061,400	645,300

Consolidated Income Statement

Years Ended Dec. 31	Operating Income	Operating Expenses	Net Income
1996	$1,489,500	$1,207,000	$192,000
1995	1,307,000	1,091,400	147,900
1994	1,111,400	924,800	130,100
1993	932,200	764,700	121,100
1992	920,800	766,900	111,500

General Counsel:	Peter L. Rossiter, Exec. V.P.	Auditors:	Arthur Andersen LLP
Trust Counsel:	J. Timothy Ritchie	Employees:	5,053
Human Resources:	William L. Setterstrom, Sr. V.P.	Member:	FDIC; Federal Reserve System
Chf. Tech. Off.:	Timothy J. Theriault		

Oak Brook Bank

1400 Sixteenth Street, Oak Brook, Illinois 60521

Telephone: (630) 571-1050

Oak Brook Bank, a wholly owned subsidiary of First Oak Brook Bancshares, Inc., is engaged in the general retail and commercial banking business. The services offered include demand, savings, and time deposits, corporate cash management services, commercial lending products such as commercial loans, mortgages and letters of credit, and personal lending products such as residential mortgages, home equity lines, auto loans, and credit card products. In addition, related products and services are offered, including discount brokerage, mutual funds and annuity sales, and foreign currency and precious metals sales. Oak Brook Bank has a full-service trust and land trust department. The bank has seven locations in DuPage County and two locations in Cook County.

Directors (In addition to indicated officers)

Anthony De Santis	Andrew T. Heytow	Geoffrey R. Stone
Miriam Lutwak Fitzgerald	Eugene P. Heytow	Bruce Wechsler
Charles J. Gries	Barry S. Kerstein	Alton M. Withers
Thomas J. Hartigan	Michael Segal	

Officers (Directors*)

* Richard M. Rieser, Jr., Chm. & C.E.O.
* Frank M. Paris, V. Chm.
* George C. Clam, Pres.
  Rosemarie Bouman, Sr. Exec. V.P. & C.F.O.
  William E. Navolio, Sr. Exec. V.P. & Gen. Coun.
  Katharine E. Blumenthal, Exec. V.P. & Trust Off.
  Jeffrey W. Brown, Exec. V.P.
  Mary C. Carnevale, Exec. V.P. & Chf. Hum. Res. Off.
  Melvin H. Gilfillan, Exec. V.P.
  Susanne C. Griffith, Exec. V.P. & Auditor

Glenn R. Krietsch, Exec. V.P.
James D. Leckinger, Exec. V.P., Treas. & Chf. Trust Off.
Dennis E. O'Hara, Exec. V.P.
Ed Berkheimer, Sr. V.P.
Patrick L. Doland, Sr. V.P.
Brian C. England, Sr. V.P.
Lola Donofrio, First V.P. & Controller
* Robert M. Wrobel, Asst. to the Chm.

Consolidated Balance Sheet As of December 31, 1996 (000 omitted)

Assets		Liabilities & Stockholders' Equity	
Cash & due from banks	$ 61,255	Deposits	$ 648,115
Securities	264,208	Funds borrowed	62,260
Net loans	416,055	Other liabilities	4,658
Properties & equipment	17,290	Stockholders' equity	51,740
Other assets	7,965		
Total	$766,773	Total	$ 766,773

Years Ended Dec. 31	Thousands Total Deposits	Demand Deposits	Time Deposits	Net Loans	Capital Accounts
1996	$648,115	$147,298	$500,817	$416,055	$51,740
1995	555,253	128,393	426,860	358,796	46,405
1994	513,729	109,271	154,430	305,822	38,034
1993	508,248	113,820	129,237	274,946	41,423
1992	436,677	94,190	111,963	262,648	32,457

Consolidated Income Statement

Years Ended Dec. 31	Thousands Operating Income	Operating Expenses	Net Income
1996	$56,880	$49,358	$7,522
1995	52,348	45,104	7,244
1994	45,081	38,280	6,801
1993	41,320	35,337	5,983
1992	39,128	34,334	4,794

General Counsel:	William E. Navolio, Sr. Exec. V.P.	Employees:	272
Human Resources:	Mary C. Carnevale, Exec. V.P.	Member:	FDIC
Mgt. Info. Svcs.:	Ed Berkheimer, Sr. V.P.	Internet:	www.obb.com
Auditors:	Ernst & Young LLP		

St. Paul Federal Bank For Savings

6700 West North Avenue, Chicago, Illinois 60707

Telephone: (773) 622-5000

St. Paul Federal Bank For Savings, a wholly owned subsidiary of St. Paul Bancorp, Inc., is primarily engaged in attracting checking, savings, and certificates of deposit accounts from the general public and investing those funds in a variety of mortgage and consumer loan products and high quality investment securities. In addition, St. Paul offers its customers a variety of allied services. Fifty-two branch offices are located in Addison, Arlington Heights, Aurora, Berkeley, Berwyn, Blue Island, Bridgeview, Buffalo Grove, Carol Stream, Chicago, Cicero, Crestwood, Downers Grove, Elgin, Elmhurst, Elmwood Park, Evanston, Evergreen Park, Franklin Park, Glendale Heights, Hanover Park, Harwood Heights, Lombard, McHenry, Melrose Park, Morton Grove, Mount Prospect, Niles, Oak Lawn, Oak Park, Orland Park, Rolling Meadows, Round Lake Beach, Skokie, Villa Park, Waukegan, Westchester, Wood Dale, and Woodridge, Illinois. SPF Insurance Agency, Inc., a wholly owned general insurance agency, provides a wide range of insurance services. Investment Network, Inc., a discount brokerage firm, offers execution and clearance services for stocks, bonds, and mutual funds. St. Paul Financial Development Corp. and Annuity Network, Inc., other wholly owned subsidiaries of St. Paul Bancorp, Inc., engage in single-family real estate development in the Chicago metropolitan area and the sale of annuity products, respectively.

Directors   (In addition to indicated officers)

William A. Anderson	Alan J. Fredian	Kenneth J. James	John J. Viera
John W. Croghan	Paul C. Gearen	Jean C. Murray, O.P.	

Officers   (Directors*)

* Joseph C. Scully, Chm. & C.E.O.
* Patrick J. Agnew, Pres. & C.O.O.
  James R. Lutsch, Sr. V.P.—Info. Services
  Robert N. Parke, Sr. V.P.—Fin. & C.F.O.
  Robert N. Pfeiffer, Sr. V.P.—Hum. Res.

Thomas J. Rinella, Sr. V.P.—Community Lend.
Donald G. Ross, Sr. V.P.—Retail Banking
Clifford M. Sladnick, Sr. V.P.—Corp. Secy. &
  Gen. Coun.

Consolidated Balance Sheet   As of December 31, 1996 (000 omitted)

Assets		Liabilities & Stockholders' Equity	
Cash & cash equivalents	$ 175,754	Deposits	$ 3,341,597
Investments	48,904	FHLB advances	456,399
Mortgage-backed securities	1,162,982	Other borrowed funds	71,032
Loans receivable (net of reserves)	2,790,867	Advanced payments for taxes &	21,562
Properties & equipment	47,160	insurance	
FHLB stock	35,211	Other liabilities	48,066
Other assets	62,872	* Stockholders' equity	385,094
Total	$4,323,750	Total	$ 4,323,750

*1,000 shares common stock outstanding.

Years Ended Dec. 31[a]	Total Assets	Mortgage Loans & Mortgage-backed Securities	Total Deposits	Stockholders' Equity
	Thousands			
1996	$4,323,750	$3,953,848	$3,341,597	$385,094
1995	4,069,311	3,657,654	3,238,915	365,891
1994	4,092,136	3,689,282	3,237,632	347,470
1993	3,671,882	3,032,758	3,256,319	351,092
1992	3,491,370	2,900,450	2,985,485	280,212

[a]Restated.

Consolidated Income Statement

Years Ended Dec. 31[a]	Gross Income	Interest Expenses	Operating Expenses[b]	Net Income
	Thousands			
1996	$326,609	$168,648	$116,078[c]	$26,573
1995	305,479	158,933	87,355	35,820
1994	276,345	131,997	84,361	34,076
1993	285,386	130,385	80,680	41,798
1992	303,915	165,900	69,956	36,561

[a]Certain financial data restated.

[b]Excludes federal and state income taxes.

[c]Includes $21,000,000 SAIF recapitalization.

General Counsel:	Clifford M. Sladnick, Sr. V.P.	**Auditors:**	Ernst & Young LLP
Human Resources:	Robert N. Pfeiffer, Sr. V.P.	**Employees:**	1,051
Mgt. Info. Svcs.:	James R. Lutsch, Sr. V.P.	**Member:**	FDIC

Standard Federal Bank for savings

4192 South Archer Avenue, Chicago, Illinois 60632-1890
Telephone: (773) 847-1140

Standard Federal Bank for savings has a total of 14 offices serving Chicago's southwest side, Downers Grove, Evergreen Park, Hickory Hills, Lombard, Naperville, Oak Lawn, Orland Park, Palos Heights, and Willowbrook. A major subsidiary is SFB Insurance Agency, Inc. Standard Federal was founded on February 22, 1909, by Justin Mackiewich, Sr., and a small group of fellow Lithuanian immigrants. The organization was known as the D.K.L. Gedimino Building & Loan until 1934 when a federal charter was received and the name Standard Federal Savings and Loan Association was chosen; present name adopted in May 1990. In January 1994, the bank formed a holding company in preparation for its conversion to a federally chartered stock savings bank, which occurred in July 1994.

Directors   (In addition to indicated officers)

Stasys J. Baras	Tomas A. Kisielius, M.D.	Albert M. Petkus
Fred V. Gwyer, M.D.	George W. Lane	Sharon A. Reese

Officers   (Directors*)

* David H. Mackiewich, Chm. & Pres.
* Thomas M. Ryan, Exec. V.P., C.O.O., & C.F.O.
  Kurtis D. Mackiewich, Sr. V.P.
  Ruta M. Staniulis, Sr. V.P.
  John Ahearn, V.P.
  Patricia Barrera, V.P.
  Michael F. Barrett, V.P.
  James T. Chippas, V.P.
  Mark Collins, V.P.
  George Cvack, V.P.

Luann Hennessy, V.P.
James Kopacz, V.P.
Donald Kowalski, V.P.
Michael Kowalski, V.P.
Jean Krusinski, V.P.
Leonard Metheny, V.P. & Corp. Sec'y.
Jack Oskvarek, V.P.
David Schaefer, V.P.
Randall R. Schwartz, V.P. & Gen. Counsel

Consolidated Balance Sheet   As of December 31, 1996 (000 omitted)

Assets		Liabilities & Stockholders' Equity	
Cash	$ 43,132	Total deposits	$ 1,719,728
Investment securities	108,258	Advances from FHLB	385,000
Mortgage-backed certs.	641,237	Advance payments by borrowers	11,470
Loans	1,485,454	for taxes & insur.	
Other assets	71,925	Other liabilities	32,182
		Stockholders' Equity	201,626
Total	$2,350,006	Total	$ 2,350,006

Years Ended Dec. 31	Thousands Total Assets	Mortgage Loans	Total Deposits	General Reserves
1996	$2,350,006	$1,485,454	$1,719,728	$201,626
1995	2,013,783	1,010,162	1,539,310	202,239
1994	1,660,037	593,047	1,393,274	185,261
1993	1,508,840	523,637	1,371,214	96,069
1992	1,506,132	492,220	1,379,605	92,201

Consolidated Income Statement

Years Ended Dec. 31	Thousands Interest Income	Interest Expense	Other Income	Other Expense	Net Income
1996	$154,292	$94,919	$6,666	$50,558	$ 9,114
1995	127,444	72,866	4,768	46,146	13,200
1994	99,044	51,879	4,593	41,677	10,081
1993	98,399	52,839	5,557	47,249	3,868
1992	109,098	65,479	5,722	39,334	10,007

Human Resources:	Patricia Barrera, V.P.	Depositors:	113,741
Mgt. Info. Svcs.:	Mark Collins, V.P.	Employees:	600
Auditors:	Ernst & Young LLP	Member:	FDIC

Index

Index to Operations by Product Classification
Using Standard Industrial Classification Numbers

MAJOR GROUP 01

0100 AGRICULTURAL PRODUCTION— CROPS
0115 Corn
DEKALB Genetics Corporation
0116 Soybeans
DEKALB Genetics Corporation
0119 Cash grains, not elsewhere classified
DEKALB Genetics Corporation

MAJOR GROUP 02

0200 AGRICULTURAL PRODUCTION— LIVESTOCK AND ANIMAL SPECIALTIES
0213 Hogs
DEKALB Genetics Corporation
0751 Livestock services, except veterinary
DEKALB Genetics Corporation

MAJOR GROUP 10

1000 METAL MINING
1011 Iron ores
Inland Steel Industries, Inc.
1041 Gold ores
FMC Corporation

MAJOR GROUP 12

1200 COAL MINING
1221 Bituminous coal and lignite mining
Zeigler Coal Holding Company
1222 Bituminous coal undergroundmining
Zeigler Coal Holding Company

MAJOR GROUP 13

1300 OIL AND GAS EXTRACTION
1311 Crude petroleum and natural gas
Amoco Corporation
1321 Natural gas liquids
Amoco Corporation

MAJOR GROUP 14

1400 MINING AND QUARRYING OF NONMETALLIC MINERALS, EXCEPT FUELS
1422 Crushed and broken limestone
Continental Materials Corporation
1442 Construction sand and gravel
Continental Materials Corporation
1459 Clay, ceramic, and refractory minerals, not elsewhere classified
AMCOL International Corporation
1474 Potash, soda, and borate minerals
IMC Global Inc.
1475 Phosphate rock
IMC Global Inc.
1479 Chemical and fertilizer mineral mining, not elsewhere classified
IMC Global Inc.
Morton International, Inc.
1499 Miscellaneous nonmetallic minerals, not elsewhere classified
Oil-Dri Corporation of America

MAJOR GROUP 15

1500 BUILDING CONSTRUCTION— GENERAL CONTRACTORS AND OPERATIVE BUILDERS
1521 General contractors—single-family houses
Sundance Homes, Inc.
1522 General contractors—residential buildings, other than single-family
Amerihost Properties, Inc.

MAJOR GROUP 16

1600 HEAVY CONSTRUCTION OTHER THAN BUILDING CONSTRUCTION - CONTRACTORS
1623 Water, sewer, pipe line, communi cation and power line construction
MYR Group Inc.
1629 Heavy construction, not elsewhere classified
MYR Group Inc.

MAJOR GROUP 17

1700 CONSTRUCTION—SPECIAL TRADE CONTRACTORS
1731 Electrical work
MYR Group Inc.
1761 Roofing, siding, and sheet metal work
Diamond Home Services, Inc.
1796 Installation or erection of building equipment, not elsewhere classified
MYR Group Inc.

MAJOR GROUP 20

2000 FOOD AND KINDRED PRODUCTS
2011 Meat packing plants
Rymer Foods Inc.
2013 Sausages and other prepared meat products
Rymer Foods Inc.
Sara Lee Corporation
2024 Ice cream and frozen desserts
Dean Foods Company
2026 Fluid milk
Dean Foods Company
2033 Canned fruits, vegetables, preserves, jams, and jellies
Dean Foods Company
The Quaker Oats Company
2035 Pickled fruits and vegetables, vegetable sauces and seasonings, and salad dressings
Dean Foods Company
2037 Frozen fruits, fruit juices, and vegetables
Dean Foods Company
2041 Flour and other grain mill products
Archer-Daniels-Midland Company
The Quaker Oats Company
2043 Cereal breakfast foods
The Quaker Oats Company
2044 Rice milling
The Quaker Oats Company
2046 Wet corn milling
Archer-Daniels-Midland Company

2053	Frozen bakery products, except bread	
	Sara Lee Corporation	
2062	Cane sugar refining	
	Archer-Daniels-Midland Company	
2064	Candy and other confectionery products	
	John B. Sanfilippo & Son, Inc.	
	Tootsie Roll Industries, Inc.	
	Wm. Wrigley Jr. Company	
2067	Chewing gum	
	Wm. Wrigley Jr. Company	
2068	Salted and roasted nuts and seeds	
	John B. Sanfilippo & Son, Inc.	
	Sara Lee Corporation	
2075	Soybean oil mills	
	Archer-Daniels-Midland Company	
2076	Vegetable oil mills, except corn, cottonseed, and soybean	
	Archer-Daniels-Midland Company	
2086	Bottled and canned soft drinks and carbonated waters	
	The Quaker Oats Company	
	Whitman Corporation	
2087	Flavoring extracts and flavoring syrups, not elsewhere classified	
	Wm. Wrigley Jr. Company	
2095	Roasted coffee	
	Sara Lee Corporation	
2096	Potato chips, corn chips, and similar snacks	
	John B. Sanfilippo & Son, Inc.	
2099	Food preparations, not elsewhere classified	
	Abbott Laboratories	
	Alberto-Culver Company	
	John B. Sanfilippo & Son, Inc.	

MAJOR GROUP 22
2200   TEXTILE MILL PRODUCTS
2251   Women's full length and knee length hosiery, except socks
Sara Lee Corporation
2253   Knit outerwear mills
Fruit of the Loom, Inc.
2254   Knit underwear and nightwear mills
Fruit of the Loom, Inc.
2273   Carpets and rugs
Shelby Williams Industries, Inc.

MAJOR GROUP 23
2300   APPAREL AND OTHER FINISHED PRODUCTS MADE FROM FABRICS AND SIMILAR MATERIALS
2311   Men's and boy's suits, coats, and overcoats
Hartmarx Corporation
2322   Men's and boys' underwear and nightwear
Fruit of the Loom, Inc.
2337   Women's, misses', and juniors' suits, skirts, and coats
Hartmarx Corporation
2341   Women's, misses', children's, and infants' underwear and nightwear
Fruit of the Loom, Inc.
2392   House furnishings, except curtains and draperies
Newell Co.

MAJOR GROUP 25
2500   FURNITURE AND FIXTURES
2521   Wood office furniture
Shelby Williams Industries, Inc.
2531   Public building and related furniture
Shelby Williams Industries, Inc.
2542   Partitions, shelving, lockers, and office and store fixtures, except wood
The Interlake Corporation
2599   Furniture and fixtures, not elsewhere classified
Shelby Williams Industries, Inc.

MAJOR GROUP 26
2600   PAPER AND ALLIED PRODUCTS
2611   Pulp mills
Stone Container Corporation
2621   Paper mills
Gaylord Container Corporation
Stone Container Corporation
2631   Paperboard mills
Gaylord Container Corporation
Stone Container Corporation
2653   Corrugated and solid fiber boxes
Gaylord Container Corporation
Stone Container Corporation
2656   Sanitary food containers, except folding
CLARCOR Inc.
Premark International, Inc.
2657   Folding paperboard boxes, including sanitary
Gaylord Container Corporation
Stone Container Corporation
2671   Packaging paper and plastics film, coated and laminated
ARTRA GROUP Incorporated
CFC International, Inc.
Envirodyne Industries, Inc.
2674   Uncoated paper and multiwall bags
Gaylord Container Corporation
Stone Container Corporation
2675   Die-cut paper, paperboard and cardboard
Gaylord Container Corporation

MAJOR GROUP 27
2700   PRINTING, PUBLISHING AND ALLIED INDUSTRIES
2711   Newspapers: publishing, or publishing and printing
Hollinger International Inc.
Tribune Company
2721   Periodicals: publishing, or publishing and printing
Pittway Corporation
Playboy Enterprises, Inc.
R.R. Donnelley & Sons Company
2731   Books: publishing, or publishing and printing
Successories, Inc.
The Goodheart-Willcox Company, Inc.
Tribune Company
2741   Miscellaneous publishing
Ameritech Corporation
Playboy Enterprises, Inc.
2752   Commercial printing, lithographic
R.R. Donnelley & Sons Company
Successories, Inc.
Wallace Computer Services, Inc.

2759 Commercial printing, not elsewhere classified
HA-LO Industries, Inc.
Successors, Inc.
Wallace Computer Services, Inc.
2761 Manifold business forms
Wallace Computer Services, Inc.
2789 Bookbinding and related work
R.R. Donnelley & Sons Company
2791 Typesetting
R.R. Donnelley & Sons Company
Schawk, Inc.
2796 Platemaking and related services
R.R. Donnelley & Sons Company
Schawk, Inc.

MAJOR GROUP 28
2800 CHEMICALS AND ALLIED PRODUCTS
2816 Inorganic pigments
Lawter International, Inc.
2819 Industrial inorganic chemicals, not elsewhere classified
Amoco Corporation
FMC Corporation
IMC Global Inc.
Nalco Chemical Company
Oil-Dri Corporation of America
2821 Plastics materials, synthetic resins, and nonvulcanizable elastomers
AMCOL International Corporation
Lawter International, Inc.
McWhorter Technologies, Inc.
Stepan Company
2833 Medicinal chemicals and botanical products
Abbott Laboratories
2834 Pharmaceutical preparations
Abbott Laboratories
UNIMED Pharmaceuticals, Inc.
2835 In vitro and in vivo diagnostic substances
Abbott Laboratories
AccuMed International, Inc.
2842 Specialty cleaning, polishing and sanitation preparations
Alberto-Culver Company
Minuteman International, Inc.
2843 Surface active agents, finishing agents, suffonated oils and assistants
Stepan Company
2844 Perfumes, cosmetics, and other toilet preparations
Abbott Laboratories
Alberto-Culver Company
2851 Paints, varnishes, lacquers, enamels and allied products
Lawter International, Inc.
2869 Industrial organic chemicals, not elsewhere classified
Amoco Corporation
Nalco Chemical Company
Stepan Company
2873 Nitrogenous fertilizers
IMC Global Inc.
2874 Phosphatic fertilizers
IMC Global Inc.

2879 Pesticides and agricultural chemicals, not elsewhere classified
FMC Corporation
Oil-Dri Corporation of America
2891 Adhesives and sealants
Lawter International, Inc.
Morton International, Inc.
USG Corporation
2893 Printing ink
Lawter International, Inc.
2899 Chemicals and chemical preparations, not elsewhere classified
Morton International, Inc.
Nalco Chemical Company
Oil-Dri Corporation of America

MAJOR GROUP 29
2900 PETROLEUM REFINING AND RELATED INDUSTRIES
2911 Petroleum refining
Amoco Corporation
2992 Lubricating oils and greases
Safety-Kleen Corp.

MAJOR GROUP 30
3000 RUBBER AND MISCELLANEOUS PLASTICS PRODUCTS
3069 Fabricated rubber products, not elsewhere classified
Woodhead Industries, Inc.
3081 Unsupported plastics film & sheet
Envirodyne Industries, Inc.
General Binding Corporation
Material Sciences Corporation
3083 Laminated plastics plate, sheet, and profile shapes
General Binding Corporation
Material Sciences Corporation
3087 Custom compounding of purchased plastics resins
Allied Products Corporation
3089 Plastics products, not elsewhere classified
AptarGroup, Inc.
CLARCOR Inc.
Envirodyne Industries, Inc.
General Binding Corporation
Home Products International, Inc.
Illinois Tool Works Inc.
Premark International, Inc.
Quixote Corporation
Shelby Williams Industries, Inc.
U.S. Can Corporation
USG Corporation
3143 Men's footwear, except athletic
Florsheim Group Inc.

MAJOR GROUP 32
3200 STONE, CLAY, GLASS AND CONCRETE PRODUCTS
3221 Glass containers
Newell Co.
3229 Pressed and blown glass and glassware, not elsewhere classified
Newell Co.

3231	Glass products, made of purchased glass
	Stimsonite Corporation
3253	Ceramic wall and floor tile
	Premark International, Inc.
3273	Ready-mixed concrete
	Continental Materials Corporation
3275	Gypsum products
	USG Corporation
3295	Minerals and earths, ground or otherwise treated
	Oil-Dri Corporation of America

MAJOR GROUP 33

3300 PRIMARY METAL INDUSTRIES

3312	Blast furnaces (including coke ovens), steel works, and rolling mills
	ABC Rail Products Corporation
	Acme Metals Incorporated
	Inland Steel Industries, Inc.
	Northwestern Steel and Wire Company
	Ryerson Tull, Inc.
	Titan International, Inc.
3315	Steel wiredrawing and steel nails and spikes
	Northwestern Steel and Wire Company
3317	Steel pipe and tubes
	Acme Metals Incorporated
	UNR Industries, Inc.
3339	Primary nonferrous metals, not elsewhere classified
	Fansteel Inc.
	Metal Management, Inc.
3357	Nonferrous wiredrawing & insulating
	Andrew Corporation
	General Instrument Corporation
3363	Aluminum die-castings
	Lindberg Corporation
	Varlen Corporation
3369	Nonferrous foundries, except aluminum and castings
	Lindberg Corporation
3398	Metal heat treating
	Lindberg Corporation
3399	Primary metal products, not elsewhere classified
	Material Sciences Corporation

MAJOR GROUP 34

3400 FABRICATED METAL PRODUCTS, EXCEPT MACHINERY AND TRANSPORTATION EQUIPMENT

3411	Metal cans
	CLARCOR Inc.
	U.S. Can Corporation
3423	Hand and edge tools, except machine tools and handsaws
	Acme Metals Incorporated
3429	Hardware, not elsewhere classified
	ABC Rail Products Corporation
	IDEX Corporation
	Newell Co.
3433	Heating equipment, except electric and warm air furnaces
	Continental Materials Corporation
3441	Fabricated structural metal
	UNR Industries, Inc.

3443	Fabricated plate work (boiler shops)
	Fansteel Inc.
3444	Sheet metal work
	Quixote Corporation
3449	Miscellaneous structural metal work
	Varlen Corporation
3452	Bolts, nuts, screws, rivets and washers
	Chicago Rivet & Machine Co.
	Illinois Tool Works Inc.
3462	Iron and steel forgings
	ABC Rail Products Corporation
	Fansteel Inc.
	PORTEC, Inc.
3465	Automotive stampings
	Acme Metals Incorporated
	Varlen Corporation
3466	Crowns and closures
	AptarGroup, Inc.
3469	Metal stampings, not elsewhere classified
	Allied Products Corporation
	Newell Co.
3471	Electroplating, plating, polishing, anodizing, and coloring
	Material Sciences Corporation
3479	Coating, engraving and allied services, not elsewhere classified
	Material Sciences Corporation
	Morton International, Inc.
3489	Ordnance and accessories, not elsewhere classified
	FMC Corporation
3492	Fluid power valves and hose fittings
	Binks Sames Corporation
	Lawson Products, Inc.
3496	Miscellaneous fabricated wire products
	Chicago Rivet & Machine Co.
	Lindberg Corporation
	Northwestern Steel and Wire Company
	UNR Industries, Inc.
3499	Fabricated metal products, not elsewhere classified
	Acme Metals Incorporated
	The Interlake Corporation

MAJOR GROUP 35

3500 INDUSTRIAL AND COMMERCIAL MACHINERY AND COMPUTER EQUIPMENT

3511	Steam, gas, and hydraulic turbines and turbine generator set units
	Caterpillar Inc.
	Sundstrand Corporation
	Woodward Governor Company
3519	Internal combustion engines, not elsewhere classified
	Brunswick Corporation
	Caterpillar Inc.
	Deere & Company
	IDEX Corporation
	Outboard Marine Corporation
	Woodward Governor Company
3523	Farm machinery and equipment
	Allied Products Corporation
	Deere & Company
	FMC Corporation

3524 Lawn and garden tractors and home lawn and garden equipment
Allied Products Corporation
Deere & Company

3531 Construction machinery and equipment
ABC Rail Products Corporation
Caterpillar Inc.
Deere & Company
PORTEC, Inc.

3532 Mining machinery and equipment, except oil and gas field machinery and equipment
Caterpillar Inc.

3535 Conveyors and conveying equipment
PORTEC, Inc.
The Interlake Corporation

3537 Industrial trucks, tractors, trailers, and stackers
AAR CORP.
Caterpillar Inc.
Navistar International Corporation

3541 Machine tools, metal cutting types
Fansteel Inc.

3542 Machine tools, metal forming types
Allied Products Corporation
Chicago Rivet & Machine Co.

3544 Special dies and tools, die sets, jigs and fixtures, and industrial molds
Federal Signal Corporation

3545 Cutting tools, machine tool accessories and machinists' precision measuring devices
Chicago Rivet & Machine Co.
Federal Signal Corporation

3548 Electric and gas welding and soldering equipment
Illinois Tool Works Inc.

3555 Printing trades machinery and equipment
Lawter International, Inc.
Multigraphics, Inc.
Zebra Technologies Corporation

3556 Food products machinery
Premark International, Inc.
Scotsman Industries, Inc.
The Middleby Corporation

3559 Special industry machinery, not elsewhere classified
Varlen Corporation

3561 Pumps and pumping equipment
Binks Sames Corporation
IDEX Corporation
Sundstrand Corporation

3562 Ball and roller bearings
Binks Sames Corporation

3563 Air and gas compressors
Binks Sames Corporation
Newell Co.

3564 Industrial and commercial fans and blowers and air purification equipment
Binks Sames Corporation
MFRI, Inc.
W.W. Grainger, Inc.

3566 Speed changers, industrial high speed drives, and gears
Illinois Tool Works Inc.
Sundstrand Corporation

3567 Industrial process furnaces and ovens
Continental Materials Corporation

3569 General industrial machinery and equipment, not elsewhere classified
CLARCOR Inc.
IDEX Corporation
MFRI, Inc.
Woodhead Industries, Inc.

3571 Electronic computers
Motorola, Inc.

3572 Computer storage devices
Cerion Technologies Inc.

3575 Computer terminals
General Instrument Corporation
Molex Incorporated
Wells-Gardner Electronics Corporation

3577 Electronic computing equipment
Multigraphics, Inc.
The Cherry Corporation
Zebra Technologies Corporation

3579 Office machines, not elsewhere classified
Bell & Howell Company
General Binding Corporation
Multigraphics, Inc.

3585 Air conditioning, warm air heating equipment and commercial and industrial refrigeration equipment
Continental Materials Corporation
Premark International, Inc.
Scotsman Industries, Inc.
Specialty Equipment Companies, Inc.
The Middleby Corporation
Whitman Corporation

3589 Service industry machines, not elsewhere classified
Culligan Water Technologies, Inc.
Minuteman International, Inc.
Specialty Equipment Companies, Inc.
The Middleby Corporation

3592 Carburetors, pistons, piston rings, and valves
Champion Parts, Inc.

3594 Fluid power pumps and motors
Binks Sames Corporation

MAJOR GROUP 36
3600 ELECTRONIC AND OTHER ELECTRICAL EQUIPMENT AND COMPONENTS, EXCEPT COMPUTER EQUIPMENT

3612 Power, distribution, and specialty transformers
Littelfuse, Inc.
Woodhead Industries, Inc.

3613 Switchgear and switchboard apparatus
Littelfuse, Inc.
Methode Electronics, Inc.
Molex Incorporated
Tellabs, Inc.
The Cherry Corporation

3621 Motors and generators
Brunswick Corporation
Outboard Marine Corporation

3625 Relays and industrial controls
Littelfuse, Inc.
Methode Electronics, Inc.
Woodhead Industries, Inc.
Woodward Governor Company

3634 Electric housewares and fans
Premark International, Inc.
Salton/Maxim Housewares, Inc.

3641 Electric lamp bulbs and tubes
Juno Lighting, Inc.

3643 Current-carrying wiring devices
Littelfuse, Inc.
Methode Electronics, Inc.
Molex Incorporated
The Cherry Corporation
Woodhead Industries, Inc.

3645 Residential electric lighting fixtures
Juno Lighting, Inc.

3646 Commercial, industrial and institutional
electric lighting fixtures
Juno Lighting, Inc.

3648 Lighting equipment, not elsewhere classified
First Alert, Inc.
Juno Lighting, Inc.

3651 Household audio and video equipment and
audio recordings
Salton/Maxim Housewares, Inc.
Wells-Gardner Electronics Corporation
Zenith Electronics Corporation

3661 Telephone and telegraph apparatus
Ameritech Corporation
Anicom, Inc.
Cobra Electronics Corporation
Motorola, Inc.
Tellabs, Inc.
Teltrend Inc.
Telular Corporation
Westell Technologies, Inc.

3663 Radio and television broadcasting and
communications equipment
Andrew Corporation
Anicom, Inc.
Anixter International Inc.
ANTEC Corporation
Cobra Electronics Corporation
Corcom, Inc.
General Instrument Corporation
Motorola, Inc.
M~Wave, Inc.
Richardson Electronics, Ltd.
Tellabs, Inc.
Telular Corporation
Zenith Electronics Corporation

3669 Communications equipment, not elsewhere
classified
Anicom, Inc.
Federal Signal Corporation
First Alert, Inc.
Pittway Corporation
Tellabs, Inc.

3671 Electron tubes
Richardson Electronics, Ltd.
Zenith Electronics Corporation

3672 Printed circuit boards
Circuit Systems, Inc.
M~Wave, Inc.
SigmaTron International, Inc.

3674 Semiconductors and related devices
Juno Lighting, Inc.
Motorola, Inc.

Richardson Electronics, Ltd.
SigmaTron International, Inc.
The Cherry Corporation
Zenith Electronics Corporation

3676 Electronic resistors
Methode Electronics, Inc.

3678 Electronic connectors
Methode Electronics, Inc.
Molex Incorporated

3679 Electronic components, not elsewhere
classified
Andrew Corporation
Corcom, Inc.
Federal Signal Corporation
General Instrument Corporation
Littelfuse, Inc.
Methode Electronics, Inc.
Molex Incorporated
Motorola, Inc.
M~Wave, Inc.
PORTEC, Inc.
SigmaTron International, Inc.
The Cherry Corporation
Wells-Gardner Electronics Corporation
Woodhead Industries, Inc.
Zenith Electronics Corporation

3694 Electrical equipment for internal combustion
engines
Borg-Warner Automotive, Inc.
Champion Parts, Inc.

MAJOR GROUP 37
3700 TRANSPORTATION EQUIPMENT

3711 Motor vehicles and passenger car bodies
Federal Signal Corporation
Navistar International Corporation

3713 Truck and bus bodies
Navistar International Corporation

3714 Motor vehicle parts and accessories
Borg-Warner Automotive, Inc.
Champion Parts, Inc.
CLARCOR Inc.
Titan International, Inc.
Universal Automotive Industries, Inc.
Whitman Corporation

3724 Aircraft engines and engine parts
AAR CORP.
Sundstrand Corporation
The Interlake Corporation

3728 Aircraft parts and auxiliary equipment, not
elsewhere classified
AAR CORP.
Fansteel Inc.
Sundstrand Corporation
Woodward Governor Company

3732 Boat building and repairing
Brunswick Corporation
Outboard Marine Corporation

3743 Railroad equipment
ABC Rail Products Corporation
Johnstown America Industries, Inc.
PORTEC, Inc.
Varlen Corporation

3769 Guided missile and space vehicle parts and auxiliary equipment, not elsewhere classified
Fansteel Inc.

3799 Transportation equipment, not elsewhere classified
Outboard Marine Corporation

MAJOR GROUP 38

3800 MEASURING, ANALYZING AND CONTROLLING INSTRUMENTS PHOTOGRAPHIC, MEDICAL AND OPTICAL GOODS; WATCHES AND CLOCKS

3812 Search, detection, navigation, guidance, aeronautical, and nautical systems and instruments
Andrew Corporation
Sundstrand Corporation

3821 Laboratory apparatus and furniture
Baxter International Inc.
Varlen Corporation

3823 Industrial instruments for measurement display, and control of process variables and related produc
Total Control Products, Inc.

3825 Instruments for measuring and testing of electricity and electrical signals
Cobra Electronics Corporation
SigmaTron International, Inc.

3826 Laboratory analytical instruments
Landauer, Inc.

3827 AccuMed International, Inc.
Stimsonite Corporation

3829 Measuring and controlling devices, not elsewhere classified
Landauer, Inc.

3841 Surgical and medical instruments and apparatus
Abbott Laboratories
Allegiance Corporation
Baxter International Inc.

3842 Orthopedic, prosthetic, and surgical appliances and supplies
Allegiance Corporation
Baxter International Inc.

3845 Electromedical and electrotherapeutic apparatus
Allegiance Corporation
Baxter International Inc.
Bio-logic Systems Corp.
Sabratek Corporation

3851 Ophthalmic goods
Wesley Jessen VisionCare, Inc.

3861 Photographic equipment & supplies
Multigraphics, Inc.

MAJOR GROUP 39

3900 MISCELLANEOUS MANUFACTURING INDUSTRIES

3911 Jewelry, precious metal
IWI Holding Limited

3944 Games, toys and children's vehicles except dolls and bicycles
WMS Industries Inc.

3949 Sporting and athletic goods, not elsewhere classified
Brunswick Corporation

3993 Signs and advertising specialties
Federal Signal Corporation

3999 Manufacturing industries, not elsewhere classified
First Alert, Inc.
Midway Games Inc.
Oil-Dri Corporation of America
WMS Industries Inc.

MAJOR GROUP 40

4000 RAILROAD TRANSPORTATION

4011 Railroads, line-haul operating
Illinois Central Corporation
Pioneer Railcorp
Wisconsin Central Transportation Corporation

4013 Railroad switching and terminal establishments
Illinois Central Corporation

MAJOR GROUP 42

4200 MOTOR FREIGHT TRANSPORTATION AND WAREHOUSING

4212 Local trucking, without storage
United Stationers Inc.
USFreightways Corporation

4213 Trucking, except local
Aasche Transportation Services, Inc.
AMCOL International Corporation
United Stationers Inc.
USFreightways Corporation

4226 Special warehousing and storage, not elsewhere classified
GATX Corporation

MAJOR GROUP 44

4400 WATER TRANSPORTATION

4424 Deep sea domestic transportation of freight
NICOR Inc.

4432 Great Lakes-St. Lawrence Seaway transportation
GATX Corporation

4489 Water transportation of passengers, not elsewhere classified
American Classic Voyages Co.

MAJOR GROUP 45

4500 TRANSPORTATION BY AIR

4512 Air transportation, scheduled
UAL Corporation

4513 Air courier services
UAL Corporation

6159 Miscellaneous business credit institutions
 Caterpillar Inc.
 Community Financial Corp.
 Deere & Company
 First Merchants Acceptance Corporation
 GATX Corporation
 Mercury Finance Company
 Navistar International Corporation
 Trans Leasing International, Inc.
6162 Mortgage bankers and loan correspondents
 Calumet Bancorp, Inc.
 Fidelity Bancorp, Inc.
 First Midwest Bancorp, Inc.
 Household International, Inc.
 Standard Financial, Inc.
6163 Alliance Bancorp
 Hemlock Federal Financial Corporation
 SuburbFed Financial Corp.
6172 GATX Corporation
 Prime Capital Corporation

MAJOR GROUP 62
6200 SECURITY AND COMMODITY BROKERS,
 DEALERS, EXCHANGES AND SERVICES
6211 Security brokers, dealers and flotation
 companies
 AMCORE Financial, Inc.
 EVEREN Capital Corporation
 Fidelity Bancorp, Inc.
 Firstbank of Illinois Co.
 Rodman & Renshaw Capital Group, Inc.
 St. Paul Bancorp, Inc.
 The John Nuveen Company
6221 Commodity contracts brokers and dealers
 EVEREN Capital Corporation
 Rodman & Renshaw Capital Group, Inc.
6282 Investment advice
 Rodman & Renshaw Capital Group, Inc.
 The John Nuveen Company
6289 Services allied with the exchange of securities
 or commodities, not elsewhere
 classified
 PC Quote, Inc.

MAJOR GROUP 63
6300 INSURANCE CARRIERS
6311 Life insurance
 Aon Corporation
 CNA Financial Corporation
 Grand Premier Financial, Inc.
 Horace Mann Educators Corporation
 Old Republic International Corporation
 The Allstate Corporation
 Unitrin, Inc.
 Washington National Corporation
6321 Accident and health insurance
 Aon Corporation
 CNA Financial Corporation
 Horace Mann Educators Corporation
 MMI Companies, Inc.
 Old Republic International Corporation
 Unitrin, Inc.

6324 Hospital and medical service plans
 CNA Financial Corporation
 First Commonwealth, Inc.
 Unitrin, Inc.
6331 Fire, marine, and casualty insurance
 Aon Corporation
 Capsure Holdings Corp.
 CNA Financial Corporation
 Deere & Company
 Grand Premier Financial, Inc.
 Horace Mann Educators Corporation
 Intercargo Corporation
 Navistar International Corporation
 Old Republic International Corporation
 RLI Corp.
 The Allstate Corporation
 Trans Leasing International, Inc.
 Unitrin, Inc.
6351 Surety companies
 Amerin Corporation
 Capsure Holdings Corp.
 CNA Financial Corporation
 First Merchants Acceptance Corporation
 Intercargo Corporation
 Mercury Finance Company
 MMI Companies, Inc.
 Old Republic International Corporation
 RLI Corp.
 The Allstate Corporation
 Trans Leasing International, Inc.
6361 Title insurance
 Old Republic International Corporation
6399 Insurance carriers, not elsewhere classified
 Aon Corporation
 First Enterprise Financial Group, Inc.
 Intercargo Corporation

MAJOR GROUP 64
6400 INSURANCE AGENTS, BROKERS, AND
 SERVICE
6411 Insurance agents, brokers, and service
 Aon Corporation
 Arthur J. Gallagher & Co.
 CCC Information Services Group Inc.
 Eagle Finance Corp.
 HealthCare COMPARE Corp.
 MAF Bancorp, Inc.
 MMI Companies, Inc.
 RLI Corp.
 Standard Financial, Inc.
 Unitrin, Inc.

MAJOR GROUP 65
6500 REAL ESTATE
6531 Real estate agents and managers
 Grubb & Ellis Company
6552 Land subdividers and developers, except
 cemeteries
 NIPSCO Industries, Inc.
 Pittway Corporation
 St. Paul Bancorp, Inc.

MAJOR GROUP 67

6700 HOLDING AND OTHER INVESTMENT COMPANIES

6712 Offices of bank holding companies
Alliance Bancorp
AMCORE Financial, Inc.
Avondale Financial Corp.
Beverly Bancorporation, Inc.
Calumet Bancorp, Inc.
Charter Financial, Inc.
Community Financial Corp.
CORUS BANKSHARES, INC.
Damen Financial Corporation
Fidelity Bancorp, Inc.
First Bankers Trustshares, Inc.
First Busey Corporation
First Chicago NBD Corporation
First Evergreen Corporation
First Financial Bancorp, Inc.
First Midwest Bancorp, Inc.
First National Bancorp, Inc.
First Oak Brook Bancshares, Inc.
Firstbank of Illinois Co.
Grand Premier Financial, Inc.
Great American Bancorp, Inc.
Hemlock Federal Financial Corporation
Heritage Financial Services, Inc.
HomeCorp, Inc.
MAF Bancorp, Inc.
Merchants Bancorp, Inc.
North Bancshares, Inc.
Northern States Financial Corporation
Northern Trust Corporation
Pinnacle Banc Group, Inc.
Princeton National Bancorp, Inc.
Southwest Bancshares, Inc.
St. Paul Bancorp, Inc.
Standard Financial, Inc.
SuburbFed Financial Corp.
The Northern Trust Company
UnionBancorp, Inc.
Westco Bancorp, Inc.
Wintrust Financial Corporation

6719 Offices of holding companies, not elsewhere classified
Aasche Transportation Services, Inc.
Acme Metals Incorporated
American Classic Voyages Co.
Amerihost Properties, Inc.
Amerin Corporation
Ameritech Corporation
Aon Corporation
Archer-Daniels-Midland Company
Argosy Gaming Company
ARTRA GROUP Incorporated
Borg-Warner Security Corporation
Capsure Holdings Corp.
CILCORP Inc.
CIPSCO Incorporated
CLARCOR Inc.
CNA Financial Corporation
Diamond Home Services, Inc.
General Instrument Corporation

Grubb & Ellis Company
Hartmarx Corporation
Help At Home, Inc.
Horace Mann Educators Corporation
Household International, Inc.
Illinois Central Corporation
Illinova Corporation
Intercargo Corporation
IWI Holding Limited
Johnstown America Industries, Inc.
Metal Management, Inc.
MFRI, Inc.
MMI Companies, Inc.
MYR Group Inc.
Navistar International Corporation
NICOR Inc.
NIPSCO Industries, Inc.
Old Republic International Corporation
Peoples Energy Corporation
Pioneer Railcorp
PLATINUM technology, inc.
Quixote Corporation
RLI Corp.
Rodman & Renshaw Capital Group, Inc.
Ryerson Tull, Inc.
SPS Transaction Services, Inc.
Telephone and Data Systems, Inc.
Tellabs, Inc.
The Allstate Corporation
The John Nuveen Company
The Leap Group, Inc.
The Middleby Corporation
Tootsie Roll Industries, Inc.
U.S. Can Corporation
UAL Corporation
Unicom Corporation
USFreightways Corporation
USG Corporation
Walgreen Co.
Waste Management, Inc.
Wisconsin Central Transportation Corporation
WMS Industries Inc.
Zeigler Coal Holding Company

6726 Unit investment trusts, face-amount certificate offices, and closed-end management investment office
Baker, Fentress & Company
The John Nuveen Company

6733 Trusts, except educational, religious and charitable
Beverly Bancorporation, Inc.

6794 Patent owners and lessors
BAB Holdings, Inc.
McDonald's Corporation
OPTION CARE, Inc.
Platinum Entertainment, Inc.

MAJOR GROUP 70

7000 HOTELS, ROOMING HOUSES, CAMPS AND OTHER LODGING PLACES

7011 Hotels and motels
American Classic Voyages Co.
Amerihost Properties, Inc.

LaSalle Banks Guide

337

MAJOR GROUP 76

7600   MISCELLANEOUS REPAIR SERVICES
7629   Electrical and electronic repair shops, not elsewhere classified
AAR CORP.

MAJOR GROUP 78

7800   MOTION PICTURES
7812   Motion picture and video tape production
Playboy Enterprises, Inc.
7822   Motion picture and video tape distribution
Playboy Enterprises, Inc.
7841   Video tape rental
Eagle Food Centers, Inc.

MAJOR GROUP 79

7900   AMUSEMENT AND RECREATION SERVICES, EXCEPT MOTION PICTURES
7933   Bowling centers
Brunswick Corporation
7941   Professional sports clubs and promoters
Tribune Company
7991   Physical fitness facilities
Bally Total Fitness Holding Corporation
7993   Coin-operated amusement devices
Argosy Gaming Company
WMS Industries Inc.
7999   Amusement and recreation services, not elsewhere classified
Argosy Gaming Company

MAJOR GROUP 80

8000   HEALTH SERVICES
8011   Offices and clinics of doctors of medicine
National Surgery Centers, Inc.
8049   Offices and clinics of health practitioners, not elsewhere classified
OPTION CARE, Inc.
8082   Home health care services
Help At Home, Inc.
OPTION CARE, Inc.
8093   Specialty outpatient clinics, not elsewhere classified
OPTION CARE, Inc.
8099   Health and allied services, not elsewhere classified
Vitalink Pharmacy Services, Inc.

MAJOR GROUP 82

8200   EDUCATIONAL SERVICES
8221   Colleges, universities, and professional schools
DeVRY INC.
8222   Junior colleges and technical institutes
DeVRY INC.
8243   Data processing schools
DeVRY INC.
TRO Learning, Inc.
8244   Business and secretarial schools
DeVRY INC.
8299   Schools and educational services, not elsewhere classified
TRO Learning, Inc.

MAJOR GROUP 87

8700   ENGINEERING, ACCOUNTING, RESEARCH, MANAGEMENT, AND RELATED SERVICES
8711   Engineering services
CILCORP Inc.
8731   Commercial physical and biological research
DEKALB Genetics Corporation
8732   Commercial economic, sociological, and educational research
HealthCare COMPARE Corp.
Market Facts, Inc.
8734   Testing laboratories
Landauer, Inc.
8741   Management services
Amerihost Properties, Inc.
Donnelley Enterprise Solutions Incorporated
HealthCare COMPARE Corp.
Market Facts, Inc.
ServiceMaster Limited Partnership
The Metzler Group, Inc.
8742   Management consulting services
Amerihost Properties, Inc.
APAC TeleServices, Inc.
Diamond Technology Partners Incorporated
Donnelley Enterprise Solutions Incorporated
HealthCare COMPARE Corp.
MMI Companies, Inc.
True North Communications Inc.
8743   Management and public relations services
True North Communications Inc.
8744   Facilities support management services
ServiceMaster Limited Partnership
8748   Business consulting services, not elsewhere classified
Information Resources, Inc.

Rankings

_____

_____

_____

_____

_____

_____

_____

_____

_____

_____

_____

_____

_____

_____

_____

_____

_____

_____

_____

_____

_____

_____

_____

Industrial, Retail, Transportation, Utility, Insurance, and Diversified Financial Companies

Company	Rank by Sales or Revenues '96	'95	Sales or Revenues (000 Omitted)	Rank by Assets '96	'95	Assets (000 Omitted)	Year End
Sears, Roebuck and Co.	1	1	$38,326,000	3	3	$36,167,000	12/96
Amoco Corporation	2	2	36,112,000	4	4	32,100,000	12/96
Motorola, Inc.	3	3	27,973,000	6	7	24,076,000	12/96
The Allstate Corporation	4	4	24,299,000	1	1	74,508,000	12/96
Sara Lee Corporation	5	5	18,624,000	15	14	12,602,000	06/96
CNA Financial Corporation	6	8	16,987,776	2	2	60,734,732	12/96
UAL Corporation	7	7	16,362,000	14	15	12,677,000	12/96
Caterpillar Inc.	8	6	15,814,000	9	11	18,728,000	12/96
Ameritech Corporation	9	9	14,917,000	7	8	23,707,000	12/96
Archer-Daniels-Midland Company	10	10	13,314,049	17	16	10,449,869	06/96
Walgreen Co.	11	11	11,778,408	34	38	3,633,646	08/96
Deere & Company	12	15	11,229,393	12	13	14,652,685	10/96
Abbott Laboratories	13	13	11,013,460	16	18	11,125,600	12/96
McDonald's Corporation	14	14	10,687,000	11	12	17,386,000	12/96
Waste Management, Inc.	15	12	9,186,970	10	10	18,366,592	12/96
Unicom Corporation	16	17	6,937,024	8	6	23,387,970	12/96
R.R. Donnelley & Sons Company	17	18	6,598,958	26	23	4,849,004	12/96
Navistar International Corporation	18	20	5,754,000	23	22	5,326,000	10/96
Baxter International Inc.	19	21	5,438,000	18	17	7,596,000	12/96
The Quaker Oats Company	20	19	5,199,000	29	27	4,394,400	12/96
Stone Container Corporation	21	16	5,141,800	20	20	6,353,800	12/96
FMC Corporation	22	24	5,080,600	24	28	4,989,800	12/96
Illinois Tool Works Inc.	23	25	4,996,681	27	33	4,806,162	12/96
Inland Steel Industries, Inc.	24	22	4,584,100	35	34	3,541,600	12/96
Allegiance Corporation	25	*	4,387,200	42	*	2,799,200	12/96
Aon Corporation	26	23	4,181,000	13	9	13,722,700	12/96
Morton International, Inc.	27	28	3,612,500	43	42	2,771,500	06/96
Household International, Inc.	28	26	3,538,200	5	5	29,594,500	12/96
W.W. Grainger, Inc.	29	29	3,537,207	48	56	2,119,021	12/96
ServiceMaster Limited Partnership	30	30	3,458,328	53	57	1,846,841	12/96
Brunswick Corporation	31	32	3,160,300	41	44	2,802,400	12/96
Whitman Corporation	32	33	3,111,300	47	43	2,409,400	12/96
Spiegel, Inc.	33	31	3,014,620	50	46	1,945,625	12/96
IMC Global Inc.	34	34	2,981,000	36	36	3,436,800	06/96
Newell Co.	35	36	2,872,817	38	40	3,005,054	12/96
Dean Foods Company	36	35	2,814,268	67	68	1,222,240	05/96
General Instrument Corporation	37	39	2,689,688	44	45	2,706,851	12/96
USG Corporation	38	38	2,590,000	55	50	1,818,000	12/96
Dominick's Supermarkets, Inc.	39	*	2,511,962	68	*	1,152,985	10/96
Anixter International Inc.	40	44	2,475,300	65	69	1,261,000	12/96
Fruit of the Loom, Inc.	41	40	2,447,400	45	41	2,547,000	12/96
Comdisco, Inc.	42	43	2,431,000	22	24	5,591,000	09/96
Tribune Company	43	42	2,405,705	33	37	3,700,900	12/96
Ryerson Tull, Inc.	44	37	2,394,000	75	76	932,200	12/96
United Stationers Inc.	45	48	2,298,170	69	73	1,109,867	12/96
Premark International, Inc.	46	27	2,267,600	58	49	1,660,800	12/96
Boise Cascade Office Products Corp.	47	58	1,985,564	77	96	905,362	12/96
Hollinger International Inc.	48	71	1,862,714	37	60	3,189,088	12/96

Company	Rank by Sales or Revenues '96	'95	Sales or Revenues (000 Omitted)	Rank by Assets '96	'95	Assets (000 Omitted)	Year End
NICOR Inc.	49	53	$1,850,700	46	47	$2,438,600	12/96
Wm. Wrigley Jr. Company	50	47	1,835,987	66	70	1,233,543	12/96
NIPSCO Industries, Inc.	51	49	1,821,626	30	31	4,274,343	12/96
Old Republic International Corp.	52	50	1,803,900	19	19	6,656,200	12/96
Borg-Warner Security Corporation	53	45	1,711,200	87	79	760,800	12/96
Illinova Corporation	54	51	1,688,700	21	21	5,712,800	12/96
Alberto-Culver Company	55	56	1,590,409	76	81	909,266	09/96
Borg-Warner Automotive, Inc.	56	57	1,540,100	60	65	1,623,600	12/96
Unitrin, Inc.	57	55	1,523,100	25	25	4,871,100	12/96
Sundstrand Corporation	58	54	1,521,000	61	59	1,595,000	12/96
GATX Corporation	59	60	1,414,400	28	30	4,750,200	12/96
BT Office Products International, Inc.	60	65	1,412,514	89	98	742,819	12/96
Molex Incorporated	61	63	1,382,673	62	62	1,460,999	06/96
USFreightways Corporation	62	64	1,330,972	93	93	688,508	12/96
Nalco Chemical Company	63	62	1,303,500	63	64	1,394,500	12/96
Zenith Electronics Corporation	64	59	1,287,900	86	85	765,300	12/96
Telephone and Data Systems, Inc.	65	72	1,214,636	31	35	4,200,969	12/96
Peoples Energy Corporation	66	67	1,198,657	56	54	1,783,750	09/96
Outboard Marine Corporation	67	61	1,121,500	79	77	873,700	09/96
Pittway Corporation	68	73	1,111,575	81	87	839,093	12/96
360° Communications Company	69	77	1,095,872	40	48	2,812,069	12/96
Eagle Food Centers, Inc.	70	69	1,014,889	134	132	254,748	01/97
CDW Computer Centers, Inc.	71	93	927,895	145	163	198,830	12/96
Safety-Kleen Corp.	72	75	923,126	72	72	1,044,823	12/96
Gaylord Container Corporation	73	66	922,000	73	74	933,000	09/96
Bell & Howell Company	74	79	902,797	84	86	800,518	12/96
CIPSCO Incorporated	75	76	896,715	52	53	1,871,656	12/96
Federal Signal Corporation	76	80	896,357	90	89	703,901	12/96
Tellabs, Inc.	77	92	868,975	88	95	743,823	12/96
Wallace Computer Services, Inc.	78	84	862,257	91	91	695,850	07/96
Wickes Inc.	79	70	848,535	130	125	272,842	12/96
Andrew Corporation	80	96	793,575	97	102	631,229	09/96
U.S. Can Corporation	81	95	761,429	96	107	643,616	12/96
Hub Group, Inc.	82	179	754,243	144	167	201,225	12/96
Zeigler Coal Holding Company	83	82	731,624	71	71	1,050,625	12/96
The Interlake Corporation	84	78	709,585	106	105	457,723	12/96
United States Cellular Corporation	85	106	707,820	49	52	2,085,899	12/96
Horace Mann Educators Corporation	86	83	703,800	32	32	3,861,026	12/96
A.M. Castle & Co.	87	94	672,600	133	141	261,370	12/96
Northwestern Steel and Wire Co.	88	91	661,069	108	110	442,518	07/96
Illinois Central Corporation	89	90	657,500	51	63	1,911,400	12/96
Envirodyne Industries, Inc.	90	89	651,356	78	78	873,747	12/96
Titan International, Inc.	91	98	634,553	102	101	558,592	12/96
CILCORP Inc.	92	99	628,392	64	66	1,285,693	12/96
Bally Total Fitness Holding Corp.	93	87	625,640	82	80	813,480	12/96
AptarGroup, Inc.	94	101	615,808	101	94	576,136	12/96
Hartmarx Corporation	95	100	610,180	110	115	430,239	11/96
ANTEC Corporation	96	88	604,382	109	106	437,238	12/96
Central Steel & Wire Company	97	97	591,400	137	136	236,300	12/96
AAR CORP.	98	105	589,328	105	108	529,584	05/97
EVEREN Capital Corporation	99	*	570,555	54	*	1,824,345	12/96
IDEX Corporation	100	108	562,561	100	104	583,773	12/96
Johnstown America Industries, Inc.	101	86	559,972	103	92	555,283	12/96

Company	Rank by Sales or Revenues '96	'95	Sales or Revenues (000 Omitted)	Rank by Assets '96	'95	Assets (000 Omitted)	Year End
General Binding Corporation	102	110	$536,836	112	126	$393,706	12/96
Stepan Company	103	102	536,635	115	116	381,012	12/96
Sportmart, Inc.	104	107	514,611	132	128	266,597	01/97
Acme Metals Incorporated	105	103	498,242	83	84	805,749	12/96
True North Communications Inc.	106	111	493,050	74	83	932,660	12/96
PLATINUM technology, inc.	107	132	468,065	98	109	610,541	12/96
Arthur J. Gallagher & Co.	108	113	456,679	99	103	590,424	12/96
The Cherry Corporation	109	112	439,592	126	124	295,646	02/97
Woodward Governor Company	110	118	417,290	122	118	348,798	09/96
Varlen Corporation	111	116	409,475	111	138	393,878	01/97
Information Resources, Inc.	112	114	405,603	124	119	334,493	12/96
AMCOL International Corporation	113	120	405,347	121	121	350,708	12/96
Specialty Equipment Cos., Inc.	114	*	401,230	152	*	176,916	01/97
DEKALB Genetics Corporation	115	123	387,500	116	120	363,300	08/96
Culligan Water Technologies, Inc.	116	128	371,018	123	127	337,362	01/97
Scotsman Industries, Inc.	117	122	356,373	128	131	283,264	12/96
Methode Electronics, Inc.	118	127	343,092	138	148	233,646	04/97
Tootsie Roll Industries, Inc.	119	124	340,909	113	117	391,456	12/96
System Software Associates, Inc.	120	115	340,800	114	111	384,400	10/96
WMS Industries Inc.	121	117	338,625	117	113	356,445	06/96
ELEK-TEK, Inc.	122	121	333,498	187	173	81,041	12/96
CLARCOR Inc.	123	129	333,338	136	140	243,964	11/96
Washington National Corporation	124	85	328,707	39	39	2,869,196	12/96
SPS Transaction Services, Inc.	125	125	320,920	57	55	1,760,785	12/96
McWhorter Technologies, Inc.	126	126	315,925	158	161	153,254	10/96
MYR Group Inc.	127	134	310,577	174	171	98,486	12/96
Binks Sames Corporation	128	135	296,686	139	137	230,229	11/96
John B. Sanfilippo & Son, Inc.	129	131	294,404	143	142	205,352	12/96
Insurance Auto Auctions, Inc.	130	*	281,893	141	*	211,804	12/96
Metromail Corporation	131	143	281,445	107	114	443,406	12/96
Material Sciences Corporation	132	145	278,017	135	147	254,089	02/97
Playboy Enterprises, Inc.	133	140	276,587	159	162	150,869	06/96
APAC TeleServices, Inc.	134	173	276,443	163	181	141,381	12/96
Allied Products Corporation	135	137	274,414	154	153	171,949	12/96
Wisconsin Central Transportation Co.	136	136	262,160	92	97	691,275	12/96
DeVRY INC.	137	146	260,007	151	166	178,089	06/96
HA-LO Industries, Inc.	138	156	254,888	182	185	87,634	12/96
Lawson Products, Inc.	139	147	250,289	153	155	175,162	12/96
HealthCare COMPARE Corp.	140	150	247,804	120	134	353,338	12/96
Midway Games Inc.	141	*	245,423	167	*	118,262	06/96
Florsheim Group Inc.	142	130	244,855	147	149	185,238	12/96
Argosy Gaming Company	143	138	244,817	104	123	532,159	12/96
MMI Companies, Inc.	144	149	243,178	70	75	1,058,018	12/96
Littelfuse, Inc.	145	148	241,446	142	146	209,951	12/96
ABC Rail Products Corporation	146	142	240,664	155	157	170,104	07/96
Richardson Electronics, Ltd.	147	151	239,667	149	151	180,158	05/96
The John Nuveen Company	148	144	232,347	118	112	355,251	12/96
First Alert, Inc.	149	141	205,607	146	144	186,491	12/96
Alternative Resources Corporation	150	159	196,728	199	196	64,403	12/96
Lawter International, Inc.	151	152	193,814	127	133	293,123	12/96
Grubb & Ellis Company	152	*	193,728	234	*	29,658	06/96
American Classic Voyages Co.	153	154	191,542	140	135	211,864	12/96
Shelby Williams Industries, Inc.	154	158	172,431	185	174	84,678	12/96

Company	Rank by Sales or Revenues '96	'95	Sales or Revenues (000 Omitted)	Rank by Assets '96	'95	Assets (000 Omitted)	Year End
Zebra Technologies Corporation	155	161	$169,715	156	165	$163,283	12/96
Multigraphics, Inc.	156	104	168,052	175	130	97,962	07/96
Technology Solutions Company	157	174	165,088	164	175	133,866	05/97
Diamond Home Services, Inc.	158	166	157,068	204	214	58,793	12/96
Wesley Jessen VisionCare, Inc.	159	*	156,752	148	*	180,600	12/96
Marks Bros. Jewelers, Inc.	160	*	155,474	177	*	93,533	01/97
RLI Corp.	161	153	155,354	80	82	845,474	12/96
UNR Industries, Inc.	162	162	154,434	178	154	93,372	12/96
Oil-Dri Corporation of America	163	160	153,787	169	169	117,692	07/96
Vitalink Pharmacy Services, Inc.	164	171	141,115	176	178	95,923	05/96
Juno Lighting, Inc.	165	165	131,479	150	156	178,181	11/96
CCC Information Services Group Inc.	166	*	130,977	205	*	58,268	12/96
The Middleby Corporation	167	163	124,765	184	176	85,968	12/96
Woodhead Industries, Inc.	168	169	123,680	189	182	78,385	09/96
Sundance Homes, Inc.	169	190	120,948	183	172	86,406	09/96
Fansteel Inc.	170	172	120,834	186	180	82,127	12/96
ARTRA GROUP Incorporated	171	168	120,699	191	179	77,379	12/96
Anicom, Inc.	172	222	115,993	181	205	87,954	12/96
Lindberg Corporation	173	167	114,020	190	183	78,095	12/96
Capsure Holdings Corp.	174	170	110,650	125	100	313,139	12/96
Salton/Maxim Housewares, Inc.	175	183	99,202	202	206	59,481	06/96
PORTEC, Inc.	176	175	97,338	198	191	65,950	12/96
Donnelley Enterprise Solutions Inc.	177	*	96,464	192	*	76,176	12/96
Factory Card Outlet Corp.	178	*	94,589	203	*	59,080	06/96
MFRI, Inc.	179	180	93,573	193	190	75,328	01/97
Continental Materials Corporation	180	184	92,768	208	197	53,893	12/96
Schawk, Inc.	181	157	90,763	157	150	160,840	12/96
Cobra Electronics Corporation	182	178	90,324	216	195	42,596	12/96
Whittman-Hart, Inc.	183	*	87,491	180	*	90,613	12/96
Teltrend Inc.	184	193	85,913	206	217	57,284	07/96
Universal Outdoor Holdings, Inc.	185	*	84,939	94	*	678,319	12/96
SPSS Inc.	186	191	83,989	209	204	52,035	12/96
Market Facts, Inc.	187	189	83,796	222	211	38,385	12/96
Stimsonite Corporation	188	187	82,712	194	186	71,870	12/96
Evans, Inc.	189	176	82,704	215	199	42,622	02/97
American Medserve Corporation	190	*	82,027	171	*	113,298	12/96
Westell Technologies, Inc.	191	181	79,385	173	189	108,049	03/97
Amerin Corporation	192	210	79,381	119	122	354,824	12/96
Aasche Transportation Services, Inc.	193	188	77,365	210	187	49,326	12/96
National Surgery Centers, Inc.	194	196	77,359	162	177	142,252	12/96
May & Speh, Inc.	195	194	77,223	170	198	115,218	09/96
OPTION CARE, Inc.	196	192	70,521	213	192	44,041	12/96
SigmaTron International, Inc.	197	203	69,600	223	219	38,315	04/96
Amerihost Properties, Inc.	198	199	68,342	196	194	66,901	12/96
Intercargo Corporation	199	177	68,241	165	170	133,710	12/96
Racing Champions Corporation	200	*	65,999	172	*	109,080	12/96
Metal Management, Inc.	201	*	65,196	195	*	70,125	03/97
Circuit Systems, Inc.	202	195	65,130	212	207	45,816	04/96
Universal Automotive Industries, Inc.	203	200	63,060	224	220	38,027	12/96
Rodman & Renshaw Capital Group	204	186	60,574	214	168	43,783	12/96
JG Industries, Inc.	205	185	60,198	246	21	15,675	01/97
American Disposal Services, Inc.	206	*	56,804	161	*	144,986	12/96
Duff & Phelps Credit Rating Co.	207	202	53,083	218	203	42,126	12/96

Company	Rank by Sales or Revenues '96	'95	Sales or Revenues (000 Omitted)	Rank by Assets '96	'95	Assets (000 Omitted)	Year End
Enterprise Systems, Inc.	208	215	$52,316	197	200	$66,231	12/96
Minuteman International, Inc.	209	201	49,120	231	215	30,968	12/96
Quixote Corporation	210	155	46,750	168	152	117,985	06/96
Rymer Foods Inc.	211	182	44,329	237	223	26,074	10/96
First Commonwealth, Inc.	212	214	44,099	226	229	34,454	12/96
Brookdale Living Communities, Inc.	213	*	41,463	160	*	146,498	12/96
TRO Learning, Inc.	214	209	41,405	217	212	42,327	10/96
SoftNet Systems, Inc.	215	227	41,387	238	210	25,586	09/96
Total Control Products, Inc.	216	*	40,821	229	*	31,462	03/97
Home Products International, Inc.	217	207	38,200	179	222	92,131	12/96
Diamond Technology Partners Inc.	218	*	37,557	239	*	25,494	03/97
CFC International, Inc.	219	211	37,227	235	225	28,206	12/96
Wells-Gardner Electronics Corp.	220	223	36,668	248	233	14,125	12/96
Trans Leasing International, Inc.	221	219	36,618	131	139	269,427	06/96
Cerion Technologies Inc.	222	224	36,540	241	235	23,333	12/96
Landauer, Inc.	223	212	36,516	220	208	41,603	09/96
Successories, Inc.	224	204	35,483	228	216	32,166	04/96
Corcom, Inc.	225	218	33,166	242	232	23,227	12/96
Eagle Finance Corp.	226	221	32,438	200	160	63,768	12/96
Medicus Systems Corporation	227	213	31,065	236	209	27,780	05/96
IWI Holding Limited	228	206	30,840	233	201	29,768	12/96
Peapod, Inc.	229	*	29,172	251	*	13,919	12/96
First Enterprise Financial Group, Inc.	230	*	28,000	166	*	119,756	12/96
Delphi Information Systems, Inc.	231	205	27,714	243	228	22,577	03/97
Champion Parts, Inc.	232	197	27,556	245	218	19,666	12/96
Telular Corporation	233	216	27,271	219	193	41,939	09/96
Platinum Entertainment, Inc.	234	*	25,488	201	*	62,091	05/96
Stericycle, Inc.	235	*	24,542	207	*	55,155	12/96
General Employment Enterprises, Inc.	236	229	23,241	256	241	9,581	09/96
Vita Food Products, Inc.	237	*	22,688	253	*	11,340	12/96
M~Wave, Inc.	238	220	22,644	244	224	21,836	12/96
Chicago Rivet & Machine Co.	239	225	22,511	230	227	31,326	12/96
Spyglass, Inc.	240	234	22,307	211	202	48,769	09/96
The Metzler Group, Inc.	241	*	22,093	225	*	37,581	12/96
Sabratek Corporation	242	*	17,696	227	*	32,951	12/96
NeoMedia Technologies, Inc.	243	*	17,518	254	*	11,266	12/96
Prime Capital Corporation	244	241	17,482	188	184	81,012	12/96
PC Quote, Inc.	245	232	17,032	252	238	11,554	12/96
The Goodheart-Willcox Company, Inc.	246	230	16,631	249	237	14,065	04/97
The Leap Group, Inc.	247	*	16,088	221	*	39,860	01/97
Bio-logic Systems Corp.	248	231	14,857	250	236	13,924	02/97
Help At Home, Inc.	249	239	11,885	257	242	9,172	06/96
Pioneer Railcorp	250	238	10,979	240	231	25,008	12/96
Baker, Fentress & Company	251	237	10,670	85	90	773,673	12/96
Aerial Communications, Inc.	252	*	7,924	95	*	672,827	12/96
UNIMED Pharmaceuticals, Inc.	253	240	7,649	232	234	30,747	12/96
BAB Holdings, Inc.	254	*	6,324	255	*	11,148	11/96
AccuMed International, Inc.	255	*	6,222	247	*	14,480	12/96
Lifeway Foods, Inc.	256	*	5,295	258	*	5,260	12/96

*   New listing.

N.B. Due to the unavailability of current financial data at this publication's press time, First Merchants Acceptance Corporation and Mercury Finance Company are not included in these rankings.

Bank and Savings Institution Holding Companies

Company	Rank by Operating Income '96	'95	Operating Income (000 Omitted)	Rank by Assets '96	'95	Total Assets (000 Omitted)	Year End	
First Chicago NBD Corporation	1	1	$10,117,000	1	1	$104,619,000	12/96	
Northern Trust Corporation	2	2	1,929,400	2	2	21,608,300	12/96	
St. Paul Bancorp, Inc.	3	3	331,976	3	3	4,357,170	12/96	
First Midwest Bancorp, Inc.	4	4	268,604	5	4	3,119,238	12/96	
AMCORE Financial, Inc.	5	5	231,507	6	5	2,814,550	12/96	
CORUS BANKSHARES, INC.	6	7	213,702	8	6	2,218,528	12/96	
Standard Financial, Inc.	7	9	166,376	7	7	2,405,221	12/96	
Firstbank of Illinois Co.	8	8	162,409	9	10	2,005,204	12/96	
First Evergreen Corporation	9	11	133,160	10	9	1,910,013	12/96	
MAF Bancorp, Inc.	10	10	124,786	4	11	3,230,341	12/96	a
Grand Premier Financial, Inc.	11	18	114,370	11	19	1,642,538	12/96	
Heritage Financial Services, Inc.	12	12	91,548	12	12	1,229,020	12/96	
First Busey Corporation	13	14	69,966	14	13	864,918	12/96	
Pinnacle Banc Group, Inc.	14	13	63,995	13	14	1,048,376	12/96	
First National Bancorp, Inc.	15	15	60,203	15	15	824,570	12/96	
Merchants Bancorp, Inc.	16	19	60,001	17	21	724,409	12/96	
First Oak Brook Bancshares, Inc.	17	17	57,197	16	18	768,655	12/96	
Avondale Financial Corp.	18	23	56,284	22	20	595,571	12/96	
Beverly Bancorporation, Inc.	19	*	51,698	21	*	630,044	12/96	
Wintrust Financial Corporation	20	*	46,569	18	*	706,037	12/96	
Calumet Bancorp, Inc.	21	22	41,911	23	23	510,217	12/96	
Northern States Financial Corp.	22	24	34,910	24	24	426,564	12/96	
UnionBancorp, Inc.	23	*	34,259	20	*	642,024	12/96	
Fidelity Bancorp, Inc.	24	27	32,511	27	26	393,664	09/96	
Princeton National Bancorp, Inc.	25	25	31,974	25	25	420,407	12/96	
SuburbFed Financial Corp.	26	29	29,738	26	27	404,092	12/96	
Southwest Bancshares, Inc.	27	26	28,537	29	28	382,361	12/96	
HomeCorp, Inc.	28	28	28,512	30	29	335,824	12/96	
Charter Financial, Inc.	29	32	26,660	28	31	388,431	09/96	
Westco Bancorp, Inc.	30	30	24,247	31	30	310,992	12/96	
Damen Financial Corporation	31	35	16,843	32	33	234,555	09/96	
Community Financial Corp.	32	33	14,652	33	34	185,799	12/96	
Alliance Bancorp	33	16	14,254	19	16	667,964	12/96	b
First Bankers Trustshares, Inc.	34	34	13,412	34	35	178,644	12/96	
Great American Bancorp, Inc.	35	*	11,448	36	*	132,369	12/96	
Hemlock Federal Financial Corp.	36	*	10,524	35	*	146,406	12/96	
North Bancshares, Inc.	37	36	8,769	37	36	117,473	12/96	
First Financial Bancorp, Inc.	38	37	6,495	38	37	94,515	12/96	

* New listing.
a Six month period only. In 1996, the company adopted calendar year reporting.
b Three month period only, prior to the merger with Liberty Bancorp., Inc. In 1996, the company adopted calendar year reporting.

Banks and Savings Institutions

Company	Rank by Total Assets '96	'95	Total Assets (000 Omitted)	Rank by Total Deposits or Savings Accts. '96	'95	Total Deposits (000 Omitted)	Year End
The First National Bank of Chicago	1	1	$51,622,906	1	1	$32,894,653	12/96
The Northern Trust Company	2	4	18,126,900	3	3	11,143,300	12/96
Citibank, Federal Savings Bank	3	3	16,787,361	2	2	12,695,868	12/96
Harris Trust and Savings Bank	4	5	14,206,667	4	7	9,726,205	12/96
LaSalle National Bank	5	6	13,386,946	5	5	8,975,557	12/96
LaSalle Bank FSB	6	7	10,842,446	6	6	7,728,803	12/96
American National Bank & Trust Co.	7	9	8,208,949	7	9	6,476,985	12/96
First of America Bank—Illinois, N.A.	8	8	6,609,403	8	8	5,303,565	12/96
St. Paul Federal Bank For Savings	9	10	4,323,750	9	10	3,341,597	12/96
Bank One, Illinois, NA	10	*	3,647,657	10	*	2,906,122	12/96
Mid America Federal Savings Bank	11	17	3,102,014	11	17	2,287,207	06/96
First Midwest Bank, N.A.	12	11	3,069,287	12	11	2,285,287	12/96
Standard Federal Bank for savings	13	13	2,350,006	14	14	1,719,728	12/96
LaSalle Bank N.A.	14	15	2,279,334	13	15	1,797,801	12/96
LaSalle Bank NI	15	19	2,017,761	16	19	1,493,692	12/96
First National Bank of Evergreen Park	16	14	1,909,937	15	13	1,696,632	12/96
Cole Taylor Bank	17	16	1,813,591	17	16	1,406,900	12/96
Liberty Federal Bank	18	*	1,310,110	19	*	1,006,570	12/96
Heritage Bank	19	22	1,221,450	18	20	1,053,385	12/96
Marquette National Bank	20	23	1,090,304	20	23	911,684	12/96
LaSalle Bank	21	*	958,548	21	*	849,571	12/96
First Bank National Association	22	20	928,210	22	22	700,945	12/96
Oak Brook Bank	23	26	766,773	24	26	648,115	12/96
The Mid-City National Bank of Chicago	24	25	756,790	23	24	679,024	12/96

Changes from Last Year's Edition

New Listings in the 1997-98 Edition

AccuMed International, Inc.
Aerial Communications, Inc.
Allegiance Corporation
American Disposal Services, Inc.
American Medserve Corporation
BAB Holdings, Inc.
Bank One, Illinois, NA
Beverly Bancorporation, Inc.
Brookdale Living Communities, Inc.
CCC Information Services Group Inc.
Diamond Technology Partners Incorporated
Dominick's Supermarkets, Inc.
Donnelley Enterprise Solutions Incorporated
EVEREN Capital Corporation
Factory Card Outlet Corp.
First Enterprise Financial Group, Inc.
Great American Bancorp, Inc.
Grubb & Ellis Company
Hemlock Federal Financial Corporation
Insurance Auto Auctions, Inc.
LaSalle Bank

The Leap Group, Inc.
Liberty Federal Bank
Lifeway Foods, Inc.
Marks Bros. Jewelers, Inc.
Metal Management, Inc.
The Metzler Group, Inc.
Midway Games Inc.
NeoMedia Technologies, Inc.
Peapod, Inc.
Platinum Entertainment, Inc.
Racing Champions Corporation
Sabratek Corporation
Specialty Equipment Companies, Inc.
Stericycle, Inc.
Total Control Products, Inc.
UnionBancorp, Inc.
Universal Outdoor Holdings, Inc.
Vita Food Products Inc.
Wesley Jessen VisionCare, Inc.
Whittman-Hart, Inc.
Wintrust Financial Corporation

Company Name Changes

AM International, Inc.	to	Multigraphics, Inc.
Binks Manufacturing Company	to	Binks Sames Corporation
CELEX Group, Inc.	to	Successories, Inc.
The Florsheim Shoe Company	to	Florsheim Group Inc.
Hinsdale Financial Corporation	to	Alliance Bancorp
LaSalle Northwest National Bank	to	LaSalle Bank N.A.
Premier Financial Services, Inc.	to	Grand Premier Financial, Inc.
Selfix, Inc.	to	Home Products International, Inc.
Tital Wheel International, Inc.	to	Titan International, Inc.
Wickes Lumber Company	to	Wickes Inc.
WMX Technologies, Inc.	to	Waste Management, Inc.

Companies No Longer Listed

Bally Entertainment Corporation	Acquired by Hilton Hotels Corp.
Bankers Life Holding Corporation	Merged with Conseco Inc.
Ben Franklin Retail Stores, Inc.	Liquidating
Caremark International Inc.	Acquired by MedPartners/Mullikin Inc.
CFI Industries, Inc.	Privately held
Circle Fine Art Corporation	Liquidating
Cole Taylor Financial Group, Inc.	Headquarters moved to Texas
DeSoto, Inc.	Merged with Keystone Consolidated Industries, Inc.
Dyna Group International, Inc.	Headquarters moved to Texas
Enviropur Waste Refining and Technology, Inc.	Liquidating
Ero, Inc.	Acquired by Hedstrom Corporation
Falcon Building Products, Inc.	Acquired by Investcorp

–continues on next page

Companies No Longer Listed (continued)

Financial Security Corp.	Merged with Pinnacle Banc Group, Inc.
FluoroScan Imaging Systems, Inc.	Acquired by Hologic Inc.
Fort Dearborn Income Securities, Inc.	Business outside this publication's parameters
International Jensen Incorporated	Acquired by Recoton Corp.
Liberty Bancorp, Inc.	Merged with Hinsdale Financial Corporation
Pioneer Financial Services, Inc.	Merged with Conseco Inc.
Rykoff-Sexton, Inc.	Headquarters moved to Pennsylvania
TODAY'S BANCORP, INC.	Merged with Mercantile Bancorporation
U.S. Robotics Corporation	Merged with 3Com Corp.

Financial Institutions No Longer Listed

Bank of America Illinois	No longer chartered in Illinois
Bank One, Chicago, N.A.	Merged to form Bank One, Illinois, NA
Columbia National Bank of Chicago	Merged with LaSalle Northwest National Bank
Northwestern Savings Bank	Merged with Mid America Federal Savings Bank
Old Kent Bank	No longer chartered in Illinois

Notes

Notes